Fodor's 1st Edition

W9-CQV-197

Central America

The Guide
for All Budgets

Completely
Updated

Where to Stay, Eat,
and Explore

On and Off
the Beaten Path

When to Go,
What to Pack

Maps, Travel Tips,
and Web Sites

Fodor's Travel Publications • New York, Toronto, London, Sydney, Auckland
www.fodors.com

Fodor's Central America

EDITORS: Melisse Gelula and Mark Sullivan

Editorial Contributors: Patricia Alisau, Gregory Benchwick, Michael de Zayas, Wayne Hoffman, Satu Hummasti, Barbara Kastelein, Gillian Notton, Dorothy MacKinnon, Sandra Sampayo, Lan Sluder, George Soriano, Jeffrey Van Fleet

Maps: David Lindroth, *cartographer*; Rebecca Baer, Robert Blake, *map editors*

Design: Fabrizio La Rocca, *creative director*; Guido Caroti, *art director*; Jolie Novak, *senior picture editor*; Melanie Marin, *photo editor*

Cover Design: Pentagram

Production/Manufacturing: Colleen Ziemba

Cover Photo (Kite festival in Guatemala): © Sheryln Bjorkren/Latin Focus.com

Copyright

Important Tip

Although all prices, opening times, and other details in this book are based on information supplied to us at press time, changes occur all the time in the travel world, and Fodor's cannot accept responsibility for facts that become outdated or for inadvertent errors or omissions. So **always confirm information when it matters,** especially if you're making a detour to visit a specific place.

Special Sales

Fodor's Travel Publications are available at special discounts for bulk purchases for sales promotions or premiums. Special editions, including personalized covers, excerpts of existing guides, and corporate imprints, can be created in large quantities for special needs. For more information, contact your local bookseller or write to Special Markets, Fodor's Travel Publications, 1745 Broadway, New York, NY 10019. Inquiries from Canada should be directed to your local Canadian bookseller or sent to Random House of Canada, Ltd., Marketing Department, 2775 Matheson Boulevard East, Mississauga, Ontario L4W 4P7. Inquiries from the United Kingdom should be sent to Fodor's Travel Publications, 20 Vauxhall Bridge Road, London SW1V 2SA, England.

PRINTED IN THE UNITED STATES OF AMERICA

10 9 8 7 6 5 4 3 2 1

CONTENTS

Maps

ON THE ROAD WITH FODOR'S

A TRIP TAKES YOU OUT OF YOURSELF. Concerns of life at home completely disappear, driven away by more immediate thoughts—about, say, what marvels will beguile the next day, or where you'll have dinner. That's where Fodor's comes in. We make sure that you know all your options, so that you don't miss something that's around the next bend just because you didn't know it was there. Mindful that the best memories of your trip might have nothing to do with what you came to Central America to see, we guide you to sights large and small all over the region. You might set out to hike the rain forests of Costa Rica, but back at home you find yourself unable to forget diving at night off the coast of Honduras or climbing an active volcano in Guatemala. With Fodor's at your side, serendipitous discoveries are never far away.

About Our Writers

Our success in showing you every corner of Central America is a credit to our extraordinary writers. Although there's no substitute for travel advice from a good friend who knows your style, our contributors are the next best thing—the kind of people you would poll for travel advice if you knew them.

Patricia Alisau discovered the mystique of the cultures south of the border during a 20-year stint as a travel correspondent in Mexico. For this book, she went back to one of her favorite places, Panama, where she first visited in the 1970s after an adventurous road trip down the Pan-American Highway all the way from the Mexican border. Patricia continues to visit and write about the region—she wrote the Panama chapter for *upCLOSE Central America*.

Freelance writer **Gregory Benchwick** first fell in love with Latin America when he traveled via chicken bus from Costa Rica to Belize in 1995. Returning to Latin America in 1999, this time to Chile, Gregory first glimpsed the rugged, enchanting, and often inhospitable landscape of El Norte Chico and El Norte Grande, which he wrote about for *Fodor's Chile*. A former editor of the *Bolivian Times*, Gregory has written extensively about travel in Latin America.

After earning a master's degree in poetry from Sarah Lawrence College, **Michael de Zayas** spent a year backpacking around Spain. He returned to Spain to write several chapters for *upCLOSE Spain*, then headed south to check out Uruguay for *Fodor's South America*, the Pampas for *Fodor's Argentina*, and Santiago for *Fodor's Chile*. A travel writer for the *New York Post* and the *Miami Herald*, de Zayas wrote about El Salvador for this book.

Melisse Gelula loves Central America. She has cave-tubed in Belize, white-water rafted in Guatemala, joined a patron saint parade in Nicaragua, traversed the rain-forest treetops on a Costa Rican canopy tour, and driven a rental car across El Salvador. In addition to editing this book, she has contributed to many Fodor's guides as an editor and travel writer, including *Fodor's Costa Rica* and *upCLOSE Central America*, respectively.

When **Wayne Hoffman** first visited Central America, he brought home a clay toucan from Costa Rica as a memento of his trip through the jungle. He soon added a tin rooster from Mexico and a wooden duck from Colombia, and thus began his flock of Latin American birds. His most recent addition is a hand-carved chicken from the Guatemalan market town of Chichicastenango. He is embarking on a six-month journey across Central America, where he hopes to greatly expand his collection. Wayne also contributed to *Fodor's South America*.

Barbara Kastelein made her way to Latin America from Holland via Great Britain, under whose gray skies she obtained a doctorate in literary studies. A freelance writer with special interests in travel, environment, and politics, she has been living in Latin America for five years. She enjoys her colorful country of choice with her partner, daughter, and baby son. For this book she returned to Honduras, which she also explored for *upCLOSE Central America*.

Seasoned traveler and prolific journalist **Dorothy MacKinnon** took up a post in San José, from which to contribute to the *Tico Times* on travel, restaurants, and nonprofit development stories—and to update the Nicoya Peninsula section of Costa Rica for this guide. She has written on travel and other topics for several North American newspapers, including the *Toronto Star* and *The Washington Post*.

A British expatriate, **Gillian Notton** wanted a little more sunshine than London could offer. She found it off the coast of Honduras. A veterinary nurse with a post graduate degree in marketing, she is now a dive shop owner on Roatán. She contributed to the section on the Bay Islands.

A native of South Africa, **Sandra Sampayo** spent three years traveling the world in search of the perfect island. She found it on the Bay Islands. She runs a marketing company and writes for a number of local and international travel publications.

Belize First magazine editor and publisher **Lan Sluder** has been banging around that country for more than a decade. In addition to writing the *Belize First Guide to Mainland Belize* and *Adapter Kit: Belize,* he has written about the country for *Caribbean Travel & Life,* the *Bangkok Post,* and Canada's *Globe & Mail,* among other publications.

George Soriano began exploring Costa Rica four years ago and hasn't stopped yet. Based in San José, he has worked as an editor at the English-language *Tico Times* and has written for several publications on Central America and Mexico. In addition to researching and updating the San José and Central Valley sections of the Costa Rica chapter, he works as a naturalist guide.

Editor **Mark Sullivan** has spent much time in Central America, scaling the heights of Volcán Pacayá in Guatemala and discovering the depths of the coral reef surrounding the Bay Islands in Honduras while editing the latest edition of *upCLOSE Central America.* He has also traveled farther south, editing *Fodor's Chile* and *Fodor's South America* along the way. His latest work, *Fodor's Kenya and Tanzania,* took him to East Africa.

Costa Rica–based freelance writer **Jeffrey Van Fleet** has spent the better part of the last decade enjoying Costa Rica's long rainy seasons and Wisconsin's winters. (Most people would try to do it the other way around.) This year he also revisited Nicaragua, a country which he's written about for Fodor's and for Costa Rica's English-language *Tico Times,* for which he's a regular contributor. Jeff has also written for Fodor's guides to Costa Rica, Chile, and Central and South America.

You can rest assured that you're in good hands—and that no property mentioned in the book has paid to be included. Each has been selected strictly on its merits, as the best of its type in its price range.

How to Use This Book

Up front is **Smart Travel Tips A to Z,** arranged alphabetically by topic and loaded with tips, Web sites, and contact information. Destination: Central America helps get you in the mood for your trip. Subsequent chapters are arranged geographically. All city sections begin with exploring information, with a section for each neighborhood (each recommending a good tour and listing sights alphabetically). All regional chapters are divided geographically; within each area, towns are covered in logical order, and attractive stretches of road between them are indicated by the designation En Route. To help you decide what you'll have time to visit, all chapters begin with our writers' favorite itineraries. (Mix itineraries from several chapters, and you can put together a really exceptional trip.) The A to Z section that ends every chapter lists additional resources.

Icons and Symbols

★   Our special recommendations

✕   Restaurant

🏨   Lodging establishment

✕🏨   Lodging establishment whose restaurant warrants a special trip

⚿   Campgrounds

☺   Good for kids (rubber duck)

☞   Sends you to another section of the guide for more information

✉   Address

☎   Telephone number

⊙   Opening and closing times

💳   Admission prices (those we give apply to adults; substantially reduced fees are almost always available for children, students, and senior citizens)

Numbers in white and black circles ③ ❸ that appear on the maps, in the margins, and within the tours correspond to one another.

For hotels, you can assume that all rooms have private baths, phones, TVs, and air-conditioning unless otherwise noted and that all hotels operate on the European Plan (with no meals) if we don't specify another meal plan. We always list a property's facilities but not whether you'll be charged extra to use them, so when pricing accommodations, do ask what's included. For restaurants, it's always a good idea to book ahead; we mention reservations only when they're essential or are not accepted. All restaurants we list are open daily for lunch and dinner unless stated otherwise; dress is mentioned only when men are required to wear a jacket or a jacket and tie.

Look for an overview of local dining-out habits in Smart Travel Tips A to Z and in the Pleasures and Pastimes section that follows each chapter introduction.

Don't Forget to Write

Your experiences—positive and negative—matter to us. If we have missed or misstated something, we want to hear about it. We follow up on all suggestions. Contact the Central America editor at editors@fodors.com or c/o Fodor's at 1745 Broadway, New York, NY 10019. And have a fabulous trip!

Karen Cure

Karen Cure
Editorial Director

Central America

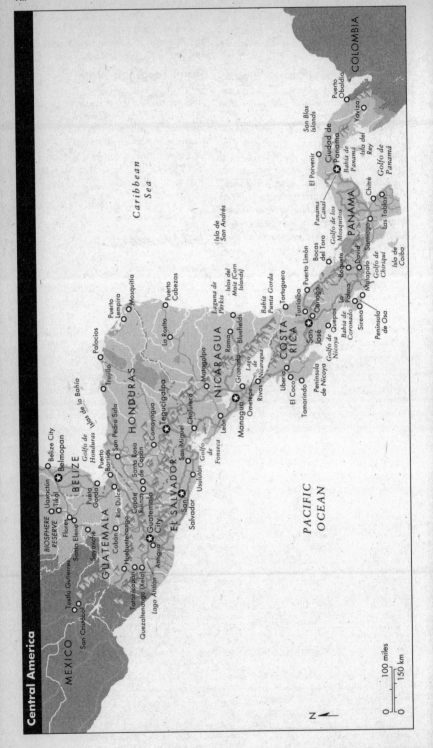

ESSENTIAL INFORMATION

ADDRESSES

In cities and larger towns, most streets are named and most buildings have numbers—whether these names and numbers are posted is a different matter. In smaller towns and villages, streets often have no formal names. Don't be afraid to ask for help, as locals are used to giving directions. Give the name of the place you are looking for, the address (including a cross street), and any nearby landmark, such as a park or church.

The most common street terms in Spanish are *calle* (street), *avenida* (avenue), and *bulevar* (boulevard). The latter two terms are often abbreviated (as *av.* and *bul.*); calle is either spelled out or, in some countries, dropped entirely so the street is referred to by proper name only.

The practice of numbering buildings doesn't enjoy wide popularity outside larger towns and cities. In some of this guide's listings, establishments have been identified by the street they're on and the nearest cross street. In extreme cases, where neither an address nor a cross street is available, you may find the notation "s/n," meaning *sin número* (no street number).

Most Central Americans must go to the post office to pick up their mail. *Apartado* (usually abbreviated *apdo.*), which you will see in many mailing addresses, means post office box.

AIR TRAVEL

Most countries in Central America have one or two international airports. Make sure you are flying into the airport nearest to the part of the country you intend to visit. Also remember that an airport in another country might be more convenient. For example, many people visiting Tikal and the other ruins in northern Guatemala choose to fly into Belize.

Definitely **pay attention to your arrival time** when selecting a flight. It's generally safer to arrive or depart during the day.

BOOKING

When you book **look for nonstop flights** and **remember that "direct" flights stop at least once.** Try to avoid connecting flights, which require a change of plane. Two airlines may operate a connecting flight jointly, so ask if your airline operates every segment of the trip; you may find that the carrier you prefer flies you only part of the way. For more booking tips and to check prices and make online flight reservations, log on to www.fodors.com.

Ask your airline for an electronic ticket. Since it eliminates all paperwork, there's no ticket to pick up or misplace; after passing through security checks, you may be able to go directly to the gate and give the agent your confirmation number, or in some cases use an electronic check-in system.

CARRIERS

Most major American carriers—American, Continental, Delta, United, and US Airways—fly to Central America. Some offer direct flights from New York or Los Angeles, while others connect through Miami, Houston, or Dallas. COPA, Panama's national airline, has flights from Los Angeles and Miami and through other U.S. cities on Continental. Grupo Taca, an alliance of Central American airlines, offers additional flights from the United States to major cities in the region. Mexicana also has flights to the region, most connecting through Mexico City.

Travelers from the United Kingdom, Australia, and New Zealand generally make connections in the United States. Those from the United Kingdom can also fly to Spain, where they can transfer to an Iberia flight to Central America.

Flying from one Central American city to another is quite inexpensive (although not when compared to the bargain-basement bus fares). Air travel can save you a lot of time, a real plus if you are only visiting for a week or two. Buying a ticket is wonderfully uncomplicated; just go to a travel agent or the airline's office. You seldom have to book in advance.

The Visit Central America program, offered by Grupo Taca, lets you buy discount coupons outside Central America. Each coupon is good for one flight within the region. The price depends on how many coupons you buy, where you start and end up, and the time of year, but usually you save up to 40%.

➤ AIRLINES: **American** (☎ 800/433–7300). **Continental** (☎ 800/231–0856). **COPA** (☎ 800/359–2672). **Delta** (☎ 800/221–1212). **Grupo Taca** (☎ 800/535–8780). **Iberia** (☎ 800/772–4642). **Mexicana** (☎ 800/531–7921). **United** (☎ 800/241–6522). **US Airways** (☎ 800/428–4322).

CHECK-IN AND BOARDING

Always **ask your carrier about its check-in policy.** Plan to arrive at the airport about 2 hours before your scheduled departure time for domestic flights and 2½ to 3 hours before international flights. For domestic flights *within* Central American countries you typically needn't arrive earlier than 1 hour.

Assuming that not everyone with a ticket will show up, airlines routinely overbook planes. When everyone does, airlines ask for volunteers to give up their seats. In return, these volunteers usually get a certificate for a free flight and are rebooked on the next flight out. If there are not enough volunteers, the airline must choose who will be denied boarding. The first to get bumped are passengers who checked in late and those flying on discounted tickets, so **get to the gate and check in as early as possible,** especially during peak periods.

Always **bring a government-issued photo ID to the airport;** even when it's not required, a passport is best.

CUTTING COSTS

The least expensive airfares to Central America are priced for round-trip travel and must usually be purchased in advance. Airlines generally allow you to change your return date for a fee; most discount tickets, however, are nonrefundable. It's smart to **call a number of airlines,** and when you are quoted a good price, **book it on the spot**—the same fare may not be available the next day. Always **check different routings** and look into using alternate airports. Also, price off-peak flights, which may be significantly less expensive than others. Travel agents, especially low-fare specialists (☞ Discounts and Deals, *below*), are helpful.

Consolidators are another good source. They buy tickets for scheduled international flights at reduced rates from the airlines, then sell them at prices that beat the best fare available directly from the airlines. Sometimes you can even get your money back if you need to return the ticket. Carefully read the fine print detailing penalties for changes and cancellations, purchase the ticket with a credit card, and **confirm your consolidator reservation with the airline.**

When you **fly as a courier,** you trade your checked-luggage space for a ticket deeply subsidized by a courier service. Many have flights to Central America; Trans Air System, for example, has flights from Miami to Guatemala City. There are restrictions on when you can book and how long you can stay. Some courier companies list with membership organizations, such as the Air Courier Association and the International Association of Air Travel Couriers; these require you to become a member before you can book a flight.

➤ CONSOLIDATORS: **Cheap Tickets** (☎ 800/377–1000 or 888/922–8849, WEB www.cheaptickets.com). **Discount Airline Ticket Service** (☎ 800/576–1600). **Pino Welcome Travel** (☎ 800/247–6578, WEB www.pinotravel.com). **Unitravel** (☎ 800/325–2222, WEB www.unitravel.com). **Up & Away Travel** (☎ 212/889–2345, WEB www.upandaway.com). **World Travel Network** (☎ 800/409–6753).

➤ COURIER RESOURCES: **Air Courier Association** (☎ 800/282–1202, WEB www.aircourier.org). **International Association of Air Travel Couriers** (☎ 352/475–1584, WEB www.courier.org). **Now Voyager Travel** (☎ 212/431–1616). **Trans Air System** (✉ 7264 N.W. 25th St., Miami, FL 33122, ☎ 305/592–1771).

ENJOYING THE FLIGHT

State your seat preference when purchasing your ticket, and then repeat it when you confirm and when you check in. For more legroom, you can request one of the few emergency-aisle seats at check-in, if you are capable of lifting at least 50 pounds—a Federal Aviation Administration requirement of passengers in these seats. Seats behind a bulkhead also offer more legroom, but they don't have under-seat storage. Don't sit in the row in front of the emergency aisle or in front of a bulkhead, where seats may not recline.

Ask the airline whether a snack or meal is served on the flight. If you have dietary concerns, **request special meals when booking.** These can be vegetarian, low-cholesterol, or kosher, for example. It's a good idea to pack some healthy snacks and a small bottle (plastic) of water in your carry-on bag. On long flights, try to maintain a normal routine, to help fight jet lag. At night, **get some sleep.** By day, **eat light meals, drink water** (not alcohol), and **move around the cabin** to stretch your legs. For additional jet-lag tips consult *Fodor's FYI: Travel Fit & Healthy* (available at bookstores everywhere).

Smoking policies vary from carrier to carrier. Most airlines prohibit smoking on all of their flights; smaller airlines and charter services allow smoking only on certain routes or certain departures. Ask your carrier about its policy.

FLYING TIMES

Flying nonstop to Central America takes 2–4 hours from Houston or Miami, 5–7 hours from New York, and 7–9 hours from Los Angeles, depending on destination. Trips from London can take 13–15 hours.

HOW TO COMPLAIN

If your baggage goes astray or your flight goes awry, complain right away. Most carriers require that you **file a claim immediately.** The Aviation Consumer Protection Division of the Department of Transportation publishes *Fly-Rights,* which discusses airlines and consumer issues and is available on-line. At PassengerRights.com, a Web site, you can compose a letter of complaint and distribute it electronically.

➤ AIRLINE COMPLAINTS: **Aviation Consumer Protection Division** (✉ U.S. Department of Transportation, Room 4107, C-75, Washington, DC 20590, ☎ 202/366–2220, WEB www.dot.gov/airconsumer). **Federal Aviation Administration Consumer Hotline** (☎ 800/322–7873).

RECONFIRMING

Check the status of your flight before you leave for the airport. You can do this on your carrier's Web site, by linking to a flight-status checker (many Web booking services offer these), or by calling your carrier or travel agent. Always confirm international flights at least 72 hours ahead of the scheduled departure time.

AIRPORTS

International flights to Belize arrive at the Philip Goldson International Airport in Ladyville, 15 km (9 mi) north of Belize City. The international airports in Guatemala are Aeropuerto Internacional La Aurora in Guatemala City and the smaller Aeropuerto Internacional Santa Elena, located in El Petén.

Costa Rica has three international airports—Aeropuerto Internacional Daniel Oduber in Liberia, Aeropuerto Internacional Juan Santamaría in San José, and Aeropuerto Internacional Tobías Bolaños in Pavas, 3 km (2 mi) west of San José.

El Salvador's Aeropuerto Internacional Comalapa is located 44 km (27 mi) south of San Salvador. International flights to Nicaragua land at Aeropuerto Internacional de Managua, 12 km (7 mi) east of Managua. Those to Panama head to Aeropuerto Internacional de Tocumen, about 26 km (13 mi) northeast of Panama City.

➤ BELIZE AIRPORTS: **Belize City Municipal Airport** (✉ North of Belize City). **Philip Goldson International Airport** (✉ Ladyville, ☎ 501/25–2014).

➤ COSTA RICA AIRPORTS: **Aeropuerto Internacional Daniel Oduber** (✉ Liberia, ☎ 506/668–1032). **Aeropuerto Internacional Juan Santamaría** (✉ San José, ☎ 506/443–2622). **Aeropuerto Internacional Tobías Bolaños** (✉ Pavas, ☎ 506/232–2820).

➤ EL SALVADOR AIRPORT: **Aeropuerto Internacional Comalapa** (✉ Comalapa, ☎ 339–9138).

➤ GUATEMALA AIRPORTS: **Aeropuerto Internacional La Aurora** (✉ Guatemala City, ☎ 502/332–6084 or 502/332–6085). **Aeropuerto Internacional Santa Elena** (✉ El Petén, ☎ 502/950–1289).

➤ HONDURAS AIRPORTS: **Aeropuerto Internacional Golosón** (Carretera La Ceiba–Tela, La Ceiba, ☎ 441–3025). **Aeropuerto Internacional Ramón Villeda Morales** (Carretera La Lima, San Pedro Sula, ☎ 668–3260 or 668–4864). **Aeropuerto Internacional Roatán** (✉ Coxen Hole, ☎ 445–1874/1875/1876/1881). **Aeropuerto Internacional Toncontín** (Bul. Comunidad Económica Europea, Tegucigalpa, ☎ 233–1115 or 233–7613).

➤ NICARAGUA AIRPORT: **Aeropuerto Internacional de Managua** (✉ Managua, ☎ 505/233–1624).

➤ PANAMA AIRPORT: **Aeropuerto Internacional de Tocumen** (✉ Panama City, ☎ 507/263–8777).

BIKE TRAVEL

Because of Central America's hot and humid climate, mountainous terrain, and less-than-perfect roads, biking isn't a popular means of transportation in most of the region. That said, there are a few spots that can be explored on mountain bikes, which are usually available to rent for $5 to $20 a day.

BIKES IN FLIGHT

Most airlines accommodate bikes as luggage, provided they are dismantled and boxed; check with individual airlines about packing requirements. Airlines sell bike boxes, which are often free at bike shops, for about $15 (bike bags start at $100). International travelers often can substitute a bike for a piece of checked luggage at no charge; otherwise, the cost is about $100. Domestic and Canadian airlines charge $40–$80 each way.

BUS TRAVEL

Bus travel in Central America is the equivalent of trains in Europe and cars in the United States. Buses are inexpensive (often less than a dollar for an hour-long journey) and run surprisingly often (many times departing several times an hour). However, comfort is minimal; roads are bumpy, seats are lumpy, and on longer trips, people are grumpy. In most places, you can flag down a bus along the road; if there's room, the driver will let you on.

Keep a close eye on your belongings on buses, as pickpockets take advantage of the crowds. Hold purses and backpacks close to your body.

CLASSES

Expect to ride on retired school buses imported from the United States. If the buses are crowded, you may have to stand for part of the journey. On some routes, you'll find express buses with air-conditioning and other comforts. These cost a few dollars more, but you'll be guaranteed a seat. Many tourists take advantage of minivans that run between popular tourist destinations. These shuttles are far more expensive, but will often get you there much faster.

PAYING

Tickets are usually sold on the buses themselves. A fare collector will pass through periodically to take your fare. They have an amazing ability to keep track of all riders who have not paid, even on a jam-packed bus. The only way to reserve a seat, even on an international route, is to buy your ticket ahead of time or simply **show up early for departure.**

CAMERAS AND
PHOTOGRAPHY

Central America, with its majestic landscapes and fascinating ruins, is a photographer's dream. People here seem amenable to having picture-taking tourists in their midst, but you should always **ask permission before taking pictures of individuals.**

You'll want to **invest in a telephoto lens** to photograph wildlife, as even standard zoom lenses won't capture a satisfying amount of detail. Always **bring high-speed film** to compensate for low light in the jungle. The thick tree canopy blocks out more light than you realize. Film is also typically cheaper outside Central America.

Casual photographers should **consider using inexpensive disposable cameras** to reduce the risks inherent in traveling with expensive equipment. One-use cameras with panoramic or underwater functions can be nice supplements to a standard camera. The *Kodak Guide to Shooting Great Travel Pictures* (available at bookstores everywhere) is loaded with tips.

➤ PHOTO HELP: **Kodak Information Center** (☎ 800/242–2424, WEB www.kodak.com).

EQUIPMENT PRECAUTIONS

Don't pack film and equipment in checked luggage, where it is much more susceptible to damage. Try to **ask for hand inspection of film,** which becomes clouded after repeated exposure to airport X-ray machines, and **keep videotapes and computer disks away from metal detectors.** Always **keep film, tape, and computer disks out of the sun.** Carry an extra supply of batteries, and **be prepared to turn on your camera, camcorder, or laptop** to prove to airport security personnel that the device is real.

CAR RENTAL

Renting cars is not common among Central American travelers. The reasons are clear: in larger cities, traffic is bad and car theft is rampant (look for guarded lots or hotels with private parking); in rural areas, roads are often unpaved, muddy, and dotted with potholes. On top of all this, the cost of gas can be steep. However, with your own car you don't have to worry about bus schedules, and you have a lot more control over your itinerary and the pace of your trip.

Decide which type of vehicle you want to rent. A *doble-tracción* (four-wheel-drive) vehicle is often essential to reach the more remote parts of Central America, especially during the rainy season. They should be booked well in advance. Most destinations are easily reached with a standard vehicle. **Reserve several weeks ahead** of time if you plan to rent any kind of vehicle in peak season or during holidays.

All the countries of Central America have larger companies as well as local agencies that are often cheaper and friendlier. Rates in Central America begin at around $30 a day and $150 a week for an economy car with air-conditioning, manual transmission, and unlimited mileage. Double that amount for a four-wheel drive vehicle.

➤ MAJOR AGENCIES: **Alamo** (☎ 800/327–9633, WEB www.alamo.com). **Avis** (☎ 800/331–1084; 800/879–2847 in Canada; 0870/606–0100 in the U.K.; 02/9353–9000 in Australia; 09/526–2847 in New Zealand, WEB www.avis.com). **Budget** (☎ 800/527–0700; 0870/156–5656 in the U.K., WEB www.budget.com). **Dollar** (☎ 800/800–6000; 0124/622–0111 in the U.K., where it's affiliated with Sixt; 02/9223–1444 in Australia, WEB www.dollar.com). **Hertz** (☎ 800/654–3001; 800/263–0600 in Canada; 020/8897–2072 in the U.K.; 02/9669–2444 in Australia; 09/256–8690 in New Zealand, WEB www.hertz.com). **National Car Rental** (☎ 800/227–7368; 020/8680–4800 in the U.K., WEB www.nationalcar.com).

CUTTING COSTS

For a good deal, **book through a travel agent who will shop around.** A recent proliferation of companies has led to competitive pricing in parts of Central America. Always **look for discount coupons** in the local tourist publications.

INSURANCE

When driving a rented car you are generally responsible for any damage to or loss of the vehicle. You may also be liable for any property damage or personal injury that you may cause while driving. Before you rent, see what coverage you already have under the terms of your personal auto-insurance policy and credit cards.

RULES AND REGULATIONS

Your driver's license may not be recognized outside your home country. International driving permits are available from the American and Canadian automobile associations and, in the United Kingdom, from the Automobile Association and Royal Automobile Club. These international permits, valid only in conjunction with your regular driver's license, are universally recognized; having one may save you a problem with local authorities.

SURCHARGES

Before you pick up a car in one city and leave it in another, **ask about drop-off charges or one-way service fees,** which can be substantial. Note, too, that some rental agencies charge extra if you return the car before the time specified in your contract. To avoid a hefty refueling fee, **fill the tank just before you turn in the car,** but be aware that gas stations near the rental outlet may overcharge. It's almost never a deal to buy the tank of gas in the car when you rent it; the understanding is that you'll return it empty, but some fuel usually remains.

CAR TRAVEL

Driving in Central America may be a bit of a challenge, but it's a great way to explore destinations off the beaten track. Keep in mind that poor road conditions can make most trips longer than you would expect. Always **make sure you have a spare tire and a jack** before setting off.

It is possible to drive between countries in Central America, but it must be done in a private vehicle. Rental cars cannot be driven to another country. There will often be a vehicle tax of up to $20 for taking your car across a border.

EMERGENCY SERVICES

Rental agencies usually provide customers with a list of numbers to call in case of car trouble, although these may not always lead to a rapid response. Locals are very good about stopping for people whose cars have broken down.

GASOLINE

Depending on which country you're in, gasoline costs between $1.40 and $2 per gallon. The next gas station may be miles away, so always fill up when you have the chance.

INSURANCE

Don't leave home without valid insurance. Always **check your insurance policy** to see if it covers you when driving abroad. If not, you may have to insure through another company.

PARKING

Car theft is not rare in Central America. Because you may be held liable if your rental car is stolen, be certain to **park overnight in a locked garage or a secure lot.** Most hotels, except for the least expensive ones, offer secure parking with a guard or locked gates.

CHILDREN IN
CENTRAL AMERICA

Central Americans love children, and having yours along may prove to be your special ticket to meeting the locals. Children are welcomed in hotels and in restaurants, especially on weekends, when Central American families go out for lunch in droves.

Let older children join in on planning as you outline your trip. **Scout your local library** for picture books, storybooks, and maps about places you'll be going. Try to **explain the concept of foreign language;** some kids, who may have just learned to talk, are confused when they can't understand when people talk. On sightseeing days try to **schedule activities of special interest to your children.**

If you are renting a car, don't forget to **arrange for a car seat** when you reserve. For general advice about traveling with children, consult *Fodor's FYI: Travel with Your Baby* (available in bookstores everywhere).

FLYING

If your children are two or older, **ask about children's airfares.** As a general rule, infants under two not occupying a seat fly at greatly reduced fares or even for free. When booking, **confirm carry-on allowances** if you're traveling with infants. In general, for babies charged 10% of the adult fare you are allowed one carry-on bag and a collapsible stroller; if the flight is full, the stroller may have to be checked or you may be limited to less.

Experts agree that it's a good idea to use safety seats aloft for children weighing less than 40 pounds. Airlines set their own policies: U.S. carriers usually require that the child be ticketed, even if he or she is young enough to ride free, since the seats must be strapped into regular seats. Do **check your airline's policy about using safety seats during takeoff and landing.** Safety seats are not allowed everywhere in the plane, so get your seat assignments as early as possible.

When reserving, **request children's meals or a freestanding bassinet** (not available at all airlines) if you need them. But note that bulkhead seats, where you must sit to use the bassinet, may lack an overhead bin or storage space on the floor.

LODGING

Most hotels in Central America allow children under a certain age to stay in their parents' room at no extra charge, but others charge for them as adults. Be sure to **find out the cutoff age for children's discounts.**

PRECAUTIONS

Children must have all their inoculations up to date before traveling abroad. Make sure that health precautions, such as what to drink and eat, are applied to the whole family. If you **don't cram too much into each day** you will keep the whole family healthier while on the road.

SIGHTS AND ATTRACTIONS

There's plenty for children to do in Central America. They can romp on the beaches, hike up volcanoes, and learn about animals in their natural habitats. Museums are a challenge, as many have explanations only in Spanish. You can make the experience more interesting for kids if you **hire an English-speaking guide.** Places that are especially appealing to children are indicated by a rubber-duckie icon (☺) in the margin.

COMPUTERS ON THE ROAD

If you're traveling with a laptop, **carry a spare battery, a universal adapter plug, and a converter** if your computer isn't dual voltage. Ask about electrical surges before plugging in your computer. Keep your computer out of the sun and avoid excessive heat for both your computer and your disks. In many areas, carrying a laptop computer could make

you a target for thieves; conceal your laptop in a generic bag, and keep it close to you at all times.

CONSUMER PROTECTION

Whether you're shopping for gifts or purchasing travel services, **pay with a major credit card** whenever possible, so you can cancel payment or get reimbursed if there's a problem (and you can provide documentation). If you're doing business with a particular company for the first time, **contact your local Better Business Bureau and the attorney general's offices** in your state and (for U.S. businesses) the company's home state as well. Have any complaints been filed? Finally, if you're buying a package or tour, always **consider travel insurance** that includes default coverage (☞ Insurance, *below*).

➤ BBB: **Council of Better Business Bureaus** (✉ 4200 Wilson Blvd., Suite 800, Arlington, VA 22203, ☎ 703/276–0100, ℻ 703/525–8277, 🌐 www.bbb.org).

CRUISE TRAVEL

Many people combine a cruise with a stay in Central America. Belize and Panama are especially popular destinations, and Costa Rica has a few small lines. To learn how to plan, choose, and book a cruise-ship voyage, consult *Fodor's FYI: Plan & Enjoy Your Cruise* (available in bookstores everywhere).

CUSTOMS AND DUTIES

When shopping abroad, **keep receipts** for all purchases. Upon reentering the country, **be ready to show customs officials what you've bought.** If you feel a duty is incorrect, appeal the assessment. If you object to the way your clearance was handled, note the inspector's badge number. In either case, first ask to see a supervisor. If the problem isn't resolved, write to the appropriate authorities, beginning with the port director at your point of entry.

IN AUSTRALIA

Australian residents who are 18 or older may bring home A$400 worth of souvenirs and gifts (including jewelry), 250 cigarettes or 250 grams of tobacco, and 1,125 milliliters of alcohol (including wine, beer, and spirits). Residents under 18 may bring back A$200 worth of goods. Prohibited items include meat products. Seeds, plants, and fruits need to be declared upon arrival.

➤ INFORMATION: **Australian Customs Service** (Regional Director, ✉ Box 8, Sydney, NSW 2001, ☎ 02/9213–2000, ℻ 02/9213–4000, 🕸 www.customs.gov.au).

IN CANADA

Canadian residents who have been out of Canada for at least seven days may bring in C$750 worth of goods duty-free. If you've been away fewer than seven days but more than 48 hours, the duty-free allowance drops to C$200; if your trip lasts 24 to 48 hours, the allowance is C$50. You may not pool allowances with family members. Goods claimed under the C$750 exemption may follow you by mail; those claimed under the lesser exemptions must accompany you. Alcohol and tobacco products may be included in the seven-day and 48-hour exemptions but not in the 24-hour exemption. If you meet the age requirements of the province or territory through which you reenter Canada, you may bring in, duty-free, 1.5 liters of wine *or* 1.14 liters (40 imperial ounces) of liquor *or* 24 12-ounce cans or bottles of beer or ale. If you are 19 or older you may bring in, duty-free, 200 cigarettes and 50 cigars. Check ahead of time with the Canada Customs and Revenue Agency or the Department of Agriculture for policies regarding meat products, seeds, plants, and fruits.

You may send an unlimited number of gifts (only one gift per recipient, however) worth up to C$60 each duty-free to Canada. Label the package UNSOLICITED GIFT—VALUE UNDER $60. Alcohol and tobacco are excluded.

➤ INFORMATION: **Canada Customs and Revenue Agency** (✉ 2265 St. Laurent Blvd. S, Ottawa, Ontario K1G 4K3, ☎ 204/983–3500 or 506/636–5064; 800/461–9999, 🕸 www.ccra-adrc.gc.ca/).

IN NEW ZEALAND

All homeward-bound residents may bring back NZ$700 worth of souvenirs and gifts; passengers may not pool their allowances, and children can claim only the concession on goods intended for their own use. For those 17 or older, the duty-free allowance also includes 4.5 liters of wine or beer; one 1,125-milliliter bottle of spirits; and either 200 cigarettes, 250 grams of tobacco, 50 cigars, *or* a combination of the three up to 250 grams. Meat products, seeds, plants, and fruits must be declared upon arrival to the Agricultural Services Department.

➤ INFORMATION: **New Zealand Customs** (Head office: ✉ The Customhouse, 17–21 Whitmore St., Box 2218, Wellington, ☎ 09/300–5399 or 0800/428–786, 🕸 www.customs.govt.nz).

IN THE U.K.

From countries outside the European Union, including those in Central America, you may bring home, duty-free, 200 cigarettes or 50 cigars; 1 liter of spirits or 2 liters of fortified or sparkling wine or liqueurs; 2 liters of still table wine; 60 milliliters of perfume; 250 milliliters of toilet water; plus £145 worth of other goods, including gifts and souvenirs. Prohibited items include meat products, seeds, plants, and fruits.

➤ INFORMATION: **HM Customs and Excise** (✉ Portcullis House, 21 Cowbridge Rd. E, Cardiff CF11 9SS, ☎ 029/2038–6423 or 0845/010–9000, 🕸 www.hmce.gov.uk).

IN THE U.S.

U.S. residents 21 and older may bring back 2 liters of alcohol duty-free, as long as one of the liters was produced in a CBI country. In addition, regardless of your age, you are allowed 200 cigarettes and 100 non-Cuban cigars. Antiques, which the U.S. Customs Service defines as objects more than 100 years old, enter duty-free, as do original works of art done entirely by hand, including paintings, drawings, and sculptures. You may also send packages home duty-free, with a limit of one parcel per addressee per day (except alcohol or tobacco products or perfume worth more than $5). You can mail up to $200 worth of goods for personal use; label the package PERSONAL USE and attach a list of its contents and their retail value. If the package contains your used personal belongings, mark it PERSONAL GOODS RETURNED to avoid paying duties. You may send up to $100 worth of goods ($200 from the U.S. Virgin Islands) as a gift; mark the package UNSOLICITED GIFT. Mailed items do not affect your duty-free allowance on your return.

➤ INFORMATION: **U.S. Customs Service** (for inquiries, ✉ 1300 Pennsylvania Ave. NW, Washington, DC 20229, ☎ 202/354–1000, 🌐 www.customs.gov; for complaints, ✉ Customer Satisfaction Unit, 1300 Pennsylvania Ave. NW, Room 5.5A, Washington, DC 20229; for registration of equipment, ✉ Office of Passenger Programs, 1300 Pennsylvania Ave. NW, Room 5.4D, Washington, DC 20229, ☎ 202/927–0530).

DINING

You can eat very well in Central America. The gastronomic gumbo of Mexican, Caribbean, Maya, Garífuna, and other cuisines provides a tasty variety of dining choices. On the coast, seafood—especially lobster, conch, and locally caught fish such as snapper and grouper—is fresh, inexpensive, and delicious. In the mountains you couldn't do better than a platter of black beans and rice accompanied by thick corn tortillas. Finish with *pan de banana* (banana bread) or *flan* (a crème caramel dessert).

Food is much less expensive than in the United States or Canada. It's possible to have a wonderful *comida típica* (which means "typical food") for just a couple of dollars. Even choosing fancier places to dine won't break the bank; in most of Central America, you can enjoy a three-course meal at an upscale restaurant and still walk away with change from your $20 bill. The restaurants we list are the cream of the crop in each price category. Properties indicated by an ✕🏨 are lodging establishments whose restaurants warrant a special trip.

MEALTIMES

Central America keeps a fairly early eating schedule. *Desayuno* (breakfast) usually runs from 7 to 9 AM. *Almuerzo* (lunch), the most substantial meal of the day, can last from noon until 2 or 3 in the afternoon. *Cena* (dinner) starts soon after sunset, which means that few restaurants stay open past 9 PM (except in Panama, where dinner starts later). Major tourist destinations and large cities are more likely to provide a few dining establishments that stay open later, especially in high season. A fair number of restaurants close on Sunday, but just as many remain open. Unless otherwise noted, the restaurants listed in this guide are open for lunch and dinner.

PAYING

Credit cards are accepted at some of the more expensive restaurants, but otherwise cash is required.

RESERVATIONS AND DRESS

Reservations are always a good idea; we mention them only when they're essential or not accepted. Book ahead for upscale restaurants, and reconfirm as soon as you arrive. We mention dress only when men are required to wear a jacket or a jacket and tie. Casual clothing is fine for the vast majority of Central American establishments.

WINE, BEER, AND SPIRITS

Cerveza (beer) is the most popular alcoholic beverage in Central America. Each country has its own national brands, which means you'll find Gallo in Guatemala and Pilsener in El Salvador. Most bars will also offer a few American brands. Tourists tend toward fruity drinks, especially along the coast of Honduras and on the cays of Belize.

DISABILITIES AND ACCESSIBILITY

Accessibility in Central America is extremely limited. Wheelchair ramps are practically nonexistent. Exploring most of the region's attractions involves negotiating cobblestone streets, steep trails, or muddy paths. Buses are not equipped to carry wheelchairs, so it's a good idea to hire a van to get about and have someone along to help out. There is a growing awareness of the needs of people with disabilities, and some hotels and attractions have made the necessary provisions.

RESERVATIONS

When discussing accessibility with an operator or reservations agent, **ask**

hard questions. Are there any stairs, inside *or* out? Are there grab bars next to the toilet *and* in the shower/tub? How wide is the doorway to the room? To the bathroom? For the most extensive facilities meeting the latest legal specifications, **opt for newer accommodations.** If you reserve through a toll-free number, consider also calling the hotel's local number to confirm the information from the central reservations office. Get confirmation in writing when you can.

SIGHTS AND ATTRACTIONS

Few sights in Central America were designed with travelers in wheelchairs in mind, and fewer still have been renovated to meet their needs. Newer destinations may have the necessary facilities, but don't count on it. Call ahead or ask someone who has visited before.

TRANSPORTATION

Central America presents serious challenges to travelers with disabilities. Although the more developed areas can be managed in a wheelchair, most rural areas are tougher. The tour company Vaya con Silla de Ruedas, Spanish for "Go with a Wheelchair," provides transportation and guided tours for travelers in wheelchairs in Costa Rica and neighboring countries and specializes in accessibility, with emphasis on comfort and safety.

➤ TOUR COMPANY: **Vaya con Silla de Ruedas** (✉ Apdo. 1146-2050, San Pedro Montes de Oca, Costa Rica, ☎ 506/225–8561 or 506/253–0931).

➤ COMPLAINTS: **Aviation Consumer Protection Division** (☞ Air Travel, *above*) for airline-related problems. **Departmental Office of Civil Rights** (for general inquiries, ✉ U.S. Department of Transportation, S-30, 400 7th St. SW, Room 10215, Washington, DC 20590, ☎ 202/366–4648, FAX 202/366–9371, WEB www.dot.gov/ost/docr/index.htm). **Disability Rights Section** (✉ U.S. Department of Justice, Civil Rights Division, Box 66738, Washington, DC 20035-6738, ☎ 202/514–0301 or 800/514–0301; 800/514–0383 TTY, for ADA inquiries; WEB www.usdoj.gov/crt/ada/adahom1.htm).

TRAVEL AGENCIES

In the United States, the Americans with Disabilities Act requires that travel firms serve the needs of all travelers. Some agencies specialize in working with people with disabilities.

➤ TRAVELERS WITH MOBILITY PROBLEMS: **Access Adventures** (✉ 206 Chestnut Ridge Rd., Scottsville, NY 14624, ☎ 716/889–9096, dltravel@prodigy.net), run by a former physical-rehabilitation counselor. **Flying Wheels Travel** (✉ 143 W. Bridge St., Box 382, Owatonna, MN 55060, ☎ 507/451–5005 or 800/535–6790, FAX 507/451–1685, WEB www.flyingwheelstravel.com).

DISCOUNTS AND DEALS

Be a smart shopper and **compare all your options** before making decisions. A plane ticket bought with a promotional coupon from travel clubs, coupon books, and direct-mail offers or on the Internet may not be cheaper than the least expensive fare from a discount ticket agency. And always keep in mind that what you get is just as important as what you save.

DISCOUNT RESERVATIONS

To save money, **look into discount reservations services** with Web sites and toll-free numbers, which use their buying power to get a better price on hotels, airline tickets, even car rentals. When booking a room, always **call the hotel's local toll-free number** (if one is available) rather than the central reservations number—you'll often get a better price. Always ask about special packages or corporate rates.

When shopping for the best deal on hotels and car rentals, **look for guaranteed exchange rates,** which protect you against a falling dollar. With your rate locked in, you won't pay more, even if the price goes up in the local currency.

➤ AIRLINE TICKETS: ☎ 800/AIR–4LESS.

➤ HOTEL ROOMS: **Turbotrip.com** (☎ 800/473–7829, WEB www.turbotrip.com).

PACKAGE DEALS

Don't confuse packages and guided tours. When you buy a package, you travel on your own, just as though you had planned the trip yourself. Fly/drive packages, which combine airfare and car rental, are often a good deal.

ECOTOURISM

Ecotourism, green tourism, environmental tourism: these terms have been flying around Costa Rica, Panama, and Belize for more than a decade. Many of the tour companies currently operating in these countries make preserving the environment a priority. More recently the ideas have spread to the less tourist-developed countries in the region. Find out whether a tour company practices "eco-friendly" policies, such as hiring and training local people as guides; controlling the numbers of visitors on each trip; avoiding areas damaged by overuse; and discouraging disruptive behavior (i.e., making loud noises to scare birds into flight). All of this can mitigate the effects of intense tourism.

ELECTRICITY

With the exception of Belize, the electrical current in Central America, 110 volts (ac), and plugs are the same as in the United States.

To use electric-powered equipment purchased in the United States or Canada in Belize, bring a converter and adapter. The electrical current in Belize is 220 volts, 50 cycles alternating current; some wall outlets in Belize take Continental-type plugs, with two round prongs.

If your appliances are dual-voltage, you'll need only an adapter. Don't use 110-volt outlets marked FOR SHAVERS ONLY for high-wattage appliances such as blow-dryers. Most laptops operate equally well on 110 and 220 volts and so require only an adapter.

ETIQUETTE AND BEHAVIOR

Many of Central America's rules of etiquette are simply common sense. This is a conservative region, so **dress modestly.** Revealing clothing is frowned upon, especially in more rural areas. Be quiet when visiting a house of worship, and don't photograph people praying. **Ask permission** before you walk across someone's property, sit next to them on a bus, or take their picture. When on a bus, **give up your seat** to an elderly person or a woman carrying a child. Strangers still rely on a handshake for first introductions—although a hearty *abrazo* (hug) will sometimes replace the handshake on your second meeting. Other customs are more nuanced and vary from country to country, so you should **observe locals and follow their lead.**

BUSINESS ETIQUETTE

Business matters are most often discussed over breakfast or lunch; if you are invited to someone's home for dinner—typically with your spouse—this is an opportunity to socialize, not to discuss business. For Central Americans, getting to trust you on a social level is all part of business. In someone's home, you will generally serve yourself food. (It is considered rude to take food and leave it on your plate.) Talking about family with business associates is perfectly polite; raising sensitive issues like politics is not. If you dine in a restaurant, men will generally resist letting women pay for meals. Wherever you meet business associates, you should remember that punctuality is less of an issue in Central America than in the United States or Europe. This doesn't mean that *you* should be late, but rather that you shouldn't be shocked or visibly perturbed if your host is up to a half hour late.

GAY AND LESBIAN TRAVEL

Harassment of gays and lesbians is infrequent in Central America, but so are public displays of affection between same-sex couples. That said, you probably won't encounter any problems with harassment on the streets or in securing a hotel room.

As a result of its history of tolerance, Costa Rica has a relatively large gay community. Here you'll find a number of amenities aimed at gay visitors—bars, hotels, and even a beach. El Salvador has a handful of gay bars, as does Guatemala City. The rest of the Central America, however, has few establishments for gays.

➤ GAY- AND LESBIAN-FRIENDLY TRAVEL AGENCIES: **Different Roads Travel** (⊠ 8383 Wilshire Blvd., Suite 902, Beverly Hills, CA 90211, ☎ 323/651–5557 or 800/429–8747, FAX 323/651–3678, lgernert@tzell.com). **Kennedy Travel** (⊠ 314 Jericho Turnpike, Floral Park, NY 11001, ☎ 516/352–4888 or 800/237–7433, FAX 516/354–8849, WEB www.kennedytravel.com). **Now Voyager** (⊠ 4406 18th St., San

Francisco, CA 94114, ☎ 415/626–1169 or 800/255–6951, FAX 415/626–8626, WEB www.nowvoyager.com).

➤ PUBLICATION: One of the best gay and lesbian travel newsletters is **Out and About** (☎ 800/929–2268, WEB www.outandabout.com), with listings of gay-friendly hotels and travel agencies plus health cautions for travelers with HIV. A 10-issue subscription costs $49; single issues are $5.

GUIDEBOOKS

Plan well and you won't be sorry. Guidebooks are excellent tools—and you can take them with you. You may want to purchase color-photo-illustrated *Fodor's Exploring Costa Rica,* which is thorough on culture and history and is available at on-line retailers and bookstores everywhere. Also consider our two in-depth guides to the region *Fodor's Belize and Guatemala* and *Fodor's Costa Rica.* Budget travelers can check out *upCLOSE Central America.*

HEALTH

Use your upcoming trip as an opportunity to **update routine immunizations,** including measles, diphtheria, and tetanus. You should also consider getting inoculated against rabies, typhoid, and hepatitis A and B. Other required vaccines will be determined by your specific destinations, along with a careful weighing of effectiveness versus side effects. Always **check with your physician or a travel clinic** for a complete list of all the shots you need. If you're not familiar with a travel clinic in your area, ask your doctor to suggest one.

Finally, compared to the risks of malaria and dengue fever, sunburn may not seem very important, but you're much more likely to suffer from a painful sunburn than any exotic disease. Even if you have a dark complexion, **bring plenty of sunscreen** and slather it on at every opportunity to protect yourself from the bright sunshine.

DIVERS' ALERT

Do not fly within 24 hours of scuba diving. Neophyte divers should have a complete physical exam before undertaking a dive. If you have travel insurance, **make sure your policy applies to scuba-related injuries,** as not all companies provide this coverage.

FOOD-BORNE DISEASES

In Central America, disease spread through contaminated food and water is the primary cause of illness to travelers. Standards of hygiene vary throughout the region. Although food-related illnesses are rare in Belize, Costa Rica, and Panama, it's always a good idea to watch what you eat and drink.

The most important preventative measure it to **drink only purified water.** In most places it is labeled *agua pura* or *agua purificada.* You can buy purified water just about anywhere. Always **watch out for ice**—it's rarely made from purified water, so it can contaminate otherwise safe beverages. To be especially safe, brush your teeth with purified water.

Also be careful in selecting your foods. Raw produce is often contaminated, so **be wary of salads** and uncooked vegetables. (Lettuce is particularly problematic, as water clings to the leaves.) Fruit is fine as long as you can peel it yourself. Don't eat cooked foods that have been allowed to cool, and **avoid raw seafood** in dishes such as ceviche. Think twice about consuming suspect foods just because you see locals doing so. These people have developed immune systems to combat illnesses that could knock you flat. The best strategy is to give your body a little time to get used to local foods by exercising restraint during the first week or so of your trip.

Cholera: This intestinal infection is caused by a bacterium carried in contaminated water or food. Cholera is characterized by profuse diarrhea, vomiting, cramping, and dehydration. If you think you may have contracted cholera, seek medical attention right away. Most people recuperate with simple fluid and electrolyte-replacement treatment. Outbreaks are more common in Guatemala and El Salvador but can happen in any country. The vaccine is only 50% effective, and the U.S. Centers for Disease Control does not recommend it as a standard vaccine for all travelers.

Diarrhea: For many people, a trip to Latin America means at least one case of traveler's diarrhea. Contaminated food and drink are the major causes. The problem, sometimes accompanied by nausea, bloating, and achiness, usually lasts a few days. For mild cases the main concern is dehydration, so drink lots of fluids. Drugs such as Bactrim and Septra may help shorten the time you suffer. Lomotil or Imodium may decrease the symptoms. If diarrhea lasts longer than a few days or is accompanied by cramping, vomiting, or mild fever, you probably have something more complicated, like a stomach infection, amoebas, giardia, or in extreme cases, cholera. In most places, you can get an inexpensive test at a clinic.

Hepatitis A: A viral infection that attacks the liver, Hepatitis A is transmitted through contaminated food. It causes achiness, exhaustion, fever, loss of appetite, queasiness, jaundice, vomiting, light stools, and dark urine. There is no specific treatment available, so it's a good idea to be immunized before you leave home.

Typhoid Fever: This bacterial infection can be spread through contaminated food and water and through contact with contaminated people. Fever, headaches, exhaustion, loss of appetite, and constipation all indicate an onslaught of typhoid. If you think you have contracted typhoid, seek medical attention immediately. Typhoid is a risk throughout Central America, but it is most common in Mexico. A typhoid vaccine is available in oral form, taken over a week, and as a series of injections spread over a month. The vaccine is only about 70%–90% effective.

INSECT-BORNE DISEASES

Mosquitoes and other insects carry a variety of diseases, so be careful to reduce your exposure. After sunset wear light-color, loose-fitting, long-sleeve shirts; long pants; and shoes and socks. Always sleep in a mosquito-proof room or tent, and if possible, keep a fan going in your room. Beyond that, bring a strong insect repellent and use it consistently. The CDC recommends products with DEET. There are 100% DEET repellents, but they're so strong that they can melt your watchband. A 25%–50% repellent can be more effective because you won't be afraid to slather it on.

If all of this sounds a bit too much like chemical warfare to you, you can try a few other options. Some people—including the U.S. Marine Corps—swear by Avon Skin-So-Soft, which was discovered to repel bugs. It works for many people, but not others. Others recommend taking extra doses of Vitamin B, as insects seem to dislike it.

Dengue Fever: This disease is transmitted by the aedes mosquito, which is most active during the day and around dawn and dusk. Dengue usually flourishes during the rainy season. It is most common in urban areas, but it's found in rural areas as well. Dengue manifests itself with flu-like symptoms—high fever, severe headache, joint and muscle aches, nausea, and vomiting. About three or four days after the fever appears, a rash develops. There is no vaccination for dengue, and treatment consists of rest and fluids. Dengue lasts for up to 10 days, but full recovery may take as long as a month. There is no vaccine.

Malaria: Transmitted by the bite of the anopheles mosquito, which is out sundown to sunup, malaria usually resembles the flu. The symptoms can include chills, aches, and fatigue. It can lead to anemia, kidney failure, and other serious problems. If you experience any of the telltale symptoms up to a year after exposure, seek medical attention. If you are going to a high-risk area, consider taking an antimalarial drug. At time of writing Malarone is the preferred drug, with almost none of the possible side effects of once popular Lariam (mefloquine).

Yellow Fever: A viral disease spread by the bite of evening-feeding mosquitoes, yellow fever is a very rare problem these days. Characterized by headaches, chills, fever, and vomiting, yellow fever can develop into jaundice, internal bleeding, and kidney failure. There is no specific drug to treat this disease, so you may want to consider getting a vaccine before you leave. Currently, the countries of Central America do not require a yellow-fever certificate unless you are traveling from a country infected with the disease.

PARASITES

In addition to all the diseases and viruses Central America has to offer, parasites abound. They are transmitted through bad food and water, through direct contact with infected water and soil, or by insect bites. Again, take precautions against insect bites, drink and eat foods you know are safe, and be sure to wear shoes to avoid direct penetration.

RABIES

Rabies is a concern in most Central American countries. Contracted by the bite of a rabid animal, this viral infection attacks the central nervous system. Avoid handling animals, including dogs. If you are bitten, wash the wound thoroughly with soap and water and seek immediate medical attention. You can be vaccinated before you leave the United States, but you'll still have to seek medical attention and get injections after you are bitten.

MEDICAL PLANS

No one plans to get sick while traveling, but it happens, so **consider signing up with a medical-assistance company.** Members get doctor referrals, emergency evacuation or repatriation, hot lines for medical consultation, cash for emergencies, and other assistance.

➤ MEDICAL-ASSISTANCE COMPANY: International SOS Assistance (WEB www.internationalsos.com; ✉ 8 Neshaminy Interplex, Suite 207, Trevose, PA 19053, ☎ 215/245–4707 or 800/523–6586, FAX 215/244–9617; ✉ 12 Chemin Riantbosson, 1217 Meyrin 1, Geneva, Switzerland, ☎ 22/785–6464, FAX 22/785–6424; ✉ 331 N. Bridge Rd., 17-00, Odeon Towers, Singapore 188720, ☎ 338–7800, FAX 338–7611).

OVER-THE-COUNTER REMEDIES

Farmacias (pharmacies) in Central America carry *aspirina* (aspirin) and other pain relievers, Pepto-Bismol, Imodium and other diarrhea treatments, and a range of other over-the-counter treatments. It's best to **bring basic medications from home,** in case you're staying in a remote area far from any pharmacies.

➤ HEALTH WARNINGS: **National Centers for Disease Control and Prevention** (National Center for Infectious Diseases, Division of Quarantine, Traveler's Health Section, ✉ 1600 Clifton Rd. NE, M/S E-03, Atlanta, GA 30333, ☎ 888/232–3228 general information, 877/394–8747 travelers' health line, FAX 888/232–3299, WEB www.cdc.gov).

HOLIDAYS

Do not plan on conducting any official business on the following days: **New Year's Day; Semana Santa** (the week before Easter) and **Easter** itself; **All Saints' Day** and **All Souls' Day** (November 1 and 2); and **Christmas Eve** and **Christmas** (December 24 and 25).

INSURANCE

The most useful travel-insurance plan is a comprehensive policy that includes coverage for trip cancellation and interruption, default, trip delay, and medical expenses (with a waiver for preexisting conditions).

Without insurance you will lose all or most of your money if you cancel your trip, regardless of the reason. Default insurance covers you if your tour operator, airline, or cruise line goes out of business. Trip-delay covers expenses that arise because of bad weather or mechanical delays. Study the fine print when comparing policies.

If you're traveling internationally, a key component of travel insurance is coverage for medical bills incurred if you get sick on the road. Such expenses are not generally covered by Medicare or private policies. U.K. residents can buy a travel-insurance policy valid for most vacations taken during the year in which it's purchased (but check preexisting-condition coverage). British and Australian citizens need extra medical coverage when traveling overseas.

Always **buy travel policies directly from the insurance company**; if you buy them from a cruise line, airline, or tour operator that goes out of business you probably will not be covered for the agency or operator's default, a major risk. Before making any purchase, **review your existing health and home-owner's policies** to find what they cover away from home.

➤ TRAVEL INSURERS: In the United States: **Access America** (⊠ 6600 W. Broad St., Richmond, VA 23230, ☎ 800/284–8300, FAX 804/673–1491 or 800/346–9265, WEB www.accessamerica.com). **Travel Guard International** (⊠ 1145 Clark St., Stevens Point, WI 54481, ☎ 715/345–0505 or 800/826–1300, FAX 800/955–8785, WEB www.travelguard.com).

➤ INSURANCE INFORMATION: In Australia: **Insurance Council of Australia** (⊠ Level 3, 56 Pitt St., Sydney, NSW 2000, ☎ 02/9253–5100, FAX 02/9253–5111, WEB www.ica.com.au). In Canada: **RBC Travel Insurance** (⊠ 6880 Financial Dr., Mississauga, Ontario L5N 7Y5, ☎ 905/791–8700 or 800/668–4342, FAX 905/813–4704, WEB www.rbcinsurance.com). In New Zealand: **Insurance Council of New Zealand** (⊠ Level 7, 111–115 Customhouse Quay, Box 474, Wellington, ☎ 04/472–5230, FAX 04/473–3011, WEB www.icnz.org.nz). In the United Kingdom: **Association of British Insurers** (⊠ 51 Gresham St., London EC2V 7HQ, ☎ 020/7600–3333, FAX 020/7696–8999, WEB www.abi.org.uk).

LANGUAGE

Spanish is the predominant language in every Central American country except for English-speaking Belize. Pockets of other languages exist—Garífuna along the Caribbean coast, creole dialects in Panama, and Maya offshoots in Guatemala —but Spanish is almost always spoken in these places as well. Wherever tourism and commerce are heaviest—major cities, beach towns, mountain resorts—English is most widely understood. But even here, English is not spoken universally or particularly well. You'll do better to **bring along a phrase book** and **learn a few expressions** you'll use often.

LANGUAGES FOR TRAVELERS

A phrase book and language-tape set can help get you started. *Fodor's Spanish for Travelers* (available at bookstores everywhere) is excellent.

LODGING

In Central America you can stay in dirt-cheap cabanas on the beach, luxury resorts in the mountains, and pretty much everything in between. Charming colonial-era houses are often a choice in smaller towns, while opulent mansions converted into hotels are common in larger cities. If there is one shortage, it's medium-price lodgings. If you'll be arriving during the high season, you may want to **reserve your first few nights' stay in advance** to avoid the stress of looking for a room on a few hours of sleep.

The lodgings we list in this book are the ones we think give you the most for your money. We always list the facilities that are available—but we don't specify whether they cost extra. When pricing accommodations, always ask what's included. Properties are assigned price categories based on the range from their least-expensive standard double room at high season to the most expensive. Properties marked ✕☰ are lodging establishments whose restaurants warrant a special trip.

Assume that hotels operate on the **European Plan** (EP, with no meals) unless we specify that they use either the **Continental Plan** (CP, with a Continental breakfast), **Breakfast Plan** (BP, with a full breakfast), the **Modified American Plan** (MAP, with breakfast and dinner) or are **all-inclusive** (including all meals and most activities).

APARTMENT AND VILLA RENTALS

If you want a home base that's roomy enough for a family and comes with cooking facilities, **consider a furnished rental.** These can save you money, especially if you're traveling with a group. Home-exchange directories sometimes list rentals as well as exchanges.

CAMPING

Many, though not all, national parks in Central America have designated areas for camping. Some popular beaches have camping areas with bathrooms and showers. If you camp in unguarded areas, you risk being robbed if you leave your tent unattended.

Permits are usually required if you plan on exploring the backcountry. Always check on permits before you go to make sure you won't be turned away. While camping, travel on marked trails and choose previously used sites to avoid trampling vegetation and causing soil erosion.

Lakes or streams might look clean enough, but all water should be purified for drinking or cooking. Boil it for at least five minutes or use the purification kits and filters available at most sporting goods stores.

HOSTELS

No matter what your age, you can **save on lodging costs by staying at hostels.** In some 4,500 locations in more than 70 countries around the world, Hostelling International (HI), the umbrella group for a number of national youth-hostel associations, offers single-sex, dorm-style beds and, at many hostels, rooms for couples and family accommodations. Membership in any HI national hostel association, open to travelers of all ages, allows you to stay in HI-affiliated hostels at member rates; one-year membership is about $25 for adults (C$35 for a two-year minimum membership in Canada, £12.50 in the United Kingdom, A$52 in Australia, and NZ$40 in New Zealand); hostels run about $10–$25 per night. Members have priority if the hostel is full; they're also eligible for discounts around the world, even on rail and bus travel in some countries.

➤ ORGANIZATIONS: **Hostelling International–American Youth Hostels** (✉ 733 15th St. NW, Suite 840, Washington, DC 20005, ☎ 202/783–6161, FAX 202/783–6171, WEB www.hiayh.org). **Hostelling International–Canada** (✉ 400–205 Catherine St., Ottawa, Ontario K2P 1C3, ☎ 613/237–7884; 800/663–5777 in Canada, FAX 613/237–7868, WEB www.hihostels.ca). **Youth Hostel Association Australia** (✉ 10 Mallett St., Camperdown, NSW 2050, ☎ 02/9565–1699, FAX 02/9565–1325, WEB www.yha.com.au). **Youth Hostel Association of England and Wales** (✉ Trevelyan House, 8 St. Stephen's Hill, St. Albans, Hertfordshire AL1 2DY, U.K., ☎ 0870/870–8808, FAX 01727/844126, WEB www.yha.org.uk). **Youth Hostels Associa-**tion of New Zealand (✉ Level 3, 193 Cashel St., Box 436, Christchurch, ☎ 03/379–9970, FAX 03/365–4476, WEB www.yha.org.nz).

HOTELS

There are a handful of luxury high-rises in the larger cities and in the most popular tourist destinations, but most hotels are smaller establishments that offer more personalized service. Remember that most hotels drop their rates during the rainy season from May through December. Ask about deals when you book.

Assume that hotels reviewed in the book take credit cards unless otherwise noted. All hotels listed have private baths unless otherwise noted.

➤ TOLL-FREE NUMBERS: **Best Western** (☎ 800/528–1234, WEB www.bestwestern.com). **Choice** (☎ 800/424–6423, WEB www.choicehotels.com). **Comfort Inn** (☎ 800/424–6423, WEB www.choicehotels.com). **Hilton** (☎ 800/445–8667, WEB www.hilton.com). **Holiday Inn** (☎ 800/465–4329, WEB www.sixcontinentshotels.com). **Howard Johnson** (☎ 800/654–4656, WEB www.hojo.com). **Inter-Continental** (☎ 800/327–0200, WEB www.intercontinental.com). **Marriott** (☎ 800/228–9290, WEB www.marriott.com). **Quality Inn** (☎ 800/424–6423, WEB www.choicehotels.com). **Radisson** (☎ 800/333–3333, WEB www.radisson.com). **Westin Hotels & Resorts** (☎ 800/228–3000, WEB www.starwood.com/westin).

MAIL AND SHIPPING

Mail from the States or Europe can take two or three weeks to arrive in a Central American country (occasionally it never does). Within these countries, mail service is even less reliable. Outgoing mail is marginally quicker, especially when sent from the capitals. Always use airmail for overseas cards and letters; delivery may take anywhere from five days to two weeks or more. Mail theft is a chronic problem, so do not mail checks, money, or anything else of value.

OVERNIGHT SERVICES

If you need to send important documents, checks, or other valuables, you can use overnight services such as Federal Express and DHL or one of the less expensive airline courier companies.

RECEIVING MAIL

If you need to receive a letter or package while traveling in Central America, you have several options. You can have your mail sent to your hotel or to the local post office by marking it *poste restante* (which means "left mail"). Anyone using an American Express card or traveler's checks can have mail sent to the company's offices offices in major cities.

A better alternative for business letters, particularly those confirming reservations and the like, is the fax machine, which is nearly ubiquitous throughout the region.

MONEY MATTERS

Central America remains a good value for travelers, although costs vary widely depending on your destination and the time of year. Prices throughout this guide are given for adults. Substantially reduced fees are often available for children, students, and senior citizens.

ATMS

You'll find *cajeros automáticos* (automatic teller machines) in many major cities. Some ATMs, especially those in Belize, do not accept foreign cards. Note that PIN numbers longer than four digits might not work at all machines. Remember to **change your PIN number** before you leave, if necessary.

In smaller towns where ATMs are not available, you can often find a bank that will give you a cash advance on your credit card. Since smaller branches have limited hours, be sure to stop in before you run out of money. Larger hotels may also give you a credit card advance; smaller hotels that accept credit cards may add a small amount to your bill and give you the cash.

Although transaction fees may be higher abroad than at home, ATM rates are excellent because they are based on wholesale rates offered only by major banks.

CREDIT CARDS

Major credit cards are accepted at most of the larger hotels and more expensive restaurants throughout Central America. As the phone system improves, many smaller hotels, restaurants, and other facilities are accepting credit cards. Still, **don't count on using plastic**—carry enough cash or traveler's checks when traveling outside of the major cities. Some hotels, restaurants, tour companies, and other businesses will give you a 5%–15% discount if you pay cash.

Throughout this guide, the following abbreviations are used: **AE**, American Express; **DC**, Diners Club; **MC**, MasterCard; and **V**, Visa.

➤ REPORTING LOST CARDS: **American Express** (☎ 336/393–1111 collect to U.S.). **Diners Club** (☎ 303/799–1504 collect to U.S.). **MasterCard** (☎ 0800/011–0184 toll-free; 314/542–7111 collect to the U.S.). **Visa** (☎ 0800/011–0030 toll-free; 410/581–9994 collect to U.S.).

CURRENCY EXCHANGE

It's best to **avoid people who offer to exchange money.** They are notorious for shortchanging tourists unfamiliar with the local currency.

For the most favorable rates, **change money through banks.** You won't do as well at exchange booths in airports or rail and bus stations, in hotels, in restaurants, or in stores. To avoid lines at airport exchange booths, always **get a bit of local currency before you leave home.**

➤ EXCHANGE SERVICES: **International Currency Express** (☎ 888/278–6628 for orders, WEB www.foreignmoney. com). **Thomas Cook Currency Services** (☎ 800/287–7362 for telephone orders and retail locations, WEB www. us.thomascook.com).

TRAVELER'S CHECKS

Do you need traveler's checks? It depends on where you're headed. If you're going to rural areas and small towns, go with cash; traveler's checks are best used in cities. Lost or stolen checks can usually be replaced within 24 hours. To ensure a speedy refund, buy your own traveler's checks—don't let someone else pay for them: irregularities like this can cause delays. The person who bought the checks should make the call to request a refund.

OUTDOORS AND SPORTS

Central America is famous for its water sports. World-class snorkeling and diving are popular off the coast of Belize, while surfing is more common on El Salvador's Pacific side. Equipment for all these activities is generally available for rent on-site, but **check for details at your specific destination** before you pack. Between the coasts, hiking is travelers' favorite pastime—whether up a volcano or through a tropical rain forest. Beyond a pair of hiking boots and some rain gear, no equipment is necessary for these excursions. Be aware that thieves sometimes target tourists who venture off the beaten path. Inexpensive excursions to the most popular destinations are a good way to go, as a local guide usually accompanies you.

PACKING

Make sure to **pack light.** For sightseeing and leisure, casual clothing and good walking shoes are appropriate. For the beach, you'll need lightweight sportswear, a bathing suit, a sun hat, and sunscreen. Travel in the forests requires long-sleeve shirts, long pants, socks, sneakers, a hat, a light waterproof jacket, and plenty of insect repellent. Light colors are best, since mosquitoes avoid them. If you're visiting the highlands or volcanoes, bring a jacket and sweater.

Other useful items include a screw-top water bottle that you can fill with bottled water, a money pouch, a travel flashlight and extra batteries, a Swiss Army knife with a bottle opener, a medical kit, binoculars, and a pocket calculator to help with currency conversions. A sarong or light cotton blanket can have many uses: beach towel, picnic blanket, and cushion for hard seats, among other things. You can never have too many large resealable plastic bags (bring a whole box), which are ideal for storing film, protecting things from rain and damp, quarantining stinky socks, and more.

In your carry-on luggage, **pack an extra pair of eyeglasses or contact lenses and enough of any medication** to last you a few days longer than the entire trip. You may also ask your doctor to write a spare prescription using the drug's generic name, since brand names may vary from country to country. In luggage to be checked, **never pack prescription drugs or valuables.** And don't forget to carry with you the addresses of offices that handle refunds of lost traveler's checks. Check *Fodor's How to Pack* (available in bookstores everywhere) for more tips.

To avoid customs and security delays, carry medications in their original packaging; don't pack any sharp objects, including knives of any size or material, scissors, manicure tools, and corkscrews, or anything else that might arouse suspicion. If you need such objects on your trip, consider shipping them to your destination or buying them there.

CHECKING LUGGAGE

How many carry-on bags you can bring with you to the airline. Most allow two, but not always, so make sure that everything you carry aboard will fit under your seat or in the overhead bin. Get to the gate early, so you can board as soon as possible. Note that if you have a seat at the back of the plane, you'll probably board first, while the overhead bins are still empty.

If you are flying internationally, note that baggage allowances may be determined not by piece but by weight—generally 88 pounds (40 kilograms) in first class, 66 pounds (30 kilograms) in business class, and 44 pounds (20 kilograms) in economy.

Airline liability for baggage is limited to $2,500 per person on flights within the United States. On international flights it amounts to $9.07 per pound or $20 per kilogram for checked baggage (roughly $640 per 70-pound bag) and $400 per passenger for unchecked baggage. You can buy additional coverage at check-in for about $10 per $1,000 of coverage, but it excludes a rather extensive list of items, shown on your airline ticket.

Before departure, **itemize your bags' contents** and their worth, and label the bags with your name, address, and phone number. (If you use your home address, cover it so potential thieves can't see it readily.) Inside each bag, **pack a copy of your itinerary.** At check-in, **make sure that each bag is correctly tagged** with the destination airport's three-letter code. If your bags arrive damaged or fail to arrive at all, file a written report with the airline before leaving the airport.

PASSPORTS AND VISAS

When traveling internationally, **carry your passport** even if you don't need one (it's always the best form of ID) and **make two photocopies of the data page** (one for someone at home and another for you, carried separately from your passport). If you lose your passport, promptly call the nearest embassy or consulate and the local police.

U.S. passport applications for children under age 14 require consent from both parents or legal guardians; both parents must appear together to sign the application. If only one parent appears, he or she must submit a written statement from the other parent authorizing passport issuance for the child. A parent with sole authority must present evidence of it when applying; acceptable documentation includes the child's certified birth certificate listing only the applying parent, a court order specifically permitting this parent's travel with the child, or a death certificate for the nonapplying parent. Application forms and instructions are available on the Web site of the U.S. State Department's Bureau of Consular Affairs (www.travel.state.gov).

PASSPORT OFFICES

The best time to apply for a passport or to renew is in fall and winter. Before any trip, check your passport's expiration date, and, if necessary, renew it as soon as possible.

➤ AUSTRALIAN CITIZENS: **Australian State Passport Office** (☎ 131–232, WEB www.passports.gov.au).

➤ CANADIAN CITIZENS: **Passport Office** (to mail in applications: ✉ Department of Foreign Affairs and International Trade, Ottawa, Ontario K1A 0G3, ☎ 819/994–3500 or 800/567–6868, WEB www.dfait-maeci.gc.ca/passport).

➤ NEW ZEALAND CITIZENS: **New Zealand Passport Office** (☎ 04/474–8100 or 0800/22–5050, WEB www.passports.govt.nz).

➤ U.K. CITIZENS: **London Passport Office** (☎ 0870/521–0410, WEB www.passport.gov.uk) for application

procedures and to request an emergency passport.

➤ U.S. CITIZENS: **National Passport Information Center** (☎ 900/225–5674; calls are 35¢ per minute for automated service, $1.05 per minute for operator service; WEB www.travel.state.gov).

SAFETY

The situation is slowly improving, but crime is still a problem in most Central American cities. (Fortunately, most visitors leave the cities for the natural sights, where theft is less common.) The main concern is pickpocketing or petty theft. Stay on your guard, especially in markets and other crowded areas. **Keep an eye on your backpack or handbag,** since some thieves can slash your bag and remove your belongings without you noticing. **Keep your cash in your pocket** rather than a wallet, which is easier to steal. Never handle money in public. Wherever you go, **don't wear expensive clothing** and **don't wear flashy jewelry.**

WOMEN IN CENTRAL AMERICA

Machismo still holds sway here, and women may be subject to unwanted looks or comments. Catcalls rarely escalate into actual physical harassment—ignoring the remarks generally ends them quickly. Local women tend to dress conservatively, so clothing that makes you stand out—revealing tops, shorts, miniskirts—makes you a more visible target for leers and jeers. If you're traveling to remote areas, it's a good idea to travel in a group. And if you're heading out for the night in a large city, it's wise to take a taxi.

SENIOR-CITIZEN TRAVEL

Many businesses give discounts to senior citizens with either proof of age or American Association of Retired Persons (AARP) discount cards. To qualify for age-related discounts, **mention your senior-citizen status up front** when booking hotel reservations (not when checking out) and before you're seated in restaurants (not when paying the bill). Be sure to have identification on hand. When renting a car, ask about promotional car-rental discounts, which can be cheaper than senior-citizen rates.

➤ EDUCATIONAL PROGRAM: **Elderhostel** (⊠ 11 Ave. de Lafayette, Boston, MA 02111-1746, ☎ 877/426–8056, FAX 877/426–2166, WEB www.elderhostel.org).

SHOPPING

Central American capitals have department stores and shopping malls where you can buy the products you know from home. But the region's main shopping centers are its markets, where rows of stalls feature everything from handwoven textiles to handcrafted pottery. These markets are typically open daily in larger cities, and one or two days a week in more remote villages.

Bargaining is accepted at markets, although it is not an essential part of the transaction as it is in some Middle Eastern countries. Look around the market for similar items to get an idea of an item's value. When you find what you're looking for, follow a few basic rules of etiquette. First, **don't haggle over items you don't intend to buy.** The vendor could be making another sale. Second, **remain polite at all times.** Simply demurring with a gentle "No, gracias" is more likely than a rude comment or an unrealistic counteroffer to lead to a reduced price. You'll be able to bargain prices down to a small extent—perhaps settling on $25 for a $30 sweater, or getting a pair of mittens thrown in for the original $30—but if you're hoping to cut the price in half, you're better off moving on.

STUDENTS IN
CENTRAL AMERICA

Central America is a fantastic place for young people on a budget. Although prices are on the rise, it is still possible to travel on less than $20 a day. With the exception of Costa Rica, there are not that many hostels in the region, but there are many inexpensive hotels. One of the cheapest ways to spend the night is camping. As long as you have your own tent, it's easy to set up camp anywhere. (If it looks like you're near someone's home, it's always a good idea to inquire first.) Central America is popular with backpackers, so you'll have no problem hooking up with other like-minded travelers in major cities or along popular travel routes.

To get good tips and advice on traveling within a budget, chat with other backpackers.

To save money, look into deals available through student-oriented travel agencies and the various other organizations involved in helping out student and budget travelers. Typically, you'll find discounted airfares, rail passes, tours, lodgings, or other travel arrangements, and you don't necessarily have to be a student to qualify.

➤ IDs AND SERVICES: **STA Travel** (☎ 212/627–3111 or 800/781–4040, FAX 212/627–3387, WEB www.sta.com). **Travel Cuts** (⊠ 187 College St., Toronto, Ontario M5T 1P7, Canada, ☎ 416/979–2406 or 888/838–2887, FAX 416/979–8167, WEB www.travelcuts.com).

TELEPHONES

Telecommunication services in Central America are reasonably dependable, notwithstanding the usual quirks (delays, echoes, and strange beeps). Public phones are traditionally clustered in centrally located offices run by telephone companies. Pay phones are fairly common, too. You can also rent cell phones in most Central American cities for use during your trip.

TIME

When the United States is observing standard time between October and April, Panama shares a time zone with New York, while the rest of Central America is one hour behind, sharing a time zone with Chicago. Unlike the United States, however, Central America does not observe daylight saving time, so from April through October, Panama is on the same time as Chicago, while the rest of the region is one hour behind, on the same time as Denver.

TOURS AND PACKAGES

Because everything is prearranged on a prepackaged tour or independent vacation, you spend less time planning—and often get it all at a good price.

BOOKING WITH AN AGENT

Travel agents are excellent resources. But it's a good idea to collect brochures from several agencies as some agents' suggestions may be influenced by relationships with tour and package firms that reward them for volume sales. If you have a special interest, **find an agent with expertise in that area**; the American Society of Travel Agents (ASTA; ☞ Travel Agencies, *below*) has a database of specialists worldwide.

Make sure your travel agent knows the accommodations and other services of the place being recommended. Ask about the hotel's location, room size, beds, and whether it has a pool, room service, or programs for children, if you care about these. Has your agent been there in person or sent others whom you can contact?

Do some homework on your own, too: local tourism boards can provide information about lesser-known and small-niche operators, some of which may sell only direct.

BUYER BEWARE

Each year consumers are stranded or lose their money when tour operators—even large ones with excellent reputations—go out of business. So **check out the operator.** Ask several travel agents about its reputation, and try to **book with a company that has a consumer-protection program.** (Look for information in the company's brochure.) In the United States, members of the National Tour Association and the United States Tour Operators Association are required to set aside funds to cover your payments and travel arrangements in the event that the company defaults. It's also a good idea to choose a company that participates in the American Society of Travel Agents' Tour Operator Program (TOP); ASTA will act as mediator in any disputes between you and your tour operator.

Remember that the more your package or tour includes the better you can predict the ultimate cost of your vacation. Make sure you know exactly what is covered, and **beware of hidden costs.** Are taxes, tips, and transfers included? Entertainment and excursions? These can add up.

➤ TOUR-OPERATOR RECOMMENDATIONS: **American Society of Travel Agents** (☞ Travel Agencies, *below*). **National Tour Association** (NTA; ⊠ 546 E. Main St., Lexington, KY 40508, ☎ 859/226–4444 or 800/682–8886, WEB www.ntaonline.com). **United States Tour Operators Association** (USTOA; ⊠ 275 Madison Ave., Suite 2014, New York, NY 10016, ☎ 212/599–6599 or 800/468–7862, FAX 212/599–6744, WEB www.ustoa.com).

TRAVEL AGENCIES

A good travel agent puts your needs first. Look for an agency that has been in business at least five years, emphasizes customer service, and has someone on staff who specializes in your destination. In addition, **make sure the agency belongs to a professional trade organization.** The American Society of Travel Agents (ASTA)—the largest and most influential in the field with more than 24,000 members in some 140 countries—maintains and enforces a strict code of ethics and will step in to help mediate any agent-client disputes involving ASTA members if necessary. ASTA (whose motto is "Without a travel agent, you're on your own") also maintains a Web site that includes a directory of agents. (If a travel agency is also acting as your tour operator, *see* Buyer Beware *in* Tours and Packages, *above*.)

➤ LOCAL AGENT REFERRALS: **American Society of Travel Agents** (ASTA; ⊠ 1101 King St., Suite 200, Alexandria, VA 22314 ☎ 800/965–2782 24-hr hot line, FAX 703/739–3268, WEB www.astanet.com). **Association of British Travel Agents** (⊠ 68–71 Newman St., London W1T 3AH, U.K., ☎ 020/7637–2444, FAX 020/7637–0713, WEB www.abtanet.com). **Association of Canadian Travel Agents** (⊠ 130 Albert St., Suite 1705, Ottawa, Ontario K1P 5G4, Canada, ☎ 613/237–3657, FAX 613/237–7052, WEB www.acta.ca). **Australian Federation of Travel Agents** (⊠ Level 3, 309 Pitt St., Sydney, NSW 2000, Australia, ☎ 02/9264–3299, FAX 02/9264–1085, WEB www.afta.com.au). **Travel Agents' Association of New Zealand** (⊠ Level 5, Tourism and Travel House, 79 Boulcott St., Box 1888, Wellington 10033, New Zealand 6001, ☎ 04/499–0104, FAX 04/499–0827, WEB www.taanz.org.nz).

VISITOR INFORMATION

➤ U.S. GOVERNMENT ADVISORIES: **U.S. Department of State** (⊠ Overseas Citizens Services Office, Room 4811,

2201 C St. NW, Washington, DC 20520, ☎ 202/647–5225 interactive hot line or 888/407–4747, WEB www.travel.state.gov); enclose a business-size SASE.

VOLUNTEER AND EDUCATIONAL TRAVEL

Volunteer programs typically provide room and board in exchange for labor. Most exact application fees and many require significant contributions or fund-raising commitments to defray program costs. Plan ahead: the best (and cheapest) programs and placements are booked solid up to a year in advance.

Amigos de las Americas runs well-established programs throughout Latin America focused on improving health and education. Volunteers live with families and work in communities for four to eight weeks. Council Travel's International Voluntary Services Department offers two- to four-week environmental or community-service projects in 22 countries around the globe. Participants must be 18 or older. The organization publishes *Volunteer! The Comprehensive Guide to Voluntary Service in the U.S. and Abroad*, which describes nearly 200 organizations around the world that offer volunteer positions. Volunteers for Peace sponsors two- to three-week camps in Africa, Asia, and Central America. Its *International Workcamp Directory* lists more than 800 volunteer opportunities.

Archaeological Fieldwork Opportunities and *Volunteer Vacations* are two books that list volunteer opportunities in Central America.

➤ CONTACTS: **Amigos de las Americas** (✉ 5618 Star La., Houston, TX 77057, ☎ 800/231–7796, WEB www.amigoslink.org). **International Voluntary Services Department** (✉ 205 E. 42nd St., 14th floor, New York, NY 10017, ☎ 212/822–2600, Ext. 2695). **Volunteers for Peace** (✉ 1034 Tiffany Rd., Belmont, VT 05730, ☎ 802/259–2759, FAX 802/259–2922, WEB www.vfp.org).

WEB SITES

Do **check out the World Wide Web** when planning your trip. You'll find everything from weather forecasts to virtual tours of famous cities. Be sure to **visit Fodors.com** (www.fodors.com), a complete travel-planning site. You can research prices and book plane tickets, hotel rooms, rental cars, vacation packages, and more. In addition, you can post your pressing questions in the Travel Talk section. Other planning tools include a currency converter and weather reports, and there are loads of links to travel resources.

WHEN TO GO

CLIMATE

Central Americans divide their year into two seasons: *invierno* (hot and rainy) and *verano* (hot and dry). Invierno, which literally means "winter," takes place during what most of us would consider summer, generally from April to November. The vegetation is at its best during this period. Keep in mind, however, that more than a few roads will be washed out. Some destinations will be unreachable, even with a four-wheel-drive vehicle. Verano, the "summer" season, is more popular among travelers because traveling around the region is much easier. There are correspondingly higher airfares and hotel rates.

Cities at higher altitudes have comfortable weather year-round; some, like Tegucigalpa in Honduras and San José in Costa Rica, are so mild that they are known as cities of "eternal spring." Towns in the mountains are cool during the day and downright chilly at night. Remember that temperatures can vary widely within short distances; one minute you're sweating so much your thighs stick to the vinyl bus seat, while the next you're making a mad scramble for a sweater.

➤ FORECASTS: **Weather Channel Connection** (☎ 900/932–8437), 95¢ per minute from a Touch-Tone phone.

1 DESTINATION: CENTRAL AMERICA

A Study in Contrasts

What's Where

Pleasures and Pastimes

Fodor's Choice

A STUDY IN CONTRASTS

F THE FIRST IMAGE that comes to mind when you think of travel in Central America is of scruffy students with duffel bags slung over their shoulders pitching tents in tropical jungles, think again. This destination isn't just for backpackers anymore.

True, Central America offers unequaled opportunities for the adventurous visitor, but enjoying the region's natural wonders doesn't necessarily mean sacrificing your creature comforts. In Guatemala, you can spend an afternoon hiking up the imposing Volcán Pacayá, peering into pools of boiling lava from the narrow rim, then pamper yourself that evening with a mug of rich coffee before a crackling fireplace in one of nearby Antigua's luxurious hotels. In Costa Rica, you can grab your binoculars at the crack of dawn to go bird-watching in the Monteverde Cloud Forest Biological Reserve and still have time to kick up your heels at midnight in one of downtown San Jose's chic discos. In Panama, you can run the rapids on a white-water rafting weekend in Chiriquí and then recuperate during the week while sampling nouvelle cuisine at Panama City's finer restaurants. You could even skip the "adventure" altogether and enjoy a cozy holiday relaxing on sandy beaches on the coast of Belize or shopping for handmade baskets in western Honduras.

This was not always the case. Until recently, a rather tiny pool of backpackers, scuba divers, and anthropology buffs were likely to choose Central America as a vacation destination. These savvy travelers found they could explore ancient relics, traverse tropical rain forests, snorkel through magnificent coral reefs, or surf the Pacific's waves—and come away with an experience unspoiled by the crowds and high prices common in more developed tourist destinations. Central America has long been the Western Hemisphere's best-kept travel secret. But as travelers started coming to the region in larger numbers—the number of tourists visiting the region rose 69% between 1994 and 1999—these seven tiny countries began to diversify their tourism offerings. Central America still beckons ecotourists, budget travelers, and those in search of a more outdoorsy vacation—but now it also offers a unique getaway to people whose idea of a good time has nothing to do with "roughing it."

The biggest reason Central America hasn't been an obvious choice among travelers for long, despite its exceptional natural beauty and rich cultural heritages, is that the most of the region has been plagued by a volatile political legacy. In the early 1960s, Central America was thrust into a grisly descent of revolutionary violence. Caught up in a complex web of growing poverty, rapid urbanization, foreign manipulation, and wicked dictatorships, Central America grabbed headlines throughout the world. Throughout the 1970s and 1980s, the situation was consistently dangerous in Nicaragua, El Salvador, and Guatemala, and incipiently volatile in Honduras and Panama. Costa Rica was the only secure country because a stable democracy and equitable economy had permitted it to dismantle its army in 1948. Belize was spared the kind of political corruption visited upon other nations, but it too was affected by political unrest when refugees—particularly from Guatemala—fled there when violent spasms gripped their homelands.

But in the 1990s a gentler wind finally blew across the region. The transformation from guerrilla warfare to political dialogue, which in the mid 1990s gave Central America a desperately needed break from the violence, has since brought about democratic elections, plans for land redistribution, and some acknowledgment of human rights abuses in those volatile countries—reconstruction *de cabo a rabo* (from head to toe).

Given these signs of progress, it seemed a cruel joke when in late October 1998, Hurricane Mitch, the region's most devastating hurricane in two centuries, struck the coast. Severe flooding and mud slides quickly covered most of Honduras and much of Nicaragua, washing away homes, infrastructure, 70% of crops, and hopes for political recovery. More than 15,000 people were killed, and millions more were left homeless. An international aid response included the scaling back of debts owed by Honduras and Nicaragua to Austria and Cuba, for example, and millions of dollars were donated by Sweden, Spain, the United States, and others. Parts of Guatemala, Belize, and El Salvador were also affected, but for Honduras and Nicaragua, the storm created long-term problems influencing nearly every aspect of life.

Natural disasters continue to take their toll on the region. A massive earthquake rocked El Salvador in January 2001, leaving more than 1 million people homeless and 1,000 people dead. Some of the country's oldest buildings were also destroyed. Just nine months later, Hurricane Iris struck Belize, destroying villages along the Placencia Peninsula and killing dozens. Although storms and tremors can wreak havoc wherever they strike, in Central America they can wipe out entire towns and disrupt the whole continent's economy.

It's fair to say that much of Central America will continue to feel the crippling effects of economic instability well into the 21st century, and that poverty is still a pervasive problem. Yet you will not find a defeated people. Life does not only go on, it positively vibrates with humor and vitality. The tourist is welcomed with a friendly, if somewhat shy kind of curiosity. Well, the local thinking goes, things must be getting better if the gringos are coming here on vacation.

But increased tourism is in some ways a mixed blessing for Central America. As a traveler it's important to recognize the influence you exert, particularly in developing countries. Although tourism injects much-needed hard currency into the coffers of struggling nations, a sudden influx of cash can upset fragile economies, introducing greed and resentment where there was once harmony and interdependence. Tourists, with all their glittering toys and wealth, can alter locals' self-perceptions and accentuate the division between those who have and those who don't. Be a responsible tourist: Respect local customs and be deferent to locals' sensibilities. Walk lightly, with a sense of humility, and try not to disturb the cultures and landscapes that brought you to Central America in the first place.

History and Culture

The history of Central America is built on a tumultuous foundation. The statues of Spanish conquistadors that adorn plazas throughout the continent serve as constant reminders of the roots of Central America's "civilization." An abundance of silver, gold, indigo, and other resources was Central America's curse. Spanish fortune seekers began colonization in the early 1500s. Textbooks will tell you that independence was reinstated some 300 years later, but U.S. intervention soon became its functional equivalent. William Walker, the persistent invader from the United States, was only the most outlandish in a subsequent parade of unsavory American characters who sought to transform Central America into their own personal Land of Opportunity.

American corporations linked the fate of much of Central America to a certain yellow, oblong fruit—Honduras, after all, was the original "banana republic." Foreign interests, such as the United Fruit Company, laid claim to the provinces and enlisted locals to build their empire. Today, the banana companies wield far less political power and contribute far less to the local economies, rendering the region increasingly dependent upon other sources of revenue, like tourism. Another source of income is logging—legal and otherwise. According to an international conservation organization called the Rainforest Action Network, more than 95% of Central America's 523,000 square km (202,000 square mi) was once covered in tropical forests. Today forests cover only about a tenth of the land, and 3,300 square km (1,274 square mi) more are destroyed each year. Needless to say, logging is a particularly contentious issue locally and internationally, as immediate economic necessities are pitted against the long-term effects of compromising the world's rain forests and the millions of plant and animal species that depend upon them. Governments, slowly realizing that an acre of intact forest has more benefit in the long run than one that has been cut down for timber or cleared for farming, have begun passing laws to protect some of the remaining forests. Often, however, the laws lack teeth, and trees are constantly being felled even in areas designated as national parks.

Religion plays a prominent role in the cultural blueprint of Central America. Catholicism is still the largest social institution, and the church has long held sway over the daily lives of the Central American faithful. (When the Spanish arrived in a community, a central cathedral—constructed by the indigenous people themselves—was always the first building erected.) In a world where you must improvise daily to feed your family (and where, at one time, family members could suddenly be made to "disappear" by a clandestine military faction), the church is a necessary source of stability and spiritual sustenance. The regimen, the rules, and the promise of a better life after death bring structure to a region that until recently has been lacking in just that. Not that the native religions have been totally lost. For example, many people living on the Bay Islands of Honduras still attend the torch-lit ceremonies of Caribbean religions, while Guatemala's Tzutuhil people still make daily offerings to ancient Maya gods. And in many communities, religious leaders look the other way as their congregations incorporate ancient rituals into Catholicism.

If you exercise healthy amounts of patience and sensitivity, you might have the privilege of discussing Central America's intriguing recent history with those who have experienced it. Few life experiences can compare to knowing the people, understanding why passion for their homeland runs so deep, and sharing their pain resulting from years of enduring warfare, commercial oppression, and slavery. Taking this all into consideration, an appreciation of their unparalleled enthusiasm and genuine respect for life itself is enough to monumentally shake your world view.

–Wayne Hoffman

WHAT'S WHERE

All together, Central America is only the size of Arizona and Utah combined. But each of its seven countries has a distinct identity, with its own culture, traditions, and flavor. The land itself—an isthmus fusing North and South America—contains far more than the beaches and rain forests that most people imagine. The sun beats down over lowland fields of sugarcane and cotton that seem to expand, then melt away in the wavy, dreamlike heat. In the highlands, the invigorating mountain air provides a respite from the taxing climate. The fertile volcanic soils of these looming peaks yield most of the region's material wealth. Evanescent clouds hover over the agricultural patchwork, lending an opaque, mystical twist. On a clear day, climb high enough and you may be treated to a view of both the Caribbean Sea and the Pacific Ocean, a sight so stimulating it leaves your knees weak.

Belize

Wedged between Guatemala and the Yucatán Peninsula, Belize is a sliver of land along the Caribbean Sea. Along its 278-km (174-mi) coastline coast are 175 cayes, some no larger than a tennis court. In the Maya Mountains—the central highlands that form the watershed for Belize's thousands of streams and rivers—there is dense rain forest; in the north, savannas and fields of sugarcane. Because it has the lowest population density of any Central American nation—El Salvador, though far smaller, has 10 times the population—most of this green interior is still the province of scarlet macaws, tapirs, kinkajous, pumas, and howler monkeys. Even reduced to vapid statistics—300 species of birds, 250 varieties of orchids, dozens of kinds of butterflies—the sheer variety of Belize's wildlife is breathtaking. The same goes for its nearly 600 Maya ruins, which range from the metropolitan splendor of Caracol to the humble burial mounds sprinkled throughout the countryside.

Guatemala

Belize may have the beaches, but Guatemala has just about everything else—misty cloud forests, tremendous mountains ranges, smoldering volcanoes, and rain forests of massive mahogany trees draped with mosses, bromeliads, and rare orchids. In the highlands around Lake Atitlán are sleepy villages that come to life each week with vibrant markets. Here you'll find Antigua, the colonial capital filled with quaint cobblestone streets, crumbling monasteries, and the country's finest restaurants and hotels. Take a white-water rafting trip to the Pacific coast, or go bathing in the Atlantic Lowlands. Water sports are popular on the Atlantic coast, which spices things up with its distinctive

Caribbean flavor. Everywhere are traces of the Maya, especially in El Petén, where the stately pyramids of Tikal rise from the steamy jungle.

El Salvador

Only 200 km (124 mi) from end to end, El Salvador is the smallest country in Central America—but it is also the most densely populated. This relative crowding is most apparent in the centrally located capital city, but respite is available only a short distance away in any direction. A quick drive from San Salvador, two beautiful lakes—Lago de Coatepeque to the west and Lago de Ilopango to the east—lure visitors with swimming, boating, and scuba diving. Farther east stretches a mountain chain where volcanic pools, hot springs, and some serious off-the-beaten-path hiking await. The rugged grandeur of the thinly populated northwest is home to the beautiful Montecristo cloud forest and the stunning Lago de Güija. The Pacific coast is a long and relaxing string of good beaches ranging from the surfing mecca of La Libertad to the quaint fishing village of Las Playitas.

Honduras

Once dubbed the "Athens of Central America," the ancient Maya city of Copán lies in the western jungles of Honduras, where its soaring pyramids are today guarded by a team of scarlet parrots. But all of this country's attractions are not historical. Populated by the Garífuna people, the northern coast has a distinctly Caribbean flavor. Towns like La Cieba are sleepy during the day, but come awake at night with music and dancing. Not far from shore are the Bay Islands, surrounded by pristine coral reefs that are a scuba diver's dream. Mountainous central Honduras has national parks and reserves that are well worth the effort it takes to reach them. In the undisturbed lowland forests you might see a jaguar or a tapir, while in the highland cloud forests you can still spot the holy grail of bird-watchers, the emerald-plumed quetzal.

Nicaragua

No one lists Managua, arguably the world's most peculiar capital, as their favorite place in Nicaragua, but it's easy to get from the city to the country's more compelling spots. Only one hour away, the Pacific Ocean laps at miles of desolate, unspoiled beaches. Even closer are the colonial towns of León, an hour north, and Granada, which borders Lago Nicaragua, with its islands, large and small. The largest and most spectacular is Isla de Ometepe, a volcanic island perfectly suited for hiking, wildlife spotting, and investigating the pre-Columbian stone carvings. Also near Granda is Volcán Mombacho Natural Reserve, a gorgeous cloud forest. The north-central region's pleasant climate, soaring mountains, and coffee farms around Matagalpa and Jinotega fuse to create the ideal environment for hiking. Off the Caribbean coast, on the laid-back Corn Islands, you'll find Creole and indigenous Miskito fisherman to be your only companions.

Costa Rica

The variety of Costa Rica's landscape belies its compact size. The Pacific coast contains a beach to satisfy everyone from nature lovers (Manuel Antonio) to party animals (Quepos). On the more remote Caribbean coast, you'll find smaller crowds and opportunities for snorkeling and sportfishing. Between the shores you'll find a variety of stunning locales. The rain forests in the north provide an ideal spot for a morning spent bird-watching as a colorful kaleidoscope of birds—scarlet-rumped tanagers and yellow-billed toucans, bright blue honeycreepers and great white egrets—floats before your eyes. (With 25% of its land set aside as nature reserves and national parks, Costa Rica is home to more species of birds than the United States and Canada combined.) A visit to the cool, damp Monteverde Cloud Forest after dark reveals creatures less flamboyant but no less intriguing, from frogs the size of your fingernail to tarantulas the size of your fist. If you want to stretch your legs, you can climb Volcán Arenal, which still shoots lava into the air on a regular basis; or, if you'd prefer to relax, you can soak in the hot springs at the volcano's base and watch the fireworks against the night sky.

Panama

Of course, the defining feature in Panama's landscape is the canal—one of the world's greatest engineering marvels, and well worth a visit. But there's more to this narrow isthmus than that all-important waterway. In fact, some of the world's most accessible rain forests line the canal itself, reachable in minutes from Panama City. Farther east, the Darién Gap offers one of the region's most pristine jungles. Tropical beaches and coral reefs line the Caribbean coast, while the sedate villages along the shores of the Azuero Peninsula in the south offer sunbathing and surfing in relative seclusion. The western part of the country has cool mountains cut through by raging rivers, ideal for rafting enthusiasts who want to ride the rapids.

PLEASURES AND PASTIMES

Exploring Nature

Central America's national parks and nature reserves are the region's most astounding tourist attraction. Whether you're exploring the Jungle Trail through Honduras or taking a canopy tour above a Costa Rican cloud forest, you're sure to spot a dazzling array of wildlife, from elusive sloths to sociable capuchin monkeys, endangered jaguarundis to omnipresent coatis. Hikers can check out a waterfall in southwestern Nicaragua, or a cave in western Honduras. Climbers can tackle the mountains of El Salvador or the volcanoes of Guatemala. Don't think you're a nature lover? Central America will change your tune.

Getting Wet

Blessed with two extensive coastlines, Central America offers a wealth of options for anyone who wants to make a big splash. On the Caribbean side, the Barrier Reef—the Western Hemisphere's longest reef system—runs from Belize to Honduras. The diving is spectacular around Belize's Turneffe Island and Lighthouse Reef. Here you'll find the famous Blue Hole; first dived by Jacques Cousteau in 1970, this breathtaking vertical chute has become something of a pilgrimage site for divers from all over the world. Snorkelers will want to head to Belize's Hol Chan Marine Reserve and Shark-Ray Alley—you'll be amazed at what you can see without a tank. For serious anglers, Belize and Costa Rica have world-class sportfishing. Diving lessons are one of the big draws at the Bay Islands of Honduras, where you can swim alongside friendly dolphins once you master your technique. On the Pacific coast, surfers can maneuver the swells near Jacó in Costa Rica or check out the perfect right-hand break at El Salvador's Punta Roca. Even if you never see the Pacific or the Caribbean, there are other ways to make waves in Central America. Take a ferry to isolated Isla de Ometepe in the middle of Lago de Nicaragua, or spend a day watching the astounding cloud formations above Guatemala's Lago Atitlán. Traverse the Panama Canal on a ship, or hop in a raft and ride the white waters of Río Cangrejal in Honduras. Just bring a towel.

Taking It Easy

One of travelers' favorite things to do in Central America is nothing at all. Stretch out on a ribbon of sand in the remote Honduran village of Limón or Panama's Bocas del Toro. Take the time to sit in the shaded plazas in the center of colonial-era towns like Granada in Nicaragua or Antigua in Guatemala, where the sounds of cathedral bells fill the air. Soak in the volcanic thermal pools at Tabacón in Costa Rica, or spend an afternoon making tiny new friends at one of Belize's butterfly farms. Whatever you decide to do, take a break to enjoy a siesta outdoors, catching warm tropical breezes from the comfort of a hammock—you'll finally understand what the word "vacation" truly means.

Uncovering the Past

The ancient Maya empire, which once occupied much of present-day Guatemala and stretched north into Mexico, east into Belize, and south into Honduras and El Salvador, disintegrated in the middle of the 16th century, leaving one of the richest cultural and archaeological legacies in the world. Only a fraction of the thousands of Maya ruins have been excavated from the jungle that over the centuries has swallowed the once-splendid cities. Tikal in Guatemala is majestic, its spectacular temples towering above the pristine rain forest; a visit to the top of Temple IV at sunrise is an unforgettable experience. Copán in Honduras contains a treasure trove of Maya sculptures, with an impressive museum that explains their cultural significance. The historical impact of Spanish colonialism is evident across the region, in the grand cathedrals of León in Nicaragua or the baroque facades of Panama City's Casco Viejo. You can even visit Trujillo, the spot in Honduras where explorer

Christopher Columbus first set foot on the American mainland.

FODOR'S CHOICE

Dining

Belize

Capricorn, Ambergris Caye. You'll have to take a water taxi to this romantic seaside eatery, but the excellent seafood makes it worth the trip. *$$$*

Smoky Mermaid, Belize City. This oasis of flowering plants is set in the garden courtyard of the Great House, an old colonial inn in Belize City. This is Belize at its most sophisticated. *$$$*

Elvi's Kitchen, Ambergris Caye. Massive mahogany doors lead you into this seaside favorite. The banner states that this is DI PLACE FOR SEAFOOD, and we cannot but agree. *$$*

Guatemala

Jake's, Guatemala City. The best wine list in Central America is the biggest draw at this Guatemala City restaurant. Twenty-five daily specials augment the excellent international menu featuring such creative dishes as smoked chicken tortellini. *$$$*

Welten, Antigua. The handmade pasta, topped with inspired sauces and organic vegetables, couldn't be more satisfying. Enjoy your meal on the plant-filled patio, where orchids cascade from above. *$$$*

El Bistro, Panajachel. Hummingbirds dart among flowering vines at this romantic eatery on the shores of Lake Atitlán. Enjoy homemade Italian pastas in the lovely garden. *$$*

Las Puertas, Flores. Six sets of swinging doors give Las Puertas its name. Fresh ingredients for the sandwiches and just-picked fruit for the smoothies give this popular spot its lasting appeal. *$*

El Salvador

Cuattro Gatti, San Salvador. Even the simplest of dishes, such as spaghetti with shrimp, is handled with grace at this Italian eatery in the Zona Rosa. It's superb from *antipasti* to *dolci*. *$$$–$$$$*

Alo Nuestro, San Salvador. Hands down the country's best restaurant, Alo Nuestro makes magic from the finest local ingredients. It forges a new standard for contemporary Salvadoran cuisine. *$$–$$$$*

Ultima Alucinación, San Salvador. A score of delicate savory and sweet crepes highlight the menu at this French-Belgian eatery found in the chef's living room. There's also a bar where you can select from among a dozen Belgian brews. *$$–$$$$*

Honduras

Casa María, Tegucigalpa. Don't ask to have the recipes for *camarones María* or any of the other specialities at this genteel restaurant. Passed down for generations, they are guarded zealously by the family. *$$*

Theo's, Tegucigalpa. Forget the tapas—this romantic restaurant in Colonia Palmira serves up rich and complex Spanish cuisine. Don't pass up the heady seafood stew called *zarzuela de mariscos*. *$$*

César Mariscos, Tela. If you like seafood, it doesn't get any fresher than at this eatery on the Caribbean. Try the catch of the day as it comes hot off the grill, or try the shellfish in one of the delicious seafood soups. *$–$$*

Nicaragua

La Marseillaise, Managua. An elegant French restaurant and art gallery have shared this house in Los Robles since the days of revolution. The menu reveals seafood specialties and a full selection of French, Spanish, Italian, and Chilean wines. *$$$–$$$$*

Mediterráneo, Granada. Candlelit tables arranged around an interior garden and quietly flowing fountains make this a local favorite. Serving the finest Spanish fare, the restaurant is known for its exceptional paella. *$$–$$$*

Costa Rica

Ambrosia, San José. Just a short drive from downtown, this eclectic restaurant has long been popular among local epicureans thanks to its inventive cuisine. *$$$*

The Garden, Puerto Viejo de Talamanca. Chef Vera Mabon's Indian-Canadian-Trinidadian background inspires this eatery's sophisticated Costa Rican fusion cooking. *$$–$$$*

Lazy Wave Food Company, Tamarindo. For serious global cuisine at laughable prices, you can't go wrong here for lunch or dinner. *$$*

Panama

Mar del Sur, David. If there were no other reason to visit David, this restaurant's Peruvian-style entrées, like *picante de langostinos* (prawns in a spicy cream sauce) would still draw crowds. *$$–$$$*

El Trapiche, Panama City. Freshly prepared Panamanian dishes are served in generous portions at this sweet indoor–outdoor restaurant in El Cangrejo. *$–$$*

Historical Sites

Belize

Actun Tunichil Muknal, Belize. Some of country's most interesting Maya sites are underground, as is this cavern on Roaring Creek near Belmopan. "The Cave of the Stone Sepulcher" holds remarkable artifacts and well-preserved skeletons of human sacrifices.

Caracol, Belize. The most spectacular Maya site in Belize, Caracol had five plazas and 32 large structures covering nearly a square mile. As many as 200,000 people are believed to have lived here.

Lamanai, Belize. Nearly 60 Maya structures are spread over this 950-acre reserve, including a massive temple that is the largest Preclassic building in the country.

Guatemala

Quiriguá, Guatemala. This important erstwhile trading center is renowned for its massive stelae, the largest in the Maya world.

Tikal, Guatemala. Guatemala's most famous ruin is the best embodiment of the extraordinary accomplishments of the Maya. This vast array of awesome temples was once a teeming metropolis.

El Salvador

Parque Libertad, Santa Ana. Surrounding the main square in El Salvador's second-largest city are the country's best-preserved colonial buildings, including a city hall, a cathedral, and a sumptuous national palace. It's a taste of bygone elegance.

San Andrés. One of El Salvador's largest archaeological sites, San Andrés is a Maya community that was inhabited between AD 600 and AD 900, about the same time as Tikal in Guatemala and Copán in Honduras.

Honduras

Copán, Western Highlands. There are many astounding archaeological sites in Central America, but none with stone carvings as well preserved as at this ancient Maya city. Most intriguing is the squat altar that shows a long line of Copán's rulers passing power down to their heirs.

Galería Nacional de Arte, Tegucigalpa. Housed in a former convent, the National Art Gallery dazzles visitors with an extensive collection of pre-Columbian treasures, including some wonderful pieces from Copán.

Museo de Antropología, Comayagua. This elegant old building served as the presidential palace during the early days of Honduras. Today it features the world's most complete exhibition of Lenca culture. There's also a splendid display of jade.

Nicaragua

Iglesia de San Francisco, Granada. Services are still held in this church dating to 1529. The old convent, now a museum, has stunningly carved stone artifacts dating from around AD 800, found on islands in Lago de Nicaragua.

Isla de Ometepe, Lago de Nicaragua. When he visited in 1866, Mark Twain described this pair of volcanoes rising from Lago de Nicaragua as "isolated from the world and its noise." Take him at his word, and board a boat for a trip among archaeological ruins and virgin forests.

Costa Rica

Monumento Nacional Guayabo, Turrialba. Once home to more than 20,000 people, this ancient city was abandoned in the 15th century. It lay undiscovered until 1968.

Panama

Museo Antropológico Reina Torres de Arauz, Panama City. Housed in an old train station, this museum holds an amazing array of artifacts dating back thousands of years and spanning numerous cultures. Look for the painted ceramics from before the Spanish conquest.

Panama Canal. Finished in 1914, this engineering marvel connecting the Pacific Ocean and the Caribbean is rich in history. Plenty of tours cover the nearby sights, from the 16th-century Spanish settlement of Casco Viejo to the 20th-century zone inhabited by the tens of thousands who built the magnificent canal.

Plaza de Francia and Las Bovedas, Panama City. The plaza at the end of the Casco Viejo peninsula is dedicated to the Frenchmen who perished while trying to build the canal in the 19th century. The square is also the site of the infamous dungeons, Las Bovedas, in use until the early 20th century.

Lodging

Belize

Hamanasi, Hopkins Village. Most dive resorts pay little attention to the accommodations. This one has stylish suites, a beautiful pool, and, as mascots, cats that came from Moscow. The diving isn't bad, either. $$$–$$$$

Inn at Robert's Grove, Seine Bight Area. The terrific food—mostly tropical takes on Continental dishes—and the attention to every detail mean that this lodging on the coast near Placencia won't be a secret for long. $$$–$$$$

Chan Chich Lodge, Gallon Jug. Built atop the plaza of a Maya temple, this lodge is one of the most scenic in Central America. It's so close to nature that your neighbors are howler monkeys and toucans, and so safe that your cabaña door doesn't have a lock. $$$

The Lodge at Chaa Creek, The Cayo. A mixture of the seclusion of the jungle and the conviviality of candlelit dinners make Chaa Creek the queen of the jungle resorts. Add to this impeccable service, delicious food, and a decadent spa. $$$

Guatemala

Ni'tun Ecolodge, San Andrés. Hidden in the forest on the shores of Lago Petén Itzá is this cluster of thatch-roof cabins. Culinary considerations are brought to the forefront, so you won't miss out on wonderful meals. $$$$

Posada del Ángel, Antigua. This truly angelic inn, set around a sparkling blue pool, may be the most charming lodging in Central America. The rooms are spacious and luxurious, with lovely corner fireplaces to keep out the chill. $$$$

Hotel La Posada, Cobán. You won't be able to resist the lovely café on the porch of this simple colonial inn off Cobán's main square. Nap in one of hammocks swing-

ing in the breeze, or retreat to your tastefully decorated room with exposed hardwood beams and fireplace. $$

Posada de Santiago, Santiago Atitlán. Sandwiched between two volcanoes on the shores of a lagoon, this hotel brings you every modern convenience while preserving the traditional Indian-village environment. $$

El Salvador

Hotel Princess Zona Rosa, San Salvador. This European-style hotel surrounds you with elegance, from the beautiful tapestries to the rich carpets. It has unparalleled views of Volcán San Salvador in the distance. $$$$

Hotel Vista Marella, San Salvador. With architectural flourishes that call to mind the colonial period, this charming bed-and-breakfast makes you feel as if you have a place of your own in Central America. Have breakfast in the cheery courtyard. $$

La Posada de Suchitoto, Suchitoto. Four villas at this colonial-era hacienda have spectacular views of Lago de Coatepeque. Wander around the fine gardens and enjoy the peaceful surroundings. $$

Honduras

Anthony's Key Resort, Roatán. On a private island, this cluster of bungalows is the most comfortable place to stay in the Bay Islands. Take a water taxi to the main building, where you can go diving or enjoy a dolphin show. $$$$

The Lodge at Pico Bonito, La Ceiba. In the shadow of Pico Bonito, this luxurious lodge is steps away from a rain forest filled with waterfalls that plummet into crystal-clear pools. You won't be able to resist diving in. $$$$

Portal del Ángel, Tegucigalpa. The family that runs the capital's most elegant inn goes out of its way to make you feel right at home. The cozy rooms call to mind the country's heritage with displays of hand-hewn pottery. $$$$

Hacienda San Lucas, Copán Ruinas. The little details, from the carefully crafted wood furniture in the simple but elegant rooms to the hammocks swinging from the porches outside, make this one of the country's most charming lodgings. $

Nicaragua

Selva Negra Mountain Resort, Matagalpa. The Black Forest, on a working coffee farm, is the country's most famous hotel. The luxurious bungalows have private porches with spectacular views. *$–$$$*

Hotel Los Robles, Managua. Evocative of a colonial-era convent, this hotel has walkways arranged around a tropical garden. Modern rooms have wrought-iron furnishings, proffering a dignified elegance unmatched in Managua. *$$*

Hotel Alhambra, Granada. The second-story rooms overlooking shady Parque Colón are simply wonderful. So is people-watching from a cane-back chair on the restaurant's breezy porch. *$–$$*

Costa Rica

Lapa Ríos, Cabo Matapalo. Perched on a ridge in a private rain forest reserve, this small hotel brings you close to nature without skimping on the amenities. Rooms overlook the surrounding jungle and the ocean beyond. *$$$$*

Villa Caletas, Tárcoles. Each of these bungalows perched on a promontory seems to enjoy a better view than the last. From the open-air restaurant you can spot Puntarenas in the distance. *$$$$*

Xandari, Alajuela. Whether you fix your vision on the clever design of the spacious villas or just watch birds and butterflies flit through the surrounding tropical gardens, it's hard not to be enchanted by this unique inn and spa. *$$$$*

Hotel Giada, Sámara. Giada, which means jade, is truly an Italian gem. The Mediterranean look, feel, and fare—when combined with the tropical garden surroundings—make this artful little hotel peerless. *$$*

Panama

Caesar Park, Panama City. Cuba's Fidel Castro and Spain's King Juan Carlos have stayed here, but you don't need to run a country to experience the same level of service. This hotel in the Westin chain has four exceptional restaurants. If you're here for business, watching TV in the sauna counts as staying on top of your game. *$$$$*

Canopy Tower Ecolodge, Parque Nacional Chagres. Is that a giant soccer ball? No, it's actually a funky lodge built above the rain forest in an abandoned radar tower.

A deck on top has outstanding views of the Panama Canal. *$$$$*

Los Establos, Boquete. True to its name, this small inn started out as a horse stable. With stirring views of the cloud-capped volcano, the light-filled rooms cater to a very different class of lodger in search of, say, lovely rattan furniture and animal-skin rugs. *$$$$*

Punta Caracol Acqua Lodge, Bocas del Toro. Balancing tip-top service and a nature-friendly philosophy, these two-story cabañas at Isla Colón are built on stilts over the ocean. They are accessible only by boat, meaning this is a very private getaway. *$$$$*

Outdoor Activities

Belize

Dive by moonlight, Hol Chan Marine Reserve. If you're a strong swimmer, this is a special treat. Nocturnal animals, including long-legged spider crabs, casually go about their business in water that sparkles with bioluminescence.

Explore a secluded lagoon, Lamanai. This secluded jungle paradise wrapping around a romantic lagoon is the perfect place to greet the dawn. Nearby Maya ruins beckon to be explored.

Guatemala

Look for dolphins, Río Dulce. You will probably only get to see these magical mammals from a canoe, but the paddling will be well worth it as you float quietly between banks of jungle foliage, with egrets and iguanas perched overhead.

See sunrise atop a temple, Tikal. Imagine that you're Maya royalty—or an intrepid archaeologist—as the emerging rays wake the jungle into its noisy daily activity.

Soak in the clear pools, Semuc Champey. Here the beautiful white water of the Río Cahabón momentarily comes to a pause at a land bridge: the universe's intention it seems, is serene soaking for the weary traveler.

El Salvador

Hike up volcanoes, Santa Ana. El Salvador's string of volcanoes is irresistible for those who love the great outdoors. Near Santa Ana you'll encounter two of the country's most formidable peaks, Volcán Santa Ana and Volcán Izalco.

Meander through misty mountains, Parque Nacional Montecristo. The trails winding through this cloud forest reserve bring you past some remarkable plants, from towering ferns to delicate orchids.

Honduras

Discover a deserted island, The Bay Islands. To really get away from it all, here you'll find dozens of palm-covered islands where you won't see another soul.

Find your feathered friends, Parque Nacional Pico Bonito. More than 275 species of birds—from long-tailed manakins to red-legged honeycreepers—have been spotted in this stretch of virgin rain forest.

Nicaragua

Descend into a dormant volcano, Granada. A unique cloud-forest reserve surrounds the verdant crater of Volcán Mombacho. Here you can spot more than 80 varieties of orchids and over 100 species of birds—some of which exist nowhere else.

Wander through open-air markets, Masaya. The country's center for handicrafts has two markets, both good places to haggle for leather goods, hammocks, pottery, and paintings in the style first developed in the Solentiname Archipelago.

Costa Rica

Meet a macaw, Corcovado National Park. If you already own a few field guides, you have probably planned your trip with our feathered friends in mind. If not, borrow some binoculars and get up at dawn—you won't regret your search for a keel-billed toucan or red-rump tanager.

Soak your troubles away, Tabacón. From these gorgeously landscaped hot springs you can take in magnificent views of rumbling Volcán Arenal.

Swing through the trees, Monteverde. Do as the monkeys do on a canopy tour. With mountain-climbing gear fastening you in, you'll have a perspective of the rain forest from the top down.

Panama

Beat the heat, Volcán Barú National Park, Boquete. In Panama's cool highland area are cloud forests with resplendent quetzals encircling the base of a magnificent volcano.

Ride the rapids, Chiriquí. Río Chiriquí can get downright challenging for white-water rafters during the rainy season, while its cousin, Río Viejo, is a consistently invigorating ride. Both will get your adrenaline flowing—and without the crowds you'd find in Costa Rica.

Submerge yourself, Bocas del Toro. The seemingly endless reefs in this vast lagoon have an array of marine life that ranges from lugubrious sea turtles to hyperactive tropical fish.

2 BELIZE

Most visitors to this tiny country head out to the cayes and atolls that dot the Caribbean Sea, lying on the brilliant white beaches or discovering the colorful coral that begins just a few feet from shore. But Belize has much more to offer—hundreds of Maya ruins, ranging from ancient cities to humble individual dwellings, make this a magical place. Nowhere else can dedicated divers and archaeology addicts find as much to invigorate their spirits.

By Lan Sluder
and Simon
Worrall

Updated by
Lan Sluder

ASLIVER OF LAND wedged between Guatemala and the Caribbean Sea, Belize is only 109 km (68 mi) wide at its broadest point. But don't let its diminutive size fool you. Within its borders Belize probably has the greatest variety of flora and fauna of any country of its size in the world.

In the Maya Mountains, the central highlands that form the watershed for thousands of streams and rivers, there is dense rain forest; in the north there are savannas and vast fields of sugarcane. Because Belize has the lowest population density of any country in Central America—El Salvador, the only smaller country, has 10 times as many people—and because Belizeans are by temperament and tradition town dwellers, most of the interior remains uninhabited.

Less than an hour's flight from the mainland is the Barrier Reef, a great wall of coral stretching the entire length of the coast. Dotting the reef like punctuation marks are hundreds of cayes, and farther out to sea are three coral atolls—all superb for diving and snorkeling. Some of the cayes are no more than Robinson Crusoe islets of white coral sand and mangroves, inhabited by frigate birds, pelicans, and the occasional fisherman, who will spend a few days diving for conch and lobster, sleeping under a sheet of canvas strung between two trees. Others, like Ambergris Caye, are becoming increasingly popular, and with the crowds comes an ample supply of bars, restaurants, and inns.

In many ways a landlocked island, Belize has more in common with Trinidad or St. Kitts than with Guatemala or El Salvador. English, the official language here, aligns the nation with the British Caribbean ("tea" here refers to just about any meal, for example, as it does in the West Indies and cockney London). Only in a few aspects is Belize like its Central American neighbors: Spanish is widely spoken in the north and west, while Maya dialects are heard mainly in the south. Moreover, the population is 62% Roman Catholic and only 12% Anglican.

If you're intent on finding a sprawling beach resort or a golfer's paradise, look elsewhere. If, on the other hand, you want to take a night dive through a tunnel of living coral, explore a jungle resounding with the call of howler monkeys, or clamber on ancient Maya ruins, the "adventure coast"—as Belize is rightly called—will not disappoint. Experiencing the rich diversity of colorful birds and animals that make their homes here, and perhaps showing them to your children, is another of this friendly, easygoing country's richest gifts. Clever Belize will probably remain a nature lover's haven for decades to come.

Pleasures and Pastimes

Beaches

Much of the mainland coast is fringed with mangrove swamps and therefore has few beaches. The few that do exist are not spectacular. This changes dramatically on the islands off the coast, particularly Ambergris Caye. The beaches are not expansive—generally a small strip of sand at the water's edge—but their white coral sand, palm trees, and mint-green water assure you that you're in the Caribbean. The best beach on the mainland is in Placencia, in the south. The Hopkins/Sittee Point area also has a good beach.

Caving

Belize is riddled with hundreds of caves, many of them unexplored in modern times. The most easily visited are those in Cayo, in Western Belize. Near San Ignacio are the caves at Barton Creek. Near Belmopan is Footprint Cave, where you can spend hours floating through underground rivers in an inner tube. Also in the area is Actun Tunichil Muknal, with its wealth of Maya artifacts, and many others. The remote Chiquibul system along the Guatemala border contains Cebeda, thought to be the country's largest cave. You don't need a guide to visit open caverns such as Rio Frio, but others require an experienced guide.

Dining

Belizean cuisine is not one of the world's greatest, but it might be the best Central America has to offer. Tasty treats—like the johnnycake, a sconelike cornmeal roll fried to a golden crisp and served at breakfast—rice and beans, fried chicken, and tasty creole "stew chicken" are the staples. Added to these are such acquired tastes as iguana, known as "bush chicken" or "bamboo chicken," and gibnut, a small rodent christened the "royal rat" after Queen Elizabeth dined on it during a state visit, and oddities of the British culinary heritage, like bread-and-butter pudding and cow-foot soup. But with the world's second-largest coral reef running the length of the coast, Belize whips up seafood as tasty as any in the Caribbean. Belizean chefs have learned how to prepare fish for a lighter northern palate (everything is *not* deep fried), and at their best dishes like grilled red snapper in a papaya-pineapple sauce, shrimp coated with coconut, or blackened shark steak squirted with fresh lime can be sublime. Throughout the country meals are washed down with delicious fresh-squeezed juices, such as lime, watermelon, and mango. However, you may decide that the national drink of Belize is orange Fanta or Belikin beer.

Belize is a casual place and demands little in the way of a dress code. A few expensive restaurants and clubs in Belize City prefer but do not require a jacket and tie for men; otherwise, you'll probably get served if you're wearing shoes and a shirt. On the cayes, you won't even need shoes at most restaurants. Reservations are advisable, as cooks buy ingredients for the evening's meal based on the number of guests expected.

CATEGORY	COST*
$$$$	over BZ$34 (over US$17)
$$$	BZ$20–BZ$34 (US$10–US$17)
$$	BZ$10–BZ$20 (US$5–US$10)
$	under BZ$10 (under US$5)

per person for a main course at dinner

Fishing

Some of the most exciting sportfishing in the world lies off Belize's coast and cayes. Fly-fishing is excellent on the shallow flats between the mainland and the reef, giving anglers a rare opportunity to achieve the "grand slam" of tarpon, bonefish, and permit in one day. Farther out to sea, sailfish, wahoo, and marlin abound. Several specialty resorts and fishing camps, such as Turneffe Flats, El Pescador, and the Lillpat Sittee River Lodge, cater to the angler, but most hotels can help you organize excellent fishing trips. Belize's attention to ecology means that catch-and-release fishing is usually the rule.

Lodging

Chain hotels are the exception rather than the rule in Belize. Here you'll find smaller establishments shaped by the personalities of their owners, most of whom are American or British. Because of the salt and humidity, operating a hotel in the tropics is an art in itself, the closest thing to keeping house on the deck of a ship. Without constant maintenance, things start to rust, the thatch (a frequently used natural building material from either the bay palm or cohune palm) leaks, and the charms of paradise quickly fade.

Rooms tend to be more expensive in Belize than elsewhere in Central America. The priciest places are in Belize City and Ambergris Caye, but they also offer more for your money because there is more competition. Hardest to find are good accommodations at moderate prices. Lodgings tend to leap from spartan to luxurious, with the middle ground occupied by either grand hotels that have fallen on hard times or small ones that are overcharging. Budget travelers, however, have a wide selection.

CATEGORY	COST*
$$$$	over BZ$400 (over US$200)
$$$	BZ$250–$400 (US$175–US$200)
$$	BZ$100–$250 (US$50–US$175)
$	under BZ$100 (under US$50)

*All prices are for a standard double room, including 7% hotel tax.

Scuba Diving and Snorkeling

The Barrier Reef, a coral necklace of 320 km (198 mi) stretching from the Yucatán Peninsula to the tip of Guatemala, is the longest in the western hemisphere. If you include the three coral atolls farther out to sea—Lighthouse Reef, Glover's Reef, and the Turneffe Islands—Belize has more than 560 km (347 mi) of reef just waiting to be explored. That's more than Bonaire, Cozumel, and all the Caymans put together. The cast of aquatic characters here is endless. One moment you can come upon an enormous spotted eagle ray, its needlelike tail streaming out behind; the next you may find the feisty little damselfish, a bolt of blue no bigger than your little finger.

Wildlife

Within this tiny country you'll find animals like scarlet macaws, tapirs, jaguars, kinkajous, mountain lions, and howler monkeys, making Belize one of the best places on earth to get close to the color and variety of tropical wildlife. Most hotels can book you a wildlife tour, and many jungle lodges, especially in Cayo, have their own guides to lead you into the wild.

Exploring Belize

Although it's not the capital, Belize City still serves as the country's transportation hub. From here you can reach the Maya ruins of the north; the mountainous Cayo district in the west; the villages along the coast to the south, and the cayes and atolls in the Caribbean. The majority of travelers, having heard the (somewhat exaggerated) rumors about Belize City, choose to move on quickly. You may want set up a base near San Ignacio or Belmopan to explore the western part of the country, in Placencia to explore the country's southern coast, or even on Ambergris Caye or Caye Caulker, from which you can make day trips to the mainland.

Great Itineraries

IF YOU HAVE 2–4 DAYS

If your international flight arrives early enough, say by 4:30 PM, head directly to one of the cayes. Otherwise, spend your first night in **Belize City** and take a morning flight or ferry to **Ambergris Caye.** Spend a few days poking around San Pedro, the island's main town, and exploring the nearby Barrier Reef. If you fancy a laid-back tropical paradise with fewer tourists and less development, travel to the southern town of **Placencia,** where you can also dive and snorkel.

IF YOU HAVE 5–6 DAYS

It's said that Belize is the only country where you can scuba dive before breakfast and hike in the rain forest after lunch, but to do this

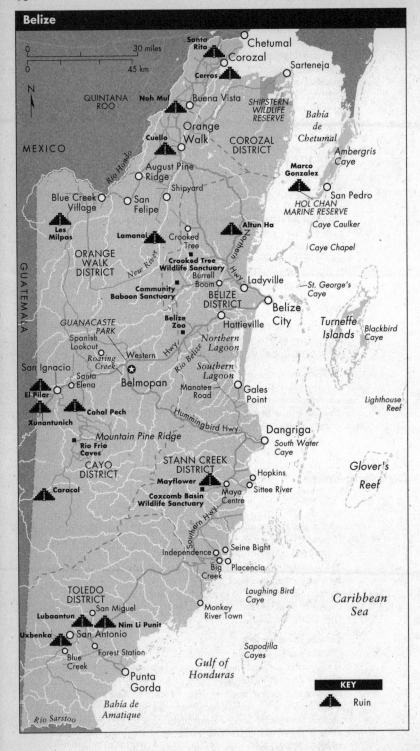

Belize

0 ——— 30 miles
0 ——— 45 km

N

MEXICO

QUINTANA
ROO

GUATEMALA

Santa
Rita
Cerros
Corozal
Chetumal
Sarteneja

Noh Mul
Buena Vista

SHIPSTERN
WILDLIFE
RESERVE

Bahía
de
Chetumal

Cuello
Orange
Walk

COROZAL
DISTRICT

Ambergris
Caye

August Pine
Ridge
Shipyard

Marco
Gonzalez

San Pedro

HOL CHAN
MARINE RESERVE

Blue Creek
Village
San
Felipe

Les
Milpas

Lamanai

Crooked
Tree

Altun Ha

Caye Caulker

Caye Chapel

ORANGE
WALK
DISTRICT

New River

Crooked Tree
Wildlife Sanctuary
Burrell
Boom

Community
Baboon Sanctuary

BELIZE
DISTRICT

Ladyville

St. George's
Caye

Belize
City

Turneffe
Islands

Blackbird
Caye

Río Hondo

Belize
Zoo

Hattieville

GUANACASTE
PARK

Spanish
Lookout
Roaring
Creek

Western
Hwy.

Northern
Lagoon

Río Belize

Northern Hwy.

San Ignacio

Santa
Elena

Belmopan

Southern
Lagoon

Manatee
Road

Gales
Point

Lighthouse
Reef

El Pilar

Cahal Pech

Xunantunich

Mountain Pine Ridge

Rio Frio
Caves

CAYO
DISTRICT

Hummingbird Hwy.

Dangriga

South Water
Caye

Glover's
Reef

Caracol

STANN CREEK
DISTRICT

Mayflower

Coxcomb Basin
Wildlife Sanctuary

Hopkins
Sittee River

Maya
Centre

Southern Hwy.

Independence

Seine Bight

Big
Creek
Placencia

Laughing Bird
Caye

Caribbean
Sea

TOLEDO
DISTRICT

Lubaantun

San Miguel

Nim Li Punit

Uxbenka
San Antonio

Blue
Creek
Forest Station

Monkey
River Town

Sapodilla
Cayes

Punta
Gorda

Gulf of
Honduras

Bahía de
Amatique

KEY

Río Sarstoo

Ruin

you have to plan carefully. Spend your first night in **Belize City**, then head to **Ambergris Caye** for a few days of fun in the sun. If you would like to extend your underwater adventures, move on to one of the remote coral atolls such as **Turneffe Atoll** or **Lighthouse Reef Atoll.** For the jungle experience, head to the **San Ignacio,** in the Cayo district, and take excursions from one of the lodges in the area. From here you can canoe down the Macal River, hike through the rain forest, or explore the Maya ruins at **Xunantunich.**

IF YOU HAVE 7–10 DAYS

If you have more than a week, it's worth spending a bit more time around **Belize City.** For Maya ruins put **Altun Ha** or **Lamanai** on your list. If it's nature you want, visit the **Crooked Tree Wildlife Sanctuary** and **Community Baboon Sanctuary.** Fly to **Ambergris Caye** for two or three days of diving and sunbathing; then fly back to Belize City and head for the resorts around **San Ignacio** to see the rain forests that make Belize a naturalist's paradise. Finally, head south to **Placencia** or **Hopkins** for a luscious last few days of snorkeling and relaxing under palm trees.

When to Tour Belize

Belize is a year-round destination, but some seasons are better than others. The dry season, from February or March to May, can be the least attractive time for inland trips, with dust and wilting vegetation, but this is a fine time to visit the coast. The rainy season is June–September, extending in some areas through October. The wet weather varies dramatically depending on where you are—in the deep south as much as 160 inches of rain falls each year, but in the rest of the country there's much less. Moreover, the rain is not continuous; sudden thunderstorms are followed by sun. On the cayes the wet season can be accompanied by lashing winds, known here as "Joe North."

Scuba enthusiasts can dive all year, but the water is at its clearest from April to June. Between November and February cold fronts from North America can push southward, producing blustery winds known as "northers" that bring rain and rough weather and tend to churn up the sea, reducing visibility. Water temperatures rarely stray from 27°C (80°F), so many people dive without a wet suit.

BELIZE CITY

From the air you realize how small Belize City is—with a population of about 60,000, it is really more of a town than a city. Few of the ramshackle buildings you'll find here are taller than the palm trees. After a couple of miles, streets simply give way to a largely uninhabited country where animals still outnumber people.

Perhaps because of its strange history, Belize was one of the most neglected colonies of the Pax Britannia. The British, who were generally generous in such matters, left little of either great beauty or interest in the capital of their former colony—no parks or gardens, no university, no museums. Indeed, one of the clichés about Belize City is that the most exciting thing that happens here is the opening of the rusty swing bridge on Haulover Creek.

In 1961 the city was almost annihilated by Hurricane Hattie, and authorities decided to move Belize's capital to Belmopan, robbing Belize City of its reason for being. In the mid-1990s both the government and private sector began a concerted effort to stop the hemorrhage of travelers, and thus money, away from the city. In 1995 a Tourism Police Unit was created to help cut down on crime, and officers on foot patrol are now a familiar sight. To make getting around the city easier, roads were resurfaced and traffic lights were installed. A new water-front walkway was built along Eve Street.

At the turn of the millennium other changes were underway. More and more colonial buildings were restored, making the Fort George area an increasingly pleasant place to stay. Late 2001 saw the unveiling of a new cruise-ship terminal and a shopping area called Fort Point Tourist Village. Though shallow water in the harbor means passengers must be brought ashore in tenders, the city expects about a quarter of a million cruise-ship passengers annually. There's still a lot of work to be done, but Belize City *is* slowly re-creating itself.

Numbers in the margin correspond to points of interest on the Belize City map.

Exploring Belize City

If you're prepared to take the time and trouble, Belize City will repay your curiosity. Belizeans are natural city dwellers, and there is an infectious sociability on streets like Albert and Queen, the main shopping strips. The finest British colonial houses—graceful white buildings with wraparound verandas, painted shutters, and fussy Victorian woodwork—are on the North Shore, near the Radisson Fort George, the most pleasant part of the city in which to stroll.

A Good Walk

A good place to start a tour of Belize City is at the **Swing Bridge** ①, which crosses the Haulover River. If you happen to be here at 5:30 AM or 5:30 PM, you can watch it in action. Close to the Swing Bridge on North Front Street is the **Marine Terminal** ②, where you catch water taxis to the cayes. Here you'll find the Coastal Zone Museum, which has displays on the Barrier Reef, and the Marine Museum, which has displays about the country's maritime history. Walk southeast along the water on Front Street to reach the **Fort George Lighthouse** ③. You'll find a view of the bustling city harbor just over the promontory. Walk north on Marine Parade and behold the Radisson Fort George Hotel, guarded by white-helmeted attendants. Next door is the Chateau Caribbean, a beautiful colonial mansion that was once Belize's only private hospital. It adjoins Memorial Park, a tranquil respite with welcome sea breezes. Farther inland are most of the embassies, housed in well-preserved mansions; the impressive American Embassy is on Gabourel Lane just south of Queen Street. While on Gabourel Lane, stop in at the new **Museum of Belize** ④, a small space in the Central Bank Building with an eclectic collection of Belizeana.

Some beautiful buildings lie south of the Swing Bridge on Regent Street. The courthouse here is a cement reconstruction of the original wooden structure, which burned down in 1926. Along the colorfully named Southern Foreshore is a cultural center called the **Bliss Institute** ⑤. At the end of Regent Street you'll find **St. John's Cathedral** ⑥, built by slaves with bricks that served as ballast in the hulls of ships arriving from Europe. One block southwest lies Yarborough Cemetery, where the inscriptions on the headstones once hinted at tales of deceit, murder, and derring-do, though you'd be hard-pressed to find any legible inscriptions after the passing of a century. Nearby is the **Government House** ⑦, the former residence of the governor-general of Belize.

TIMING
Belize City is fairly compact, so this walk should take only a few hours.

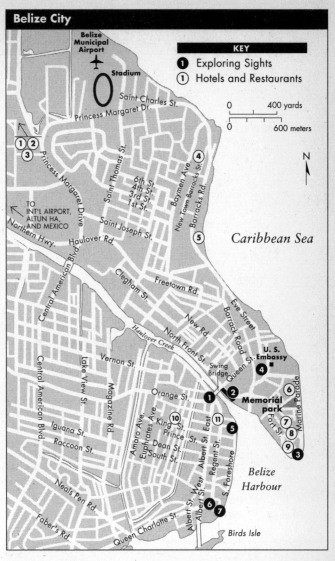

Sights to See

⑤ Bliss Institute. Overlooking the harbor from the south bank of Haulover Creek, this building houses the National Arts Council and hosts cultural events throughout the year. There are a drama series (April), Children's Festival of the Arts (May), dance festival (June and July), and a variety of musical and cultural performances during the month-long celebration of independence in September. A few Maya artifacts from Caracol are on display in the entryway. ⊠ *2 Southern Foreshore, between Church and Bishop Sts.,* ☎ *227/2110.* ☉ *Weekdays 8:30–noon and 1–5.*

③ Fort George Lighthouse. Towering over the entrance to Belize Harbor, this lighthouse stands guard on the tip of Fort George Point. It was designed and funded by the country's greatest benefactor, Baron Bliss. A memorial to him is nearby. ⊠ *Fort St.*

⑦ Government House. The finest colonial structure in the city is said to have been designed by the illustrious British architect Sir Christopher

Wren. Built in 1812, it was once the residence of the governor general, the queen's representative in Belize. After he and the rest of government moved to Belmopan, it housed visiting VIPs. (Queen Elizabeth stayed here in 1985, Prince Philip in 1988.) It is now open to the public, and you can peruse its archival records, silver, glassware, and furniture and mingle with the tropical birds that frequent the gardens. ⊠ *Regent St. at Southern Foreshore,* ☎ *227/3050.* ⌨ *BZ$5.* ☉ *Weekdays 8:30–4:30.*

❷ Marine Terminal. Housed in a former firehouse dating from the 1920s, this white clapboard building is where you can catch a boat to the cayes. While you wait, you can browse around the two museums on the premises. On the main level is the **Coastal Zone Museum,** which tells all about the reef and the creatures that make it their home. On the second floor is the **Marine Museum,** where you can wander among models of boats that have sailed these waters and displays of tools used by shipwrights. One ticket gets you into both museums. ⊠ *10 N. Front St., at Queen St.,* ☎ *223/1969.* ⌨ *BZ$4.* ☉ *Mon.–Sat. 8–4:30.*

❹ Museum of Belize. Debuting in 2002, this small but interesting museum has displays on Belize history and culture ranging from ancient Maya artifacts to a cell from the old jail built in 1853. ⊠ *Gabourel La.,* ☎ *223/4524.* ⌨ *BZ$10.* ☉ *Tues.–Fri. 10–6, Sat. 10–3.*

❻ St. John's Cathedral. At the south end of Albert Street, this lovely structure is the oldest Anglican church in Central America and the only one outside England where kings were crowned. From 1815 to 1845 four kings of the Mosquito Coast (a British protectorate along the coast of Honduras and Nicaragua) were crowned here. ⊠ *Albert St.,* ☎ *227/2137.*

❶ Swing Bridge. As you may have guessed, the bridge spanning Haulover Creek actually swings. Each day at 5:30 AM and 5:30 PM, four men handwinch the bridge a quarter-revolution so a bevy of waiting boats can continue their journeys upstream (when it was the only bridge in town, this snarled traffic for blocks). The bridge, made in England, opened in 1923; it was renovated and upgraded in 1999. It's the only one of its kind left. ⊠ *Haulover Creek where Queen and Albert Sts. meet.*

Dining and Lodging

$–$$ ✕ **Sea Rock.** This unprepossessing restaurant has the best Indian food in Belize—period. The spicy tandoori fare is cooked in a clay oven and served in a comfortable dining room enlivened by a few trinkets from India. It's a good first stop for vegetarians, as it serves many meatless dishes. ⊠ *190 New Town Barrack Rd., near Princess Hotel,* ☎ *223/4105. AE, MC, V. Closed Sun.*

$ ✕ **Dit's Saloon.** Nobody does beans and rice better than Dit's, a Belize City institution. More café-cum-saloon than restaurant, it's a real local place. (Like many other older Belizean restaurants, it has a sink right in the dining room.) Cheery striped tablecloths lend the place a homey feel. The sticky and sweet baked goods are delicious, especially the three-milks cake and the coconut tarts. Stop by for breakfast—the platters of eggs, beans, and toast, washed down with ample mugs of tea, are an excellent value. ⊠ *50 King St.,* ☎ *227/3330. No credit cards.*

$ ✕ **Macy's Café.** You've seen the wildlife? Now you can eat it. Wrap your mouth around armadillo, brocket deer, gibnut, and, by request, stewed iguana, known locally as bamboo chicken. Macy, the Jamaican-born proprietor, says it's tough to prepare—it has to be scalded, then washed in lime juice and vinegar—but delicious to eat. Macy proudly displays a letter from the bishop of Belize congratulating the staff on its catering feats and a photo of Harrison Ford, who commandeered the table by the door during the making of *The Mosquito Coast.* ⊠ *18 Bishop St.,* ☎ *227/3419. No credit cards.*

$$$ ✕🖸 **Princess Hotel & Casino.** Big-time gambling arrived in Belize when the country's first Las Vegas–style casino opened at this sprawling hotel in 2000. The hotel, by far the largest in Belize, is still being expanded to house the new facilities. More than 60 new rooms are being built, while some of the older ones are awaiting much needed renovation. It's not quite the MGM Grand, but it's as serious. As you enter the casino, more than 400 slot, video poker, and other machines fill the central part of the room. Black jack, roulette, craps, and poker tables are toward the back. Even if you don't gamble, the hotel's all-you-can-eat buffet at lunch and dinner, of surprising quality for the price, is a bargain at just BZ$15. For the same price you can get sloshed at the all-you-can-drink happy hour from 5 to 7 on Friday. ⊠ *Kings Park,* ☎ *223/2670,* ℻ *223/2660,* 𝖶𝖤𝖡 *www.princessbelize.com. 179 rooms, 5 suites. Restaurant, room service, cable TV, pool, gym, hair salon, dive shop, marina, fishing, bowling, casino, theater, bar, laundry service, business services, meeting rooms, car rental, travel services; no-smoking rooms. AE, MC, V.*

$$$ ✕🖸 **Radisson Fort George.** Porters in pith helmets keep British colo-
★ nialism in the air at Belize City's finest hotel. Lush red and ocher fab-
rics, faux-leopard carpets, and reproduction rattan and hardwood antiques re-create the British raj of the 1880s. Rooms in the main build-ing have private verandas overlooking the pool and gardens; those in the six-story tower have panoramic views of the sea through tinted glass; while those in the executive wing across the road overlook the river and one of the hotel's two pools. Service is always sprightly, and hotel staffers are relentlessly efficient and friendly. A marina can handle ves-sels of up to 250 ft, and one of Belize's top dive operations, Hugh Parkey's Dive Belize, is on the hotel's dock. The Bayman's Tavern is one of the city's premier watering holes. ⊠ *2 Marine Parade,* ☎ *227/7400; 800/ 333–3333 in the U.S.,* ℻ *227/3820,* 𝖶𝖤𝖡 *www.radissonbelize.com. 102 rooms. Restaurant, room service, in-room data ports, some in-room safes, minibars, cable TV, 2 pools, gym, dive shop, marina, fishing, bar, shops, laundry service, business services, meeting rooms, car rental, travel services; no-smoking rooms. AE, MC, V.*

$$ 🖸 **Belize Biltmore Plaza.** Once sinking into lodging oblivion, this hotel is staging a comeback. Manager Teresa Parkey, who formerly ran Fort Street Guesthouse, has made much needed improvements to the pool and grounds and also upgraded many of the rooms. The "deluxe premier" rooms, with new carpets and mattresses, are worth the extra cost. Also turning around is the Victorian Room, which serves entrées like stew chicken and New York strip. It's a now a popular lunch spot for local businesspeople. Themed evenings, such as Thursday jazz night and Fri-day happy hour (5–7), draw sizable crowds. ⊠ *Mile 3½, Northern Hwy.,* ☎ *223/2302,* ℻ *223/2301,* 𝖶𝖤𝖡 *www.belizebiltmore.com. 80 rooms. Restaurant, room service, cable TV, pool, 2 bars, shops, laundry service, business services, meeting rooms, travel services. AE, MC, V.*

$$$ ✕🖸 **The Great House.** The grand colonial facade of this house, one of
★ the largest wooden structures in Belize, is one of the most pleasing sights in the Fort George area. Owner Steve Maestre has turned his house into a fine little inn that holds one of the city's best restaurants. The large rooms have polished pine floors and beds piled with decorative pillows and colorful quilts. The wraparound verandas are pleasant places to sit and read as you catch the breeze from the sea. On the ground floor a tiny gallery of shops leads to the Smoky Mermaid, where you can dine under the stars. In a large courtyard shaded by breadfruit and sapodilla trees, the amiable servers bring Caribbean-influenced seafood dishes, inventive pasta, and savory barbecues. ⊠ *13 Cork St.,* ☎ *223/*

3400, FAX 223/3444, WEB *www.greathousebelize.com. 12 rooms. Restaurant, fans, in-room fax, in-room safes, refrigerator, cable TV, shops, laundry service, travel services. AE, DC, MC, V.*

$$ ✕🔲 **Chateau Caribbean.** The bright colors of the Caribbean enliven the rooms in this handsome colonial-style hotel. The suites have balconies overlooking the harbor. As this is Belize, don't expect everything to work perfectly—the louvered windows in your room may not close, defeating the air-conditioning. Fortunately, all rooms have phones, so you can call the front desk. Chateau Caribbean is best known for its second-floor restaurant. With white tablecloths, gleaming cutlery, and great ocean views, it's a charming place to eat. The menu is an unusual combination of Chinese and Caribbean dishes, so you could have grilled snapper with rice and beans while your dining companion enjoys sweet and sour pork. ⊠ *6 Marine Parade,* ☎ 223/0800, FAX 223/0900, WEB *www.chateaucaribbean.com. 20 rooms. Restaurant, room service, cable TV, bar, laundry service, meeting rooms. AE, MC, V.*

$$ 🔲 **Colton House.** This beautiful 1920s West Indian–style house, in a prime
★   location in Fort George, is Belize City's best small inn. Proprietors Alan and Ondina Colton take loving care of this charmer. Alan, who came here with the British armed forces, has an enormous collection of ecology books he's happy to share. He also is an enthusiastic amateur beer brewer and owner of the "Swamp Water Brewery of Belize," consisting of 5-gallon buckets in a washroom. Ondina, originally from Caye Caulker, handled the interior decoration. The wraparound veranda is furnished with hammocks and white rattan furniture; the interior has antiques and cool, polished wood floors. ⊠ *9 Cork St.,* ☎ 224/4666, FAX 223/0451, WEB *www.coltonhouse.com. 5 rooms, 1 suite. Some rooms with fans, library, travel services; no room phones, no TV in some rooms, no kids under 10, no smoking. No credit cards.*

$–$$ 🔲 **Embassy Hotel.** If you want a place to stay en route to somewhere else, this hotel is just steps from the international airport. It has little charm, and some of the rooms look down at heel, but it's safe, clean, and convenient. There are a restaurant and a sunny roof deck where you can relax in a hammock or challenge a friend to a game of table tennis. Staying longer? Consider one of the one-bedroom apartments. The hotel will also store your luggage or dive gear. ⊠ *Philip S. W. Goldson International Airport,* ☎ 225/3333, FAX 225/2267, WEB *www.embassyhotelbelize.com. 40 rooms, 7 suites, 8 apartments. Restaurant, bar, travel services. MC, V.*

$$ 🔲 **Villa Boscardi.** If you're edgy about Belize City, this B&B in Belize's northern suburbs might be your cup of herbal tea. Franco and Francoise Boscardi (he's Italian, she's Belgian) opened their home in a quiet residential area to guests. Four rooms are bright, sunny, and stylishly decorated, with a hint of Europe here, a taste of Belize there. A new detached bungalow in the back has a refrigerator and coffeemaker. Breakfast is included. ⊠ *6043 Manatee Dr. (turn toward sea off Northern Hwy. at Golding Ave., then left on 2nd lane to 5th house on right),* ☎ FAX 223/1691, WEB *www.villaboscardi.com. 4 rooms, 1 cottage. Fans, some refrigerators, cable TV, free airport shuttle, car rental. AE, MC, V.*

Outdoor Activities and Sports

Operated for years by Hugh Parkey, **Belize Dive Connection** (⊠ 2 Marine Parade, Belize City, ☎ 223/4526, FAX 27/8808) runs trips to suit your every whim from the Radisson Fort George dock. Dive trips to Hol Chan Marine Reserve near Ambergris Caye run around BZ$180 per person.

Shopping

For Belizean souvenirs try the **National Handicraft Center** (⊠ Fort St., ☎ 223/3636). Popular items include hand-carved figurines, pottery, and woven baskets. Belize's beautiful stamps are available from the **Philatelic Society** (✉ Queen St., behind post office). Many feature lovely images of the country's wildlife. The **Book Centre** (✉ 4 Church St., ☎ 227/7457) sells magazines and the classics.

If you want to stock up on picnic supplies, head to **Brodies** (✉ Mile 2½, Northern Hwy., ☎ 223/5587). **Save-U** (✉ Belikin Area Plaza, ☎ 223/1291) is a good place to browse for local bargains.

Side Trips from Belize City

Altun Ha

If you've never visited an ancient Maya city, make a trip to Altun Ha. It's not the most dramatic site in Belize, but it is the most thoroughly excavated and the most accessible. People resided here for nearly two millennia; the first inhabitants settled here before 900 BC, and their descendants finally abandoned the site around AD 900. A team from the Royal Ontario Museum that first excavated the site in the mid-1960s found 250 structures spread over more than 1,000 square yards. In the Temple of the Masonry Altars, the archaeologists found the grandest and most valuable piece of Maya art ever discovered—the head of the sun god Kinich Ahau carved from a solid block of green jade. As there's no national museum, the head is kept in a solid steel vault in the central branch of the Bank of Belize. ✉ *45 km (28 mi) north of Belize City,* ☎ *No phone.* ⌑ *BZ$5.* ☉ *Daily 9–5.*

Belize Zoo

It comprises just 29 acres, but the Belize Zoo packs a lot of nature in a small space. Housing only animals native to the region, the zoo has habitats as natural as its budget allows. As you stroll the trails on a self-guided tour, you visit several Belizean ecosystems—rain forest, lagoons, and riverine forest—and spot more than 125 species. Besides the rare black jaguar, you'll also see the country's four other wild cats: the puma, margay, ocelot, and jaguarondi. Probably the most famous resident of the zoo is named April. She's a Baird's tapir, the national animal of Belize. This relative of the horse and rhino is known to locals as the mountain cow. ✉ *48 km (30 mi) west of Belize City,* ☎ 220/8004, WEB *www.belizezoo.org* ⌑ *BZ$15.* ☉ *Daily 9–4:30.*

Community Baboon Sanctuary

One of the country's most interesting wildlife conservation projects, the Community Baboon Sanctuary is actually a haven for black howler monkeys. The reserve, encompassing a 32-km (20-mi) stretch of the Belize River, was established in 1985 by a group of local farmers. The howler monkey—an agile bundle of black fur with a deafening roar—was then being zealously hunted throughout Central America and was facing extinction. Today there are nearly 1,000 black howler monkeys in the sanctuary, as well as numerous other species of birds and mammals. Thanks to ongoing conservation efforts, you can also see howler monkeys in a number of other areas, including at Lamanai in northern Belize, along the Macal and Belize rivers in western Belize, and near Monkey River in southern Belize. Exploring the Community Baboon Sanctuary is made easy by about 5 km (3 mi) of trails that start near a small museum. ✉ *50 km (31 mi) west of Belize City,* ☎ 227/7369. ⌑ *BZ$10.* ☉ *Dawn–dusk.*

Crooked Tree Wildlife Sanctuary

A paradise for animal lovers, this wildlife sanctuary encompasses a chain of inland waterways covering more than 3,000 acres. Traveling through by canoe, you're likely to see iguanas, crocodiles, coatis, and turtles. The sanctuary's most prestigious visitor, however, is the jabiru stork.

With a wingspan up to 9 ft, it is the largest flying bird in the Americas. For birders the best time to come is in the dry season, roughly from February to early June, because lowered water levels mean birds tend to group together to find water and food, making them easy to spot. Snowy egrets, snail kites, ospreys, and black-collared hawks, as well as two types of duck—Muscovy and black-bellied whistling—and all five species of kingfisher native to Belize can be spotted. ⊠ *Turn west off Northern Hwy. at Mile 30.8, then drive 3 km (2 mi),* ☏ *223–4987 for Belize Audubon Society.* ☑ *BZ$8.*

Lamanai

The longest-occupied Maya site in Belize, Lamanai was inhabited until well after Christopher Columbus discovered the New World in 1492. Archaeologists have found signs of continuous occupation from 1500 BC until AD 1700. In all, 50 or 60 Maya structures were spread over what is now a 950 acres. The most impressive of these is the largest Preclassic structure in Belize—a massive, stepped temple built into the hillside overlooking the river. Many structures at Lamanai have been only superficially excavated. Trees and vines grow from the tops of the temples, the sides of one pyramid are covered with vegetation, and another pyramid rises abruptly from the forest floor. ⊠ *39 km (24 mi) south of Orange Walk.* ☑ *BZ$5.* ☉ *Daily 9–5.*

Belize City A to Z

AIR TRAVEL TO AND FROM BELIZE CITY

Philip S. W. Goldson International Airport is near Ladyville, 14 km (9 mi) north of the city. In addition to international flights, it has a domestic terminal with flights to Ambergris Caye and Caye Caulker and the coastal towns of Dangriga and Placencia. Taxis to town cost BZ$35. The Belize City Municipal Airport, on the seafront about 2 km (1 mi) north of the city center, also has flights to these destinations. Fares from the municipal airport are about 10%–45% cheaper than similar flights departing from the international airport.

BUS TRAVEL TO AND FROM BELIZE CITY

Belize City is the hub of the country's fairly extensive bus network, so there's regular service to various regions of Belize and connections to the Guatemalan and Mexican borders. Novelo's is the dominant carrier in the country, especially on Western and Northern highways. ➤ BUS INFORMATION: **Novelo's** (⊠ W. Collet Canal, Belize City, ☏ 227/ 2025).

BUS TRAVEL WITHIN BELIZE CITY

There is no bus service within Belize City. If you are headed for another part of the city, your best option is taking a taxi. Don't walk around the city at night except in the Fort George area.

CAR RENTAL

Most international rental-car agencies have locations at Philip S. W. Goldson International Airport as well as in downtown Belize City. Branches at the airport are usually closed on Sunday. Avis has a branch at Belize City Municipal Airport as well.

Budget, offering the best service in town, has a fleet of low-mileage vehicles. Some locally owned companies, such as Crystal Auto Rental, are less expensive than many of the international chains and offer service that is just as good. ➤ LOCAL AGENCIES: **Avis** (⊠ Municipal Airport, Belize City, ☏ 223/ 4619; ⊠ Philip S. W. Goldson International Airport, Ladyville, ☏

225/2385). **Budget** (✉ 771 Bella Vista, Belize City, ☎ 223/2435; ✉ Philip S. W. Goldson International Airport, Ladyville, ☎ 223/2435). **Crystal Auto Rental** (✉ Mile 1½, Northern Hwy., Belize City, ☎ 223/1600; ✉ Philip S. W. Goldson International Airport Ladyville, ☎ 223/1600). **Hertz** (✉ 11A Cork St., Belize City, ☎ 223/5395; ✉ Philip S. W. Goldson International Airport, Ladyville, ☎ 223/5395). **Thrifty** (✉ Central American Blvd. and Fabers Rd., Belize City, ☎ 227/1271).

CAR TRAVEL

There are only two highways to Belize City—the Northern Highway, which leads from the Mexican border, 165 km (102 mi) away, and the Western Highway, which runs 131 km (81 mi) from Guatemala. Both are paved and in good condition. Recently installed signs point you to nearby destinations such as the Belize Zoo.

Finding your way around the city itself, however, is much more difficult. The downtown area's narrow one-way streets, usually without signs identifying where you are, often end abruptly because of construction work or an inconveniently located river. Save your nerves and explore the city by taxi or, in safer sections such as the Fort George area, on foot.

EMERGENCIES

Karl Heusner Memorial, a public hospital, and Belize Medical Associates, a private facility, both have 24-hour emergency rooms. Brodie's Pharmacy, at Market Square, is open Monday, Tuesday, Thursday, and Saturday 8:30–7, Wednesday 8:30 AM–12:30 PM, Friday 8:30 AM–9 PM and Sunday 9 AM–12:30 PM. Community Drug, with several locations in Belize City, is open daily 8–8.

Dr. Osbert Usher, a dentist, sees patients on short notice.
➤ DOCTORS AND DENTISTS: **Osbert Usher** (✉ 16 Magazine Rd., ☎ 227/3415).
➤ HOSPITALS: **Belize Medical Associates** (✉ 5791 St. Thomas St., ☎ 223/0303). **Karl Heusner Memorial** (✉ Princess Margaret Dr., ☎ 223/1548).
➤ PHARMACIES: **Brodie's Pharmacy** (✉ Regent St. at Market Sq.). **Community Drug** (✉ Farmers' Market and 18 Albert St.).

MAIL AND SHIPPING

The main post office is inside the historic Paslow Building, just north of the Swing Bridge. It is open weekdays 8–noon and 1–4:30. Mail service from Belize City to the United States and other countries is generally fast and reliable (airmail to the United States usually takes about five days). For faster service use DHL and FedEx, both of which have offices in Belize City.
➤ OVERNIGHT SERVICES: **DHL** (✉ 38 New Rd., ☎ 223/4350). **Federal Express** (✉ 32 Albert St., ☎ 227/3507).
➤ POST OFFICES: **Main Post Office** (✉ N. Front St. at Queen St., ☎ 223/2201).

MONEY MATTERS

U.S. dollars are accepted everywhere in Belize, but if you need to exchange another currency, you can do so at one of the five banks operating in Belize City—Alliance Bank, Atlantic Bank, Bank of Nova Scotia, Barclays, and Belize Bank. Most banks have their main offices on Albert Street in downtown Belize City, with smaller branches scattered around the city. Should you exchange U.S. dollars at a bank, expect to be charged a 1%–2% fee.

The good news is most banks in Belize City have ATMs. The bad news is many of these do not accept cards issued outside Belize. Exceptions are those at Barclays Bank branches in Belize City, Dangriga, and Belmopan. Even these machines may be out of order, so do not depend on ATMs for your cash. Most banks offer cash advances on cards issued by Visa and MasterCard for a fee ranging from BZ$5 to BZ$30.

➤ BANKS: **Alliance Bank** (✉ Princess Margaret Dr., ☎ 223/5698). **Atlantic Bank** (✉ Freetown Rd., ☎ 223/4123). **Bank of Nova Scotia** (✉ Albert St., ☎ 227/7027). **Barclays Bank** (✉ 21 Albert St., ☎ 227/7211). **Belize Bank** (✉ 60 Market Sq., ☎ 227/7132).

SAFETY

Belize City earned a reputation for street crime in the early '90s, but the government has made great strides in cleaning up the problem. Remember to take the same precautions you would take in any city—don't wear expensive jewelry or watches, avoid handling money in public, and leave valuables in a safe. On buses and in crowded areas hold purses and backpacks close to the body. Check with the staff at your hotel before venturing into any unfamiliar areas, particularly at night.

TAXIS

Cabs cost BZ$5 for one person between any two points in the city, plus BZ$1 for each additional person. Outside the city you're charged by the distance you travel. There are no meters, so be sure to agree on a price before you leave. Pick up a taxi at Market Square or by the Swing Bridge. Cinderella Taxi and Caribbean Taxi are reputable local companies.

➤ TAXI COMPANIES: **Cinderella Taxi** (☎ 224/5240). **Caribbean Taxi** (☎ 227/2888).

TOURS OPERATORS

Discovery Expeditions is a well-known tour operator with offices at the Philip S. W. Goldson International Airport and at several hotels in Belize City. In addition to sightseeing tours, it provides airport transfers and transportation to other parts of the country. Maya Travel's Katie Valk, a New Yorker with attitude (softened by some 15 years' residency in Belize), can organize a trip to just about anywhere in the country. She also has good connections at most hotels and can get you a room even when everything seems to be booked. S&L Travel is another long-established tour operator.

➤ TOUR COMPANIES: **Discovery Expeditions** (✉ 5916 Manatee Dr., ☎ 223/0748). **Maya Travel Services** (✉ Belize City Municipal Airport, ☎ 223/1623). **S&L Travel** (✉ 91 N. Front St., ☎ 227/7593).

VISITOR INFORMATION

The Belize Tourist Board, in the New Central Bank Building, is open weekdays 8–noon and 1–5.

➤ CONTACTS: **Belize Tourist Board** (✉ New Central Bank Building, Level 2, Gabourel La., Box 325, Belize City, ☎ 223/1913 or 800/624–0686, FAX 223/1943, WEB www.travelbelize.org).

THE CAYES AND ATOLLS

Imagine heading back to shore after a day's snorkeling, the white prow of your boat pointing up into the billowing clouds, the base of the sky darkening to a deep lilac, the spray from the sea-green water pouring over you like warm rain. To the left San Pedro's pastel buildings huddle among the palm trees like a detail from a Paul Klee canvas. To the right the surf breaks in a white seam along the reef. Over the surface of the water flying fish scamper away.

This and many other delicious experiences lie off the coast of Belize, where more than 400 cayes (pronounced "keys," as in the Florida Keys) dot the Caribbean Sea like punctuation marks in a long, liquid sentence. Most cayes lie inside the Barrier Reef, which allowed them to develop undisturbed by the tides and winds that would otherwise have swept them away. The vast majority are uninhabited except by pelicans, brown- and red-footed boobies, and some lewd-sounding creatures called wish-willies (actually a kind of iguana). The names of the islands are evocative and often humorous: there are Wee Wee Caye, Laughing Bird Caye, and—why ask why?—Bread and Butter Caye. Some names suggest the kind of company you should expect: Mosquito Caye, Sandfly Caye, and even Crawl Caye, which is supposedly infested with boa constrictors. Many, like Cockney Range or Baker's Rendezvous, simply express the whimsy or nostalgia of the early British settlers. The battle fought for control of the high seas spilled over into nomenclature. With the rout of the Spanish at the Battle of St. George's Caye, in 1798, English names took precedence: Turneffe, for Terre Nef; Lighthouse Reef, for Quattro Cayos; Glover's Reef, for Longorif.

Farther out to sea, between 48 km and 96 km (between 30 mi and 60 mi) off the coast, are the atolls, which from the air look impossibly beautiful. At their center the water is mint green: the white sandy bottom reflects the light upward and is flecked with patches of mangrove and rust-color sediment. Around the fringe of the atoll the surf breaks in a white circle before the color changes abruptly to ultramarine as the water plunges to 3,000 ft.

Scuba Diving

Dive destinations are often divided into two broad categories—the reef and the atolls. Most reef diving is done on the northern section, particularly off Ambergris Caye. Here the reef is just a few hundred yards from shore, making access to your dive site extremely easy: the journey by boat usually takes as little as 10 minutes. Coast and coral are farther apart as you head south, which mean a greater dependence on weather. On Ambergris Caye you might be stuck in your hotel during a morning storm, but you still have a good chance of getting out in the afternoon. Most of the cayes' dive shops are attached to hotels, and the quality of dive masters, equipment, and facilities varies considerably.

Many resorts offer diving courses. A one-day basic familiarization course costs between BZ$250 and BZ$350. A four-day PADI certification course costs BZ$700–BZ$800. A popular variant is a referral course, in which you do the academic and pool training at home, then do the required dives here; the cost for two days is about BZ$500.

If you want to experience something truly dramatic, head to the atolls, which make for some of the world's greatest diving. The only problem with the atolls is that they're awfully far from the accommodations. If you're staying on Ambergris Caye, Glover's Reef is out of the question for a day trip by boat. Even when the weather is perfect— which it often isn't in winter—a trip to Lighthouse Reef takes between two and three hours. Turneffe is more accessible, but even that is a long and comparatively costly day trip, and you're unlikely to reach the atoll's southern tip, which has the best diving. If you're determined to dive the atolls, you can stay at one of the island resorts or spend time on a live-aboard dive boat.

Numbers in the margin correspond to points of interest on the Cayes, Atolls, and Barrier Reef map.

Ambergris Caye

❶ *56 km (35 mi) northeast of Belize City.*

At 40 km (25 mi) long and 7 km (4½ mi) wide, Ambergris is the queen of the cayes. On early maps it was often referred to as Costa de Ambar, or the Amber Coast, a name supposedly derived from the blackish substance secreted by the sperm whale that often washes up on beaches. No proof exists, however, that ambergris was ever found here, although there's also an Ambergris Caye in the Bahamas.

A few years ago, when you flew into the caye's main town, San Pedro, the tips of the plane's wings almost touched the laundry hanging in people's backyards. Once landed, you could walk from one end of town to the other in 10 minutes. Today you need a bike just to get from one end of the airstrip to the other. Every year there are more cars, more souvenir shops, and more tourists. Ambergris will never be like Cancún, but it is the most developed—some would say overdeveloped—of the cayes. In 1999, the town paved one of the island's sandy streets for the first time.

The heart of the town is still the same: a couple of rows of brightly painted wooden houses with the ocean on one side and the lagoon on the other. Old men still lean over their balconies in the evenings to watch the world go by, and many people stroll down the roads barefoot. The stores and restaurants still have names like Lily's, Alice's, or Martha's. With a population around 4,400, San Pedro remains a small, friendly, and prosperous village. It has one of the highest literacy rates in the country and an admirable level of awareness about the fragility of the reef. The large number of substantial private houses being built on the edges of town is proof of how much tourism has enriched San Pedro.

Tourism on the island was slowed down temporarily in 2000, when Hurricane Keith slammed the island with 140 mph winds. The storm killed three people on the caye and caused millions of dollars in damage. Visiting the island today, however, you won't even realize a hurricane swept through. The hotels and other businesses quickly reopened, and even the palm trees have recovered. Because the winds came in from the west, beaches actually accreted sand. Hurricane Iris, which followed in 2001, did severe damage to parts of southern Belize, but had absolutely no effect on Ambergris Caye.

One of the biggest decisions you'll make about Ambergris Caye is where to stay. You have three basic options: in or near the town of San Pedro, in the South Beach or South End area beyond town, or on the North Beach or North End of the island beyond the channel. If you prefer easy access to restaurants, bars, and other activities, you'll likely be happier in San Pedro. Accommodations in town are generally simple and not too expensive (BZ$30–BZ$200). Rooms on the main streets can be noisy, not so much from cars as from late-night revelers. There are also numerous small bistros in town where, as often as not, you'll be eating with your feet in the sand. The fish arrives at your table fresh from the ocean. If you want silence and sand, you have to go out of town for resort-style accommodations. For privacy and the feeling of being away from it all, consider the South End, which is a golf cart ride away, or the even more remote North End, which is reachable only by water taxi.

Whether you arrive in San Pedro by air or by ferry from Belize City, you'll be met by a small crowd of cab drivers, friendly but a little pushy, offering cheap deals on lodging. Keep in mind that hotels pay a commission to these drivers, and the commission is reflected in the hotel

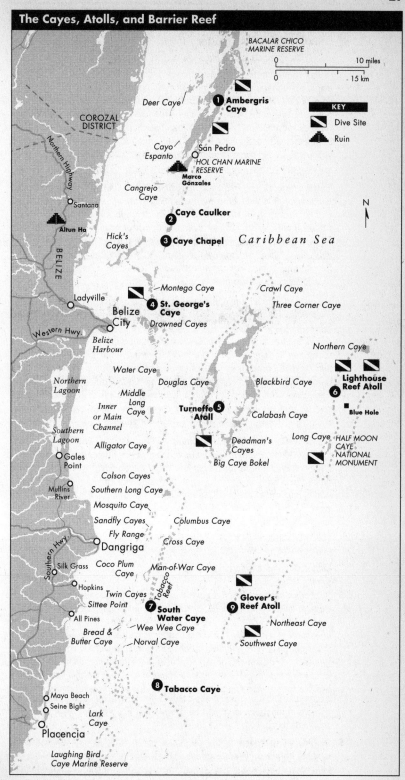

The Cayes, Atolls, and Barrier Reef

BACALAR CHICO
MARINE RESERVE

0 _____ 10 miles

0 _____ 15 km

KEY

Dive Site

Ruin

Deer Caye

1 Ambergris Caye

COROZAL
DISTRICT

Northern Highway

Cayo
Espanto

San Pedro

HOL CHAN MARINE
RESERVE

Marco
Gonzales

Cangrejo
Caye

Santana

Hick's
Cayes

2 Caye Caulker

3 Caye Chapel

Caribbean Sea

Altun Ha

B E L I Z E

Ladyville

Montego Caye

Crawl Caye

Three Corner Caye

4 St. George's Caye

Belize
City

Drowned Cayes

Western Hwy.

Belize
Harbour

Water Caye

Northern
Lagoon

Middle
Long
Caye

Douglas Caye

Blackbird Caye

Northern Caye

Lighthouse Reef Atoll 6

Blue Hole

Inner
or Main
Channel

Turneffe Atoll 5

Calabash Caye

Southern
Lagoon

Alligator Caye

Deadman's
Cayes

Long Caye

HALF MOON
CAYE
NATIONAL
MONUMENT

Gales
Point

Big Caye Bokel

Mullins
River

Colson Cayes

Southern Long Caye

Mosquito Caye

Columbus Caye

Sandfly Cayes

Fly Range

Cross Caye

Southern Hwy.

Dangriga

Silk Grass

Coco Plum
Caye

Man-of-War Caye

Hopkins

Twin Cayes

Tobacco Reef

Sittee Point

Glover's Reef Atoll 9

All Pines

7 South Water Caye

Northeast Caye

Bread &
Butter Caye

Wee Wee Caye

Norval Caye

Southwest Caye

8 Tabacco Caye

Maya Beach

Seine Bight

Lark
Caye

Placencia

Laughing Bird
Caye Marine Reserve

N

rate. For the best rates call the hotel directly when you arrive. During the off-season (May–October), hotels offer walk-in rates that are often a third less than the advertised rates.

Although development on Ambergris continues relentlessly, the far north of the island remains pristine, or close to it. At the top of the caye, butting up against Mexico, **Bacalar Chico National Park** encompasses 105 square km (41 square mi) of land, reef, and sea. Here you can still find white-tail deer, ocelots, saltwater crocodiles, and, according to some reports, pumas and jaguars. Diving, snorkeling, and fishing are excellent, especially off Rocky Point. You'll need a boat and a guide to take you here. ⊠ *North end of Ambergris Caye.* 🎟 *BZ$5.*

The highlight of the reef is the **Hol Chan Marine Reserve** (Maya for "little channel"), 6 km (4 mi) from San Pedro at the southern tip of Ambergris. It's a 20-minute boat ride from the island. Basically, Hol Chan is a break in the reef about 100 ft wide and 20 ft–35 ft deep, through which tremendous volumes of water pass with the tides. The 13-square-km (5-square-mi) park has a miniature Blue Hole, a 12-ft-deep cave whose entrance often attracts the fairy basslet, an iridescent purple-and-yellow fish frequently seen here. The reserve is also home to a large population moray eels.

Varying in depth from 50 ft to 100 ft, Hol Chan's canyons lie between buttresses of coral running perpendicular to the reef, separated by white, sandy channels. Some sides are very steep; others comprise gently rolling undulations. You'll occasionally find tunnel-like passageways from one canyon to the next. Not knowing what's in the next "valley" as you come over the hill can be pretty exciting. Because fishing is off-limits here, divers can see teeming marine life, including spotted eagle rays. You'll identify large numbers of squirrel fish, butterfly fish, parrot fish, and queen angelfish as well as Nassau groupers, barracuda, and large shoals of yellowtail snappers.

Shark-Ray Alley, a sandbar where you can snorkel with nurse sharks and rays (who gather here to be fed) and even larger numbers of daytrippers, was added to the reserve in 1999. Sliding into the water is a feat of personal bravery, as sight of the sharks and rays brushing past you is daunting yet spectacular. A night dive here is a special treat: the water lights up because of bioluminescence, and many nocturnal animals emerge, such as octopus and spider crab. You need above-average swimming skills, especially at night, as the current is very strong. ⊠ *Southern tip of Ambergris Caye.* 🎟 *BZ$10.*

Dining and Lodging

SAN PEDRO

$$$ ✕ **Elvi's Kitchen.** Elvi Staines started out selling burgers from the win-
★ dow of her house in 1974. Soon she added a few tables on the sand under a flamboyant tree. A quarter century later the tree is still here (cut back to fit inside the roof), but everything else is changed. Enter through massive mahogany doors and you'll be tended to by a staff of a couple of dozen in snappy black-and-white outfits. The burgers at lunch are still good—if you're hungry, order the macho burger with double meat—but the place now specializes in upmarket dishes such as shrimp in watermelon sauce or crab claws with garlic butter. For dessert the coconut pie is a must. ⊠ *Pescador Dr.,* ☎ *226/2176. AE, MC, V. Closed Sun.*

$$–$$$ ✕ **Fido's Courtyard.** Sooner or later you're sure to end up at Fido's, sipping something cold and contemplating the ocean views. This casual restaurant and bar is one of the most popular places in San Pedro, serving up everything from fish-and-chips to slices of pizza. It's open every day for lunch and dinner, and some nights, depending on the season, there's live music. ⊠ *Barrier Reef Dr., just north of Catholic church,* ☎ 226/3176.

$$ ✕ **Estel's Dine by the Sea.** Estella's father-in-law was a World War II flier with a squadron called Di Nah Might (his flight jacket is displayed on the wall). Not surprisingly, this is one of the best places in town to get a hearty American-style breakfast complete with bacon, fried potatoes, and freshly squeezed juice. Later in the day you can order burgers, Mexican meals, and excellent seafood dishes. The little white-and-aqua building is right on the beach, as you might guess from the sandy floor and porthole-shape windows. There's a terrace outside where you can sit under a thatch umbrella and watch pelicans. ⊠ *Barrier Reef Dr.,* ☎ 226/2019. *No credit cards.*

$$ ✕ **JamBel Jerk Pit.** The spicy jerk-style dishes here are the way to go at this eatery that combines the cuisines of Jamaica and Belize (hence the name). This casual spot is in the middle of town next door to Big Daddy's. You can relax in the main dining room, where reggae is always playing, or upstairs on the roof, which is often so windy you'll have to hang on to your napkin. The ocean views make it worth the trouble. ⊠ *Barrier Reef Dr., next to Central Park and Big Daddy's,* ☎ 226/3303. *AE, MC, V.*

$–$$ ✕ **Papi's Diner.** Atmosphere is in short supply at Papi's, as are views of the sea. Hardly more than a screened porch with a few wooden tables, Papi's is an unpretentious place tucked away at the north end of town. The seafood and other dishes are expertly prepared and served at some of the most reasonable prices in town. The grilled fish, served with all the usually side dishes, goes for BZ$16. ⊠ *Pescador Dr. at north end of town behind Seven Seas Resort,* ☎ 226/2047. *No credit cards.*

$–$$ ✕ **The Reef.** There's no sea view here, and not much else beside heaping portions of fresh fish, chicken, and beans and rice. The lunch menu has Mexican dishes at rock-bottom prices. Avoid the specials at dinner, which are overpriced. ⊠ *Pescador Dr., just north of Elvi's,* ☎ 226/3212. *No credit cards.*

$$$ ▥ **Mayan Princess.** This pink hotel, sitting pretty right in the middle of town, has rattan furniture covered with pastel-color fabrics. Sliding doors open onto verandas where you can eat the meals you've prepared in your well-equipped kitchenette. In the low season—and sometimes even the high season, as well—managers Sheila and Rusty Nale drop room prices dramatically. When making reservations, it doesn't hurt to ask for a deal. ⊠ *Barrier Reef Dr.,* ☎ 226/2778, FAX 226/2784, WEB *www.mayanprincesshotel.com.* 23 apartments. Fans, kitchenettes, cable TV, beach, travel services. AE, MC, V.

$$ ▥ **San Pedro Holiday Hotel.** This quartet of colonial-style houses, with cheery pink-and-white trim, is right in the heart of town. Owned by Celi McCorkle, one of the first Belizeans to open a hotel here, the San Pedro is always spic-and-span. All rooms have polished wood floors, and many have views of the small in-town beach. Celi's, one of the Caye's better restaurants, serves salads, sandwiches, and other light fare. ⊠ *Barrier Reef Dr.,* ☎ 226/2014, FAX 226/2295, WEB *www.sanpedroholiday.com.* 16 rooms, 1 suite. Restaurant, fans, beach, dive shop, bar, shops, laundry service, travel services. AE, MC, V.

$$ ▥ **Tides Beach Resort.** One of the island's most experienced dive masters, Patojo Paz, opened this hotel with his wife, Sabrina, in 1999. The three-story wood-frame structure harks back to a time before everybody built with reinforced concrete. When you're ready to get wet, the dive boat is only a few feet away. When you return, there's a beach bar in which you can quench your thirst and swap stories. Standard rooms are attractive, if a bit on the small side. For a few bucks more you can upgrade to a bigger room with a king-size bed. The best are the four seafront rooms on the second and third floors, which have balconies overlooking the beach. The hotel is north of town, but it's possible to walk along the beach to San Pedro's bars and restaurants. ⊠ *Boca del Rio Dr., north of town,* ☎ *226/2283,* FAX *226/3797,* WEB *www.ambergriscaye.com/tides. 12 rooms. Fans, refrigerators in some rooms, beach, dive shop, dock, bar, laundry service; no a/c in some rooms, no room phones, no TVs in some rooms. AE, MC, V.*

$ 🏠 **Ruby's.** If you're a tightwad, you'll like this clean hotel on the beach. No wonder budget-minded travelers flock here—air-conditioned rooms with private baths and balconies facing the ocean go for under BZ$100. Try the breakfast burritos at the hotel's little restaurant, which opens early for the fishing and diving crowd. ⊠ *South end of Barrier Reef Dr., at Tarpon St.,* ☎ *226/2063,* FAX *226/2434,* WEB *www. ambergriscaye.com/rubys. 17 rooms, 11 with bath. Restaurant, beach, fishing; no a/c in some rooms, no room phones, no room TVs. AE, MC, V.*

$ 🏠 **San Pedrano.** Painted mint green, blue, and white, this is the cheeriest budget hotel in San Pedro. Each of the spotless rooms has crisp linens. The owners, members of the Gonzalez family, are friendly folks. ⊠ *Barrier Reef Dr.,* ☎ *226/2054,* FAX *226/2093. 6 rooms. Fans; no a/c in some rooms, no room phones, no room TVs. AE, MC, V.*

NORTH OF SAN PEDRO

$$$$ ✕ **Capricorn.** Almost from the day it opened in 1996, this small seaside bistro has been widely considered the best restaurant on the island. Clarence and Annabel Burdes (he's French-Canadian, she's British) serve up delights like rosemary focaccia, medallion of beef with grilled lobster, and crepes with seafood. For dessert there are equally dreamy tropical treats such as key lime pie or coconut ice cream. You'll have to arrange a water taxi to get here, but once you've settled on the veranda, just steps from the sea, you'll be glad you made the trip. If you don't want to leave, there are three little cabanas on the beach. ⊠ *5 km (3 mi) north of San Pedro,* ☎ *226–2809. Reservations essential. AE, MC, V.*

$$$$ ✕ **Mambo Cuisine.** "Food and love are the most important things in the world," says the warm, exuberant Italian co-owner, Nadia Torcelli. The variety and delectability of the meals served at this restaurant in the Mata Chica resort reflect this dictum, particularly the seafood and pasta dishes. A new menu debuted in 2001 that emphasizes seafood specials such as chilled stone crabs. The dining room, in a soaring *palapa* (thatch-covered structure), has charming decorative touches, like the seashells used as salt and pepper shakers. ⊠ *8 km (5 mi) north of San Pedro,* ☎ *220/5010. AE, MC, V.*

$$$$ ✕ **Rendezvous Restaurant & Bar.** Next door to Journey's End is Belize's first and only restaurant serving Thai-French fusion. The *som tum* (shredded papaya) and *cho cho* (a local squash) in a tangy sauce with peanuts, coriander, and dried shrimp make a great starter. Follow that with chicken in a spicy red curry sauce, smoothing it out with chocolate truffle cake with Belizean *wongla* (sesame) seed candy. The owners, who have lived and worked in Thailand and Singapore, also make and bottle their own wines using imported grape concentrate. A honeymoon suite above the restaurant can be rented if you can't bear the water-taxi ride back to your hotel. ⊠ *8 km (5 mi) north of San Pedro,* ☎ FAX *226/3426. AE, MC, V.*

$$–$$$ ✕ **Sweet Basil.** In a quiet residential area on North Ambergris, Sweet Basil is the place to get everything you need for an epicurean picnic. You'll have to take your bike or golf cart up Pescador Drive and across the "cut," a cross-caye channel where a hand-pulled ferry will take you

and your vehicle across for BZ$5. Look for the pink-and-blue house a quarter of a mile on, where you can relax on the upstairs veranda eating some of Belize's scarcer commodities, like lox, prosciutto, and imported cheese. Salade *niçoise* or tapenade is served here 10–5 daily except Monday. ⊠ *Tres Cocos area, North Ambergris,* ☎ *226/3870. No credit cards. Closed Mon.*

$$$$ ⊞ **Captain Morgan's Retreat.** Featured prominently on *Temptation Island,* this resort hasn't been shy about touting it (or in boosting rates to take advantage of the exposure). But instead of scantily clad beauties, here you'll find a long, quiet stretch of sand beside thatch-roof cabanas. Each has windows that let in lots of light and a porch with unobstructed ocean views. Good-size tile showers are welcome in the otherwise narrow baths. Newer condos have a sitting room and kitchen. The pool, surrounded by a hardwood deck, offers an alternative to a dip in the ocean, which is not at its best here. Despite the attractive setting, the staff here seems to change frequently, making for less than tempting service. The rates aren't much of a bargain, either. ⊠ *6 km (4 mi) north of San Pedro,* ☎ *226/2567; 888/653–9090 in the U.S.,* FAX *307/587–8914,* WEB *www.belizevacation.com. 14 cabanas, 12 condos. Restaurant, fans, pool, beach, dive shop, dock, bicycles, volleyball, bar, laundry services, travel services; no TVs in some rooms. AE, DC, MC, V.*

$$$$ ⊞ **Mata Chica.** A dozen or so casitas in shades of mango, banana, and
★ blueberry accentuated by the brilliance of the white sand make this resort look like something out of a Gauguin painting. Fabrics inside echo these brilliant colors, as do the murals in each bedroom and the Mexican tiles in the uniquely styled baths. Delectable meals are served at Mambo Cuisine, which excels at seafood. Nadia Torcelli and her husband, Philippe, worked in the fashion business for a decade before coming here. They brought with them a guest list that has included such stars as Mick Jagger, but you'll feel special even if your 15 minutes haven't arrived. If you crave the water, Philippe can take you on day or overnight cruises on his catamaran. The beach here is postcard pretty, so you might not mind that there's no pool. A new beachside minispa with a hot tub opened in 2001. ⊠ *8 km (5 mi) north of San Pedro,* ☎ *220–5010,* WEB *www.matachica.com. 12 casitas, 2 cabanas. Restaurant, fans, beach, snorkeling, boating, fishing, bar, laundry service, travel services; no room TVs. AE, MC, V.*

$$$$ ⊞ **Portofino.** After a long series of delays, this new resort on the site of
★ the former Green Parrot finally opened in late 2001. With an eye on the success of nearby Mata Chica, it targets the tony side of the market. Here you'll find lushly landscaped grounds, an international-style restaurant called Coralino, and an "ocean pool" (a bit of dockside shore that has been scooped out to accommodate swimmers). Rooms are in thatch-roof buildings facing the ocean. Eight cabanas have bamboo four-poster beds draped with linen mosquito nets (although mosquitoes are rarely a problem). Two "tree house" suites are perched on wooden stilts above the sand. A deluxe honeymoon suite has a private whirlpool. ⊠ *10 km (6 mi) north of San Pedro,* ☎ *221/2096,* FAX *226/4272,* WEB *www. portofinobelize.com. 8 rooms, cabanas. Restaurant, room service, fans, minibars, beach, snorkeling, boating, fishing, bar, laundry service, travel services; no in-room phones, no in-room TVs. AE, MC, V.*

$$$–$$$$ ✕⊞ **El Pescador.** Every place on Ambergris Caye claims to offer fishing trips, but if you want some of the best guides, boats, and gear in Belize, this is the place for you. Occasionally described as a "fishing camp," the main lodge here is actually a handsome colonial house with comfortable, if not luxurious, rooms with mahogany floors. Adjoining the lodge are deluxe two- and three-bedroom villas (with prices to match). Other recent additions include a pool. You can enjoy a fine meal, served

family style in the dining room, or a drink on the veranda. Most guests are here as part of a fishing package whose price starts at BZ$1,696 per person for three nights. ⊠ *5 km (3 mi) north of San Pedro,* ☎ *226/ 2398,* 𝖥𝖠𝖷 *226/2977,* 𝖶𝖤𝖡 *www.elpescador.com. 13 rooms, 4 villas. Restaurant, fans, kitchens, pool, beach, dock, boating, fishing, bar, fly shop, laundry service, travel services; no TV in some rooms. MC, V.*

$$$–$$$$ 🏨 **Journey's End.** The caye's largest resort, Journey's End caters to families who like to keep busy. There are activities day and night, from windsurfing and kayaking to snorkeling and diving. The reef is a little closer to shore here, so there's no need for snorkelers to pay for a boat trip. Come back for dinner, followed by live music. Journey's End is one of the few resorts in Belize that offers an all-inclusive option, letting you pay in advance for all meals and drinks. The landscaped grounds with coconut palms and cedar trees are well maintained, though some of the seafront cottages could use some sprucing up. The rooms facing the lagoon comfortably sleep groups of 10. And if you're lucky, you might see a crocodile from your patio. ⊠ *8 km (5 mi) north of San Pedro,* ☎ *226/2173; 800/460–5665 in the U.S.,* 𝖥𝖠𝖷 *713/780– 1726,* 𝖶𝖤𝖡 *www.journeysendresort.com. 70 rooms. Restaurant, fans, refrigerators in some rooms, 2 tennis courts, pool, beach, dive shop, snorkeling, windsurfing, boating, fishing, bar, laundry service, travel services; no TVs in some rooms. AE, MC, V.*

$$$–$$$$ 🏨 **Playa Blanca.** Run by Gary "Gaz" Cooper, a British expatriate who is a well-known dive operator in San Pedro, Playa Blanca feels like a private home. The pièce de résistance is the penthouse, a 2,200-square-ft suite with three bedrooms and two baths and great views of the water—it's ideal for a large family or group of friends. Packages include dives in the area. ⊠ *8 km (5 mi) north of San Pedro,* ☎ *226/ 5206,* 𝖶𝖤𝖡 *www.playablancabelize.com. 3 suites. Fans, kitchens, refrigerators, pool, beach, dive shop, snorkeling, windsurfing, boating, fishing, bar. MC, V.*

SOUTH OF SAN PEDRO

$$ ✕ **Jade Garden.** Classic Cantonese dishes have a Caribbean twist at Jade Garden, as in the fish chow mein and the conch kebabs. You'll find American-style 12-ounce T-bone steaks and Belizean-style pork chops on the menu, too. This attractive restaurant fills the top two floors of a white colonial-style building just outside town. It's outfitted with handsome rattan furniture and pastel tablecloths, making this one of the caye's more comfortable restaurants. ⊠ *¼ mi south of airstrip, Coconut Dr.,* ☎ *226/2126. AE, MC, V.*

$$$$ 🏨 **Cayo Espanto.** After you arrive at this tiny private island west of Ambergris Caye, you may find that you don't want to leave. And why should you? Your luxurious villa comes complete with amenities like a splash pool, Egyptian cotton linens, and even a personal butler (the staff-to-guest ratio here is two to one). The walls on several of the villas literally fold back to let in the Caribbean sun. Meals, prepared by chefs who took home awards from Caribbean Culinary Federation competitions, are delivered to your own waterside table. You can expect entrées from local rock crab to grilled breast of duck. For all this personal care you'll pay a small fortune, so why not enjoy it? ⊠ *5 km (3 mi) west of Ambergris Caye, Box 90, San Pedro,* ☎ *888/666–4282 in U.S.,* ☎ 𝖥𝖠𝖷 *221/3001,* 𝖶𝖤𝖡 *www.aprivateisland.com. 5 villas. Restaurant, fans, room service, cable TV, 4 pools, beach, dock, snorkeling, boating, fishing, laundry service, travel services. AE, MC, V. AP.*

$$$$ 🏨 **Victoria House.** With its bougainvillea-filled gardens, this beautiful
★   property 3 km (2 mi) south of San Pedro has the style and seclusion of a diplomatic residence. In the white colonial-style house with airy verandas and tile walkways are three ample suites with mahogany fur-

nishings. They share a wraparound veranda that looks over the tree-tops to the turquoise sea. Stone-and-thatch casitas with private porches overlooking the sea are arranged around a lawn shaded by palm trees. A luxury suite on the beach has a king-size bed with silver headboard. Victoria House has made a lot of improvements over the past two years, the biggest of which is a gorgeous pool. The hotel's restaurant has also improved—dreary buffets have been replaced by dishes like shrimp beignets and conch fritters. Sea kayaks, catamarans, and a full array of diving tours are available. ⊠ *Coconut Dr., 3 km (2 mi) south of San Pedro,* ☎ *226/2067; 800/247–5159 in the U.S.,* ℻ *404/373–3885,* WEB *www.victoria-house.com. 13 rooms, 10 casitas, 3 suites, 2 villas. Restaurant, fans, kitchens, pool, beach, dive shop, dock, snorkeling, windsurfing, boating, fishing, bar, laundry service, travel services; no TVs in some rooms. AE, MC, V.*

$$$$ 🏨 **Villas at Banyan Bay.** If you like little luxuries like a whirlpool bath in your room, this complex about 3 km (2 mi) south of town will suit you splendidly. The red-tile-roof buildings hold stylishly furnished two-bedroom condos that have verandas overlooking the sea. You won't feel cramped here—these are some of the largest and most luxe apartments on the island. The cathedral ceilings in the main living area sport a stunning array of tropical hardwoods. The pool is one of the largest on the island, and Mar de Tumbo is at the top of a short list of the island's best beaches. Rico's Bar & Grill, which opened in 2001, has friendly service and a beautiful setting on the water. ⊠ *Coconut Dr., 3 km (2 mi) south of San Pedro,* ☎ *26/3739,* ℻ *226/2766,* WEB *www.banyanbay.com. 42 apartments. Restaurant, fans, in-room hot tubs, kitchens, cable TV, pool, beach, dive shop, dock, bar, laundry service, travel services. AE, MC, V.*

$$$–$$$$ 🏨 **Ramon's Village Resort.** One of the first resorts to open on the cayes, Ramon's keeps on growing. In 2001 it unveiled a new collection of cottages across the street called Steve and Becky's Cute Little Hotel. Guests in the pink-and-lime cottages have access to all the resort's amenities. The cabanas in the older part of the complex are a bit too close together, but are certainly comfortable—the best are those closest to the water. A small artificial reef near the 420-ft pier brings fish to snorkelers. A new pool is gorgeous, but it's smaller than it looks in the brochures. Ramon's has a well-regarded dive operation, sending out guests in seven dive boats. Evening means margaritas at the poolside bar or a beach barbecue featuring live music. ⊠ *Coconut Dr.,* ☎ *226/2071; 800/624–4315 in the U.S.,* ℻ *226/2214,* WEB *www.ramons.com. 61 rooms, 8 cottages. Restaurant, fans, some kitchens, cable TV, pool, beach, dive shop, dock, boating, snorkeling, bar, shop, laundry service, travel services. AE, MC, V.*

$$$ 🏨 **SunBreeze Beach Hotel.** This midsize resort at the southern edge of town has always enjoyed an unbeatable location. Under the no-nonsense hand of manager Julia Edwards, the place has truly blossomed. The rooms, surrounding a plant-filled courtyard, are quite large. Five deluxe rooms have whirlpool baths. All units are equipped for guests with disabilities. The hotel also has a small beach area (there's a seawall you must cross to reach the water), a shaded pool, and a dive shop. The Blue Water Grill serves Pan-Asian fare, including—a first for San Pedro—sushi. The first paved street on the island, a short strip of cobblestone put down in 1999, is just outside the front door. ⊠ *Coconut Dr.,* ☎ *226/2191,* ℻ *226/2346,* WEB *www.sunbreeze.net. 36 rooms. Restaurant, some refrigerators, cable TV, pool, beach, dive shop, dock, laundry service, travel services. AE, MC, V.*

$$$ 🏨 **Caribbean Villas.** Mixing Caribbean and Spanish styles, these two
★ graceful villas are set on a lovely stretch of beach south of San Pedro. An intelligent and creative design—luggage hides beneath built-in sofas

and spacious lofts sleep six—make these apartments feel larger than they are. A four-story bird-watching tower has made the place an oasis for birders, with as many as 100 species flitting about at any one time. This sanctuary was the brainchild of owner Susan Lala, an avid birder. A tiny artificial reef helps attract schools of fish. If relaxation by the sea is what you're seeking, few spots are better. There's no bar or restaurant, but a nice grocery store, Island Supermarket, is handy if you want to do your own cooking. ⊠ *Coconut Dr., 1 km (¾ mi) south of San Pedro,* ☎ *226/2715; 785/776–3738 in the U.S.,* FAX *226/2885,* WEB *www.caribbeanvillashotel.com. 10 suites. Fans, kitchenettes, outdoor hot tub, beach, dock, snorkeling, bicycles, travel services; no room phones, no TV in rooms. AE, MC, V.*

$$$ 🏨 **Xanadu Island Resort.** It's billed as the "world's first monolithic dome resort," a description that might appeal only to engineers. Happily, these domes look nicer than they sound. Owner Ivan Sheinbaum says construction is costly, but the result is a structure that can withstand winds of up to 300 mph. Covered with thatch, the buildings contain suites with bedrooms and baths on two levels. They are attractively furnished in earth tones and have all the modern amenities. There are a nice little stretch of beach, a 350-ft pier, and a pool. You also get free use of bikes, canoes, and kayaks. ⊠ *Coconut Dr., 2 km (1 mi) south of San Pedro,* ☎ *226/2814,* FAX *226/3409,* WEB *www.xanaduresort-belize.com. 10 suites. Fans, kitchens, cable TV, pool, beach, dock, snorkeling, travel services. AE, MC, V.*

$$–$$$ 🏨 **Banana Beach Resort.** Inspired by the architecture of the Mexican town of Mérida, this three-story resort is set on a sandy beach that happens to be one of the island's nicest. The expansive one-bedroom apartments surround a courtyard with swimming pool and a breezeway leading to the sea. Many have balconies just feet from the sea, while others have ocean views. Ask for one of the corner units on the second and third floors. The rates are surprisingly low, considering the quality. Flush with the success of Banana Beach, owner Tim Jeffers has added another 28 units next door, along with another pool, a restaurant, and dive shop. The staff, among the friendliest on the island, is glad to arrange diving and snorkeling trips, fishing excursions, and other activities. ⊠ *Coconut Dr., 3¼ km (2 mi) south of San Pedro,* ☎ *226/3890,* FAX *226/3891,* WEB *www.bananabeach.com. 63 suites. Restaurant, fans, kitchens, cable TV, 2 pools, beach, dive shop, dock, boating, bicycles, laundry service, travel services. AE, MC, V.*

$$ 🏨 **Changes In Latitudes.** The sign out front, depicting an igloo melting under a tropical sun, is an in-joke about Canadian owner Lori Reed's decision to move south to run this little bed-and-breakfast. A relaxed spot, this inn is close to San Pedro's restaurants and bars. The rooms are all on the small side, but they're clean and have louvered windows to let in the ocean breezes. The three garden-side rooms get the most light; others face a concrete wall. A full breakfast is served in the common room, but you can also prepare your own meals and store beer upstairs in Lori's fridge. Diving, snorkeling, and boating trips are easy to arrange. ⊠ *Coconut Dr., ¼ mi south of San Pedro,* ☎ FAX *226/2986,* WEB *www.ambergriscaye.com/latitudes. 6 rooms. Fans, travel services; no room phones, no room TVs. AE, MC, V.*

$$ 🏨 **Coconuts Caribbean Hotel.** Operated by the same folks who run Banana Beach, this inn by the ocean stays busy year-round thanks to low rates and employees who always seems to be smiling. They are eager to arrange diving and snorkeling trips or help with restaurant selections. The two-story building has big, airy rooms, some with L-shape sleeper sofas. The bar on the sandy beach serves refreshing rum drinks. This is one of the best deals on the island, especially off-season. ⊠ *Coconut Dr., ¾ mi south of San Pedro,* ☎ *226/3500,* FAX *226/3501,* WEB

www.coconutshotel.com. 14 rooms. Snack bar, fans, beach, snorkeling, bicycles, bar, travel services; no TVs in some rooms. AE, MC, V.

Outdoor Activities and Sports

BOATING

For sailing Belize will never rival the British Virgin Islands. The shallow water kicks up a lot of chop, and hidden coral heads and tidal currents pose a danger to even those who know the area. When you charter a boat you have to stay inside the barrier reef, but there's a lot of beautiful territory to explore. The top outfit here is **Tortola Marine Management** (✉ Coconut Dr., ☎ 226/3026, FAX 226/3072, WEB www.sailtmm.com), which has a small fleet of catamarans and a yacht with three staterooms. Rates vary, depending on the type of boat and time of year, but range from around BZ$5,000 to more than BZ$14,000 a week, not including provisions. Skippers and cooks are an additional BZ$200 per day each. Split among three to eight people, the prices are competitive with hotel rates.

SCUBA DIVING

Sensing that their future lay in tourism, the people of Ambergris Caye were the first to cater to those who wanted to witness Belize's undersea world. In its profusion of dive shops, experience of dive masters, and range of equipment and facilities, Ambergris Caye remains ahead of the rest. San Pedro even has a hyperbaric chamber and an on-site doctor to tend to divers with the bends, paid for by contributions from all the dive shops.

Most dive masters are former fishermen, locals who began diving as a sideline and eventually began to do it full time. The best of them have an intimate knowledge of the reef and a superb eye for coral and marine life. They are also quite ecologically aware, knowing full well that the destruction of the reef would not only be a great tragedy in itself but would leave them without a way to support their families. It was a group of dive masters who fastened a network of buoys to the bedrock to prevent further destruction of the coral. In bad weather one anchor dragged across the bottom can destroy more coral than a 1,000 divers.

Speedboats take divers out to their destinations. Power generally comes from two hefty outboards mounted on the back, and with the throttle open it's an exhilarating ride. If you don't want to get splashed, sit in the middle. Many boats are constructed from solid mahogany. As they represent the major investment of the dive companies, the boats are lovingly maintained.

Dives off Ambergris are usually single-tank dives at depths of 50 ft–80 ft, giving you approximately 35 minutes of bottom time. Most companies offer two single-tank dives per day, one in the morning and one in the afternoon. Snorkeling generally costs BZ$30–BZ$50 per person for two or three hours or BZ$70–BZ$100 for a day trip, including lunch. Diving trips run BZ$70–BZ$80 for a single-tank dive, BZ$100–BZ$130 for a double-tank dive, and BZ$300–BZ$380 for day trips with dives to Turneffe Atoll or Lighthouse Reef.

Amigos del Mar (✉ Off Barrier Reef Dr., near Mayan Princess Hotel, ☎ 226/2706, WEB amigosdive.com) is probably the most consistently recommended dive operation on the island. It offers a range of local dives as well as trips to Turneffe Atoll and Lighthouse Reef in a fast 42-ft dive boat. The well-regarded **Gaz Cooper's Dive Belize** (✉ 5 mi north of town at Playa Blanca Resort, ☎ 226/3202, WEB www.divebelize.com) boasts about having the smallest dive operation on the island, preferring to keep it exclusive. **Larry Parker's Reef Divers** (✉ Spindrift Hotel,

Barrier Reef Dr., ☎ 226/3134, WEB www.reefdivers.com), a long-established company, offers a full range of dives and instruction. The owner
has been diving in Belize since 1977. Among those offering atoll trips
are **Blue Hole Dive Center** (⊠ Barrier Reef Dr., San Pedro, Ambergris
Caye, ☎ 226/2982, FAX 226/2810).

Nightlife

With live music most nights, **Barefoot Iguana** (⊠ Coconut Dr., ¾ km
south of town) is the loudest bar on the island. Known for its burgers,
BC's Beach Bar (⊠ South of SunBreeze Hotel) is a popular oceanfront
bar that hosts all-you-can-eat barbecues on Sunday afternoon. **Big
Daddy's** (⊠ Barrier Reef Dr., north side of Central Park) is where the
action is in downtown San Pedro. Since it's right on the water, there's
a beachside barbecue some nights. The music and real boozing here
don't usually get started until around 11. Across the street from Big
Daddy's is **Jaguar** (⊠ Barrier Reef Dr.), another popular San Pedro
disco.

Shopping

At **Belizean Arts** (⊠ Fido's Courtyard, off Barrier Reef Dr., ☎ 226/
2638) you'll find a selection of works by local painters. Also on display are handicrafts from the region, including hand-painted animal
figures from Mexico, masks and fabrics from Guatemala, and brilliantly
colored tropical fish made of coconut wood. For clothing and such the
best place to stop is **D&G Gift Shop** (⊠ Angel Coral St., behind Elvi's,
☎ 226/2069). The store also sells custom-made jewelry. About 3 km
(2 mi) south of town, **Hummingbird Rattan** (⊠ Coconut Dr., at Mar
de Tumbo, ☎ 226/2960) sells high-quality furniture. At **Sea Gal Boutique** (⊠ Barrier Reef Dr., in Holiday Hotel, ☎ 226/2431) the owner
has an artist's eye. Everything is beautiful, even the T-shirts.

Caye Caulker

❷ *8 km (5 mi) south of Ambergris Caye, 29 km (18 mi) northeast of Belize City.*

For many years Caye Caulker had a reputation as a haven for British
"squaddies" looking for a fight and backpackers in search of a cheap
place to crash. As more upscale lodgings begin to open, its charms are
beginning to shine through. Brightly painted houses on stilts line the
coral sand streets. Flowers outnumber cars ten to one (golf carts, bicycles, and bare feet are the preferred means of transportation). The
living is easy, as you might guess from all the NO SHIRT, NO SHOES, NO
PROBLEM signs at the bars. This is the kind of place where most of the
listings in the telephone directory give addresses like "near football field."

A plethora of dive and snorkel operators offers reef tours (some of them
are "cowboys," so make sure you use a reputable company). Plan on
spending about BZ$25–BZ$40 for a snorkeling trip around the island
or to Hol Chan Marine Reserve. If you run out of money, don't worry.
One of the island's newer amenities is a bank.

Dining and Lodging

$$ ✕ **The Sandbox.** The names of regulars are carved on the backs of the
chairs at this popular eatery. Whether outside under the palms or in-
doors under the lazily turning ceiling fans, you'll always have your feet
in the sand here. Open from 7 AM to 9 PM, the Sandbox serves a lob-
ster omelet for breakfast, a roast beef sandwich for lunch, and red snap-
per in a mango sauce for dinner. The chowders are very good, and the
conch fritters are suitably spicy. Prices are reasonable, and the portions
are enormous. At night the bar gets very lively. ⊠ *Front St. at public
pier,* ☎ *226/0200. AE, MC, V.*

$$ ✕ **Sobre Las Olas.** The surf-and-turf specials are the reason to head to this beachfront barbecue spot. The cooks toss lobster or whatever other seafood is in season on the grill, along with steaks and chicken. All the seating is outdoors under a canopy, the better to enjoy the sea breezes. ⊠ *Front St., near Rainbow Hotel,* ☎ *226/0243. No credit cards.*

$–$$ ✕ **CocoPlum Gardens.** It's a bit of a hike to this little restaurant at the south end of the island, but the breakfasts are worth the effort—enjoy wholesome breads, fresh-made granola, and homemade jams, all in a lovely garden setting (not surprising, as the owners also operate a nursery.) It's currently open only in the morning, but popular demand may convince them to start serving dinner. While you're here, browse the small gallery and gift shop with Belizean-made crafts. ⊠ *South end of island, near airstrip,* ☎ *226–0226. MC, V. Closed Monday.*

$–$$ ✕ **Jolly Roger.** If you're in the mood for juicy lobster at a modest price, this place serves some of the best in the islands. There's delicious barbecued fish, too. Seating is at little tables beside the owner's house. ⊠ *Front St. near Health Center,* ☎ *no phone. No credit cards.*

$ ✕ **Glenda's.** Glenda's has been around for years, and it's as good as ever for cheap, filling breakfasts or lunches. The classic eye-opener is a cinnamon roll, johnnycake (ask for one, as they're not on the menu), and fresh-squeezed orange juice. You just have to order the tasty rice and beans for lunch. ⊠ *Back St., toward south end of village,* ☎ *no phone. No credit cards. No dinner.*

$ ✕ **YooHoo Deli.** This is the best place to grab a Cuban sandwich and a Fanta before your afternoon snorkeling trip. It's open from 10 until around sunset. The restaurant is standing room only, meaning there's no seating. ⊠ *Front St. next to police station,* ☎ *226/0232. No credit cards.*

$$ ▥ **Chocolate's.** A 70-something Belizean named Chocolate rents out one of the best rooms on Caye Caulker—a romantic retreat with a four-poster bed, vaulted mahogany ceiling with fan, and a screened-in veranda that looks out to the sea. The tile bath has a very large shower (terry cloth robes are nearby). Halogen reading lamps, a refrigerator, and a coffeemaker are nice little extras. Chocolate's manatee-watching trips to Goff Caye and his alligator-spotting cruises in the coastal lagoons are terrific. He says he's planning on building a couple more rooms because the one he has stays full much of the time. ⊠ *At north end of island, near the Split,* ☎ *226–0151. 1 room. Fans, refrigerator, shop, snorkeling; no a/c, no room phones, no room TVs. MC, V.*

$$ ▥ **Iguana Reef Inn.** Far and away Caye Caulker's most upmarket lodging, Iguana Reef has just about everything but a concierge. The suites are colorfully furnished with handmade furniture and local artwork. Unusual for the island, all are air-conditioned. Upstairs suites have vaulted ceilings with skylights. The latest addition is a thatch-roof bar. Because the inn is on the lee side of the island, you have the benefit of sunset views from your veranda. Considering the amenities, the rates are quite reasonable. The manager is a wealth of information about the island. ⊠ *Near end of Middle St., next to soccer field,* ☎ *226/0213,* FAX *226–0000,* WEB *www.iguanareefinn.com. 12 suites. Fans, refrigerator, snorkeling, fishing, bar, travel services; no room phones, no room TVs. AE, MC, V.*

$$ ▥ **Lazy Iguana B&B.** This B&B may be the tallest structure on any of the cayes. The views of the sunsets from the rooftop terrace are terrific, though the hotel's location on the back side of the island means you may have to swat an occasional mosquito while you watch. The rooms are furnished with attractive wicker and tropical hardwood furniture. Feel free to make yourself at home in the common room—owner Mo Miller says no shoes are required. Breakfast is included in the rate. ⊠

South of main public pier, ☎ *226/0350,* FAX *226/0320,* WEB *www. lazyiguana.net. 4 rooms. Fans; no room phones, no room TVs. MC, V.*

$$ 🏠 **Seaside Cabanas.** Just to the left of the public pier is this cluster of thatch cabanas. Though a bit pricey for Caye Caulker, they've proven to be quite popular and often are full. All have private baths, and some have air-conditioning. Hummingbird Tours can arrange dive, snorkel, and sightseeing trips. ✉ *Near Front St., at public dock,* ☎ *226/0498,* WEB *www.seasidecabanas.com. 10 cabanas. Fans, refrigerators, cable TV, beach, dive shop, snorkeling, fishing, bar, travel services; no a/c in some rooms, no room phones, no room TVs. MC, V.*

$$ 🏠 **Shirley's Guest House.** At the southernmost tip of the caye, this little inn has four green-trimmed wooden cottages raised up on stilts and a cabana with a covered veranda. All the rooms look out to sea. Shirley's place is quiet and safe because, according to her, she runs a tight ship and no one would mess with her. We have to agree. ✉ *South end of island, on waterfront,* ☎ *226/2145,* FAX *226/0145,* WEB *www.geocities.com/ shirleysguesthouse. 10 rooms. Fans, refrigerators, beach, laundry service; no a/c, no room phones, no room TVs, no kids under 18. MC, V.*

$ 🏠 **Treetops.** Three miniature security guards—Jack Russell terriers— guard this comfortable hotel. The rooms are generously proportioned and so clean you could eat off the floor. Sporting probably the most unusual decor of any on the islands is the Premier Room, which has an East African theme, complete with authentic masks and spears (the owner was in Africa with the British armed forces). The white-sand garden lost much of its bougainvillea during Hurricane Keith, but it's still a peaceful place to curl up on a chaise lounge and read. The staff is happy to arrange water sports and tours. ✉ *Caye Caulker,* ☎ *226/ 0008,* FAX *226/0115,* WEB *www.treetopsbelize.com. 4 rooms, 2 with bath. Fans, refrigerators, cable TV, beach, snorkeling, laundry service, travel services; no a/c in some rooms, no room phones. MC, V.*

$ 🏠 **Trends Beachfront Hotel.** The first thing you see when you arrive at the pier is this little hotel, painted a tropical pink and green. Thanks to its location and its bright rooms, it stays full much of the time. TVs are available on request. ✉ *Near Front St., at public dock,* ☎ *226/ 0094,* FAX *226/0097,* WEB *www.cayecaulker.com/trends.htm. 6 rooms. Fans, refrigerators; no a/c, no room phones, no room TVs. MC, V.*

Outdoor Sports and Activities

If you're looking for someone to take you out to the reef, **Frenchie's Diving Services** (✉ Front St., ☎ 226/0234) is a well-regarded local operator.

Shopping

Annie's Boutique (✉ North end of island, near the Split, ☎ 226/0151) has the best women's and children's clothes in Belize. Here you'll find dresses and sarongs made with fabrics from Bali, some unique silver jewelry, and Guatemalan bags that somehow don't make you look like a backpacker. **Galleria Hicaco** (✉ Front St., ☎ 226/0178) has Belizean arts and crafts, including jewelry, dolls, carvings, and pottery.

Caye Chapel

➌ *2 km (½ mi) south of Caye Caulker, 10 km (6 mi) south of Ambergris Caye.*

Not since the days of British colonialism has there been a real 18-hole golf course in Belize. But for traveling duffers, a new course opened on Caye Chapelin in late 1999. It's a beautiful par-72 course, flat but long, with four par-5 holes. Challenges include brisk prevailing winds and the occasional crocodile. If golf is your game, this is the best Belize has to offer (smaller 9-hole courses are also located near Altun Ha ruins on the Old Northern Highway and at Jaguar Reef Lodge near Hopkins). There has been considerable controversy over the construction of this course, as some environmentalists believe that a golf course—which typically requires large applications of fertilizer and pesticides—could pose an ecological danger to the nearby reef. However, the course uses a special hybrid grass that requires half the fertilizers, pesticides, and irrigation of ordinary grass.

Dining and Lodging

$$$$ ☷ **Caye Chapel Golf Resort.** This resort was designed as a corporate retreat, but you can stay here if you've got the dough. The expansive villas, which stand at imperial attention along the seafront, are similar to what you might see in exclusive gated communities in Boca Raton, Florida. Inside you'll find every luxury—whirlpool baths, expansive wet bars, and kitchens with the latest German appliances. New in 2002 are a dozen "budget" casitas with a price tag that's significantly less than the villas. The golf course's clubhouse has a restaurant with indoor and open-air dining and stunning views of the sea. ⊠ *Caye Chapel,* ☎ *226/8250,* ℻ *226–8201,* ᗐᗐ *www.belizegolf.cc. 8 villas, 12 casitas. Restaurant, fans, some in-room hot tubs, kitchens, cable TV, pool, gym, beach, dive shop, dock, boating, marina, fishing, basketball, tennis courts, marina, bar, laundry service, airstrip, travel services. AE, MC, V.*

St. George's Caye

4 *15 km (9 mi) northeast of Belize City.*

Just a stone's throw from Belize City, this small caye is steeped in history. The state of Belize had its origins here, as St. George's Caye held the first capital of the original British settlement. Later the island was the site of a decisive battle with the Spanish. Islanders had a total of one sloop, while the Spanish had 31 ships. Their knowledge of the sea, however, helped them to defeat the invaders in two hours.

Getting to St. George's Caye couldn't be easier, as the boat trip from Belize City takes little more than 20 minutes. Although St. George's Caye has some great places to dive, many serious scuba enthusiasts choose to head out to the more pristine atolls.

Dining and Lodging

$$$$ ☷ **St. George's Lodge.** In colonial days this long-established resort was a favorite with the British because of its proximity to Belize City. Today St. George's Caye is a favorite of divers, undoubtedly because of the diving program led by Fred Good. You have a choice of basic rooms in the main building or thatch cottages by the water. Electricity comes from the lodge's own windmills, and your shower water is heated by the sun. The lodge doesn't have a liquor license, but you can bring your own booze to the beautiful rosewood bar. The restaurant serves homemade bread and grilled snapper or grouper, and coffee is delivered to your door in the morning. Weekly dive packages start at around BZ$3,400 per person, including meals. ⊠ *1604 Maple St., Nokomis, FL 34275,* ☎ *800/678–6871 in the U.S.,* ℻ *941/488–3953,* ᗐᗐ *www.gooddiving.com. 6 cabanas, 10 rooms. Restaurant, fans, beach, dive shop, snorkeling, travel services; no a/c, no room phones, no room TVs. AE, MC, V. AP.*

Turneffe Atoll

5 *40 km (25 mi) east of Belize City.*

This chain of tiny islands and mangrove swamps makes up an atoll the size of Barbados. The largest of the three atolls, Turneffe Atoll is the closest to Belize City. It's one of the best spots for diving, thanks to several steep drop-offs. Only an hour from Lighthouse Reef and 45 minutes from the northern edge of Glover's Reef, Turneffe Atoll is a good base for exploring the atolls.

Turneffe Atoll's best-known attraction, and probably the most exciting wall dive in Belize, is the **Elbow**, at the southernmost tip of the atoll. You may encounter eagle rays swimming nearby. Sometimes as many as 50 flutter together, forming a rippling herd that will take your breath away. This is generally considered an advanced dive because of the strong currents, which sweep you toward the deep water beyond the reef.

Though it's most famous for its spectacular wall dives, the atoll has dives for every level. The atoll's leeward side, where the reef is wide and gently sloping, is a good place for shallower dives and snorkeling; you'll see large concentrations of tube sponges, soft corals such as forked sea feathers and sea fans, and plenty of fish. Also on the atoll's western side is the wreck of the *Sayonara*. No doubloons to be scooped up here—it was a small passenger and cargo boat that went down in 1985—but it's a good place to practice wreck diving.

Dining and Lodging

$$$$ 🏨 **Turneffe Flats.** The sound of the surf is the only thing you'll hear at these smart blue-and-white beachfront cabins. The rooms, fitted with elegant hardwoods, are a far cry from the bare-bones fishing camp that occupied this site in the early '80s. You can dive here—the reef is only 200 yards from the shore—but the ubiquitous fishing-pole racks suggest that snook, bonefish, and permit are still the dominant lure. If you don't love fishing, you may feel like a bit of an outsider, as 75% of the clientele comes expressly to fish. You pay a pretty penny to indulge your passion, however—a weekly fishing package for two is around BZ$10,000. ⊠ *Northern Bogue (Box 36, Deadwood, SD 57732),* ☏ *800/815–1304 or 605/578–1304,* 𝖥𝖠𝖷 *605/578–7540,* 𝖶𝖤𝖡 *www.tflats. com. 6 rooms. Restaurant, dive shop, snorkeling, fishing; no room phones, no room TVs. No credit cards.*

$$$$ 🏨 **Turneffe Island Lodge.** White dive tanks serving as fence posts and
   ★   a rusty anchor from an 18th-century British warship set the tone at this shipshape resort at the south end of Turneffe Atoll. This was the first dive lodge on Turneffe Atoll, and it bagged the best spot a few hundred yards from the legendary Elbow. But if you came to Belize for the diving, this is an ideal base. The rooms, in palm-shaded cottages with views of the sea, have been refurbished without spoiling the cozy feeling created by the varnished hardwood fittings. The two-story colonial-style house, which holds the bar and the dining room, glows from the original mahogany trim installed by Mennonite craftsmen in the early '60s. ⊠ *Coco Tree Caye,* ☏ *713/313–4670 or 800/874–0118,* 𝖥𝖠𝖷 *713/313–4671,* 𝖶𝖤𝖡 *www.turneffelodge.com. 7 cabanas, 12 rooms. Restaurant, fans, dive shop, snorkeling, fishing, bar, travel services; no room phones, no room TVs. AE, MC, V.*

Lighthouse Reef Atoll

   ❻ *80 km (50 mi) east of Belize City.*

If Robinson Crusoe had been a man of means, he would have repaired here for a break from his desert island. It's the most distant of Belize's atolls, but it's the closest you'll get to paradise. Lighthouse Reef is also the most accessible, thanks to an airstrip.

Lighthouse Reef is about 29 km (18 mi) long and less than 2 km (1 mi) wide and is surrounded by a seemingly endless stretch of coral. Here you'll find two of the country's five-star dives. From the air the **Blue Hole,** a breathtaking vertical chute that drops several hundred feet through the reef, looks like a dark blue eye in the center of the shallow lagoon. The Blue Hole was first dived by Jacques Cousteau in 1970 and has since become a diver's pilgrimage site. Just over 1,000 ft wide at the surface and dropping almost vertically to a depth of 412 ft, the Blue Hole is like swimming down a mine shaft. It is this excitement, rather than the marine life, that has led to the thousands of stickers reading, "I Dived the Blue Hole."

The best diving on Lighthouse Reef is at **Half Moon Caye.** A classic wall dive, Half Moon Caye begins at 35 ft and drops almost vertically to blue infinity. Floating out over the edge is a bit like free-fall parachuting. Magnificent spurs of coral jut out to the seaward side, looking like small tunnels; they're fascinating to explore and invariably full of fish. An exceptional variety of marine life hovers around this caye. On the gently sloping sand flats behind the coral spurs, a vast colony of garden eels stirs, their heads protruding from the sand like periscopes. Spotted eagle rays, sea turtles, and other underwater wonders frequent the drop-off.

Although difficult to reach and lacking accommodations, **Half Moon Caye National Monument,** Belize's easternmost island, offers one of the greatest wildlife encounters in Belize. Part of the Lighthouse Reef system, Half Moon Caye owes its protected status to the presence of the red-footed booby. The species is here in such numbers that it's hard to believe it has only one other nesting ground in the entire Caribbean (on Tobago Island, off the coast of Venezuela). Some 4,000 of these birds hang their hats on Half Moon Caye, along with iguanas, lizards, and loggerhead turtles. The entire 40-acre island is a nature reserve, so you can either explore the beaches or head into the bush on the narrow nature trail. Above the trees at the center of the island is a small viewing platform—at the top you're suddenly in a sea of birds that will doubtless remind you of a certain Alfred Hitchcock movie. Several dive operators and resorts arrange day trips and overnight camping trips to Half Moon Caye.

Dining and Lodging

$$$$ ⊞ **Lighthouse Reef Resort.** Once a spartan dive camp, Lighthouse Reef
★ has gradually been transformed into one of the most exclusive resorts in Central America. You'll probably feel like you're the only person on the island. You have a choice of simple cabanas, suites with pine-plank floors, and handsome colonial-style villas with Queen Anne–style furnishings. The setting—palm trees lining the mint green ocean—is breathtaking, and the diving, under expert supervision, is as good as any in the world. Seven-night packages cost BZ$3,100–BZ$3,700 per person, including meals, dives, and air transfer from Belize City. ⊠ *Northern Caye,* ☎ *800/423–3114 in the U.S.,* ⅎ*X 941/439–2118 in the U.S.,* ⩗ *www.scuba-dive-belize.com. 11 rooms. Restaurant, fans, some refrigerators, beach, dock, dive shop, fishing, travel services; no room phones, no room TVs. MC, V.*

South Water Caye

❼ *23 km (14 mi) southeast of Dangriga.*

The first island in the south to have been developed for tourism, tiny South Water Caye makes for good off-the-beaten-reef diving. The reef is only a short swim from shore. The nearby **Smithsonian Institution's Marine Research Laboratory** (⊠ Carrie Bow Caye) welcomes visitors by appointment; contact the Blue Marlin Lodge for more information.

Dining and Lodging

$$$$ 🏨 **Blue Marlin Lodge.** This picturesque resort makes an excellent base for fishing, snorkeling, and diving trips, as the reef is only 50 yards away. World-class destinations such as Turneffe Atoll and Glover's Reef are easily accessible. The Belizean-run place is child-friendly, with activities to please everyone on your trip. Accommodations, which spread out over half the caye, range from thatch cabanas to larger cabins perched on stilts to three lemon-yellow concrete dome buildings. All rooms are close enough to the sea that the sound of the waves may lull you to sleep. A restaurant and bar are great places to swap stories with other travelers. The minimum stay is four days. ⊠ *South Water Caye,* ☎ *522/2243; 800/ 798–1558 in the U.S.,* FAX *522/2296,* WEB *www.bluemarinlodge.com. 16 rooms. Restaurant, beach, dive shop, snorkeling, fishing, bar, baby-sitting, travel services; no a/c in some rooms, no room phones, no room TVs. MC, V.*

$$$–$$$$ 🏨 **Pelican Beach Cottages.** If you like to snorkel, get thee to this former nunnery. Once a convent belonging to the Sisters of Mercy, this colonial-era house called Pelican's Pouch has five large rooms on the second floor. There also are two cottages; if you're with a group ask for the Osprey's Nest, a three-bedroom house with two large verandas. At the center of the island, at what's called "Pelicans' University," student groups can rent a large house with bunk beds. The resort has a great beach, where you can swim and snorkel to your heart's content. The fishing's good, too. You may occasionally have to combat sandflies and mosquitoes, so bring along strong repellent. ⊠ *South Water Caye,* ☎ *522/2044,* FAX *522/2570,* WEB *www.pelicanbeachbelize.com. 5 rooms, 2 cottages, 1 dormitory. Restaurant, beach, dive shop, snorkeling, boating, fishing, travel services; no a/c, no room phones, no room TVs. AE, MC, V.*

Tobacco Caye

❽ *18 km (11 mi) southeast of Dangriga.*

If you don't want to pay a lot for your place in the sun, Tobacco Caye may be for you. It's a tiny island—barely three acres—but it's right on the reef, so you can snorkel just a few feet from shore. All the accommodations here are budget places, basically just rough wood cabins. Periodically they get blown away by storms but are rebuilt, usually a little nicer than they were before. But the prices remain low, around BZ$70–BZ$125 a day per person, including meals. Boats leave from Dangriga for the 30-minute trip to Tobacco Caye.

Dining and Lodging

$–$$ 🏨 **Tobacco Caye Lodge.** This little cluster of pastel blue cabins sits just feet from the turquoise sea. There's a bit more room here for stretching out than at the other lodges on the island, as the property extends from the sea to the lagoon. A thatch-roof bar is set away from the cabins, and three simple but filling meals are included in the rate. ⊠ *Tobacco Caye,* ☎ *520/5033,* WEB *www.tclodgebelize.com. 6 cabins. Fans, beach, snorkeling, fishing, bar; no a/c, no room phones, no room TVs. MC, V.*

Glover's Reef Atoll

❾ *113 km (70 mi) southeast of Belize City.*

Named after the pirate John Glover, this coral necklace strung around a 208-square-km (80-square-mi) lagoon is the southernmost of Belize's three atolls. The diving rates as some of the best in Belize. Visitors to

Glover's Reef are charged BZ$5 a day, paid to the Belize Fisheries Department.

Although most of the finest dive sites are along the atoll's southeastern side, one exception is **Emerald Forest Reef,** named for its masses of huge green elkhorn coral. Because the most exciting part of the reef is only 25 ft down, it's excellent for novice divers. **Long Caye Wall,** another exciting wall, has a dramatic drop-off hundreds of feet down. Overhangs covered in sheet and boulder coral make it a good place to spot turtles, rays, and barracuda.

Southwest Caye Wall is an underwater cliff that falls quickly to 130 ft. It's briefly interrupted by a narrow shelf, then continues its near-vertical descent to 350 ft. This dive gives you the exhilaration of flying in blue space, so it's easy to lose track of how deep you are going. Both ascent and descent require careful monitoring.

Dining and Lodging

$ ⛺ **Glover's Atoll Resort.** This little group of cabins is a lesson in laid-back living. Forget about electricity and running water and surrender to a life of nothing but fishing, diving, and cooking your own meals. You bring your tackle for the boat or shore fishing and your own food supplies (and anything else you'll need). This is as close as they come to a *Gilligan's Island*–style vacation spot. ⌧ *Box 563, Belize City,* ☎ *520/5016,* WEB *www.glovers.com.bz. MC, V.*

The Cayes and Atolls A to Z

AIR TRAVEL TO AND FROM THE CAYES AND ATOLLS

Maya Island Airways and Tropic Air operate flights to Ambergris Caye and Caye Caulker from both the municipal and international airports in Belize City. Each has hourly service every day to Ambergris Caye between 7:30 and 5:30. In high season, additional flights are sometimes added to accommodate demand. Round-trip fares for the 20-minute flight are about BZ$104 (municipal) and BZ$188 (international).

The airstrip on Ambergris Caye is in San Pedro. You'll always find taxis waiting at the airstrip, and most hotels run shuttles. If you're proceeding on foot, it's about two minutes, around the edges of the soccer field, to the hotels in town. The airstrip on Caye Caulker is at the south end of the island. Hotels may send a golf cart to pick you up. Otherwise, you'll find that taxis are available.

There are no scheduled flights to the other cayes, although Lighthouse Reef and Caye Chapel both have airstrips where charter flights can land. ➤ AIRLINES AND CONTACTS: **Maya Island Airways** (⌧ Box 458, Belize City, ☎ 223/1403; 800/521–1247 in the U.S., WEB www.mayaairways.com). **Tropic Air** (⌧ Box 20, San Pedro, ☎ 226/2012; 800/422–3435 in the U.S., WEB www.tropicair.com).

BOAT AND FERRY TRAVEL

A variety of boats connects Belize City with Ambergris Caye. The cost is about BZ$25 one-way. The most dependable, operated by the Caye Caulker Water Taxi Association, leave from the Belize Marine Terminal on North Front Street. The speedy open boats depart Belize City at 9, noon, and 3 and return from San Pedro at 8 AM, 11:30 AM, and 2:30 PM. Caye Caulker Water Taxi Association boats bound for Caye Caulker take 45 minutes and cost BZ$15 each way. Departures are every 90 minutes between 9 and 5, with return trips departing the Public Pier in Caulker between 6:30 and 3.

To reach the more remote cayes, you are left to your own devices. You can charter boats in either San Pedro or Belize City, but they're not cheap. The resorts on the atolls run their own planes or boats, but these are not available to the general public. Ask your hotel if it provides transportation. For the southern cayes, inquire about boats departing from Dangriga. Pelican Beach Hotel sends a boat to its resort on South Water Caye. Several boats make the run from Dangriga to Tobacco Caye for BZ$30 each way. Check at the Riverside Restaurant in Dangriga or ask at your hotel on Tobacco Caye.

➤ CONTACTS: **Caye Caulker Water Taxi Association** (✉ Marine Terminal, N. Front St. at Swing Bridge, Belize City, ☎ 223/1969).

EMERGENCIES

For medical care on Ambergris Caye try the Lions Club Clinic or Dr. Lerida Rodriguez, who (as is often the case with physicians in Belize) operates a pharmacy from her office. On Caye Caulker, the Caye Caulker Health Center, usually staffed by a volunteer doctor, is open weekdays 8–11:30 and 1–4:30. For dental care or serious ailments you need to go to Belize City.

➤ DOCTORS: **Lerida Rodriguez** (✉ Galleria Bldg., San Pedro, ☎ 226/3197).

➤ HOSPITALS: **Lions Clinic** (✉ Near airstrip, San Pedro, ☎ 226/2073). **Caye Caulker Health Center** (✉ Front Street, near Lena's Hotel, Caye Caulker, ☎ 226/0166).

HEALTH

Visiting Ambergris Caye is like a vacation in Florida—you'll face few health concerns worse than sunburn. San Pedro's water, from a treated municipal water supply, is safe to drink. On Caye Caulker, the water, usually from brackish shallow wells, often smells of sulfur. To be safe, drink only bottled water. On other remote cayes the water usually comes from cisterns. You'll want to stick to the bottled stuff.

MAIL AND SHIPPING

On Ambergris Caye the post office in San Pedro is open weekdays 8–noon and 1–5. On Caye Caulker the post office is on Back Street on the south side of town. It is open weekdays 9–noon and 2–5 and Saturday 9–noon.

➤ POST OFFICES: **Caye Caulker** (✉ Back St., ☎ 226/0325). **San Pedro** (✉ Barrier Reef Dr., ☎ 226/2250).

MONEY MATTERS

Atlantic Bank, on Barrier Reef Drive in San Pedro, is open Monday, Tuesday, Thursday, and Friday 8–noon and 1–3, Wednesday 8–1, and Saturday 8:30–noon. Belize Bank, on Barrier Reef Drive in San Pedro, is open Monday–Thursday 8–1 and Friday 8–1 and 3–6. There is just one bank on Caye Caulker, Atlantic Bank on Back Street, south of Chan's Market. It is open weekdays 9–1. Although all these banks have ATMs, they don't accept cards issued outside Belize. Cash advances on your Visa or MasterCard are available at these banks.

➤ BANKS: **Atlantic Bank** (✉ Barrier Reef Dr., San Pedro, ☎ 226/2195; ✉ Back St., Caye Caulker, ☎ 226/0207). **Belize Bank** (✉ 49 Barrier Reef Dr., San Pedro, ☎ 226/2482).

TOUR OPERATORS

All tour guides in San Pedro and on Caye Caulker should be members of their respective associations—if in doubt, ask to see identification. Among the top tour operators in San Pedro are Tanisha Tours, which offers excellent trips to Altun Ha and Lamanai, and SEAduced by Belize, which is unmatched for its nature and kayak tours. On Caye Caulker,

Chocolate is the best-known guide and tour operator and is known for his full-day manatee trips.

➤ TOUR COMPANIES: **Chocolate Tours** (✉ Front St., Caye Caulker, ☎ 226/0151). **SEAduced by Belize** (✉ Tarpon St., San Pedro, ☎ 226/2254). **Tanisha Tours** (✉ San Pedro, ☎ 226/2314).

VISITOR INFORMATION

Ambergris Caye, Caye Caulker, and the other cayes are in some ways stepchildren of Belize's official tourist industry. Though these islands draw more visitors than any other area, the Belize Tourist Board and Belize Industry Tourist Association seem to give short shrift to the cayes. There may or may not be an official tourist information office open in San Pedro when you're there, and there isn't one on Caye Caulker. In any case, by far the best source of information on the island is on-line. The Web site www.AmbergrisCaye.com, operated by Marty Casado, has more than 6,000 pages of facts and figures on San Pedro, along with a good bit of information on Caye Caulker and other parts of the country.

THE CAYO

When the first jungle lodges opened in the Cayo, not many people thought this wild district on the country's western border would become a magnet for travelers. The region was too remote, the weather too unpredictable. Today more than half of those touring Belize visit the Cayo sometime during their trip, making this the country's second most popular destination. Comprising more than 5,200 square km (2,000 square mi) but with fewer than 15,000 inhabitants, the mountainous region is both Belize's largest district and one of its least populated.

You'll know you are entering the Cayo a few miles west of Belmopan. Having run along the Belize River for miles, the road winds out of the valley and heads into a series of sharp bends. In a few minutes you'll see cattle grazing on steep hillsides and horses flicking their tails. If it weren't for the Fanta orange sunsets and palm trees, this could be the Auvergne.

Other things change as you enter the Cayo. The heavyset Creole people who live along the coast give way to light-footed Maya; English is replaced by Spanish as the predominant language; and four-wheel-drive vehicles become a necessity. The lost world of the Maya begins to come alive through majestic, haunting ruins. And the Indiana Jones in you can now hike through the jungle, ride horseback, canoe down the Macal or Mopan rivers, and explore incredible caves.

Most wildlife featured on Belize's currency lives in the Cayo—the mountain lion, the jaguar and its diminutive cousin the ocelot, and the even smaller margay. Ornithologists in search of the country's 400-plus avian species carry telescopes, cameras, and tape recorders with microphones the size of Larry King's, but for most people a pair of binoculars will do. Even if you've never been bird-watching, setting off through the jungle in search of motmots, masked tityras, violaceous trogons, and scaly throated leaf-tossers as the sun begins to burn off the early morning mist will soon have you hooked.

National Geographic filmed *Journey to the Underworld* in the Cayo's Caves Branch River area, where fascinating limestone caves are found in lush tropical forests. Many of these caverns, hung with glistening white stalactites, have barely been explored. Resorts such as Caves Branch, Pook's Hill, and Jaguar Paw are arranging more and more expeditions for guests who want to see the caves from an inner tube or

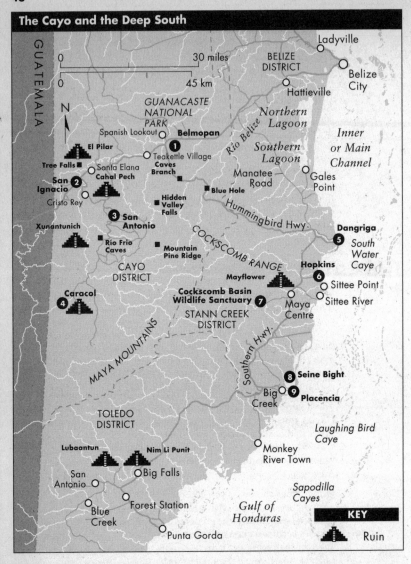

The Cayo and the Deep South

a boat. Serious spelunkers can even explore with scuba gear. Before trying either, though, inquire about histoplasmosis, a fungal infection of the lungs that can threaten explorers who venture into caves containing large numbers of bats.

Numbers in the margin correspond to points of interest on the Cayo and the Deep South map.

Belmopan

① *80 km (50 mi) southwest of Belize City.*

The best way to see Belize's capital is through the rearview mirror as you head toward the Cayo. The brainchild of Belize's longest-serving prime minister, George Price, Belmopan was to be Belize's answer to Brasilia and Canberra—a resplendent, modern capital city. Instead, it's a dreary cluster of concrete office buildings plunked down in the middle of nowhere, proving that cities cannot be created overnight but must come into being over centuries. It's a great shame because that money could have been spent on revamping the seaside town of Belize City, which could have been greatly transformed.

Worth a quick visit on the way out of Belmopan is Belize's small nature reserve, **Guanacaste National Park,** named for the huge guanacaste trees that grow here. Also called monkey's ear tree because of their oddly shaped seedpods, the trees tower to more than 100 ft. Locals use them for dugout canoes called dorries. The 50-acre park has a rich population of tropical birds, including smoky brown woodpeckers, black-headed trogons, red-lored parrots, and white-breasted wood wrens. You can try one of the eight hourly tours every day, or you can also wander around on your own. ☉ *Daily, tours every hr 8:30–3:30.* 🖃 *BZ$5.*

The small hilltop village of **Spanish Lookout,** about 19 km (12 mi) north of the Western Highway, is one of the centers of the Mennonite community in Belize. At first the village's blond-haired, blue-eyed residents seem out of place in this tropical country. In fact, they are thriving. Carpenters and dairy farmers, they build nearly all the resorts in the area, and most of the eggs and milk you'll consume during your stay will have come from their farms. The women dress in cotton frocks and head scarves, and the men wear straw hats, suspenders, and dark trousers. Many still travel in horse-drawn buggies. The cafés and small shops in Spanish Lookout offer a unique opportunity to mingle with these world-wary people, but note that they do not appreciate being gawked at or photographed any more than you do.

Less than half an hour south of Belmopan, **Blue Hole** is a natural turquoise pool surrounded by mosses and lush vegetation, excellent for a cool dip. The Blue Hole is actually part of an underground river system. On the other side of the hill is St. Herman's Cave, once inhabited by the Maya. A path leads up from the highway, right near the Blue Hole, but it's quite steep and difficult to climb unless the ground is dry. To explore the cave, it's best to wear sturdy shoes and bring a flashlight. Some years ago there were some unfortunate incidents at the site, with tourists robbed and, in one case, raped. A full-time attendant was subsequently appointed to patrol the area. ⊠ *Hummingbird Hwy.* 🖃 *BZ$8.*

Dining and Lodging

$$$$ 🏨 **Jaguar Paw.** Although this lodge is down a long dirt road, it's anything but rustic. Inside the massive structure you're struck by the eye-popping Maya murals painted by American Pam Braun. Each room has a theme—the Victorian Room, with a country armoire and sheer curtains; the Pioneer Room, with a pebble-lined shower and rough-hewn wooden bed; and others. There's 24-hour a/c, thanks to Big Gennie, the generator. Surrounding all of this is 215 acres of jungle that contains caves that you (and day-trippers from Ambergris Caye) can float through on an inner tube. Several jaguars have also been spotted here—hence, the name. ⊠ *Off Western Hwy., turn south at Mile 37 and follow dirt road 11 km (7 mi),* ☎ *888/775–8645 in the U.S.,* 🕸 *www.jaguarpaw. com. 16 rooms. Restaurant, fans, pool, fishing, hiking, bar, travel services; no room phones, no room TVs. AE, DC, MC, V.*

$$$ 🏨 **Pook's Hill.** When the lamps are lighted each night on the polished rosewood veranda, this low-key jungle lodge is one of the most pleasant places in the Cayo. Owners Vicki and Ray Snaddon used to be beekeepers, but when African bees wiped out their hives, they decided to become hoteliers. Their stone-and-thatch cabanas are laid out on a grassy clearing around a small Maya site. The circular ones at the top are smaller, but they make up for it with treetop views. The larger ones below sit

on a grassy terrace facing the jungle. During the day you can swim, ride horses through a 6,800-acre reserve teeming with wildlife, or boat up the Roaring River to a series of caves, many of which contain Maya burial sites. ⊠ *At Mile 52 of Western Hwy., head south for 8 km (5 mi),* ☎ FAX *820/4017,* WEB *www.pookshillbelize.com. 9 cabanas. Restaurant, hiking, bar; no a/c, no room phones, no room TVs. MC, V.*

$$–$$$ 🏠 **Banana Bank Ranch.** This isn't the most luxurious of the jungle lodges, ★ but it's one of the best values. It's also one of the best spots for families with kids. Riding enthusiasts of all skill levels can choose from 50 fine horses. Owners John and Carolyn Carr, both American expats, arrange canoeing, bird-watching, and other trips. A hand-pulled ferry takes you across the Belize River to the lodge. Several domesticated animals live on the property, including a monkey named Simon and a ravishingly beautiful jaguar named Tika. The newly restored century-old house, called the Headquarters, serves as a café and lounge. ⊠ *Off Western Hwy., turn north at Mile 48,* ☎ *820/2020,* FAX *820/2026,* WEB *www.bananabank.com. 7 cabanas, 3 rooms. Restaurant, a/c in some rooms, fans, horseback riding, bar, travel services; no room phones, no room TVs. MC, V.*

$–$$$ 🏠 ⛰ **Caves Branch Adventure Co. & Jungle Camp.** Those with Indi- ★ ana Jones fantasies should look no farther than this 58,000-acre private reserve. The most intrepid will head to the bunkhouse, while those in search of creature comforts will appreciate the cabanas of mahogany and bamboo. Owner Ian Anderson offers more than a dozen different wilderness adventures. On the tubing expedition to Footprint Cave you'll spend hours floating around underground lakes and crawling past stalagmites into dry chambers. Unbelievable Maya relics are scattered about, seemingly ignored by archaeologists. Just when you think you've left your world behind, your guide will unpack a lunch that you'll eat where Maya performed bloodletting rituals. Cold Belikins await you when you return, followed by a delicious family-style meal. Don't fill up on the fresh-baked bread, though, as at least two entrées are sure to follow. ⊠ *19½ km (12 mi) south of Belmopan at Mile 41½ of Hummingbird Hwy.,* ☎ FAX *822/2800,* WEB *www.cavesbranch.com. 12 cabanas, 6 with bath; 8 beds in bunkhouse; camping. Restaurant, fans, hiking, caving, bar, travel services; no a/c, no room phones, no room TVs. No credit cards.*

$$ 🏠 **Warrie Head Ranch & Lodge.** On arrival you're greeted with fresh fruit punch served by Miss Lydia, the personable Creole woman who manages this peaceful lodge. The elegant grounds, with seemingly every tree and shrub ablaze with color, have the look of a botanical garden. It's a short walk across the property to a small waterfall on Warrie Head Creek and to the beautiful Old Belize River. A monstrous steam tractor, once used to drag mahogany logs to the river, a horse-drawn sugar mill, and several old chicle pots enhance the historic atmosphere of this former logging camp. Owners John and Bia Searle have stocked the cozy rooms with 18th-century antiques. Dinner is special at Warrie Head, with guests lining up at the buffet to enjoy big helpings of Miss Lydia's tasty home-style cooking, which draws on creole, Spanish, and North American recipes. ⊠ *Western Hwy.,* ☎ *227/ 0755,* FAX *227/5213,* WEB *www.warriehead.com. 10 rooms. Restaurant, fans, hiking, bar, travel services; no a/c, no room phones, no room TVs. AE, MC, V.*

San Ignacio

❷ *37 km (23 mi) southwest of Belmopan.*

When you hear the incredible commotion made by grackles in the trees of the town square, you'll know that you've arrived at San Ignacio, the hub of the Cayo district. It's worth coming here at sunset to listen to the eerily beautiful sound made by these iridescent birds.

With its well-preserved wooden structures, dusty little San Ignacio is one of the few Belizean towns where you might wish to linger. Evenings are cool and mosquito free, and the colonial-era streets are lined with a few funky bars and restaurants. The location, in a pretty valley nestled between the Macal and Mopan rivers, makes San Ignacio an excellent base for exploring western Belize. Nearby are three Maya ruins, as well as a few national parks and a cluster of butterfly farms.

★ After crossing the Mopan River near the village of San José Succotz on a hand-pulled ferry—ask to work the crank yourself, if you'd like— you'll reach the archaeological site of **Xunantunich** (pronounced *zoo-nan-too-nitch*), which means "stone maiden." As you hike through the profusion of maidenhair ferns to the ruins, you'll encounter numerous butterflies flitting through the air. A magnificent avenue of cohune palms announces your arrival at an important ceremonial center from the Maya Classic Period. Drinks and snacks are available at a visitor center that provides the the history of the site. El Castillo, the massive 120-ft-high main pyramid, was built on a leveled hilltop. Though it's not as excavated as Altun Ha, the pyramid furnishes a spectacular 360-degree panorama of the Mopan River valley. On the eastern wall is a reproduction of one of the finest Maya sculptures in Belize, a frieze decorated with jaguar heads, human faces, and abstract geometric patterns that tells the story of the Moon's affair with Morning Light. *Southwest of San Ignacio.* ✉ *BZ$5.* ⊙ *Weekdays 8–5, weekends 8–4.*

El Pilar, a less frequented archaeological site, is still being excavated under the direction of Anabel Ford, a professor at the University of California. Excavations of Maya ruins have traditionally concentrated on public buildings, but at At El Pilar the emphasis has been on domestic architecture—everything from reconstructing houses to replanting gardens with crops used by the Maya. El Pilar, occupied from 700 to 1000, shows evidence of sentry posts in some areas, suggesting that this was a community of high-ranking officials surrounded by a hostile population. Two well-marked trails take you around the site. Because the structures have not been stripped of vegetation, you may feel like you're walking through a series of shady orchards. Don't forget your binoculars: in the 5,000-acre nature reserve there's some terrific bird-watching. Behind the main plaza a lookout grants a spectacular view across the jungle to El Pilar's sister city, Pilar Poniente, on the Guatemalan border. ✉ *13 km (8 mi) west of Bullet Tree Falls.*

Just outside San Ignacio is a third major Maya ruin, the unfortunately named **Cahal Pech** (meaning "place of the ticks"). It was occupied from around 900 BC to AD 1100. At its peak, around AD 600, Cahal Pech was a medium-size settlement with some three dozen structures huddled around seven plazas. It is thought that it functioned as a kind of guard post, standing watch over the nearby confluence of the Mopan and Macal rivers. It may be somewhat less compelling than the area's other ruins, but it's really no less mysterious, given that these structures mark the presence of a civilization we still know so little about. You can try to get some answers at the small museum. *South of San Ignacio.* ✉ *BZ$5.* ⊙ *Tues.–Sat. 9–noon and 1–4:30, Sun. 9–noon.*

The **Ix Chel Tropical Research Center,** founded by Rosita Arvigo, is a center for traditional Maya medicine. Arvigo met Don Elijio Pantí, a Belizean shaman, and in 1985 became his apprentice by promising to preserve traditional healing practices. The center, run by Arvigo and her husband, has established itself as a special botanical garden: the beautiful Rainforest Medicine Trail takes you on a short, self-guided walk through the rain forest, providing you with a chance to study the symbiotic nature of its plant life. Learn about the healing properties of such indigenous plants as gumbo-limbo and man vine and see some of the endangered medicinal plants that Arvigo and her colleagues have rescued. The center has sent about 3,000 species of Belizean plants to the U.S. National Institutes of Health for analysis. The shop here sells Maya medicinal products like Belly Be Good and Flu Away, as well as Arvigo's excellent books. Arvigo and her staff offer aromatherapy and herbal and mineral-water therapies, as well as Maya massage, manicures, and pedicures. ⊠ *Next to Chaa Creek,* ☎ *824/3870,* WEB *www. rainforestremedies.com.* ☞ *BZ$12 for Rainforest Medicine Trail.*

The **Chaa Creek Natural History Center** is a small but always expanding museum of Belize's flora and fauna. It has a tiny library and displays of everything from butterflies to snakes (thankfully pickled in jars). Just outside is a screened-in blue morpho butterfly breeding center. If you haven't encountered blue morphos in the wild, you can see them up close here and even peer at their slumbering pupae, which resemble jade earrings. Once you're inside the double doors, the blue beauties, which look boringly brown when their wings are closed, flit about or remain perfectly still, sometimes on your shoulder or head, and open and close their wings to what seems like an innate rhythm akin to inhaling and exhaling. Hourly tours are led by a team of naturalists. ⊠ *The Lodge at Chaa Creek,* ☎ *824/2037,* FAX *824–2501,* WEB *www.chaacreek.com.* ☞ *BZ$10.* ⊙ *Daily 9–4.*

The life's work of Ken duPlooy, an ornithologist who died in 2001, and the personable Judy duPlooy is the 45-acre **Belize Botanical Gardens,** a collection of hundreds of trees, plants, and flowers from all over Central America. Enlightening tours are given by local Maya who can tell you the names of the plants in Mayan, Spanish, and English and explain their medicinal uses. An orchid house holds the duPlooys' collection of 180 orchid species. ⊠ *duPlooy's, San Ignacio, head 7½ km (5) mi west on Benque Rd., turn left on Chial Rd.,* ☎ *824/3101,* FAX *824/3301,* WEB *www.duplooys.com.* ☞ *BZ$10.*

Besides thoughtful displays on Cayo flora and fauna, **Tropical Wings,** a little nature center, has 20 species of butterflies including the blue morpho, owl, giant swallowtail, and monarch varieties. The facility, at the Trek Stop, has a small restaurant and gift shop. ⊠ *10 km (6 mi) west of San Ignacio,* ☎ *823/2265.* ☞ *BZ$5.*

Dining and Lodging

IN SAN IGNACIO

$$ ✕ **Sanny's Grill.** Belizean basics such as chicken or pork chops are the staples here, but they are transformed into something wonderful with a hot grill and equally hot spices. Try the champagne shrimp or lime-thyme red snapper, served with the tastiest, spiciest rice and beans in the Cayo. You can enjoy them outside on a covered deck or inside in a casual dining room. And the prices? The restaurant's democratic motto proclaims: PRICES ANYONE CAN AFFORD. In a residential area off Benque Road, Sanny's can be hard to find after dark. ⊠ *23rd St., heading west of San Ignacio, look for a sign just beyond the Texaco station,* ☎ *824–2988. No credit cards. No lunch Sun.*

$ ✕ **Eva's.** Not just a bustling café and bar, Eva's is a Cayo institution—it's an Internet café, bulletin board, information center, trading post, and meeting place all in one. The food is honest-to-goodness Belizean fare, with some bacon and eggs, omelets, and sandwiches thrown in for good measure. Mugs of wickedly strong black tea are always available. No one is in much of a hurry, making this an excellent place to write post-cards, catch up on your journal, or just soak up some authentic Belizean atmosphere. Presiding over the colorful chaos is Bob Jones, a garrulous British ex-serviceman, who can tell you everything from where to rent a canoe to what to do if you get bitten by a fer-de-lance to where to find a room. You can use Eva's computers to catch up on your e-mail. ✉ 22 *Burns Ave.*, ☎ 824–2267, WEB *www.evasonline.com. No credit cards.*

$$$ 🏨 **San Ignacio Resort Hotel.** Queen Elizabeth stayed here when she visited the Cayo in 1994. If you want a hotel in San Ignacio itself, this could be the place for you. It doesn't look like much from the road, but the large and comfortable rooms have verandas facing the jungle. There are a small pool and an iguana hatchery. The Running W restaurant specializes in steak, and the bar is big and usually busy. The staff can arrange birding and other excursions. Next door is a small casino packed with video poker machines, one-armed bandits, and a few live tables. ✉ *Buena Vista Rd., San Ignacio*, ☎ 824/2034, FAX 824/2134, WEB *www.sanignaciobelize.com. 25 rooms. Restaurant, cable TV, pool, bar, casino, laundry service, meeting rooms, travel services. AE, MC, V.*

$$ 🏨 **Windy Hill Resort.** You don't have to drive for hours to get to this lodge—it's on a 100-acres just south of San Ignacio. The cabanas, all with private verandas, are perched on a low hill across the landscaped grounds. Furnishings are custom-made from local hardwoods, and decorations include handwoven Guatemalan rugs. Each is cooled by a lazily turning ceiling fan. The resort runs many tours to Tikal (a favorite here), Caracol, and other destinations. It recently added a popular night jungle-walk tour. ✉ *Benque Rd., 1½ km (1 mi) west of San Ignacio*, ☎ 824/2017; 800/946–3995 in the U.S., FAX 824/3080, WEB *www.windyhillresort.com. 25 cabanas. Restaurant, fans, minibars, pool, horseback riding, travel services; no a/c, no room phones, no room TVs. AE, MC, V.*

NEAR SAN IGNACIO

$$$$ 🏨 **Ek 'Tun.** Imagine water as blue as a sapphire gushing from a natu-★ ral mineral spring. Imagine a pool constructed not of concrete but of limestone and other natural materials set among towering palms. Then imagine being here in complete solitude—even going skinny-dipping, if you like—with only the howler monkeys for company. With only two cottages, Ek 'Tun is more of a bed-and-breakfast in the jungle than a traditional lodge. After arriving on a river skiff, you step onto the 600-acre grounds, which have giant ceiba trees and flowering shrubs. Both cabanas are constructed of thatch and hardwood poles, with rough-hewn staircases leading up to the sleeping lofts. On the extensive network of trails you can spot orange-breasted falcons and toucans. Go exploring in several of Belize's most interesting caves. The excellent meals, included in the price, are served in a stucco-and-thatch dining room overlooking the river. ✉ *On Macal River*, ☎ 820/3002; 303/442–6150 in the U.S., WEB *www.ektunbelize.com. 2 cabanas. Restaurant, river beach, pool, hiking, horseback riding, caving, bar, travel services; no a/c, no room phones, no room TVs. MC, V.*

$$$$ 🏨 ♨ **The Lodge at Chaa Creek.** This is the queen of jungle resorts.★ Everything about the place, from the beautiful hardwood furniture to the friendly staff of 70, is simply better than anywhere else. The setting, on 330 acres of rolling hills above the Macal River, is magnificent. The whitewashed stone cottages manage to be both extremely simple and extremely elegant. Surrendering to progress, the lodge has installed electricity throughout. For the budget traveler Chaa Creek has the Macal River Safari Camp in a clearing above the Macal River. Small A-frame rooms are set up on individual wooden platforms. The resort's new spa, on a hill above the lodge, has an unspeakably gorgeous view

of the Mayan Mountains and is by far the best-equipped facility in Belize. Treatments include mud and herbal body wraps, scrubs, massages, and facials. As if all this weren't enough, Chaa Creek's safari-style tours are among the finest in the country. ⊠ *West of San Ignacio, drive 7½ km (5 mi on Benque Rd., turn left on Chial Rd.,* ☎ *824/2037,* ℻ *824/ 2501,* WEB *www.chaacreek.com. 20 rooms, 2 suites, 10 casitas. Restaurant, room service, fans, hiking, horseback riding, spa, laundry service, meeting rooms, travel services; no a/c, no room phones, no room TVs. AE, DC, MC, V.*

$$$$ ⭐ **Mopan River Resort.** Belize's first true all-inclusive resort includes everything from meals to tours to lodging in one reasonably priced package. Once you've taken the short ferry trip across the Mopan River to the resort's manicured, palm-studded grounds, you're in your own private bit of paradise. The facades of the cabanas look traditional, but inside are amenities like cable TVs and minibars stocked with complimentary soft drinks and beer. Birders will enjoy the new 20-ft-tall bird-watching tower. Owner Jay Picon is affable and well traveled. Over drinks or a barbecue, Jay will regale you with tales of his days as a pilot and corporate executive. Dinners are often Thai themed, with recipes his wife picked up from cooking courses taken in Bangkok. ⊠ *Benque Viejo del Carmen,* ☎ *823–2047,* ℻ *823/3272,* WEB *www.mopanriverresort.com. 12 cabanas. Restaurant, refrigerators, minibars, some kitchens, cable TV, pool, laundry service, travel services; no a/c, no room phones, no smoking in cabanas. D, MC, V. All-inclusive. Closed July–Oct.*

$$–$$$$ ⭐ **duPlooy's.** High above a bend in the Macal River called Big Eddy is the spectacular location of this resort. From the deck, 30 ft above the forest floor, you look straight out to a dramatic sweep of limestone cliffs. From the sandy beach below you can swim and dive off the rocks. Bungalows are filled with hardwood furnishings. A new two-story cottage has wraparound porches, king-size beds, whirlpool bath, fridge, and great views. There are less expensive rooms in the jungle lodge. The food is terrific, and there's always a vegetarian option. On the premises is the 45-acre Belize Botanical Gardens. By canoe this resort is only a few minutes upstream from Chaa Creek; by car it's a 15 minute-drive over a bumpy track. ⊠ *San Ignacio, head 7½ km (5 mi west on Benque Rd., turn left on Chial Rd.,* ☎ *824/3101,* ℻ *824/3301,* WEB *www.duplooys.com. 8 rooms, 2 with bath. Restaurant, fans, hiking, horseback riding, laundry service, travel services; no a/c, no room phones, no room TVs. MC, V.*

$$$ ⭐ **Royal Mayan Resort & Spa.** If you can get up the stupendously steep hill and ignore the closet-size guest rooms, you might enjoy this alternative to the region's jungle lodges. The view—from the top of that darn hill—is nothing short of breathtaking. The hotel, owned by the same well-connected people who developed Fort Point Tourist Village in Belize City, has a gorgeous pool and two outdoor hot tubs (one overlooking the ruins of Xunantunich). The staff at the spa delivers a range of soothing services, including massages. Guest rooms are nicely furnished, with custom-made cabinets and designer linens that give the rooms an upscale atmosphere. ⊠ *Benque Viejo del Carmen,* ☎ *888/271–3483 in the U.S.,* ℻ *305/969–7946 in the U.S.,* WEB *www.royalmayan.com. Restaurant, cable TV, fans, pool, gym, spa, travel services.*

$$ ⭐ **Green Heaven Lodge.** What's a nice young couple from the south of France doing in Belize? Dominique Agius and Anne-Karine Chappaz say one day they were looking for the Costa Rican consulate but stumbled upon the Belize consulate instead. That led to a trip to a country they knew almost nothing about. They now provide personal attention to their guests, who are usually outnumbered by the staff. Scattered around a low hill are four yellow-stucco cabins with red-tin roofs, all modestly appointed with Belizean-made furniture. Take a dip

in one of the nicest pools in the Cayo, or relax in the hammocks under the poolside palapa. Dominique runs the restaurant, La Vie En Rose, serving French classics like beef bourguignon. It's open daily 7 AM–10 PM. ⊠ *Chial Rd., 8 km (5 mi) west of San Ignacio,* ☎ *820/2034; 800/ 889–1512 in the U.S.,* WEB *www.ghlodgebelize.com. 4 cabins. Restaurant, fans, pool, volleyball, bar, travel services; no a/c, no room phones, no room TVs. AE, MC, V.*

$$ ⊞ **Maya Mountain Lodge.** This hilltop lodge is not luxurious, but that's not its intention. In recent years the lodge has focused on family-oriented activities. Owner Suzi Mickler, who has a master's degree in curriculum management, is the lodge's "headmistress." In addition to designing the nature trails (one trail passes 150 species of edible jungle plants, the other concentrates on ornamentals), she has created a host of courses at different levels, particularly for children, covering everything from Belizean history to ornithology. The lodgings are whitewashed cottages with private patio. A large wooden building has rooms for budget-conscious travelers. A pleasant open-air dining room serves up food that is tasty and plentiful. The staff is agreeable, and the grounds are thriving thanks to more than a decade of tender loving care. ⊠ *Cristo Rey Rd., outside San Ignacio,* ☎ *824/2164,* FAX *824/ 2029,* WEB *www.mayamountain.com. 8 cottages, 6 rooms with shared baths. Restaurant, fans, pool, hiking, laundry service, travel services; no a/c in some rooms, no room phones, no room TVs. AE, MC, V.*

$–$$ ⊞ **Clarissa Falls.** The rumbling low falls are the first and last sounds of the day at Clarissa Falls. It's a well-known place among Belizeans, who head here for tasty meals of enchiladas and black bean soup served under the open-air palapa overlooking the Mopan River. Chena Galvez, the charming owner, and her sister Anna create the simple, delicious food the friendly staff serves in copious quantities. This is their family ranch, a rolling 900-acre expanse of grassy pasture. Chena has spent her life on the ranch, and over the years she has built a small colony of homey thatch cabanas with electricity and private baths. Two are big enough for large families. The pet parrot, Larry, enjoys drinking coffee. ⊠ *Western Hwy., 9 km (5½ mi) west of San Ignacio,* ☎ FAX *824/3916. 11 cabanas, 9 with bath. Restaurant, bar, hiking; no a/c, no room phones, no room TVs. MC, V.*

$ ⊞ **Aguada.** When you can get a room in a clean, attractive hotel that's this cheap, go for it. This hotel in Santa Elena, a low-key town near San Ignacio, has proved so popular that the owners, an American man and his Belizean wife, have added more rooms overlooking the pool. The hotel has a friendly restaurant serving Belizean dishes as well as American standards like burgers. The large common room has a television and games. If you're carless, the hotel is within walking distance of downtown San Ignacio. There are also a real London taxi cab, used for trips around the Cayo, and vans that run to and from the airports in Belize City. ⊠ *Santa Elena,* ☎ *824/3609,* WEB *www.aguada.com. 14 rooms. Restaurant, pool, travel services; no room phones, no room TVs. MC, V.*

$ ✕⊞ ⚠ **The Trek Stop.** A cold Belikin and filling Mexican and Belizean dishes await you when you return to this cluster of neat-as-a-pin cabins. Tents or just campsites are also available, as is a common kitchen for cooking your own grub. American expats Judy and John Yaeger and their Belizean partners opened this spot on top of a hill near San José Succotz in 1998. It's a fine find, particularly for budget travelers. *San José Succotz, 9.6 km (6 mi) west of San Ignacio,* ☎ *823/2265,* WEB *www.tbcnet.com/dyaeger/susa/trekstop.htm. 6 cabins without bath. Restaurant, bar, travel services; no a/c, no room phones, no room TVs. MC, V.*

Outdoor Activities and Sports

CANOEING

The Cayo's many rivers, especially the Mopan and Macal, make it an excellent place for canoeing. Most of the larger resorts, like Chaa Creek and duPlooy's, have canoes. You can easily rent canoes in San Ignacio from **Toni Canoes** (☎ 824/3292).

CAVING

Over the millennia, as dozens of swift-flowing rivers bored through the soft limestone, the Maya Mountains became pitted with miles of caves. The Maya used them as burial sites and, according to one theory, as subterranean waterways that linked the Cayo with communities as far north as the Yucatán. Then the caves fell into a 1,000-year slumber, disturbed only by the nightly flutter of bats. In recent years the caves have been rediscovered by spelunkers. First on the scene was Ian Anderson, owner of **Caves Branch Adventure Co. & Jungle Camp** (⊠ 19½ km [12 mi] south of Belmopan, ☎ FAX 822/2800, WEB www.cavesbranch.com). He and his friendly staff of trained guides run exhilarating Indiana Jones–style caving, tubing, and hiking trips from a tiki-torchlighted jungle camp just south of Belmopan. David Simson, of **David's Adventure Tours** (⊠ San Ignacio, ☎ 824/3674, WEB www.belizex.com/davidstours.htm) was the first to do tours of the now-popular Barton Creek Cave. **Mayawalk Adventures** (⊠ San Ignacio, ☎ 824/3070, WEB www.mayawalk.com) specializes in tours to the spectacular, and spooky, cave of Actun Tunichil Muknal.

HORSEBACK RIDING

When it comes to horseback riding adventures, the undisputed local experts are found at the lodges of Mountain Equestrian Trails and Chaa Creek. **Easy Rider** (⊠ Collins Ave., San Ignacio, ☎ 824/3734) also runs equestrian tours of the Maya ruins and other points of interest in the region.

Shopping

Caesar's Place (⊠ Western Hwy., east of San Ignacio, ☎ 824/2341) has T-shirts, hammocks, postcards, and jewelry for last-minute shoppers. Don't expect a deal, though.

San Antonio

❸ *27 km (17 mi) south of San Ignacio.*

Heading southeast from San Ignacio, the road winds up from the Macal Valley through fertile farming country where corn, peanuts, and beans grow in small roadside clearings. A few miles beyond the village of Cristo Rey, the vegetation gets wilder as the road swings south and southeast away from the river. Cohune palms, trumpet trees, wild papayas, and strangler vines grow in profusion, while here and there a crop of bananas or corn cuts into the hillside. Shortly before the village of San Antonio, you emerge onto a plateau with fine views of the Maya Mountains. With its sheep, goats, and orange trees, San Antonio's cluster of brightly painted wooden houses clinging to the hillside at 1,000 ft looks like a tropical version of a Greek hilltop community.

A rugged dome of granite and limestone containing some of the most ancient rocks in Central America, the 780-square-km (300-square-mi) ★ **Mountain Pine Ridge Forest Reserve** is a highlight of any journey to Belize and an adventure to reach. Along with the Cockscomb Basin Wildlife Sanctuary and the Maya ruins at Lamanai, it's one of the sights no visitor should miss.

As you leave the lush tropical forest, the road circles the western slopes of the mountains. Baldy Beacon, at just over 3,000 ft, lies to the east. After the heat and humidity of lowland Belize, the cooler air is enormously refreshing. Unfortunately, much of the savanna here is marked by dead trees. A southern pine beetle infestation in 2000 and 2001 killed thousands of acres of mountain pines. The dead pines, besides being an eyesore, are also potential fuel for the forest fires common in this region during the dry season, from around February or March through May.

But there is more to see in Mountain Pine Ridge than pines. You'll see lilac-color mimosa, St. John's wort, and occasionally a garish red flower known as hotlips. There's also a huge variety of ferns, ranging from the tiny maidenhair fern to giants the size of coconut palms, and a fair selection of Belize's 154 species of orchids. Look out, too, for a wild tree called craboo, whose berries are used for making a brandylike liqueur believed to have aphrodisiac properties. Birds love this fruit, too, so any craboo is a good place to look for orioles and woodpeckers.

The roads—there are about 2,400 km (1,500 mi) of them—were built by the British army, which, with U.S. and Belize forces, still uses this area for training in jungle warfare. Some roads have names, but most have numerical monikers, like A10. Of course, the best way to see this area is on a mountain bike or by the power of your own feet, not bouncing around in an Isuzu Trooper. The village of Augustine is home to the headquarters of the forest reserve. It's the only place in the area where you're allowed to camp.

Inside Mountain Pine Ridge Forest Reserve is **Hidden Valley Falls.** Also known as the Thousand Foot Falls (although in fact it drops nearly 1,600 ft), it's the highest in Central America. A thin plume of spray plummets over the edge of a rock face into a seemingly bottomless gorge below. All this isn't as appealing as it sounds, as the viewing area is some distance from the falls. To climb closer requires a major commitment. A shelter, some benches, and a public rest room provide creature comforts. The nearby **Río On** has flat granite boulders on which to sunbathe and a series of crystal-clear pools and waterfalls in which to dunk yourself.

Just outside the reserve proper are the **Río Frío Caves.** They're only a few miles down a steep track, but ecologically speaking these caves are a different world. In the course of a few hundred yards, you drop from pine savanna to tropical forest. Nothing else in Belize illustrates the country's extraordinary geological variety so clearly as this startling transition. A river runs right through the center and over the centuries has carved the rock into fantastic shapes. Swallows fill the place, and at night ocelots and margays pad silently across the cold floor in search of slumbering prey. Seen from the dark interior, the light-filled world outside seems more intense and beautiful than ever. Rising vertically through the mouth of the cave is a giant hardwood tree, *Pterocarpus officialis,* its massive paddle-shape roots anchored in the sandy soil of the riverbank and its green crown straining toward the blue sky.

More than 30,000 pupae are raised each year at this facility, the largest of Belize's six butterfly farms. if you want to get a closer look at the creatures, **Green Hills Butterfly Farm** hosts about 30 butterfly species in a 2,700-square-ft flight area. Jan Meerman, who has published a book on the butterflies of Belize, runs the place with Dutch partner Tineke Boomsma. ⊠ *Mile 8, Pine Ridge Rd.,* ☎ ℻ *820/4034.* ⌦ *BZ$8.* ☉ *Daily 8–4:30.*

The newly established **Elijio Panti National Park,** created in 2001 and named after the famed Guatemala-born herbal healer who died in Cayo in 1996 at the age of 106, is a wonderful addition to the already extensive Belize national parks system. It comprises 100,000 acres of land around the villages of San Antonio, Cristo Rey, and El Progreso. The hope is that the elimination of hunting in this park will encourage the return of more wildlife to western Belize. At this early stage the park boundaries are as yet ill-defined, no admission fee is charged, an official welcome center and other park formalities are absent.

Dining and Lodging

$$$$ ⊞ **Blancaneaux Lodge.** You may detect a whiff of Beverly Hills as you
★   sweep down the hibiscus- and palm-lined driveway of this upscale Mountain Pine Ridge resort and pass a well-groomed croquet lawn. This is hardly surprising, as Blancaneaux Lodge is owned by Francis Ford Coppola. Laid out on a hillside above the Privassion River, the lodge's five villas have been featured in *Architectural Digest*. They have soaring thatch ceilings, Japanese-style tile baths, and screened porches overlooking the river. The filmmaker's own villa, one of the finest Cayo residences, is available when he's not here. A fleet of Land Rovers takes you to remote Maya ruins or on shopping trips to Guatemala. Bring your plane, as this resort has its own landing strip. ⊠ *Near San Antonio,* ☎ 824/3878; 800/746–3743 *in the U.S.,* FAX *824/3919,* WEB *www.blancaneauxlodge.com. 7 cabanas, 5 villas. Restaurant, fans, hiking, horseback riding, bar, laundry service, airstrip, travel services; no a/c, no room phones, no room TVs. AE, MC, V.*

$$$ ⊞ ⛰ **Mountain Equestrian Trails.** Even if you don't ride, Mountain Equestrian Trails is a gorgeous place to stay. The setting, in the bottom of a lush valley with views of the jungle-covered flanks of the Mountain Pine Ridge, is second to none. Owners Jim and Marguerite Bevis, back in the saddle after a stint in the United States, have expanded the lodge to include 10 Spanish-style cabanas with lighting from kerosene lamps. Budget travelers like the tents, each built on a permanent wooden platform. Home-style meals are served in the "cantina," which doubles as a bar and reception area. Surefooted Texas quarter horses pick their way over the resort's 97 km (60 mi) of jungle trails, some of which wind up and down quite precipitous slopes. Nearby is Green Hills Butterfly Ranch. ⊠ *Mountain Pine Ridge Rd., off Western Hwy.,* ☎ 800/838–3918 *in the U.S.,* FAX *941/488–3953 in the U.S.,* WEB *www.metbelize.com. 10 cabanas, 8 tents. Restaurant, hiking, horseback riding, bar; no a/c, no room phones, no room TVs. MC, V.*

$$–$$$ ⊞ **Five Sisters Falls & Lodge.** It's unfair to call this place a poor man's Blancaneaux Lodge. This resort, run by retired Belizean customs officer Carlos Javier Popper, has its own laid-back style, and the setting is possibly even more dramatic than that of its neighbor. Perched on a steep hill, it looks down on the waterfall that gives the place its name. Accommodations are in thatch cabanas with screened porches, as well as in boxy rooms in the main building. A tram will take you down to the river if you don't fancy walking down the 286 steps. After your swim the thatch-roof bar is a great place to unwind. The restaurant, with a beautiful view of the falls, serves Belizean food. ⊠ *Near San Antonio,* ☎ 800/447–2931 *in the U.S.,* ☎ FAX *820/4005,* WEB *www.fivesisterslodge.com. 8 cabanas, 7 rooms, 5 with bath. Restaurant, fans, hiking, bar, meeting room; no a/c, no room phones, no room TVs. AE, MC, V.*

$$ ⊞ **Crystal Paradise.** In the village of Cristo Rey, this resort is one of the area's few Belizean-owned family operations. And what a family this is! The Tuts, an equal mix of Creole, Maya, and Spanish cultures, have 10 children. Eldest son Jeronie can identify more than 200 bird species and is an expert on medicinal plants; younger brother Evrald knows the surrounding jungle of the beautiful Mountain Pine Ridge area about as well as anyone. The Tuts have a good variety of very reasonably priced tours, including jungle camping, river excursions, and horseback riding. The whitewashed cabanas have Guatemalan bedspreads and other nice touches. ⊠ *Cristo Rey Rd., 6¼ km (4 mi) from San Ignacio,* ☎ FAX *824/2772,* WEB *www.crystalparadise.com. 8 cabanas, 12 rooms. Restaurant, fans, hiking, horseback riding; no a/c, no room phones, no room TVs. MC, V.*

Shopping

The village of San Antonio is home to the **Tanah Art Museum** (⊠ San Antonio, ☎ 824/3310), run by four sisters with clever hands and great heads for business. Look for the eye-catching slate carvings. At the other end of the village is the Magana family's arts-and-crafts shop, **Magana Zaac-tunich Art Gallery** (⊠ San Antonio, ☎ no phone), which specializes in wood carvings.

Caracol

★ ❹ *65 km (40 mi) south of San Ignacio, a 3-hr journey by road.*

Caracol (Spanish for "snail") is the most spectacular Maya site in Belize, as well as one of the most impressive in Central America. It was once home to as many as 200,000 people, nearly the population of modern-day Belize. It was a Maya Manhattan, a metropolis with five plazas and 32 large structures covering nearly a square mile. Once Caracol has been fully excavated it may dwarf even the great city of Tikal, which lies only a few dozen miles away. The latest evidence suggests that Caracol won a crushing victory over Tikal in the mid-6th century, a theory that Guatemalan scholars have not quite accepted. Until a group of *chicleros* (collectors of gum base) stumbled on the site in 1936, Caracol was buried under the jungle of the remote Vaca Plateau. It's hard to believe it could have been lost for centuries, as the great pyramid of Canaa is the tallest structure in Belize. The road to Caracol is decent, but if you want to drive on your own, be sure to inquire about road conditions first. A visitor center has opened here. ⊠ *From Mountain Pine Forest Ridge reserve entrance, head south 23 km (14 mi) to village of Douglas De Silva; turn left and go 58 km (36 mi).* ▨ *BZ$10.* ☉ *Daily 8–4.*

The Cayo A to Z

AIRPORTS AND TRANSFERS

Most people bound for the Cayo fly into Belize City. Discovery Expeditions, with a location at the international airport, picks up Cayo-bound passengers at both the international and municipal airports. Many resorts provide transportation to the Cayo from both airports in Belize City for about BZ$70 each way. Several hotels in San Ignacio, including Aguada, also run shuttles to and from Belize City and San Ignacio, for around BZ$50 a person. Call ahead for reservations.

➤ AIRLINES AND CONTACTS: **Discovery Expeditions** (⊠ 126 Freetown Rd., Belize City, ☎ 223/0748, FAX 223/0750).

BUS TRAVEL TO AND FROM THE CAYO

Novelo's has frequent service between Belize City and San Ignacio. The journey on the Western Highway takes about three hours and costs BZ$5–BZ$6, depending on whether the bus is a local or express.

➤ BUS INFORMATION: **Novelo's** (⊠ 1 Wyatt St., San Ignacio, ☎ 824/2508).

CAR RENTAL

Safe Tours Belize is a well-regarded rental agency in Santa Elena, just east of San Ignacio.

➤ LOCAL AGENCIES: **Safe Tours Belize** (✉ Western Hwy., Santa Elena, ☎ 824/3731, WEB www.belizex.com/safetours.htm).

CAR TRAVEL

To get to the Cayo, simply follow the Western Highway from Belize City. The Western Highway is a well-maintained two-lane highway. Watch out for "sleeping policemen" (speed bumps) near villages along the way.

EMERGENCIES

In case of emergency you'll find La Loma Luz Hospital, in Santa Elena, just east of San Ignacio.

➤ HOSPITALS: **La Loma Luz Hospital** (✉ Western Hwy., Santa Elena, ☎ 824/3253).

➤ HOT LINES: **Police** (☎ 824/2111).

➤ PHARMACIES: **The Pharmacy** (✉ 24 West. St., San Ignacio, ☎ 824/2510).

HEALTH

Health standards in the Cayo are fairly high. The water in San Ignacio and Santa Elena comes from a treated municipal system, so it's safe to drink. Resorts in the region have their own safe water systems. There are relatively few mosquitoes or other insects in the Cayo, as the porous limestone terrain means that rain does not stand in puddles. Some cases of dengue fever and malaria have been reported in the Cayo, however, so you may want to slather yourself with repellent that contains DEET.

MAIL AND SHIPPING

The San Ignacio post office is on Hudson Street. It's open weekdays 8–noon and 1–4:30 and Saturday 8–noon.

➤ POST OFFICES: **San Ignacio** (✉ Hudson St., San Ignacio, ☎ 824/2049).

MONEY MATTERS

Although American dollars are accepted everywhere, you can exchange money at the border crossing in Benque Viejo del Carmen. Banks in San Ignacio include Atlantic Bank, Belize Bank, and Bank of Nova Scotia. They are all downtown on Burns Avenue. All have ATMs, but none accepts cards issued outside the country.

➤ BANKS: **Atlantic Bank** (✉ 17 Burns Ave., San Ignacio, ☎ 824/2596). **Bank of Nova Scotia** (✉ Burns Ave. at Riverside St., San Ignacio, ☎ 824/4190). **Belize Bank** (✉ 16 Burns Ave., San Ignacio, ☎ 824/2031).

SAFETY

Being close to the El Petén region of Guatemala, thousands of Cayo visitors make short trips over the border to see the fantastic ruins of Tikal. Its proximity to this tourist attraction is a boon for the Cayo but also a burden, as the poverty-stricken population of northern Guatemala spills over the border into relatively affluent Belize. Armed gangs from Guatemala have on several occasions robbed tourists around San Ignacio. But despite these events, the Cayo has comparatively little crime. As a visitor, you are unlikely to encounter any problems.

TOUR OPERATORS

Most jungle lodges offer a full range of day trips. Among the largest and best lodge-affiliated tour operations are Chaa Creek Expeditions and Windy Hill Tour Company. For cave tours, David's Adventure Tours, Mayawalk Adventures, and Caves Branch Adventure Company are the best. International Archeological Tours runs good expeditions to Maya sites in Belize and Guatemala. Toni's River Adventures is the leading operator for canoe trips.

➤ TOUR COMPANIES: **Chaa Creek Expeditions** (✉ 77 Burns Ave., San Ignacio, ☎ 824/2037, WEB www.chaacreek.com). **Caves Branch Adventure Company** (✉ Mile 41½, Hummingbird Hwy., Belmopan, ☎ 824/2800, WEB www.cavesbranch.com). **David's Adventure Tours** (✉ Savannah St., San Ignacio, ☎ 824/3674, WEB www.belizex.com/davidstours.htm). **International Archeological Tours** (✉ West St., San Ignacio, ☎ 824/3391). **Windy Hill Tour Company** (✉ Western Hwy., San Ignacio, ☎ 824/2017, WEB www.windyhillresort.com).

VISITOR INFORMATION

There is a Belize Tourist Industry Association office at the Cahal Pech ruins, but the best way to find out what's happening is to stop by Eva's in San Ignacio, a café that doubles as an unofficial visitor center. Owner Bob Jones, a tattooed ex-British soldier, knows the Cayo like the back of his hand. You can also contact local tour operators.

➤ TOURIST INFORMATION: **Belize Tourist Industry Association** (✉ Cahal Pech, San Ignacio, ☎ 824/4236). **Eva's** (✉ 22 Burns Ave., San Ignacio, ☎ 824/2267).

PLACENCIA AND ENVIRONS

As always in Belize, the transition from one landscape to another is swift and startling. When you approach Placencia, the lush, mountainous terrain of the north gives way to flat plains bristling with orange trees. The Stann Creek Valley is Belize's San Fernando Valley, the place where most of its fruit is grown. Bananas were the original bumper crop here, and banana plantations are still an important industry today. Equally startling is the cultural segue: whereas San Ignacio has a Spanish feeling, this area is strongly Afro-Caribbean.

Tourist dollars, the staple of contemporary Belize, have largely slipped passed Dangriga, but they are rapidly transforming Placencia, the region's most picturesque spot. Several years ago there were only three small resorts north of town. Now there are about 20, stretching up to the village of Seine Bight and beyond. The paving of the Southern Highway from Dangriga to the turnoff for Placencia and the construction of a airstrip north of Placencia have made the region more accessible (once you arrive, however, most roads consist of red dirt and potholes). Real estate sales are a driving force here. A section of the road down the peninsula was moved west in 1999 so that more land would be on the valuable side facing the sea. Much of the land north of Placencia has been divided up into lots awaiting development; if things continue at this pace, the area will one day rival Ambergris Caye as Belize's top beach destination.

Numbers in the margin correspond to bullets on the Cayo and the Deep South map.

Dangriga

❺ *160 km (99 mi) southeast of Belmopan.*

With a population of 8,800, Dangriga is the largest town in the south and the home of the Garífuna (or Black Caribs, as they are also known). They are perhaps the most unusual of the many ethnic groups that have found a home in this tiny country. The Garífunas' story is a bizarre and moving one, an odyssey of exile and dispossession in the wake of the confusion wrought in the New World by the Old. They are descended from a group of Nigerian slaves who were shipwrecked on the island of St. Vincent in 1635. At first the Caribs, St. Vincent's indigenous population, fiercely resisted the outsiders, but they soon overcame their initial distrust.

In the eyes of the British colonial authorities, the new ethnic group that developed after years of intermarriage was an illegitimate and troublesome presence. Worse still, the Garífuna sided with, and were succored by, the French. After nearly two centuries of guerrilla warfare, the British decided that the best way to solve the problem was to deport them en masse. After a circuitous and tragic journey across the Caribbean, during which thousands perished of disease and hunger, the exiles arrived in Belize.

That the Garífuna have managed to preserve their cultural identity is one more example of Belize's extraordinary ability to maintain rather than suppress diversity. They have their own religion, a potent mixture of ancestor worship and Catholicism; their own language, which, like Carib, has separate male and female dialects; their own music, a percussion-oriented sound known as punta rock; and their own social structure, which dissuades young people from marrying outside their own community. In writer Marcella Lewis, universally known as Auntie Madé, they also had their own poet laureate.

For the traveler there's not much to keep you in Dangriga. But for one day each year, November 19, the town is all color and exuberance—this is Garífuna Settlement Day, when these proud people celebrate their arrival in Belize and remember their roots. Dangriga then cuts loose with a week of Carnival-style celebrations.

Dining and Lodging

$$ 🏨 **Mama Noots Backabush Resort.** Being environmentally aware doesn't mean you can't also be comfy. Instead of a diesel motor behind your cabana, here you have a combination solar, wind, and hydro system to generate electricity. Most produce served in the open-air dining room is grown on the grounds. Rooms, in thatch cabanas or a modern concrete building, have views of the rugged Maya Mountains. Because the resort is *backabush* (in the forest), owners Kevin and Nanette Denny advise guests to bring lightweight "jungle clothing," along with a poncho, plenty of insect repellent, and an adventuresome spirit. Nearby is the Mayflower archeological site, where a long-awaited excavation and restoration have begun, and miles of jungle trails and waterfalls. Wildlife spotting and birding here are excellent. ✉ *Near Mayflower archaeological site,* ☎ *520/2050,* WEB *www. mamanoots.com. 6 rooms, 2 dorm rooms. Restaurant, fans, hiking, bar; no a/c, no room phones, no room TVs. AE.*

$$ 🏨 **Pelican Beach Resort.** It has linoleum floors and thin wood walls, but this waterfront hotel outside Dangriga is the best the town has to offer. There are a dock and a little beach area, but you won't find the water appealing for swimming. Most rooms are in a two-story colonial-style building with a veranda. Some have porches with sea views, and all have real tubs rather than showers. The restaurant is a bit pricey for what you get, but the food and service are dependable. The resort is close to Cockscomb Basin Wildlife Sanctuary and has an annex on Southwater Caye, 20 minutes away by boat. ✉ *Northeast of Dangriga,* ☎ *522/2044,* FAX *522/2570,* WEB *www.pelicanbeachbelize.com. 20 rooms. Restaurant, fans, dock, boating, bar, laundry service, meeting rooms, travel services; no a/c in some rooms, no phones in some rooms, no TVs in some rooms. AE, MC, V.*

Hopkins

❻   *17 km (10 mi) south of Dangriga on the Southern Hwy., then 3⅓ km (2 mi) east on a dirt road.*

Hopkins is an interesting Garífuna village on the coast about halfway between Dangriga and Placencia. Garífuna culture is more accessible here than in Dangriga. Hopkins has the same toast-color beaches as those you'll find in Placencia, and a number of new resorts have opened to take advantage of them. Americans, Canadians, and Europeans are snapping up beachfront land here at prices lower than in Placencia or on Ambergris Caye, but so far only a few vacation homes have been built. If there's a downside to the area, it is the sandflies, which can be vicious here.

Dining and Lodging

$$$$ 🏨 **Kanantik Reef & Jungle Resort.** Are you looking to experience the barrier reef and the jungle without having to make decisions more difficult than whether to have the fish or the steak for dinner? Intent on frolicking on a palm-lined private beach? Want an active vacation with all the snorkeling, sailing, kayaking, and fishing that you can handle? Then this luxurious all-inclusive resort that opened in early 2002 may be your place. Kanantik—a Mopan Maya word meaning "to take care"—has air-conditioned cabanas hidden away on 300 acres just north of Hopkins. The large and luxuriously outfitted cabanas, echoing African themes, are striking round structures with conical roofs. The resort took years to build; construction included bulldozing a lengthy road and building an airstrip. Rates are at the top end of the Belize spectrum, at BZ$1,200 a day double. ⊠ *Southern Hwy., 23 km (14 mi) south of Dangriga,* ☎ *520/8048; 800/965–9689 in the U.S.,* 🕸 *www.kanantik.com. 25 cabanas. Restaurant, fans, refrigerators, pool, beach, dive shop, dock, snorkeling, boating, fishing, horseback riding, bar, laundry service, airstrip, travel services. All-inclusive. AE, MC, V.*

$$$$ 🏨 **Jaguar Reef Lodge.** At night, with a row of torches burning on the beach and the thatch-covered dining room glowing in the lamplight, this lodge has an East African feel. Nestled on the coast, it has views over the water in one direction and of the green slopes of the Maya Mountains in the other. Cottages of whitewashed stone have soaring pitched ceilings with exposed wooden beams. Inside you'll find Mexican-tile baths with mahogany-encased basins. Even those items that are less essential, like the mahogany-and-canvas beach umbrellas, are held to the same high standards. The resort can arrange dive trips, cruises on the nearby Sittee River, or excursions to nearby wildlife reserves. The beach is only so-so for swimming, but there's a seaside pool. About the last thing you'd expect to find in this area is a golf course, but 9 holes will be completed in 2002. The food is good, served in a waterside dining room with indoor and outdoor seating. The Garífuna staff is polite and easygoing. ⊠ *Hopkins,* ☎ *800/289–5756 in the U.S.,* 🕸 *www.jaguarreef.com. 12 rooms, 4 suites. Restaurant, fans, refrigerators, 9-hole golf course, pool, beach, dive shop, dock, snorkeling, fishing, bar, laundry service, travel services. AE, MC, V.*

$$$–$$$$ 🏨 **Hamanasi.** The name is Garífuna for "almond," and Hamanasi has quickly become one of the top beach resorts in Belize. The hotel looks unprepossessing from the dirt road, but once you arrive, you see the manicured grounds and the lobby lined with original art. The "zero effect" pool that seems to stretch to infinity is one of the most appealing in Belize. Choose from regular rooms, gorgeous suites with king-size four-poster beds of barba jolote wood, and "tree houses" raised on stilts. Diving is why most people come to the resort—owners Dana and

David Krauskopf have dived all over the world, from Bali to Zanzibar—but you won't feel out of place here if you want to snorkel or just laze around the pool. The restaurant serves delicious seafood and an eclectic blend of American and Belizean dishes. ✉ *Hopkins,* ☎ *520/ 7073; 877/552–3483 in the U.S.,* WEB *www.hamanasi.com. 8 rooms, 8 suites. Restaurant, fans, refrigerators, pool, beach, dive shop, dock, boating, fishing, bar, travel services. MC, V.*

$$$–$$$$ ⌂ **Lillpat Sittee River Lodge.** This lodge, on 50 acres near the Sittee River, is devoted to a single passion. The fishing—on the river, on the flats, or out at Glover's Reef—is superb. The staff takes you where the bonefish, tarpon, permit, and snook are biting. You get a lot more than a fishing shack, as native hardwoods and Guatemalan furnishings are used throughout the lodge. The curved mahogany table in the dining room, where you eat family-style meals, is a thing of beauty. If you just want to relax, there's a beautiful new pool. If you don't fish, the lodge can also arrange bird-watching and snorkeling trips. ✉ *Sittee River,* ☎ FAX *520/7019,* WEB *www.lillpat.com. 4 rooms. Restaurant, fans, cable TV, pool, boating, fishing, hiking, bar, travel services. AE, MC, V.*

$$ ⌂ **Beaches and Dreams.** New hotels are popping up all around the region, but Beaches and Dreams has managed to secure one of the area's nicest tan-color stretches of shoreline. Like many other innkeepers in the area, Sharon and Dave Helgesen left their jobs behind to build a beachside bungalow in Belize. Their B&B, completed in late 1998, has two octagonal cottages, each with a vaulted ceiling, rattan furnishings, and a small veranda just a few feet from the sea. The pub-style restaurant serves some of the best food and coldest drinks in Hopkins. Try the seafood-and-fruit kebabs or the Cajun chicken pizza. Diving trips can be arranged. ✉ *Sittee Point,* ☎ FAX *523/7078,* WEB *www.beachesanddreams.com. 4 rooms. Restaurant, fans, beach, bar, travel services; no a/c, no room phones, no room TVs. MC, V.*

$ ⌂ **Tipple Tree Beya Inn.** Tiny Tipple Tree Beya Inn provides a comfortable alternative to the upmarket resorts along the coast. Here you can relax on the beach or kick back in a hammock. Run by a friendly British woman, the inn has three rooms that are simple but shiny clean, as well as a separate private cabin with a kitchenette. You can even pitch a tent on the beach. Bicycles and kayaks are available for rent. Tipple Tree also operates a small lodge in nearby Sittee River village, where you can relax by the river under the jungle canopy. You might even see a jaguar. ✉ *Hopkins,* ☎ *520/7006,* WEB *www.tippletree.net. 1 cabin, 3 rooms without bath. Beach, snorkeling, camping; no a/c, no room phones, no room TVs. MC, V.*

$ ⌂ **Toucan Sittee.** Neville Collins used to run a store in San Ignacio before he retired here to a 20-acre farm where he grows 10 varieties of mangoes. He and his wife, Yoli, now run this retreat on the Sittee River. Each of the four cottages on stilts has living and dining rooms and one or two bedrooms. Collins can arrange all kinds of activities (canoeing, hiking, bird-watching) if you tire of just hanging around in a peaceful place filled with birds flying among the ginger plants. Delicious meals use organic ingredients grown on the farm. Like all lodges in these parts, this one can get a bit buggy, so bring repellent. ✉ *Sittee River,* ☎ *523/ 7039,* WEB *www.freespace.virgin.net/david.griggs. 3 apartments, 2 rooms without bath. Fishing, camping; no a/c, no room phones, no room TVs. No credit cards.*

Outdoor Activities and Sports

The best diving operation in the area is at **Hamanasi** (✉ Hopkins, ☎ 520/7073). Here you'll find the newest equipment and the biggest boats. **Second Nature Divers** ✉ Sittee River, ☎ FAX 523/7038, WEB www. belizenet.com/divers.html) has a good reputation.

Shopping

Jaguar Reef Resort (⊠ Hopkins, ☎ 800/289–5756 in the U.S.) has a fine little gift shop filled with pottery and embroidery as well as Garífuna crafts. The store also carries Marie Sharp's superb hot sauces, New Age music, and drugstore items like sunscreen and the very necessary no-see-um repellent.

Cockscomb Basin Wildlife Sanctuary

★ ❼ *48 km (30 mi) southwest of Dangriga.*

The mighty jaguar, once the undisputed king of the Central and South American jungles, is now endangered. But it has a haven in the Cockscomb Basin Wildlife Sanctuary, which covers 102,000 acres of lush rain forest in the Cockscomb Range of the Maya Mountains. Because of this reserve, as well as other protected areas around the country, Belize has the highest concentration of jaguars in the world.

Jaguars are shy, nocturnal animals that prefer to keep their distance from humans, so the possibility of sighting one in the wild is small. The jaguar, or *el tigre,* as it's known in Spanish, is nature's great loner, a supremely free creature that shuns even the company of its own kind. Except during a brief mating period and the six short months the female spends with her cubs before turning them loose, jaguars live alone, roaming the rain forest in splendid isolation. At certain times of year, however, jaguars are routinely spotted here. In November 2001 visitors saw jaguars, including mothers with cubs, nearly every day of the month on the road to the visitor center. They had to get up early, as the sightings occurred between 5:30 and 6.

In the 1980s, in a misguided attempt by an American naturalist to track their movements, seven jaguars were tagged with radio collars. Special steel cages were built to catch them because they had smashed several wooden ones to pieces. A jaguar would enter a cage, trip a door behind it, and find itself captive. What followed was a conflagration of fur and fury of almost unbelievable proportions. The captured jaguars were so powerful that in their desperate attempts to escape they threw the 300-pound cages around like matchboxes. They sheared off most of their teeth as they tried to bite through the steel. Within a year all seven had died.

Other conservation efforts have been more successful. Today there are an estimated 25–30 jaguars—8–10 adult males, 9–10 adult females, and the rest young animals—spread over about 400 square km (154 square mi). This is the world's largest jaguar population. In contrast, the jaguar was hunted to extinction in the United States by the late 1940s.

Cockscomb Basin has a wonderful array of Belize's wildlife other than jaguars. You might see other cats—pumas, margays, and ocelots—plus coatis, kinkajous, deer, peccaries, and, last but not least, tapirs. Also known as the mountain cow, this shy, curious creature appears to be half horse, half hippo, with a bit of cow and elephant thrown in. Nearly 300 species of birds have been identified in the Cockscomb Basin, including the keel-billed toucan, the king vulture, several species of hawks, and the scarlet macaw.

The reserve boasts Belize's best-maintained system of jungle and mountain trails, most of which lead to at least one outstanding swimming hole. The sanctuary also offers spectacular views of Victoria Peak and the Cockscomb Range. Bring some serious bug spray with you—the reserve is alive with mosquitoes and tiny biting flies called no-see-ums, and wear long-sleeve shirts and long pants. The best times to hike anywhere in Belize are early morning, late afternoon, and early evening, when temperatures are lower and more animals are on the prowl.

You have to register in a hut by the entrance before proceeding several miles to the visitor center. The road winds through dense vegetation, including splendid cahune palms, purple mimosas, orchids, and big-leaf plantains. The marvelous sound of tropical birds, often resembling strange windup toys, grows stronger and stronger. This is definitely four-wheel-drive terrain. You may have to ford several small rivers as well as negotiate deep, muddy ruts. At the end, in a clearing with hibiscus and bougainvillea bushes, you'll find a little office where you can buy maps of the nature trails, along with rest rooms, several picnic tables, cabins, and a campground.

You're not likely to see jaguars here, as they have exceptionally good senses of smell and hearing. But walking along these 12 well-marked nature trails is a good way to get to know the region. Most are loops of 1–2 km (½–1½ mi), so you can do several in a day. The most strenuous trail takes you up a steep hill, from the top of which there is a magnificent view of the entire Cockscomb Basin. ⊠ *Outside Maya Centre*, ☎ 227/7369. ⊠ *BZ$10*. ⊙ *Daily 8–5*.

Dining and Lodging

You can camp in the reserve for BZ$10 a night per person, or you can stay in pleasant new rooms in cabins with solar-generated electricity for BZ$44 per person. Book in Belize City through Belize Audubon Society (☎ 223/5004).

$ 🏠 **Tutzil Nah Cottages.** Gregoria Chun and his family, Mopan Maya people who have lived in this area for generations, provide accommodations in simple thatch cabanas. Meals also are available, and the Chuns provide a range of tours to Cockscomb and to Maya sites. ⊠ *Near Maya Centre, Km 13 1/2, Southern Hwy.*, ☎ *520/3044*, WEB *www.mayacenter.com. 5 cabanas. No a/c, no room phones, no room TVs. No credit cards.*

Seine Bight

⑧ *44 km (27 mi) south of Dangriga.*

Like Placencia, its Creole neighbor to the south, Seine Bight is a sleepy coastal fishing village. It may not be like this for long, because Placencia's resorts are stretching north to this Garífuna community. The beach is among the best in Belize, even though garbage sometimes mars the view. Hotels do rake and clean their beachfronts, and several community cleanups have been held to try to solve this problem. All the businesses catering to tourists are off the main road (actually, it's the only road) that leads to Placencia. Like Placencia village, Seine Bight was devastated by Hurricane Iris in October 2001, and many of the simple wooden homes in the village were destroyed. Maya Beach, to the north of Seine Bight, is a collection of homes and hotels along the shore.

Dining and Lodging

$–$$ ✕ **Mango of Maya Beach.** Owner and chef Chris Duffy, a painter from Connecticut, serves something different every day in her tiny thatch-top restaurant. All the entrées are sophisticated by Belizean standards—field greens with Dijon vinaigrette, lobster scampi, and tropical fruit fondue are often on the menu. Lunch and dinner are served daily, but she appreciates your letting her know you're coming. ⊠ *Maya Beach, 2 km (1 mi) north of Seine Bight, on main road*, ☎ *614/7023. No credit cards.*

$$$$ ⊞ **Inn at Robert's Grove.** Imagine that you've met an energetic New
★ York couple named Bob and Risa Frackman, and they invite you to
stay at their place on a palm-lined stretch of beach. You can play a few
games of tennis and swim in one of the beachside pools or in the sea.
Their chef, Frank Da Silva, will cook you large breakfasts, pack picnic lunches for boat rides to deserted cayes, and serve dinner in the
seaside dining room. This personal attention is what you get at this resort, often full in season. The choicest digs are the suites, featuring verandas overlooking the ocean. On the roof of each building is a
whirlpool, also with a view. You can even work out in the new gym.
The hotel has its own dive center, with three boats; and a private caye
for picnics. ⊠ *1 km (½ mi) south of Seine Bight,* ☎ *523/3565; 800/
565–9757 in the U.S.,* FAX *523/3567,* WEB *www.robertsgrove.com. 20
rooms, 12 suites. Restaurant, fans, some refrigerators, 2 pools, gym,
beach, dive shop, dock, snorkeling, windsurfing, boating, fishing, 2 tennis courts, bars, gift shop, laundry service, travel services. AE, MC, V.*

$$$–$$$$ ✕⊞ **Luba Hati.** From the widow's walk above the central wing of the
★ two-story main house there's a great view of the lagoon in one direc-
tion and the ocean in the other. The red-tile roofs and tree-filled court-
yard below feel a bit like Umbria—no accident, as owners Franco and
Mariuccia Gentile are originally from Italy. No thatch-covered huts
here—accommodations are in substantial structures of stone and mor-
tar. Creative touches include staircases supported by giant tree trunks.
Each room is decorated with African and Guatemalan fabrics. New
beachfront cottages are the most popular digs. You'll eat well here, too;
Franco is an excellent chef, and his selection of classic Italian dishes
and wines has brought a touch of the dolce vita to Placencia. The staff
is happy to arrange tours and other activities. ⊠ *1 km (½ mi) south of
Seine Bight village,* ☎ *523/3402,* FAX *523/3403,* WEB *www.lubahati.com.
3 cottages, 8 rooms. Restaurant, fans, saltwater pool, beach, dock,
snorkeling, fishing, laundry service; no a/c in some rooms, no room
TVs. AE, MC, V.*

$$$ ⊞ **Green Parrot.** This cluster of Mennonite-built cottages on a pretty
beach is great for families with small kids, as each has a dining area
and a fully stocked kitchenette. The sleeping quarters are upstairs in
a loftlike space with a pitched wooden roof. One nifty feature is an
octagonal-shape wall panel, operated by pulleys, that can be opened
for a bedside view of the ocean. Two thatch cabanas have outdoor showers. The beachfront restaurant and bar are decorated with high-back
chairs of varnished cane that were made by local craftspeople. It's best
if you have a car here, as it's an expensive cab ride from Placencia. ⊠
Maya Beach, 6½ km (4 mi) north of Seine Bight, ☎ *523/8009,* FAX *523/
2488,* WEB *www.greenparrot-belize.com. 6 cabins, 2 cabanas. Restaurant, fans, beach, dock, snorkeling, bar; no a/c, no room phones, no
room TVs. AE, MC, V.*

$$$ ⊞ **Nautical Inn.** "It's not for campers" is how owner Ben Ruoti de-
scribes this inn, which consists of two-tier octagonal cottages brought
here from North Carolina. He and his wife, Janie, are proud of their
American-style fixtures, such as firm mattresses and glass-wall show-
ers. The Oar House restaurant serves good Belizean home cooking as
well as barbecues right on the beach. The pool is one of the nicest on
the peninsula. The inn has some canoes as well as a dive boat to get
you to the reef. If you just want to hang out, a pretty beach awaits.
Janie will show you her baby iguanas, which she raises and releases.
On Wednesday evening the hotel hosts Garífuna drummers and coconut
bowling. There's nothing like a milk-filled ball to throw off your game.
⊠ *Seine Bight,* ☎ *523–3595; 800/688–0377 in the U.S.,* FAX *523/3594,*
WEB *www.nauticalinnbelize.com. 12 rooms. Restaurant, fans, pool,*

beach, dock, dive shop; no room phones, no TVs in some rooms. AE, MC, V. FAP.

$$$ 🏨 **Singing Sands.** The six wood-and-thatch cabanas here are small and simply decorated with Guatemalan needlecrafts. They were relocated after Hurricane Iris and now have better views. Singing Sands has its own 25-ft boat for snorkeling, a treat of a beach, a dock with a nice area for swimming, and a pool for those who'd rather take a dip in freshwater. ✉ *Seine Bight,* ☎ *800/649–3007 in U.S.,* WEB *www.singingsands.com. 6 cabanas. Restaurant, fans, refrigerators, pool, beach, dock, dive shop, bar, travel services; no a/c, no room phones, no room TVs. AE, MC, V.*

$$ 🏨 **Barnacle Bill's.** If you're the independent type, this property on Maya Beach has a pair of wooden cottages set among the palm trees about 60 ft from the surf. Each cottage has fully equipped kitchen where you can make your own meals and a private deck. ✉ *23 Maya Beach Way,* ☎ FAX *523/8010,* WEB *www.gotobelize.com/barnacle. 2 cottages- Fans, beach, snorkeling, fishing; no a/c, no room phones, no room TVs. MC, V.*

Shopping

Painter and writer Lola Delgado moved to Seine Bight from Belize City in the late 1980s. Her workshop, **Lola's Art,** displays her cheerful acrylic paintings of local scenes (BZ$100 and up). She also sells hand-painted cards and some of her husband's wood carvings. Espresso and pastries are available. Open 9 AM–10 PM, the workshop is up a flight of steps in a tiny wooden house off the main street, behind the football field.

Placencia

9 *8 km (5 mi) south of Seine Bight, 52 km (32 mi) south of Dangriga.*

Set in a sheltered half-moon bay with crystal-clear water and almost 5 km (3 mi) of palm-dotted white sand, this fishing village is straight out of a Robert Louis Stevenson novel. Founded by pirates, the community is now inhabited by an extraordinary mélange of people. To the west the Cockscomb Range ruffles the tropical sky with its jagged peaks; to the east a line of uninhabited cayes grazes the horizon. From here you can dive along the reef, hike into the jungle, explore the Maya ruins at Lubantuun, or treat yourself to some of the best sportfishing in the country. Once you arrive, you'll probably just want to lie in a hammock with a good book, perhaps getting up long enough to cool off in the waves.

Placencia is so small that it doesn't even have a main street—it has a concrete path just wide enough for two people. Setting off purposefully from the southern end of town, the path meanders through everyone's backyard, passes wooden cottages on stilts overrun with bougainvillea and festooned with laundry, then, as if it had forgotten where it was headed in the first place, peters out abruptly in a little clearing filled with lovely white morning glories. Stroll along the sidewalk and you've seen the town. If you don't mind it being a little rough around the edges, you'll be utterly enchanted by this rustic village, where the palm trees rustle, the waves lap the shore, and no one is in a hurry.

Dining and Lodging

$$–$$$ ✕ **Pickled Parrot Bar & Grill.** This popular feet-in-the-sand restaurant and bar is in the heart of Placencia. Fresh seafood is the main draw, but owner Wende Bryan also offers pizza on Friday and American-style burgers every day. She has converted the Barracuda and Jaguar Inn to

long-term rentals. ✉ *Off main road, behind Wallen's Market,* ☎ *523/ 3330. AE, MC, V.*

$$$ 🏨 **Rum Point Inn.** When they first came to Placencia, George and
★ Coral Bevier had to cut their way through the undergrowth to find the
old colonial-style house they'd bought. Today this beachfront inn is
one of southern Belize's best-known resorts. The domelike original build-
ings—a bit like flying saucers—are all about space and light. Each has
a unique set of windows—some are portholes, others geometric pat-
terns cut into the walls. A cluster of two-story buildings have four high-
ceilinged rooms with baths equipped with double sinks and Japanese-style
tubs. The library has one of Belize's best collections of books on the
Maya, piles of novels and magazines, and a raft of CDs and videos.
The *Auriga*, the inn's jet-powered dive boat, can anchor beside the most
remote caye. Tours and activities abound, including a splendid trip up
the Monkey River. ✉ *2½ km (1½ mi) north of Placencia,* ☎ *523/3239;
800/747–1381 in the U.S.,* FAX *523/3240,* WEB *www.rumpoint.com. 22
rooms. Restaurant, pool, dock, dive shop, snorkeling, travel services;
no a/c in some rooms, no room phones, no room TVs. AE, DC, MC,
V. FAP, MAP.*

$$–$$$ 🏨 **Kitty's Place.** Kitty's has stood the test of time. It's not the fanciest
resort on the peninsula, but it has a barefoot feel that the newer places
can't duplicate. On the same beautiful stretch of soft sand as Rum Point
Inn, it offers a mixed bag of accommodations, from single rooms to
studios. Three newer cottages face the sea, but some of the nicest
rooms are in the colonial-style house. The upstairs restaurant, deco-
rated with Bob Marley posters, is lively and serves good local fare. The
gift shop sells everything from suntan lotion to Guatemalan crafts. If
you need to check your e-mail, Kitty's has one of the village's two In-
ternet cafés. Sea kayaking, diving, and fishing are popular activities,
and for BZ$100 per person Kitty will pack you off to a remote caye
for the night. ✉ *2½ km (1½ mi) north of Placencia,* ☎ *523/3227,* FAX
523/3226, WEB *www.kittysplace.com. 3 cabanas, 8 rooms. Restaurant,
beach, dive shop, boating, gift shop, travel services; no a/c, no room
phones, no room TVs. AE, MC, V.*

$$$ 🏨 **Mariposa.** No sign marks the entrance to this brace of oceanfront
suites in a private home just north of Placencia. You only know you're
at Mariposa (Spanish for "butterfly") when you see all the wings
painted on posts and doorways along the driveway. Low-key is the catch-
word here. Owners Peter and Marcia Fox let you lounge in your own
palapa near the private beach or relax on your secluded veranda. If
you like, they'll stock your kitchen with all the groceries you need. Mariposa is quite the opposite of a big full-service beach resort, but it's an
appealing spot if you are searching for a home away from home. ✉
2½ km (1½ mi) north of Placencia, ☎ *523/4069,* FAX *523/4076,* WEB
www.mariposabelize.com. 2 suites. Fans, beach. D, MC, V.

$$ 🏨 **Harry's Cozy Cabanas.** Harry Eiler's three varnished-wood cabanas
with screened porches are as nice as Harry is, though they don't have
quite as much character. Each has a kitchenette with a fridge. The lo-
cation is quieter than the main part of the village. ✉ *Placencia Har-
bor, just south of Tentacles,* ☎ *523/3155. Fans, kitchenettes; no a/c,
no room phones, no room TVs. No credit cards.*

$–$$ 🏨 **Tradewinds.** If you're yearning for a secluded cottage directly on the
★ beach but don't want to pay a lot of money, then this little colony is
for you. Five cabins, painted in Caribbean pastels, are small but pleasant. Rebuilt after Hurricane Iris, they enjoy just about the best location
in the village, off to themselves on the beach at the south point of the
peninsula. The owner is the village's former postmistress, Janice Leslie.
✉ *South Point, Placencia,* ☎ *523/3122. 5 cabins. Fans, refrigerators,
beach, snorkeling; no a/c, no room phones, no room TVs. MC, V.*

$ ⊞ **Manatee Inn.** Run by a friendly young Czech couple, the Manatee Inn offers top value for your money. The rooms on the second floor of this wood-frame two-story lodge, new in 2001, are simply furnished but extremely clean and have hardwood floors and private baths. Larger apartments, perfect for families, are on the first floor. The hotel isn't on the beach, but it has a freshwater pool. ⊠ *At north end of village,* ☏ FAX *523/4083,* WEB *www.manateeinn.com. 6 rooms, 2 apartments. Fans, pool; no a/c, no room phones, no TVs in some rooms. AE, MC, V.*

Outdoor Activities and Sports

FISHING

The fly-fishing on the flats off the cayes east of Placencia is some of Belize's best. You'll encounter plentiful tarpon—they flurry 10 deep in the water at times—as well as permit, bonefish, and snook. Most of the better hotels can arrange guides. If you want a local guide, call **Kevin Modera** (☏ 523/3243, WEB www.kevinmodera.com). He has great information about fishing in Placencia.

SAILING

In late 2001, **Moorings** (⊠ Placencia Harbor, Placencia, ☏ 888/952–8420 in the U.S.) opened a branch in Placencia. It offers bareboat catamaran charters, with a week's sailing going for around BZ$9,000.

SCUBA DIVING

Most of the larger resorts, like Nautical Inn, the Inn at Robert's Grove, and Rum Point Inn, have good dive shops. For been-there-done-that divers, Rum Point also has a new program that lets you take part in a marine wildlife survey run out of Key Largo. Divers are asked to fill out survey forms listing the number of bar-fin blennies or mimic triplefins they spot, and the information is forwarded to Florida for cataloging. Brian Young runs the **Seahorse Dive Shop** (☏ 523/3166), which has a good reputation. For snorkeling trips and gear there's **Ocean Motion** (☏ 523/3363), near the grocery store.

Placencia and Environs A to Z

AIR TRAVEL TO AND FROM PLACENCIA AND ENVIRONS

Both Tropic Air and Maya Island Air have regular service to Placencia from Belize City (BZ$118 from the municipal airport, BZ$140 from the international one). You can purchase tickets at some of the region's resorts, such as Kitty's and the Inn at Robert's Grove. The airstrip is about 3 km (2 mi) north of the center of Placencia, so you'll probably want to take a taxi (BZ$10 from the center of town) if your hotel doesn't provide a shuttle.

➤ AIRLINES AND CONTACTS: **Maya Island Air** (⊠ Placencia airstrip, ☏ 523/3475, WEB www.mayaairways.com). **Tropic Air** (⊠ Placencia airstrip, ☏ 523/3410, WEB www.tropicair.com).

BUS TRAVEL TO AND FROM PLACENCIA AND ENVIRONS

For routes south to Belmopan and Dangriga, try Southern Transport, a successor to Z-Line. The main bus stop in Placencia is near the Shell station. The bus station in Dangriga is seven blocks south of town on the main road, near the Texaco and Shell stations.

➤ BUS INFORMATION: **Southern Transport** (⊠ 3 Havana St., Dangriga, ☏ 522/2160).

CAR RENTAL

Budget and other rental agencies in Belize City will deliver a car to Placencia for a fee of around BZ$130.

CAR TRAVEL

To get to Placencia, head southeast from Belmopan on the Hummingbird Highway. Once a potholed nightmare, the thoroughfare is now the best route in Belize, if not in all of Central America. It's also the most scenic road in Belize. On your right rise the jungle-covered Maya Mountains, largely free of signs of human habitation except for the occasional field of corn or beans.

If you want to drive directly from Belize City to Placencia, take the turnoff at Mile 30 on the Western Highway for Dangriga and the south. The 60-km (36-mi) Manatee Road is unpaved—dusty in dry weather, sometimes flooded after rains—but it saves about an hour on the drive south. The Southern Highway is now beautifully paved from Dangriga to Independence south of Placencia, and another 42 km (25 mi) is paved from Punta Gorda north. Eventually the 50 km (30 mi) of remaining dirt on the Southern Highway will be paved, according to the Belize government. From the Southern Highway to Placencia most of the 42 km (25 mi) is unpaved and can be treacherous after rains, even for four-wheel-drive vehicles.

EMERGENCIES

Although Placencia now has a nurse, an acupuncturist, a part-time chiropractor, and a natural healer, for serious medical attention you should go to Dangriga or Independence.

➤ HOSPITALS: **Dangriga Regional Hospital** (⊠ Stann Creek District Hwy., Dangriga, ☎ 52/2078). **John Price Memorial Clinic** (⊠ Independence, ☎ 62/2167).

HEALTH

Malaria and dengue fever are present in the region's more remote reaches. The water supply in Dangriga is not dependable, so make sure to drink bottled water. Placencia and Hopkins have safe, treated water.

MAIL AND SHIPPING

The Placencia post office is on the second floor of a wooden building at the south end of the sidewalk. It is usually open 8:30–noon and 1–4 weekdays.

➤ POST OFFICES: **Placencia** (⊠ South end of sidewalk, ☎ 62/3104).

MONEY MATTERS

In Placencia, Atlantic Bank is open weekdays 8–noon. There are no ATMs in town that accept foreign-issued cards in Placencia. Amazingly, the Barclays Bank in Dangriga has an ATM that (usually) accepts foreign cards.

➤ BANKS: **Atlantic Bank** (⊠ at end of main road, Placencia, ☎ 523/3386). **Barclays Bank** (⊠ Commerce St., Dangriga, ☎ 522/2015).

TAXIS

If you need a ride to the airport in Dangriga, call Neal's Taxi. Fare from downtown to the airstrip at the north end of town should be about BZ$6. In Placencia taxis are more expensive, given the relatively short distances involved. It's BZ$30–BZ$40 one way from Placencia to Maya Beach, BZ$10 from downtown to the airstrip.

➤ TAXI COMPANIES: **Neal's Taxi** (⊠ 1 St. Vincent St., Dangriga, ☎ 522/3309).

TOURS OPERATORS

Many tour guides and operators offer dive and snorkel trips to Laughing Bird, Ranguana, or other cayes, wildlife tours to Monkey River, and excursions to Maya ruins such as Nim Li Punit or Lubaantun. For the more adventurous traveler, Toadal Adventures has excellent biking, hiking, and kayaking tours.

➤ Tour Companies: **Toadal Adventures Belize** (✉ Point Placencia, Placencia, ☎ 253/3207).

VISITOR INFORMATION

The Placencia office of the Belize Tourism Industry Association is in a building near the gas station at the south end of the village. The agency publishes the *Placencia Breeze,* an informative monthly newspaper. Placencia has a very helpful Web site listing all accommodations, restaurants, and bars, www.placencia.com. Hopkins has an interesting Web site put together by local people, www.hopkinsbelize.com.

➤ Tourist Information: **Belize Tourism Industry Association** (✉ Point Placencia, Placencia, ☎ 523/4045).

BELIZE A TO Z

AIR TRAVEL TO AND FROM BELIZE

The main airlines serving Belize from the United States are American, with daily flights from Miami and Dallas–Fort Worth; Continental, which has daily nonstop flights from Houston; and Taca, which has nonstop flights from Houston. It is often cheaper to fly into the Mexican city of Cancún, but the journey to Belize will take a full day away from each end of your Belize vacation. AeroCaribe no longer flies to Belize City from Cancún.

Planes on domestic routes are usually single- or twin-engine island hoppers. Depending on where you depart, you may endure several takeoffs and landings. Most domestic flights leave from the municipal airport, near the center of Belize City, which is easier to reach than the international airport. Domestic fights from the municipal airport tend to be cheaper than from the international one. The main carriers are Tropic Air and Maya Island Air, both of which fly to Ambergris Caye and Caye Caulker, as well as Dangriga, Placencia, and Corozal.

➤ Airlines and Contacts: **Maya Island Airways** (✉ Belize Municipal Airport, Belize City, ☎ 226–3838, 800/225–6732 in the U.S., WEB www.mayaairways.com). **Tropic Air** (✉ San Pedro, ☎ 226/2012, 800/ 422–3435 in the U.S., WEB www.tropicair.com).

AIRPORTS AND TRANSFERS

Philip S. W. Goldson International Airport is 14 km (9 mi) north of the city. Taxis to town cost BZ$35. The Belize City Municipal Airport has flights to San Pedro and down the coast to Dangriga and Placencia.

➤ Airports: **Belize City Municipal Airport** (✉ North of Belize City). **Philip S. W. Goldson International Airport** (✉ Ladyville).

BUS TRAVEL TO AND FROM BELIZE

There is daily bus service from the Guatemalan and Mexican borders. Buses cross from Chetumal, Mexico, and stop in Corozal, Belize, where you can catch another bus to Belize City or a plane to San Pedro. Buses from Guatemala (via Flores) stop in the border town of Melchor de Mencos. Cross the border and take a bus or taxi to San Ignacio, 13 km (8 mi) away, or continue on the bus to Belize City.

BUS TRAVEL WITHIN BELIZE

Although there is no rail system in Belize, there is fairly extensive bus service by private companies. The quality of the buses and the roads on which they travel vary considerably. Novelo's, the dominant carrier in the country, especially on the Western and Northern highways, has acquired several competing companies. Because of consolidations in the industry that created Novelo's and other companies, you'll find that schedules are in flux. However, buses are still extremely cheap (about BZ$5–BZ$22 from Belize City to other points in the country) and remain an excellent way to experience Belize as the Belizeans do. Outside the cities you can flag them down like cabs, and the driver will let you off whenever you want. Expect to ride on old U.S. school buses or retired Greyhound buses. On the Northern and Western highways there are a few express buses with air-conditioning and other comforts; these cost a few dollars more.

Novelo's buses stop in Belmopan and San Ignacio and go north to Orange Walk and Corozal, while Southern Transport covers Dangriga and points south.

➤ BUS INFORMATION: **Novelo's** (✉ W. Collet Canal, Belize City, ☎ 227/2025). **Southern Transport** (✉ 3 Havana St., Dangriga, ☎ 522/2211.

CAR RENTAL

Belize City now has branches of most international car-rental agencies, as well as several local operators. Prices vary from company to company, but all are high by U.S. standards (BZ$120–BZ$230 per day). Some cars rented out by the local operators—V-8 gas-guzzlers driven down from Texas—will cost you dearly for gas alone, whereas the international agencies have modern, dependable fleets. A four-wheel-drive Suzuki with unlimited mileage from Budget costs about BZ$150 per day. Off-season rates are lower. For serious safaris a four-wheel-drive vehicle (preferably a Land Rover or an Isuzu Trooper) is invaluable. Some major hotels offer all-terrain vehicles with guides for about BZ$400 per day.

CAR TRAVEL

Belize is one of the few countries left in the Americas where off-road conditions are still the norm on many of the major roads. Getting somewhere is never a question of simply going from A to B; there are always a bit of adventure involved and a few detours to Y and Z.

Only the Northern Highway (to Orange Walk and Corozal), the Western Highway (to Belmopan and San Ignacio), and the Hummingbird Highway (from Belmopan to Dangriga) are fully paved. The Southern Highway is now about three-fourths of the way along, with only about 50 km (30 mi) still unpaved. Once you get off the main highways, distances don't mean that much—it's time that counts. You might have only 20 km (12½ mi) to go, but it can take you a grueling 90 minutes. If you bring your own car, you'll need to buy insurance in Belize.

GASOLINE

Unleaded premium gasoline costs around BZ$5.50 per gallon. There are modern service stations, even a few open 24 hours, in Belize City and in most of the north and west. In remote areas fill up whenever you see a gas station.

EMBASSIES AND CONSULATES

There are no Australian or New Zealand embassies or consulates in Central America.

➤ CONTACTS: **British High Commission** (✉ Embassy Square, Belmopan, ☎ 822/2146). **Canadian Consulate** (✉ 29 Southern Foreshore, Belize City, ☎ 223/1060). **U.S. Embassy** (✉ 29 Gabourel La., Belize City, ☎ 227/7161).

MONEY MATTERS

The greenback is accepted everywhere in Belize, so if you are carrying U.S. dollars you do not need to exchange money. Other currencies, including Canadian dollars, are generally not accepted in Belize. If you need to exchange another currency you can do so at one of the five banks operating in Belize—Alliance Bank, Atlantic Bank, Bank of Nova Scotia, Barclays, and Belize Bank. Most banks have their main offices on Albert Street in Belize City, with branches in larger towns around the country. Should you exchange U.S. dollars at a bank, expect to be charged a 1%–2% fee.

TOUR OPERATORS

Many tour companies stick to their local area, but several venture farther afield. One of the best is Discovery Expeditions, which has several offices in Belize City hotels. The staff is friendly and well informed and can help you arrange expeditions virtually anywhere in the country. Maya Travel Services, in Belize City, is knowledgeable about the country and can book hotels, tours, and transportation. S&L Travel Services, in Belize City, is also reputable. Amigo Travel, the largest tour company on Ambergris Caye, offers both mainland and island tours and snorkeling excursions.

➤ TOUR COMPANIES: **Amigo Travel** (⊠ Barrier Reef Dr., San Pedro, ☎ 226/2180). **Discovery Expeditions** (⊠ 5916 Manatee Dr., Buttonwood Bay, Belize City, ☎ 223/0748, FAX 23/0750). **Maya Travel Services** (⊠ Belize City Municipal Airport, Belize City, ☎ 223/1623). **S&L Travel Services** (⊠ 91 N. Front St., Belize City, ☎ 227/7593).

3 GUATEMALA

With incomparable ancient ruins, graceful colonial churches, and colorful highland markets, Guatemala is the center of the Maya heartland. This landscape is known for its rushing white-water rivers and expansive stretches of rain forest that hide spider monkeys, toucans, and iguanas among massive mahogany trees draped with mosses, ferns, and rare orchids.

Updated by
Gregory
Benchwick

CAPTIVATING TRAVELERS FOR CENTURIES, Guatemala has lost none of its charm. From conquistador Pedro de Alvarado, who stopped between battles to marvel at the beauty of Lago Atitlán, to writer Aldous Huxley, who waxed poetic on the same lake's shores centuries later, this intricate jewel of a country has intrigued and inspired its share of foreigners. With a territory of just 108,900 square km (42,046 square mi), Guatemala encompasses palm-lined beaches, luxuriant cloud forests, rugged mountain ranges, scrubby desert valleys, and rain forests chock-full of tropical flora and fauna.

Guatemala's landscape may be fascinating, but its population of more than 12.5 million people is even more compelling. All the indigenous peoples are Maya, but they comprise at least 22 ethnicities, differentiated by sometimes subtle distinctions in language, dress, and customs. The rest of the population is divided among mestizos (Spanish-speaking descendants of Spaniards and Indians), Garífunas (descendents of escaped African slaves), and those of predominantly Spanish ancestry who have maintained their imported bloodline and their lease on power. Though Spanish is Guatemala's official language, it's the mother tongue of only about half the population. Many people in the highlands and along the coast speak one of the many indigenous languages.

Guatemala's recent history has largely been the story of a struggle for land and political equality in the face of military rule. By the late 1970s guerrilla groups had begun to tap into the long-held grievances of Guatemala's indigenous peoples. The right-wing government unleashed a brutal campaign not just against the guerrillas, but against civilians. During the worst years of the violence—the "scorched-earth" campaigns of the early 1980s—the military razed hundreds of villages in an effort to flush out a handful of guerrillas. A peace accord finally put an end to the 36-year civil war in 1996.

Guatemala has entered a period of slow recovery. With peace has come increased international investment, and evidence of this economic growth appears throughout the country in the form of new roads, better communication systems, and more electrical power reaching isolated regions. All these improvements have made the country much more attractive to visitors.

Pleasures and Pastimes

Archaeological Treasures

The department of El Petén, much of which is covered with tropical rain forest, was the heart of the ancient Maya empire. Only a fraction of the estimated 1,500 ruins have been explored, and even those that have been excavated remain surrounded, if not actually covered, by vegetation. Aside from Tikal, traveling to the archaeological sites often involves maneuvering a four-wheel-drive vehicle down muddy roads. More isolated sites require taking a boat, riding a mule, or hacking you way through the trees. No matter how you get there, it's likely to be an adventure.

Dining

The basis of Guatemalan food is corn, usually eaten as a tortilla, as a tamale, or on the cob. Black beans accompany most meals, either whole beans cooked in a broth or mashed and refried. Meats are often served in *caldos* (stews) or cooked in a spicy chili sauce. Thin and tender *lomito,* a popular cut of beef, is on the menu in most restaurants. The most popular fish is the delicious *robálo,* known elsewhere as snook. Along the coast you'll find *tapado,* a coconut stew made with plantains, shrimp, crab, and fish.

CATEGORY	COST*
$$$$	over Q100 (over US$13)
$$$	Q70–Q100 (US$9–US$13)
$$	Q40–Q70 (US$5–US$9)
$	under Q40 (under US$5)

per person for a main course at dinner

Lodging

Guatemala now has a wide range of lodging options, from suites at luxurious high-rises to stark rooms in budget hotels. Guatemala City has the most options, but the much more appealing city of Antigua is a better base for exploring the country. Rooms often fill up on weekends, so make reservations well in advance. Panajachel has the widest selection of accommodations in the highlands, and Chichicastenango and Quetzaltenango can claim some creditable lodgings. Most remote villages offer only spartan lodgings, if any at all.

CATEGORY	COST*
$$$$	over Q600 (over US$77)
$$$	Q360–Q600 (US$46–US$77)
$$	Q160–Q360 (US$20–US$46)
$	under Q160 (under US$20)

All prices are for a standard double room, excluding tax.

Shopping

Nearly all of Guatemala's handicrafts come from the highlands, so it's no surprise that this region is a shopper's paradise. Most famous are the handwoven fabrics—in every highland village you'll see women weaving traditional patterns. But Guatemala's indigenous population creates countless other kinds of handicrafts; just as each region has its traditional fabrics, it has other specialties, such as ceramics, baskets, toys, statues, bags, or hats. Don't worry if you forget to buy that souvenir in Sololá, as most of these items are also available in the markets of Antigua and Guatemala City.

Exploring Guatemala

Great Itineraries

Guatemala is a rugged country where major roads are few and far between and highways are nonexistent. But because there are only two airports—one in Guatemala City, the other in Flores—you're forced to do most of your travel by land. All but the hardiest travelers will want to stay in the larger towns and explore the more isolated regions on day trips. A trip to Guatemala should last no less than five days, during which you can take in the most popular sights and still get off the beaten path. Eight days allow a better look at Tikal and El Petén.

IF YOU HAVE 5 DAYS

Fly into **Guatemala City,** departing immediately for the colonial city of ⌂ **Antigua.** Spend at least two nights here. If you're in Antigua on Thursday or Sunday, plan an early morning excursion to the mountain village of **Chichicastenango,** where the region's best handicrafts are found at a lively market. On your fourth day take an early morning plane to **Flores,** a pastel-painted town in El Petén. Head straight to the ruins at nearby **Tikal.** Depending on your schedule, you may choose to spend the night either here so you can see the ruins in the morning (a must for birders) or in Flores so you'll be closer to the airport for your flight back to Guatemala City.

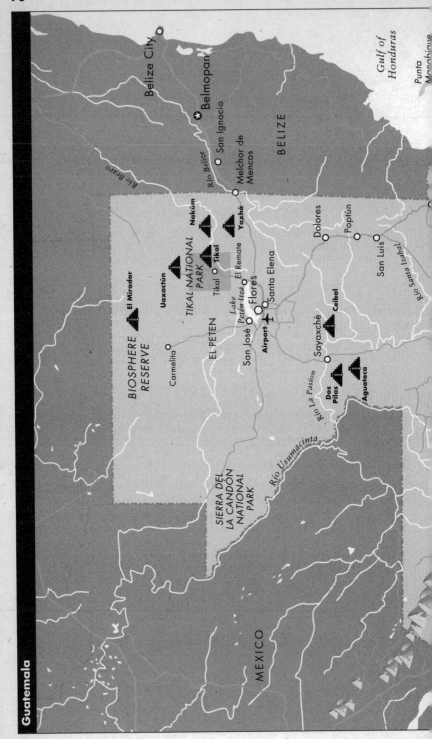

Guatemala

Spend your first day in **Guatemala City,** visiting the museums and dining in Zona Viva. On day two head for **Antigua** so you can tour the remarkable ruins of 16th-, 17th-, and 18th-century monasteries and convents. Spend two nights here, and then head for **Panajachel.** Spend day five visiting the villages surrounding picture-perfect Lago Atitlán or head to the renowned market in the colonial village of **Chichicastenango.** On day six fly north to **Flores,** where you can spend the afternoon shopping, strolling, and sipping cappuccino. Make arrangements for a taxi to pick you up at your hotel the next morning—you'll want to leave before dawn for the breathtaking ruins of **Tikal.** Climb the rustic ladder to the top of the tallest temple, then watch the sunrise over the rain forest that engulfs the ancient city. Spend your last morning hiking the terrific trails of the **Biotopo Cerro Cahuí** before returning to Guatemala City.

When to Tour Guatemala

Most come to Guatemala from June to August and from January to April. The rainy season runs from May to November, with a few dry spells in July and August. A typical day in the rainy season is sunny in the morning, cloudy at midday, and pouring throughout the afternoon and evening. Guatemala's climate depends more on altitude than season. El Petén is hot, while the mountains enjoy warm days and cool nights.

GUATEMALA CITY

Once hailed as the "jewel of Central America," Guatemala City has certainly lost its luster. The country's capital, a tangle of streets and alleyways, retains little of its colonial charm. With few of the country's most popular attractions—no ancient ruins, flamboyant markets, or spectacular mountains—there's little reason to stay longer than necessary. But as it's the country's transportation hub, you're likely to end up here. Fortunately, the city has some decent restaurants and hotels, as well as several excellent museums and a lively nightlife.

The sprawling metropolis can be intimidating, as it is divided between the Old City and the New City as well as into 21 different *zonas.* But there is virtually no reason to stray from the four central zones, which makes getting around—and getting your bearings—quite manageable. The Old City covers Zona 1, in the north, and the New City spans Zona 9 and Zona 10, in the south. Between them is Zona 4, notable only because it contains the bus terminals. Otherwise, this seedy section is best avoided.

In the Old and New cities, numbered *avenidas* (avenues) run south to north, while *calles* (streets) run west to east. Addresses are usually given as a numbered avenida or calle followed by two numbers separated by a dash: the first number is a nearby cross street or avenue and the second is a specific building. The building numbers increase as they approach the higher-numbered cross streets and then start over at the next block, so 9 Avenida 5–22 is on 9 Avenida near 5 Calle, and 9 Avenida 5–74 is on the same block, only closer to 6 Calle. A word of warning: make sure you're in the right zone. Different zones often contain identical addresses.

Numbers in the text correspond to numbers in the margin and on the Guatemala City map.

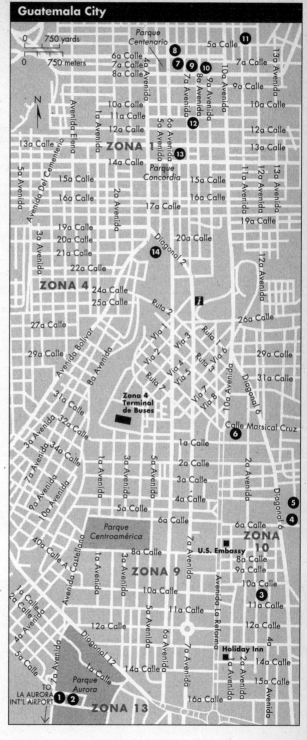

Guatemala City

The New City

Whereas the Old City is the real Guatemala, the New City's modern look and pace are reminiscent of upscale districts in North American cities. This is especially the case in Zona Viva, the posh center of Zona 10, where dozens of smart restaurants, bars, and clubs stay open long after the rest of the city goes to bed. During the day the New City's museums and cultural sites draw an equally affluent and savvy crowd.

A Good Tour

Begin at the **Museo Nacional de Arqueología y Etnología** ① for a crash course in Maya history. Next door, the **Museo Nacional de Arte Moderno** ② will ricochet you into the present with exhibitions of contemporary Guatemalan art. Taxi over to **Zona Viva** ③ for lunch at one of the several terrific restaurants. Afterward, head downhill on 6 Calle past 6 Avenida to the **Museo Ixchel** ④, arguably the city's best museum, where you'll learn about traditional Maya textiles. Next door is the **Museo Popol Vuh** ⑤, which holds a collection of remarkable archeological objects. From here the **Jardines Botánico** ⑥ is about seven blocks away: walk north on 6 Avenida and turn left on 1 Calle. Strolling here is a great way to wind up your afternoon before heading back to your hotel to rest before dinner.

TIMING

If you visit all the museums and stop for lunch, this tour will easily fill a day. Because the Zona 13 museums are somewhat far from the rest of the attractions in the Zona 10 environs, you'll likely want to get a lift. A taxi is about 40 quetzales.

Sights to See

⑥ **Jardines Botánico.** At the northern end of Zona 10, the small but lovely Botanical Gardens contain an impressive collection of plants and a little natural history museum. ⊠ *Calle Mariscal Cruz, near Av. La Reforma, Zona 10,* ☎ *331–0904.* ☉ *Weekdays 8–4.*

★ ④ **Museo Ixchel.** The city's best museum focuses on textiles of Guatemala's indigenous community. An impressive array of handwoven fabrics from 120 highland communities, some of which date from the 19th century, is displayed here. You'll also find sculptures, photographs, and paintings, including work by Andres Curruchich, an important and influential Guatemalan folk painter. Multimedia and interactive weaving displays make it engaging for all ages. ⊠ *End of 6 Calle, at 6 Av., Zona 10,* ☎ *331–3739.* ☐ *Q20.* ☉ *Weekdays 8:30–5:50, Sat. 9–1.*

★ ① **Museo Nacional de Arqueología y Etnología.** Dedicated to the ancient and modern Maya, the National Museum of Archaeology and Ethnology has a large and excellent collection of Maya pottery, jewelry, masks, and costumes, as well as models of the ancient cities themselves. ⊠ *Edificio 5, La Aurora Park, Zona 13,* ☎ *472–0478.* ☐ *Q40.* ☉ *Tues.–Sun. 9–4.*

② **Museo Nacional de Arte Moderno.** Surrealism and multimedia work are among the wide range of styles represented at the National Museum of Modern Art. Many of Guatemala's most distinguished artists are represented here, including Efraín Recinos and Zipacna de León. ⊠ *Edificio 6, La Aurora Park, Zona 13,* ☎ *472–0467.* ☐ *Q16.* ☉ *Tues.–Fri. 9–4.*

★ ⑤ **Museo Popol Vuh.** Though much smaller than the city's other museums, Popol Vuh has an interesting display of stone carvings from the Preclassic period, with the earliest pieces dating from 1500 BC. Religious figures, animals, and mythological half-animal–half-man creatures all have stolid eyes, hawkish noses, and fierce poses. Statues range widely in size, but some are quite big, which is particularly impressive given that they were each cut from a single stone. ✉ *6 Calle at 6 Av., Zona 10,* ☎ *361–2301.* ⌑ *Q20.* ☉ *Weekdays 9–5, Sat. 9–1.*

③ Zona Viva. Upscale restaurants and nightclubs have popped up here around the office towers and high-rise hotels. Undoubtedly the most cosmopolitan area of town, Zona Viva is filled with well-dressed people flaunting their electronics (cell phones and handheld computers are ubiquitous). Avenues accommodate pedestrians overflowing from the narrow sidewalks on which restaurants have somehow introduced outdoor seating. Lines extend from popular discos and bars, where the thumping music sometimes gets people dancing in the streets. ✉ *Zona 10.*

The Old City

Older and grittier than the New City, the Old City has the hustle and bustle of many Central American capitals. But walking around the area, especially around the Plaza de las Armas, is quite pleasant.

A Good Walk

Start at the **Plaza Mayor** ⑦, the heart of the Old City. Clustered around the square are some of the city's oldest landmarks, including the **Palacio Nacional** ⑧ and **Catedral Metropolitano** ⑨. A block east is the **Mercado Central** ⑩, an underground maze of stalls selling goods from the highlands. Walk two blocks east to 11 Avenida, then head north until you reach **La Merced** ⑪. The tiny church is worth a look for its ornate interior.

Three blocks south of Plaza Mayor is the **Edificio de Correos Central** ⑫, a lovely colonial structure that houses the main post office. Two blocks farther is a lovely old church, the **Iglesia de San Francisco** ⑬. History buffs will want to continue south to the **Centro Cultural Miguel Ángel Asturias** ⑭.

TIMING
A few hours should suffice to see the Old City sights.

Sights to See

⑨ Catedral Metropolitano. Built between 1782 and 1868, Metropolitan Cathedral is a rare example of colonial architecture in the Old City. Standing steadfast on the eastern end of Plaza Mayor, it is one of the city's most enduring landmarks. The ornate altars hold outstanding examples of colonial religious art, including an image of the Virgen de la Asunción, the city's patron saint. ✉ *8 Calle and 7 Av.,* ☎ *no phone.* ⌑ *Free.* ☉ *Daily 8–6.*

⑭ Centro Cultural Miguel Ángel Asturias. The imposing Teatro Nacional and the Teatro del Aire Libre are parts of this cluster of buildings named for Guatemala's Nobel Prize–winning novelist. Asturias opposed the dictatorship and therefore spent much of his life in exile. ✉ *24 Calle 3–81, Centro Cívico,* ☎ *232–4041.* ⌑ *Free.* ☉ *Weekdays 10–4.*

⑫ Edificio de Correos Central. You can mail packages from your hotel, but it's far more fun to come to this cantaloupe-color structure dating from the colonial era. ✉ *7 Av. 12–11,* ☎ *332–6101.* ☉ *Weekdays 8–7, Sat. 8–3.*

⑬ Iglesia de San Francisco. Built between 1800 and 1851, the Church of St. Francis is known for its ornate wooden altar. Here you'll find a small museum explaining the church's history. ✉ *6 Av. and 13 Calle.*

⑩ Mercado Central. A seemingly endless maze of underground passages is home to the Mercado Central, where handicrafts from the highlands are hawked from overstocked stalls. It's not as appealing as the open-air markets in Antigua or Chichicastenango, but the leather goods, wooden masks, and woolen blankets found here are often cheaper. ⊠ *8 Calle and 8 Av.,* ☏ *no phone.* ☉ *Mon.–Sat. 9–6, Sun. 9–noon.*

⑪ **La Merced.** If religious iconography is one of the reasons you're in Guatemala, step inside this lovely church dating from 1813 to see its baroque interior. Many of the elaborate paintings and sculptures found in the baroque structure originally adorned La Merced in Antigua but were moved here after earthquakes devastated that city. ⊠ *5 Calle and 11 Av.* ☉ *Daily 6 AM–7 PM.*

⑧ **Palacio Nacional.** Built between 1939 and 1944, the grandiose National Palace was built to satisfy the monumental ego of President Jorge Ubico Castañeda. It once held the offices of the president and his ministers, but now its 320 rooms house an art museum. The collection of paintings and sculptures by well-known Guatemalan artists was moved here from Antigua after that city's devastating earthquakes. Look for Alfredo Gálvez Suárez's murals illustrating the history of the city above the entry. ⊠ *6 Calle and 7 Av.,* ☏ *no phone.* ▨ *Free.* ☉ *Daily 9–noon and 2–5:30.*

⑦ **Plaza Mayor.** Clustered around this historic square are landmarks that survived the 19th century's earthquakes. In the center of the park is a fountain where children sometimes splash, always within sight of their parents on the nearby benches. ⊠ *Between 6 and 8 Calles and 6 and 7 Avenidas.*

Dining

The New City
CONTEMPORARY

$$$–$$$$ ✕ **Jake's.** If you only have one meal in Guatemala City, head to this
★ excellent eatery. Jake Denburg, a painter-turned-restaurateur, has used his creative talents to produce dishes ranging from handmade smoked chicken tortellini to robálo in a green-pepper sauce. The crowning achievement is the robálo *Venecia royal* (with a creamy shrimp sauce over spinach). ⊠ *17 Calle 10–40, Zona 10,* ☏ *368–0351. AE, DC, MC, V. No dinner Sun.*

$$–$$$ ✕ **Siriacos.** Modern art adorns the walls of this cheerful bistro, which serves excellent pasta in a vaguely art deco setting. Take a seat in one of the black high-back chairs and enjoy the tasty Caesar salad. ⊠ *1 Av. 12–12, Zona 10,* ☏ *334–6316. AE, DC, MC, V. Closed Sun. No lunch Sat.*

$$ ✕ **Tamarindos.** Guatemala City's best new restaurant, Tamarindos
★ serves up innovative, decidedly eclectic fare ranging from duck in tamarind sauce to Thai-style curries. Curlicue lamps and whimsical sofas that seem straight out of *Alice in Wonderland* lend the place a post-modern ambience. It's an exhilarating destination for dinner, but the reasonably-priced menu also makes this an excellent choice for lunch. ⊠ *11 Calle 2–19A, Zona 10,* ☏ *360–2815. AE, DC, MC, V. No lunch Sat., closed Sun.*

GUATEMALAN

$$$–$$$$ ✕ **Hacienda Real.** Small stone pedestals containing hot coals warm the
★ dining room, so even on a chilly day you needn't pass up this charming restaurant serving authentic Guatemalan fare. Choose from platters of robálo, steak, or pork, all served with a variety of savory condiments like fresh salsa, pickled carrots, and jalapeños. The attentive servers bring endless baskets of warm tortillas, but try not to eat every last one—the truly incomparable caramel flan shouldn't be missed. ⊠ *13 Calle 1–10, Zona 10,* ☏ *335–5409. AE, MC, V.*

$$$–$$$$ ✕ **Los Ranchos.** A pretty blue colonial facade with big picture windows
★ welcomes you to Guatemala's best steak house. Most meat, including
the rib-eye and chateaubriand, comes from the United States, but the
specialty of the house, a skirt steak called the *churrasco los ranchos,*
is a hearty cut that hails from Argentina. Ask your server to recom-
mend one of the excellent wines from Chile and France. Save room for
the desserts, which range from tiramisu to *tres leches,* a type of cake
injected with sweetened condensed milk, evaporated milk, and cream.
⊠ *2 Av. 14–06, Zona 10,* ☎ *363–5028. AE, DC, MC, V.*

$$$–$$$$ ✕ **Romanello's.** As the name suggests, Italian influences creep into the
★ cooking at this Zona Viva eatery. There's no set menu, but you can
usually choose from tenderloin, lobster, and robálo. There's always a
pasta dish that can be prepared with a variety of sauces. The decor is
simple but elegant, with a few antiques set here and there. There is no
sign outside, but it's next door to De Mario. ⊠ *1 Av. 12–70, Zona 10,*
☎ *361–1116. AE, DC, MC, V. Closed Sun.*

$$–$$$$ ✕ **Hacienda de los Sanchez.** This Zona Viva steak house is known for
its quality cuts of beef, yet the atmosphere has won over more than
one vegetarian. The brick-floored dining room calls to mind the American West, with such touches as sturdy wooden tables and old saddles.
Eat inside or on the plant-filled patio. Grilled and barbecued meats dominate the menu, but you can also order chicken and seafood. ⊠ *12 Calle
2–25, Zona 10,* ☎ *334–8448. AE, DC, MC, V.*

$$–$$$ ✕ **Jake's Tomato Pies.** Serving up the best pizza this side of the Río
Grande, this place is a winner. The recipe hails from New Jersey, which
the eponymous owner claims is where the best pizza in the world is
made. Here you'll be able to find tried-and-true favorites, or you can
go out on a limb and try a duck-sausage-and-pepper or shrimp-and-
pesto pizza. ⊠ *13 Calle and Av. Reforma, Zona 10,* ☎ *367–1760. AE,
DC, MC, V. Closed Sun.*

$$ ✕ **Tre Fratelli.** Run by three hip Guatemalans, this bustling restaurant
caters to the city's young professionals. The food is definitely Italian, but
there are plenty of local touches. Favorites like fettuccine *frutti di mare*
(with seafood), ravioli *alla Bolognese* (with a variety of meats), and the
quattro stagione (four-season) pizza are all served with freshly baked bread.
⊠ *2 Av. 13–25, Zona 10,* ☎ *366–2678. AE, MC, V. No dinner Sun.*

$$–$$$ ✕ **Olivadda.** An ideal lunch spot, this cozy eatery in the Hotel Santa
Clara serves up tasty Mediterranean fare. Take a table on the tranquil
patio, where a melodic fountain is surrounded by flowers filled with
hummingbirds. Start with traditional Middle Eastern appetizers such
as tabbouleh, *baba ghanouj,* and falafel, then move on to *kafta* (deli-
cately spiced beef patties served in pita bread with tahini). Finish with
an orange-and-honey baked apple stuffed with almonds and cinnamon.
⊠ *12 Calle 4–21, Zona 10,* ☎ *339–1811. AE, DC, MC, V.*

$$$–$$$$ ✕ **De Mario.** The cuisine at this Zona Viva favorite is firmly rooted in
Spanish traditions, so you can enjoy such entrées as paella and roast
suckling pig. But the menu here is one of the country's most original,
combining flavors from both sides of the Atlantic. Entrées like robálo
with mushroom sauce are standouts. ⊠ *1 Av. 12–98, Zona 10,* ☎ *339–
2329. AE, DC, MC, V. No dinner Sun..*

The Old City

$$ ✕ **Arrin Cuan.** Ask locals to recommend a place to eat in the Old City,
and chances are they will send you to this spirited Guatemalan favorite.

The decor couldn't be simpler—wooden masks adorn the walls and soda-bottle flower vases add a touch of color to each table. The flavorful cuisine, typical of the Cobán region, includes *kak-ik* (a spicy turkey stew), *gallo en chicha* (chicken in a slightly sweet sauce), and *sopa de tortuga* (turtle soup). ⊠ *5 Av. 3–27, Zona 1,* ☎ *238–0784 or 238–0242. AE, DC, MC, V.*

MEXICAN

$$–$$$ ✕ **Los Cebollines.** The decor is nothing special, but the attraction here is the delicious Mexican food. Sangria or beer is the typical accompaniment to traditional tacos, burritos, fajitas, and, less predictably, *caldo tlalpeño de pollo* (a chicken stew with chickpeas and avocado). There's another in Zona 10. ⊠ *6 Av. 9–75, Zona 1,* ☎ *232–7750;* ⊠ *1 Av. 13–42, Zona 10,* ☎ *368–0663. AE, DC, MC, V.*

$–$$ ✕ **El Gran Pavo.** You can't miss this restaurant—it's housed in a pink building with a gaudy neon sign on top. Inside is just as flashy. Bright colors dazzle you as you walk past hats, blankets, and other Mexican kitsch. The standard tacos and enchiladas are on the menu, but you'll also run across items like *aujas norteñas* (grilled beef strips covered with a red sauce and surrounded by avocado slices) and *camarones siempre joven* (shrimp in a spicy black chili sauce). ⊠ *13 Calle 4–41, Zona 1,* ☎ *232–9912. AE, DC, MC, V.*

SPANISH

$$–$$$ ✕ **Altuna.** A few blocks south of Plaza Mayor, this popular restaurant
★   serves Spanish and Basque cuisine in a pleasantly bustling atmosphere. Waiters in white jackets and ties move briskly around the covered courtyard that serves as the main dining room. If you want a bit more privacy, ask to be seated in one of several adjacent rooms decorated with Iberian paintings, photographs, and posters. The menu is fairly limited; consider the calamari, paella, or filet mignon with mushroom sauce. ⊠ *5 Av. 12–31, Zona 1,* ☎ *251–7185 or 232–0669. AE, DC, MC, V. Closed Mon.*

$$ ✕ **El Mesón de Don Quijote.** In the heart of the Old City, this colorful restaurant serves respectable cuisine from northern Spain (Asturias, to be exact). Popular with old-timers, it's a favorite late-night spot because it's open until 1 AM. The long bar adjoining several dining rooms hosts live musicians who play under a flashy painting of a flamenco dancer. The extensive menu is filled with such palate pleasers as seafood casserole, sliced Spanish ham, lentils with sausage, and paella big enough for four people. ⊠ *11 Calle 5–27, Zona 1,* ☎ *232–1741. AE, DC, MC, V. Closed Sun.*

Lodging

The New City

$$$$ 🏨 **Camino Real.** With every imaginable amenity and a staff that aims
★   to please, it isn't surprising that the immense Camino Real has hosted everyone from rock stars to heads of state. The spacious reception area lies just beyond a long foyer lined with comfortably overstuffed leather chairs. Stately rooms are furnished with carved French provincial–style pieces. French doors provide views of the nearby volcanoes. ⊠ *14 Calle and Av. La Reforma, Zona 10,* ☎ *333–4633; 800/228–3000 in the U.S.,* FAX *337–4313,* WEB *www.westin.com. 388 rooms. 2 restaurants, in-room safes, minibars, cable TV, 2 pools, spa, 2 tennis courts, 3 bars, 8 shops, concierge, business services, meeting rooms, travel services. AE, DC, MC, V.*

$$$$ 🏨 **Guatemala City Marriott.** Although its facade won't win any awards, this hotel does earn points for its excellent location not far from the Zona Viva. The lovely lounge offers rest to the weary; relax with a cocktail in one of the comfortable armchairs as you listen to jazz. You can always head to the Cabaña Club, a spacious spa and sports facility. Rooms are nicely furnished, with desks designed for business travelers. ⊠ *7 Av. 15–45, Zona 9,* ☎ *339–7777; 800/228–9290 in the U.S.,* FAX *332–1877,* WEB *www.marriotthotels.com. 385 rooms. 3 restaurants, minibars, cable TV, pool, spa, health club, bar, meeting room, travel services. AE, DC, MC, V.*

$$$$ ⊞ **Hotel Santa Clara.** This colonial house has character that most other hotels can't match. Ivy-covered walls give way to a cozy reception area. Some rooms surround a breezy courtyard overflowing with potted plants, while others share a balcony reached by a spiral staircase. The softly lighted rooms have wooden paneling and tile floors, as well as elegant touches like dried flowers. ⊠ *12 Calle 4–51, Zona 10,* ☎ *339–1811,* FAX *332–0775,* WEB *www.hotelcasasantaclara.com. 14 rooms. Restaurant, room service. AE, DC, MC, V.*

$$$$ ⊞ **Mansión San Carlos.** This modest colonial structure puts a little space between you and the bustling Zona Viva. Floor-to-ceiling windows in the reception area look out onto a sunny courtyard dotted with statues. Sloping stairs lead up to the individually decorated rooms, where hardwood floors add lots of character. Other rooms in an annex are newer, but they lack the charm of those in the main house. ⊠ *Av. La Reforma 7–89, Zona 10,* ☎ *362–9077,* FAX *331–6411. 21 rooms. Restaurant, bar, business services. AE, DC, MC, V.*

$$$$ ⊞ **Meliá Guatemala.** Giant glass elevators in the atrium-style lobby ascend to a dizzying view of the city. With 22 meeting rooms and 16 ballrooms, the hotel is designed to accommodate large conventions. Executives can also take advantage of the array of business services. Rooms on the south side have the most impressive views of the surrounding volcanoes— even the health club overlooks these soaring peaks. ⊠ *Av. Las Américas 9–08, Zona 13,* ☎ *339–0666; 800/339–3542 in the U.S.,* FAX *339– 0690,* WEB *www.solmelia.com. 194 rooms, 2 suites. 2 restaurants, minibars, cable TV, health club, sauna, spa, bar, business services, convention center, meeting rooms, car rental. AE, DC, MC, V.*

$$$$ ⊞ **Real Inter-Continental.** In the center of the Zona Viva, the towering Inter-Continental has a decidedly modern feel. A giant statue of bartering Mayas greets you at the entrance, where massive columns of rough stone rise majestically. On either side are sweeping staircases. The comfortable rooms, where modern art adorns the walls, follow this theme. The very good French restaurant imported its chef from Paris. ⊠ *14 Calle 2–51, Zona 10,* ☎ *379–4446,* FAX *379–4447,* WEB *www.interconti.com. 239 rooms. Restaurant, café, minibars, pool, spa, bar, meeting room, travel services. AE, DC, MC, V.*

$$$ ⊞ **Casa Grande.** This stately hotel, housed in a former residence, is one of the best lodging options in the New City. You enter through iron gates, then step into a small reception area that leads to a comfortable lounge with a fireplace to keep out the chill. The restaurant spills out into the courtyard; its cast-iron chairs are surrounded by arches covered with dangling philodendrons. Traditional tile floors grace the rooms, which are furnished with antiques. Rooms in the front open onto a balcony. ⊠ *Av. La Reforma 7–67, Zona 10,* ☎ FAX *332–0914. 28 rooms. Restaurant, bar. AE, DC, MC, V.*

$$$ ⊞ **Stofella.** For those who feel more at home in smaller hotels, Stofella is a real find. A short staircase leads to a flower-filled reception area. Charming rooms have sitting areas that afford a bit of privacy. Ask for one of the original rooms, as those added during a recent renovation lack character. If you're feeling social, join the other guests in the cozy bar. ⊠ *2 Av. 12–28, Zona 10,* ☎ *334–6191,* FAX *331–0823. 102 rooms. Gym, bar, laundry service, business services. AE, DC, MC, V.*

The Old City

$$$$ ⊞ **Hotel Royal Palace.** A diamond in the rough, this classy hotel is a welcome retreat from the frantic pace of the streets outside. The hotel has a great sense of style—a tile fountain reminiscent of Andalusia graces the central courtyard. The rooms are slightly musty but are nevertheless comfortable and quiet. Ask for one with a view of 6 Avenida—it's a great way to view the action without having to fight the crowds. ⊠ *6 Av. 12–66, Zona 1,* ☎ *220–8970,* FAX *238–3715,* WEB *www.hotelroyalpalace.com. 74 rooms. Restaurant, gym, sauna, concierge, travel services, airport shuttle. AE, DC, MC, V.*

$$$ ⊞ **Pan American.** The grande dame of downtown hotels, the Pan American was for many years the most luxurious lodging in town. To step ★ into the lobby of this former mansion is to leave the confusion of the city behind. A covered courtyard with attractive wrought-iron chandeliers spills out from the restaurant, whose servers wear traditional highland dress. The rooms are small but attractive, with walls adorned with traditional paintings. ⊠ *9 Calle 5–63, Zona 1,* ☎ *251–8713; 800/448–8355 in the U.S.,* FAX *232–6402,* WEB *www.hotelpanamerican.com. 56 rooms. Restaurant, concierge, travel services, airport shuttle. AE, DC, MC, V.*

$$ ⊞ **Chalet Suizo.** This quiet hotel has been popular with budget travelers for more than 40 years. An attractive central courtyard behind the reception area is a great place to relax. Facing a series of smaller courtyards, the rooms are all fairly plain. The staff is friendly and will happily store your extra luggage while you travel around the country. ⊠ *14 Calle 6–82, Zona 1,* ☎ *251–3786,* FAX *232–0429. 51 rooms, 15 with bath. Restaurant, travel services. No credit cards.*

$$ ⊞ **Posada Belén.** This little bed-and-breakfast is exceptional, thanks to the couple that runs it. Built in 1873, it has been renovated just enough ★ to combine old-world charm with modern comfort. Rooms have tile floors, handwoven bedspreads, and walls decorated with Guatemalan paintings and weavings. A small but impressive collection of Mayan artifacts graces the dining room. Family-style meals are made to order by the owners, who are also a font of information about the city. ⊠ *13 Calle A 10–30, Zona 1,* ☎ *232–9226 or 254–5430,* FAX *251–3478,* WEB *www.guatemalaweb.com. 10 rooms. Dining room, library, travel services, airport shuttle. AE, DC, MC, V.*

$ ⊞ **Hotel Ajau.** This slightly faded hotel has an interior courtyard and three floors of balconied rooms. The rooms are clean, with tile floors and a few pieces of wooden furniture. Rooms facing away from the street are quieter. ⊠ *8 Av. 15–62, Zona 1,* ☎ *232–0488,* FAX *251–8097. 43 rooms, 23 with bath. No credit cards.*

Nightlife and the Arts

The Zona Viva is the city's nightlife center, offering everything from sedate bars to noisy discos. Strolling the streets is especially entertaining, as people come here to see and be seen. Old City nightspots have more character than those in the New City, so they shouldn't be passed up just because the area isn't the greatest. At night it's always best to take a cab for any destination more than a few blocks away.

The New City

The **Brass Beer Company** (⊠ 3 Av. 12–48, Zona 10) serves a variety of excellent microbrews to a mellow crowd. **Giuseppe Verdi** (⊠ 14 Calle at Av. La Reforma, Zona 9) is an upscale bar that caters mostly to tourists. Attracting an international crowd, **Sesto Senso** (⊠ 2 Av. 12–81, Zona 10) offers live music ranging from Guatemalan folk to American pop. A longtime favorite, **El Establo** (⊠ Av. La Reforma 10–31, Zona 9) has been playing rock and roll for more than two decades.

Discos come and go, but the place to be right now is **Q** (⊠ 4 Av. 15–53, Zona 10). **Rich and Famous** (⊠ upstairs at Los Proceres Mall, Av. La Reforma and Blvd. de los Proceres, Zona 9) is a decent club in a mall. A fun crowd heads to **Salambo** (⊠ 1 Av. 13–70, Zona 10), where the ambience is decadently camp.

The Old City

Drawing an intellectual crowd, **La Bodeguita del Centro** (⊠ 2 Calle 3–55, Zona 1) hosts live music and poetry readings. If you feel like dancing, go to **El Gazabo** (⊠ 6 Calle at 3 Av., Zona 1).

Outdoor Activities and Sports

Fishing

Guatemala's southern coast is arguably one of the best billfishing spots in the world, especially during fall and spring. **Artmarina** (⊠ Iztapa, ☎ 881–4035, WEB www.artmarina.com) offers outings on well-equipped vessels. **Villas del Pacifico** (⊠ Iztapa, ☎ 316–1741) is one of the best companies in the area, offering a variety of excursions from the Iztapa area.

White-Water Rafting

On an exhilarating white-water rafting trip down the Río Coyolate, offered June–October, you'll pass iguanas sunning themselves, toucans resting on overhanging branches, and flitting morpho butterflies. **Area Verde Expeditions** (⊠ 4 Av. Sur 8, Antigua, ☎ 832–3863) offers trips that range from easy to challenging. **Clark Tours** (⊠ 6 Diagonal 10–01, 7th floor, Zona 10, ☎ 339–2888) offers a range of trips.

Shopping

If you're in the market for *típica,* a term that roughly translates as "typical goods," head to **Mercado Central** (⊠ 8 Calle and 8 Av.). There's also a **Mercado de Artesanías** (⊠ 6 Calle in La Aurora Park, Zona 13), where you can find goods made by highland artisans.

A number of stores east of Avenida La Reforma sell handmade goods. It's small, but **El Gran Jaguar** (⊠ 14 Calle 7–49, Zona 9) has a decent selection. The spacious **San Remo** (⊠ 14 Calle 7–60, Zona 9) has a wide variety of handcrafted items. **Típicos Reforma Utatlán** (⊠ 14 Calle 7–77, Zona 13) has an excellent selection of textiles made in highland villages.

Across Avenida La Reforma is a cluster of souvenir shops. **Topis** (⊠ Calle 12 and Diagonal 6, Zona 10) has a fine selection of pottery by artists from Antigua. The elegant **Casa Solares** (⊠ Av. La Reforma 11–07, Zona 10) is pricey, but you can be certain that you are buying the best-quality goods. **In Nola** (⊠ 18 Calle 21–31, Zona 10) specializes in textiles, but you will also find items in leather and wool. It's your best bet if you only have time to pop into one shop.

In the Old City, **Lin Canola** (⊠ 5 Calle 9–60, Zona 1) has an excellent selection of típica and other goods. The prices are often cheap.

Side Trips from Guatemala City

Biotopo del Quetzal

A 2,849-acre tract of cloud forest along the road to Cobán, the Biotopo del Quetzal was created to protect Guatemala's national bird. The resplendent quetzal, known for its brilliant plumage, is endangered because of the indiscriminate destruction of the country's forests. Since it is easier to spot quetzals around dawn or dusk, it's worth spending a night in the area. Even if you don't catch a glimpse of the legendary bird, there are plenty of other species to spot, and the luxuriant greenery of the cloud forest is gorgeous in its own right.

One of the last remaining cloud forests in Guatemala, the Biotopo del Quetzal is a vital source of water for the region's rivers. Moisture that evaporated from Lago Izabal settles here as fog, which provides sustenance for the towering old-growth trees. Plants like lichens, hepaticas, bromeliads, and orchids abound. If you're lucky, you can see howler monkeys swinging above the two well-maintained trails, the 2-km (1-mi) Los Helechos (The Ferns) and the 4-km (2-mi) Los Musgos (The Mosses). ⊠ *164 km (102 mi) northeast of Guatemala City,* ☎ *no phone.* ☞ *Free.*

DINING AND LODGING

$$ ×🏠 **Posada Montaña del Quetzal.** This comfortable country inn near
★   the Biotopo del Quetzal is the area's best lodging. Choose between small rooms in the main building and spacious bungalows with two bedrooms and a sitting room warmed by a fireplace. The restaurant overlooks a pool and serves a limited selection of Guatemalan and Continental cuisine. ⊠ *4 km (2½ mi) south of the Biotopo del Quetzal,* ☎ *335–1805 in Guatemala City. 8 rooms, 10 bungalows. Restaurant, bar, coffee shop, pool, hiking, fishing. No credit cards.*

Biotopo Monterrico

The Biotopo Monterrico encompasses 6,916 acres along Guatemala's Pacific coast that include everything from mangrove swamps to dense tropical forests. This is a haven for ornithologists, as the reserve is home to more than 100 species of migratory and indigenous birds. Turtles swim ashore from July to February, and you can often see them digging nests for their eggs at night. The nearby village of Monterrico even has a decent beach, but be careful about the rough current. ⊠ *48 km (30 mi) south of Guatemala City,* ☎ *no phone.* ☞ *Free.*

Quiriguá

Unlike the hazy remnants of chiseled images you see at most other archaeological sites in Central America, Quiriguá has some that are seemingly untouched by winds and rain. They emerge from the rock faces in breathtaking detail. Quiriguá is famous for the amazingly well-preserved stelae, or carved pillars, that are the largest yet discovered. They depict Quiriguá's ruling dynasty, especially the powerful Cauac Sky. Several monuments, covered with interesting zoomorphic figures, still stand, and the remains of an acropolis and other structures have been partially restored.

In ancient times Quiriguá was an important Maya trading center that stood on the banks of the Río Motagua (the river has since changed its course). The ruins are surrounded by a lush stand of rain forest—an untouched wilderness in the heart of banana country. ⊠ *186 km (115 mi) northeast of Guatemala City,* ☎ *no phone.* ☞ *Q25.* ⊙ *Daily 7:30–5.*

Guatemala City A to Z

AIR TRAVEL TO AND FROM GUATEMALA CITY

Most international flights into Guatemala head to Aeropuerto Internacional La Aurora, an unusually friendly airport where a marimba band often greets you as you step off the plane. The international airlines serving the airport are American, Aviateca, Continental, Copa, Iberia, KLM, Mexicana, Taca, Tapsa, and United.

Domestic carriers fly between the capital and Flores/Santa Elena, in El Petén; Puerto Barrios and Río Dulce, on the Atlantic coast; and Quetzaltenango and Huehuetenango, in the highlands. Serving these routes are Aeroquetzal, Aerovias, and Tikal Jets.

➤ DOMESTIC CARRIERS: **Aeroquetzal** (☎ 334–7689). **Aerovias** (☎ 332–7470 OR 332–5686). **Tikal Jets** (☎ 334–5568).

➤ INTERNATIONAL CARRIERS: **Aerovias** (☎ 332–7470 or 332–5686). **American** (☎ 334–7379). **Continental** (☎ 366–9985). **Copa** (☎ 361–1577). **Iberia** (☎ 332–0911). **KLM** (☎ 367–6179). **Mexicana** (☎ 333–6001). **Taca** (☎ 331–8222). **Tapsa** (☎ 331–9180). **United** (☎ 336–9900).

AIRPORTS AND TRANSFERS

Less than a mile from the New City, Aeropuerto Internacional La Aurora is a bit too close for comfort. A taxi to the airport from downtown runs $6–$8.

➤ AIRPORTS: **Aeropuerto Internacional La Aurora** (☎ 332–6084 or 332–6085).

BUS TRAVEL TO AND FROM GUATEMALA CITY

The *terminal de buses,* or main bus station, is in Zona 4. From here you can catch a bus to almost anywhere in the country. Autobuses de Oriente has service to El Petén. Transgalgos travels to the highlands.

Some companies run small minivans, which are a much more comfortable way to travel. Atitrans, Turansa, and Vision Travel offer shuttle service to most cities.

➤ BUS INFORMATION: **Atitrans** (☎ 832–0644). **Autobuses de Oriente** (☎ 238–3894). **Transgalgos** (☎ 253–4868). **Turansa** (☎ 832–2928). **Vision Travel** (☎ 832–3293).

BUS TRAVEL WITHIN GUATEMALA CITY

The bus system can be quite confusing, but locals are usually happy to point you to the one you need. After a while you'll get to know the system. Buses that serve La Reforma say REFORMA on the windshield; likewise, buses that say TERMINAL all pass by the main bus station in Zona 4. Only the buses marked AEROPUERTO go to the airport. Bus service pretty much ends at 8 PM. Watch your belongings at the bus station, as well as while boarding, riding, and exiting the bus.

CAR RENTAL

If you're not intimidated by Guatemala City's winding mountain roads, renting a car is a great way to see the countryside. There are several international agencies at Aeropuerto Internacional La Aurora and dozens in the New City. Reputable local companies include Tabarini and Tikal.

➤ LOCAL AGENCIES: **Avis** (✉ 6 Av. 11–24, Zona 9, ☎ 332–7744). **Budget** (✉ Av. Hincapié 11–01, Zona 13, ☎ 332–2024). **Hertz** (✉ 7 Av. 14–76, Zona 9, ☎ 332–2242). **National** (✉ 12 Calle Montúfar 7-69, Zona 9, ☎ 360–2030, WEB national@intelnet.net.gt). **Tabarini** (✉ 2 Calle A 7–30, Zona 10, ☎ 331–9814). **Tikal** (✉ 2 Calle 6–56, Zona 10, ☎ 361–0257).

CAR TRAVEL

Driving in Guatemala City is a headache. You can expect narrow streets jammed with traffic at just about any time of day. Things get better once you move out of the center of the city. Drives to nearby destinations like Antigua, for example, can be quite pleasant.

Breaking into cars is common in the capital, so it's best to park in a guarded lot. All expensive and most moderate hotels have protected parking areas. Avoid leaving anything of value in the car.

EMERGENCIES

If you're a little out of sorts, there's no reason to leave your hotel because Farmacias Klee delivers 24 hours a day. El Sauce Las Americas, with branches in the Old City and the New City, is open 24 hours a day. Osco and Meykos also have reputable pharmacies in the New City's Zona 10.

➤ EMERGENCY SERVICES: **Ambulance** (☎ 128). **Fire** (☎ 122 or 123). **Police** (☎ 110 or 120).

➤ HOSPITALS: **Centro Médico** (✉ 6 Av. 3–47, Zona 10, ☎ 332–3555). **Hospital Herrera Llerandí** (✉ 6 Av. 8–71, Zona 10, ☎ 334–5959 or 332–5455).

➤ PHARMACIES: **El Sauce Las Americas** (✉ 23 Calle and Av. Las Américas, Zona 13, ☎ 331–5996; ✉ 4 Av. and 16 Calle, Zona 1, ☎ no phone). **Osco** (✉ 16 Calle and 4 Av., Zona 10, ☎ 337–1566). **Meykos** (✉ Blvd. Los Próceres, Zona 10, ☎ 363–5903; ✉ 6 Av. 5–01, Zona 9, ☎ 334–1962). **Farmacias Klee** (☎ 360–8383).

MAIL AND SHIPPING

To ship important packages, use Federal Express or United Parcel Service. Both have offices in the New City. You can also send packages from the Correos Central.

➤ OVERNIGHT SERVICES: **United Parcel Service** (✉ 12 Calle 5–53, Zona 10, ☎ 360–6460). **Federal Express** (✉ 14 Av. 7–12, Bodega 20, Zona 14, ☎ 80/472–2222 in the U.S.).

➤ POST OFFICES: **Correos Central** (✉ 7 Av. 12–11, Zona 1, ☎ 332–6101).

MONEY MATTERS

You can exchange currency at almost any bank in Guatemala City. Bancared, one of the most popular banks, has 150 ATMs around the city. Many hotels even have ATMs on the premises.

➤ BANKS: **Bancared** (✉ 7 Av. 15–45, Zona 9). **Banco Industrial** (✉ 7 Av. 5–10, Zona 4, Guatemala City).

SAFETY

Guatemala City is no more dangerous than any other large city. To avoid being preyed upon by pickpockets and other unsavory characters, leave expensive jewelry and watches at home, carry purses and camera bags close to the body, and take along only as much cash as you'll need. At night stick to well-lighted areas.

TAXIS

Taxis can be found waiting at hotels and intersections or can be flagged down on the street. Most do not have meters, so negotiate a price before getting in. Within a single zone, a ride should cost Q16–Q24; between zones expect to pay Q32–Q48. Taxis Intercontinental is a reputable firm.

➤ TAXI COMPANIES: **Taxis Intercontinental** (☎ 336–9624 or 202–09800).

TOURS OPERATORS

Many major tour operators offer half- and full-day tours of the capital as well as day trips outside the city. Area Verde offers white-water rafting and kayaking trips. Other reputable companies are Clark Tours, Jaguar Tours, Tropical Tours, Turansa, and Unitours.

➤ TOUR COMPANIES: **Clark Tours** (✉ 6 Diagonal 10–01, 7th floor, Zona 10, ☎ 339–2888). **Jaguar Tours** (✉ 13 Calle 3–40, Edificio Atlantis, 3rd floor, Zona 10, ☎ 363–2640). **Maya Expeditions** (✉ 15 Calle 1–91, Zona 10, ☎ 363–4955; 800/733–3350 in the U.S., WEB www.mayaexpeditions.com). **Tropical Tours** (✉ 3 Calle A 3–22, Zona 10, ☎ 339–3662). **Turansa** (✉ Km 15 Carretera Roosevelt, Zona 11, locale 69, ☎ 595–3575). **Unitours** (✉ 12 Calle 9–35, Edificio Ermita, Zona 1, ☎ 230–0696).

Inguat, Guatemala's ever-helpful government tourism office, is open
weekdays 8–4 and Saturday 8–1.
➤ TOURIST INFORMATION: **Inguat** (✉ 7 Av. 1–17, Zona 4, ☎ 331–1333
or 331–1334, WEB www.guatemala.travel.com).

ANTIGUA

45 km (28 mi) west of Guatemala City.

Filled with vestiges of its colonial past—cobblestone streets, enchanting squares, and deserted convents—Antigua instantly transports you
back hundreds of years to when the Spanish ruled this land. Founded
in 1543, the city was initially called Santiago de los Caballeros de
Guatemala after the patron saint of the conquistadors. For 200 years
it was the capital of a region that included what is now Central America and part of Mexico. Along with Lima and Mexico City, it was one
of the greatest cities of the Americas.

By the late 18th century the city had been destroyed by earthquakes
several times. Because it was a major political, religious, and intellectual center—it had 32 churches, 18 convents and monasteries, seven
colleges, five hospitals, and a university—it was always rebuilt. Powerful tremors struck again in late 1773, reducing much of the city's painstakingly restored elegance to rubble. The government reluctantly
relocated to a safer site in the Ermita Valley, 45 km (28 mi) east, where
Guatemala City now stands.

Today you'll find a mountainside enclave that is vastly more pleasant
than Guatemala City. An ever-increasing influx of visitors has brought
in some of the country's finest hotels and restaurants, a collection of
boutiques and galleries, and several dozen Spanish-language schools
that attract students from all over the world. Antigua is also a favored
escape for wealthy Guatemalans. Its higher prices mean that many people cannot afford to live here, so they travel to the city each day to sell
their wares.

*Numbers in the text correspond to numbers in the margin and on the
Antigua map.*

A Good Walk

Any tour of Antigua must start at **Plaza Mayor** ①, the tree-shaded central park. As in most other Central American communities, this is a
place that always buzzes with activity. On the north side of the square
stands the **Palacio del Ayuntamiento** ②, an imposing structure that once
served as the city hall. Facing it is the **Palacio de los Capitanes Generales** ③. The most impressive building on the square is the **Catedral
de San José** ④, one of the loveliest of the city's many churches. Across
5 Calle Oriente from the cathedral is the **Museo de Arte Colonial** ⑤,
where you'll find religious art dating from the 17th century. Between
2 and 4 PM you can visit **Casa Popenoe** ⑥, a private residence and a
restored and beautifully furnished colonial mansion, two blocks east.
Close by are the ruins of **Convento Santa Clara** ⑦, with hidden passages and mysterious underground rooms, and the **Monasterio San Francisco** ⑧, where you can knock on the tomb of Friar Pedro de San José
de Betancur to have your prayers answered.

Head north on 2 Avenida to reach the labyrinthine ruins of the **Convento de las Capuchinas** ⑨. Two blocks east, spanning 5 Avenida
Norte, is the graceful **Arco de Santa Catalina** ⑩. Half a block north is
the **Nuestra Señora de La Merced** ⑪, an ornate church painted the same
brilliant yellow as the arch. Walk west to walk around the impressive

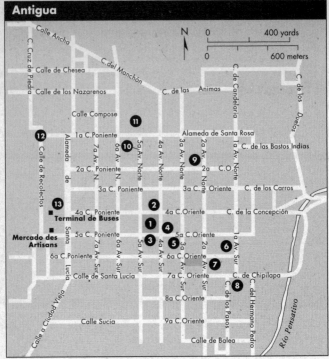

ruins of **La Recolección** ⑫. Just to the south is a covered market called **Mercado Central** ⑬. Women from nearby villages come here to sell fruits and vegetables.

TIMING

This tour, taken at a leisurely pace, can fill a day. Remember that most sights close promptly at 5 PM and that some ruins are closed on Sunday and Monday.

Sights to See

★ ⑩ **Arco de Santa Catalina.** The only remnant of the once-enormous Convent of St. Catherine is this beautiful yellow arch that spans 5 Avenida Norte, a street locals call Calle de Santa Catalina. The convent was founded in 1613 with only four nuns, but by 1693 its growing numbers forced it to expand across the street. ⊠ *5 Av. Norte and 2 Calle Poniente,* ☎ *832–0184.* ✆ *Q30.*

Casa K'Ojom. K'Ojom means "music" in three indigenous languages, and this very modest museum highlights the musical traditions of Guatemala's vastly diverse indigenous population. An interesting 15-minute documentary film is a good introduction for the newcomer touring the collection of musical instruments and other artifacts. ⊠ *Calle del Cemetario Final, Jocotenango,* ☎ *832–0907.* WEB *www.centroazotea.com.gt.* ✆ *Q25.* ☉ *Weekdays 8:30–4, Sat. 8:30–2.*

⑥ **Casa Popenoe.** A short loop through this beautifully restored colonial mansion takes you through courtyards and several rooms containing decorative items, including original oil paintings, fine ceramic dishes, and other items that have been in the house since its original construction in 1636. Since this is a private home, hours are limited. ⊠ *1 Av. Sur at 5 Calle Oriente,* ☎ *no phone.* ✆ *Q10.* ☉ *Mon.–Sat. 2–4.*

④ Catedral de San José. Only two chapels remain in what was once the city's main house of worship. The lovely white cathedral was completed in 1680 but destroyed in an earthquake less than 100 years later. As in most other Latin American churches, the cross and altar are toward the east so that worshipers face the Holy Land. ⊠ *4 Av. Sur, east side of Plaza Mayor,* ☎ *no phone.* 🖭 *Q3.*

★ **⑨ Convento de las Capuchinas.** Antigua's largest convent was built in 1736 by the Capuchins, whose number had swelled because they did not require young women to pay dowries to undertake the religious life. The convent was abandoned after the earthquake of 1773, even though damage to the structure was relatively light. In the 1940s the convent was restored and opened to the public. The ruins, which are quite well preserved, include several lovely courtyards and gardens, the former bathing halls, and a round tower lined with the nuns' cells. ⊠ *2 Av. Norte at 2 Calle Oriente,* ☎ *832–0184.* 🖭 *Q30.* ☉ *Daily 9–5.*

⑦ Convento Santa Clara. Shortly after it was founded in 1699, the Convent of St. Clara grew to be a rather elaborate complex housing nearly 50 nuns. When it was destroyed by an earthquake in 1717, the sisters quickly rebuilt it with the intention of having it exceed its former glory. It was struck by violent tremors again in 1773, and the site was finally abandoned. The remaining arches and courtyards make a pleasant place to roam. ⊠ *2 Av. Sur at 6 Calle Oriente,* ☎ *832–0184.* 🖭 *Q30.* ☉ *Daily 9–5.*

⑬ Mercado Central. The smell of fresh fruits and vegetables will lead you to this unassuming market. Women in colorful skirts sell huge piles of produce grown in their own gardens. Their husbands are nearby, chatting with friends or watching a soccer match. ⊠ *Between Amaeda de Santa Lucia and Calle de Recolectos.*

⑧ Monasterio San Francisco. Pedro de San José de Betancur, a friar who lived in the 17th and 18th centuries, was beatified by Pope John Paul II for his good works, which has made his tomb at the Monastery of St. Francis an important local landmark. Many miracles are ascribed to Friar Pedro, who has answered the prayers of petitioners who knocked gently on his casket. The remainder of the ruins, dating from 1579, is worth a visit for the views of the surrounding areas from the upper floor. ⊠ *7 Calle Oriente and 1 Av. Sur,* ☎ *no phone.* 🖭 *Q2.* ☉ *Daily 9–5.*

⑤ Museo de Arte Colonial. On the former site of the University of San Carlos, the Museum of Colonial Art, its cloisters left largely intact through the shakier centuries, holds a collection of mostly 17th-century religious paintings and statues commissioned by the Castilians. ⊠ *Calle de la Universidad and 4 Av. Sur,* ☎ *832–0429.* 🖭 *Q25.* ☉ *Tues.–Fri. 9–4, weekends 9–noon and 2–4.*

★ **⑪ Nuestra Señora de La Merced.** Our Lady of Mercy is one of Antigua's most eye-catching attractions, known far and wide for its fanciful yellow stucco facade. Architect Juan Luis de Dios Estrada wisely designed the church to be earthquake resistant. The squat shape, thick walls, and small, high windows are responsible for La Merced surviving the 1773 quake with barely a crack. The attached monastery, which has an immense stone fountain in the central courtyard, has excellent views of surrounding volcanoes. ⊠ *1 Calle Poniente and 6 Av. Norte,* ☎ *no phone.* 🖭 *Q2.* ☉ *Daily 9–noon and 3–6.*

② Palacio del Ayuntamiento. As in colonial times, the City Hall continues to serve as the seat of government. Today it also houses two museums, the Museo de Santiago (Museum of St. James) and Museo del

Libro Antiguo (Museum of Antique Books). The former, which adjoins what was once the city jail, displays colonial art and artifacts; Central America's first printing press is displayed in the latter. ⌂ *4 Calle Poniente, north side of Plaza Mayor,* ☎ *832–5511.* ▭ *Q10.* ☉ *Tues.–Fri. 9–4, weekends 9–noon and 2–4.*

❸ **Palacio de los Capitanes Generales.** Although it has not yet been fully restored, the Palace of the Captains General is easily recognized by its stately archways. It houses the city's tourism office and other governmental agencies. ⌂ *5 Calle Poniente, south side of Plaza Mayor.*

❶ **Plaza Mayor.** Surrounded by old colonial buildings, this tree-lined square is where locals and travelers alike pass quiet afternoons on shady benches listening to the trickling fountain. ⌂ *4 Calle Poniente and 5 Av. Norte.*

⑫ **La Recolección.** Despite opposition from the city council, which felt the town already had plenty of monasteries, La Recolección was inaugurated in 1717, the same year it was destroyed by an earthquake. Like many others, it was quickly rebuilt but shaken to the ground again in 1773. A stone arch still graces the church stairway, but the ceiling did not fare so well—it lies in huge jumbled blocks within the nave's crumbling walls. ⌂ *1 Calle Poniente at Calle de Recolectos,* ☎ *no phone.* ▭ *Q30.* ☉ *Daily 9–5.*

Dining and Lodging

$$$$ ✕ **Welten.** You feel like a guest in a private home when you arrive at
★   this restaurant—you even have to knock to get in. Take your pick of tables, which are set on a patio with cascading orchids, by a small pool in the rear garden, or in one of the elegantly appointed dining rooms. The menu includes homemade pasta dishes, such as semi-circular *anolini* served with a creamy pepper-and-cognac sauce, as well as fish and meat dishes served with a variety of sauces. ⌂ *4 Calle Oriente 21,* ☎ *832–0630. AE, DC, MC, V. Closed Tues.*

$$–$$$ ✕ **Cafe Letras.** With its stark white walls and modern lines, Cafe Letras calls to mind the cool minimalism of northern Europe. The only color in the restaurant comes from the blue of the striped tablecloths and the red of the roaring fire. The menu, like the ambience, is spare, featuring such Scandinavian favorites as Swedish meatballs. ⌂ *1 Calle Poniente 3,* ☎ *832–0277. V. Closed Tues.*

$$–$$$ ✕ **La Casserole.** The chef at this restaurant serves up classic French fare with subtle Guatemalan influences, incorporating local flavors and colors into classic dishes. Although the menu changes every week or so, there are a few constants—seafood bouillabaisse cooked in a slightly spicy tomato sauce and steak tenderloin with a salsa made from spicy *chiltepe* peppers are two standouts. The restaurant is housed in a renovated colonial mansion. ⌂ *Callejón de la Concepción 7,* ☎ *832–0219. AE, DC, MC, V. Closed Mon. No dinner Sun.*

$$–$$$ ✕ **Fonda de la Calle Real.** An old Antigua favorite, this place now has two locations serving the same Guatemalan and Mexican fare. The original restaurant, on 5 Avenida Norte near Plaza Mayor, has pleasant views from the second floor. It tends to be a bit cramped, however. The newer space, around the corner on 3 Calle, is in a colonial home spacious enough to offer both indoor and outdoor seating. The menu includes queso fundido and a famous *caldo real* (a hearty chicken soup). ⌂ *3 Calle Poniente 7, at 6 Av. Norte,* ☎ *832–0507.* ☉ *Daily noon–10;* ⌂ *5 Av. Norte 5, at 4 Calle Poniente,* ☎ *832–2696. AE, DC, MC, V.*

$$ ✕ **Café Flor.** Once this homey restaurant switched from Mexican to Asian cuisine, it never looked back. The friendly proprietors serve a menu that includes Thai curries, Chinese noodles, and Indian vegetable dishes. Be careful—some of the dishes, especially the curries, are quite

spicy. Asian food aficionados will find the food not at all like the real thing, but Antigua is, after all, about as far from the source as you can get. ⊠ *4 Av. Sur 1, at 5 Calle Oriente,* ☎ *832–5274. AE, MC, V.*

$$ ✕ **El Mediterraneo.** Step into this tiny restaurant and you're transported
★ to northern Italy. Delicious antipasti, delicate homemade pastas, and other favorites are among the best Italian dishes in the city. Wash it all down with a selection from the affordable wine list. The atmosphere and decor are low-key, but the service is first rate. ⊠ *6 Calle Poniente 6-A,* ☎ *832–7180. V. Closed Tues.*

$$ ✕ **Quesos y Vino.** This small Italian restaurant serves up homemade pastas, pizzas from a wood-burning oven, and a variety of home-baked breads. Choose from an impressive selection of cheeses and wines sold by the bottle. ⊠ *5 Av. Norte 32, near Arco de Santa Catalina,* ☎ *832–7785. No credit cards. Closed Tues.*

$$ ✕ **Restaurante Don Martín.** For old-world charm, head to this intimate restaurant in a restored colonial home. The spare menu features local and international favorites, including a variety of salads and desserts—the mango salad and five-pepper steak are highly recommended. The service is always impeccable, and the food is delicious. ⊠ *4 Av. Norte 27,* ☎ *832–1063. V.*

$–$$ ✕ **Frida's.** Looking for a place where you and your friends can knock back a few margaritas? At this festive cantina the whole group can fill up on classic Mexican fare, including *taquitos,* enchiladas, and burros, the diminutive siblings of the American-style burrito. Things really get going when the mariachi band shows up. Fans of Frida Kahlo and Diego Rivera will find a great selection of prints. ⊠ *5 Av. Norte 29, near Arco de Santa Catalina,* ☎ *832–0504. AE, DC, MC, V.*

$ ✕ **Café Condesa.** Homemade pies and pastries make this a popular spot. Beginning at 6:45 AM, breakfast is known for daily specials such as toast topped with strawberries, papaya, or mango and sprinkled with sugar, and omelets made with fresh vegetables. For lunch try the quiche or the brie plate. You can eat in the café's airy dining room or grab a cappuccino and a sweet roll at Café Condesa Express next door. ⊠ *5 Av. Norte, west side of Plaza Mayor,* ☎ *832–0038. MC, V.*

$ ✕ **Café de la Fuente.** This popular vegetarian eatery takes over the courtyard of La Fuente, a classy collection of shops in a renovated colonial estate. Classical music creates a peaceful atmosphere. The international breakfasts, served until 11 AM, range from New York-style bagels and cream cheese to Mexican-style tofu *ranchero.* La Fuente also makes one of the best desserts in town—a decadently rich chocolate brownie topped with coffee ice cream. ⊠ *4 Calle Oriente 14, at 2 Av. Norte,* ☎ *832–4520. No credit cards.*

$ ✕ **Doña Luisa Xicotencatl.** Named after the mistress of Spanish con-
★ quistador Pedro de Alvarado, Doña Luisa Xicotencatl is something of a local institution. Tables are scattered throughout a dozen rooms and on the balcony and terrace of this former colonial residence, but it's still not easy to get a seat. Sandwiches and other light fare make for ample lunch and dinner options. ⊠ *4 Calle Oriente 12, at 3 Av. Norte,* ☎ *832–2578. MC, V, DC.*

$$$$ ✕▥ **Hotel Posada de Don Rodrigo.** A night in this restored colonial mansion, some 250 years old, is a journey back in time. All the rooms, with soaring ceilings and gorgeous tile floors, are set around two large courtyards and several smaller gardens. A tile fountain trickles in the dining room, which is set on a garden terrace. To the side a woman with a piping hot grill prepares the tortillas for your traditional Guatemalan meal. Light sleepers, beware: the lively marimba band can sometimes play long into the night. ⊠ *5 Av. Norte 17,* ☎ *832–0291,* **WEB** *posadadedonrodrigo.centroamerica.com. 35 rooms. Restaurant, bar. AE, DC, MC, V.*

$$–$$$ ✕▯ **Mesón Panza Verde.** A beautiful courtyard with a fountain sur-
★ rounded by colorful gardens welcomes you to this restful retreat. The
elegant rooms downstairs open onto small gardens, while the romantic suites upstairs have four-poster beds piled high with down comforters
and terraces where hammocks swing in the breeze. The rooftop patio
is wonderful in late afternoon or early morning, and the restaurant is
one of the best in town. The meat dishes are particularly good, such
as the *lomito* bourguignonne with escargot. ⊠ *5 Av. Sur 19,* ☎ FAX *832–
2925. 3 rooms, 3 suites. Restaurant. AE, DC, MC, V.*

$$$$ ▯ **Casa Azul.** Not many hotels have guest books filled with recommendations for specific rooms, but those on the second floor are so
good that people want to share them with others. The upstairs rooms
with views of the volcanoes are more expensive, but they are also larger
and brighter. With sitting rooms that open onto a pleasant courtyard,
centrally located Casa Azul has a serene atmosphere. ⊠ *4 Av. Norte
5,* ☎ *832–0961 or 832–0962,* FAX *832–0944,* WEB *www.casazul.guate.
com. 10 rooms. Pool, hot tub, sauna, bar. AE, DC, MC, V.*

$$$$ ▯ **La Casa de Los Sueños.** This stunning colonial mansion, recently converted into a bed-and-breakfast, may truly be the house of your dreams.
With a lovely patio surrounded on all sides by hanging plants, this little inn is a perfect romantic getaway. A joyful antique hobbyhorse and
a square grand piano add character to the sitting room. The rooms are
painted the washed-out hues that typify Antigua. A pool out back is a
refreshing retreat. ⊠ *1 Av. Sur 1,* ☎ FAX *832–0802 or 832–2177,* WEB
www.lacasadelossuenos.com. 8 rooms. Pool. AE, DC, MC, V.

$$$$ ▯ **Casa Santo Domingo.** This elegant hotel was built around the ruins
★ of the ancient Monasterio Santo Domingo, taking advantage of its long
passageways and snug little courtyards. Dark carved-wood furniture,
yellow stucco walls, and iron sconces preserve the monastic atmosphere.
Luxurious amenities abound, such as private hot tubs in the baths, but
these do not detract from the historical feel. ⊠ *3 Calle Oriente 28,* ☎
832–0140, FAX *832–4155,* WEB *www.casasantodomingo.com.gt. 97
rooms. Restaurant, pool, massage, sauna, spa, bar, concierge. AE,
DC, MC, V.*

$$$$ ▯ **Hotel Antigua.** As a tasteful combination of colonial elegance and
modern comfort, Hotel Antigua is one of the city's most popular lodgings. The sparkling pool, set amid lush gardens, is a treat after a day
exploring the dusty city streets. Standard rooms have plenty of space
for two, while one- and two-level suites can house a whole family quite
comfortably. The oldest part of the hotel is a colonial-style building
with a restaurant, bar, and a beautiful sitting room. ⊠ *8 Calle Poniente
1, at 5 Av. Sur,* ☎ *832–0288 or 832–0331,* FAX *832–2807,* WEB *www.
hotelantigua.com.gt. 60 rooms. 2 restaurants, bar, pool, playground,
convention center. AE, DC, MC, V.*

$$$$ ▯ **Posada del Ángel.** You'd never know from the unassuming wooden
★ gate that you're at the threshold of Antigua's most beautiful lodging.
It's all part of the ruse at this truly angelic inn. Large corner fireplaces
warm the rooms, each of which is decorated with well-chosen antiques.
Those on the main floor look out onto a plant-filled courtyard, while
the one above has a private rooftop terrace. Early morning light
bounces off the long reflecting pool and into the windows of the cozy
breakfast room. The staff has catered to presidents and prime ministers, but you'll receive the same fine service. ⊠ *4 Av. Sur 24A,* ☎ *832–
5303; 800/934–0065 in the U.S.,* WEB *www.posadadelangel.com. 5
rooms. Dining room, room service, bar, library, concierge, airport
shuttle. AE, DC, MC, V.*

$$$ ▯ **Hotel Aurora.** This genteel inn, still run by the same family that opened
it in 1923, has an unbeatable location in the heart of the city. The dimly

lighted colonial-style rooms face a beautifully tended garden. You can relax on a tiled portico strewn with plenty of comfortable rattan chairs. Rooms have wooden furniture and old-fashioned armoires. ⊠ *4 Calle Oriente 16,* ☎ FAX *832–0217/5515. 16 rooms. AE, MC, V.*

$$$ 🔂 **Hotel Convento.** This hotel was built among the ruins of an old con-
★ vent where only the often-photographed Arco de Santa Catalina remains. The spacious rooms, all a bit dimly lighted, are tastefully decorated with handicrafts and handwoven bedspreads. Most face a verdant courtyard where a smattering of tables and chairs encourages you to venture out with a good book. ⊠ *5 Av. Norte 28, at 2 Calle Poniente,* ☎ *832–3879,* FAX *832–3079,* WEB *www.convento.com. 18 rooms. Restaurant, some kitchenettes, Internet, shop. No credit cards.*

$$$ 🔂 **Quinta de las Flores.** With views of three volcanoes from the well-
★ tended gardens and the open-air dining room, this luxury hotel takes advantage of its location southeast of the city. It's great for those in search of peace and quiet. This 19th-century hacienda combines colonial comfort with a sense of whimsy—the decor includes modern takes on traditional crafts. All the high-ceilinged rooms have fireplaces to keep you cozy on chilly evenings. ⊠ *Calle del Hermano Pedro 6,* ☎ *832–3721 or 832–3722,* FAX *832–3726,* WEB *www.quintadelasflores.com. 9 rooms, 5 bungalows. Restaurant, some kitchenettes, minibars, pool, bar, playground. AE, DC, MC, V.*

$$ 🔂 **Posada Asjemenou.** There are plenty of charming hotels in colonial mansions, but the difference here is that you won't pay through the nose. The rooms are clean and comfortable, and the staff is friendly and eager. The small café serves breakfast and snacks. If you hanker for more substantial fare, head to the nearby pizzeria run by the same family. ⊠ *5 Av. Norte 31, at 1 Calle Poniente,* ☎ FAX *832–2670,* WEB *www.antiguacolonial.com/asjemenou.htm. 12 rooms, 9 with bath. Café. AE, DC, MC, V.*

Nightlife and the Arts

You won't have trouble finding a bar in Antigua, as the city is filled with watering holes. Many of these you'll find within a few blocks of Plaza Mayor are favored by young people studying Spanish at one of the many language schools. Head a bit farther afield, and you can raise a glass with the locals.

Bars and Clubs

Locals swear that the place to be is **Ricky's** (⊠ 4 Av. Norte 4). The conversation is convivial and the cocktails are inexpensive. Homesick Brits should head to **Hogshead** (⊠ 1 Calle Poniente 23), where pub food is served in a relaxed atmosphere. The staff is warm and attentive. For live music, seek out **Jazz Gruta** (⊠ Calzada de Santa Lucía Norte 17), an intimate club where local groups perform every night except Sunday.

The ever popular **Chimenea** (⊠ 4 Calle Poniente and 7 Av. Sur) caters to students who crowd the small dance floor. If you want to dance the night away, **Casbah** (⊠ 5 Av. Norte 45) is Antigua's only real disco. Latin rhythms make the place popular.

Outdoor Activities and Sports

From mountain biking to white-water rafting, Antigua has plenty of activities for those who want to explore the great outdoors. Don't just head out solo, however. Some of the most popular destinations have been the sites of robberies. Choose a knowledgeable tour operator who will set you up with a guide who knows the area.

Biking

The rolling hills that surround Antigua make for great mountain biking. Local agencies rent bikes as well as equipment like helmets and water bottles. **Mayan Bike Tours** (⊠ 3 Calle Poniente and 7 Av. Norte, ☎ 832–3743, WEB www.mayanadventures.com) offers trips ranging from easy rides in a morning or afternoon to more challenging treks lasting several days. **Old Town Outfitters** (⊠ 5 Av. Sur 12, ☎ 832–4171, WEB www.bikeguatemala.com) caters to a backpacker crowd, but its trips are suitable for people of all ages.

Hiking

Hikers head to the volcanoes surrounding Antigua. Of the four reachable from Antigua, only Volcán Pacayá is still active (although Volcán Fuego smokes fairly often). Antigua's best volcano expeditions are offered by **Eco-Tours Chejos** (⊠ 3 Calle Poniente 24, ☎ 832–5464), whose friendly owner has climbed Volcán Pacaya more than 1,800 times. The prices are higher than most, but there are usually fewer people. **Sin Fronteras** (⊠ 3 Calle Poniente 12, ☎ 832–1017) will take you on a one-day trip to Pacayá or a two-day trip to Fuego or Acatenango. **Voyageur** (⊠ 4 Calle Oriente 14, ☎ 832–4237) is another reputable outfitter.

Shopping

Antigua is a shopper's paradise. The single largest concentration of shops can be found in the **Mercado de Artisanías** (⊠ 4 Calle Poniente and Alameda de Santa Lucía), but stroll down any street and you'll find boutiques selling everything from finely embroidered blouses to beautiful ceramics.

With a wide selection of *artisanía*, **Casa de Artes** (⊠ 4 Av. Sur 11) is a nice place to browse. **Casa de los Gigantes** (⊠ 7 Calle Oriente 18) has a good selection of quality items, including genuine antique festival masks. For hand-painted pottery by local artisans, try **Topis** (⊠ 5 Av. Norte 20B).

Antigua A to Z

AIR TRAVEL TO AND FROM ANTIGUA

The nearest airport is Guatemala City's Aeropuerto Internacional La Aurora, a little less than an hour's drive away. If your hotel does not offer a transfer from the airport, there are plenty of shuttle buses that run this route.

BUS TRAVEL TO AND FROM ANTIGUA

A variety of companies runs frequent shuttle buses between Guatemala City and Antigua. Transportes Turisticos Atitrans and Turansa are both reputable companies. Buses leave every 15 minutes from 18 Calle and 4 Avenida in Zona 1 in Guatemala City. They depart on a similar schedule from the bus station in Antigua. It's best to call ahead for reservations, but you can also purchase tickets on board.

Transportes Turisticos Atitrans and Turansa also offer service to the Western Highlands, with the cost ranging from 100 quetzales for Chichicastenango and Panajachel to 200 quetzales for Quetzaltenango. You can also catch a public bus at the terminal, which is cheaper but much less comfortable. There are one or two direct buses to Panajachel and Quetzaltenango each day, as well as five or six bound for Chichicastenango. Tickets cost about 16 quetzales.

➤ BUS COMPANIES: **Transportes Turisticos Atitrans** (⊠ 6 Av. Sur 8, ☎ 832–1381). **Turansa** (⊠ 5 Calle Poniente 11B, ☎ 832–4691).

➤ Bus Stations: **Terminal de Buses** (✉ Alameda Santa Lucía at 4 Calle Poniente).

CAR RENTAL

If you want to rent a car to explore Antigua, it's a good idea to do so in Guatemala City's Aeropuerto Internacional La Aurora. In Antigua a reputable local agency is Tabarini Rent-A-Car.
➤ Local Agencies: **Tabarini Rent-A-Car** (✉ 2 Calle Poniente 19A, ☎ FAX 832–3091).

CAR TRAVEL

The roads around Antigua are mostly well paved, so drives through the countryside can be quite pleasant. Keep on your guard, though, as other drivers may ignore traffic laws and common sense. As one jovial man behind the wheel of a bus recently said, "All drivers in Guatemala are crazy."

To reach Antigua, drive west out of Guatemala City via the Calzada Roosevelt, which becomes the Pan-American Highway. At San Lucas turn right off the highway and drive south to Antigua. If you're coming from the Western Highlands, head south near Chimaltenango.

EMERGENCIES

For all emergencies call the police department. Contact the tourist police for free escorts, information, and minor matters.
➤ Emergency Services: **Police** (✉ 5 Calle Poniente, west end of Palacio del Capitán, ☎ 832–0251). **Tourist police** (✉ 4 Av. Norte, Palacio del Ayuntamiento, ☎ 832–7290 or 832–0532).
➤ Hospitals: **Pedro de Betancourt Hospital** (✉ Calle de Los Peregrinos and 4 Av. Sur, ☎ 831–1319).
➤ Pharmacies: **Farmacia Roca** (✉ 4 Calle Poniente 11, ☎ 832–0612).

INTERNET

With its sizable population of expatriates, Antigua has a good supply of Internet cafés. The competition is fierce, so expect very low prices. Enlaces and Enlinea have conveniently located offices. Antigua Post also has a scanner, so you can send photos to friends and family back home.
➤ Internet Cafés: **Enlaces** (✉ 6 Av. Norte 1). **Enlinea** (✉ 1 Calle Poniente 9; 1 Av. Sur 17; 5 Av. Sur 12). **Antigua Post** (✉ 6 Av. Sur 12).

MAIL AND SHIPPING

Antigua's main post office is across from the bus station. You can drop off your letters here, or ask the staff at your hotel to mail them for you. For packages try Envios Etc.
➤ Overnight Services: **Envios Etc.** (✉ 3 Av. Norte 26).
➤ Post Offices: **Correos Central** (✉ 4 Calle Poniente and Alameda Santa Lucía).

MONEY MATTERS

You won't have a problem finding ATMs in Antigua. Bancared, near Plaza Mayor, has one that accepts cards issued in the United States.
➤ Banks: **Bancared** (✉ 4 Calle Poniente 22).

SAFETY

Antigua is one of Guatemala's safest cities, as the streets around Plaza Mayor are patrolled by the tourist police. Farther from the square you should walk in groups or take taxis after the sun goes down. Be careful in the countryside, where there have been some robberies. If you plan to tackle one of the nearby volcanoes, hire a reputable guide.

TAXIS

A taxi between Guatemala City and Antigua should cost about 200 quetzales. Many run between Aeropuerto Internacional La Aurora and Antigua. Mijandos has a good reputation.

➤ TAXI COMPANIES: **Mijandos** (☎ 832–5051 or 832–5049).

TOURS OPERATORS

There are a number of travel agencies that can book you on trips around the region and throughout the country. Among the better known are Rainbow Travel Center, Vision Travel, and Turansa. One of the best is Antigua Tours, run by independent guide Elizabeth Bell. It offers all sorts of personalized trips, from walking tours of Antigua to excursions to Tikal.

A number of *fincas* (farms) in the hills around Antigua offer tours. Finca Los Nietos, a coffee plantation, and Finca Valhalla, a macadamia farm, are both southwest of the city.

➤ TOUR COMPANIES: **Antigua Tours** (⊠ 3 Calle Oriente 28, in the Hotel Casa Santo Domingo, ☎ 832–5821, WEB www.antiguatours.net). **Finca Los Nietos** (⊠ 6 km [4 mi] from Antigua, ☎ 831–5438). **Finca Valhalla** (⊠ 7 km southwest of Antigua, ☎ 831–5799). **Rainbow Travel Center** (⊠ 7 Av. Sur 8, ☎ 832–4202). **Turansa** (⊠ 5 Calle Poniente 11B, ☎ 832–4691). **Vision Travel** (⊠ 3 Av. Norte 3, ☎ 832–3293, WEB www.guatemalainfo.com).

VISITOR INFORMATION

Inguat, the national tourism agency, has an office in the Palacio de los Capitanes Generales, on the south side of Plaza Mayor. It is open daily 8–noon and 2–5.

➤ TOURIST INFORMATION: **Inguat** (⊠ 5 Calle Poniente, Palacio de los Capitanes Generales, ☎ 832–0763).

THE WESTERN HIGHLANDS

Beginning near the colonial capital of Antigua, the Western Highlands run all the way to the border of Mexico. This is a spectacular landscape where grumbling volcanoes rise above broad alpine lakes and narrow river ravines, lush tropical valleys and misty cloud forests, pine-draped hillsides and wide pastoral plains. Many people come to the Western Highlands to experience its natural beauty, and few are disappointed.

This region is home to the majority of Guatemalan's indigenous people, who live in small villages you'll find nestled in the valleys and perched on the hillsides. Most survive on subsistence farming, selling what little is left over. Entire families pack fruits, vegetables, and whatever else they have onto their backs and head to market. Held at least once a week in most communities, market day is as much a social gathering as anything else. Activity starts in the wee hours, when there is still a chill in the air. The momentum wanes around late afternoon as the crowds depart, eager to head home before the sun sinks behind the mountains.

The heart of the Western Highlands is undoubtedly Lago Atitlán. At the foot of three massive dormant volcanoes—San Pedro (9,920 ft), Tolimán (10,340 ft), and Atitlán (11,560 ft)—the lake is one of the loveliest spots in Guatemala. More than a dozen communities are found along its shores. To the north is the charming village of Chichicastenango. Quiet for most of the week, it explodes with activity on Thursday and Sunday, when a sprawling open-air market takes over its main square. West of Lago Atitlán lies Quetzaltenango, Guatemala's second-largest

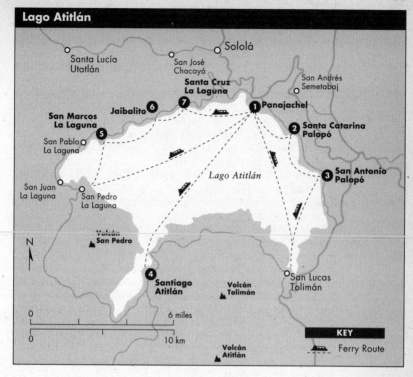

Lago Atitlán

○ Sololá

○ Santa Lucía Utatlán

○ San José Chacayá

Santa Cruz La Laguna ⑦

Jaibalito ⑥

San Marcos La Laguna ⑤

San Pablo La Laguna

San Andrés Semetabaj ○

① **Panajachel**

② **Santa Catarina Palopó**

③ **San Antonio Palopó**

Lago Atitlán

San Juan La Laguna ○

San Pedro La Laguna ○

▲ *Volcán San Pedro*

N

④ **Santiago Atitlán**

Volcán Tolimán ▲

○ San Lucas Tolimán

0 — 6 miles
0 — 10 km

Volcán Atitlán ▲

KEY

🚢 Ferry Route

---

city. The Sierra de Chuacús, a string of active and dormant volcanoes just outside the city limits, makes this an ideal place for outdoor activities.

Numbers in the text correspond to numbers in the margin and on the Lago Atitlán map and the Western Highlands map.

Panajachel

❶ *110 km (68 mi) northwest of Antigua.*

A few decades ago Panajachel was just a quiet Cakchiquel village on the northern shore of Lago Atitlán, but it has since grown into a hangout for foreigners who came here and loved the region so much that they never left. And who can blame them? Bordered by three volcanoes that drop off into the crystalline waters of Lago Atitlán, Panajachel's setting could hardly be more dramatic.

The **Reserva Natural Atitlán** (✉ 2 km [1 mi] west of Panajachel, ☎ 762–2565) has a walking trail that loops through a small river canyon, crossing suspension bridges and passing a butterfly atrium and enclosures of spider monkeys and coatimundis. There's also a beach for a bit of posteducational relaxation. Campsites are available in the park.

Dining and Lodging

$$$–$$$$ ✕ **Casablanca.** Panajachel's most elegant restaurant, Casablanca has a white-walled dining room with windows overlooking the main street. The handful of tables on the upper level is much more intimate. The menu is ample, if a bit overpriced, and includes a few seafood standouts such as lobster. ✉ *Calle Principal 0–93, at Calle Santander,* ☎ *762–1015. AE, DC, MC, V.*

$–$$ ✕ **El Bistro.** Hummingbirds dart among flowering vines at this romantic eatery on the shores of Lago Atitlán. Enter though an iron gate that leads into a garden hidden behind a low wall. Eat at one of the tables outside or choose between the pair of intimate dining rooms. Two standout specialties are the fettuccine *arrabiata* (with a slightly spicy tomato sauce) and the steak au poivre (cooked in a wine sauce and black pepper). ⊠ *End of Calle Santander,* ☎ *762–0508. AE, MC, V. Closed Tues.*

$–$$ ✕ **El Patio.** Although it's known by the outdoor patio that gives the place its name, most of the restaurant's tables are inside a large dining room with little ambience. Nevertheless, it's a popular spot for breakfast. The lunch and dinner menus offer greater variety, including such items as filet mignon, roast pork, and chicken à la king. ⊠ *Calle Santander,* ☎ *762–2041. AE, DC, MC, V.*

$ ✕ **Pájaro Azul.** Tired of *frijoles* for breakfast? There isn't a single bean
★ to be found at this pastel-hue café, which serves up outstanding crepes. Choose from a small but creative menu of savory dinner crepes and sweet dessert crepes, or pick and choose among your favorite ingredients. ⊠ *Calle Santander, next to the post office,* ☎ *762–2596. No credit cards.*

$$$$ ✕🏠 **Hotel Atitlán.** In a quiet cove east of Panajachel, this Spanish-style
★ inn consists of a main building flanked by two-story wings that surround a pool. The extensive grounds border on a long stretch of shoreline and the Reserva Natural Atitlán, a wooded reserve crossed by footpaths and hanging bridges. The tile-floor rooms have balconies overlooking the gardens or the lake. Even if you don't stay here, stop by for views of the lake at sunset. The menu is reliable, offering entrées such as baked chicken. ⊠ *2 km (1 mi) west of Panajachel,* ☎ *762–0048 in Panajachel; 360–8405 in Guatemala City.* 🌐 *www. hotelatitlan.com. 64 rooms. Restaurant, pool, beach tennis court, bar, shop. AE, DC, MC, V.*

$$$ ✕🏠 **Cacique Inn.** A collection of little buildings about a block from the main street, Cacique Inn is a relaxing retreat. Spacious, if sparsely furnished, rooms have sliding-glass doors that open onto the lovely garden. The rooms have fireplaces that warm you up in a snap. The grounds are surrounded by a wall, which makes the terraces by the pool a private place to sunbathe. The restaurant is one of the best in town, serving an wide selection of Guatemalan dishes. ⊠ *Calle del Embarcadero, near Calle Principal,* ☎ 📠 *762–1205 or 762–2053. 35 rooms. Restaurant, pool, bar. AE, DC, MC, V.*

$$$$ 🏠 **Hotel Posada de Don Rodrigo.** This hotel possesses some of the best views of the lake (they would be even better if the giant waterslide wasn't in the way). The nicely decorated rooms make use of handwoven fabric from the local communities. Ask for one of the newer rooms, which have better views. The restaurant, which serves good standard fare, never seems crowded. Relax in one of the hammocks hung along a breezy corridor. ⊠ *End of Calle Santander,* ☎ *762–2326 or 762– 2329,* 📠 *331–6838.* 🌐 *posadadedonrodrigo.centroamerica.com. 39 rooms. Restaurant, pool, sauna, squash. AE, DC, MC, V.*

$$$$ 🏠 **Porta Hotel del Lago.** Panajachel's biggest hotel, the Porta Hotel del Lago also has the most amenities. Although it lacks the character of smaller hotels, it's comfortable and conveniently located and has topnotch service. Rooms have balconies overlooking the public beach on Lago Atitlán. The huge restaurant next door looks out onto the pool. ⊠ *End of Calle Rancho Grande, at Calle Buenas Nuevas,* ☎ *762–1555,* 📠 *762–1562,* 🌐 *www.portahotels.com. 100 rooms. Restaurant, cable TV, pool, gym, hot tub, massage, sauna, bar, meeting room. AE, DC, MC, V.*

$$$ 🏠 **Hotel Dos Mundos.** Set amid colorful gardens, this hotel gives you comfortable accommodations without the hefty price tag of more deluxe digs. The medium-size rooms are simply and tastefully furnished. Most open onto the pool area, where you can spend your afternoon on a lounge chair with a cocktail. The restaurant has a certain elegance, with tables set beneath a soaring thatch roof. ✉ *Calle Santander 4–72,* ☎ *762–2078 or 762–2140,* FAX *762–0127,* WEB *www.atitlan.com. 21 rooms. Restaurant, pool, travel services. AE, DC, MC, V.*

$$$ 🏨 **Rancho Grande Inn.** A German immigrant by the name of Milly Schleisier opened this string of bungalows back in the 1940s. In so doing, she created what is still one of the most charming of Panajachel's accommodations, melding the designs of country houses in her homeland with the colorful culture of her adopted country. Each of the bungalows is unique, but all have king-size beds covered with locally woven spreads. The largest bungalow, which can sleep up to five, also has a fireplace. ✉ *Calle Rancho Grande,* ☎ *762–1554,* FAX *762–2247,* WEB *www.travellog.com. 11 bungalows, 1 bungalow suite. Breakfast room. AE, DC, MC, V.*

$$ 🏨 **Müllers Guest House.** On the quiet street parallel to Calle Santander, this little inn is set in a pretty garden. The rooms call to mind a European bed-and-breakfast with their honey-hued wood floors and pastel walls. Breakfast is in the homey sitting room, the same place where you will enjoy wine and cheese in the late afternoon. ✉ *Calle Rancho Grande 1–82,* ☎ *762–2442 or 762–2392,* FAX *337–0656 3 rooms, 1 bungalow. MC, V.*

$ 🏨 **Hotel Galindo.** Separate sitting rooms with fireplaces make the suites at this budget-minded hotel worth the money. They surround a courtyard filled with greenery. The restaurant is breezy and attractive. ✉ *Calle Principal,* ☎ *762–1168 or 762–2071. 14 rooms, 4 suites. Restaurant. No credit cards.*

Nightlife and the Arts

Because Panajachel is a resort town, it probably has the liveliest nightlife in the highlands. Most bars are clustered near the intersection of Avenida de los Arboles and Calle Principal. The **Circus Bar** (✉ Av. de los Arboles, ☎ 762–2056) is a popular spot for locals and travelers alike. There's often live music. The dimly lighted **Chapiteau Disco** (✉ Av. de los Arboles) plays mostly rock.

Outdoor Activities and Sports

Water sports are becoming more popular at Lago Atitlán, giving the lake a Club Med feel. You can rent a canoe from **Diversiones Acuáticas Balom** (✉ on the public beach near ferry terminals, ☎ 762–2242). It's best to get out early and be back by noon, as the afternoon winds can be fierce.

For exploring the countryside you can rent a mountain bike at **Moto Servicio Quiché** (✉ Av. de los Arboles at Calle Principal) and pedal over to nearby villages.

Shopping

Calle Santander is one long open-air market, lined on both sides with vendors who hang their wares from fences and makeshift stalls. An outdoor market called **Tinimit Maya** (✉ Calle Santander) is easily the best place for reasonably priced artesanía. **El Guipil** (✉ Calle Santander) is a large boutique with a varied selection of handmade items from highland villages. **Ojalá** (✉ Av. de los Arboles) has a small but excellent selection of antiques.

Santa Catarina Palopó

2 *4 km (2½ mi) east of Panajachel.*

You'll be surrounded by the brilliant blues and greens of huipiles worn by local women as you walk down the cobblestone streets of this picturesque town. From here you'll be treated to magical views of the trio of volcanoes that looms over the lake. In Santa Catarina you'll see ramshackle homes standing within sight of luxury chalets whose owners arrive as often by helicopter as they do by car.

Dining and Lodging

$$$ ✕🏨 **Villa Santa Catarina.** In a long yellow building with an adobe-tile roof, Villa Santa Catarina has magical views. Rooms are small, but each has a private balcony overlooking the lake. The restaurant serves typical Guatemalan dishes such as *pepian de pollo* (chicken in a spicy sauce). You can relax in the pool or head to a series of natural hot springs that are only a few hundred feet away. ⌧ *Calle de la Playa,* ☎ ℻ *334–8136. 36 rooms. Restaurant, bar, pool, waterskiing. AE, DC, MC, V.*

$$$$ 🏨 **Casa Palopó.** By far the best B&B on the lake, luxurious Casa
★ Palopó has an almost mystical atmosphere. Each of the six rooms, decorated with religious-themed artworks from around the world, offers incredible views of the volcanoes. Muted blues run throughout this former villa, mirroring the colors of the lake. Most baths have giant tubs perfect for soaking. ⌧ *South of Santa Catarina Palopó,* ☎ *762–2270,* ℻ *762–2721.* 🆆🅴🅱 *www.casapalopo.com. 2 rooms, 2 suites. Restaurant, pool, library, Internet, no kids under 15. AE, DC, MC, V.*

San Antonio Palopó

❸ *6½ km (4 mi) east of Santa Catarina Palopó.*

Slightly larger than neighboring Santa Catarina Palopó, San Antonio Palopó is a quiet farming village centered around a beautiful adobe church. Most people have tiny plots of land where they grow green onions, which you may see them cleaning down by the lake. This is one of only a handful of regions in Latin America where men still dress in traditional costumes on a daily basis. Their pants have geometric motifs and calf-length woolen wraparounds fastened by leather belts or red sashes.

Lodging

$$ 🏨 **Terrazas del Lago.** This charming hotel overlooking the lake is notable for its floral-pattern stone tiles. Simply decorated rooms have wooden tables and iron candlesticks. Those in front have patios with great vistas. A small restaurant serves simple breakfasts and lunches, while several terraces are perfect for a quiet cup of afternoon tea. ⌧ *Calle de la Playa,* ☎ *762–0157,* ℻ *762–0037. 12 rooms. No credit cards.*

Santiago Atitlán

★ **❹** *21 km (13 mi) west of San Antonio Palopó.*

Across the lake from Panajachel, Santiago Atitlán has a fascinating history. With a population of about 48,000, this capital of the proud and independent Tzutuhil people is one of the largest indigenous communities in Guatemala. They resisted political domination during the country's civil war, which meant that many residents were murdered by the military. After a 1990 massacre in which 12 people were killed, the villagers protested the presence of the army in their town. To everyone's surprise, the army actually left, and Santiago Atitlán became a model for other highland towns fighting governmental oppression.

A road that leads up from the dock is lined on both sides with shops selling artesanía—take a good look at the huipiles embroidered with elaborate depictions of fruits, birds, and spirits. Many local women wear a "halo," which is a 12-yard-long band wrapped around their forehead. Older men also wear traditional dress, sporting black-and-white-stripe calf-length pants with detailed embroidery below the knee.

The main road leads to the squat white **Iglesia de Santiago Atitlán,** the church where Tzutuhil deities can be seen in the woodwork around the pulpit. It was on this very pulpit that Father Stanley Francis Rother was assassinated by right-wing death squads in July 1981 for his outspoken support of the Tzutuhil cause. Beloved by the local parishioners, he is remembered with a plaque near the door.

As you get off the boat, small children may offer to lead you to the **Casa de Maximón** in exchange for a few quetzales. Santiago Atitlán is one of the few places where people actively worship Guatemala's cigar-smoking Maximón, a local deity who also goes by the name San Simón. Every year a different member of the local *cofrade* (religious society) houses the wooden idol and accommodates his many faithful followers. When you locate the right house, you'll be ushered inside to see the shrine. If you haven't brought a cigar to leave in his collection plate, a few quetzales will do just fine.

Dining and Lodging

$$ ╳⌐ **Bambú.** Run by a Spanish expatriate with a penchant for fine food, Bambú is known for its excellent restaurant. You'll be served Spanish fare in an A-frame dining room warmed by a stone fireplace. On the beautifully tended grounds are a string of thatch-roof bungalows with private patios overlooking the lake. Immaculate stone pathways loop through a series of taxonomically arranged gardens (cacti in one, flowers in the next, and so on), while most of the restaurant's fruits, vegetables, and herbs are cultivated out back. ⊠ *1 km (½ mi) east of town,* ☎ *721–7332,* FAX *721–7197. 5 bungalows. Restaurant, boating, bar. AE, DC, MC, V.*

$$ ╳⌐ **Posada de Santiago.** This longtime favorite has deluxe accom-
★ modations in private bungalows with volcano views. Pass through the carved-wood doors into the stone-wall bungalows and you'll find fireplaces and beds piled high with thick wool blanket. The restaurant serves exquisite food, such as smoked chicken píbil in a tangy red sauce and Thai coconut shrimp. The wine list is surprisingly extensive. ⊠ *1 km (½ mi) south of town,* ☎ *410–2444,* FAX *721–7167,* WEB *www.atitlan. com, 12 bungalows. Restaurant, boating, mountain bikes, shop. AE, DC, MC, V.*

Outdoor Activities and Sports

Horseback riding around the lake is arranged by Americans Jim and Nancy Mattisson at **Aventura en Atitlán** (⊠ 10 km [6 mi] from town, ☎ 201–5527). Various rides, including an exhilarating torchlighted night-time outing, wind through lush lowlands and spectacular cloud forests.

San Marcos La Laguna

➎ *15 minute boat trip from Panajachel.*

San Marcos is a tiny village catering mostly to tourists. From the dock you can reach the center of the village by walking uphill along a narrow cobblestone path. The village itself has one or two stores and a restaurant around the central square. If you plan on staying in San Marcos you should remember to bring a flashlight, as most of the town does not have electricity.

Lodging

$$ ⌐ **Posada Schumann.** Full of old-fashioned charm, this little inn has bungalows set along a narrow swath of garden stretching down to the lake. Exposed stonework and unfinished wood paneling lend the place a slightly rustic feel, but the rooms are enlivened by the festive colors from local weaving. The hot water can be unreliable. ⊠ *San Marcos La Laguna,* ☎ *202–2216. 4 rooms without bath, 3 bungalows. Restaurant. No credit cards.*

$ ▢ **Hotel Jinava.** Set in a secluded cove, the small hotel is a great place to get away from it all. Each of the bungalows, shaded by avocado and papaya trees, has excellent views of the volcanoes. Ask the friendly German owner to make you a tropical drink, one of his favorite pastimes. If piña coladas are not your thing, then request a massage—he is rumored to be the best masseur on the lake. The restaurant serves up great curries and other international dishes. ✉ *San Marcos La Laguna,* ☎ *705–6035, 406–5986.* WEB *www.jinava.de 5 bungalows. Restaurant, massage. No credit cards.*

Jaibalito

❻ *10-min boat trip west of Panajachel.*

So small that it rarely appears on maps of the region, Jaibalito is the most undisturbed of the villages surrounding Lago Atitlán. Santa Cruz La Laguna is a short walk away, but otherwise Jaibalito is quite isolated. There is no boat service after 6 PM, so this village is only for those seeking peace and quiet.

Dining and Lodging

$$ ✕▢ **Casa del Mundo.** Built atop a cliff overlooking the azure waters, this gorgeous inn has unquestionably the best vantage point for gazing at Lago Atitlán. All the rooms have views, but those from Number 1 and Number 3 are the most breathtaking. If you can tear yourself away from the windows you'll notice the beautifully decorated rooms have wood-beam ceilings, red-tile floors, and stucco-and-stone walls hung with local handicrafts. Meals are served family style in the cozy restaurant. ✉ *Jaibalito dock,* ☎ *204–5558,* WEB *www.virtualguatemala.com/casadelmundo. 8 rooms, 4 with bath. Restaurant, boating. No credit cards.*

$–$$ ✕▢ **Vulcano Lodge.** Set on a coffee plantation, this lodge has well-tended gardens with hammocks that make nice retreats in the afternoon. The tastefully decorated rooms are on the small side, but they all have private terraces. Alas, there are no views of the lake. The restaurant serves up international favorites. ✉ *Jaibalito,* ☎ *410–2237. 5 rooms, 1 suite. Restaurant. No credit cards.*

Santa Cruz La Laguna

❼ *10-min boat ride west of Panajachel.*

It's a steep walk to the hillside village of Santa Cruz La Laguna, but the hale and hearty are rewarded with a stroll through a community that most travelers overlook. The square adobe houses are positioned precariously on the slopes, looking as if they might be washed away by the next heavy rain. A highlight of this little village is a squat adobe church in the main plaza.

Dining and Lodging

$$ ✕▢ **Arca de Noé.** Magnificent views are the big draw at this rustic retreat. Housed in several bungalows constructed of wood and stone, the rooms are small but neat. The delicious home cooking is served family style in the main building, which resembles a New England farmhouse. The menu changes constantly, but each meal comes with fresh vegetables and bread hot out of the oven. ✉ *Santa Cruz La Laguna,* ☎ *306–4352. 10 rooms, 6 with bath. Restaurant, boating. No credit cards.*

Outdoor Activities and Sports

Lago Atitlán's wealth of underwater wonders draws divers from around the world. **ATI Divers** (✉ Iguana Perdida, ☎ 762–2621) is a certified diving school that offers courses for all levels, from basic certification to dive master.

The Western Highlands

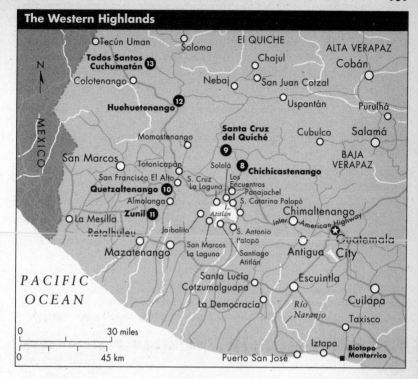

Chichicastenango

★ ❽ *37 km (23 mi) north of Panajachel, 108 km (67 mi) northwest of Antigua.*

Perched on a hillside, Chichicastenango is in many ways a typical highland town. The narrow cobblestone streets converge on a wide plaza where most days you'll find a few old men passing the time. You'd hardly recognize the place Thursday and Sunday, when row after row of colorful stalls fill the square and overflow into the adjoining alleys. There's a dizzying array of handmade items, from wooden masks to woolen blankets to woven baskets. Much of the artesanía is produced for tourists, but walk a few blocks in any direction and you'll find where the locals do their shopping. South of the square you'll see a narrow street where stern-faced women sell chickens. To the east you might run across a family trying to to coax a just-purchased pig up a rather steep hill.

Try to get to Chichicastenango at dawn, when the early morning mist swirls around the vendors as they set up shop. Better yet, come late in the day on Wednesday or Saturday. Not only will you get better deals before the tourists arrive, but you'll witness the town's amazing transformation. Arriving by bus or by foot, the people of the surrounding villages come with what they have to sell strapped to their backs. Men balance heavy wooden tables across their shoulders, while old women bend over under the weight of wrought-iron machines for making shaved ice. Even little children help, balancing bundles bigger than they are.

A Good Walk

Any tour of Chichicastenango begins in the tranquil **Parque Central,** which is transformed twice each week when hundreds of vendors arrive from villages near and far. Don't forget to wander along the neighboring streets, as the market long ago outgrew the square. Presiding over Parque Central is the gleaming white **Iglesia de Santo Tomás,** where Christian ceremonies and Maya mysticism intertwine. Across the square is the smaller but no less lovely **Capilla de Calvario.** On the south side of the square is **Museo Regional,** which provides a look at the culture of the region before the arrival of the Spanish. Head west down a street hill to the colorful **cementerio,** just outside town. You'll be treated to wonderful views of the city's red rooftops. If you're intrigued by the evidence of ancient rituals found in the cemetery, head south of town to the Maya shrine of **Pascual Abaj,** which is still used today. If you're lucky, you might see locals praying before the stone head.

TIMING

After a morning wandering around the market, you can see the rest of the sights in this little town in the course of an afternoon. Wear comfortable shoes, as the walk uphill to Pascual Abaj can be challenging.

Sights to See

Capilla de Calvario. Across from the Iglesia de Santo Tomás is this squat little chapel. It doesn't attract the attention that its much larger neighbor does, but from its steep steps you'll have a nice view of the market. ⊠ *West end of Plaza Mayor.*

Cementerio. Filled with mausoleums painted brilliant shades of teal, yellow, and orange, the town's cemetery is one of the most colorful in the Western Highlands. In the midst of headstones topped with crosses you'll doubtless find candles and incense—evidence of Maya rituals. ⊠ *West end of 8 Calle.*

Iglesia de Santo Tomás. Standing watch over the square is this gleaming white church, busy with worshipers all day and late into the night. Enter through a door on the right side. The church was built in 1540 on the site of an ancient temple, and locals say a block of stone near the massive front doors is all that remains of the altar. The Quiché people still consider Chichicastenango their holy city. Church officials look the other way as Maya ceremonies are still practiced here today. Some worshipers wave around pungent incense during the day, while at night others toss rose petals and pine needles into a raging fire right on the steps of the church. ⊠ *East end of Plaza Mayor.*

Pascual Abaj. This ancient Maya shrine, perched on a hilltop south of town, is often vandalized by overzealous Christians. The elongated stone face of the waist-high idol is always restored so that believers can return to their daily prayers. *Brujos,* the local shamans, lead villagers in special rites that occasionally include slaughtered chickens. To see the shrine, follow 9 Calle until you see the signs for the narrow footpath up the hill. ⊠ *South of Chichicastenango.*

Parque Central. As in most colonial villages, the heart of Chichicastenango is its central square. All the major sights are either here or on the nearby streets. Three blocks north is Arco Gucumatz, an arch over 5 Avenida where you watch vendors heading to the square. ⊠ *5 Av. and 7 Calle.*

Museo Regional. If you want to learn more about the history of Chichicastenango, this little colonial-era building displays pre-Columbian artifacts that came from the private collection of a local priest. ⊠ *Next to Iglesia de Santo Tomás.*

Dining and Lodging

$–$$ ✕ **Las Brasas.** An eclectic collection of local handicrafts brightens the walls of this excellent second-floor steak house. The chef, formerly of Hotel Santo Tomás, grills up a great steak, but there are plenty of other options, including a delicious *longaniza* (a sausage similar to chorizo). ⊠ *6 Calle 4–52, second level,* ☎ *756–2226. AE, DC, MC, V.*

$–$$ ✕ **La Fonda del Tzijolaj.** This restaurant's second-story balcony overlooking Plaza Mayor is a great place to watch the vendors set up on the eve of the market. The *pollo chimichurri* (chicken in an herb sauce) is one of the best choices from the mostly traditional menu. There are also a few surprises, such as spinach gnocchi. ⊠ *7 Calle and 4 Av.,* ☎ *756–1013. AE, DC, MC, V.*

$–$$ ✕ **La Villa de los Cofrades.** With two locations within a block of each other, it's hard to miss this longtime favorite. The smaller of the two has patio seating right on Plaza Mayor, where you can watch the vendors setting up their stalls while you feast on Belgian waffles or sip one of the finest cappuccinos in the country. The other location, a block away on 5 Calle, has a less hectic atmosphere. ⊠ *7 Calle and 5 Av., 5 Calle and 6 Av.,* ☎ *756–1643. AE, MC, V.*

$$$$ ✕🏨 **Hotel Santo Tomás.** Built in the Spanish style around a central courtyard, Hotel Santo Tomás is one of the town's best lodgings. Breezy passageways in which hundreds of plants spring from rustic clay pots lead past two trickling fountains. Spacious rooms are decorated with traditional textiles and antique reproductions. Each has a fireplace to warm you when the sun goes down. The large restaurant serves an excellent lunch buffet on market days. ⊠ *7 Av. 5–32,* ☎ *756–1316 or 756–1061,* FAX *756–1306. 43 rooms. Restaurant, pool, gym, hot tub, sauna, bar. AE, DC, MC, V.*

$$$ ✕🏨 **Mayan Inn.** Intricate woodwork and solid adobe construction make
★ the luxurious Mayan Inn one of the country's loveliest hotels. Rooms with corner fireplaces surround a series of beautifully maintained garden courtyards. Most have wide windows overlooking the pine-covered hills. The service is excellent—an attendant in traditional costume is assigned to each room and does everything from lighting the fire to serving dinner. Meals are taken in stately dining halls, with a set menu that changes daily. The restaurant is open from 7 AM to 9 AM, noon to 2 PM, and 7 PM to 9 PM. ⊠ *3 Av. at 8 Calle, 1 block west of plaza,* ☎ *756–1179; 339–2888 in Guatemala City,* FAX *756–1212; 339–2909 in Guatemala City. 30 rooms. Restaurant, bar. AE, DC, MC, V.*

$$ ✕🏨 **Hotel Chugüila.** In an older building a few blocks north of the plaza, this hotel has a variety of rooms facing a nice cobblestone courtyard. The plant-filled portico leading to most rooms is scattered with inviting chairs and tables. Rooms are simply furnished, and a few have fireplaces. The oddly shaped and warmly lighted dining room is perhaps the hotel's best feature, especially since its windows look out onto the main street. Lunch and dinner menus offer standard Guatemalan fare. ⊠ *5 Av. 5–24,* ☎ FAX *756–1134. 25 rooms, 20 with bath, 2 suites. Restaurant. AE, DC, MC, V.*

$ 🏨 **Hospedaje Salvador.** Looking like something out of the game Chutes and Ladders, this colorful mishmash of a hotel is a favorite among budget travelers. Rooms are aligned along three and four levels of incongruously curved breezeways, with steep stairs zigzagging all about. Though the rooms are a bit musty, the beds are a bit lumpy, and hot water is available only for a couple of hours in the morning, what the hotel lacks in comfort it compensates for with lots of character. ⊠ *10 Calle at 5 Av., 3 blocks south of the plaza,* ☎ *756–1329. 46 rooms, 10 with bath. No credit cards.*

$ 🏨 **Hotel Chalet.** The Alps are nowhere to be seen, but the sun-splashed breakfast room at the heart of this cozy little hotel somehow makes the name work. The rooms are smallish but not cramped. Wooden masks and other handicrafts adorn the walls. A pleasant terrace is a great place for relaxing after a taxing day of shopping. ⊠ *3 Calle 7–44,* ☎ FAX *756–1360. 7 rooms. AE, DC, MC, V.*

$ 🏨 **Posada El Arco.** This great little hotel has a distinctly homey feel. The spacious rooms, with their slightly corny decor, are happily reminiscent of the '70s. All rooms have fireplaces for the chilly evenings. To get here, climb up the stairs to the top of the arch that crosses 5 Avenida and turn left. ⊠ *4 Calle 4–36,* ☎ *756–1255. 7 rooms. Laundry facilities. No credit cards.*

Nightlife and the Arts

Nightlife in limited in hard-working Chichicastenango, although there are many tiny bars along the streets surrounding the plaza where you can join the locals for a beer. **Las Brasas** (⊠ 6 Calle 4–52, ☎ 756–2226) occasionally has live music.

Santa Cruz del Quiché

❾ *19 km (12 mi) north of Chichicastenango.*

Adventurous travelers may want to continue north from Chichicastenango for further glimpses of the region called El Quiché, where you'll find traditional villages set on the pine-covered hills. A half hour north of Chichicastenango lies the provincial capital of Santa Cruz del Quiché, which serves as a base for exploring the area. Quiché, as the town is commonly called, is known for its pretty white church on the east side of the Parque Central. It was built from the stones taken from a Maya temple destroyed by the Spanish.

North of town is **K'umarcaaj,** the ancient capital of the Quiché kingdom. This once-magnificent site was destroyed by Spanish conquistadors in 1524. The ruins haven't been restored, but they are frequently used for Maya rituals. A taxi to and from the ruins should cost less than 60 quetzales.

Dining and Lodging

$ ✕ **Comedor Flipper.** A cage of lively birds lends a cheerful atmosphere to this small eatery, which serves good Guatemalan fare. The *avena* (a warm wheat beverage) is delicious, especially on a cold morning. There is no sign of the restaurant's trusty cetaceous namesake, though a ceramic sailfish atop the refrigerator comes close. ⊠ *1 Av. 7–31, around the corner from Hotel San Pasqual,* ☎ *no phone. No credit cards.*

$ ⊞ **Hotel San Pasqual.** This little hotel has a definite charm, most of it emanating from the engaging couple that runs it. The simple rooms, with handwoven bedspreads, surround a sunny courtyard. Clotheslines full of the day's laundry stretch to the roof next door. The shared baths are clean, but hot water is available only in the morning. ⊠ *7 Calle 0–43, Zona 1,* ☎ *755–1107. 37 rooms, 11 with bath. No credit cards.*

Quetzaltenango

❿ *91 km (56 mi) southwest of Chichicastenango.*

Originally part of the Maya empire, Quetzaltenango was captured in the 14th century by the Quiché people, who called it Xelajú. It remained part of the Quiché kingdom until 1524, when Spaniard Pedro de Alvarado defeated the great warrior Tecún Umán in battle. The conquistador destroyed the city and used the stones for a new city called Quetzaltenango, which means "place of many quetzals." Locals have never gotten used to the name and still refer to Quetzaltenango as Xelajú, or simply Xela.

In a valley guarded by Volcán Santa María, Quetzaltenango has long had an economy based on agriculture. The rolling hills are particularly good for growing coffee. More recently, it has begun to attract travelers, who come here to purchase the intricate weavings from the surrounding villages. The first Sunday of each month is the main market day, and the central square is filled with women selling their wares.

A Good Walk

Begin your stroll aroun Quetzaltenango in the beautiful **Parque Centroamérica,** pausing to admire the facade of the colonial-era **Catedral del Espíritu Santo.** Be sure to visit the **Museo de Historia Natural** and the **Museo del Arte.** Save your ticket stub for an afternoon visit to the **Museo del Ferrocarril de los Altos.** From the central plaza head north, stopping along the way at Mercado La Democracia for a little shopping. Two blocks north is the shady **Parque Benito Juarez.** Enjoy an ice cream cone, then check out the **Iglesia de San Nicolás.**

TIMING

Quetzaltenango is fairly compact, so it's possible to see the major sights in a sunny afternoon. Remember that although most sights are in Zona 1, Parque Benito Juarez is to the north in Zona 3.

Sights to See

Catedral del Espíritu Santo. On the southeastern corner of Parque Centroamérica, this cathedral dates from 1535. The crumbling facade, which features life-size saints that look down upon those headed here to pray, is currently undergoing reconstruction. ⊠ *11 Av. and 7 Calle, Zona 1.*

Iglesia de San Nicolás. This blueish church, on the east side of Parque Benito Juarez, is known for its unusual baroque design. Although lovely, it looks a bit out of place in the town's mix of Greek and colonial structures. ⊠ *15 Av. and 3 Calle, Zona 3.*

Museo de Historia Natural. To the south of Parque Centroamérica, the Museum of Natural History is interesting mainly for its neoclassic flourishes. Inside are some mildly interesting examples of pre-Columbian pottery. ⊠ *7 Calle and 11 Av., Zona 1,* ☎ *761–6427.*

Museo del Arte. On the southwest corner of the main square is the Museum of Art, whose eclectic collection ranges from realist oils to abstract and multimedia works. The building also houses a school of art. ⊠ *12 Av. and 7 Calle, Zona 1,* ☎ *no phone.*

★ **Museo del Ferrocarril de Los Altos.** In the same building that houses the Museum of Art, the Los Altos Railroad Museum tells the history of the railroad that once connected Quetzaltenango with other towns in the Western Highlands. ⊠ *12 Av. and 7 Calle, Zona 1,* ☎ *no phone.*

Parque Benito Juarez. About 10 blocks north of Parque Centroamérica is this palm-lined park where many families spend their Sunday afternoons. Ice cream stands are in glorious abundance. ⊠ *15 Av. and 3 Calle, Zona 3.*

Parque Centroamérica. The central plaza in Quetzaltenango is one of the most beautiful in Central America. It's surrounded by architectural masterpieces, such as the magnificent building called Pasaje Enríquez. ⊠ *12 Av. and 4 Calle, Zona 1.*

Dining and Lodging

$$ ✕ **Da Valentino.** White walls sparsely adorned with watercolor paintings provide a subdued setting for this Italian eatery. The food does all the talking, and the handmade egg noodles and delicious gnocchi covered with rich sauces speak volumes. Da Valentino advertises its "high-quality slow food," and for good reason: expect to wait a while for the steaming platters of pasta to arrive. ⊠ *14 Av. A 1–37, Zona 1,* ☎ *761–4494. No credit cards. Closed Mon.*

$–$$ ✕ **Royal Paris.** This bistro caters to the foreign students who have come to Quetzaltenango to study Spanish, so it offers a wide selection of dishes. Some aren't the least bit Parisian, such as the succulent chicken curry. They're all prepared with flair, however. The ambience is definitely imported, with a slightly bohemian feeling courtesy of the paintings of cabaret scenes on the walls. ⊠ *Calle 14A 3–06, Zona 1,* ☎ *761–1942. AE, DC, MC, V.*

$ ✕ **El Kopetin.** Good food, attentive service, and reasonable prices make this place popular with the locals, so it can be tough to get a table later in the evening. It couldn't be described as fancy, but the long polished bar and wood paneling give it a comforting atmosphere. The menu has a number of delicious appetizers, including traditional queso fundido. ⊠ *14 Av. 3–51, Zona 1,* ☎ *761–8381. AE, DC, MC, V.*

$$$ ✕🏨 **Hotel Villa Real Plaza.** Surrounding a covered courtyard illuminated by skylights, the spacious rooms at Hotel Villa Real Plaza all have fireplaces that you'll appreciate on cool evenings. Those in a newer wing are superior to those in the dimly lighted older section. Ask for a room away from the bar, as the crowd can be noisy as the night winds down. The restaurant's interesting menu options range from chicken cordon bleu to a variety of meaty stews. ⊠ *4 Calle 12–22, Zona 1,* ☎ *761– 6270,* 🖷 *761–6780. 58 rooms. Restaurant, bar. AE, DC, MC, V.*

$$$ ✕🏨 **Pensión Bonifáz.** Don't let the name fool you into thinking this is a modest establishment—Pensión Bonifáz is Quetzaltenango's most upscale hotel. Housed in a stately old building at the central plaza's northeast corner, it has a modern interior that doesn't quite live up to its exterior. Still, it is a comfortable, well-run establishment. The nicest rooms are in the older building, where small balconies offer nice views of the plaza. A small café serves light fare, while the larger restaurant has a Continental menu; both share a devilishly tempting pastry cart. ⊠ *4 Calle 10–50, Zona 1,* ☎ *761–4241 or 761–2182,* 🖷 *763–0671. 74 rooms. Restaurant, café, pool, hot tub, bar. AE, DC, MC, V.*

$$$ 🏨 **Casa Mañen.** West of the central plaza, this romantic little B&B blends colonial comforts with modern conveniences. The rooms are spacious and homey, with handmade wall hangings and throw rugs and the occasional rocking chair. On the roof is a two-level terrace with a fantastic view of the city. Breakfast is served in a small dining room downstairs. The staff is happy to help you with travel plans. ⊠ *9 Av. 4–11, Zona 1,* ☎ *765–0786,* 🖷 *765–0678,* 🌐 *www.comeseeit.com. 9 rooms. AE, DC, MC, V.*

$$ 🏨 **Hotel Modelo.** Founded in 1892, this family-run establishment is run by a wizened man who was actually born on the premises. Over the years the distinguished hotel has maintained its tradition of good service. The wood-floor rooms, furnished with antiques, surround a few small courtyards leading off the lobby. ⊠ *14 Av. A 2–31, Zona 1,* ☎ *761–2529,* ☎🖷 *763–1376. 24 rooms. Restaurant. AE, DC, MC, V.*

$ 🏨 **Casa Kaehler.** A few blocks off the plaza, this slightly ramshackle hotel is a popular spot with travelers on a budget. Rooms on two floors of a converted residence face a small courtyard overflowing with plants. Though simple, they are clean and comfortable. There's a separate lounge where you can chat with other guests. ⊠ *13 Av. 3–33, Zona 1,* ☎ *761–2091. 7 rooms, 1 with bath. No credit cards.*

Nightlife

Aside from the lounges in the big hotels, there are only a few nightspots in Xela. Right off the central square, **Salon Tecún** (⊠ Pasaje Enrique, Zona 1) is a small pub that is popular with students. Catering to the university crowd, **El Duende** (⊠ 14 Av. between 1 Calle and 2 Calle, Zona 1) is the place to go dancing on the weekends. There's also dancing at **Cuba Disco** (⊠ Blvd. Minerva, Zona 3).

Outdoor Activities and Sports

BICYCLING

There's great mountain biking through the hills and villages surrounding Quetzaltenango. **Vrisa Bicicletas** (⊠ 15 Av. 3–64, Zona 1,

☎ 761–3237) rents both on-road and off-road bikes by the day or week and has maps so you can take self-guided tours of the countryside.

HIKING

Quetzaltrekkers (✉ Casa Argentina, 12 Diagonal 8–67, Zona 1, ☎ 761–2470, WEB beef.brownrice.com/streetschool) is a nonprofit company that supports three major social-service programs by coordinating truly unforgettable hiking trips. The three-day trek to Lago Atitlán and the two-day ascent of Volcán Tajamulco both pass through spectacular countryside and several remote villages.

Shopping

The bustling **Mercado Minerva** (✉ 6 Calle, Zona 3), next to the main bus terminal, is the best of the city's markets. There are plenty of interesting handicrafts to be found here. Artisanía from most of the villages in the region can be found in the **Mercado La Democracia** (✉ 1 Calle and 15 Av., Zona 3). Since there are relatively few shoppers, prices tend to be lower than elsewhere in the city. Near Parque Centroamérica, the **Centro Comercial Municipal** (✉ 7 Calle and 11 Av., Zona 1) has a more limited selection of souvenirs.

Quetzaltenango is famous for its beautiful glass. **Vitra** (✉ 13 Av. 5–27, ☎ 763–5091) is one of the most noted stores. You'll find excellent hand-blown glass at affordable prices.

Zunil

★ ⑪ *9 km (5½ mi) south of Quetzaltenango.*

At the base of an extinct volcano, the radiant village of Zunil is one of the prettiest in the highlands. Mud and adobe houses are clustered around the whitewashed church that marks the center of town. On the outskirts of the village you'll find the local cemetery, which is lined with tombstones painted in soft shades of pink and blue.

Zunil is surrounded by the most fertile fields in the valley, so it's no surprise most people make their living off the land. The best day to visit is Monday, when women wearing vivid purple shawls crowd the covered market hawking produce grown in their own gardens.

High in the hills above Zunil are the wonderful hot springs of **Fuentes Georginas.** There are four pools, two of which remain in their natural basins. The water ranges from tolerable to near scalding. The springs are tucked in a lush ravine in the middle of a cloud forest, so hikers should take advantage of the beautiful trails that begin here. To get here, take the first left off the main road after passing Zunil.

Lodging

$ 🏨 **Fuentes Georginas.** Although they are a bit rundown, these dozen bungalows have fireplaces that keep you cozy at night. The best part of staying here is having round-the-clock access to the hot springs, which close to the public at 5 PM. ✉ *8 km (5 mi) from main road,* ☎ *no phone. 8 bungalows. Restaurant. No credit cards.*

Huehuetenango

⑫ *94 km (58 mi) north of Quetzaltenango.*

At the foot of a mountain range called Los Cuchumatanes, Huehuetenango was once part of the powerful Mam Empire, which dominated most of the highland area. It wasn't until much later that the Guatemalan Quiché came into the area to stir things up, pushing the Mam up into the mountains.

Today Huehuetenango is a quiet town, serving mostly a gateway to the magnificent Cuchumatanes and the isolated villages scattered across them. The town surrounds **Parque Central,** where you'll find a pretty fountain and shell-shape bandstand. The butter yellow **Catedral de la Immaculada Concepción** stands guard over the main square.

The ancient city of **Zaculeu,** 4 km (2 mi) from Huehuetenango, was built around AD 600 by the Mam tribe. The site was chosen for its strategic location, as it has natural barriers on three sides. The defenses worked all too well against the Spanish. Realizing they could not take the Zaculeu people by force, the Spaniards chose instead to starve them out. Within two months they surrendered. Today the ruins consist of a few pyramids, a ball court, and a two-room museum that gives a few insights into the world of the Mam.

Dining and Lodging

$–$$ ✕ **Las Brasas.** Grilled meats are the specialty at Huehuetenango's best restaurant. Simple red-and-white tablecloths are the only nod toward decor, but because it's the sole place in town with any atmosphere, this is a fairly reassuring sight. The menu has a surprisingly broad range of options. There are even Chinese entrées, which you certainly won't find anywhere else. ⊠ *2 Calle 1–55,* ☎ *764–6200. AE, DC, MC, V.*

$ ✕ **Jardín Café.** This colorful little corner restaurant has a friendly atmosphere that makes it popular among the locals. Come early for the excellent pancakes served at breakfast, or stop by for beef and chicken dishes at lunch or dinner. The menu includes a few Mexican favorites as well. ⊠ *4 Calle and 6 Av.,* ☎ *769–0769. No credit cards.*

$ ✕ **Pizza Hogareña.** Put together your own pizza from a long list of
★   fresh ingredients at this simple little eatery. If you prefer, you can opt for spaghetti, grilled meat, or sandwiches. ⊠ *6 Av. 4–49,* ☎ *764–3072. No credit cards. Closed Mon.*

$$ ▥ **Hotel Casa Blanca.** Who would've thought that Huehuetenango would have such a top-notch hotel? Spacious rooms, excellent service, and a central location make it the town's best lodging option. Third-floor rooms have great views, especially when the bougainvillea are in full bloom. At the restaurant you can choose between a table in the shady courtyard or in the cozy dining room warmed by a fireplace. ⊠ *7 Av. 3–41,* ☎ FAX *769—0777. 15 rooms. Restaurant, cable TV, meeting rooms. MC, V.*

$$ ▥ **Hotel Zaculeu.** This hotel north of the main square has welcomed guests for more than a century. When you pass through the front doors, you enter a courtyard overflowing with greenery. The older rooms, set around a portico, are brightened by locally made fabrics. They can be a bit noisy, however, especially those facing the street. The newer ones in the back lack character. ⊠ *5 Av. 1–14,* ☎ *764–1086,* FAX *764–1575. 38 rooms. Restaurant. V.*

$ ▥ **Hotel Mary.** This four-story hotel in the heart of town offers clean, if spartan, accommodations. Ask to see a few rooms, as some are much better than others. ⊠ *2 Calle 3–52,* ☎ *764–1618,* FAX *764–7412. 27 rooms. Cable TV. No credit cards.*

Todos Santos Cuchumatán

⓭ *40 km (24 mi) north of Huehuetenango.*

Although it takes about three hours to cover the short distance from Huehuetenango to Todos Santos Cuchumatán, the bumpy ride is probably the best way to experience the tremendous height of Los Cuchumatanes. The winding dirt road can be anxiety provoking when one side of the road drops off into a deep ravine. Despite the arduous journey, Todos Santos Cuchumatán is the most frequently visited mountain village. Many people come between October 21 and November 1, when the villagers celebrate the Festival de Todos Santos. The highpoint is a horse race in which the competitors ride bareback.

Market day is Thursday. Men wear the traditional candy-cane-stripe pants and shirts with long embroidered collars. The women wear stunning red, pink, and purple huipiles with indigo skirts.

The Western Highlands A to Z

AIR TRAVEL TO AND FROM THE WESTERN HIGHLANDS

Both Quetzaltenango and Huehuetenango have small airports with service to and from Guatemala City. Taca is the only airline that flies these routes.

➤ AIRLINES AND CONTACTS: **Taca** (☎ 261–2144).

BOAT AND FERRY TRAVEL

With the exception of the service between Panajachel and Santiago Atitlán, Lago Atitlán's public ferries have been replaced by private water taxis. Although they don't follow a schedule, the private boats are much faster and cost about the same. Panajachel has two primary docks, one at the end of Calle del Embarcadero and one at the end of Calle Rancho Grande. The first is for private boats on the San Pedro route, stopping at Santa Cruz, Jaibalito, San Marcos, Santa Clara, and San Pedro. It's about 10 quetzales, no matter where you get off.

The other dock is for hour-long journeys to Santiago, with departures at 8:30, 9, 9:30, 10, 4, and 5 and returns at 6, 11:45, 12:30, 1, 2, and 5. The cost is about 10 quetzales. Private boats occasionally take passengers to Santiago in about half the time.

BUS TRAVEL TO AND FROM THE WESTERN HIGHLANDS

Transportes Rebuli travels from Guatemala City to Panajachel hourly from 5 to 4 daily. Buses bound for Guatemala City leave Panajachel hourly from 6 to 3 daily. The 6 AM and 3 PM buses are more expensive, but they're much more comfortable. Count on a four-hour trip.

To get to Chichicastenango and Santa Cruz del Quiché, take Veloz Quichelense, which departs from the capital on the half hour between 5 AM and 6 PM and returns on a similar schedule. For Quetzaltenango, take Galgos buses, which leave Guatemala City at 5:30, 8:30, 11, 12:45, 2:30, 5, 6:30, and 7. They depart from Quetzaltenango at 4, 5, 8:15, 9:45, 11:45, 2:45, and 4:45. The trip takes four hours.

To travel to Huehuetenango, you can choose from several companies for the five-hour run from Guatemala City. Los Halcones has departures at 7 and 2. Rápidos Zaculeu runs buses at 6 and 3. Transportes Velasquez also has daily departures at the same time.

Transportes Turisticos Atitrans and Turansa have buses that travel from Antigua to towns in the Western Highlands. You can also catch a public bus at the terminal, which is cheaper but much less comfortable. The one or two direct buses to Panajachel and Quetzaltenango each day, as well as five or six bound for Chichicastenango.

➤ BUS INFORMATION: **Galgos** (✉ 7 Av. 19–44, Zona 1, Guatemala City, ☎ 253–4868). **Los Halcones** (✉ 7 Av. 15–27, Zona 1, ☎ 238–1979). **Rápidos Zaculeu** (✉ 9 Calle 11–42, Zona 1, ☎ 232–2858). **Transportes Rebuli** (✉ 21 Calle 1–34, Zona 1, Guatemala City, ☎ 251–3521). **Transportes Velasquez** (✉ 20 Calle 1–37, Zona 1, ☎ 221–1084). **Veloz Quichelense** (✉ Terminal de Buses, Zona 4, Guatemala City, ☎ no phone).

CAR RENTAL

There is only one national car-rental agency in the Western Highlands, Tabarini Rent-A-Car. If you are considering renting a car, a good option is to do so in Guatemala City.

➤ LOCAL AGENCIES: **Tabarini Rent-A-Car** (✉ 9 Calle 9–21, Zona 1, Quetzaltenango, ☎ 763–0418; ✉ Hotel Los Cuchumatanes, Sector Brasil Zona 7, Huehuetenango, ☎ 764–1951).

CAR TRAVEL

The Pan-American Highway—more country road than highway, really—heads northwest out of Guatemala City, where it is called the Calzada Roosevelt. It passes through Chimaltenango before reaching a crossroads called Los Encuentros. Here you can head north to Chichicastenàngo, Santa Cruz del Quiché, and Nebaj. Continue on the Pan-American Highway, and you'll pass a turnoff to Panajachel and then another for San Marcos La Laguna and other towns on Lago Atitlán. The Pan-American Highway continues over some impressive ridges and then descends to a crossroads called Cuatro Caminos, about 200 km (124 mi) from the capital. Here the road to Quetzaltenango heads off to the south. About 60 km (37 mi) north of Cuatro Caminos, the road to Huehuetenango cuts off to the right. Many roads to the north of Huehuetenango and Santa Cruz del Quiché are unpaved and pretty rough—this is nerve-racking mountain driving relieved intermittently by memorable views.

EMERGENCIES

In Panajachel, Panamedic Centro Clínico Familiar offers 24-hour medical attention. The doctors, Francisco Ordoñez and his wife, Zulma Ordoñez, both speak English.

➤ EMERGENCY SERVICES: **Ambulance** (☎ 762–4121 in Panajachel; 761–2956 in Quetzaltenango). **Police** (☎ 762–1120).

➤ HOSPITALS: **Panamedic Centro Clínico Familiar** (✉ Calle Principal 0–72, Panajachel, ☎ 762–2174).

➤ PHARMACIES: **Farmacia Nueva Unión** (✉ Calle Santander near Calle Principal, Panajachel). **Farmacia Nueva** (✉ 6 Calle and 10 Av., Zona 1, Quetzaltenango, ☎ 762–4531).

INTERNET

MayaNet is the best Internet café in Panajachel. It is open daily until 9 PM and charges about 20 quetzales per hour.

➤ INTERNET CAFÉS: **MayaNet** (✉ Calle Santander, Panajachel).

MAIL AND SHIPPING

All the villages in the Western Highlands have post offices, but you are probably better off posting your letters from the larger towns. If you are sending something valuable, go with DHL or one of the local companies that will ship packages. Alternativas is in Quetzaltenango, while Get Guated Out is in Panajachel.

➤ OVERNIGHT SERVICES: **Alternativas** (✉ 16 Av. 3–35, Zona 3, Quetzaltenango).**Get Guated Out** (✉ Comercial Pueblito, upstairs, Panajachel). **DHL** (✉ Calle Santander, Panajachel, ☎ 762–1474).

➤ POST OFFICES: **Chichicastenango** (✉ 7 Av. 8–47). **Panajachel** (✉ Calle Santander and Calle 5 de Febrero). **Quetzaltenango** (✉ 15 Av. and 4 Calle, Zona 1).

MONEY MATTERS

All the larger towns in the Western Highlands have ATMs where you can use your bank card. Bancared has branches in Panajachel, Chichicastenango, Quetzaltenango, and Huehuetenango.

➤ BANKS: **Bancared** (✉ 5 Av. and 6 Calle, Chichicastenango; 4 Calle

6–81, Zona 1, Huehuetenango; Calle Principal 0–78, Zona 2, Panajachel; 4 Av. 17–40, Zona 3, Quetzaltenango).

SAFETY

Several groups of travelers have been robbed while hiking around the
Lago Atitlán area. It is always a good idea to hire a guide, especially
when you are not familiar with your destination.

TOURS OPERATORS

In Panajachel, Atitrans and Centroamericana Tourist Service are both
reputable companies. Chichicastenango's only tour company, Chichi
Turkaj–Tours, is well-regarded. In Quetzaltenango, Quetzaltrekkers support social service programs in the area. Union Travel in Quetzaltenango also offers tours to just about everywhere in the region.
➤ TOUR COMPANIES: **Atitrans** (⊠ 3 Av. 1–30, Zona 2, Panajachel, ☎ 762–
2336). **Centroamericana Tourist Service** (⊠ 3 Av. 4–70, Zona 2, Panajachel, ☎ 762–2496). **Chichi Turkaj–Tours** (⊠ 5 Calle 4–42, Zona 1,
Chichicastenango, ☎ 756–2111). Quetzaltrekkers (⊠ Casa Argentina,
Diagonal 12 8–67, Zona 1, Quetzaltenango, ☎ 761–2470). **Union
Travel** (⊠ In Los Pinos Av. Santander, Zona 2, Panajachel, ☎ 762–2426).

VISITOR INFORMATION

The Guatemala tourism agency Inguat has offices in Panajachel, Quetzaltenango, and San Miguel Totonicapán. The staff at the office in Panajachel is particularly helpful.
➤ TOURIST INFORMATION: **Inguat** (⊠ Calle Santander, Panajachel, ☎
762–1392; ⊠ Parque Centro América, Quetzaltenango, ☎ 761–4931;
⊠ Casa de Cultura, 8 Av. 2–17, next to Hospedaje San Miguel, Zona
1, San Miguel Totonicapán, ☎ 766–1575).

TIKAL AND THE MAYA RUINS

The jungles of El Petén were once the heartland of the Maya civilization. The sprawling empire—including parts of present-day Mexico,
Belize, Honduras, and El Salvador—was once made up of a network
of cities that held hundreds of thousands of people, but a millennium
ago this fascinating civilization vanished without a trace. The temples
that dominated the horizon were swallowed up by the jungle.

The first major Maya society dates to 2000 BC, based largely on the
traditions of the Olmecs, a people living in what is now Mexico. Over
the next 2,000 years the Maya proved to be an intellectually curious
people. They developed a type of writing (one of the earliest) and a sophisticated system of mathematics (the first to use a zero). The Maya
were particularly adept astronomers, mapping the orbits of the sun,
moon, and planets with incredible accuracy—the Maya lunar cycle differs from today's calculations by only seven minutes.

From about 250 BC to AD 900 the Maya developed complex social systems, agricultural practices, and religious beliefs, reaching their zenith
with the construction of temples like Tikal. Around AD 1000, the
Maya suffered repeated attacks from rival civilizations, followed by a
sudden and mysterious period of decline. The arrival of conquistadors
like Hernán Cortés and Pedro de Alvarado in the early 1500s marked
the beginning of the subjugation of what was left of the Maya people.

Today El Petén is a sparsely populated backwater where ancient ruins
just seem to crop up from the landscape. Nature reigns supreme, with
vines and other plants quickly covering everything that stands still a
little too long. Whatever your primary interest—archeology, history,
birding, biking—you'll find plenty to do and see in this remote region.

Tikal and the Maya Ruins

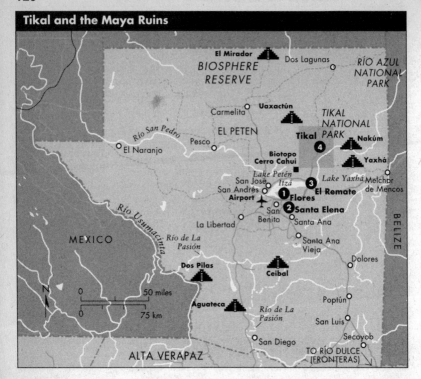

Numbers in the text correspond to numbers in the margin and on the Tikal and the Maya Ruins map.

Flores

★ **①** *206 km (133 mi) north of Río Dulce, 61 km (38 mi) northeast of Sayaxché.*

The red-roof town of Flores, on an island surrounded by the waters of Lago Petén Itzá, is on the site of the ancient city of Tatyasal. This was the region's last unconquered outpost of Maya civilization, until finally falling to the Spanish in 1697. The conquerors destroyed the city's huge pyramids.

Today the provincial capital is a pleasant place to explore, with its narrow streets lined with thick-walled buildings painted pink, blue, and purple. Flowering plants droop over balconies, giving the town a tropical flavor. There's a central square presided over by a colonial church. Connected to the mainland by a bridge, the city serves as a base for travelers to El Petén.

Dining and Lodging

$–$$ ✕ **Floating Restaurant Don Quijote.** Set on a small boat that is permanently docked on the town's southern shore, Don Quijote is a great place to watch the sunset. The curiously charming owner, Eduardo Frutos, serves up a tasty paella made from a recipe from Valencia. He's proud to announce that travelers have come all the way from Japan bearing pictures of his most famous dish, which appears in a guidebook. ⊠ *2 blocks west of bridge,* ☎ *712–6514. MC, V.*

$–$$ ✕ **La Luna.** With its homemade paper lamp shades illuminating the lovely blue walls, La Luna inspires romance on any moonlit night. You can just as easily fall in love with the place when you stop in for a delicious lunch. Choose from inventive dishes, including wonderful vegetarian options like the stuffed squash in white sauce. Many people drop by for a drink at the bar. ⊠ *Calle 30 de Junio,* ☎ *926–3346. AE, DC, MC, V. Closed Mon.*

$–$$ ✕ **Las Puertas.** On a quiet side street, Las Puertas was named for its
★ six screened doors. It's a favorite hangout for locals and travelers alike. The friendly couple who run the place take great pride in serving only the freshest foods. They are famous for their delicious sandwiches made with homemade bread and mozzarella cheese and their giant goblets of incredible iced coffee. In the afternoon you can relax with a fruit drink as you play one of the many board games. ⊠ *Calle Central at Av. Santa Ana,* ☎ *926–1061. AE, DC, MC, V. Closed Sun.*

$–$$ ✕ **El Tucán.** Toucans and parrots, part of the menagerie belonging the owner, share the breezy terrace with diners at this pleasant eatery. The small dining room, decorated with highland weavings, also has good views of one of Flores's cobblestone streets. The menu includes a variety of traditional meals, though Mexican cuisine is the specialty here. ⊠ *Av. 15 de Septiembre and Calle Centroamérica,* ☎ *926–0536. AE, DC, MC V.*

$ ✕ **Pizzeria Picasso.** If you find yourself returning to Pizzeria Picasso, it's because the pizza that is baked in a huge brick oven comes out incomparably hot and delicious. The decor, featuring a print of Picasso's *Guernica,* is another draw. If you're not in the mood for pizza, there is a variety of pastas as well. Save room for cheesecake or tiramisu and a cup of steaming cappuccino. ⊠ *Calle Centroamérica,* ☎ *926–0673. AE, DC, MC, V.*

$$$–$$$$ ✕⊡ **Ni'tun Ecolodge.** After hiking through the jungle, you'll love re-
★ turning to this charming cluster of cabins. The point is to disturb the environment as little as possible, so the buildings are constructed of stone and wood left behind by farmers clearing land for fields. The common areas, including an airy bar and reading room upstairs, make it difficult not to sit inside and watch the hummingbirds dance around the gardens. The owners also run Monkey Eco Tours, so you can choose from itineraries ranging from one-day trips to nearby villages to seven-day journeys to El Mirador, the Maya site with the highest temples. ⊠ *2 km (1 mi) west of San Andres,* ☎ *201–0759,* FAX *926–0807; 978/945–6486 in the U.S.,* WEB *www.nitun.com. 4 cabins. Restaurant, travel services. MC, V.*

$$ ✕⊡ **Hotel Sabana.** On the northern tip of Flores, this small hotel offers simple rooms that open onto a terrace overlooking the pool. A sundeck has nice views of the lake. This is a good choice if you want a few creature comforts like air-conditioning and television. ⊠ *Calle Union and Av. Libertad,* ☎ FAX *926–3323,* WEB *www.sabanahotel.com. 28 rooms. Restaurant, cable TV, pool, bar. AE, DC, MC, V.*

$$ ✕⊡ **Hotel Santana.** Sitting right on the water, this bright pink hotel is the best lodging on the island. All the rooms open up onto wide balconies with wicker chairs where you can enjoy the view. The sunny central courtyard surrounds a pleasant pool. ⊠ *Calle 30 de Junio,* ☎ FAX *926–0662,* WEB *www.santanapeten.com. 32 rooms. Restaurant, a/c, in-room safes, pool. AE, DC, MC, V.*

$ ✕⊡ **Posada Doña Goya.** A rooftop terrace with hammocks swinging in the breeze is the best part of staying at this budget lodging. If you prefer, grab a good book and sink into one of the comfortable lounge chairs. The hotel is clean and well run, which explains why it is so popular. Come early in the day to secure a room. Stop by for the famous breakfast from 6 to 10. ⊠ *Calle Union,* ☎ *926–3538. 6 rooms, 3 with bath. Restaurant, fans. No credit cards.*

$$ ☷ **Hotel Petén.** An arabesque plunge pool graces the central courtyard of this lovely lodging. Taking a dip to escape the midday heat is a treat not to be missed. The rooms are simply furnished. Ask for one facing the lake, as the views are incredible. ⊠ *Off Calle 30 de Junio,* ☎ 926–0593. *21 rooms. Restaurant, a/c, pool, travel agency, Internet. AE, DC, MC, V.*

Nightlife

Discoteca Raices (Av. Periferico) is the island's only true disco. The bar at the **Mayan Princess** (⊠ Av. La Reforma and Av. 14 de Noviembre) shows nightly movies on a big-screen TV.

Las Puertas (⊠ Calle Central at Av. Santa Ana, ☎ 926–1061) has live music every night. The artsy **La Luna** (⊠ Calle 30 de Junio, ☎ 926–3346) has a pleasant atmosphere.

Santa Elena

❷ *½ km (¼ mi) south of Flores.*

Although it lacks the charms of neighboring Flores, gritty Santa Elena is pretty much unavoidable. Most services that you'll need for your trip to El Petén, from currency exchange to travel planning, are usually offered here. There are also nicer hotels here than in Flores.

Dining and Lodging

$$$$ ✕☷ **Petén Espléndido.** You're not on Flores, but the views of that pretty island from your private balcony are the next best thing. Every possible amenity is available at this lakeside hotel, from cable TV to Internet access. The pool, surrounded by palm trees, is a great place to spend an afternoon sunbathing. Sit at one of the shaded tables on the terrace or in the pretty dining room and enjoy the *especial del día* (daily special). Families enjoy the paddleboats on the lake. ⊠ *At foot of bridge leading to Flores,* ☎ 926–0880, ℻ 926–0866, ℠ *www.petenesplendido. com. 62 rooms. Restaurant, cable TV, pool, convention center, airport shuttle. AE, DC, MC, V.*

$$$$ ✕☷ **Villa Maya.** You could lie in bed and count the birds flying by your
★ window at these modern villas on beautiful Lago Petén Itzá. Some 50 species have been spotted in the region. If you're more interested in mammals, ask an attendant where to find the troop of spider monkeys that roams the grounds and the adjacent rain forest. Explore the jungle by following one of the nature trails or see more of the lake by renting a rowboat. All the rooms, tastefully decorated with colorful weavings and mahogany accents, have terrific views. ⊠ *12 km (7 mi) east of Santa Elena,* ☎ 926–0086; 334–8136 in Guatemala City, ℻ 334–8134 in Guatemala City, ℠ *www.villasdeguatemala.com. 36 rooms. Restaurant, pool, horseback riding, boating, travel services. AE, DC, MC, V.*

$$$ ✕☷ **Maya International.** This string of thatch bungalows built over Lago Petén Itzá has lost a bit of its former grandeur. The simple accommodations are surrounded by water lilies, which were sacred to the Maya. From the private balconies you can watch waterfowl forage for their dinner. For your own meals there's the moderately priced restaurant, housed in a round building set out over the water. The set menu changes daily. ⊠ *3 blocks east of bridge to Flores,* ☎ 334–8136, ℻ 334–8134. *20 bungalows. Restaurant. AE, DC, MC, V.*

$$ ✕☷ **Casa Elena Hotel.** An attractive lobby paneled with lots of dark wood welcomes you to this centrally located hotel. Just beyond the entrance is a pretty restaurant that lets the breeze in through lace curtains. There's a wide range of dinner options, from fresh fish to grilled steak. The rooms lack the charm of others in the area, but they are clean and comfortable. There are no balconies—for a view, head to the meeting room on the top floor. The pool has a small waterslide that kids love. ⊠ *6 Av.,* ☎ *926–2239,* FAX *926–0097. 28 rooms. Restaurant, pool, meeting room. AE, DC, MC, V.*

$$$ ⊞ **Hotel del Patio-Tikal.** Built in traditional Spanish style, this modern hotel is known by its barrel-tile roof. Rooms face a small patio with a trickling fountain. All have nice touches like writing desks and ceiling fans. Ask for a room on the first floor, as these have much larger windows. The patio restaurant sits under big arches leading to a grassy courtyard, making it a much more pleasant place to relax than the musty bar. ⊠ *2 Calle and 8 Av., Santa Elena,* ☎ *926–0104,* FAX *926–3030. 21 rooms. Restaurant, pool, gym. AE, DC, MC, V.*

Outdoor Activities and Sports

There are several caves in the hills behind Santa Elena with interesting stalactite and stalagmite formations and subterranean rivers. The easiest to visit is Aktun Kan, just south of town. The bilingual guides of the **Tourist Guide Association of Santa Elena** (⊠ Hotel Tayasal, St. Elena and San Benito, ☎ 926–3133) can take you to Aktun Kan and other sites.

El Remate

❸   *30 km (18½ mi) northeast of Flores.*

A mellow little town on the eastern shore of Lago Petén Itzá, El Remate is known mostly for its wood carvings by families that have dedicated themselves to this craft for generations. Because it's less than one hour from both Tikal and Yaxhá, El Remate makes a good base for exploring the area.

With more than 1,500 acres of rain forest, **Biotopo Cerro Cahuí** (⊠ west of El Remate, ☎ Q20) is one of the most accessible wildlife reserves in El Petén. It protects a portion of a mountain that extends to the eastern edge of Lago Petén Itzá, so there are plenty of opportunities for hiking. Two well-maintained trails put you in proximity of birds like oscillated turkeys, toucans, and parrots. As for mammals, look up to spot the long-armed spider monkeys or down to see squat rodents called *tepezcuintles.* Tzu'unte, a 6-km (4-mi) trail, leads to two lookouts with views of nearby lakes. Both begin at a ranger station, where English-speaking guides are sporadically available.

Dining and Lodging

$$ ✕ **La Estancia Cafetería.** Locals keep this one a secret because the low-key La Estancia Cafetería serves up incredibly flavorful fare. Owner Victor Morales's specialty is an exquisite whitefish served with vegetables sautéed in butter on a wooden platter. Every once in a while he cooks up some fresh venison. Even though the driveway is usually filled with cars, this eatery is easy to miss. Look for the Orange Crush sign. ⊠ *2 km (1¼ mi) south of El Remate,* ☎ *no phone. No credit cards.*

$$$$ ✕⊞ **Camino Real Tikal.** To experience the natural beauty of the jun-
★   gles surrounding Lago Petén Itzá without sacrificing creature comforts, many people head to Camino Real Tikal. It's possible to spend several days at the hotel without exhausting the possibilities—kayaking on the lake, hiking in a private reserve, swimming in the beautiful pool, lounging in the lakeside hammocks, and experiencing a traditional Maya sauna. A dozen thatch-roof villas set high on the hillside hold the rooms. A fine terrace restaurant serves international dishes as well as local specialties. Particularly tasty is the sea bass, cooked in a plantain leaf and covered with a delicate tomato-based sauce. ⊠ *5 km (3 mi) west of El Remate,* ☎ *926–0204; 800/228–3000 in the U.S.,* FAX *926–0222. 72 rooms. Restaurant, bar, coffee shop, pool, boating, shop, gym, travel services, airport shuttle, car rental. AE, DC, MC, V.*

\$\$ ✕⌸ **La Mansión del Pajaro Serpiente.** Perched high on the hillside, La Mansión del Pajaro Serpiente has what are perhaps the prettiest accommodations in El Petén. Canopy beds add a festive touch to the bedrooms, each of which adjoins a sitting room. Finished in dark tropical woods, all have big windows that let in lots of light. You can throw open the windows to catch the lake breezes, so sleeping is comfortable. Up a nearby hill is a swimming pool and a covered terrace with several hammocks. The open-air restaurant serves local and international dishes. ✉ *On main highway south of El Remate,* ☎ FAX *926–4246. 10 rooms. Restaurant, pool, travel services. No credit cards.*

\$ ✕⌸ **La Casa de Don David.** As you chat with David Kuhn, the owner of this cluster of bungalows, keep an eye out for his pet parrot. The little fellow sometimes gets jealous. But talking with Kuhn is worth it, as he and his wife, Rosa, have lived in the area for more than 25 years and are a great source of travel tips. Rooms are simple and clean, with private baths. Hammocks are everywhere, including the covered terrace that overlooks the tropical fruit orchard. Perhaps La Casa is most famous for its second-story restaurant, which has good home cooking. Have dinner for two in a booth, or eat at the "friendship table" and make some new acquaintances. ✉ *On road to Biotopo Cerro Cahuí,* ☎ *306–2190.* WEB *www.lacasadedondavid.com. 15 rooms. Restaurant. No credit cards.*

Outdoor Activities and Sports

The fun folks at **Tikal Canopy Tour** (✉ Near entrance to Tikal, ☎ 708–0674) have expeditions that take you to the true heart of the rainforest—not on ground level, but more than 100 ft up in the air. In the canopy you'll see monkeys and maybe even a sloth. The tour ends with an exhilarating 300-ft-long ride down a zip line.

Tikal

★ ❹ *35 km (22 mi) north of El Remate.*

You rise shortly before dawn, instinctively aware that creatures out there in the darkness are doing the same. It isn't long before you hear the muffled roars of howler monkeys in the distance. After a quick cup of coffee you and your fellow adventurers follow your guide through the deserted plazas toward the pyramid that towers over everything else. The climb up the side is difficult in the dark, but after scrambling up rickety ladders and over roots and vines you find yourself at the top. You glance to the east, past the endless expanse of jungle, just as the sun starts to rise.

The high point of any trip to Guatemala is a visit to Central America's most impressive ruins. Tikal is one of the most popular tourist attractions in Central America—and with good reason. Smack in the middle of the 575-square-km (222-square-mi) Parque Nacional Tikal, the towering temples are ringed on all sides by miles of virgin forest. The area around the ruins is great for checking out creatures that spend their entire lives hundreds of feet above the forest floor in the dense canopy of trees. Colorful birds like yellow toucans and scarlet macaws are common sights.

Although the region was home to Maya communities as early as 600 BC, Tikal itself wasn't established until sometime around 200 BC. One of the first structures to be built here was a version of the North Acropolis. Others were added at a dizzying pace for the next three centuries. By AD 100 impressive structures like the Great Plaza had already been built. But even though it was a powerful city in its own right, Tikal was still ruled by the northern city of El Mirador. It wasn't until the arrival of a powerful dynasty around AD 300 that Tikal arrogated itself to full power. King Great Jaguar Paw sired a lineage that would build Tikal into a city rivaling any of its time.

By the 6th century Tikal governed a large part of the Maya world, thanks to a leader called Caan Chac (Stormy Sky), who took the throne around AD 426. Under Caan Chac, Tikal became an aggressive military and commercial center that dominated the surrounding communities with a power never before seen in Mesoamerica. The swamps protected the city from attack and allowed troops to spot any approaching enemy. Intensive agriculture in the *bajos* (lowlands) provided food for the huge population. A valuable obsidian trade sprang up, aided by the city's strategic position near two rivers.

Tikal thrived for more than a millennium, forming strong ties with two powerful centers: Kaminal Juyu, in the Guatemalan highlands, and Teotihuacán, in Mexico City. The city entered a golden age when Ah-Cacao (Lord Chocolate) acscended the throne in AD 682. It was Ah-Cacao and his successors who commissioned the construction of most of the city's most important temples. Continuing the tradition of great structures, Ah-Cacao's son commissioned Temple I, which he dedicated to his father, who is buried beneath it. He also ordered the construction of Temple IV, the tallest temple at Tikal. By the time of his death in 768, Tikal was at the peak of its power. It would remain so until its mysterious abandonment around 900.

For almost 1,000 years Tikal remained engulfed by the jungle. The native Peténeros certainly knew of the ancient city's existence, but no one else ventured near until 1848, when the Guatemalan government dispatched archaeologists to the region. Tikal started to receive international attention in 1877, when Swiss researcher Gustav Bernoulli commissioned locals to remove the carved wooden lintels from across the doorways of Temples I and IV. In 1881 and 1882 English archaeologist Alfred Percival Maudslay made the first map showing the architectural features of this vast city. In 1951 the Guatemalan air force cleared an airstrip near the ruins to improve access for large-scale archaeological work. Today, after more than 150 years of digging, researchers say that Tikal includes some 3,000 buildings. Countless more are still covered by the jungle. ⊠ *Parque Nacional Tikal,* ☎ *no phone.* ▢ *Q50.* ☉ *Daily 6–6.*

The Tikal Ruins

As you enter the Tikal, keep to the middle trail. You'll soon arrive at the ancient city's center, filled with awe-inspiring temples and intricate acropolises. The pyramid that you approach from behind is **Temple I,** known as the Temple of the Great Jaguar because of the feline represented on one of its carved lintels. It's in what is referred to as the **Great Plaza,** one of the most beautiful and dramatic in Tikal. The Great Plaza was built around AD 700 by Ah-Cacao, one of the wealthiest rulers of his time. His tomb, comparable in magnitude to that of Pa Cal at the ruins of Palenque in southern Mexico, was discovered beneath the Temple of the Great Jaguar in the 1960s. The theory is that his queen is buried beneath **Temple II,** called the Temple of the Masks for the decorations on its facade. It's a twin of the Temple of the Great Jaguar. In fact, construction of matching pyramids distinguishes Tikal from other Maya sites.

The **North Acropolis,** to the west of Ah-Cacao's temple, is a mind-boggling conglomeration of temples built over layers and layers of previous construction. Excavations have revealed that the base of this structure is more than 2,000 years old. Be sure to see the stone mask of the rain god at Temple 33. The **Central Acropolis,** south of the Great Plaza, is an immense series of structures assumed to have served as administrative centers.

If you climb to the top of one of the pyramids, you'll see the gray roof combs of others rising above the rain forests canopy but still trapped within it. **Temple V,** to the south, is waiting to be restored to some semblance of its former grandeur. In 2001 about $3 million was allocated for its reconstruction. **Temple IV,** to the west, is the tallest-known structure built by the Maya. Although the climb to the top is difficult, the view is unforgettable.

To the southwest of the plaza lies the **South Acropolis,** which hasn't been reconstructed, and a 105-ft-high pyramid, similar in construction to those at Teotihuacán. A few jungle trails, including the marked Interpretative Benil-ha Trail, offer a chance to see spider monkeys and other wildlife. Outside the park, a somewhat overgrown trail halfway down the old airplane runway on the left leads to the remnants of old rubber-tappers' camps and is a good spot for bird-watching.

At park headquarters you'll find two archaeological museums that display Mayan artifacts. They are a good resource for information on the enigmatic rise and fall of the Maya people.

Other Nearby Sites

Although Tikal is the most famous, El Petén has hundreds of archaeological sites, ranging from modest burial chambers to sprawling cities. The vast majority have not been explored, let alone restored. Within a few miles of Tikal are several sites that are relatively easy to reach. Because they are in isolated areas, it's a good idea to go with a guide.

Nakúm lies deep within the forest, connected to Tikal via jungle trails used for horseback expeditions. You cannot visit during the rainy season, as you'll sink into mud up to your ankles. Two building complexes and some stelae are visible. ✉ *26 km (16 mi) east of Tikal.*

The 4,000-year-old city of **Uaxactún** was once a rival to Tikal's supremacy in the region. It was conquered by Tikal in the 4th century and lived in the shadow of that great city for centuries. Inscriptions show that Uaxactún existed longer than any other Mayan city, which may account for the wide variety of structures. Here you'll find, if you can imagine, a Maya observatory. You'll need to secure a free permit to visit Uaxactún from the administration building near Tikal. ✉ *24 km (16 mi) north of Tikal.*

Overlooking a beautiful lake of the same name, the ruins of **Yaxhá** are divided into two sections of rectangular structures that form plazas and streets. The city was probably inhabited between the Preclassic and Postclassic periods. The ruins are currently being restored by a German organization. Lago Yaxhá, surrounded by virgin rain forest, is a good bird-watching spot. During the rainy season only a four-wheel-drive vehicle—or setting out on horseback or on foot—will get you to Yaxhá; the rest of the year the road is passable. ✉ *10 km (6 mi) east of Tikal.*

A popular ecotourism destination, **El Zotz** is where you'll find the remnants of a Maya city. On a clear day you can see the tallest of the ruins at Tikal from these unexcavated ruins. The odd name, which means "the bat" in Q'eqchí, refers to a cave from which thousands of bats make a nightly exodus. Troops of hyperactive spider monkeys seem to have claimed this place for themselves, swinging through the treetops and scrambling after each other like children playing a game of tag. ✉ *24 km (15 mi) west of Tikal.*

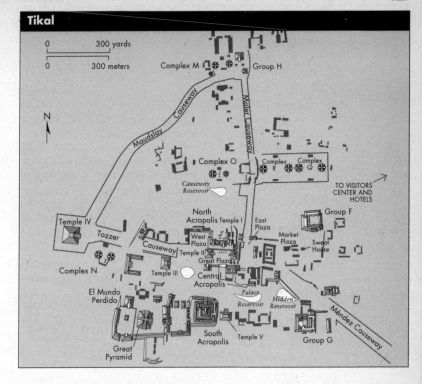

Dining and Lodging

$$ **✕⊞ Tikal Inn.** This cluster of comfortable bungalows wraps around
★ a well-manicured garden and a pool. It's set apart from the other lodg-
ings, affording a bit of privacy. The rooms have a modern feel, yet they
have thatch roofs and stucco walls decorated with traditional fabrics.
A small restaurant has a menu that changes daily. Rates include break-
fast and dinner. ⊠ *Parque Nacional Tikal,* ☎ *926–1917,* ☎ ⨳ *926–
0065. 22 rooms. Restaurant, pool. No credit cards.*

$$$ **⊞ El Campamento del Sombrero.** This cluster of wooden cabins is a
restful place to spend the night. There's no electricity in the rooms, but
they each have two double beds and a private bath. The restaurant serves
three meals a day. ⊠ *Yaxká,* ☎ *926–5229,* ⨳ *926–5198. 9 rooms.
Restaurant. No credit cards.*

$$$ **⊞ Jungle Lodge.** Built to house archaeologists working at Tikal, this
hotel has cute duplexes. There's a lack of privacy, as the dividing wall
between the rooms does not meet the ceiling. The rooms are clean, but
the furnishings are dated. ⊠ *Parque Nacional Tikal,* ☎ *477–0570,* ⨳
476–0294. 46 rooms, 34 with bath. Restaurant, pool. V.

Tikal and the Maya Ruins A to Z

AIR TRAVEL TO AND FROM EL PETÉN

Grupo Taca, Racsa, and Tikal Jets operate flights from Guatemala City
to Santa Elena that take less than an hour and cost about $60 each
way. Several daily flights leave the capital around 7 AM and return around
4 PM. Air service between Santa Elena and the Mexican resort of Can-
cún is offered by Aviateca and Aerocaribe. Aerocaribe also offers
flights to the ruins of Pelenque.

Aeropuerto Internacional Santa Elena is less than 1 km (½ mi) outside
town. Taxis and shuttles meet every plane and charge about 20 quet-

zales to take you into town. Plans to build a new runway are on the drawing boards. This would allow direct international flights from the United States to land in Santa Elena.

➤ AIRLINES AND CONTACTS: **Aerocaribe** (☎ 926–0923). **Grupo Taca** (☎ 926–1238). **Racsa** (☎ 926–1477). **Tikal Jets** (☎ 926–0386 or 332–5070).

BUS TRAVEL TO AND FROM EL PETÉN

Linea Dorada offers direct bus service between Guatemala City and Santa Elena and Flores. The 10-hour trip on air-conditioned buses with comfortable reclining seats, TVs, and bathrooms costs $30–$50 round-trip. Call at least one day ahead for reservations. Inexpensive local service is available, but these buses stop in every village along the way, which adds hours to the trip.

➤ BUS INFORMATION: **Linea Dorada** (✉ Calle Principal, Santa Elena; ✉ Calle de la Playa, Flores, ☎ 926–0528 in Santa Elena, 232–9658 in Guatemala City).

BUS TRAVEL WITHIN EL PETÉN

In Santa Elena the San Juan Hotel serves as the local bus terminal. Here you can catch a bus operated by San Juan Travel that makes the two-hour trip to Tikal at 6, 8, 10 AM and return trips at 2, 4 and 5 PM. Local buses serving other destinations like Sayaxché depart from the market in Santa Elena. They are inexpensive but very slow.

➤ BUS INFORMATION: **San Juan Travel** (✉ San Juan Hotel, Santa Elena, ☎ 926–0041).

CAR RENTAL

If you're not booked on a tour, the best way to get around El Petén is by renting a four-wheel-drive vehicle. The major rental agencies, including Budget and Hertz, have offices at Aeropuerto Internacional Santa Elena. Koka, a local company, rents four-wheel-drive vehicles from an office in the Camino Real Tikal near El Remate. San Juan Travel, at the San Juan Hotel in Santa Elena, rents four-wheel-drive vehicles and passenger vans.

➤ LOCAL AGENCIES: **Budget** (✉ Aeropuerto Internacional Santa Elena, ☎ 950–0741). **Koka** (✉ Camino Real Tikal, El Remate, ☎ 926–1233). **Hertz** (✉ Aeropuerto Internacional Santa Elena, ☎ 950–0204). **San Juan Travel** (✉ San Juan Hotel, Santa Elena, ☎ 926–2013).

CAR TRAVEL

Roads in El Petén are often in poor repair and not very well marked. Some are impassable during the rainy season, so check with the tourist office before heading out to the ruins surrounding Tikal. A four-wheel-drive vehicle is highly recommended.

EMERGENCIES

Medical facilities in El Petén are not as modern as in the rest of the country. If you're really sick, consider getting on the next plane back to Guatemala City.

➤ EMERGENCY SERVICES: **Police** (☎ 926–1365).

➤ HOSPITALS: **Hospital del Instituto Guatemalteco de Seguridad Social** (✉ Santa Elena, ☎ 926–0619).

➤ PHARMACIES: **Farmacia Nueva** (✉ Av. Santa Ana, Flores, ☎ 926–1387). **Farmacia San Carlos** (✉ 4 Calle 1–92, Zona 1, Santa Elena, ☎ 926–0753).

MAIL AND SHIPPING

The main post office in Flores is a half block east of the main square. In Santa Elena the post office is a block east of the bridge leading to

Flores. Mail service is slow, so expect to get back home before your letter does.

➤ POST OFFICES: **Flores** (✉ Calle 10 de Noviembre, Flores). **Santa Elena** (✉ 2 Calle and 7 Av., Flores).

MONEY MATTERS

There are several banks in Santa Elena, but nowhere else in the region. Make sure to exchange your money before heading off on your jungle adventure. Some high-end hotels will exchange dollars for a small commission.

➤ BANKS: **Banco Industrial** (✉ Calle Principal, Santa Elena, ☎ 926–0281).

TOURS OPERATORS

Flores-based Martsam Travel, run by Lileana and Benedicto Grijalva, offers many different types of tours in the area. The El Petén environmental group ProPetén offers adventure trips led by rubber-tappers who once worked at plantations in the forest.

Guatemala City-based Adventuras Naturales and Flores-based Expedition Panamundo specialize in tours of the Maya world and bird-watching expeditions. Guatemala City–based Maya Expeditions has trips down Sayaxché area rivers and the nearby archaeological sites. From Antigua, Inter Quetzal, Sin Fronteras, and Vision Travel all offer tours of El Petén.

➤ TOUR COMPANIES: **Adventuras Naturales** (✉ 9 Calle 18–17, Zona 14, Guatemala City, ☎ FAX 333–6051). **Expedition Panamundo** (✉ Av. Reforma, Flores, ☎ 926–0501). **Inter Quetzal** (✉ 7 Av. 1–20, Zona 4, Guatemala City, ☎ 331–9282). **Martsam Travel** (✉ Calle Centroamérica and Av. 30 de Junio, Flores, ☎ 926–0346, ☎ FAX 926–3225). **Maya Expeditions** (✉ 15 Calle 1–91, Zona 10, Guatemala City, ☎ 363–4955). **Sin Fronteras** (✉ 3 Calle Poniente, Antigua, ☎ 832–1226). **Vision Travel** (✉ 3 Av. Norte 3, Antigua, ☎ 832–3293, WEB www.guatemalainfo.com).

VISITOR INFORMATION

Arcas, which returns illegally captured animals to the wild, is a great resource on the flora and fauna of El Petén. Inguat has two offices in El Petén, one in Flores and one at Aeropuerto Internacional Santa Elena.

➤ TOURIST INFORMATION: **Arcas** (✉ 10 km [6 mi] east of Santa Elena, ☎ 591–4731). **Inguat** (✉ On Parque Central, Flores, ☎ 926–0669; ✉ Aeropuerto Internacional Santa Elena, ☎ 926–0533 at the airport).

GUATEMALA A TO Z

AIR TRAVEL TO AND FROM GUATEMALA

Guatemala has two international airports: Aeropuerto Internacional La Aurora, at the edge of Guatemala City, and the smaller Aeropuerto Internacional Santa Elena, in El Petén.

Domestic carriers fly between Guatemala City and Santa Elena, Puerto Barrios and Río Dulce on the Atlantic coast, and Quetzaltenango and Huehuetenango in the highlands.

BUS TRAVEL TO AND FROM GUATEMALA

There is bus service from Guatemala City to cities on the Mexican and Honduran borders, as well as to destinations in Belize and El Salvador. To La Mesilla, on the Mexican border, El Condor departs at 4, 8, 10, 1, and 5 for the seven-hour trip. To Tecún Umán, on the Mexican border, Fortaleza has hourly departures from 1 AM to 6 PM; the journey takes five hours. For service to El Carmen/Talismán, also on the Mexican border, contact Galgos. Departures are at 5:30, 10, 1:30, and 5. Maya Mundo runs buses to Quintana Roo, Mexico.

Melva International has service to San Salvador. Eight buses a day depart between 4 AM and 6 PM for the five-hour journey. For service to Esquipulas, on the border of Honduras, try Rutas Orientales. Buses run almost hourly from 5 AM to 6 PM and take four hours. For El Florido take the bus to Chiquimula at 7 AM, 10 AM, or 12:30 PM and change there. Linea Dorada operates from Santa Elena to destinations in Belize.

➤ BUS INFORMATION: **El Condor** (✉ 19 Calle 2–01, Zona 1, Guatemala City, ☎ 232–8504). **Fortaleza** (✉ 19 Calle 8–70, Zona 1, Guatemala City, ☎ 220–6730). **Galgos** (✉ 7 Av. 19–44, Zona 1, Guatemala City, ☎ 253–4868). **Melva International** (✉ 3 Av. 1–38, Zona 9, Guatemala City, ☎ 331–0874). **Rutas Orientales** (✉ 19 Calle 8–18, Zona 1, Guatemala City, ☎ 238–3894). **Mundo Maya** (✉ Calle de la Playa, Edificio Hotel Itza 1, Flores, ☎ 926–0070).

BUS TRAVEL WITHIN GUATEMALA

Buses are the most widely used form of public transportation, with myriad companies running buses to almost every community that can be reached by road. Buses range from comfortable coaches with reclining seats and rest rooms to run-down school buses carrying twice as many people as they were built to hold, as well as a few animals.

If you decide to travel point to point without a plan, be sure the bus driver knows where you're going, and ask several times during the trip where you should get off. If you're friendly and give reminders you're there, the driver will almost always be helpful.

CAR TRAVEL TO AND FROM GUATEMALA

It's possible to enter Guatemala by land from Mexico, Belize, El Salvador, and Honduras. The Pan-American Highway, which passes through most major cities, connects the country with Mexico at La Mesilla and with El Salvador at San Cristobal Frontera. It's also possible to travel to El Salvador via the coastal highway, crossing at Ciudad Pedro de Alvarado, or Valle Nuevo. Pacific routes to Mexico pass through Tecún Umán and El Carmen/Talismán.

To reach Belize, take the highway east from Flores, passing El Cruce before reaching the border town of Melchor de Mencos. There are also two routes into Honduras, through El Florido or Esquipulas.

CAR TRAVEL WITHIN GUATEMALA

You need a valid driver's license from your own country to drive in Guatemala. Most roads leading to larger towns and cities are paved; those leading to small towns and villages are generally dirt roads. *Doble-tracción,* or four-wheel drive, is a necessity in many remote areas, especially at the height of the rainy season. Gas stations can be also scarce, so be sure to fill up before heading into rural areas. Consider bringing some extra fuel along with you. Don't count on finding repair shops outside the major towns.

DISABILITIES AND ACCESSIBILITY

People with disabilities will find Guatemala's cobbled streets and lack of wheel-chair access nearly impossible to negotiate. This said, most high-end hotels and tour providers are able to accommodate people with disabilities.

EMBASSIES

➤ EMBASSIES: **Canada** (✉ Edificio Edyma Plaza, 8th floor, 13 Calle 8–44, Zona 10, Guatemala City, ☎ 333–6102). **United Kingdom** (✉ Centro Financiero Torre II, 7th floor, 7 Av. 5–10, Zona 4, Guatemala City, ☎ 332–1601). **United States** (✉ Av. La Reforma 7–01, Zona 10, Guatemala City, ☎ 331–1541).

HEALTH

The most common health hazard for visitors to Guatemala is traveler's diarrhea. To avoid this problem, drink only bottled water. Remember to avoid raw vegetables unless you know they've been thoroughly washed and disinfected. Be wary of strawberries and other unpeeled fruits for the same reason. Heat stroke is another risk, but one that can easily be avoided. The best way to steer clear of heat stroke is to do as the locals do (wake early and retire at midday for a siesta) and drink lots of water.

MAIL AND SHIPPING

There are post offices in most communities, but the best way to mail letters and packages is often through your hotel. If at all possible, bring the items home with you, as Guatemala brings new meaning to the concept of "snail mail."

MONEY MATTERS

You can exchange U.S. dollars at any bank and in most hotels. It's far more difficult to exchange other currencies. If you are traveling with currency other than U.S. dollars, it would be wise to change the money into dollars or quetzales before you arrive. Traveler's checks are accepted only in larger hotels.

ATMS

There are ATMs that work on the Cirrus and Plus systems in most major cities. In smaller cities you will be hard pressed to find an ATM, but you should be able to go to the bank to withdraw money from your account using your ATM card. Make sure you only have a four-digit pin number, as many ATMs only take four digits.

CREDIT CARDS

In smaller cities you will be hard pressed to find an ATM, but you should be able to go to the bank to withdraw money from your account using your debit card. Make sure you have a four digit pin number, as many ATMs will not accept those with five or more digits.

CURRENCY

Guatemalan currency is called the quetzal, after the resplendent national bird. There are 1-, 5-, 10-, and 25-centavo coins. Bills come in denominations of one-half, 1, 5, 10, 20, 50, and 100 quetzales. At press time $1 was worth roughly Q8.

SAFETY

Most crimes directed at tourists have been pickpocketings and muggings, as well as thefts from cars. In the cities you should do the same as you would in any metropolitan area—leave flashy jewelry and watches at home, keep your camera in a secure bag, and don't handle money in public. Hire taxis only from official stands at the airport, outside hotels, and at major intersections. When traveling outside the cities, it's a good idea to hire a guide. Some of the volcanoes near Antigua and Lago Atitlán have been frequented by muggers.

TELEPHONES

Public phones are few and far between in Guatemala, but most towns have offices where you can place both national and international calls. The easiest way to place a call is from your hotel.

Guatemala's country code is 502; there are no local area codes.

TIPPING

A tip of about 10 percent is standard at most Guatemalan restaurants. Bellhops and maids expect tips only in the more expensive hotels. Tip tour guides about 10 percent of the tour price.

VISITOR INFORMATION

The staff at Inguat is courteous, professional, and knowledgeable. There are offices in Guatemala City, Antigua, Quetzaltenango, Panajachel, Flores, and Santa Elena.

➤ TOURIST INFORMATION: **Inguat** (⊠ 7 Av. 1–17, Zona 4, Guatemala City, ☎ 331–1333; ⊠ Palacio de los Capitanes, Antigua, ☎ 832–0763; ⊠ 7 Calle 11–35, Zona 1, Quetzaltenango, ☎ 761–4931; ⊠ Calle Santander 1–30, Zona 2, Panajachel, ☎ 762–1392; Parque Central, Flores, ☎ 926–0669; ⊠ Santa Elena Airport, Santa Elena, ☎ 926–0533).

4 EL SALVADOR

A drive through the countryside of El Salvador reveals a majestic backdrop of volcanoes—more per square mile than anywhere else in the Americas. Amid the lush landscape you'll revel in the solitude of Lago de Coatepeque, a lake set in a 40,000-year-old crater. More than 300 km (180 mi) of beaches line the Pacific shore, shared by fisherman at La Libertad, surfers at El Sunzal, and sunseekers at Costa del Sol.

By Michael
de Zayas

BE CAREFUL WITH YOUR HEART, because you just might lose it in El Salvador. The country has subtle charms that might go unnoticed on first glance. Very little here is geared toward travelers, especially outside the capital of San Salvador, making this a perfect destination for those with an adventurous spirit. The country's lovely landscapes, fascinating history, and genuinely friendly people—not to mention the utter lack of foreigners—will win over travelers who are strong of will and long on patience. If you have the desire to experience a Central American country untainted by tourism, you will find what you are looking for in El Salvador.

One appealing aspect of El Salvador is its diminutive size. The country, the smallest in Central America, is only 200 km (124 mi) long from end to end. The major roads are well paved and reasonably maintained, so trips to even the most far-flung reaches never take more than a few hours. This means that El Salvador's most beguiling sights are more accessible than you might guess. Although the country has seen most of its old-growth forests felled for timber or to make way for farms, this age of awareness about the environment—and its potential to draw tourists—has not been lost upon the powers that be, who are struggling to make up for lost time. The verdant national parks of the northwest (including a misty cloud forest), several impressive volcanoes (some still active), and a handful of sparkling lakes are now looked on as national treasures.

San Salvador, the sprawling capital, serves as the gateway for most visitors to El Salvador. It offers the mix of good and bad found in most cities of Central America. Although it can be wretched to the eye, San Salvador also has lively markets, interesting museums, and plenty of nonstop nightlife. Not far from the capital are several azure lakes—Lago de Coatepeque, Lago de Ilopango, and Lago de Güija—that lure you with opportunities for boating, swimming, or just relaxing in the sun. To the east of San Salvador stretches a chain of mountains that beckons to those in search of some serious off-the-beaten-track hiking. The thinly populated northwestern region is home to national parks such as Parque Nacional Montecristo. The Pacific coast is an unbroken string of beaches with some of the best surfing in the world.

El Salvador's natural beauty makes its history of armed conflict seem that much more tragic. Its grim past mocks its hopeful name, which in Spanish means "The Savior." You'll meet few people in this country whose lives haven't been affected by one of the longest and bloodiest civil wars of the last century. It will never be known how many men, women, and children lost their lives, although the figure is estimated to be well over 100,000. How this peaceful place erupted into violence that shocked the world during the 1980s is a story of uninterrupted greed, corruption, and exploitation that began five centuries ago.

The original inhabitants of El Salvador belonged to several different peoples related to the Maya and the Toltecs, including the Pok'omames, Lencas, Chortis, and later the Uluas and Pipiles. Lacking the population centers found in neighboring Guatemala, the area's small indigenous communities were easily conquered by the Spanish conquistadors who arrived in the 16th century. Wealthy settlers followed, seizing huge swaths of the fertile land for haciendas to grow cotton and indigo. This way of life continued for more than two centuries.

The country's first push for independence came when José Matías Delgado, known today as the father of the country, led a revolt against the Spanish in 1811. That first uprising was unsuccessful, but the priest led another a decade later that finally severed ties with the colonial government. He became the country's first president in 1821.

At about the same time, Europeans developed a taste for a stimulating new product called coffee. The modest plots of sustenance farmers were quickly swallowed up by increasingly powerful owners of the haciendas. It worked out wonderfully for the coffee barons: the *campesinos* who no longer had their own land needed to feed their families, while the plantations required people to work the fields. Conflicts between rich and poor were the inevitable result. In 1833, Anastasio Aquino rallied indigenous peoples with the slogan: "Land for those who work it."

The Great Depression brought increasing political tensions to El Salvador. Desperate workers—losing their livelihoods as plantations fell idle—began to gravitate toward leftist leaders like Augstín Farabundo Martí. In January 1932, after the government voided the results of a series of municipal elections won by communist candidates, Martí led an uprising in the coffee center of Sonsonate. The army responded with unprecedented brutality, methodically hunting down and killing anyone suspected of supporting the insurrection. To this day, you'll see few Salvadorans wearing traditional garb—it disappeared almost overnight as indigenous people, fearing further attacks, tried to blend in with their neighbors.

In the mid-20th century, the disparity between rich and poor only increased. Agricultural exports increased tenfold in the 1960s, but the Salvadoran people ranked in the top five most undernourished populations in the world. People pressed for change. José Napoleón Duarte, a founder of the Christian Democratic Party, won the presidency in 1972, but military leaders voided his victory. Popular protest, ranging from civil disobedience to armed insurrection, followed. The government responded by organizing death squads. Workers, students, and intellectuals were targeted, but a particularly bitter battle was waged against the clergy, who openly criticized the government's treatment of the poor. In 1980, Archbishop Oscar Romero, a leading human-rights advocate, was gunned down while delivering a sermon.

Soon after Romero's assassination, four guerrilla organizations united under the leadership of the Frente Martí Liberación Nacional. U.S. President Ronald Reagan, wary of the success of communists in neighboring Nicaragua, delivered unprecedented levels of aid. Instead of addressing the needs of the poverty-stricken population, the money was used to bolster the military. One of the most tragic examples occurred in 1981, when the army marched into the village of Mozote and massacred as many as 1,000 people. Hundreds of thousands fled the war-torn country.

In the late '80s, after rebel forces pitched battles in the heart of the capital city, negotiations began making unprecedented progress. A peace accord, mediated by the United Nations, officially ended 12 cruel years of civil war in 1992.

The last decade has brought many positive changes. The repressive Policía Nacional was disbanded and replaced by the Policía Nacional Civil, and judicial and electoral reforms were initiated. Crime is still a problem in many areas, but there are signs of progress. The country now boasts Central America's strongest economy—a major accomplishment. Because of all the corporate executives headed to the country, upscale hotels such as the Inter-Continental, Marriott, and Radisson have opened for business. Salvadorans, eager to see their country move forward, are clearly pleased with the progress.

El Salvador

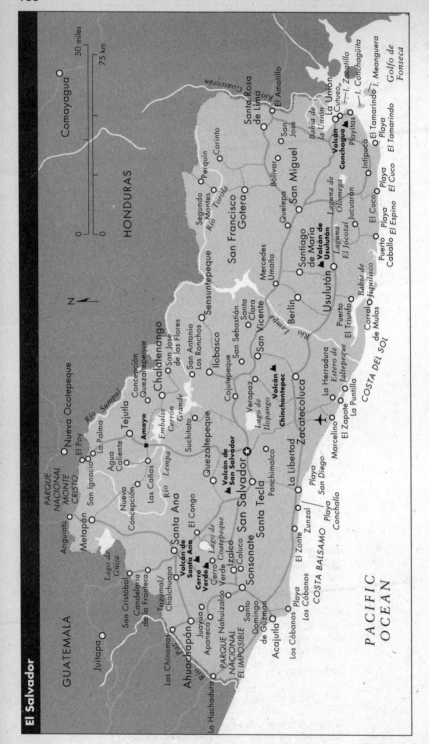

Pleasures and Pastimes

Archaeological Sites

While none are as grand as Tikal in Guatemala or Copán in Honduras, El Salvador has some interesting archaeological sites where you can wander among the remnants of Mesoamerican settlements. Temples at Tazumal and San Andrés are both well worth the trip. Joya de Cerén, just a few miles from San Andrés, provides a fascinating glimpse into the daily life of ancient peoples.

Beaches

One of El Salvador's best-kept secrets is its miles of beautiful beaches. When you head to the shore, you'll see why. The Costa del Sol, an easy drive from San Salvador, fills up with sun worshippers on the weekends. The Costa Balsamo is a favorite of surfers, who say the waves here are some of the best in Central America. Divers can explore one of the few coral reefs on the Pacific coast.

Dining

No food is more typically Salvadoran than the *pupusa,* a fried tortilla filled with beans, cheese, or *chicharón* (pork skin). A pupusa called a *revuelta* has all three fillings mixed together. These creations are found in *pupuserías,* where they are served up with tomato sauce or a type of pickled cabbage called *curtido.* The Salvadorian version of fast food, pupusas are a good way to fill up on the cheap. A breakfast here consists of eggs, beans, cheese, fried plantains, tortillas, and coffee. For something a little different, try *huevos picados* (scrambled eggs mixed with a few vegetables). For lunch, expect beef, chicken, or fish with rice, beans, tortillas, and a small salad. A delicious seafood soup called *mariscada* makes a satisfying dinner.

The most common drinks are *gaseosas* (sodas) and *refrescos* (fruit drinks with tons of sugar). Icy *minutas* are slushy drinks sweetened with honey—truly a godsend on a hot afternoon. Don't forget, however, to ask whether they are made with purified water. *Licuados* are similar to minutas, but fresh fruit and sometimes milk are added. Two omnipresent varieties of locally brewed *cerveza* (beer) are Pilsner and Suprema.

CATEGORY	COST*
$$$$	over 135 colones (over $15)
$$$	90–135 colones ($10–$15)
$$	45–90 colones ($5–$10)
$	under 45 colones (under $5)

*per person, for a main course at dinner

Lodging

There's no shortage of modern hotels in San Salvador. You'll immediately recognize names of top chains such as Inter-Continental, Marriott, and Radisson. Outside the capital, however, there are fewer comfortable lodgings. *Posadas* and *cabañas* are usually more upscale options, while *hospedajes* and *casas de huespedes* are most often lower-end lodgings; *hoteles* can be anything along the spectrum. *Moteles* are almost always seedy establishments that should be avoided. There are only a few sanctioned camping areas in the country, mostly in the west.

CATEGORY	COST*
$$$$	over 1,350 colones (over $150)
$$$	900–1,350 colones ($100–$150)
$$	450–900 colones ($50–$100)
$	under 450 colones (under $50)

*All prices are for a standard double room, excluding tax.

Outdoor Activities

The upper slopes of El Salvador's string of volcanoes are irresistible for those who love the great outdoors. Since the peaks are fairly low—El Pital, the country's highest peak, rises to only 8,950 ft—easy climbs will bring you to breathtaking views. National parks such as El Imposible in the southwest, Montecristo in the northwest, and Cerro Verde between the two, are the places to go for serious hiking through a variety of terrains. Regions like Chalatenango and Morazán have trails that bring hikers through a countryside dotted with small villages. There's plenty of opportunity for boating and other activities on lakes like Lago de Coatepeque.

Shopping

Markets and shops throughout the country are filled with locally produced crafts. In the village of Guatajiagua, near San Miguel, you can see local artisans making earthenware plates, jugs, and bowls in the same way as their ancestors. This pottery, which is then tinted with a black dye made from seeds, is used on a daily basis in most Salvadoran homes. San Sebastian, east of San Salvador, is the place for hammocks and other woven goods. La Palma, in the north, is known for the colorful designs of artist Fernando Llort. Other villagers now emulate Llort's childlike view of rural life. Kitschy *pícaras,* which originated in the village of Ilobasco, can be found in shops around the country. These egg-shape containers have little clay tableaux of subjects ranging from the sacred to the profane.

Exploring El Salvador

El Salvador is welcoming its first wave of tourists, but is ill prepared for them. You'll gain a much greater appreciation of the country, and avoid a lot of frustration, by hiring a car and driver. It's cheaper than renting a car, and you won't have to worry about bad directions, confusing signage, or poorly paved roads. Travel companies offer specialized tours of the country's archaeological sites, historical monuments, and mountain villages.

Great Itineraries

IF YOU HAVE 3 DAYS

Spend the first day in **San Salvador.** Its major sights, including the Museo de Arte Moderno and the Museo Nacional de Antropología, can easily be seen in one day. Because the country's best restaurants and hotels are located in the capital, consider making this your base and taking day trips to other parts of the country. On your second day head north to **Suchitoto,** a colonial-era village where beautifully preserved buildings line the cobblestone streets. On the third day, head west to **Lago de Coatepeque,** a beautiful lake that makes a great place to stop for lunch. Outdoors enthusiasts will want to hike up nearby Cerro Verde or Volcán Santa Ana.

IF YOU HAVE 5 DAYS

If you have a few more days to explore El Salvador you will be able to head a bit farther afield. Start with the itinerary above. On the fourth day travel west to **Santa Ana,** where you can stop by for a look around its central square. The cathedral and several museums are found along its edges. From Santa Ana you can explore the Ruta de las Flores, which takes you through mountain villages such as **Apaneca** and **Izalco.** On the fifth day, head south to the port town of **La Libertad,** enjoying the catch of the day in one of the many seaside restaurants.

When to Tour

El Salvador greets most of its visitors during the dry season between November and April. During the wet season, which runs from May to October, it rains almost every day. Fortunately, the downpours are usually short. The best time to visit is in the very beginning or end of the rainy season when the countryside is green, but the weather still manageable. Unless you're planning mountain treks, a sturdy umbrella will do fine. San Salvador and the Pacific coast are almost always hot during the day. Cooler temperature prevail at the higher elevations.

SAN SALVADOR

Growing by leaps and bounds, San Salvador offers glimpses of the future of El Salvador. This modern city is the engine that runs the strongest economy in Central America. Here you'll find the Colonia San Benito, an upscale neighborhood where you can stroll among the restaurants and galleries. To the north is Colonia Escalón, where you'll find many of the city's most popular shops boutiques. Colonia Centroamerica has some of the city's most happening bars and clubs.

But San Salvador is experiencing some growing pains. It's especially noticeable in El Centro, the city's historic center. With resources directed elsewhere (the newly opened art museum was built in Colonia San Benito), it has been sadly neglected. Although it has some lovely old buildings, the gritty neighborhood does not make visitors feel welcome.

San Salvador is easily the most densely populated city in Central America. The official count is about 1.5 million, but that figure increases by at least half when you figure in those living in the shantytowns along its edges. There are not nearly enough jobs to go around, which means pickpocketings and other petty crimes are all too common. Be on your guard, especially in markets and other crowded places.

Some visitors are surprised to find so few older buildings in this colonial city. San Salvador has been destroyed by tremors several times since it was founded in 1525, and consequently bears hardly a trace of its heritage. In 1986, much of the capital was leveled by an earthquake that left more than 1,000 people dead. Another in 2001 caused even more damage.

Exploring San Salvador

For a chaotic Central American capital, San Salvador is surprisingly easy to navigate. Like most of its neighbors, El Salvador has cities organized in grid pattern, with *avenidas* running north–south and *calles* running east–west. To make addresses easier to find, avenidas are labeled *norte* when north of the main plaza and *sur* when they are to the south (for example, Avenida 4a Norte). Ditto for calles, using *oriente* (abbreviated ote.) on the east side and *poniente* (pte.) on the west. San Salvador takes the system one step further, placing odd-numbered avenidas west of the central plaza and even ones to the east, odd calles to the north and even to the south. While confusing at first, this system makes orienting yourself easier because the main plaza will always be roughly at Avenida 1 and Calle 1.

In many Central American cities, the major streets in either direction change names as they cross the main square. San Salvador is a typical case, as Calle Arce becomes Calle Delgado as it crosses the plaza. In some cases, main roads may change names as the *colonia* (neighborhood) changes. As you head east from Colonia Escalón, Paseo Escalón becomes Alameda Roosevelt, then Calle Ruben Dario, then Calle 2a Poniente, and finally Calle 2a Oriente.

140

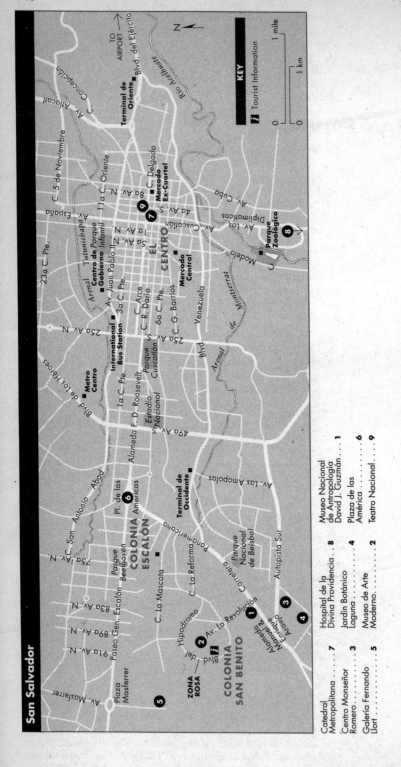

San Salvador

Catedral
Metropolitana **7**

Centro Monseñor
Romero **3**

Galería Fernando
Llort **5**

Hospital de la
Divina Providencia . . **8**

Jardín Botánico
Laguna **4**

Museo de Arte
Moderno. **2**

Museo Nacional
de Antropología
David J. Guzmán **1**

Plaza de las
América **6**

Teatro Nacional **9**

Colonia San Benito

While most of the city's graceful old buildings are found in El Centro, this neighborhood is where you'll find some of the newer attractions, such as the outstanding museums dedicated to anthropology and modern art. Also here is the vibrant Zona Rosa, a stretch of Avenida del Hipódromo lined with restaurants, bars, and nightclubs. You'll probably spend most of your time in the city here and in Colonia Escalón and Colonia Centroamerica.

A GOOD WALK

Colonia San Benito is one of the few neighborhoods in the city where you won't feel nervous walking by yourself. Start at the **Museo Nacional de Antropología David J. Guzmán** ①. From there, walk up Avenida de la Revolución, past the Plaza Italia, to the end of the street, where you'll see the Monumento de la Revolución, now incorporated into the **Museo de Arte Moderno** ②. Circle around Boulevard del Hipódromo, where you can browse in the shops and boutiques. It's a short taxi ride to the **Centro Monseñor Romero** ③ and the wonderful **Jardín Botánico La Laguna** ④.

TIMING

This walk itself will take less than an hour. If you stop in the anthropology museum and modern art museum, this walk will take a full morning or afternoon.

SIGHTS TO SEE

❸ **Centro Monseñor Romero.** In an incident that drew international outrage, a group of men broke into the rectory at the Universidad Centroamericano José Simeón Cañas in 1989 and murdered six Jesuits, their housekeeper, and her daughter. This sobering memorial displays the victims' papers and personal items, as well as graphic photos of the murder scene. The church next door is well worth visiting, as is a small rose garden. ✉ *Calle del Mediterraneo and Av. Río Amazonas, Col. Antiguo Cusclatan,* ☎ *503/210–6600.* ⌦ *Free.* ☾ *Weekdays 8–noon and 2–6, Sat. 8–noon.*

★ ❹ **Jardín Botánico La Laguna.** A huge collection of plants and flowers from around the world—including a 200-year-old ceiba tree, a large collection of orchids, and bamboo forest—is found at this botanical garden, called La Laguna because it is located in the crater of an extinct volcano that was filled with water until an earthquake drained it in 1873. You don't have to be a botanist to enjoy the shady paths and babbling streams that make this park a welcome respite from the city's hustle and bustle. ✉ *Near Universidad Centroamericano José Simeón Cañas.* ⌦ *35¢.* ☾ *Tues.–Fri. 9–5, weekends 9–5:30.*

★ ❷ **Museo de Arte Moderno.** The Museum of Modern Art, which opened in 2002, has become the country's most important cultural center. The 25,000-square-ft facility, consisting of a large main hall connected to three smaller galleries, is home to a permanent collection of works by Salvadoran artists. Two of the smaller galleries will host rotating exhibitions by national and international artists, while the third is dedicated to the work of Toño Salazar, a Salvadoran caricaturist who portrayed the most important personalities of the 20th century. The museum's importance to the country shouldn't be underestimated. Leaders say the museum "heralds a renaissance of cultural consciousness" for the country, and one senses this is not hyperbole. By incorporating into the museum's central plaza the 70-ft Monumento de la Revolución, the museum sets itself at the center of the country's intellectual and spiritual psyche. ✉ *Av. La Revolución,* ☎ *503/243–3927,* WEB *www.marteelsalvador.com.* ⌦ *$2.* ☾ *Tues.–Sun. 9–5.*

① **Museo Nacional de Antropología David J. Guzmán.** The National Museum of Anthropology, the country's most respected museum, was founded in 1883 by Salvadoran scientist David Joaquín Guzmán. After being damaged in a 1986 earthquake, it reopened in this spacious complex. Stroll through the five galleries to learn about the country's cultural history. The explanatory text is only in Spanish, but it's easy to appreciate the pottery from pre-Hispanic times, the clothing of indigenous peoples, and the looms from San Sebastian. In a garden you can follow a path to a replica of a traditional wood-and-straw hut. ⊠ *Av. La Revolución,* ☎ *503/243–3927.* 🎟 *$3.* ⊙ *Tues.–Sun. 9–5.*

Colonia Escalón

An upscale commercial and residential neighborhood, Colonia Escalón is west of the historic district. Along Paseo General Escalón, the neighborhood's main artery, you'll find several of the city's glitziest shopping centers.

SIGHTS TO SEE

⑤ **Galería Fernando Llort.** With much success at home and abroad, Fernando Llort has received the most attention of any Salvadoran artist. This popular gallery sells original paintings, prints, and posters. The staff carefully packs purchases for you flight home. ⊠ *Calle La Mascota and Av. Masferrer, Col. Maquilishuat,* ☎ *503/263–9165.*

⑥ **Plaza de las América.** Near the beginning of Colonia Escalón is a statue called *The Saviour of the World,* depicting Jesus standing on top of a globe. It sits in the center of this tree-lined park. ⊠ *Paseo General Escalón at Bul. Constitución.*

El Centro

Chaotic during the day and rough at night, the city's historic center is an intimidating place for visitors. Here you'll find some of the city's best-known landmarks, such as the colorful Catedral Metropolitana.

SIGHTS TO SEE

⑦ **Catedral Metropolitana.** The city's main cathedral, damaged by a series of earthquakes, was repainted by one of El Salvador's most famous artists, Fernando Llort. The facade is painted with bright solid colors, with rural motifs such as cattle, houses, corn, flowers, and butterflies. Archbishop Oscar Romero was buried here after being assassinated in 1980. ⊠ *Calle 2a Ote. between Av. Cuscatlán and Av. 2a Sur,* ☎ *no phone.* 🎟 *Free.*

⑧ **Hospital de la Divina Providencia.** It was at the altar of this hospital's small chapel, in the middle of mass, that Archbishop Oscar Romero was gunned down by a government death squad in March 1980. The church is simple and peaceful, with a plaque near the altar commemorating the tragedy. Ask in the office to the left of the church for a tour of Romero's living quarters, where you'll find photos, books, and even the typewriter he used to compose his famous homilies. ⊠ *Final Calle Toluca and Av. B, Col. Miramonte Pte.,* ☎ *503/260–0520.* 🎟 *Free.* ⊙ *Daily 8 AM–noon and 2–4.*

⑨ **Teatro Nacional.** Dating from 1910, the elegant National Theater is one of the most recognizable landmarks in San Salvador. Huge columns line the entrance, a favorite place for vendors selling jewelry and other items. The gilt-edged interior, lovingly restored to its original splendor, is a clue to how much wealth the coffee plantations once brought to El Salvador. ⊠ *Av. 2a Sur and Calle Delgado,* ☎ *503/222–5689.*

Dining

If you enjoy sampling *platos típicos* (typical dishes), you'll have a great time in San Salvador. Every block has at least one or two *comedores* (inexpensive eateries) serving up pupusas and other favorites. But San Salvador also has a handful of inventive restaurants where chefs combine local ingredients and international techniques to create something astounding.

$$$–$$$$ ✕ **Cuattro Gatti.** Named for a tavern in the owner's hometown in
★ Italy, Cuattro Gatti is the most attractive restaurant in the Zona Rosa. Original art hangs on the walls of the candlelit dining room. The restaurant serves up delicious Italian food; even the simplest of dishes, such as spaghetti with shrimp, is handled with grace. The carpaccios are excellent, especially the *ai fungi* with mushrooms, arugula, and Parmesan. Tagliatelle served with a porcini mushroom sauce is superb. The *zupetta di pesce,* with fish, octopus, and squid, comes in a zesty sauce made with chili, garlic, and capers. For dessert there's homemade gelato. ⊠ *La Reforma 232, Col. San Benito,* ☎ *503/223–6027. AE, DC, MC, V. Closed Sun. No lunch Sat. and Mon.*

$$$–$$$$ ✕ **Gilberto's.** Set in a comfortable home with a backyard garden, this restaurant south of Colonia Escalón is run by Gilberto and Susan Chacón. Although not formally trained as chefs, they add a personal touch to the cooking. A few minutes after ordering chocolate mousse, for example, you'll see Susan in the garden picking impatiens for a garnish. The changing menu of classic entrées—duck à l'orange, beef Stroganoff, chateaubriand—tends to be a bit bland. Little paper flags that designate the country of origin are stuck into the various dishes. ⊠ *79 Av. Sur 147, Col. La Mascota,* ☎ *503/263–7690. AE, DC, MC, V. Closed Sun. No lunch Fri. and Mon.*

$$–$$$$ ✕ **Alo Nuestro.** Hands down the best restaurant in El Salvador, Alo Nue-
★ stro is set on a softly lit terrace under a lovely *caimito.* The sticky sweet fruit from this tree is one of many Salvadoran ingredients elevated to epicurean heights by chef Tomás Regalado, who studied international cooking techniques at some of New York's top restaurants. You can lean toward your favorite influence, as do members of the French Embassy when they order the thick tenderloin with béarnaise sauce. Grilled chicken in a chili chipotle sauce is also delicious. Get the full range of flavors with the five-course tasting menu. Desserts are a specialty, so don't pass up the warm chocolate mousse cake. ⊠ *La Reforma 225, Col. San Benito,* ☎ *503/223–5116. AE, DC, MC, V. Closed Sun.*

$$–$$$$ ✕ **La Pampa Argentina.** Halfway up Volcán San Salvador, this appealing ranch house has a bougainvillea-lined garden that overlooks the city. At night the soft breezes and glittering lights make for a tranquil setting. Hot off the *parrilla* (grill) are tenderloin steaks weighing anywhere from 8 to 14 ounces. The service is formal and attentive. ⊠ *End of Paseo General Escalón, Col. Escalón,* ☎ *503/264–0892. AE, DC, MC, V.*

$$–$$$$ ✕ **Ultima Alucinación.** Belgian chef Alain Brys and his wife opened up
★ their home as a restaurant, setting up five tables in their living room. Word of his skill spread, and so they added another eight tables in the plant-filled garden. There's also a bar—select from among a dozen Belgian brews. Crepes are the star attraction, with over a dozen choices, including one filled with Brie, mushrooms, and apples. Gourmet pizzas, fired up in a wood-burning stove, attract the staff from the Italian embassy. Among the 10 sweet crepes for dessert, try the *capricieuse,* which comes with jam, almonds, and a side of sorbet. ⊠ *Av. Masferrer 5153, Col. Escalón,* ☎ *503/263–1320. AE, DC, MC, V. Closed Sun. and Mon.*

$$–$$$ ✕ **Café–Café.** San Salvador is lucky to have chef Roberto Cuadra Mora, who spent more than a decade in Peru delighting diners with his flavorful fare. Among the top choices here is the *ceviche de pescado* (fish marinated with lemon, garlic, onion, and cilantro) accompanied by *camote,* a delicious yellow sweet potato. The best course of action is to order a sampling of smaller dishes—the chef will tell you his favorites. The dining room is filled with lovely Peruvian paintings, sculptures, and weavings, all of which are for sale. ⊠ *Calle El Algodón 50, Col. Escalón,* ☎ *503/263–2413 or 503/284–3338. AE, DC, MC, V. No dinner Sun.*

$$–$$$ ✕ **El Bodegón.** You know a place is an institution when you hear Pope John Paul II dined there *twice.* Much of the reason for its fame is owner Ángel García, who has greeted patrons at the door since 1966. The Madrid native makes sure the simple Continental menu features seafood standouts like paella as well as masterful meat dishes like chateaubriand, filet mignon, and beef Stroganoff. The dining room, bordered by floral curtains, is quite intimate. With elegant touches like monogrammed plates, the restaurant has the ambience of an established gentleman's club. ⊠ *Paseo General Escalón and 77 Av. Norte, Col. Escalón,* ☎ *503/264–5143. AE, DC, MC, V. Closed Sun.*

$$–$$$ ✕ **Hunan.** Locals consider this the best of the many Chinese restaurants that pepper the city. The decor is over the top, with hand-carved seating, elaborate floral paintings, and intricate lamps. From the always-busy dining room, the city lights in the distance are an appealing glimmer. The food falls a bit short, but dishes like *pato Peking* (Peking duck), and *pollo Hunan* (Hunan chicken) are attractively presented. ⊠ *Paseo Escalón and 99 Av. Norte, Col. Escalón,* ☎ *503/263–9989. AE, DC, MC, V.*

$$–$$$ ✕ **Kamakura.** The traditional paper screens that decorate Kamakura are a clue that you've found the country's best place for hand-rolled sushi. Sit at simple wooden tables and chairs, at the sushi bar, or on the floor in the private tatami room. There's also a plant-filled back room with a running fountain. The tempura is light and flaky and sometimes comes with a pinwheel of battered lotus root. ⊠ *Paseo General Escalón and Av. 93 Norte, Col. Escalón,* ☎ *503/263–2401. AE, DC, MC, V.*

$–$$ ✕ **La Ventana.** The most unique restaurant in the capital, La Ventana
★ has a friendly and informal atmosphere. Pick up old copies of the *New York Times* from a pile by the door and head to one of the dining rooms furnished with solid wood tables. Several of these intimate spaces feature changing painting and photography exhibits. For dinner choose among filet mignon, Hungarian goulash, and *salchichas alemanes al curry* (curried wurst, the German owner's specialty). The international selection of beers features 11 from Belgium. Wines are available by the glass. ⊠ *Calle San Antonio Abad 2335, Col. Centroamerica,* ☎ *503/ 226–5129. AE, DC, MC, V. Closed Mon.*

$–$$ ✕ **Punto Literario.** This little café wouldn't attract much attention in
★ a more cosmopolitan city, but it will warm the heart of many an expatriate with its perfect crostones topped with avocado, Brie, and sundried tomatoes. The restaurant is next door to the eponymous bookstore, the best in the city. Here you can linger over a glass of wine while perusing a monograph of contemporary art or architecture. The alfresco dining area, beside a gentle waterfall, makes this a good stop while exploring the Zona Rosa. ⊠ *Bul. del Hipódromo 325, Col. San Benito,* ☎ *503/243–6619. AE, DC, MC, V. Closed Sun.*

$–$$ ✕ **Tutto Pasta.** The owner of the wonderful Cuattro Gatti also runs this informal eatery. Though inexpensive, it does not lack style; subdued lighting and yellow and green walls make the dining room pleasant. The fresh pastas are the same ones made for its sister restaurant, which means they're dependably delicious. Try the *gnocchi alle quattro stagioni* (gnocchi with tomato, olives, ham, and mushrooms in a cream sauce) or the *lasagne agli spinaci* (spinach lasagna with a cream sauce). ⊠ *Paseo General Escalón at 77 Av. Norte, Col. Escalón,* ☎ *503/257–2544. AE, DC, MC, V. No dinner Sun.*

$ ✕ **Kalpataru.** While a bit off the beaten track, this is a good place to sample pupusas with unusual fillings such as parsley, spinach, and garbanzo beans. Wash them down with an assortment of fruit juices and shakes. The café, south of Colonia Escalón, is part of a store that sells herbal medicines and such. You can also sign up for yoga classes. ⊠ *Calle La Mascota 928, Col. La Mascota,* ☎ *503/263–1204. AE, DC, MC, V. Closed Sun.*

Lodging

Colonia Escalón and Colonia San Benito are home to nearly all of the city's the top hotels, including the Marriott, Princess, and Radisson. The Inter-Continental is nearby in Colonia Los Héroes. The larger hotels, competing for guests, are quick to offer discounted rates. You may secure a corporate rate merely by showing a business card. Ask about cheaper weekend rates as well.

$$$$ 🏨 **Hotel Princess Zona Rosa.** An elegantly sloping mansard roof gives this high-rise a European flair. The interior is no less Continental, with large tapestries adorning the lobby, rich carpeting in the halls, and hunting prints in the rooms. Churchill's Bar, with comfortable leather sofas, adds a degree of sophistication. The formal restaurant looks out to the small pool through stately arches. There is a fine health club with thrice-weekly yoga and aerobics classes. Another advantage is the unbeatable location in the Zona Rosa. No wonder it has a reputation as the most luxurious hotel in the country. ⊠ *Av. Magnolias and Bul. del Hipódromo, Col. San Benito,* ☎ *503/298–4545,* ℻ *503/298–4500,* ⓦⒺⒷ *www. hotelesprincess.com. 199 rooms, 5 suites. Restaurant, in-room data ports, in-room safes, minibars, cable TV with movies and video games, pool, health club, lounge, pub, shops, dry cleaning, laundry service, business services, Internet, meeting rooms, airport shuttle, car rental, travel services, free parking, no-smoking floors. AE, DC, MC, V.*

$$$$ 🏨 **Marriott.** This low-rise hotel in the Zona Rosa ran into a bit of luck when the city's new modern art museum opened across the street. Also outside its front doors is a nice promenade where you can browse among the shops or relax at a café. You're sure to feel comfortable at this hotel, which in addition to its fine rooms, offers additional amenities like daily fax digests from the *New York Times*. All rooms have balconies, some with nice city views. ⊠ *Final Av. de la Revolución, Col. San Benito,* ☎ *503/283–4000,* ℻ *503/283–4040,* ⓦⒺⒷ *www.marriotthotels.com/saldt. 221 rooms, 4 suites. Restaurant, café, room service, in-room data ports, in-room safes, minibars, cable TV, room TVs with movies and video games, pool, gym, massage, sauna, lobby lounge, bar, shops, dry cleaning, laundry service, Internet, business services, convention center, meeting rooms, airport shuttle, car rental, travel services, free parking, no-smoking floors. AE, DC, MC, V.*

$$$ 🏨 **Real Inter-Continental San Salvador.** You'll be handed a glass of freshly squeezed orange juice as you check into this high-rise in Colonia Los Héroes. The service will never flag for the rest of your stay. Because of the large convention center, the Real Inter-Continental is considered the city's best business hotel. Rooms, with three phones and direct in-room Internet connections, are perfect for traveling executives. Tequilas, a colorful restaurant that serves up big margaritas, is one of the best in the city. You can relax with a cocktail in the lobby lounge. Metro-Centro, Central America's largest mall, is across the street. ⊠ *Bul. de los Héroes and and Av. Sisimiles, Col. Los Héroes,* ☎ *503/211–3333,* ℻ *503/211–4444,* ⓦⒺⒷ *www.interconti.com. 222 rooms, 6 suites. 2 restaurants, room service, in-room data ports, in-room safes, minibars, cable TV, room TVs with movies and video games, pool, gym, 2 bars, lounge, shops, dry cleaning, laundry service, Internet, business services,*

convention center, meeting rooms, airport shuttle, car rental, travel services, free parking, no-smoking floors. AE, DC, MC, V.

$$ ⌂ **Holiday Inn.** This business-minded lodging has amenities of the biggest hotels—Internet access, business center, meeting rooms—at half the price. While its location outside the city may be too remote for most travelers, it couldn't be more convenient for those with business at the U.S. Embassy. After you've closed the deal you can swim laps in the pool or work out in the gym. A buffet breakfast is included in the rates. ✉ *Bul. Santa Elena, Col. Santa Elena,* ☎ *503/247–7000,* FAX *503/247–7070,* WEB *www.holidayinn.com.sv. 128 rooms, 4 suites. Restaurant, in-room data ports, in-room safes, minibars, cable TV with movies and video games, pool, gym, bar, dry cleaning, laundry service, business services, convention center, Internet, meeting rooms, free parking, no-smoking floors. AE, DC, MC, V. BP.*

$$ ⌂ **Hotel Vista Marella.** With architectural flourishes that call to mind
★ the colonial period, the newly opened Vista Marella is that rarest of finds: a clean, dependable, mid-range hotel. Though it's marketed as a bed-and-breakfast, you don't have the feeling that you're staying in someone's home. Instead, it's more like a small apartment complex with cute and tidy rooms. A pleasant breakfast area, with wrought iron chairs and tables set in a courtyard, faces a trim little pool. The simplicity of a few potted trees is cheery. ✉ *Calle Juan José Cañas between 81 Av. Sur and 83 Av. Sur, Col. Escalón,* ☎ FAX *503/211–3432. 18 rooms. Restaurant, cable TV, in-room data ports, laundry service, bar, pool, Internet, business services. AE, DC, MC, V. CP.*

$$ ⌂ **Novo Apart-Hotel.** If you're in San Salvador for an extended stay, consider the Novo Apart-Hotel. Rates are reduced if you book for a week or more. It's not quite like home, but it does have nice touches like fully stocked kitchens. Relax in the hammock on your terrace, which overlooks the pool and gardens dotted with statues. ✉ *Av. 61 Norte, north of Calle 1 Pte., Col. Escalón,* ☎ *503/260–2288,* FAX *503/260–5053,* WEB *www.novoapart-hotel.com. 50 rooms. Restaurant, kitchens, refrigerators, cable TV, pool, gym, bar, conference rooms. MC, V.*

$$ ⌂ **Radisson.** Tucked away in Colonia Escalón, this hotel is a great place to get away from the noise of the city. Off the lobby you'll find an interesting array of shops. The restaurant is set beside a colonnade where a waterfall drops into the pool. The main complex offers rooms that are nearly identical to those in the city's other luxury hotels, but a second building behind the pool has suites that cost about half as much. There aren't as many amenities—no minibar, no in-room safe—but you can request a complimentary microwave, mini-refrigerator, and coffeemaker. ✉ *89 Av. Norte and 11 Calle Poriente, Col. Escalón,* ☎ *503/298–4545,* FAX *503/298–4500,* WEB *www.radisson.com/sansalvadores. 298 rooms. Restaurant, in-room data ports, in-room safes, minibars, microwaves, cable TV with movies and video games, pool, gym, 2 bars, shops, dry cleaning, laundry service, Internet, business services, convention center, meeting rooms, airport shuttle, car rental, travel services, free parking, no-smoking floors. AE, DC, MC, V.*

Nightlife and the Arts

Nightlife

If you want to party, you'll head to one of two very different neighborhoods—Colonia San Benito and Colonia Centroamerica. The former is where you'll find the Zona Rosa, the destination for young people with lots of style and lots of cash. Colonia Centroamerica, adjacent to the Universidad de El Salvador, has a more bohemian atmosphere. There are also a few watering holes along the shopping strip of Colonia Escalón.

Not surprisingly, weekends are the most popular part of the week for those for going out on the town. Dress is largely casual, with the notable exception of Mario's, where you need to look good. Last call is 2 AM.

COLONIA CENTROAMERICA

Part of San Salvador's top independent arts organization, **La Luna Casa y Arte** (⊠ 228 Calle Berlín, Col. Centroamerica, ☎ 503/260–2921) is a restaurant, bar, and performance space that hosts everything from poetry readings to film screenings. It is perhaps the city's most interesting place for drinks, with an indoor-outdoor patio and a postmodern mix of surreal and indigenous imagery. **Les Tres Diables** (⊠ Calle San Antonio Abad 2241, Col. Centroamerica, ☎ 503/225–5609) has a bohemian bent. Inside you'll find political posters and alternative music. Look for the neon "3D" sign outside. For more of a cocktail-party atmosphere, head to **La Ventana** (⊠ Calle San Antonio Abad 2335, Col. Centroamerica, ☎ 503/226–5129). All that shaking and stirring occasionally leads to dancing in the lobby. If you're bar-hopping, around the corner from La Ventana is **Los Celtas** (⊠ Calle San Antonia Abad and Calle Principal, Col. Centroamerica, ☎ 503/226–2841), a laid-back Scottish bar. The long, narrow space is perhaps liveliest of in the city.

In the neighborhood just north of Colonia Centroamerica you'll find **El Arpa** (⊠ Av. A 137, Col. San José, ☎ 503/225–0429), the most authentic place in the country for a pint of Guinness. Indoors the decor is a tribute to the old country, but the outdoor patio is the nicest place to sit. **Deja Vu** (⊠ Av. A 124, Col. San José, ☎ 503/225–0412), across from El Arpa, has tables both inside and outside.

It's a bit out of the way, but you might want to end up at **Restaurant Hey!** (⊠ 31 Pasaje Palmeral at Calle Toluca, Colonia Toluca), which has good food and music performed by its Chilean owner.

COLONIA ESCALÓN

Sports Bar & Grill (⊠ Paseo General Escalón and Av. 99 Norte, Col. Escalón, ☎ 503/263–6201) is the place for a satellite connection to the home team. You can count on good spicy chicken wings and burgers.

COLONIA SAN BENITO

While the bars and clubs in the Zona Rosa come and go, changing names every couple months, **Mario's** (⊠ Bul. El Hipódromo 2-281, Col. San Benito, ☎ 503/223–6068) looks like a permanent fixture. It has the best dance floor in the country, which means it's always packed. Things get going late, about 1 AM. When you're looking for a slightly older crowd, head up Avenida de la Revolución to **Señor Frog's** (⊠ Bul. El Hipódromo, Col. San Benito, ☎ no phone), where the action starts around 9 PM and runs past 2 AM.

One of city's liveliest night spots, **Los Rinconcitos** (⊠ Bul. El Hipódromo 310, Col. San Benito, ☎ 503/298–4799) is three bars in one—on weekends you'll find a mariachi band on the lower level, recorded music in the middle level, and a rock band playing on the back patio. This courtyard is a great place for a drink.

GAY BARS

Although they have a mostly straight clientele, Los Rinconcitos and Mario's in the Zona Rosa and Las Celtas, La Luna, and Tres Diablos in Colonia Centroamerica are "gay friendly" establishments frequented by gays and straights alike. It's easy to have a good time with the open-minded crowds.

Scape (⊠ Av. Juan Pablo II between Avs. 61 and 63 Norte, Col. Miramonte, ☎ 260–5154) is the best of the handful of gay bars in the capital. While primarily for men, it also draws a small contingent of women, especially Thursday and Friday. The basement dance floor features music that varies from techno to merengue. Strippers perform on weekends, when the bar stays open all night. Another standard is **Millennium** (⊠ Juan Pablo II between Avs. 61 and 63 Norte, Colonia Miramonte, ☎ no phone). A good choice is **Latino's** (⊠ Juan Pablo II between Avs. 61 and 63 Norte, Colonia Miramonte, ☎ no phone).

The Arts

One of the best ways to get acquainted with the local arts scene is to check out the bulletin board at the bookstore **Punto Literario** (⊠ Bul. del Hipódromo 325, Col. San Benito, ☎ 503/243–6619). **Centro Cultural de España** (⊠ La Reforma 166, Col. San Benito, ☎ 503/279–0751), which hosts a variety of cultural events, is another good place to start.

La Luna Casa y Arte (⊠ 228 Calle Berlín, ☎ 503/260–2921, WEB www.lalunacasayarte.com), the city's top independent arts organization, has a performance space where you can see cutting-edge art. Beatrice Alcaine, the young Salvadoran who runs the space from her old home, also organizes children's writing workshops. Check the calendar for specific events.

Concatur (⊠ 1 Calle Pte. 822, El Centro, ☎ 503/221–2016), the government-run cultural organization, has a downtown space with monthly poetry readings, art exhibitions, dance performances, and other events. There's also a café that's open for lunch.

DANCE

The **Ballet Folklórico de El Salvador** (⊠ 1 Calle Pte. 1233, El Centro, ☎ 221–0972), performs traditional folk dances. The country's top clasical and contemporary dance company is **Escuela Nacional de Danza** (⊠ 1 Calle Pte. 1233, El Centro, ☎ 221–0972), which performs in Teatro Presidente.

FILM

San Salvador has many cinemas where you can watch movies in English with Spanish subtitles. Movie listings are posted in *El Diario de Hoy*, the country's largest newspaper. Admission is about $2. Among the best theaters in town is the **Cinemark** (⊠ Bul. de los Héroes, Col. Miramonte, ☎ 503/261–2001), in the sprawling MetroCentro. **La Luna Casa y Arte** (⊠ 228 Calle Berlín, ☎ 503/260–2921, WEB www.lalunacasayarte.com) hosts an independent film series on Monday and Wednesday.

GALLERIES

Most of the city's best galleries are located in the Zona Rosa. Above Punto Literario, **Vila Nova** (⊠ Bul. del Hipódromo 325, Col. San Benito, ☎ 503/245–6225, WEB www.vilanovafineart.com) has two floors of gallery space. You'll see changing exhibits of contemporary painting, sculpture, and photography. **Galería 1-2-3** (⊠ Av. La Capilla 258, Col. San Benito, ☎ 503/275–9827) is the city's oldest gallery. It features shows by promising young artists.

Galería Espacio (⊠ La Reforma 209, Col. San Benito, ☎ 503/223–4807) shows works by international heavy hitters. Next door to Galería Espacio is **Galería Saravia** (⊠ La Reforma 227, Col. San Benito, ☎ 503/ 260–6383). As well as exhibitions it offers drawing classes.

MUSIC

The city has two excellent venues for classical music, the most famous being the **Teatro Nacional** (⊠ Av. 2a Sur and Calle Delgado, El Centro, ☎ 503/222–5689), a lovely building in the city's historical center.

Located in the Zona Rosa is the **Teatro Presidente** (✉ Final Av. La Revolución, Col. San Benito, ☎ 503/243–3407). The well-regarded **Orquestra Sinfonica Nacional** (☎ 503/221–2373) played its first concert in 1922. It continues to perform classical works.

Concatur (✉ 1 Calle Pte. 822, ☎ 503/221–2016), a government-run "culture house," regularly stages Spanish-language plays. It was the only theater to remain open during the civil war, and so has a special place in the hearts of Salvadorans. The excellent space is behind a café and bookshop. The **Centro Nacional de Artes** (✉ Calle Valero Lecha, Col. San Mateo, ☎ 503/298–1839) stages plays at various theaters around the city, including the restored Teatro Nacional.

Outdoor Sports and Activities

Participant Sports

ATHLETIC CLUBS

At the Hotel Princess, **El Spa** (✉ Av. Magnolias and Bul. del Hipódromo, Col. San Benito, ☎ 503/298–4545) has one of the best health clubs in the country. You can work out in the weight room, join aerobics and yoga classes, or even schedule a massage. It's free to hotel guests, but others must purchase a monthly membership costing $50.

World Gym (✉ Bul. Orden de Malta Sur, Col. Santa Elena, ☎ 503/243–4142) has large weight rooms as well as racquetball and basketball courts. **Bally Sport Center** (✉ Albert Einstein 10, Col. Lomas de San Francisco, ☎ 503/273–2290) has similar facilities.

BOWLING

With two dozen lanes, **Galaxy Bowling** (✉ 75 Av. Norte, at Parque Beethoven, Col. Escalón, ☎ 503/264–7136) is the country's only modern bowling alley. The cost varies by the day and the hour, ranging from $5 (weekdays noon–2 PM) to $15 (Saturday 10 AM–midnight). There's a six-person maximum per lane. Shoe rental is $1.

GOLF

There are two private courses that cater to those who can't make it through a trip without playing a few rounds. It only has nine holes, but **Campestre Golf Club** (✉ Paseo Gen. Escalon 5423, Col. Escalón, ☎ 503/263–0284) is the only course located within San Salvador proper. It is open daily 6–6. To play 18 holes you need to head to **Club Salvadoreño** (✉ Lago de Ilopango, ☎ 503/225–1634).

Spectator Sports

SOCCER

Like nearly every other Latin American country, El Salvador is focused on one sport: *futbol*. Matches take place Sunday from January to May and August to December. The capital has three teams that play in **Estadio Cuscatlán** (✉ Autopista Sur, Col. Altamira, ☎ 503/275–7811).

Shopping

Malls

MetroCentro (✉ Bul. De los Héroes, Col. Miramonte, ☎ 503/257–6000) is the largest shopping center in Central America. It's not as bland as suburban malls, however. Here you'll find two labyrinthine stories of laid-back shops where Salvadorans often come to spend an afternoon. **Basilea** (✉ Bul. del Hipódromo, Col. San Benito, ☎ 503/279–0056), a small shopping center in the Zona Rosa, caters to a more upscale crowd. It has a few boutiques, jewelry shops, and an art gallery. If all the shopping makes you hungry, there's also a bakery.

Galerías Escalón (✉ Paseo General Escalón, Col. Escalón, ☎ 503/245–0733), the second-biggest mall in the city, is home to a modern movie theater. Its upscale stores include Benetton and Bally. **Plaza Merliot** (✉ Paseo General Escalón, Col. Escalón, ☎ 503/229–4341) isn't quite as upscale as its neighbor. It also has a movie theater.

Markets

The rows of stalls at the **Mercado Nacional de Artesanías** (✉ Alameda Manuel Enrique Araujo, Col. San Benito, ☎ 503/243–2341), is where you can find handicrafts from all over El Salvador (and some from Guatemala, as well). This is one-stop-shopping for ceramics, hammocks, and just about anything else you can imagine. It's open daily 9–6.

Sometimes called the Mercadito de Merliot, the **Mercado Antiguo Cuscatlán** (✉ Final Calle La Cañada y Av. Las Arboledas, ☎ 503/278–7475) is a traditional market with individual areas for meats, seafood, haircutting salons, spices, piñatas, and fruits. It's open daily 8–4.

The huge downtown market, **Mercado Central** (✉ 6 Calle Ote., between 23 y 27 Av. Sur, Col. La Mermeja, ☎ 503/222–4667)is the biggest and most colorful in the country. Pickpockets like the crowds, so be on your guard. The chaotic **Mercado Ex-Cuartel** (✉ Av. 8a Sur between Calle Delgado and Calle 1a Ote., El Centro) seems to go on forever. Prices here are slightly higher than the local villages (where most of the crafts come from), but it's one-stop-shopping for ceramics, textiles, hammocks, and more.

Specialty Shops

Galería Fernando Llort is contained within a small indoor complex called **El Arbol de Dios** (✉ Calle La Mascota and Av. Masferrer, Col. Maquilishuat, ☎ 503/263–9165), meaning "God's Tree." Besides the gallery, El Arbol de Dios contains a nice gift store, a framing store, and Pupusería Margoth, a small cafeteria-style eatery with a wide range of Salvadoran food. The souvenir shop is a good place to pick up the vivid Llort-designed beach towels, shirts, ceramics, jewelry, and stationery.

The huge **Red Artesanal** (✉ 3 Calle Pte. 5351, Col. Lomas Verdes, ☎ 503/264–0673) is the best place in the country to buy quality handicrafts. The sophisticated shop features ceramics, sculptures, candles, and items made of *petate* (woven palm fronds). There's also dancing and painting workshops for kids. It's open weekdays 8–12 and 1–6, Saturday 9–11. **Arte y Madera** (✉ 3 Calle Pte. 4440, between Calle 85 and Calle 87, Col. Escalón, ☎ 503/263–7328) sells textiles from San Sebastian, baskets from Nahuizalco, and large wood trays called *bateas*. It's open Monday–Saturday 8–6.

Side Trips from San Salvador

Lago de Ilopango

Filling the crater of an extinct volcano, Lago de Ilopango is the country's largest and deepest lake, covering more than 120 square km (46 square mi). Along the beach is a line of stalls selling freshly fried fish. Locals will offer to take you on a half-hour boat ride to the island of Puntún. Another destination on the lake is Cerros Quemados (which means "Burned Hills"), an island created by an 1880 volcanic eruption. ✉ *15 km (9 mi) east of San Salvador.*

Panchimalco

South of the capital lies the picturesque village of Panchimalco. Here, surrounded by lush green mountains and dramatic boulders, descendants of the indigenous Pipil people live a surprisingly traditional life. The town's tranquil cobblestone streets lead to a small but elegant colonial church. A yearly festival, on the first Sunday of March, features a colorful parade. ✉ *15 km (9 mi) south of San Salvador.*

Joya de Cerén

About 1,500 years ago, Volcán Laguna Caldera erupted, depositing several yards of volcanic ash in the surrounding area. A Maya village at the base of the volcano was buried beneath the debris. The perfectly preserved village—everything right down to clay urns and the food inside them—was discovered by a construction worker in 1976. The site provides an intriguing look at Maya life, including the foods they ate, the crops they grew, and their social structure. Because there are no signs, it's best to see the site with a guide. You can view pieces unearthed here, including an ornate obsidian blade, at the anthropology museum in San Salvador. ✉ *36 km (22 mi) west of San Salvador,* ☎ *no phone.* ✈ *$3.* ☉ *Tues.–Sun. 9–5.*

San Andrés

El Salvador's second-largest archaeological site, San Andrés is a Maya community that was inhabited between 600 and 900, about the same time as Tikal in Guatemala and Copán in Honduras. More than 12,000 people once made their homes in and around the city. Two plazas ringed by pyramids have been carefully excavated, although the concrete used to shore up the structures is rather ugly. An interesting museum explains the history of the site and displays clay figurines found here. A scale model of the city helps you to imagine its former grandeur. The grounds are beautifully maintained, with trees set around the grass-covered terraces. Salvadorans often come here for picnics. ✉ *33 km (21 mi) west of San Salvador,* ☎ *no phone.* ✈ *$3.* ☉ *Tues.–Sun. 9–4:30.*

Volcán de San Salvador

This volcano, visible from all over the region, offers excellent perspectives of San Salvador and the entire Valle de las Hamacas. There are two craters, the most famous of which is nicknamed El Boquerón ("The Big Mouth"). A path leads to the bottom of the crater, where you'll find another cone, formed during an eruption in 1917. It's best to hire a guide, as robbers sometimes target hikers along this route. ✉ *11 km (7 mi) north of Santa Tecla,* ☎ *no phone.* ✈ *Free.*

San Salvador A to Z

AIR TRAVEL TO AND FROM SAN SALVADOR

Most people exploring this region fly into Aeropuerto Internacional Comalapa, 44 km (27 mi) south of San Salvador.

BUS TRAVEL TO AND FROM SAN SALVADOR

Most intercity buses leave from one of the two main terminals: Terminal de Oriente serves destinations north and east of the capital, while Terminal de Occidente serves those to the west.

➤ BUS TERMINALS: **Terminal de Occidente** (✉ Av. 49a Sur and Bul. Venezuela). **Terminal de Oriente** (✉ Av. Peralta).

BUS TRAVEL WITHIN SAN SALVADOR

While the government has repeatedly tried improve it, San Salvador's bus system is dangerous. Drivers compete for customers, causing frequent accidents. Buses are crowded, resulting in pickpocketings and other crimes. That said, the bus system is efficient and extremely inexpensive. It's also easy to navigate, with the route numbers posted on the front of each bus.

CAR RENTAL

Most of the major rental agencies—Avis, Budget, Hertz, and Thrifty—have offices in San Salvador. A local agency worth checking into is Union.

➤ RENTAL AGENCIES: **Avis** (✉ 43 Av. Sur 127, Col. Flor Blanca, ☎ 503/261–1212). **Best** (✉ 3 Calle Pte., Col. Escalón, ☎ 503/298–9611). **Budget** (✉ Paseo Gen. Escalón, Col. Escalón, ☎ 503/264–3888). **Hertz** (✉ 9 Calle Pte. at 91 Av. Norte, Col. Escalón, ☎ 503/264–2818). **Thrifty** (✉ Bul. Orden de Malta Sur 12, Col. Santa Elena, ☎ 503/289–2984). **Union** (✉ Calle Conchaga 22, Col. Santa Elena, ☎ 503/243–8025, WEB unionrentacar.com).

CAR TRAVEL

Those who are used to urban driving will find that the city's thoroughfares are relatively simple to negotiate, as the capital is small and easy to get around. Getting around by taxis is less of a hassle, however.

EMBASSIES

Embassies are generally open weekdays 8–4:30. Call before you visit, as many close their doors for a few hours at midday.

➤ EMBASSIES: **Canada** (✉ 63 Av. Sur and Alameda Roosevelt, Col. Escalón, ☎ 503/279–4659). **United Kingdom** (✉ 4828 Paseo General Escalón, Col. Escalón, ☎ 503/263–6527). **United States** (✉ Bul. Santa Elena, Col. Antiguo Cuscatlán, ☎ 503/278–4444).

EMERGENCIES

On Boulevard de los Héroes, Hospital Bloom is well regarded. In Colonia Escalón, Hospital de la Mujer provides general care for women. Less severe problems can often be handled at *laboratorios* or *clínicas*. Pharmacies are scattered throughout town. On Boulevard de los Héroes, Farmacia Internacional is open 24 hours.

➤ EMERGENCY SERVICES: **Ambulance** (☎ 121). **Fire** (☎ 503/271–1244). **Police** (☎ 121).

➤ HOSPITALS: **Hospital Bloom** (✉ Bul. de los Héroes, Col. Lacayo, ☎ 503/225–4481 or 503/225–4114). **Hospital de la Mujer** (✉ Av. 81a Sur and Calle Juan José Cañas, Col. Escalón, ☎ 503/263–1122).

➤ 24-HOUR PHARMACY: **Farmacia Internacional** (✉ Bul. de los Héroes and Av. Juan Pablo II).

MAIL AND SHIPPING

San Salvador's main post office is located in El Centro, just east of Parque Infantil. It's open weekdays 8–5, Saturday 8–noon. The best way to send important packages is through one of the many express services. UPS is safe and reliable. It delivers to addresses in the United States in three to six business days. DHL is the city's most professional shipping company. It costs more, but the company can deliver a package to the United States in two business days.

➤ OVERNIGHT SERVICES: **DHL** (✉ 47 Av. Norte 104, Col. Palmira, ☎ 503/260–7722). **UPS** (✉ Calle El Progreso 3139, Col. Roma, ☎ 503/245–0400).

➤ POST OFFICE: **San Salvador** (✉ Final 17 Av. Norte, El Centro, ☎ 503/271–1922).

MONEY MATTERS

Banco Cuscatlán, Banco Hipotecario, Citibank, and Scotiabank are the places to go to exchange currency. They are ubiquitous—not only in San Salvador, but throughout the country. Many branches have ATMs that accept cards issued abroad. You'll find branches of most banks along Avenida Roosevelt in Colonia Escalón and on Avenida Cuscatlán in El Centro, as well as in the Zona Rosa. Banks are usually open weekdays 9–5 and Saturday 9–noon.

➤ BANKS: **Banco Cuscatlán** (✉ Torre Cuscatlán, ☎ 503/212–2020). **Banco Hipotecario** (✉ Paseo General Escalón, Col. Escalón, ☎ 503/441–1273). **Citibank** (✉ Alameda Manuel Enrique Araujo, Col. Escalón, ☎ 503/211–2484). **Scotiabank** (✉ La Reforma 1114, Col. San Benito, ☎ 503/210–8877.

SAFETY

As with any other big city in Central America, parts of San Salvador have quite a bit of street crime. Cramped sidewalks make tourists easy targets for pickpockets. Some areas, such as El Centro, are especially dangerous. It's a good idea to take a taxi to your destination, even during the day.

TAXIS

Taxis are plentiful in San Salvador. You should always settle on a price before beginning a journey because there are no meters. A five-minute trip should run about $6.

➤ TAXI COMPANIES: **Acontaxis** (✉ 10 Av. Sur 2011, Col. América, ☎ 503/270–1176). **Radio Taxis Magdalena** (✉ Diagonal Univ. and 21 Calle Pte., Col. América, ☎ 503/235–1061).

TELEPHONES

San Salvador, along with the rest of El Salvador, uses the area code 503. To make a call to anywhere within the country, simply dial the seven-digit number.

TOUR OPERATORS

Amor Tours is a well-regarded tour operator, offering trips around the city as well as excursions to nearby archaeological sites.

➤ TOUR COMPANY: **Amor Tours** (✉ 73 Av. Sur and Av. Olímpica, Col. Escalón, ☎ 503/223–5130).

VISITOR INFORMATION

Two branches of the Corporación Salvadoreña de Turismo, one at the airport and another in the Zona Rosa, dole out simple maps, bus schedules, and pamphlets on various points of interest. Most of the information is current, but not all of it is in English. The Zona Rosa branch of Corsatur is open weekdays 8–12:30 and 1:30–5:30.

➤ TOURIST INFORMATION: **Corsatur** (✉ Bul. del Hipódromo 508, Col. San Benito, ☎ 503/243–7835, WEB www.elsalvadorturismo.gob.sv).

NORTHERN AND WESTERN EL SALVADOR

Head north or west of San Salvador and you find yourself passing through valleys carpeted in brilliant shades of green. The mild climate and fertile soil make this the country's coffee capital. The crop continues to bring in great wealth to the owners of the haciendas, but the people who live in the surrounding villages remain grindingly poor.

Toward the borders of the tiny country you'll encounter some breathtaking scenery. In the northwest, the rugged mountains near La Palma attract hikers. Here is El Pital, the country's highest peak. Parque Nacional Montecristo, El Salvador's most famous nature reserve, is perpetually shrouded in mist. This cloud forest is one of the last places in the country to see endangered animals such as the spider monkey.

Western El Salvador is also known for its dramatic natural beauty. South of the town of Santa Ana is Lago de Coatepeque, a beautiful blue lake hidden inside the crater of a long-dormant volcano. Rivers and scenic waterfalls draw many people to the region, especially near Sonsonate. To get a glimpse at how people have lived for centuries, follow the Ruta de las Flores ("Route of Flowers"). Here you'll find a handful of sleepy village set high in the mountains. The region is home to a few indigenous communities. Sadly, their distinctive dress, language, and customs are quickly dying out.

Suchitoto

★ *27 km (17 mi) north of San Salvador.*

Cobblestone streets lined with squat colonial buildings make this little town so enchanting. Its setting, along a huge reservoir called Cerrón Grande, makes it one of the most popular destinations for day-trippers from Sal Salvador. In the center of town you'll find a square called **Parque San Martín,** the heart of Suchitoto. Around the bandstand are dozens of benches that are filled with locals until late in the evening. In between are a few quirky sculptures, including one that is a replica of a *tatú,* or tunnel, used as a hiding place during the civil war. Hanging over the cave is part of an actual plane that was shot down by rebels. Look closely and you can see the bullet holes. Another piece of interesting public art is across the street at a restaurant called La Balanza. This restaurant's name, which means "The Balance," refers to the scale that rests above the entrance; on one side is part of an unexploded bomb that was dropped on the city, while on other other is a stack of tortillas.

The rather secretive **Museo Alejandro Cotto** is housed in the residence of an eccentric man known as *el brujo de Suchitoto* (the warlock of Suchitoto). A former film director, Cotto is known for his efforts to preserve his hometown's character. After letting you in through the 300-year-old front door, Cotto proudly shows off the printing equipment owned by his father, including antique presses and blocks of metal with raised letters. A number of galleries hold his family's collection of works by top Salvadoran painters. A chapel contains centuries-old wooden saints and relics. Cotto takes you down verdant paths lined with bubbling fountains he switches on and off and past such antiques as a 200-year-old sugarcane juicer. The high point of the tour is a serpentine trail that leads to a magnificent view of the nearby reservoir of Cerrón Grande. ⊠ *3 Av. Norte s/n,* ☎ *no phone.* ☞ *$3.* ☉ *Daily 9–noon and 2–5:30.*

A cooperative of young artists, **Casa de los Mestizos** is a good place to learn about the region. The former home, set around a stone courtyard, serves as a exhibition space for works by painters and sculptors, as well as a performance space for musicians, actors, and poets. Free foreign movies are screened here on weekends. The building also houses a funky restaurant and bar. ⊠ *3 Av. Norte 48,* ☎ *503/848–3438.* ☞ *Free.* ☉ *Daily 10–10.*

Dining and Lodging

$–$$ ✕ **La Balanza.** From the scale above the entrance to the prow-shape bar,
★ there's much here that's symbolic and strange. The soft-spoken owners, Carlos and Julia Rubidia, are glad to explain it all. The blue tiles near the bar, for instance, represent the nearby lake. You can see it if you dine in the tower, which is decorated with antiques and artifacts. The rest of the open-air restaurant is relaxing, even if the collection of war memorabilia—bullets, mortars, and the like—is not. A sign posted by the Rubidias that reads *Mejor es la Paz* ("Peace is Better") makes the message clear. The menu is typically Salvadoran, like *gallina india* (grilled hen) and *pan con pavo* (turkey sandwich). ⊠ *North side of Parque San Martín,* ☎ *503/335–1408. No credit cards. No dinner Mon.*

$$–$$$ ✕▥ **La Posada de Suchitlán.** The quartet of villas at this century-old
★ hacienda have private patios overlooking the lake—one of the most beautiful views in the country. The villas, set in lovely gardens, are a few dollars more than the other rooms, but they are well worth the

expense. On the premises is a small zoo with parrots and rabbits. Specialties at the restaurant include *gallo en chicha,* a deliciously sweet soup made with corn liquor. Don't pass up the homemade bread. If it's a hot day, try a refreshing fruit-flavored *licuado* (smoothie). ⊠ *Final 4 Calle Pte., Barrio San José,* ☎ *503/335–1064,* FAX *503/335–1164,* WEB *www.laposada.com.sv. 6 rooms, 4 villas. Restaurant, cable TV, playground, free parking. AE, DC, MC, V.*

Chalatenango

69 km (43 mi) from San Salvador.

On the northern shore of Cerrón Grande, the bustling town if Chalatenango makes a good base for exploring the most far-flung region of El Salvador. With a population of 30,000, it is the area's largest city. Despite being a center of conflict during the civil war—a large garrison is still found here—Chalatenango retains the easygoing charm characteristic of many northern communities. The gleaming **Catedral de Chalatenango,** newly restored, stands guard on the east side of the central square.

Many people head to Chalatenango because the surrounding country is so beautiful. Here you'll find **La Montañona,** a pine forest reserve on top of a massive hill. Getting there is a feat—it's a 5-km (3-mi) hike from the village of La Laguna—but you'll be rewarded with spectacular views.

Lodging

$ ☒ **Hotel California.** Rooms at this little hotel are somewhat sterile, but they're comfortable and have private baths. Those upstairs have nice terraces. ⊠ *Calle Morazán, between Avs. 2a and 4a,* ☎ *503/335–2170. No credit cards.*

Shopping

You can get a taste of daily life at the bustling **Mercado Central** (⊠ Calle Morazán and Av. 4a Norte). The market is also a good place to stop for lunch.

Concepción Quezaltepeque

10 km (6 mi) west of Chalatenango.

The civil war ravaged this little village, but today Concepción Quezaltepeque is one of El Salvador's most peaceful spots. Its reputation as the country's hammock capital is a testament to its mellow character. **Llano Grande,** about 8 km (5 mi) from Concepción Quezaltepeque, offers commanding views of the surrounding countryside.

Shopping

While in town, check out the **Cooperativa Inmaculada Concepción** (⊠ 1 block from the central plaza, ☎ 503/331–2229), where you can buy beautifully woven hammocks. The women who work here are happy to chat about their craft. There are also cooperatives in the nearby villages of San José de Las Flores and San Antonio Los Ranchos.

La Palma

70 km (43 mi) northwest of Concepción Quezaltepeque.

In the shadow of El Pital, the country's highest mountain, is the little town of La Palma. That peak, as well as others nearly as high, draw hikers from around the world. From the top you can see across parts of El Salvador and Honduras.

When artist Fernando Llort moved to La Palma three decades ago, he began teaching residents his distinctive, playful style of painting. Today La Palma is famous for the dozens of workshops producing wood and ceramic goods adorned with these childlike designs. The facade of the town's little church, however, is the work of Llort himself.

Dining and Lodging

$$ ✕🏨 **Entre Pinos.** Set amid towering pines, this rustic retreat is one of the country's most appealing lodgings. The reason is the unbeatable location near the highland village of San Ignacio. From here you can hike or ride horses through the mountainous terrain. The rooms, in log cabins, would be more charming if it weren't for the gaudy bedspreads and curtains. There are two restaurants serving Salvadoran favorites. ✉ *Carretera Toncal del Norte, Km 87, San Ignacio,* ☎ *503/ 335–9370,* 🅵🅰🆇 *503/335–9322. 42 rooms, 3 bungalows. Restaurant, café, minibars, cable TV, bar, meeting rooms, helipad. AE, DC, MC, V.*

$ 🏨 **Posada Real.** The best of the bunch in La Palma, Posada Real has small but clean rooms that surround a nice courtyard. The restaurant serves up traditional Salvadoran fare. ✉ *1 block south of park,* ☎ *503/ 335–9009,* 🅵🅰🆇 *503/335–9322. Restaurant. MC, V.*

Metapán

160 km (99 mi) west of Chalatenango.

Sitting high in the mountains near the Guatemalan border, Metapán is one of the most isolated Salvadoran towns. Some vestiges of the colonial era still remain, such as the **Iglesia de San Pedro.** The church's unusually ornate facade, dating from 1743, resembles a wedding cake. Rows of altars trimmed in gold line the inside of the domed structure.

Arguably the country's most beautiful lake, **Lago de Güija** straddles the border of El Salvador and Guatemala. The brilliant blue body of water is of great religious importance to both the Toltec and Pipil peoples. Legend has it that the lake was formed after several nearby volcanoes erupted, altering the paths of several rivers and destroying the towns of Zacualpa and Güija.

Fisherman will offer to take you on a two-hour tour of the lake. This should get you to the island of Tipa, where you'll be treated to great views of Volcán Chingo and Volcán Ipala, both near the Guatemalan border. On the island is Cerro Negro, a cluster of volcanic boulders that form a cave where fishermen take refuge during storms. Make sure to ask to see Las Figuras, so named for the hieroglyphics carved into boulders. Researchers came several years ago and hauled away the best of the rock carvings so they could be displayed in the national museum, but there are still a dozen or so interesting ones left.

One of the country's last remaining tracts of untouched forest is found at the breathtaking **Parque Nacional Montecristo,** part of an international conservation project administered by El Salvador, Guatemala, and Honduras. In addition to 7,600-ft Cerro Montecristo, two other peaks, 7,900-ft Cerro Miramundo and 7,100-ft Cerro El Brujo, stand nearby. With altitudes like these it can get chilly, so bring a jacket. Most people climb up to the cloud forest, where the tops of the mountains are perpetually covered with mist. The journey through the thick forest is a dark, wet odyssey. It rains more here than anywhere else in the country—more than 80 inches annually. The hothouse nurtures a wide range of plants, including an array of colorful orchids.

The number of animals found in the forest is amazing, from anteaters and porcupines to agoutis and pumas. A number of endangered species, such as long-limbed spider monkeys, have made their home in Montecristo. Also be on the lookout for rare birds, such as the brilliant green quetzal.

The park's upper reaches are closed from April through September to ensure undisturbed breeding. During these months you can still explore the other areas of the park. No matter what time of year you visit, you must obtain a permit from the Administración del Parque Nacional Montecristo in San Salvador before you can camp. ✉ *Calle El Matazano, Col. Santa Lucia, San Salvador,* ☎ *503/442–0119.* 🎫 *$5.75.*

Santa Ana

63 km (40 mi) west of San Salvador, 45 km (28 mi) south of Metapán.

Salvadoreños call Santa Ana *la segunda ciudad,* as it's the country's second-largest city. But don't worry that this will be a smaller version of San Salvador. With some of the country's best-preserved colonial buildings, Santa Ana retains much of its past elegance. **Parque Libertad,** at the intersection of Avenida Independencia and Calle Libertad, is marked by graceful white bandstand. Facing Parque Libertad is the neo-Gothic **Catedral de Santa Ana.** The ornate facade is topped by two towers. The stained glass in the rose window is broken in places, a vestige of the earthquake that devastated the region in 2001.

Facing the cathedral, the **Palacio Municipal** dates back to Santa Ana's brief stint as capital of the republic. Its neoclassical facade faces the street, but a peek inside reveals a colonial-style courtyard complete with a central fountain. Wooden balconies run around the sides.

The cream-color **Teatro Nacional de Santa Ana,** an elegant neoclassical theater, is probably the most remarkable piece of architecture in the country. The building, dating from 1910, is certainly the best preserved, as a superb restoration returned its original grandeur. Note the Volcán de Santa Ana depicted on the ornamental crest on the facade. It sits on the northern edge of Parque Libertad. Next door to the Teatro Nacional is **Casino Santaneco,** built in 1896 as a private club; unlike many such buildings in Central America, it is still used in that capacity today. Note the spiral columns that adorn the corner entrance. Ask a guard to let you inside for a peek at the polished interior. Moorish-style eight-point stars grace the woodwork of the ceiling and balconies.

On the south side of the main square is **Museo Regional de Occidente,** a regional museum with changing exhibitions dedicated to the economic, social, and cultural development of western El Salvador. Upstairs you'll find some fine examples of the artifacts from the region's archaeological sites. Downstairs is a display about the country's currency. ✉ *Av. Independencia Sur 8,* ☎ *503/441–2128 or 503/441–1215.* 🎫 *35¢.* ☉ *Tues.–Sat. 9–12 and 2–5.*

★ The Maya city of **Tazumal,** which means "place where people were burned" in the Q'eqchí language, is one of El Salvador's most important and best-preserved pre-Columbian sites. Although much smaller than Tikal in Guatemala or Copán in Honduras, Tazumal gives a glimpse into the lives of several indigenous civilizations dating back over 3,000 years. Archaeological evidence suggests that the city traded with communities as far away as present-day Mexico. Unfortunately, only a small part of the 5-square-km (3-square-mi) area has been excavated, although work continues on and off. Until more structures are uncovered, Tazumal's main attractions are the large pyramid and ball court. From atop the large pyramid, most likely a religious temple, you have a nice view of the town of Chalchuapa and the surrounding countryside.

A small museum displays a number of relics found at Tazumal, although many of the best ones have been taken to museums in the capital. Photos and placards relate the site's complex history and the difficult restoration process. All are in Spanish. ⊠ *13 km (8 mi) west of Santa Ana.* ☎ *$3.* ☉ *Tues.–Sun. 9–5.*

Dining and Lodging

The city is known for its *sorbetes,* which blend sherbet and ice cream. As you explore the city, look out for the little pushcarts run by a company called Sin Rival. The best flavors are *leche,* made with condensed milk, and *frutas,* made from different types of fresh fruit.

$–$$ ✕ **Los Horcones.** If the Swiss Family Robinson were to open a restau-
★ rant, it might look like this Santa Ana landmark. The name refers to the rough-hewn tree trunks that support the structure, giving it the feel of a tree house. Orchids and ferns hang from the rafters. The odd-size yellow and blue letters on the sign appear to be falling off, which only makes the place more endearing. Tacos and pupusas are the best bets here, although the a menu has a little of everything. Located on the main square, this is also a perfect place to stop for a licuado or a cold beer. ⊠ *Av. 1 Norte,* ☎ *503/447–2038. No credit cards.*

$–$$ ✕ **El Patio.** It's worth the trip to this wonderful spot just for a taste
★ of the Salvadoran specialty called *gallo en chicha.* The sweet soup, flavored with prunes, olives, and raisins, has rooster meat in a home-made liquor made from fermented corn. Wash down your meal with with a mammoth *fresco* (fruit smoothie)—try *piña* (pineapple) or *sandia* (watermelon). The restaurant, set around a cool courtyard, looks like a colonial-era ranch. ⊠ *21 Calle Pte. 3,* ☎ *503/440–4221. AE, DC, MC, V.*

$ ✕ **Cafetería Ban Ban.** This popular bakery has two locations facing each other on Santa Ana's main street. Both serve up espresso drinks and tasty traditional pastries such as *orejitas* (sweet, flaky, ear-shape sweets) and *merengues* (puffs of sweetened egg whites). ⊠ *Av. Independencia Sur between Calle Libertad and Calle 1a Pte.,* ☎ *503/447–9155. No credit cards.*

$$ ⌂ **Hotel Sahara.** This is the best hotel in the city, which isn't saying much. You'll have to put up with fluorescent lights, chipped paint, and tacky furnishings. The rooms are clean, however, and have soaring ceilings. A rooftop terrace has views of the surrounding volcanoes. ⊠ *Av. 10a Sur and Calle 3a Pte.,* ☎ *503/ 447–8832 or 503/447–0458,* FAX *447–8865. 18 rooms. Restaurant, cable TV, laundry service, shop, Internet, free parking. AE, DC, MC, V.*

Lago de Coatepeque

16 km (10 mi) west of Santa Ana.

Set high in the mountains, Lago de Coatepeque is one of the most beautiful sights in El Salvador. The enormous lake, set in a nearly perfectly circular crater, covers 26 square km (16 square mi). Here you'll find some of the best swimming in the country. The air is cool and fresh, and the natural springs keep the water temperature remarkably comfortable. Best of all, the lake hasn't been ruined by reckless development—in fact, all you'll find are the dozens of lovely old homes that line the shore, belonging primarily to Santa Ana coffee barons. The hotels, set back from the lake, have raised terraces that let you gaze out over the water to the looming Santa Ana and Izalco volcanoes.

Dining and Lodging

$ ✕ **Amacuilco Guest House.** Colorful murals lend a bohemian flavor to this slightly ramshackle beach house, popular with backpackers. If you just want to gaze out at the lake, there's no better place than the dock. If you feel a little more energetic, rent a canoe. Then again, you might decide to take a Spanish or Nahuatl class or browse around the artesanía made at the in-house workshop. ⊠ *Lago de Coatepeque,* ☎ *503/ 441–6239. 2 rooms. Restaurant, lake. No credit cards.*

$ ✕🏨 **Hotel Torremolinos.** On a long dock directly above the shore, Torremolinos has no real competition, which means it can get away with slightly dingy rooms. Still, it is a wonderful spot to take in the lake's majesty. The menu at the restaurant is typically Salvadoran, with specialties like *guapote* (bass) and shrimp-stuffed avocado. On Sunday afternoon, dance to live cumbia music while the sun sets over the mountains. ⊠ *Lago de Coatepeque,* ☎ *503/446–9437. 25 rooms. Restaurant, lake, bar. AE, DC, MC, V.*

Parque Nacional Cerro Verde

8 km (5 mi) west of Lago de Coatepeque.

The name is Spanish for "green hill," but Cerro Verde doesn't quite describe the towering peak that forms the centerpiece of this popular national park. This extinct volcano, with excellent views of Lago de Coatepeque, is home to a wide variety of birds—more than 125 species, including 17 types of hummingbirds, have been spotted inside the nature reserve. You can choose among several clearly marked trails. The short nature trail is a pleasant stroll to good views of Volcán de Santa Ana. Signs along the way point out unique features of the crater. The air is clean, crisp, and often chilly, so bring a jacket.

A more serious hike is up **Volcán de Santa Ana,** the highest volcano in El Salvador. Also known as Lamatepec ("father hill"), this 7,757-ft peak is still active, although it hasn't erupted for decades. A hike to its crater and back takes about four hours, but the views of Volcán Cerro Verde and Volcán Izalco make it worth the effort. From the rim you'll surely get a whiff of the sulfuric lagoon from inside the crater.

Hard-core hikers will want to take on the smaller but tougher **Volcán Izalco.** One of the world's youngest volcanoes, the 6,396-ft mound of stone was created in 1770 when molten lava began spewing so rapidly that in less than a month the debris had piled up thousands of feet high. The pyrotechnics were so intense that they could be seen from the sea, and sailors dubbed it *El Faro del Pacifico* (The Lighthouse of the Pacific). After almost two centuries of continuous activity, Izalco suddenly went dormant in 1957. Black and utterly barren, it remains an imposing sight. The climb to the crater is not as daunting as it appears, but the round-trip journey involves a good three hours of strenuous hiking. The crumbling surface—"two steps forward, one step back" the whole way—means inexperienced hikers should think twice before accepting the challenge.

Sadly, Parque Nacional Cerro Verde has become a popular spot for thieves as well. Ask a ranger to accompany you—it's free, and the details they provide about the park and its wildlife can be quite interesting. ⊠ *37 km (23 mi) from Santa Ana.* 🎫 *$2.* ☾ *Daily 8–5.*

Sonsonate

65 km (40 mi) southwest of San Salvador.

Founded in 1552, Sonsonate is one of the oldest cities in El Salvador. Today it's a major commercial center, processing much of the coffee grown in the surrounding area. The city suffered much damage in the 2001 earthquake; one of the seemingly endless aftershocks toppled the steeple of the beautiful Catedral de Sonsonate.

One of the best reasons to spend a day in Sonsonate is to visit **Santo Domingo de Guzmán.** Originally a village called Toponomia (meaning "river of thorns"), the community has preserved quite a bit of its indigenous heritage. Some residents still speak only Nahuatl. Santo Domingo Guzmán boasts two beautiful and dramatic waterfalls. Salto El Escuco, also called El Saltillo ("the little waterfall"), is the nearer of the two. It plummets more than 150 ft. The truly adventurous should continue to the 300-ft Salto La Tepechapa, also called El Saltón ("the big waterfall"). They aren't easy to find, so hire a guide in town.

One of the best-known parks in El Salvador, **Atecozol** has pre-Columbian–style architecture that's pretty enough to be on a postcard (and it is). Here you'll find trails through the forest, terraced pools, and an impressive statue of Atonatl, a Pipil chief who became a national hero when he shot an arrow into the conquistador Pedro de Alvarado in 1524.

Ruta de las Flores

5 km (3 mi) west of Sonsonate.

In the mountains of southwestern El Salvador, the Ruta de las Flores is an informal collection of villages stretching between Sonsonate and Ahuachapán. They're all along the same highway, so traveling between them is easy. This is one of the few places in the country where you'll have to break out your sweater, because the mountain air can be chilly, especially at night.

Nahuizalco is famous for its wicker workshops—a dozen or more produce baskets, chairs, tables, and other products. It's home to a large population of Pipil who came here prior to Spanish occupation. There's also a unique night market where locals buy and sell fruits and vegetables by candlelight.

Apaneca has the highest elevation of any major settlement in El Salvador. It is also one of the prettiest, with cobblestone streets lined with colorful houses. The surrounding countryside is spectacular, so it's no surprise that hikers come here from around the world. The colonial-era **Iglesia de Apaneca** is a bit run down, but the twin bell towers are still quite pretty. Curiously, the church faces away from the main square. South of town is **Finca Santa Leticia,** where you'll find three Maya sculptures. These potbellied monoliths, carved some 2,500 years ago, weigh in at 14,000 to 21,000 pounds each. They were discovered here in 1963. Hire a guide to take you to **Laguna Verde** and **Laguna de las Ninfas,** two lovely lakes.

You'll likely spot **Juayúa** if you do any hiking in the area, as the colonial church and whitewashed buildings gleam in the sun. This community is best known as the home of the *Cristo Negro* (Black Christ), a 15th-century sculpture that attracts hundred of pilgrims every year. The charming little village is surrounded by the fields of coffee that bring prosperity to the region.

Dining and Lodging

$$ ✕▥ **Finca Santa Leticia.** It's just outside Apacneca, but this family-run hotel's location within 230 acres of tropical hardwood forests makes it feel miles from civilization. To emphasize the seclusion, accommodations lack TVs and phones. The simply decorated rooms are crowned with ceiling beams made from lumber from the nearby farm. The restaurant serves three meals a day featuring grilled meats and freshly caught fish. The property is a fully functioning coffee plantation, and tours of the facilities are available through the English-speaking owner. ⊠ *Lago de Coatepeque,* ☏ *503/441–6239,* WEB *www.coffee.com.sv. 11 rooms. Restaurant, pool, hiking, bar; no room TVs, no room phones. AE, DC, MC, V. BP.*

Ahuachapán

30 km (19 mi) northwest of Sonsonate.

It may not have the charm of many of the towns in the mountains, but the bustling community of Ahuachapán is an important stop if you need to exchange currency or pick up some provisions. Ahuachapán is unique in the area, as it has two plazas and two churches. **Iglesia El Calvario,** known for its ornate altar, is on the western edge of Parque Menéndez. **Parroquía de Nuestra Señora del Asunción,** with its beautiful stained-glass windows, is to the east of Parque La Concordia.

Parque Nacional El Imposible

30 km (19 mi) west of Sonsonate.

Named for a treacherous gorge that once was indeed impassable, Parque Nacional El Imposible is El Salvador's largest national park. Covering 13,000 acres, it contains 260 types of birds (including king vultures, white hawks, and black-crested eagles) and 40 species of mammals (including pumas, wild boars, and collared anteaters). The landscape itself is truly spectacular, soaring to 4,756 ft. Eight rivers run through one of the last remaining dry tropical forests in the Americas. There are a number of trails starting at the visitor center just inside the San Benito entrance, from easy half-hour loops to grueling six-hour treks. You are required to have a ranger with you on all of the longer trails, so ask at the visitor center for information. The park is closed to most visitors, but you can obtain a permit from SalvaNatura in San Salvador. ⊠ *SalvaNatura, Av. 77a Norte and Pasaje Ismania, Col. Escalón, San Salvador,* ☏ *503/263–1111,* FAX *223–3516,* WEB *www.salvanatura.org.* ⌨ *$6.*

La Libertad

33 km (20 mi) south of San Salvador.

El Salvador's famed Costa del Bálsamo, named for the abundant balsam trees that grow along the coast, runs from Acajutla to La Libertad. If you're a surfer, you may find that you never want to leave. Those who travel in search of the perfect wave say the area offers the best surfing in Central America, and among the best in the world.

The long pier in the center of La Libertad is one of the most colorful destinations in the country. Keep your eye out for when the returning fishing boats are hoisted up onto the end of the pier with a winch—a procedure both impressive and entertaining. After the fishermen haul in the day's catch, aproned women carefully arrange it for sale.

When you drive to the coast, you'll hit the Carretera del Litoral. Head west along this road and you'll soon reach some of the best beaches. Since much of the shoreline is private, one of the best ways to see the area is to head to an oceanfront restaurant. In addition to enjoying delicious seafood, you can leave your car parked there when you venture out to the sand.

Dining and Lodging

$$–$$$ ✕ **Café Sunzal.** Fuchsia and purple bougainvillea frame soothing ocean views at this attractive little café. Chinese lanterns in bamboo cubes

are suspended from the peaked thatch roof that lets in the cool breezes and the sound of the surf. While the food doesn't quite live up to the promise of the setting, you can sample dishes such as grilled shrimp with garlic butter, fish fillet with honey-roasted almond sauce, and lobster with steamed vegetables. Wash them down with California wines. ⊠ *Playa El Sunzal, Carretera del Litoral Km 43,* ☏ *503/243–0426. AE, DC, MC, V. Closed Mon.*

$$–$$$ ✕ **Dolce Manny's Bar & Grill.** Big hopes are pinned on this place, which promises to bring nightlife to the coast. The soft glow of candles and the crash of the waves make this the place to be after the sun goes down. Striving for a more contemporary look than La Dolce Vita downstairs, the restaurant has wooden tables surrounding a raised bar. Feel free to choose whatever you like from the selection of broiled meats and seafood prepared in front of you on a large grill—owner Manny Vides says if you don't like a dish, he'll offer you another free. Try the *pescado Tahiti,* which is grilled fish served in banana leaves. ⊠ *La Libertad, Carretera El Litoral, above La Dolce Vita,* ☏ *503/346–0330. AE, DC, MC, V.*

$$–$$$ ✕ **La Dolce Vita.** This gem is most famous of the cluster of restaurants piled high above La Libertad's beach of polished stones. Italian owner Carmine Cedrola, who worked in some fine Florentine establishments, has produced an affordable menu of Mediterranean favorites. The result is you have to wait in line on weekends to get a table in the open-air dining room packed with families wrapping up their day at the beach. The menu is the most varied on the coast. The lobster is a good bet, whether served *a la plancha* (grilled) or *al ajillo* (with garlic). Wandering musical groups called *combos* entertain the crowd. ⊠ *Puerto La Libertad, Carretera El Litoral,* ☏ *503/335–3592. AE, DC, MC, V.*

$$–$$$ ✕ **La Dolce Vita 2.** The simplest way to spend a day at the Costa del Bálsamo is to head to this seaside restaurant. While not as lively as its older sibling, its location on a wide stretch of Playa San Blas makes up for that. You can eat under the shade of 15 palm trees, or request a table with an umbrella out on the sand. The clientele is mostly local families enjoying seafood accompanied by *coco natural* (fresh cocoanut milk) or *coco loco* (the same with vodka). The service here is very friendly. ⊠ *Playa San Blas, Carretera del Litoral Km 39,* ☏ *503/ 346–0136. AE, DC, MC, V.*

$$$ ✕🏨 **Suites Jaltepeque.** There are only a few hotels on the coast, and this one on the Costa del Sol is by far the best. On a long lawn lined with coconut palms, this family-oriented complex surrounds a pretty pool. If you want to explore the area, rent a horse to ride along the sandy beach. The thatch-roof restaurant serves everything from sandwiches and burgers to meats and seafood. All the rooms have small balconies. The best for groups are the double suites, which come with two bedrooms and two baths; these are also nearer the beach. Check out the weekend packages, which are even cheaper than nightly rates. ⊠ *Bul. Costa del Sol Km 70,* ☏ *503/338–0225,* FAX *503/338–0227,* WEB *www.jaltepeque.com. 33 rooms. Restaurant, room service, kitchenettes, microwaves, refrigerators, cable TV, horseback riding, bar, shop, laundry service. AE, DC, MC, V.*

Outdoor Activities and Sports

To the west side of La Libertad, the rocky spit known as **Punta Roca** is one of the world's top surf spots. With a perfect right-hand break, Punta Roca was legendary among surfers in the 1970s. Twelve years of civil war, however, drove away all but the most dedicated wave-riders. Today, Punta Roca remains relatively empty, much to the delight

of the small group of surfers who have rediscovered it. The eastern side of the wave is smaller and softer, perfect for less experienced surfers (though not first-timers).

There are a number of excellent surf spots farther west, most of them practically empty. **Playa Tunco,** the closest to La Libertad, boasts a left-hand break. Ask about renting a board and getting a few lessons. **Playa Zunzal** has consistent waves and a good right-hand point. **Playa El Zonte** has a consistent right-hand break, with a decent left-hander at the point. **Playa Chutía** has a nice right-hand break.

Northern and Western El Salvador A to Z

AIR TRAVEL
Most people exploring this region fly into Aeropuerto Internacional Comalapa, 44 km (27 mi) south of San Salvador.

BUS TRAVEL TO AND FROM NORTHERN AND WESTERN EL SALVADOR
Terminal de Occidente in San Salvador has buses headed to the western part of the country, while Terminal de Oriente serves destinations north of the capital.

CAR RENTAL
Many visitors who plan to explore this region pick up a rental car in San Salvador. You can also rent a car in Santa Ana.

MONEY MATTERS
Your best bet for financial transactions is in San Salvador, but you can get cash advances on credit cards and use ATMs at banks in Santa Ana.
➤ BANKS: **Banco Hipotecario** (✉ 2 Calle Pte. and 2 Av. Norte, Santa Ana, ☎ 503/441–1273). **Scotiabank** (✉ Av. Independencia Sur, Santa Ana, ☎ 503/440–7280).

TOUR OPERATORS
Suchitoto Tours is a cooperative run by the ecologically and historically minded volunteers at Casa de los Mestizos. The group organizes inexpensive outings on Saturdays to wildlife preserves and other scenic sights throughout the country.
➤ TOUR COMPANIES: **Suchitoto Tours** (✉ 3 Av. Norte 48, ☎ 848–3438).

EASTERN EL SALVADOR

This region is extraordinarily diverse, ranging from mountain villages to charming towns to modern cities. Some areas within this region are famous for their artesanía, others for their outdoor activities. Eastern El Salvador rarely draws the attention of tourists, but the warm and generous spirits of its people wins the hearts of many who visit.

Cojutepeque

32 km 19 mi) east of San Salvador.

The main attraction of this village is the Cerro De Pavas ("Hill of Turkeys"), where the **Santuario de la Virgen de Fátima** is found. The sanctuary holds a small statue, brought here from Portugal in 1949, that draws crowds of worshipers every Sunday. There's a great view of Lago Ilopango from the hill as well.

The towns's famous pork sausages, spicy *chorizos,* and salamis garland the quaint roadside stands.

Ilobasco

22 km (14 mi) north of Cojutepeque.

Just up the road from Cojutepeque, this village is famous for the dozens of workshops that produce brightly colored ceramic items. All along Avenida Bonilla you'll find *sorpresas,* which are hand-painted scenes of village life inside egg-shape shells. (You might indeed be surprised to behold the depictions of randy villagers inside some). Make sure to stop by the **Escuela de Capacitación Kiko** (✉ Av. Bonilla), a ceramics school that gives tours of its facility.

San Sebastián

22 km (14 mi) south of Ilobasco, 14 km (9 mi) east of Cojutepeque.

Festoons of colorfully dyed string hanging outside storefronts welcome you to San Sebastian, which, like Concepción Quetzaltepeque in the north, is famous for its textiles. This is a great place to buy radiant hammocks, place mats, tablecloths, towels, blankets, and bedspreads. You are welcome to watch the weavers at work at the local textile factories. **Textiles y Funerales Duran** (✉ 3 blocks from the plaza, ☏ no phone) has large, complicated looms, and the weavers seem happy to explain how they work.

San Vicente

11 km (7 mi) southeast of San Sebastián.

In the shadow of 7,154-ft Volcán Chichontepec sits San Vicente, a colonial town founded in 1635. The elegant architecture makes you daydream about life here centuries ago. In the 1830s, San Vicente was the country's temporary capital. Today the easygoing town is the center of an agricultural region dominated by coffee and sugarcane.

San Vicente's most notable feature is the fanciful **Torre de Reloj,** which looks likes a scaled-down Eiffel Tower. Plunked down in the middle of the leafy Parque Cañas, it offers a terrific view of the city, especially in late afternoon. The **Alcaldía de San Vicente,** which houses the local government, is a stately white building on the south side of the main square. On the eastern side of the plaza stands **Catedral de San Vicente**—earthquakes have left all but the facade in ruins. The **Iglesia El Pilar,** a gothic church dating back to the 18th century, stands two blocks south of the plaza. Inside you'll find a beautiful hand-carved wooden altar. Near the door is a plaque honoring José Simeón Cañas, remembered for abolishing slavery in El Salvador. The **Santuario San Juan Bautista,** another lovely church, is two blocks east of the cathedral on 6a Avenida Norte.

Some of the sights have a more sober history. An enormous **cuartel,** or military compound, occupies the entire block southwest of the plaza; you can't miss its fatigue-wearing sentries. This area saw many battles during the bloody civil war.

Near Verapáz, a village just west of San Vicente, you'll find a beautiful hot spring. Strong sulfuric fumes have made the affectionately named **Infiernillo,** meaning "Little Hell," a popular retreat for those who believe in the medicinal properties of the water.

A crater lake called **Laguna de Apastapeque,** about 3 km (2 mi) northeast of San Vicente, is a great place to escape the heat. Here you'll find a tidy beach, a swimming pool, and a restaurant. It can be crowded on weekends, but during the week you'll have the place practically to yourself. If you're interested in smaller, more secluded lakes, ask about nearby Laguna Bruja or Laguna Ciega.

Dining

$–$$ ✕ **Casa Blanca.** Grilled shrimp and steak are the specialties at this laid-back restaurant. Start with complimentary *bocas* (appetizers), then move on to one of the tasty chicken or fish dishes. ⊠ *11 Calle 2a Ote.,* ☎ *503/393–0549. No credit cards.*

Santiago de María

40 km (25 mi) east of San Vicente.

One of the most beautiful towns in eastern El Salvador, Santiago de María is in the middle of coffee-growing country; you'll spot the local cash crop creeping over the hills surrounding the town. The lively and attractive city was spared the ravages of the war, save for a brief occupation by rebels who looted the fields that belonged to President Alfredo Cristiani. It was not spared from the earthquakes that hit the region in the past few years; many of the buildings are still being repaired.

When visiting Santiago de María, give yourself a day or two to explore the surrounding countryside. **Cerro Tigre** (Tiger Hill) is the name given a string of overlapping hills east of town. A two-hour climb leads you to commanding views of the valley. To the west of town, Volcán de Alegría has a crater lake known as the **Laguna de Alegría,** which is known more for its medicinal properties than its recreation; the sulfur fumes emanating from the rock are said to have therapeutic value when inhaled.

Dining

$–$$ ✕ **El Marrua.** This surprisingly good Brazilian restaurant, on the north side of the central square, serves up *tortillas arabes* (fried potato patties filled with meat or vegetables) and *lomito al la plancha* (grilled beef). ⊠ *Calle Bolívar,* ☎ *no phone. No credit cards.*

San Miguel

45 km (30 mi) east of Santiago de María.

With almost 200,000 residents, San Miguel is the third-largest city in the country. On the central Parque David J. Guzmán, the huge **Catedral de Nuestra Señora de la Paz** (⊠ 4 Av. Norte) possesses a marble altar and stained-glass windows that are worth seeing. Here you'll find a statue of the Virgin Mary that supposedly saved the city from destruction during a volcanic eruption. South of the central square sits the elegant **Antiguo Teatro Nacional** (⊠ 2 Calle Ote.), a century-old building where plays are often staged from August through November. About seven blocks west of the square are the lovely gardens that house the **Capilla de la Medalla Miagrosa** (⊠ 7 Av. Norte and 4 Calle Pte.), a chapel where a religious medal once worked miracles.

The **Laguna de Olomega** is still the lifeblood of the many villages that dot its shoreline, which means fish is the main meal for miles around. (Locals favor the tasty *guapote* and the sturgeon-size tilapia.) You can reach the communities around the lake, including Olomegita and La Estrachura, on passenger boats that leave at 8 AM, return at 3 PM, and leave again at 4 PM (35¢). Another nice stop is Los Cerritos, a little island where locals bake in the sun.

Dominating the town is the 6,986-ft **Volcán Chaparrastique,** an active volcano that last erupted in 1976. It's an intense two-hour hike to the summit from the town of La Placita.

Dining and Lodging

$–$$ ✗ **Acajutla.** Great seafood dishes are served in an airy and elegant thatch-roof dining room of this San Miguel favorite. ⊠ *Av. Roosevelt Sur and 7 Calle Pte.,* ☎ *503/661–2255. AE, DC, MC, V.*

$ ✗ **Chilitas Pupuseria.** At this mammoth San Miguel institution, you'll find the service lukewarm but the pupusas always piping hot. It gets crowded on the weekends. ⊠ *Calle 8a Ote. and Av. 6a Norte,* ☎ *no phone. No credit cards.*

$ ▥ **El Mandarin.** The most comfortable accommodations in town are to be had here. The management is friendly and helpful, while the rooms are simple and clean. As a bonus, you can also get tasty Chinese food at the restaurant. ⊠ *Av. Roosevelt Norte 407,* ☎ *503/669–6969,* FAX *503/669–7912. 32 rooms. Restaurant, cable TV. MC, V.*

$ ▥ **El Viajero.** A pleasant older man runs this bright and cheerful hotel. Simple but spacious rooms surround a pretty courtyard crisscrossed with laundry lines. The beds aren't the greatest, but everything is spic and span. ⊠ *Av. 7a Norte and Calle 6a Pte.,* ☎ *503/661–1716. 12 rooms. MC, V.*

Eastern El Salvador A to Z

AIR TRAVEL

Most people exploring this region fly into Aeropuerto Internacional Comalapa, 44 km (27 mi) south of San Salvador.

BUS TRAVEL TO AND FROM EASTERN EL SALVADOR

Buses bound for San Salvador depart about every 10 minutes from dawn until dusk from San Vicente and San Miguel.

CAR RENTAL

If you find yourself in need of a car, head to San Miguel. Hertz is represented here, as are well-respected local agencies like Paradiso and Uno.
➤ LOCAL AGENCIES: **Paradiso** (⊠ San Miguel, ☎ 503/667–7767). **Hertz** (⊠ San Miguel, ☎ 503/661–1691). **Uno** (⊠ San Miguel, ☎ 503/669–0188).

MAIL AND SHIPPING

All communities of any size in eastern El Salvador have a post office somewhere near the central square. The main post office in San Miguel is on 4 Avenida Sur, about three blocks south of Parque David J. Guzmán. For important packages, try Urbano Express.
➤ POST OFFICES: **San Miguel** (⊠ 4 Av. Sur, between 3 and 5 Calles Oriente).
➤ OVERNIGHT SERVICES: **Urbano Express** (⊠ Av. Roosevelt Norte 415, San Miguel, ☎ 503/669–5324).

MONEY MATTERS

The best place for financial transactions is in San Salvador, but you can secure cash advances from credit cards and use ATM at banks in San Vicente and San Miguel. Banco Hipotecario and Scotiabank have branches in both cities.
➤ BANKS: **Banco Hipotecario** (⊠ Calle 2 Poniente 192, San Miguel, ☎ 503/661–6203; (⊠ Calle 1 Oriente 2, San Vicente, ☎ 503/393–0108). **Scotiabank** (⊠ Av. 2 Norte 106, San Miguel, ☎ 503/661–2652; ⊠ Av. 1 Norte and Calle Quiñónez de Osorio, San Vicente, ☎ 503/393–0989).

EL SALVADOR A TO Z

AIR TRAVEL TO AND FROM EL SALVADOR

Grupo Taca has a very good reputation. It flies between San Salvador and all other Central American capitals. Grupo Taca also has flights

from the United States, as do American, Continental, and United. There are no direct flights from Europe, so you should transfer in Miami or Houston.

➤ AIRLINES AND CONTACTS: **American** (✉ Alameda Roosevelt 3107, ☎ 503/298–0777). **Continental** (✉ Torre El Roble, Bul. de Los Héroes, ☎ 503/260–2180). **Grupo Taca** (✉ Edificio Caribe, Plaza Las Américas, San Salvador, ☎ 503/267–8222). **United** (✉ Paseo General Escalón, ☎ 503/279–3900).

AIRPORTS

Aeropuerto Internacional Comalapa is 44 km (27 mi) south of San Salvador. Expect a trip to the capital to take about 45 minutes.

A taxi will cost $18 from the airport to your hotel, $16 on the way back. The larger hotels, however, have shuttles waiting for flights.

➤ AIRPORT INFORMATION: **Aeropuerto Internacional Comalapa** (✉ South of San Salvador, ☎ 503/260–7920).

BUS TRAVEL

Salvadoran buses are of the school-bus variety (but decidedly more colorful) and are numbered according to their route. Intercity buses have their destination, along with important stops along the way, posted on the windshield. Bus travel is cheap—few trips cost more than $2. Departures on most routes are frequent, leaving every 10 to 20 minutes during the day. Buses rarely depart after sunset. Don't plan to arrive by bus "just in time" for anything, as delays are common.

Mastering the *desvío* (highway junction) is an important skill in Salvadoran bus travel—you'll often take one bus to a desvío, and then pick up another heading to your destination. Finally, the word *pickup* has been adopted by Salvadorans to mean any truck that carries passengers—if you don't mind the wind, this isn't a bad option (and in more remote areas where buses run infrequently, it may be your *only* option). Rates are slightly cheaper than buses.

In San Salvador, Terminal Puerto Bus is an international terminal for several bus lines, including King Quality and and Transnica. Destinations include Guatemala City (5 hrs, $23), Tegucigalpa (7 hrs, $25), and Managua (10 hrs, $30). Ticabus vehicles depart from Avenida 10a Norte and Calle Conception to Guatemala, Honduras, and Nicaragua; the buses are much more modest, but the prices are about half those of the more luxurious companies.

➤ BUS COMPANIES: **King Quality** (✉ Bul. del Hipódromo 415, Col. San Benito, San Salvador, ☎ 503/222–2158). **Ticabus** (✉ Av. 10a Norte and Calle Conception, San Salvador, ☎ 503/222–4808). **Transnica** (✉ Alameda Roosevelt and 59 Av. Sur, San Salvador, ☎ 240–1212).

➤ BUS STATION: **Terminal Puerto Bus** (✉ Av. Juan Pablo II at Av. 19a Norte, San Salvador, ☎ 503/222–2158).

CAR RENTAL

In El Salvador, you can rent cars for about $50 per day. At the airport, all the rental agencies are clustered together outside the arrivals gate. Here you'll find Avis, Budget, Hertz, Thrifty, and the reliable local agency Best, which charges about $10 less per day than other agencies.

➤ RENTAL AGENCIES: **Avis** (✉ ☎ 503/339–9268). **Best** (✉ ☎ 503/298–9611). **Budget** (✉ ☎ 503/339–9942). **Hertz** (☎ 503/339–8004). **Thrifty** (✉ ☎ 503/339–9947).

CAR TRAVEL

El Salvador has well-maintained highways, especially between the major cities. The Inter-American Highway, here called the CA-1, runs

right through the middle of the country. Some smaller roads need work, but generally are passable. You can rent cars—at rates approaching those of the United States—in the capital and some other cities. During the rainy season, many drivers prefer a four-wheel-drive vehicle or a pickup truck.

To hit the road in El Salvador, all you need is a valid U.S. or international driver's license. You should always have evidence of your rightful possession of a car; proof of insurance isn't necessary, although it's good to have.

HEALTH

The most common malady for visitors to El Salvador is travelers' diarrhea. The best way to avoid it is to be careful about what you eat. Don't drink the water—*agua purificada* (purified water) is available everywhere in bottles. Always order your drinks *sin hielo* (without ice). Avoid salads and fresh fruits that may have been washed in tainted water. Do sample foods from street vendors, but make sure they are still hot. It's a good idea to eat only what has been prepared in front of you. Prepare in advance for the possibility of becoming sick by bringing Pepto-Bismol (the chewable tablets are convenient) and Imodium (in capsules). If it doesn't blow over in a day or two, head to a doctor.

As for mosquito-borne diseases, dengue fever is much more common in El Salvador than malaria, particularly in the eastern lowlands. Socks and long pants are the best protection. Make sure your bug spray has a high DEET content. Lastly, the sun can be extremely strong, even during the rainy season. Use a good sunscreen and wear a wide-brimmed hat.

INTERNET

A company called Infocentros has 26 offices in El Salvador that provide Internet access, as well as other business services. You can count on finding an Infocentro just about anywhere in the country. In the capital, the most convenient branch is located in the Zona Rosa. Most hotels offer business services, although it can get pricey.

INTERNET CAFÉS

Infocentros (⊠ Bul. del Hipódromo 324, Col. San Benito, San Salvador, ☎ 503/223–0586; ⊠ 1a Calle Pte. and Av. José Matías Delgado, Centro Comercial Plaza Prisma, Santa Ana, ☎ 503/447–7746; ⊠ 4a Calle Pte. 105, San Miguel, ☎ 503/661–5987; ⊠ Calle San Martín 2, Suchitoto, ☎ 503/335–1736; ⊠ 1 Calle Pte. and 3a Av. Norte 9, San Vicente, ☎ 503/393–5350; ⊠ 3 Calle Pte., Sonsonate, ☎ 503/451–5243, WEB www.infocentros.com.sv).

MAIL AND SHIPPING

Mail service in El Salvador is inexpensive, but quite slow and somewhat unreliable. Letters and postcards usually arrive in two weeks. Letters to the United States cost about 50¢, and slightly more to Europe and Australia. Do not send cash, valuables, or anything else important through the mail.

MONEY MATTERS

Unlike some of its neighbors, El Salvador's currency has been rock-solid for a number of years. The official currency is the U.S. dollar. *Colónes* are still widely accepted, though the government is slowly phasing out this older currency. The exchange rate is permanently fixed at 8.75 colones to the U.S. dollar, or about 11¢–12¢ to the colón. There's a one colón coin, as well as 5, 10, and 25 *centavo* pieces. Paper bills come in 5, 10, 25, 50, 100, and 200 colón denominations. Ask for smaller bills when exchanging money, as many small shops and restaurants can't

change large bills. Upscale restaurants and hotels don't bother with colones, dealing in dollars only.

ATMS

Most branches of banks like Banco Cuscatlán, Banco Hipotecario, and Scotiabank have ATMs that accept foreign cards. Before you leave home, make sure your secret code has no more than four digits.

CURRENCY

In El Salvador, a ¢ designation before a price indicates cost in colones. A $ sign means the price is in U.S. dollars.

PASSPORTS AND VISAS

Americans, Canadians, Central Americans, and most Europeans do not need visas to enter El Salvador for stays of fewer than 90 days. If you think you might need one, call your country's embassy or bring your passport and two passport-size photos to any Salvadoran consulate or embassy to get a free visa. When you arrive in El Salvador by land or by air you will be charged $10 for a tourist card, typically good for at least 30 days (but they'll give you up to 90 days if you ask). If you need an extension, go to the Extrangería in the Centro de Gobierno on Avenida Juan Pablo II in San Salvador. It's open weekdays 8–12:30 and 1:30–4. You'll have to spend $3 on photos (which you can have taken outside the building) and another $1.50 for processing, but you can do it all in an hour or two. The mandatory airport departure tax is $25, payable in cash only.
➤ PASSPORTS: **Extrangería** (✉ Centro de Gobierno, Av. Juan Pablo II, San Salvado, ☎ 503/271–1936 or 221–2111).

SAFETY

Wherever you go, don't wear expensive clothing, don't wear flashy jewelry, and don't handle money in public. It's a good idea to keep your money in a pocket rather than a wallet, which is easier to steal. Keep cameras in a secure camera bag, preferably one with a chain or wire embedded in the strap. Always remain alert for pickpockets, and don't walk alone at night, especially in the larger cities.

TELEPHONES

There are three main phone companies: Telecom, Telefónica, and Telemóvil. Because of competition among the trio, rates stay quite reasonable. In fact, it's cheaper to call the United States from El Salvador than it is to call El Salvador from the United States.

AREA AND COUNTRY CODES

All of El Salvador uses the same area code: 503. To make a call within the country, simply dial the seven-digit number. To call El Salvador from the United States and Canada, dial 1 followed by 503 and the seven digits, just as if you were calling long distance within the United States or Canada. To make an international call from within El Salvador, dial 155, then 00, then the country code, and finally the area code and seven digit number.

PUBLIC PHONES

Most public phones require phone cards. Remember that phone cards are issued by one of the three telephone companies, so they only work in some phones. Because Telecom has the greatest number of public phones, it's advisable to purchase the company's cards, which come in denominations up to to 50 colones (about $6).

TIPPING

Hotel and upscale restaurants usually add a 10% *propina,* or gratuity, so scrutinize the check closely. Leave a bit more if you feel it's appropriate. Taxi drivers don't expect a tip.

TOURS OPERATORS

The best way to explore El Salvador is with Alligatours, an adventure travel and ecotourism company that hires English-speaking locals as guides. Alligatours runs countryside treks to gushing waterfalls; up Volcán Izalco (coming down by sliding down the ash), and through Parque Nacional El Imposible. Most tours are inexpensive, with many even cheaper than renting a car. Amor Tours is another well-regarded tour operator, offering three-hour city tours as well as other treks to archaeological sites, mountain villages, and secluded beaches.

➤ TOUR COMPANIES: **Alligatours** (⊠ Paseo General Escalón 3658, Col. Escalón, San Salvador, ☎ 503/211–0967, FAX 503/211–0968, WEB www. alligatour.com). **Amor Tours** (⊠ 73 Av. Sur and Av. Olímpica, Col. Escalón, San Salvador, ☎ 503/223–5130).

VISITOR INFORMATION

The Corporación Salvadoreña de Turismo is the major tourist board in the country. Corsatur's office in San Salvador stocks pamphlets and maps. It's open weekdays 8–noon and 1–5:30. It also operates an information desk in the airport, usually open daily 10 AM–5:30 PM. Concultura, based in San Salvador, manages archaeological sites throughout El Salvador. SalvaNatura, which runs the national parks, is also a good source for hiking information.

Good maps of El Salvador are not easily found, so keep your eyes peeled. Most official ones look like maps of Disneyland, with thick, black lines that could have been drawn with a crayon. The Instituto Geográfico Nacional in San Salvador sells decent maps at reasonable prices.

➤ TOURIST INFORMATION: **Concultura** (⊠ Av. de la Revolución, Col. San Benito, San Salvador, ☎ FAX 221–4380). **Corsatur** (⊠ 508 Bul. Hipódromo, Col. San Benito, San Salvador, ☎ 503/243–7835, WEB www. elsalvadorturismo.gob.sv). **Instituto Geográfico Nacional** (⊠ Calle 1a Pte. 310, at Av. 43 Norte, Col. Escalón, San Salvador, ☎ 503/260–6417 or 260–7920). **SalvaNatura** (⊠ Av. 77a Norte and Pasaje Ismania, Col. Escalón, San Salvador, ☎ 503/263–1111, FAX 223–3516, WEB www. salvanatura.org).

5   HONDURAS

It wasn't long ago that most visitors to
Honduras were headed to the splendid
Mayan ruins at Copán or the spectacular
diving of the Bay Islands. Now many
people are drawn to the Caribbean coast,
home of the Garífuna people, to experience
the exhilarating punta music and taste the
bitter spirit called gifiti. Others go directly to
the national parks and reserves, which are
flush with birds from dazzling quetzals to
bobbing toucans.

by Barbara
Kastelein

THE ORIGINAL "BANANA REPUBLIC," Honduras still has vast tracts of land devoted to the ubiquitous yellow fruit. But there is far more to this rugged country bordered by Guatemala, El Salvador, and Nicaragua. In its jungly cloud forests, the air is cool, the rain is abundant, and the landscape is covered with ferns, orchids, and bromeliads. Good guides will be able to point out green iguanas, white-faced monkeys, and—if you are lucky—jaguars and ocelots. The Caribbean coastline offers hundreds of miles of palm-fringed beaches, many with golden sand lapped by gentle sapphire waves. Not far from shore are coral reefs where you can swim with dozens of graceful eagle rays. Tourism here is still in its infancy, so adventurers have plenty of opportunity to enjoy the country's natural wonders in virtual solitude.

Don't wait too long to visit, though. Honduras has been pegged as a hot spot for ecotourism. Keenly aware of what is at stake, the government has been setting aside land for national parks. There are now more than 100 biological reserves and wildlife refuges in the country, such as Parque Nacional La Tigra, north of Tegucigalpa, and Parque Nacional Celaque, south of Gracias. Although many of these are "paper parks" that lack any means to keep lumber companies from chopping down acres of forests, others are going to great lengths to preserve the country's natural treasures.

Explorer Christopher Columbus landed on the northern coast in 1502, claiming the region for Spain. He was far from the first person to set foot here, however. This land had already seen great civilizations rise and fall. Nowhere is this more evident than in Copán, one of the most breathtaking archaeological sites in Central America. What makes Copán so fascinating to archaeologists is not just its astounding size, but its small details. Here they have uncovered carvings that tell the history of this great city, as well as that of others in the region. If you want to understand the ancient civilizations of Quiriguá in Guatemala or Teotihuacán in Mexico, first come to Copán.

In Honduras you will find many generous and good-humored people, especially if you are armed with at least a few words of Spanish. Unlike neighboring Guatemala, there are few indigenous communities here. Most people here are mestizo, meaning mixed-race descendants of Spaniards and Indians. The Lenca and Chortí of the western highlands and the Miskito, Pech, and Tawahka of the northeastern rain forests make up just a fraction of the population. You will have to make quite an effort to reach their isolated villages. You are likely, however, to come across the Garífuna, along the northern coast. This Afro-Caribbean people, brought to Roatán in 1797, has maintained a strong cultural identity and is famous for its traditional dances and music.

Pleasures and Pastimes

Archaeological Treasures

The country's best-known archaeological site, the ancient city of Copán, lies in the jungle near the border of Guatemala. Often dubbed the "Athens of Central America," Copán is known for its soaring pyramids, mammoth stelae, and intricately carved stairway that tells the story of the highly advanced civilization that thrived here for hundreds of years. For as yet undiscovered wonders, excavation work is finally beginning on the ruins of Los Naranjos, near Lago de Yojoa.

Bird-Watching

Veteran bird-watchers have a choice of landscapes—rain forest, cloud forest, or tropical dry forest—in which to spot over 700 different

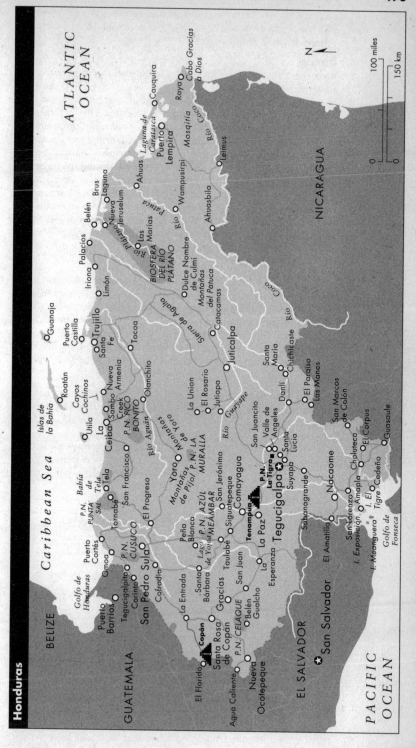

173

Honduras

species. Here you'll find everything from hummingbirds to motmots. Lago de Yojoa, a lovely lake south of San Pedro Sula, has turned many people into avid ornithologists.

Dining

Although Honduras isn't known for its cuisine, you might encounter some pleasant surprises. The national dish is said to be the *plato típico* consisting of some combination of meat, rice, beans, cheese, plantains (called *tajadas*), and perhaps eggs or avocados. This "typical dish" can always be livened up by the hot sauce on the table, often a home-made variety. The true Honduran favorite that foreigners rarely try is the rich *sopa de mondongo* (tripe and vegetable soup). A less intimidating but similarly tasty meal is centered around the *pupusa*, a golden-fried patty of corn, beans, and cheese, usually served with a vinegary blend of cabbage and onion called *repollo*. *Nacatamales* (cornmeal and chicken wrapped in banana leaves) are found all over Central America, but in Honduras they can be very moist and delicate. *Baleadas* (tortillas with beans and cheese) are cheap, pleasant snacks and handy for vegetarians, who can ask for one *sin carne* (without meat).

You'll find fruit abundant—*mango verde* or *mango tierno* (baby green mango) in the spring is not to be missed—and often dressed in novel ways, with a sweet hot sauce, or with lime and a ubiquitous mixture of cumin, pepper, and salt called *pimienta*. Street vendors' fare can also be seductive, especially charcoal-grilled corn on the cob. One of the country's best-kept secrets is *frita de elote* (a deep-fried, sizzling mash of corn and sugar), sold by competing little girls along the road near Lago de Yojoa.

Mealtimes do not vary greatly from the United States, with lunch at noon and dinner at 7 or even earlier. To combat the heat and make the most of the sunlight, Hondureños are early risers, so breakfast is likely to be at 7 or 8, a bit later if you are staying on the beach. In elegant restaurants (meaning those with tablecloths) a tip of at least 10% is about right, while anywhere else it's fine to leave small change. Reservations are rarely necessary, except where indicated.

CATEGORY	COST*
$$$$	over 225 lempiras (over US$15)
$$$	150–225 lempiras (US$10–US$15)
$$	75–150 lempiras (US$5–US$10)
$	under 75 lempiras (under US$5)

per person, for a main course at dinner

Lodging

Cities and towns usually have a wide range of hotels, and all but the tiniest villages have accommodations of some sort. Larger hotels, either parts of international chains or landmarks in their own right, are more costly than you might expect, but offer amenities such as business centers and travel offices. Another attractive alternative is the small hotel set in a colonial-era home. You'll appreciate the personalized attention from the staff.

If there isn't a hotel in town, you can probably find a *hospedaje*, an inexpensive lodging. In remote spots, such as mountain villages around Santa Rosa, locals will often help you find a place to sleep. If you are taken in by a friendly family, you'll find that there's no better way to learn about the culture.

CATEGORY	COST*
$$$$	over 2,250 lempiras (over US$150)
$$$	1,500–2,250 lempiras (US$100–US$150)
$$	750–1,500 lempiras (US$50–US$100)
$	under 750 lempiras (under US$50)

All prices are for a standard double room, excluding tax.

Scuba Diving and Snorkeling

The colorful coral surrounding the Bay Islands, 60 km (37 mi) off the northern coast, has been attracting divers for decades. There's no need to take a boat out to see the spectacular underwater world—in many places the reef begins only a few yards from shore. Farther out you'll find shipwrecks waiting to be explored. Although many novices come here to get their certification, there are plenty of dives that will challenge those who have been diving for years.

Trekking

Honduras is heaven for the intrepid traveler who doesn't mind the exertion required to reach the heart of a pristine cloud forest. Parque Nacional La Tigra, Parque Nacional Celaque, and Parque Nacional Cusuco, three of the most accessible reserves, are well worth the effort. Just be prepared to get wet and muddy, since it rains in these areas throughout the year. Throughout the country, biology students serve as guides, and they are eager to teach you about the region's natural wonders.

White-Water Rafting

Adventurous rafters are delighted to find white water, rapid and deliciously warm, throughout the jungle rivers in the northern reaches of Honduras. The Río Cangrejal, near La Ceiba, is one of the top rafting destinations in Central America, with rapids ranging from Class II to V.

Exploring Honduras

Bordered by Guatemala and El Salvador on the west and by Nicaragua to the east, Honduras has the most rugged topography of Central America. With peaks reaching over 9,345 ft, this predominantly mountainous country has been isolated from the rest of the region for much of its history. If you intend to wander even a bit off the beaten track you need to be prepared—rent a sturdy vehicle, hire a knowledgeable guide, and budget extra time for negotiating the terrain.

Great Itineraries

IF YOU HAVE 3 DAYS

Spend your first day in **Tegucigalpa,** exploring the streets of the capital. Don't miss El Picacho, a mountain that overlooks the city. The nearby villages of **Santa Lucia** and **Valle de Angeles,** with their cobblestone streets, are a great place to stroll on your second day. Get up early the next day so you have plenty of time to explore **Parque Nacional La Tigra,** considered one of the loveliest rain forests in the world.

IF YOU HAVE 5 DAYS

Start in **San Pedro Sula,** taking in the anthropology museum if you have the time. On your second day take a first-class bus to **Copán Ruinas,** where you'll find the painstakingly preserved ruins of one of the greatest ancient cities. Make sure to descend into the tunnels that wind below the pyramids to get a glimpse of what daily life was like for the Maya. Return to San Pedro Sula on your fourth day, continuing to **Tela,** a sleepy village on the northern coast. If you're here on the weekend you can attend a dance thrown by Garífuna, an Afro-Caribbean people who live along the shore.

IF YOU HAVE 7 DAYS
Head to the coastal community of **La Ceiba** to spend a day or two hiking through the pristine forests around towering Pico Bonito. If the weather is warm, cool off underneath one of the wonderful waterfalls. From La Cieba it's a short flight to **Roatán,** the largest of the Bay Islands. Here you can spend a few days learning how to scuba dive. If you crave a bit more privacy, nearby **Utila** has splendid beaches that you might have all to yourself.

When to Tour

The northern coast is hot and humid year-round. The rainy season here runs from October through January, although wet weather can come at any time of year. In the rest of the country, the altitude matters much more than the season. Tegucigalpa, nestled in the mountains, enjoys warm afternoons that fade into cool evenings. San Pedro Sula, sitting in the lowlands, is often sweltering.

TEGUCIGALPA

Tegucigalpa often receives short shrift from travelers, but on a sunny afternoon when there's a breath of a breeze you may wonder what everyone is complaining about. The city of more than 1 million people sits in a valley surrounded by beautiful pine-covered mountains. There are plenty of nearby villages to explore, and national parks filled with exotic flora and fauna are a short drive away. But the city streets, sometimes set at a sharp incline, are just as exhilarating to explore. Plaza Morazán, the lively main square, is a great place to get to know the people. In front of Iglesia Los Dolores you'll want to wander among the rows of souvenir stalls.

The city's name is the contraction of two words from the language of the area's indigenous people: *teguz* (hill) and *galpa* (silver). As the mining industry brought wealth to the region, the city spread down from the hills and across the Río Choluteca. In 1880 it became the country's capital. The same year, the Gran Hotel Central opened as the city's first public lodging. A sign on the patio reflected the pace of life: DON'T LAY ON THE HAMMOCKS WITH YOUR SPURS ON.

The city, with its winding streets lined with colorful houses built into the hillsides, retains many characteristics of a provincial town. But the surge in population has brought rumbling buses and blaring horns. Whenever possible, take side streets; it's not only a chance to see the hidden life of the city, but also to get away from major bus routes.

Exploring Tegucigalpa

Tegucigalpa is made up of dozens of different neighborhoods. Those called *barrios* are usually older and more centrally located neighborhoods than the *colonias*. As long as you know to which neighborhood you're headed, getting somewhere won't be a problem. In theory, the fact that *avenidas* run north–south and *calles* run east–west should make getting around much easier. Few maps, however, have details like street names. Familiarize yourself instead with the city's landmarks, as locals will refer to these when giving directions.

A Good Walk

The best place to begin a walk around Tegucigalpa is at **Plaza Morazán** ①, the heart of the city. **Catedral San Miguel** ②, one of the prettiest of the capital's many houses of worship, stands on the park's eastern edge. If you need to get your bearings, there's no better way than to head north on Calle Hipolito Matute, which eventually leads

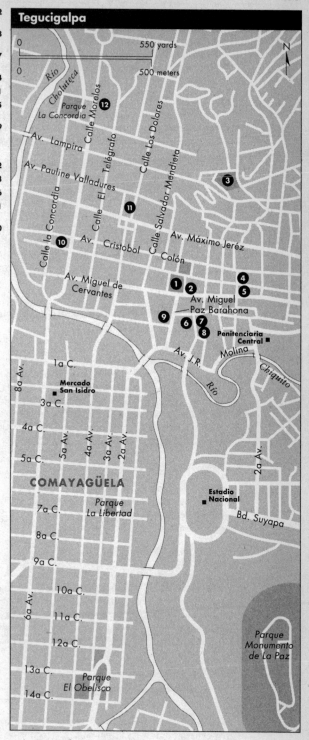

Tegucigalpa

you to pretty **Parque La Leona** ③. If you aren't up for that much walking, head east for four blocks along Calle Peatonal to Parque Valle. Facing the park is Tegucigalpa's oldest church, **Iglesia de San Francisco** ④. A block south is a museum featuring works by contemporary Honduran painters, the **Museo de Hombre** ⑤.

South of the central square is the leafy **Parque La Merced** ⑥, a great place to take a break. To the east are a lovely old church called the **Iglesia de la Merced** ⑦ and an interesting gallery called the **Galería Nacional de Arte** ⑧. To the west is a tribute to the founding fathers of the country called the **Museo Histórico de la República** ⑨.

When you're ready to face the heat again, head back to Parque Morazán, then wander the length of the Calle Peatonal, a bustling pedestrian street. Take in the fine old post office building on the left before you stop for an ice cream cone in the shady Parque Herrera. While you're here, take a peek inside the **Teatro Nacional Manuel Bonilla** ⑩. Head east again, turning north on Calle Los Dolores to admire the moving **Iglesia Los Dolores** ⑪. You will probably not want to take another step, so catch a taxi up the hill to the **Museo National de Historica y Antropologia Villa Roy** ⑫. As you wander around the exhibits, you may be surprised to find how much of the country's history you've already discovered.

TIMING

This walk will take four or five hours, depending on how long you browse around the museums.

Sights to See

❷ **Catedral San Miguel.** Presiding over the eastern edge of Plaza Morazán, this gleaming white cathedral is more formally known as the Parroquia San Miguel Arcángel, named for Tegucigalpa's patron saint. The domed structure, flanked by towering palms, has stood on this site since 1765. Sunlight streams into the apse, where you'll find the glittering gold-and-silver altar sculpted by Guatemalan artist Vicente Galvéz. ⊠ *Av. Miguel de Cervantes and Calle Hipolito Matute.* ▨ *Free.* ☉ *Daily 9–4.*

Cristo de Picacho. Standing guard over the city, this monumental statue of Christ has been a landmark since it was erected in 1997. From here there's a beautiful view of the valley. Parque de las Naciones Unidas is a great place to have a picnic. ⊠ *Cerro El Picacho,* ☏ *no phone.* ▨ *L4.* ☉ *Mon.–Fri. 8–3, Sat.–Sun. 9–4:30.*

★ ❽ **Galería Nacional de Arte.** Housed in the former Convento de San Pedro Nolasco, the bright and airy National Gallery of Art displays some wonderful artifacts, including finely detailed pre-Columbian ceramics and intricate Maya sculptures from Copán. Inaugurated in 1996, the museum has a dozen exhibition halls holding lovely examples of religious and colonial art; these serious works contrast nicely with the more comic modern works on the patio. Upstairs you'll find paintings by Pablo Zelaya Sierra and other 20th-century artists. ⊠ *Av. La Merced,* ☏ *237–9884.* ▨ *L10.* ☉ *Mon.–Sat. 9–4.*

❼ **Iglesia de la Merced.** Two *retablos,* or small religious paintings, flank the attractive altarpiece housed inside this 17th-century church. It's adjacent to the Galería Nacional de Arte. ⊠ *Av. La Merced.* ▨ *Free.*

❹ **Iglesia de San Francisco.** Three blocks east of Plaza Morazán lies the first church built in Tegucigalpa. Construction on the building, which sits on a leafy little square called Parque Valle, began in 1592. Inside are a pretty altarpiece and colonial religious paintings. ⊠ *Av. Cristobal Colón and Calle Salvador Corieto.* ▨ *Free.* ☉ *Daily 9–4.*

⑪ **Iglesia Los Dolores.** This twin-towered church dating from 1732 is dedicated to human sorrow, earning it a special place in the hearts of poverty-stricken Hondureños. On the facade you'll see carvings representing the last days of Christ, including the cock that crowed three times to signal that he had been betrayed. The interior, dominated by a colorful dome, features paintings of the crucifixion. The church faces a lively square filled with stalls selling inexpensive goods. ⊠ *Calle Los Dolores at Av. Máximo Jerez.* ☒ *Free.* ☉ *Daily 9–4.*

❺ **Museo del Hombre.** Once serving as the country's Supreme Court, this quiet building a few blocks east of Plaza Morazán houses works by contemporary Honduran painters. Airy galleries are arranged around a lovely courtyard. Recently renovated, the museum is often busy in the evening with events. ⊠ *Av. Miguel de Cervantes and Calle Las Damas,* ☎ *238–3198.* ☒ *Free.* ☉ *Mon.–Fri. 9–noon and 1–5.*

❾ **Museo Histórico de la República.** Housed in the former Casa Presidencial, the Museum of the Republic tells the history of Honduras starting with its independence from Spain. Recently renovated, the museum is filled with presidential portraits and political paraphernalia. ⊠ *Paseo Marco Aurelio Soto and Calle Salvador Mendieta,* ☎ *222–3470.* ☒ *L20.* ☉ *Mon.–Sat. 8–noon and 1–4.*

⑫ **Museo National de Historica y Antropología Villa Roy.** This hillside mansion near Plaza La Concordia, once home to President Julio Lozano, houses the National Museum of History and Anthropology. For those who read Spanish there is some quirky information on the republic's struggles after it gained its independence. ⊠ *Near Plaza de la Concordia,* ☎ *222–1468.* ☒ *L30.* ☉ *Tues.–Sun. 8:30–3:30.*

❸ **Parque La Leona.** A 20-minute walk north of Plaza Morazán, this charming park is well worth the effort to get here. Up some steep and twisting cobbled streets, it has lovely views of Tegucigalpa. It's even nicer at night, and locals say the winking lights look like a nativity display. Many of the older houses in this beautiful, but somewhat dishevelled, neighborhood once belonged to European settlers. ⊠ *Calle Hipolito Matute.* ☒ *Free.*

❻ **Parque La Merced.** A few blocks south of Plaza Morazán, this small park provides weary travelers with some shady places to sit. Older men in wide-brimmed hats tend to perch here, making the most of the relative calm to read their newspapers and gossip. The park is the site of a 19th-century university; today its auditorium houses art exhibits and music performances. Many of the city's most popular museums, including the Galería Nacional de Art, are in the area. ⊠ *Calle Bolívar.* ☒ *Free.*

❶ **Plaza Morazán.** Crowded night and day, the city's central park is where everyone comes to chat with friends, purchase lottery tickets, have their shoes polished, and listen to free afternoon concerts. You'll want to sit here for a while to admire the cathedral's facade and watch the pigeons playing peekaboo among the statues. Nearby is the Calle Peatonal, where street vendors hawk their wares and money changers haggle over rates. ⊠ *Calle Bolívar and Av. Miguel de Cervantes.*

NEED A BREAK? When you don't feel like fighting the crowds in El Centro, beat a hasty retreat into the mall called Midence Soto. The unpretentious but crowded **Espresso Americano** (⊠ Plaza Morazán, ☎ 238–2508) serves up some of the best coffee in the country.

❿ **Teatro Nacional Manuel Bonilla.** The National Theater, built in 1915, has an ornate interior that was modeled after the Athenée in Paris.

Nightly events range from classical ballet performances to rock concerts. ⊠ *Av. Miguel Paz Barahona and Calle La Concordia, Barrio El Centro,* ☎ *222–4366.* ▭ *L3.*

Dining

Tegucigalpa has a few outstanding restaurants, especially along Boulevard Morazán. Colonia Palmira, to the east of El Centro, is an up-and-coming area for dining and drinking with the smart and trendy crowd.

Barrio El Centro

$$–$$$ ✕ **El Quijote.** One of the oldest restaurants in Tegucigalpa, El Quijote has been in business for more than three decades. Straightforward Spanish dishes are the speciality, especially the *paella valenciana.* Other highly recommended dishes include the hearty *fabada asturiana* (a meaty stew). There's also a fully stocked bar. Its location in El Centro offers a pretty view of Catedral San Miguel and the other historic buildings surrounding Plaza Morazán. ⊠ *Calle a la Leona, La Pedrera,* ☎ *237–0070. AE, MC, V.*

$–$$ ✕ **Restaurante Mediterraneo.** This friendly place may remind you of a diner, especially because the extensive menu includes a large number of Greek favorites. The rice dishes are good value, as are the salads. The restaurant is also a popular watering hole in the early evening because of the free *boquitas* (appetizers). ⊠ *Av. Salvador Mendieta 511,* ☎ *237–9618. AE, MC, V. Closed Sun.*

$–$$ ✕ **'stacolossal.** With a name that's short for "está colossal," this cheap and cheerful restaurant does indeed serve up mammoth quesadillas and enchiladas. The best part is that the price isn't big at all. Stop by in the morning for waffles, omelets, and pancakes. The old photos on the wall show what Tegucigalpa looked like in the good old days. ⊠ *Av. Colón 346, west of Hondutel,* ☎ *222–8368. No credit cards. Closed Sun.*

$ ✕ **Café Paradiso.** This unpretentious little coffeehouse serves local specialties such as *carajillo* (coffee with cognac). The food is basic but filling, with locals leaning toward favorites like the *tortilla española* (Spanish omelet). While you wait, peruse the selection of books on Honduran history and politics. ⊠ *Av. Miguel Paz Barahona at Calle Las Damas,* ☎ *237–0337. No credit cards. Closed Sun.*

Colonia Palmira

$$ ✕ **Alondra.** Set in a restored colonial house, Alondra has long been regarded as one of Tegucigalpa's finest restaurants. While its reputation has slipped in recent years, it is still one of the city's most elegant eateries. Choose between one of several dining rooms or the pleasant terrace. Start with *palmito en salsa verde* (hearts of palm in green sauce), followed by *lomo de cerdo a la toscana* (Tuscan-style pork loin). ⊠ *Av República de Chile,* ☎ *232–5909. AE, DC, MC, V. Closed Sun.*

$–$$ ✕ **Casa María.** Frequented by the country's upper crust, this genteel
★   restaurant has plenty of rooms that can be closed off for presidential meetings. Yet Melba Robelo, the Nicaraguan owner, makes sure everyone feels welcome. The fish dishes, made with the freshest ingredients, all have intriguing flavors. Try the onion soup with Swiss cheese, followed by breaded *camarones* (shrimp) served with butter and tarragon. The famous *crepes de manzana* (apple crepes) are served with almonds and liqueur. The service is irreproachable. ⊠ *Blvd. Morazán at Av. Ramón Ernesto Cruz,* ☎ *239–4984. AE, MC, V.*

$–$$ ✕ **Theo's.** Forget the tapas—this distinguished eatery offers rich and
★   complex Spanish dishes prepared under the watchful eye of Spanish chef José Miguel Herrero. Sit in the romantically lit dining room or outside on the terrace. The *ensaladilla rusa* (Russian salad) is pure wizardry, combining cream, eggs, and prawns. The signature dish is the

abundant *zarzuela de mariscos* (seafood stew). If you have not had an outstanding dining experience in Honduras, this restaurant, with a list of excellent Spanish wines, will make you weep for joy. ⊠ *Av. República de Panamá 436,* ☎ *238–3575. AE, MC, V. Closed Sun.*

$ ✕ **Café Honoré.** Hearty soups and abundant salads are the draws at this restaurant in Colonia Palmira. The outdoor terrace is a good spot for a beer, or even a bottle of French wine. On a cloudy day head into the wood-paneled dining room. ⊠ *Av. República de Argentina 1941,* ☎ *239–4567 or 239–7566. AE, DC, MC, V. Closed Sun.*

$ ✕ **Tre Fratelli.** If you arrive on a Friday or Saturday night you just might think you're at a private party. That's the atmosphere at this boisterous Italian restaurant. Generous servings of pasta, tasty fish dishes, and pleasant salads at accessible prices have made this place a tremendous hit. If you're here at a quieter moment, take a table near the pleasant garden at the back. ⊠ *Av. República de Argentina 216,* ☎ *232–1942. Reservations essential. No credit cards. No dinner Sun.*

Hatillo

$$–$$$ ✕ **La Cumbre.** Long considered the city's most romantic restaurant, La Cumbre has a panoramic view of Tegucigalpa. By night or day, it is worth the trip to view the world from this privileged vantage point. The elegant dining room serves classic German dishes such as *jägerschnitzel.* ⊠ *Km 7.5 Carretera a Hatillo,* ☎ *211–9000 or 211–9001. AE, MC, V. Closed Sun.*

Lodging

There is a good range of hotels in Tegucigalpa, many in the Colonia Palmira. Choose between elegant high-rises, older favorites that are full of personality, or intimate hostels with personalized service.

Barrio El Centro

$ 🏨 **Hotel MacArthur.** Even though it's close to the center of the city, this budget-price hotel is remarkably quiet. After a day exploring the Tegucigalpa, it's nice to return for a nap in one of the spacious rooms or a dip in the pool. The manager is extremely helpful, dispensing information about the region. ⊠ *Av. Lempira 454, Barrio El Centro,* ☎ *237–5906. 45 rooms. Cable TV, pool, laundry service. AE, MC, V.*

$ 🏨 **Hotel Plaza.** Near Plaza Morazán, this moderately priced hotel is convenient to all the sights in Barrio El Centro. The attractively decorated rooms are clean and quiet. If you're hungry for a midnight snack, the cafeteria is open around the clock. ⊠ *Calle Peatonal, Barrio El Centro,* ☎ *237–2111,* 𝖥𝖠𝖷 *237–2119. 80 rooms. Restaurant, cafeteria, room service, cable TV, conference rooms, laundry service. AE, MC, V.*

Colonia Palmira

$$$ 🏨 **Hotel Honduras Maya.** The view of El Picacho Cristo, a 30-ft statue of Jesus perched on a nearby hill, is one of the best reasons to stay at this local landmark. A favorite in days gone by, this high-rise has faded a bit, with shortcomings here and there such as having to wait for hot water. The lobby is welcoming, however, and the rooms are spacious. There's a pretty pool, as well as a wading pool for the kids. Dine in the pleasant terrace restaurant, or stop by for a drink in the cozy bar. ⊠ *Av. República de Chile, Col. Palmira,* ☎ *220–5000,* 𝖥𝖠𝖷 *220–6000,* 𝖶𝖤𝖡 *www.hondurasmaya.hn. 146 rooms. Restaurant, coffee shop, room service, pool, cable TV, gym, hair salon, spa, bar, conference rooms, shops, laundry service, car rental. AE, DC, MC, V.*

$$$
★ 🏨 **Hotel Portal del Ángel.** The city's only boutique hotel, Hotel Portal del Ángel combines colonial elegance with sleek modern design. Gilt mirrors and baroque religious art bring a hallowed air to the lobby, while cool colors and clean lines brighten the courtyard. You can dine

here beneath pale blue and lemon arches where plants climb up bits of twirling wrought iron. Swathes of hand-carved mahogany are used for headboards in the generously sized rooms. In the heart of Colonia Palmira, the hotel is close to trendy bars and restaurants. ⊠ *Av. República de Perú 2115, Col. Palmira,* ☎ *239–6538 or 235–8841,* FAX *235–8839. 19 rooms, 5 suites. Restaurant, pool, bar, business services, conference rooms, laundry service. AE, DC, MC, V.*

$$ 🛏 **Hotel Plaza San Martin.** You're not far from the city's financial district at this modern high-rise, which makes it popular with a corporate clientele. Internet access is available in the full-service business center, where you can also make use of the meeting rooms and banquet facilities. It's not all work and no play, however. Each room has a terrace that overlooks leafy Colonia Palmira. For art lovers, a collection of paintings by Honduran artists hangs in the lobby. ⊠ *Plaza San Martín, Col. Palmira,* ☎ *232–8268,* FAX *231–1366,* WEB *plazasanmartinhotel. com. 110 rooms. Restaurant, room service, gym, hair salon, sauna, business services, Internet, meeting rooms, bar, children's programs, airport shuttle. AE, DC, MC, V.*

$$ 🛏 **Leslie's Place.** You'll be offered fruit-flavor beverages upon your arrival at this friendly bed-and-breakfast. That won't be the last thoughtful touch provided by the exceptionally caring staff. Rooms are spacious and cheerful, and it's a pleasure to get lost in the attractively tiled corridors of the converted house. Breakfast is served amid the green fronds that shade the patio garden, which overlooks a children's play area. ⊠ *Calzada San Martín 452, Col. Palmira,* ☎ *239–0641 or 220–5325,* FAX *232–1687,* WEB *www.dormir.com. 20 rooms. Breakfast room, fans, cable TV, gym, laundry service. AE, DC, MC, V.*

Elsewhere in the City

$$$$ 🛏 **Hotel Real Inter-Continental Tegucigalpa.** Built with business travelers in mind, this grand hotel in the heart of the city's financial district offers secretarial and courier services and conference facilities with state-of-the-art equipment. When you finish that meeting, head to the pool or the fully equipped gym. Great shopping is nearby, but you really never need to leave the area, as Mall MultiPlaza has plenty of boutiques to keep you occupied. Many of the comfortable rooms have CD players and VCRs, and one is designed for people with disabilities. ⊠ *Ave. Roble s/n, Col. Florencia,* ☎ *231–1300,* FAX *231–1400,* WEB *tegucigalpa.honduras.intercontinental.com. 167 rooms, 7 suites. Restaurant, room service, cable TV, pool, gym, bar, Internet, laundry services, business services, convention center, meeting rooms, car rental, travel services, no-smoking rooms. AE, DC, MC, V.*

$$$ 🛏 **Hotel Real Clarion.** A truly elegant lobby is your introduction to the Hotel Real Clarion, the most imposing of the capital's large hotels. Geared to business travelers, it has a floor reserved for executives where you are pampered with a drink in the evening and breakfast the next morning. Some rooms are on the small side, although all are luxuriously appointed. The pool is very attractive, and the gardens are immaculate. ⊠ *Blvd. Juan Pablo II, Col. Alameda,* ☎ *220–4500,* FAX *220–5086,* WEB *www.gruporeal.com. 186 rooms. Restaurant, room service, cable TV, pool, gym, spa, bar, business services, conference rooms, laundry services. AE, DC, MC, V.*

$$ 🛏 **Humuya Inn.** If you bristle at the thought of another hotel, consider this friendly little inn. Once a private home, it is set in a leafy neighborhood far from the center of the city. Sunlight streams through the windows of the rooms, which have what must be the comfiest beds in Honduras. High ceilings, ceramic tile floors, and pieces of locally made crafts make them feel particularly homey. Breakfast, with fresh banana and coconut breads, is included in the rate. Lunch and dinner are also

available. If you want to make your own meals, the apartments have full kitchens. ✉ *Colonia Humuya 1150,* ☎ *235–7275,* FAX *235–7276,* WEB *www.humuyainn.com. 9 rooms, 5 apartments. Restaurant, business services, Internet, laundry service, free parking. AE, MC, V. CP.*

Shopping

In Barrio El Centro, you will find a number of handicraft shops facing Avenida Miguel de Cervantes, which runs along the southern edge of Plaza Morazán. A block north is Calle Peatonal, a pedestrian street lined with shops frequented by locals.

Most residents of Tegucigalpa do their shopping in malls. One of the most glitzy is **Mall MultiPlaza** (✉ Blvd. San José Bosco, Col. Florencia, ☎ 556–7050). Stroll among the upscale shops, see the latest releases at the movie theater, and stop for a bite at the food court.

Honduran cigars, which rival those from Cuba, are a popular souvenir. In Mall MultiPlaza is **Tabaco Fino** (✉ Blvd. San José Bosco, Col. Florencia, ☎ no phone). Near the American Embassy, **Casa Havana** (✉ Blvd. Morazán, Col. Palmira, ☎ 236–6632) is another cigar shop.

In Vitro (✉ Av. República de Panamá 2139, Col. Palmira, ☎ 232–3452) sells blown glass and other crafts made by the students at the Fundación San Juancito. Decorative items made from everything from paper to wrought iron make unique gifts.

Nightlife and the Arts

Friday and Saturday nights are very lively around Colonia Palmira, where you'll find good bars and restaurants, and on Bulevar Morazán, which is home to the glitziest clubs. Pick up the current edition of *Honduras This Week* to find out what's happening around town.

Nightlife

BARS

The liveliest bar in town is **Taco Taco** (✉ Av. República de Argentina 2102, Col. Palmira, ☎ 232–2024) where you compete with the itinerant mariachi and salsa musicians to be heard. The only drawback is the location near the eastern end of Bulevar Morazán—you need to take a taxi from the center of town. One of the city's best-known hangouts is **Tobacco Road** (✉ Av. Miguel Paz Barahona, Barrio El Centro, ☎ 237–3903), a friendly place to have a beer. As the name suggests, there's a selection of Honduran cigars on sale.

To hang out with local artists, head to **Casita del Pueblo** (✉ 1 Calle, Col. Palmira, ☎ 232–6058). This cultural center hosts musicians on the weekends, and the salsa and cumbia music usually gets everyone dancing. Before the show begins, you can sample some typical Honduran dishes—the *tamalitos* and *pupusas* are highly recommended. If you're here earlier in the week, Thursday is poetry night.

CLUBS

In Colonia Palmira is a cluster of clubs that are popular with foreigners and locals alike. **Confetti's** (✉ Blvd. Morazán, Col. Palmira) is one of the city's most popular discos. A Mexican restaurant during the day, **Plaza Garibaldi** (✉ Blvd. Morazán, Col. Palmira) opens as a disco at 8 PM, but really gets going much later. It's one of the few places in Tegucigalpa that is open all night.

South of Colonia Palmira, Avenida Juan Pablo II is popular with a younger, trendier crowd. Don't be intimidated by the sign asking customers to leave their guns at the door at **Tropical Port** (✉ Av. Juan Pablo

II, Col. Alameda). Maybe the crowd just doesn't appreciate all the thumping disco music. At **Rock Castle Pub** (⊠ Av. Juan Pablo II, Col. Alameda) there's always live music on the weekends.

The Arts

Teatro Nacional Manuel Bonilla (⊠ Av. Miguel Paz Barahona and Calle La Concordia, Barrio El Centro, ☎ 222–4366) hosts frequent performances by music and dance groups.

Outdoor Activities and Sports

Soccer is akin to religion in Honduras, as it is in most countries in Latin America. The populace is so passionate about fútbol that a game with El Salvador in 1969 sparked a war—although the underlying conflicts were more serious. The season runs October to July when **Estadio Nacional** (⊠ Barrio Morazán, Col. Palmira) hosts matches Saturday, Sunday, and Wednesday. Check the local papers for times. Admission is about 25 lempiras.

Side Trips from Tegucigalpa

Suyapa

Just east of Tegucigalpa is Suyapa, home of a tiny clay statue called the *Virgen de Suyapa,* the patron saint of Honduras. Legend has it that a poor farmer was sleeping in a field when he felt a stick poking him in the back. Perplexed, he put the stick in his bag. When he arrived home, instead of the stick he found a statue of the Virgin Mary.

This is quite a miraculous Virgin, certainly in terms of getting around on her own accord. In the 1980s she went missing, reappearing some time later in the men's room of a restaurant in Tegucigalpa called La Terraza de Don Pepe. The eatery has a shrine in her honor to this day.

The statue of the Virgen de Suyapa can be found in the 16th-century **Iglesia de Suyapa,** an intimate church where the flickering of candles lit by the faithful can be quite humbling. Religious items, such as decorative prayer cards featuring the image of the Virgin, are for sale in the stalls down the steps from the church. As the morning wears on you can also buy soft drinks and snacks. ⊠ *Blvd. Suyapa.*

Overshadowing the smaller church is the mammoth white-and-gray **Basílica de Suyapa.** The beautiful stained-glass windows of translucent sky blue are inspirational, but the basilica itself has a haughty air. It was built in 1954 to house the Virgen de Suyapa, but she is not fond of it. On many occasions she has left it at night, found back at her original perch the following morning. She consents to be displayed here on her feast day, February 3, when pilgrims descend on the town to honor her. ⊠ *Blvd. Suyapa,* ☎ *no phone.* ☉ *Daily 8–12 and 2–5.*

Santa Lucía

Santa Lucía is a pleasant mining town of winding cobblestone streets, red-tile roofs, and colorful gardens. Only 12 km (7 mi) east of the capital, it is surrounded by hills thick with pines. The colonial-era church houses a wooden figure of Christ called *El Cristo Negro* brought here by the Spanish in 1574.

LODGING

$ 🏠 **Posada de las Nubes.** This pretty B&B offers a spectacular view of the pine-covered mountains. Filled with quaint touches, the Inn of the Clouds is the perfect place to watch the sunset from your private patio. Continental breakfasts are served in the café, where you can enjoy wine or beer in the evenings. ⊠ *Carretera a Valle de Angeles s/n,* ☎ *779–0441,* FAX *232–1092. 4 rooms. Café, cable TV, bar. MC, V. CP*

Parque Nacional La Tigra

One of the most accessible national parks in Honduras, Parque Nacional La Tigra protects a cloud forest considered one of the most beautiful in the world. Just 20 km (12 mi) from Tegucigalpa, the park feels worlds away. You'll forget the crowds in the capital as you wander among the orchids, bromeliads, and treelike ferns that tower above you. If you start early in the morning you can see much of the park in a day, but you'll gain even more by spending the night. With patience and a bit of luck you might spot ocelots, peccaries, and white-faced monkeys, as well as resplendent quetzals and the more than 200 species of birds.

There are currently seven different trails, including a few designed with children in mind. More challenging trails include *La Cascada*, which leads to a waterfall, and *La Esperanza*, which winds its way to the highest point in the park. Bring plenty of water and layers of clothes you can peel off when you work up a sweat. Be prepared to get wet and muddy. Paths are well marked, but a guide will help you spot creatures you would otherwise miss.

Two entrances take you into the 241-square-km (93-square-mi) park, each with a visitor center where you can talk with rangers and pick up a trail map. The western entrance at Jutiapa is more accessible from Tegucigalpa, but the one at El Rosario has an old hospital that has been converted into a hostel with dorm-style accommodations. If you want to spend the night, contact the Fundación Amigos de la Tigra. ⊠ *Amitigra, Edificio Italia, Col. Palmira,* ☎ *235-8494,* 📠 *235-8493,* WEB *www.nps.gov/centralamerica/honduras.*

DINING AND LODGING

$ ✕🏠 **Cabaña Mirador El Rosario.** This cabin in the clouds belongs to Monika and Jorg, a friendly German couple. They are happy to make you breakfast and dinner, as well as transport you to the park. They also make and sell excellent jam. The warm shower is a treat in the wilderness. ⊠ *El Rosario,* ☎ *987–5835. 2 rooms. Dining room, hiking. No credit cards.*

Valle de Angeles

It bustles with tourists from the capital on weekends, but during the week Valle de Angeles maintains an atmosphere of centuries past. Sunday is the day to arrive, when you can ride around in a horse-drawn cart or browse among the crafts found under five *pabellones* (pavilions). It's worth taking time to look for mahogany bowls, reed baskets, woven hammocks, embroidered blouses, bead necklaces, and bizarre ceramic chickens in bright shades of crimson.

The old church in the central square lacks the colonial charm of the one in Santa Lucia, but the nearby park has a painted fountain surrounded by lush trees. A comical macaw sometimes plays hide-and-seek on the roof of the bandstand. Valle de Angeles is about 11 km (8 mi) east of Santa Lucia.

DINING AND LODGING

$ ✕ **El Anafre.** This restaurant is named for a traditional mush of refried beans, cream, and cheese served with tortilla chips in a clay container. It's a great place to down a beer, as it is often open until 10 or later. ⊠ *Parque Central,* ☎ *no phone. No credit cards.*

$ ✕ **Carnes El Español.** You smell the sizzling *chorizo* (sausage) and *carnitas* (chunks of beef) cooked by Don Manolo even before you see his popular restaurant. ⊠ *Parque Central,* ☎ *no phone. No credit cards.*

$ ✕ **Golosina's Toñita.** There is probably no better place for lunch than this bare shack plastered with faded pictures of old mariachi stars. An excellent trio is usually accompanied by the cadent voice and romantic antics of Don Ruben Amador, flirtatious husband of the restaurant's

chef and namesake. Try the hot *pupusas* (filled pockets of cornmeal) and authentic *sopa de mondongo* (tripe soup). ✉ *Parque Central,* ☎ *no phone. No credit cards.*

$ 🏨 **La Posada del Ángel.** This colonial-style hotel, complete with a grassy courtyard, makes a great weekend escape. All rooms have splendid mountain views. There's a pool and plenty of activities for the kids. Reservations should be made a few days in advance for weekends. ✉ *Calle Principal s/n.* ☎ FAX *766–2233. 20 rooms. Restaurant, cable TV, pool, bar, conference room. AE, MC, V.*

Tegucigalpa A to Z

AIR TRAVEL TO AND FROM TEGUCIGALPA

Two North American airlines, American and Continental, have daily flights into Tegucigalpa. Taca flies here from many cities in Latin America. Isleña specializes in flights to and from the Bay Islands.

➤ AIRLINES AND CONTACTS: **American** (✉ Edificio Palmira, Av. República de Chile, Col. Palmira, ☎ 233–6919 or 232–1415, WEB www.aa.com). **Continental** (✉ Edificio Palic, Av. República de Chile, Col. Palmira, ☎ 220–0988 or 220–0989, WEB www.continental.com). **Isleña** (✉ Aeropuerto Internacional Toncontín, ☎ 233–1130, WEB www.flyislena.com). **Taca** (✉ Edificio Interamericana, Blvd. Morazán, Col. Palmira, ☎ 239–0148 or 233–3566, WEB www.grupotaca.com).

AIRPORTS AND TRANSFERS

About 7 km (4 mi) outside Tegucigalpa, Aeropuerto Internacional Toncontín has been nicknamed the "Stop and Drop," referring to the steep descents necessary to reach the short runway. Most international flights land here, although some fly to San Pedro Sula and Roatán.

Many taxi drivers who hang around the airport are hucksters who take advantage of unwary travelers. Don't pay more than 90 lempiras for the 20- to 30-minute ride to town.

➤ AIRPORT INFORMATION: **Aeropuerto Internacional Toncontín** (✉ Blvd. Comunidad Económica Europea, ☎ 233–1115 or 233–7613).

BUS TRAVEL TO AND FROM TEGUCIGALPA

There is no single bus station connecting the capital with the rest of the country. Many companies have their terminals in Comayagüela, the community across the Río Choluteca. It's a rougher neighborhood, so be on your guard.

If you're headed north, Viana Clase Oro and Hedman Alas travel to San Pedro Sula and La Ceiba. They offer clean, comfortable coaches with air-conditioning, snacks, and even movies. Sáenz Primera has six departures per day to San Pedro Sula. El Rey Express has a decent hourly "direct" (meaning just a couple of stops) to San Pedro Sula. Cristina offers a slightly less frequent service to La Ceiba, from which you can hop off to Tela. Cotraibal has a morning departure to Trujillo.

The only buses west are the slow ones labeled "servicio a escala," but El Rey and Los Norteños will take you to Comayagua, Siguatepeque, and Lago de Yojoa. La Sultana heads to Santa Rosa de Copán four times a day, and El Jungueño can get you to Santa Barbara.

➤ BUS COMPANIES: **Cotraibal** (✉ 7 Av., between Calles 11 and 12, Comayagüela, ☎ 237–1666). **Cristina** (✉ 8 Av., between Calles 12 and 13, Comayagüela, ☎ 220–0117 or 220–1555). **El Jungueño** (✉ 8 Av., between Calles 12 and 13, Comayagüela, ☎ 237–2921). **El Rey** (✉ Av. 6 and Calle 9, Comayagüela, ☎ 237–6609). **El Rey Express** (✉ Calle 12 and Av. 7, Comayagüela, ☎ 237–8561). **Hedman Alas** (✉ 11 Av., between Calles 13 and 14, Comayagüela, ☎ 237–7143). **La**

Sultana (⊠ 8 Av., between Calles 11 and 12Comayagüela,, ☎ 237–8101). **Los Norteños** (⊠ 12 Calle, between 6 and 7 Av., Comayagüela, ☎ 237–0706). **Sáenz Primera** (⊠ Calle 12 and Av. 7, Comayagüela, ☎ 233–4229 or 233–4249). **Viana Clase Oro** (⊠ Blvd. Fuerzas Armadas, ☎ 235–8185).

BUS TRAVEL WITHIN TEGUCIGALPA

Tegucigalpa has many bus routes that can take you to the edges of the city and back for a few lempiras. Some bus stops are marked by signposts, but the most reliable indicator is a bunch of people huddled by the curb looking expectant down the street. Buses start running at 5 AM and stop around 9 PM. Locals use buses like North Americans use cars, so they're quite knowledgeable about the routes; most are willing to show you which bus to get on. At Plaza Morazán, you'll find a bus going almost anywhere in the city.

CAR RENTAL

The vehicle of choice for exploring Honduras—especially if you are heading off the beaten path—is the four-wheel-drive double-cabin pickup. A number of international companies, including Avis, Budget, and Thrifty, are based at the airport. Rental cars are not cheap, however. They start at $50 per day.

➤ RENTAL AGENCIES: **Avis** (⊠ Aeropuerto Internacional Toncontín, ☎ 233–9548; ⊠ Av. República de Chile, Col. Palmira, ☎ 232–0088). **Budget** (⊠ Aeropuerto Internacional Toncontín, ☎ 235–9331 or 233–5170). **Hertz** (⊠ Av. República de Chile, Col. Palmira, ☎ 239–0772 or 239–1307). **Thrifty** (⊠ Aeropuerto Internacional Toncontín, ☎ 233–0933 or 233–0922; ⊠ Col. Prados Universitario, ☎ 235–6077).

CAR TRAVEL

Unless you are taking a day trip outside of the city, driving in Tegucigalpa is best avoided. In Barrio El Centro parking is an ordeal, traffic snarls are frequent, and many intersections have no signs warning that you are entering a one-way street.

EMBASSIES AND CONSULATES

The Canadian Embassy is open weekdays 8:30–12:30. The embassy for the United Kingdom is open weekdays 8–1 and 2–4:20, while its counterpart for the United States is open weekdays 8–5.

➤ EMBASSIES: **Canada** (⊠ Blvd. San Juan Bosco, Col. Payaquí, ☎ 232–6799). **United Kingdom** (⊠ Edificio Banexpo, Blvd. San Juan Bosco, Col. Palmira, ☎ 232–5429). **United States** (⊠ Edificio Embajada Americana, Av. La Paz, Col. Palmira, ☎ 236–9320).

EMERGENCIES

Clínica Viera, on Avenida Cristobal Colón, accepts walk-ins around the clock. Drugstores are found everywhere in the city. Farmacia Rosna has English-speaking staff on duty daily 9 AM–7 PM. Pharmacies take turns staying open all night, so check the schedule on the door of any shop to locate the nearest open one.

➤ HOSPITAL: **Clínica Viera** (⊠ Av. Cristobal Colón, Barrio El Centro, ☎ 237–3160).

➤ HOT LINES: **Ambulance** (☎ 195). **Fire** (☎ 198). **Police** (☎ 199).

➤ PHARMACY: **Farmacia Rosna** (⊠ Calle Peatonal, Barrio El Centro, ☎ 237–0605).

MAIL AND SHIPPING

The city's main post office is in Barrio El Centro, opposite the Ministerio de Gobernació. It is open weekdays 7–7 and Saturday 8–1. For packages, DHL, Federal Express, and UPS all have offices downtown.

➤ POST OFFICE: **Correo de Honduras** (✉ Av. Miguel Paz Barahona at Calle El Telégrafo, Barrio El Centro, ☎ 237–8353 or 237–8354).
➤ OVERNIGHT SERVICES: **DHL** (✉ Av. República de Chile 502, Col. Palmira, ☎ 220–1800, ⓦⒺⒷ www.dhl.com). **Federal Express** (✉ Plaza San Martín, Col. Palmira, ☎ 239–0340 or 239–1971, ⓦⒺⒷ www.fedex. com). **UPS** (✉ Plaza San Martín, Col. Palmira, ☎ 232–7121 or 239–4287, ⓦⒺⒷ www.ups.com).

MONEY MATTERS

U.S. cash and traveler's checks are the easiest, and usually the only, currency you can exchange in Honduras. Try Banco de Honduras near Parque Central. Most banks in the capital are open weekdays 9–5, but Bancahsa on Avenida Cristobal Colón is also open Saturday 9–noon. Visa cash advances are available at some banks, but are always given at Credomatic on Boulevard Morazán.
➤ BANKS: **Bancahsa** (✉ Av. Cristobal Colón at Calle Los Dolores, Barrio El Centro, ☎ 237–1171). **Banco de Honduras** (✉ Plaza Morazán, Barrio El Centro, ☎ 232–6122). **Credomatic** (✉ Edificio Interamericana, Blvd. Morazán, ☎ 237–4596).

SAFETY

Tegucigalpa is generally safe, provided you dress down, don't wear flashy jewelry or watches, and avoid handling money in public. It's a good idea to keep your money in a pocket rather than a wallet, which is easier to steal. In markets and other crowded areas, hold purses or handbags close to the body; thieves use knives to slice the bottom of a bag and catch the contents as they fall out. Avoid walking anywhere at night.

TAXIS

After 9 PM, taxis are basically the only transportation option. Day and night, taxis solicit your business by honking. If you take them up on it, discuss the price immediately. All prices should be around 50 to 60 lempiras. If the driver seems unimpressed by how much you'll pay, ask to be let out at the corner—that usually closes the deal. Certain taxis are colectivos, where several people going in the same general direction share a ride. It's a good compromise between the expense of a regular taxi and the inconvenience of a bus. Look for lines of people in the side streets around Plaza Morazán, or yell out your destination when a half-full taxi honks at you.

If you'd like to call a cab, RadioTaxi is prompt and efficient.
➤ TAXI COMPANY: **RadioTaxi** (☎ 225–5563).

TELEPHONES

They are often damaged or deficient, but public phones are found everywhere in the capital and operate with coins or cards. The main office of Empresa Hondureña de Telecomunicaciones, better known as Hondutel, is on Avenida Colón in Barrio El Centro. Branches are scattered around the city. Calls from your hotel will be much more expensive.

Cell phones are becoming a good option, especially if you are in Honduras on business. Two good companies are Telefónica Celular Celtel and Cellular Rental.
➤ TELEPHONES: **Cellular Rental** (✉ Blvd. Juan Pablo II, Col. Alameda, ☎ 220–4500). **Hondutel** (✉ Av. Colón, Barrio El Centro, ☎ 238–3131, ⓦⒺⒷ www.hondutel.com). **Telefónica Celular Celtel** (✉ Blvd. Suyapa, Col. Florencia Norte, ☎ 222–0250, ⓦⒺⒷ www.celtel.net).

TOUR OPERATORS

Agencies specialize in different destinations, so check around for the best price to where you are headed. Trek de Honduras organizes ad-

venture trips to remote regions. Other good companies include Destino de Exito, Go Honduras, and Honduras Travelling.

➤ TOUR COMPANIES: **Destino de Exito** (✉ Edificio Europa, Col. San Carlos, ☎ 236–9651, FAX 236–9707). **Go Honduras** (✉ 7 Calle 844, Col. El Prado, ☎ 239–2550, FAX 239–2575). **Honduras Travelling** (✉ Calle Panamá 2194, Col. Palmira, ☎ 236–8511). **Trek de Honduras** (✉ Edificio Midence 218, Barrio El Centro, ☎ 238–1944).

VISITOR INFORMATION

The friendly Instituto Hondureño de Turismo in Colonia San Carlos is worth a visit for information about the city.

➤ TOURIST INFORMATION: **Instituto Hondureño de Turismo** (✉ Edificio Europa, Col. San Carlos, ☎ 222–2124, FAX 222–6621, WEB www. letsgohonduras.com).

THE WESTERN HIGHLANDS

For 2,000 years the Mayas resided in what is now Western Honduras, creating the distinctive art and architecture that can still be seen at the ancient city of Copán. The Lencas, who are believed to have lived alongside the Mayas, had an equally vibrant, although less well known, culture. Dominating the region after the fall of the Mayas, the Lancas had no intention of being subjugated when the Spanish arrived in the 16th century. Chief Lempira brought tribes together to battle the conquistadors; his murder at the hands of the Spanish at a "peace conference" provided Honduras with its first national hero. The country's currency is named for the great warrior.

Western Honduras still shows evidence of its colonial past. Cobblestone streets are lined with whitewashed Spanish-style houses. As you explore the highlands, you will find yourself whisked back to another era. Small communities tucked into the green mountains maintain their old religious, cultural, artistic, and medicinal traditions. The people here are more outgoing than in many parts of Honduras, and they are more than happy to converse with newcomers.

With the exception of Comayagua, most of the attractions found in Western Honduras are more accessible from San Pedro Sula than from Tegucigalpa. Many people exploring the country's western and northern regions often choose to bypass the capital altogether, flying instead into Aeropuerto Internacional Ramón Villeda Morales in San Pedro Sula.

San Pedro Sula

265 km (165 mi) northwest of Tegucigalpa.

Founded in 1536 by Spanish conquistador Pedro de Alvarado, the country's second-largest city acquired the odd "Sula" at the end of its name from the word *usula*, which means "valley of birds." You might still find yourself awakened by their calls, that is if the roar of the traffic does not reach your ears first. To hear some of the 300 species that live in the area, you'll probably have to visit nearby Parque Nacional Cusuco.

Now a bustling commercial center, San Pedro Sula is the fastest-growing city between Bogotá and Mexico City. It has long been a hub for the banana, coffee, and sugar industries. Despite its single-minded focus on business, San Pedro Sula's convenient location and modern airport has made it a gateway for those intent on exploring the country's western and northern reaches. Its well-maintained roads make it easy to drive east along the coast or south into the mountains.

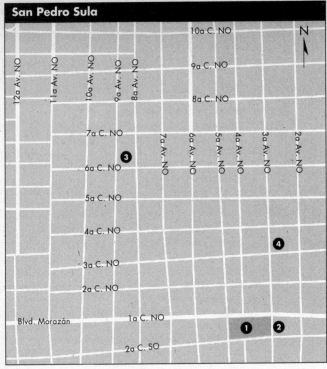

San Pedro Sula

Exploring San Pedro Sula

Built on a traditional grid pattern, San Pedro Sula is an easy city to navigate. Its intersecting calles and avenidas are divided into four quadrants—northeast (abbreviated NE), southeast (SE), northwest (NO), and southwest (SO). You'll probably spend most of your time in the southwest quadrant. Around the perimeter of the city runs Avenida Circunvalación, which has other names at different points in the city. It seems every other vehicle is a taxi, and most rides cost between 20 and 40 lempiras. San Pedro has some city buses, but they usually travel only by day to the places you might want to visit by night.

To get your bearings, start in the center of town at Parque Central, bordered by Calle 1a and Avenida 3a. The Hotel Gran Sula across the street is a prominent landmark. The town's few attractions are an easy walk north or south from here. Remember that the area called *abajo de la linea* (literally meaning "below the line") which means the southeast quadrant below Avenida 1a, is a dangerous neighborhood night or day.

A Good Walk

Begin at **Parque Central** ①, where you just might run into some street-corner evangelists anxious to save your soul. To the east is the mammoth **Catedral de San Pedro Sula** ②, where you aren't likely to encounter such a hard-sell approach. Although the neoclassical edifice resembles some of the country's older churches, it was only begun about 50 years ago. To the south you'll find a *peatonal* (paved pedestrian street). If you are feeling hungry, buy a ripe orange or green mango from a vendor. Ask for a *servilleta* (napkin), as they are delicious but messy.

From Parque Central, head one block west and five blocks north to reach the **Mercado Guamilito** ③. You'll find beautifully crafted mahogany handicrafts at excellent prices. Make sure to check out the adjacent food market. Even if you don't sample any of the local dishes, the smell

of sizzling tortillas is intriguing. Two blocks south and three blocks east you'll come face-to-face with the **Museo de Antropología e Historia.** ④. Here you can stop for lunch in the cafeteria and spend a pleasant hour or two strolling through the museum.

TIMING

This walk will take about two hours, or a bit more if you stop to browse in the museum.

Sights to See

❷ **Catedral de San Pedro Sula.** On the eastern edge of Parque Central, this massive neoclassical structure was begun in 1949 but not completed for many years. The most important church in town, it is always buzzing with activity. Locals seem to treat it as a community center, and worshippers are surprisingly friendly and talkative. ⊠ *3 Av. SO at 1 Calle.* ⊘ *Daily 8–6.*

❸ **Mercado Guamilito.** Mornings are the busiest and best time to visit this enclosed market in the northwest section of town. Besides wonderful ebony carvings, artisans also sell colorful baskets and hand-tooled leather goods. ⊠ *Calle 6a NO between Av. 8 and 9 NO,* ☏ *no phone.* ⊘ *Mon.–Sat. 7–5, Sun. 8–11:30.*

❹ **Museo de Antropología e Historia.** You will find no better introduction to the country's geography, history, and society than at this museum near Parque Central. Spread over two floors, the eye-catching exhibits examine clues about the ancient cultures that once inhabited the region, recreate daily life in the colonial era, and recount the country's more recent history. The sculptures, paintings, ceramics, and other items are labelled in Spanish (and occasionally in English). Budget a good two hours to take it all in. There is also gift shop and a cafeteria serving a tasty set lunch. ⊠ *3 Av. NO and 4 Calle NO,* ☏ *557–1496 or 557–1798.* ▣ *L15.* ⊘ *Tues.–Sun. 10–4.*

❶ **Parque Central.** Money changers, shoe shiners, watch vendors, and truant schoolchildren mill around San Pedro Sula's central square. Locals lounge about beneath the scrawny trees watching the crowds file past. ⊠ *Av. 3 and 5 SO and Calle 1 and 2 SO.*

Dining

$$$–$$$$ ✕ **Don Udo's.** Originally from Holland, Don Udo Van der Waag fell in love with the mountains around San Pedro Sula. Over the years his restaurant here has grown from a casual meeting place where the menu was scribbled on a chalkboard to one of the city's fanciest eateries. Along with excellent beers you'll find a good selection of wines. Try the stuffed crab appetizer followed by a tasty jalapeño fillet. Fresh lobster is another treat. If you want to recreate a dish at home, there's a gourmet food store next door. ⊠ *Blvd. Los Próceres, Barrio Río de Piedras,* ☏ *553–3106. AE, MC, V. Closed Sun.*

$$$–$$$$ ✕ **La Estancia Parrillada.** A repeated winner of international competitions, this Uruguayan restaurant's combination of traditional recipes and international flair has secured it a top place in this city's gastronomical scene. The service is professional, yet friendly. For starters select the mountain oysters, then move on to one of the grilled cuts of South American beef. The comfortable bar next door offers an astounding selection of liquors from all over the world. ⊠ *12 Av. NO and 6 Calle NO, Barrio Los Andes,* ☏ *552–3002. V. Closed Sun.*

$$–$$$$ ✕ **Chef Marianos.** San Pedro Sula isn't far from the Caribbean, which means you can easily find delicious seafood. This local favorite is run by a Garífuna family, so everything is as fresh as possible. Recommended are the king crab, jumbo shrimp, and the *negro bello* (a mixed plate of meat, conch, and fish). If it's available, don't pass up the lobster.

The service is attentive. ⊠ *6 Av. SO at 10 Calle SO, Barrio Suyapa,* ☎ *552–5492. AE, MC, V.*

$–$$ ✕ **Italian Grill.** San Pedro Sula has plenty of restaurants serving Italian favorites, but this European-style bistro is something special. Soft music plays in the background, making the hearty soups, flavorful pastas, and overstuffed sandwiches all the more appealing. The homemade gelatos and cakes top off a perfect meal. ⊠ *Calle 8 SO, between Av. 16 and 17, Barrio Suyapa,* ☎ *552–1770. AE, MC, V.*

$ ✕ **Cafetería Pamplona.** This cheerful eatery on Parque Central serves up inexpensive Spanish-style dishes that are a welcome change from the beans-and-rice routine. Get here early, as it's only open until 8 PM. Breakfast is a bargain, and the coffee is nice and strong. ⊠ *2 Calle SO,* ☎ *no phone. No credit cards.*

$ ✕ **Hasta La Pasta.** Homemade antipasti and hearty pastas, all at reasonable prices, make this one of the most popular Italian restaurants in town. The garden courtyard makes a pleasant place to savor a glass of wine. ⊠ *22 Av. and 2 Calle NO, Col. Moderna,* ☎ *550–5494 or 550–3048. AE, MC, V.*

Lodging

$$$$ 🏨 **Copantl Hotel & Club.** Long considered the city's finest hotel, this high-rise is a favorite among corporate travelers. There are plenty of meeting rooms and a wide range of business services available. Many of the rooms look down on the Olympic-size pool. The panoramic views of the mountains from La Churrasquería, the steak house on the seventh floor, are unforgettable. There are shops and even an art gallery where you can browse. The service is uneven, however, and the din that comes from the cocktail lounge at night doesn't ensure a good night's sleep. ⊠ *Blvd. del Sur, Col. Los Arcos,* ☎ *556–8900,* WEB *www.hotelcopantl.com. 199 rooms. Restaurant, coffee shop, cable TV, minibars, tennis courts, pool, bar, lounge, piano bar, shop, business services, meeting rooms, travel agent, free parking. AE, MC, V.*

$$$$ 🏨 **Hotel Princess.** Although it caters predominantly to business executives, this European-style hotel has personalized service that makes it a good option for any traveler. There are plenty of amenities, from the sparkling pool to the gym. The restaurant is decorated in a stark style, while the bar more closely resembles an English pub. The concierge is great for tips on restaurants. ⊠ *10 Calle SO and Av. Circunvalación, Col. Trejo,* ☎ *556–9600,* FAX *556–9595,* WEB *www.hotelesprincess.com/eng/honduras. 117 rooms, 3 suites. Restaurant, room service, cable TV, in-room safes, pool, gym, bar, shops, Internet, business services, meeting rooms, free parking, car rental. AE, MC, V.*

$$ 🏨 **Gran Hotel Sula.** This downtown high-rise offers a wide range of services you don't often find, from a bank to a travel agent to an airline reservation desk. Facing Parque Central, it is close to all of San Pedro Sula's major attractions. Business travelers will appreciate the fact that it is near the financial district. Café Skandia, overlooking the pool, is a great place for late-night dinners and early breakfasts. All the rooms have balconies with views over the city. ⊠ *1 Calle NO, between 3 and 4 Av.,* ☎ *552–9999,* FAX *552–7000,* WEB *www.cjhotels.com. 125 rooms. Restaurant, cafeteria, cable TV, pool, piano bar, shop, business services, meeting rooms. AE, MC, V.*

$$ 🏨 **Holiday Inn.** With a great location in the center of town, this elegant high-rise is among the city's best hotels. All of the comfortably furnished rooms are set up for business travelers, so there are connections for your computer and plenty of telephones. For dining there's Antonio's, which serves typical Honduran cuisine, as well as a coffee shop that stays open until midnight. The staff is always ready to help guests find their way around the city. ⊠ *Blvd. Morazán, between 10 and 11*

Av., ☎ *550–8080,* FAX *550–5353,* WEB *sanpedrosula.holiday-inn.com.*
128 rooms, 2 suites. Restaurant, cafeteria, cable TV, pool, gym, bar,
business services, meeting rooms, airport shuttle. AE, MC, V.

$$ ☒ **Hotel Saint Anthony.** This delightful hotel has splendid views from
the pretty rooftop pool. You can feel your tensions fade as you step into
the elegant lobby. If you have business needs, there is an executive floor
with computer connections. ☒ *3 Av. SO at 13 Calle SO,* ☎ *558–0744.*
90 rooms. Restaurant, cable TV, pool, business services, shop. MC, V.

$ ☒ **Hotel Bolívar.** Ideal for the budget traveler, Hotel Bolívar has ameni-
ties usually found only at more expensive lodgings, such as a restau-
rant, a bar, and a sparkling pool. The service is quite friendly. ☒ *2 Av.*
SO at 2 Calle SO, ☎ *553–3224,* FAX *553–4823. 65 rooms. Restaurant,*
bar, pool, cable TV, laundry service, laundry service. MC, V.

Nightlife and the Arts

The neighborhood where people go to party, the Zona Viva, is west
of town near Avenida Circunvalación. People begin to hit the clubs
around 10. Places come and go, so pick up a copy of *Honduras Tips*
at your hotel to find out which spot is popular at the moment.

BARS

An instant hit with the young crowd, **Frogs** (☒ Blvd. Los Próceres, near
Av. Circunvalación) is known for its great light system and good music.
There are three different bars, including one where you can order
food. If you can't stand the karaoke on weekends, you can retreat to
the second-story deck overlooking the volleyball court. A local favorite,
Shauki's Place (☒ Av. 18 SO at 8 Calle) is open late. You can listen to
a live trio playing inside, or step into the garden to swig a beer.

In the Princess Hotel, **Clancy's Bar** (☒ 10 Calle SO at Av. Circunvalación)
is one of the city's most refined bars. It's a good spot for appetizers
before dinner or for a nightcap afterwards. Set in a tropical garden with
a fountain, **El Hijo de Cuervo** (☒ 13 Calle NO, between 7 and 8 Av.)
is a bar that also serves tasty Mexican fare. The cheerful **Las Jarras**
(☒ Av. 16 NO at 2 Calle) is a great place to enjoy a few *bocas* (appe-
tizers) in the afternoon.

CLUBS

The classiest dance club in town, **Henry's** (☒ Av. Circunvalación at 11
Ave. NO) is a favorite with hip and trendy Sampedranos. Locals let
loose on the sprawling dance floor. Also popular is **Confeti's** (☒ Av.
Circunvalación, near the exit to Puerto Cortés). Attracting a slightly
older crowd, **El Quijote** (☒ 11 Calle SO, between 3 and 4 Av.) is the
most exclusive of the city's dance clubs.

THE ARTS

For cultural events, try the **Centro Cultural Sampedrano** (☒ Av. 4 NO,
at Calle 3, ☎ 553–3911), which often has art exhibitions. It also
serves as the public library. **Alianza Francesa** (☒ 23 Av. SO, between
Calles 3 and 4, ☎ 552–4359) has a range of cultural events.

Side Trips from San Pedro Sula

Parque Nacional Cusuco

This swath of subtropical forest was declared a protected area in 1959
when an ecologist reported that the pine trees here were the tallest in
Central America. It's located in the Cordillera del Merendón, a moun-
tain range that runs through Hunduras and Guatemala. The park's high-
est peak is Cerro Jilinco, which towers to 7,355 ft.

Although the park is named for the *cusuco,* or armadillo, you're un-
likely to see this shy creature. You're more apt to spot troops of howler

monkeys or white-faced monkeys. The park is a birder's paradise, with close to 300 different species, including toucans, parrots, and elusive resplendent quetzals. You can pick up a map of the four trails at the visitor center, but hiring a guide is a good idea because you'll see wildlife you might have missed.

Administered by the Fundación Ecologista Hector Rodrigo Pastor Fasquelle, Cusuco has accommodations in two small cabins. The park is 20 km (12 mi) west of San Pedro, but the trip will take 2½ hours— especially when the rain turns the roads to mush. You'll definitely need a four-wheel-drive vehicle to negotiate the terrain. ⊠ *Fundación Ecologista Hector Rodrigo Pastor Fasquelle, 7 Av. NO at 1 Calle,* ☎ *552– 1014,* FAX *557–6620.* 🖻 *L225.*

Cascadas de Pulhapanzak

The roaring Pulhapanzak Falls are the highest in the country. The thunderous noise draws you down the 128 steps to where you have a good view of the 328-ft waterfall. Local children will offer to guide you to the best spots to contemplate nature's glory. The falls are located near Peña Blanca along the highway linking Tegucigalpa and San Pedro Sula. ⊠ *Near Peña Blanca,* ☎ *no phone.* 🖻 *L20.*

Copán Ruinas

168 km (104 mi) south of San Pedro Sula.

With a squat colonial church watching over its eastern edge, the central square of Copán Ruinas calls to mind an era long past. You may think you've gone back in time, as horse-drawn wagons are not an uncommon sight on the surrounding cobblestone streets. Although most visitors come here to see the astounding Maya ruins east of town, you can also learn a bit about that culture at the **Museo Copán Ruinas.** Though most of this charming little museum's descriptions are in Spanish, the ancient tools and artworks speak for themselves. The exhibit on *el brujo* ("the witch") is especially striking, displaying the skeleton and religious artifacts of a Mayan shaman. ⊠ *West side of Parque Central,* ☎ *no phone.* 🖻 *L40.* ☉ *Daily 8–noon and 1–4.*

★ A cadre of colorful parrots greets you at the gate to **Copán,** one of the most breathtaking archaeological sites in Central America. Down a tree-lined path you'll find a series of beautifully reconstructed temples. The intricate carvings on the stone structures, especially along the Hieroglyphic Stairway, are remarkably well preserved. Here you can marvel at the artistry of a city that many have called the "Athens of the New World."

The area open to the public covers only a small part of the city's ceremonial center. Copán once extended for nearly 2 km (1¼ mi) along the river, making it as large as many Mayan archaeological sites in Guatemala. It is also just as old—more than 3,000 years ago there was an Olmec settlement on this site. Because new structures were usually built on top of existing ones, the great temples that are visible today were built during the reigns of the city's last few rulers.

The first king during the Classic Period, Yax Kuk Mo (or "Blue-Green Quetzal Macaw") came to power around AD 435. Very little is known about him or his successors until the rise of the 12th king, Smoke Jaguar (628–695). Under his rule Copán grew to be one of the largest cities in the region. His successor, King 18 Rabbit (695–738), continued the quest for complete control of the region. The city's political structure was shaken, however, when he was captured by the soldiers of Quiriguá, a city in what is today part of Guatemala. He was brought to that city and beheaded.

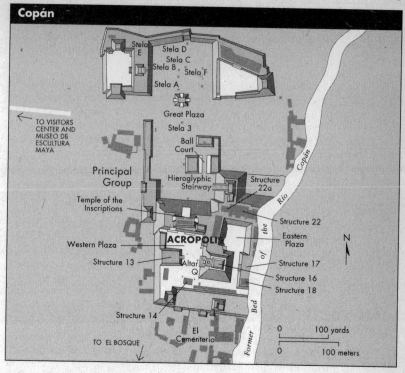

Copán

Stela E
Stela D
Stela C
Stela B
Stela F
Stela A
Great Plaza
Stela 3
Ball Court
TO VISITORS CENTER AND MUSEO DE ESCULTURA MAYA
Principal Group
Hieroglyphic Stairway
Structure 22a
Temple of the Inscriptions
Structure 22
Western Plaza
ACROPOLIS
Eastern Plaza
Structure 13
Altar Q
Structure 17
Structure 16
Structure 18
Structure 14
El Cementerio
TO EL BOSQUE
Río Copán
Former Bed of the
N
0   100 yards
0   100 meters

During his short reign, Smoke Monkey (738–749) was increasingly challenged by powerful noble families. Smoke Monkey's son, Smoke Shell (749–763), tried to justify his power by playing up the historical importance of great warrior kings. He ordered the construction of the elaborate Hieroglyphic Stairway, the longest Classic Maya inscription yet to be discovered, which emphasized the supremacy in battle of Copán's rulers. The 16th king, Dawning Sun (763–820), continued to glorify warfare in his architecture, but it was too late. By this time, Copán and its political authority were in decline.

As you stroll past towering cieba trees on your way to the archaeological site, you'll find the **Great Plaza** to your left. The stelae (meaning "tree stones") standing about the plaza were monuments erected to glorify rulers. Some stelae on the periphery are dedicated to Smoke Jaguar, but the most impressive, located in the middle of the plaza, depict 18 Rabbit. Besides stroking the egos of the kings, these monuments had religious significance as well. Vaults for ritual offerings have been found beneath most of them.

The city's most important **ball court** lies south of the Great Plaza. One of the largest of its kind in Central America, it was used for more than simple entertainment. Players had to keep a hard rubber ball from touching the ground, perhaps symbolizing the sun's battle to stay aloft. Stylized carvings of macaw heads that line either side of the court may have been used as markers for keeping score—and the score was worth keeping, since the losers were probably put to death. Near the ball court is one of the highlights of Copán, the **Hieroglyphic Stairway.** This amazing structure, covered with a canopy to protect it from the weather, contains the single largest collection of hieroglyphs in the world. Erected by King Smoke Shell, the 63 steps immortalize the battles won by Copán's kings, especially those of the much revered King Smoke

Jaguar. Once placed chronologically, the history can no longer be read because an earthquake knocked many steps free, and archaeologists replaced them in a random order. All may not be lost, however, as experts have located an early photograph of the stairway that helps unlock the proper sequence.

The **Western Court** is thought to have represented the underworld. The structures, with doors that lead to blank walls, appear symbolic. On the east side of the plaza is a reproduction of Altar Q, a key to understanding the history of Copán. The squat platform shows a long line of Copán's rulers passing power down to their heirs. It ends with the last great king, Dawning Sun, facing the first king, Yax Kuk Mo.

The **Acropolis** was partly washed away by the Río Copán, which has since been routed away from the ruins. Dawning Sun was credited with the construction of many of the buildings surrounding this grand plaza. Below the Acropolis are tunnels that lead to what archaeologists agree are some of the most fascinating discoveries at Copán. Underneath Structure 16 are the near-perfect remains of an older building, called the **Rosalila Temple.** This structure, dating from 571, was subsequently buried below taller structures. Uncovered in 1989, the Rosalila was notable in part because of the paint remains on its surface—rose and lilac—for which it was named. Another tunnel called **Los Jaguares** takes you past tombs, a system of aqueducts, and even an ancient bathroom.

Two other parts of Copán that served as residential and administrative areas are open to the public. While the architecture is not nearly as impressive as that of the larger buildings, archaeologists are fascinated by the glimpse into the daily lives of people other than kings. **El Bosque** (literally, "the Forest") lies in the woods off the trail to the west of the Principal Group. **Las Sepulturas** ("the graves"), which lies 2 km (1 mi) down the main road, is a revealing look into Maya society. Excavations have shown that the Maya had a highly stratified social system, where the elite owned houses with many rooms.

East of the main entrance to Copán, the marvelous **Museo de Escultura Maya** provides a close-up look at the best of Maya artistry. All the sculptures and replicas are accompanied by informative signs in English as well as Spanish. Here you'll find a full-scale replica of the Rosalila Temple. The structure, in eye-popping shades of red and green, offers an educated guess at what the ceremonial and political structures of Copán must have looked like at the time they were in use.

The entrance fee covers admission to the ruins, as well as to nearby sites like El Bosque and Las Sepulturas. Admission to the tunnels to Rosalila and Los Jaguares is extra, as is admission to the Museo de Escultura Maya. It's a good idea to hire a guide, as they are very knowledgable about the site. English-speaking ones charge about L300 for a two-hour tour, while Spanish-speaking guides charge about half that. A small cafeteria and gift shop are near the entrance. ⊠ *1 km (½ mi) east of Copán Ruinas,* ☎ *no phone.* ☎ *L150.* ☉ *Daily 8–4.*

Dining and Lodging

$-$$ ✕ **Carnitas Nía Lola.** Housed in a charming wooden building, this longtime favorite has sweeping views of the valley from its second-story dining room. Wonderful smells emanate from the meats on the grill, which is crowned with a stone skull reminiscent of those at the nearby ruins. One of the favorite dishes here is the *carne encebollado,* sizzling beef topped with onions and accompanied by a mound of french fries. ⊠ *2 blocks south of the Parque Central,* ☎ *no phone. AE, MC, V.*

$ ✕ **Llama del Bosque.** Named for a colorful flower, this cheerful little place is tucked away on a side street. It feels much larger than it really

is because of the sloped wooden ceiling that soars above the dining room. This is the place to come for barbecued meats—try the *pinchos,* which are chunks of beef brought to your table on long skewers. You're guaranteed not to go home hungry. ⊠ *1½ blocks west of Parque Central,* ☎ *651–4431. AE, MC, V.*

$ ✕ **Tunkul Restaurante & Bar.** If you're really hungry, this is the place to come for burritos the size of a rolled-up newspaper. The tiny tile-roof building has a few tables in the front next to the bar, but walk to the back to the delightfully overgrown garden. Mix and mingle with other travelers during the nightly happy hour from 8 to 9, when all mixed drinks are half price. Don't stumble as you leave, as the restaurant is located where the street drops steeply into the valley. ⊠ *1½ blocks west of Parque Central,* ☎ *651–4410. No credit cards.*

$$ 🏨 **Hotel Marina Copán.** Facing Parque Central, this colonial-era building has been lovingly converted into the town's prettiest hotel. The second-story restaurant overlooks the sparkling pool, shaded by clusters of banana trees. Brilliant bougainvillea lines the paths to the rooms, which are filled with hand-hewn wood furniture and cooled by lazily turning ceiling fans. At the bar you can listen to mariachi music on Friday and Saturday nights. ⊠ *Northwest corner of Parque Central,* ☎ *651–4070,* FAX *651–4477,* WEB *www.hotelmarinacopan.com. 40 rooms. Restaurant, café, cable TV, pool, gym, sauna, spa, bar, shop, laundry service, meeting rooms. AE, MC, V.*

$$ 🏨 **Hotel Posada Real de Copán.** The closest lodging to the archaeological site, this Spanish-style hotel is in the hills just outside of town. The open-air lobby, filled with tropical flowers, adds to the ambience. Inside the tile-roof buildings are generously proportioned rooms with views of the lush gardens. After a day exploring the dusty ruins, swim a few laps in the palm-shaded pool or relax in the nearby hot tub. ⊠ *2 km (1 mi) east of Copán Ruinas,* ☎ *651–4480,* FAX *651–4497,* WEB *www.posadarealdecopan.com. 80 rooms. Restaurant, room service, cable TV, pool, hot tub, hiking, bar, shop, meeting rooms. AE, MC, V.*

$$ 🏨 **Plaza Copán.** Watch horses clip-clop around the cobbled streets of Copán Ruinas from your terrace at this hotel on Parque Central. Ask for one of the rooms on the top floor, which have views of the town's red tile roofs. Relax with a drink by the little pool in the central courtyard, which is shaded by tall palm trees. The restaurant set behind a lovely colonnade, appropriately called Los Arcos, serves traditional fare. ⊠ *Southeast corner of Parque Central,* ☎ *651–4508,* FAX *651–4039. 21 rooms. Restaurant, fans, minibar, cable TV, pool, bar. AE, MC, V.*

$ 🏨 **Hacienda San Lucas.** In a century-old hacienda, this country inn is
★ one of the most charming lodgings in the area. Flavia Cueva, a descendant of the original owner, says restoring the farm was a "labor of love." Her tender care shows in all the details, from the carefully crafted wooden furniture in the simple but elegant rooms to the hammocks swinging from the porch outside. The restaurant, near the delightful old stove, serves steaming tamales, tasty adobo sauce, and aromatic coffee. Take a walk to Los Sapos, a Maya archeological site where huge stones were carved into the shape of frogs, or go horseback riding through the cool Copán Valley. ⊠ *1½ km (1 mi) south of Copán,* ☎ *651–4106,* WEB *www. geocities.com/sanlucascopan. 4 rooms. Restaurant, fans, hiking, horseback riding. No credit cards.*

Santa Rosa de Copán

153 km (95 mi) south of San Pedro Sula.

Set in one of the most beautiful regions of Honduras, Santa Rosa de Copán has a friendliness that makes you long to linger. It is the kind of highland town that still feels like a village—you get the sense you

would know everybody in town within a week or so. The hilltop *casco histórico* (historic center) is being renovated with care, with much work being put into preserving the splendid colonial-era buildings lining the narrow cobbled streets.

Tobacco still runs the local economy, and nearly everyone seems to be hard at work rolling cigars. Some prefer the strong Don Melo or the smoother Santa Rosa, but the pride of the area is the Zino, made by **Flor de Copán** (⌧ Calle Real Centenario 168, between 2 and 3 Av., ☎ 662–0111). A seductively sweet odor engulfs you as you enter the decrepit old factory west of Parque Central. In the dimly lit space you can watch workers piling tobacco leaves into *pilones* (bales). The neat shop at the entrance stocks the different brands made by the company. The factory is open weekdays 7:30–noon and 2–4.

Coffee lovers should head to **Beneficio Maya** (⌧ between 11 and 12 Av. NO, Col. San Martín, ☎ 662–1665) where they can watch the roasting and grading process. Fresh export-grade coffee is for sale on the premises. The factory is open weekdays 7:30–noon and 2–4. Take a taxi, as it's difficult to find.

Set in a lovingly restored building, the **Casa de Cultura** (⌧ Av. Alvaro Contreras, Barrio del Centro, ☎ 662–0800) buzzes with music lessons, theater, ballet, and modern dance and may well have one of the best children's libraries in Central America. The patio is a pleasant place to relax.

Dining and Lodging

$$ ✕ **El Rodeo.** Stuffed animals gaze down from the walls as you take a seat in this popular steak house. Meals are filling, accompanied by salad and plantains. There's always a crowd, as it doubles as a local watering hole. It stays open late (for Santa Rosa, anyway). ⌧ *1 Av., between 1 and 2 Calle SE, Barrio El Centro,* ☎ *662–0697. AE, MC, V.*

$–$$ ✕ **Flamingo's.** Considered one of the finest restaurants in town, this is the place to come for a quiet meal. A touch of elegance is added by the white- or melon-color tablecloths. Dishes include such specialties as pork with onion sauce. The wine list includes some decent Chilean options. ⌧ *1 Av. between Calle Real Centenario and 1 Calle SE, Barrio El Centro,* ☎ *662–0654. AE, MC, V.*

$ ✕ **Bella Italia.** A friendly Honduran-Italian couple serves up generous portions of Italian food at this eatery in the center of town. You might be surprised to find calzones in Santa Rosa de Copán. It's not quite what you'd find in Florence or Rome, but the spirit is there. ⌧ *1 Calle SE at 4 Av., Barrio El Centro,* ☎ *662–1953. No credit cards.*

$ ✕ **Pizza Pizza.** Hand-tossed pizzas with homemade sauce and locally grown toppings are given top billing at this cheery restaurant, but people come from all over for the delicious garlic bread. You can also order hamburgers, sandwiches, and other light fare. In addition to food, you can also check your e-mail, browse through a stack of books, or chat with amiable American owner Warren Post about what's going on in the area. If anyone would know, it's him. ⌧ *Calle Real Centenario, between 5 and 6 Av., Barrio El Centro (4½ blocks east of Parque Central),* ☎ *662–1104,* WEB *www.lunarpages.com/srcopan. No credit cards.*

$ 🏨 **Hotel Elvir.** Enjoy a glass of *timoshenko*, a fruity spirit flavored with cloves, at the rooftop bar of this colonial-style hotel. By far the best lodging in town, it has a beautiful patio and smart lobby. Comfortable rooms have cozy beds and modern baths. The restaurant is good, but a little overpriced. ⌧ *Calle Real Centenario, at 2 Av. SO,* ☎ *662–0805. 43 rooms. Restaurant, fans, cable TV, laundry service. MC, V*

$ 🏨 **Hotel Santa Rosa.** After entering through an attractive wooden lobby, you'll be escorted to one of the rooms surrounding a pleasant garden scattered with rocking chairs. The restaurant serves basic food.

✉ *Hwy. CA4,* ☎ *662–2365 or 662–2366,* FAX *662–2368. 26 rooms. Restaurant. No credit cards.*

Shopping

Two blocks east of Parque Central is the covered **mercado** (✉ Calle Real Centenario), an enticing market that sells everything from shawls to saddles. It is also the place to go for a great breakfast—ask for *atol chuco,* a delicious mush of fermented corn served with a few beans, lime, and roasted squash seeds.

Gracias

50 km (31 mi) from Santa Rosa de Copán.

Founded in 1536 by Gonzalo de Alvarado, brother of Spanish conquistador Pedro de Alvarado, Gracias has a fascinating history. Its original name was Gracias a Dios, after the conquistador's exclamation of gratitude that he had finally found land flat enough to build a city after wandering for days in the mountains. The town's colonial history resonates in the three churches you'll find along its cobblestone streets. A short walk up to the fort of San Cristobal provides an inspiring view of the nearby mountains.

Nearby are several indigenous communities, the largest being the Lenca people. **La Campa,** only 16 km (10 mi) from Gracias, is a lovely Lenca village set in the rugged mountains. It's well worth visiting to see the local ceramics—the same red pottery you will see for much higher prices in Tegucigalpa and San Pedro Sula. Just outside town is the home of the delicate Doña Desideria, a smiling lady who bakes red pottery in the open air. She will happily show you around. Also make sure to stop by the Iglesia de San Mattías. The statue of San Mattías was stolen a few years ago, but the uproar was so great that the thieves relented, wrapping it in rags and leaving it on a bus from Gracias to Santa Rosa de Copán, where it was discovered and returned.

Another 16 km (10 mi) away is the remote village of **San Manuel Colohete,** whose stunning colonial church is considered to be the most beautiful in the country. Sculpted saints set in niches make the facade quite unusual, while the swirling colors of the walls and ceilings inside have led people to compare it to the Sistine Chapel. The massive gold-plated altarpiece with a gleaming Cristo Negro is breathtaking. At his feet (you may have to move some lace decorations) are some paintings of sun and moon that recall the religions that Christianity hasn't managed to completely push aside. Ask in the square for Don Olvidio Mejía if you wish to see more religious treasures. He'll accompany you to the bell tower, where there's a wonderful view.

The area around Gracias is considered one of Honduras's best-kept secrets, as it's home to **Parque Nacional Celaque,** one of the largest tracts of cloud forest left in Central America. At 9,345 ft, the Montaña de Celaque is the highest peak in Honduras. The name means "box of water" in the Lenca language, after the 11 rivers flowing from this mountain. The hike to the summit, which takes seven to eight hours, is easier during the dry season. The park is home to spider monkeys, tapirs, and pumas, as well as birds such as toucans and quetzals.

Getting to the park is not a walk in the park. A 9 km (6 mi) dirt road leads from Gracias to the park's entrance, more or less a two-hour journey. The visitor center is another half hour beyond that. There is no public transport to the park, but you can hire a car in Gracias. You can stay overnight at the visitor center, where you'll find two small cabins with beds, showers, and cooking facilities. ✉ *Gracias,* ☎ *662–1459.* 💶 *L50.* ☉ *Daily 8–4.*

Dining and Lodging

$ ✕🏨 **Hotel y Restaurante Guancascos.** A hub of activity, this clean and comfortable hotel is the best in town. The restaurant doles out plentiful portions of *platos típicos* (typical dishes), heaping helpings of poultry, and huge bowls of hot vegetable soup. To escape from the midday heat, sip fresh juices made from local berries on the shady balcony overlooking the town. Owner Frony Miedama can set up trips to Parque Nacional Celaque and rents a cabin there called the Cabaña Villa Verde. ✉ *Barrio el Rosario*, ☎ 656–1219, FAX 656–1526, WEB *www.guancascos.com.* 11 rooms. Restaurant, fans, Internet. AE, MC, V.

$ 🏨 **Hotel Erick.** They are a little spare, but clean rooms at Hotel Erick have a few niceties like cable TV. The friendly owners will let you store your gear here while you explore Parque Nacional Celaque. ✉ *Barrio Mercedes*, ☎ 656–1066. 33 rooms. Fans, cable TV. No credit cards.

Lago de Yojoa

100 km (62 mi) south of San Pedro Sula.

The largest natural lake in the country, shimmering Lago de Yojoa is home to an amazing variety of birds. More than 370 different species are found in the moss-draped trees, from black-bellied whistling ducks and blue-crowned motmots to red-legged honeycreepers and keel-billed toucans. For even more unusual sights, you can grab a pair of binoculars and hire a boat to Isla del Venado.

With a name that means means "eye of water," Lago de Yojoa was once populated by Lenca, Maya, and other peoples. There are many ruins, the most significant being Los Naranjos on the northwest shore. Excavations were stalled for lack of funds, but now seem to be back on track. Of course, the main draw of the lake is purely recreational. Despite being a popular weekend recreation spot for families, the lake is still unspoiled. There are all kinds of trips you can take out onto the lake, the most popular being by catamaran.

Lodging

$–$$ 🏨 **Honduyate Marina.** If you want to relax with a gin and tonic as you gaze at Lago de Yojoa, this is *the* place. Charming expat Richard Joint, who evokes all things British, and is a wealth of information about the area. From your gleaming white cabin you can wander down to look at the boats in the marina. Enquire about the *casa de campo* (country house) on the far side of lake. Sleeping eight, it's great for a longer stays. ✉ *Km 161 Carretera del Norte, Monte Verde, Santa Cruz de Yojoa*, ☎ 982–2338 or 990–9387, FAX 239–2423. 5 cabins. Restaurant, bar, boating, marina, bar. AE, MC, V.

$–$$ 🏨 **Hotel Finca Las Glorias.** Set on a coffee and orange plantation, this flower-strewn hotel makes a perfect lakeside retreat. The picturesque bridge leading to an airy pavilion is great for bird-watching, and the catamaran trips on the lake are sublime. From the private balcony of your cabana you can watch horses and their foals trot around. Weekends tend to fill up with families, so reserve ahead. ✉ *Lago de Yojoa*, ☎ 566–0461 or 566–0462, FAX 566–0553, WEB *www.hotellasglorias.com.* 40 rooms. Restaurant, cable TV, 2 pools, boating, billiards, horseback riding, playground, shop. MC, V.

Comayagua

★ *82 km (51 mi) northwest of Tegucigalpa.*

Founded in 1537, Santa María de Comayagua was the first capital of Honduras. It was also one of the last bastions of resistance by the Lenca and Nahuatl people, who staged a revolt two years later. Pres-

ident Marco Aurelio Soto moved the seat of power to Tegucigalpa in 1880, allegedly to avenge repeated snubs by the city's haughty upper classes. After a century of decline, Comayagua was declared a national monument in 1972. The focus now is on preserving its colonial-era character. The impressive project is evidenced in the gleaming white facade of the Catedral de Comayagua and immaculately clean Parque Central.

With two of the best museums in the country, Comayagua must not be missed. Close to Tegucigalpa, you can see its major sights in a day. Most of its colonial churches are within a block of each other, and the museums are within easy walking distance. The city fills up in Semana Santa (the week leading up to Easter), when brightly colored "carpets" made of dyed sawdust decorate an entire block in the center. Processions crop up on nearly every street corner.

The largest house of worship constructed during the colonial period, **Catedral de Santa María** (⊠ Parque Central) dates from 1711. The interior is incredibly ornate, with four hand-carved wooden altars covered in gold. Note the intriguing statue of Santa Ana, the mother of the Virgin Mary, carrying a diminutive Santa María, who in turn is holding a tiny infant Jesús. Phillip II of Spain donated a clock from Alhambra for the tower, and Hondureños claim it is the oldest in the Americas. As it's over 800 years old, it could well be true. For a peek at the ancient workings, ask in the square for Don Blas Reyes, who can lead you up the belfry steps. This affable old gent may let you roam about on the cathedral roof for a truly magnificent view of the surrounding hills.

At the north end of town is **Iglesia de la Caridad** (⊠ Calle 7a Norte, at 3 Av. NO). In the back is the country's only remaining open-air chapel, originally used for the conversion of indigenous peoples. The church's interior is famous for its statue of *El Señor de la Burrita* (Lord of the Burro), which is paraded through town on Palm Sunday. Three blocks southeast of Iglesia de la Caridad is **Iglesia San Francisco** (⊠ Av. 2 de Julio, at 7 Calle NE), founded in 1560. The bell in the tower was brought from Spain and dates back to 1460, making it the oldest in the Americas. The church houses an elegantly carved baroque altarpiece from the 18th century. Dating from 1542, **Iglesia La Merced** (⊠ Calle 1a, at 2 Av. NE) was the first church to be built in Honduras. One of the oldest in the Americas, it houses a magnificent altarpiece.

★ Recently restored, the elegant old building that holds the **Museo de Antropología** served as the country's first presidential palace. Since 1940 the museum has provided a fascinating examination of Lenca culture. It contains some well-preserved artifacts from around Comayagua, from cave art to colorful ceramics. It also houses interesting fossils and an important collection of jade. A workshop at the back has been transformed into a school where men and women train as carpenters, stonemasons, blacksmiths, and in the other old trades needed to rebuild the city according to the old traditions. A small cafeteria is open for breakfast and lunch. ⊠ 6 Calle NE, at Av. 2 de Julio, ☎ 772–0386, FAX 772–2693. ☜ L20. ☉ Tues.–Sat. 8:30–4, Sun. 9–5.

Located in a building that served as Central America's first university, **Museo Colonial** holds a mysterious treasure trove guarded by cloistered nuns. The varied collection of 15th- to 18th-century artworks from local churches includes paintings, sculptures, and jewels used to adorn the statues of saints. It also houses the chair used by Pope John Paul II when he visited Tegucigalpa, the first worm-eaten statue of the Virgin Mary to reach Honduras, and a long-locked Christ sculpture with violet eyes

that, if you stare into them, are said to reawaken long-lost dreams. ✉ *Av. 2 de Julio, between Calle 3a NO and 4a NO,* ☎ 772–0169. ✉ *L15.* ⊙ *Tues.–Sun. 9–12 and 2–5.*

Dining and Lodging

\$\$ ✕ **Villa Real.** A charming 18th-century house with a horse-drawn carriage in the entranceway houses the best restaurant in the city. Tables are set in a pretty, overgrown garden beside a trickling fountain. Enjoy the hint of a breeze as you sample *pechuga marsala* (chicken breast with vegetables). The *plato típico* is also quite satisfying. Ask manager Tirso Zapata to show you around the historic building. ✉ *Calle Real 35,* ☎ ℻ 772–0101. MC, V.

\$\$ 🏨 **Hotel Santa María Comayagua.** With a pool that's a welcome respite from the heat, this hotel has all the extras that matter most. Rooms are clean and fresh. Although outside the city, the hotel is only a 10-minute walk to the historic center. ✉ *Km 82, Carretera Tegucigalpa-San Pedro Sula,* ☎ *772–7872 or 772–8934,* ℻ *772–7719. 28 rooms. Restaurant, cable TV, pool, bar, conference rooms. AE, MC, V.*

The Western Highlands A to Z

AIR TRAVEL TO AND FROM THE WESTERN HIGHLANDS

American and Continental both have daily flights from the United States into San Pedro Sula. Taca flies to the city from many capitals throughout Central America. Isleña specializes in flights to the Bay Islands. Iberia flies from Madrid to San Pedro Sula.

➤ AIRLINES AND CONTACTS: **American** (✉ 16 Av. between 1a and 2a Calle, San Pedro Sula, ☎ 553–3506 or 668–3244, WEB www.aa.com). **Continental** (✉ 1 Calle NO, between 3 and 4 Av., San Pedro Sula, ☎ 552–9770; ✉ Av Circunvalación at 8 Calle, San Pedro Sula, ☎ 557–4141 or 668–3208, WEB www.continental.com). **Iberia** (✉ 12 Calle at 2 Av., San Pedro Sula, ☎ 550–2530 or 668–3216, WEB www.iberia.com). **Isleña** (✉ 7 Av. between 1 and 2 Calles, San Pedro Sula, ☎ 552–8322 or 552–8335). **Sosa** (✉ 8 Av at 1 Calle, San Pedro Sula, ☎ 550–6545 or 668–3223). **Taca** (✉ Av. Circunvalación at 13 Av., San Pedro Sula, ☎ 550–5265 or 668–3020, WEB www.grupotaca.com).

AIRPORTS AND TRANSFERS

About 15 km (9 mi) outside San Pedro Sula, Aeropuerto Internacional Ramón Villeda Morales has connections to most international destinations. There are also frequent flights to the Bay Islands and others parts of the country.

There are no airport shuttle buses, only private taxis. A taxi to downtown San Pedro Sula should cost no more than L150.
➤ AIRPORT INFORMATION: **Aeropuerto Internacional Ramón Villeda Morales** (✉ Carretera La Lima, San Pedro Sula, ☎ 668–3260).

BUS TRAVEL TO AND FROM THE WESTERN HIGHLANDS

Buses to Comayagua, the only community in Western Honduras more accessible from Tegucigalpa than San Pedro Sula, are the slow "servicio a escala." Norteños and El Rey lines offer daily service. The same buses also stop at Lago de Yojoa. Santa Rosa de Copán is 7½ hours by bus on La Sultana. It's probably quicker to take an express bus to San Pedro Sula and head south from there.

If you're headed north, Viana Clase Oro and Hedman Alas run luxury buses to San Pedro Sula. Sáenz Primera and King Quality are other luxury services to San Pedro Sula. King Quality runs two buses daily to San Salvador and one daily to Guatemala. El Rey Express has a de-

cent "direct" (meaning just a few stops) service to San Pedro Sula that leaves every hour.

One daily bus operated by Gracianos runs from San Pedro to Gracias, but Congolón has more frequent departures.

➤ BUS COMPANIES: **Congolón** (✉ 8 Av. between 9 and 10 Calle, San Pedro Sula, ☎ 553–1174). **El Rey** (✉ 7 Av. between 5 and 6 Calle, San Pedro Sula, ☎ 553–4264). **El Rey Express** (✉ 9 Av. between 9 and 10 Calle, San Pedro Sula, ☎ 550–8355). **Gracianos** (✉ Parque Central, Gracias, ☎ no phone; ✉ 6 Calle between 6 and 7 Av., San Pedro Sula, ☎ no phone). **Hedman Alas** (✉ 3 Calle between 7 and 8 Av., San Pedro Sula, ☎ 553–1361). **King Quality** (✉ 6 Calle between 7 and 8 Av., San Pedro Sula, ☎ 553–4547). **La Sultana** (✉ Barrio Miraflores, Santa Rosa de Copán, ☎ 662–0940). **Norteños** (✉ 6 Calle between 6 and 7 Av., San Pedro Sula, ☎ 552–2145). **Sáenz Primera** (✉ 8 Av. between 5 and 6 Calle, San Pedro Sula, ☎ 553–4969). **Viana Clase Oro** (✉ Av. Circunvalación, San Pedro Sula, ☎ 556–9261).

CAR RENTAL

There is no shortage of car rental agencies in San Pedro Sula, and most have offices both in the airport and in town. Two good local companies are Maya and Molinari. There are no rental agencies in Gracias, Comayagua, or Santa Rosa de Copán.

➤ LOCAL AGENCIES: **Avis** (✉ Aeropuerto Internacional Ramón Villeda Morales, San Pedro Sula, ☎ 668–3164; ✉ 1 Calle and 6 Av., San Pedro Sula, ☎ 553–0888 or 552–2872). **Hertz** (✉ Aeropuerto Internacional Ramón Villeda Morales, San Pedro Sula, ☎ 668–3156 or 668–3157; ✉ Blvd. Morazán and Calle 1, San Pedro Sula, ☎ 550–8080). **Maya** (✉ Aeropuerto Internacional Ramón Villeda Morales, San Pedro Sula, ☎ 668–3168; ✉ 3 Av., between 7 and 8 Calles, San Pedro Sula, ☎ 552–2670 or 552–2671). **Molinari** (✉ 1 Calle, between 3 and 4 Av., San Pedro Sula, ☎ 553–2639 or 552–2704). **Thrifty** (✉ Aeropuerto Internacional Ramón Villeda Morales, San Pedro Sula, ☎ 668–3152 or 668–3153).

CAR TRAVEL

Traffic can get heavy during rush hour, but driving in San Pedro Sula is a breeze compared to the gridlock in the capital. Since this is the country's most important transportation hub, streets into and out of the city are well maintained, making driving to surrounding areas a pleasure. In the more mountainous parts of the region you will need a four-wheel-drive vehicle or a sturdy pickup.

EMBASSIES AND CONSULATES

The embassy for the United Kingdom is open weekdays 8:30–11:30 and 2–6.

➤ EMBASSY: **United Kingdom** (✉ Edificio Banexpo, Av. Circunvalación 11, San Pedro Sula, ☎ 550–7374 or 550–2288, FAX 550–7009, WEB www.fco.gov.uk).

EMERGENCIES

Clínica Bendaña, on Avenida Circunvalación, is a 24-hour clinic in San Pedro Sula that can assist you with most emergencies. Clínica Bendaña serves Comayagua, while Hospital Regional del Occidente serves Santa Rosa de Copán. Drugstores are plentiful in most towns.

➤ HOSPITALS: **Clínica Bendaña** (✉ Av. Circunvalación between 9 and 10 Calles, San Pedro Sula, ☎ 557–4429 or 553–1618). **Clínica Bendaña** (✉ 1 block from Parque Central,, Comayagua, ☎ 772–0102). **Hospital Regional del Occidente** (✉ Barrio del Calvario, Santa Rosa de Copán, ☎ 662–0107).

➤ Pharmacies: **Farmacia Central** (⊠ Calle Centenario, Barrio Mercedes, Santa Rosa de Copán, ☎ 662–0465). **Farmacia Cruz Roja** (⊠ Barrio Mercedes, Santa Rosa de Copán, ☎ 662–0050). **Farmacia Handa** (⊠ 3 Av. at 5 Calle, San Pedro Sula, ☎ 550–1068). **Farmacia María Auxiliadora** (⊠ Av. Circunvalación between 9 and 10 Calles, San Pedro Sula, ☎ 552–7282).

MAIL AND SHIPPING
There are post offices near the center of most towns in the Western Highlands. If you have a package, there are plenty of overnight services available in San Pedro Sula.
➤ Overnight Services: **Federal Express** (⊠ Av. Circunvalación at 2 Calle SO, San Pedro Sula, ☎ 557–6591, WEB www.fedex.com). **Trans Express** (⊠ Blvd. del Norte, San Pedro Sula, ☎ 553–0428). **UPS** (⊠ 16 Av. NO, between 3 and 4 Calle, San Pedro Sula, ☎ 557–8805).
➤ Post Offices: **Comayagua** (⊠ 1 block east of Parque Central, ☎ 772–0089). **San Pedro Sula** (⊠ 3 Av. SO and 9 Calle, San Pedro Sula, ☎ 552–3185). **Santa Rosa de Copán** (⊠ Barrio el Centro, ☎ 662–0030).

MONEY MATTERS
San Pedro Sula has plenty of banks, most of them open weekdays 9–3. Many are also open Saturday mornings. There are also currency exchange offices in the airport and around the central square. Most hotels also have exchange currency, but some give unfavorable rates. American Express, MasterCard, and Visa are widely accepted in San Pedro Sula, but less so outside the big city. Cash advances from your Visa or MasterCard can be arranged smoothly while in San Pedro, but the procedure will be more of a challenge in smaller towns.
➤ Banks: **Banco de Honduras** (⊠ 1 Calle, San Pedro Sula, ☎ 557–4952, WEB www.bch.hn). **Banco Sogerin** (⊠ 1 Calle at 8 Av., San Pedro Sula, ☎ 550–2002). **Credomatic** (⊠ 5 Av. NO at 2 Calle, ☎ 557–4350, WEB www.credomatic.com).

SAFETY
Lock your car doors while driving in San Pedro Sula, as there have been robberies. Certain stretches of road between San Pedro Sula and Santa Rosa de Copán are dangerous after sunset, so always travel by day.

TAXIS
Negotiate the price before you set off. Although taxis are quite safe by day, at night you should use a company recommended by your hotel.
➤ Taxi Company: **Radio Taxi** (☎ 557–8801).

TOUR OPERATORS
Santa Rosa is home to one of the most culturally informed tour operators in the country, Lenca Land Trails. Historian Max Elvir has learned local traditions by traveling to nearby villages by mule. If you want to see the more remote communities such as San Manuel de Colohete, you will get much more out of the adventure if you go with him.

Other reputable tour operators include MC Tours, which serves the region around San Pedro Sula and Copán Ruinas, and Explore Honduras, which leads trips to San Pedro Sula.
➤ Tour Companies: **Explore Honduras** (⊠ 2 Av. NO at 1 Calle, San Pedro Sula, ☎ 552–6242 or 552–6093, WEB www.explorehonduras.com). **Lenca Land Trails** (⊠ Calle Real Centenario SO and 2 Av., Santa Rosa de Copán, ☎ 662–1374). **Mayan VIP Tours** (⊠ 1 Calle at Av. Circunvalación, San Pedro Sula, ☎ 552–7862). **MC Tours** (⊠ 6 Av. SO at 10 Calle, San Pedro Sula, ☎ 552–4455, WEB www.mctours-honduras.com).

THE CARIBBEAN COAST

The northern coast of Honduras is the domain of the Garífuna people, descendants of African slaves who were shipwrecked in the Caribbean. They first settled on the island of St. Vincent in the Lesser Antilles, but in the 18th century the British forcibly moved them to Roatán in the Bay Islands. Many eventually migrated to the mainland, and they now inhabit the Caribbean coast from Belize to Nicaragua. Many Garífuna people along the coast live in thatched-roof huts next to the sea, getting by mostly by fishing.

In Garífuna music, dancing, and native language you can note a distinct West African influence. Octogenarians can still sing and dance long after younger people collapse from exhaustion. Some of their songs are filled with images of poverty and loss, while others are more like oral history put to music. Religious rituals, especially those focusing on death, are very much in evidence here, and respect for the ancestors is central to the culture.

The regional cuisine along the coast happens to be the country's best, with specialties such as *sopa de caracol* (conch soup) and *tapado de pescado* (steamed fish and coconut milk stew) served with *machuca* (mashed yucca). *Pan de coco* (coconut bread) is another favorite in the area, as is the bitter spirit *gifiti*.

Omoa

69 km (43 mi) north of San Pedro Sula.

A seductive beach and spectacular waterfalls where the Sierra de Omoa meets the Caribbean have made this former fishing village an up-and-coming vacation destination. The town is still small enough, however, that addresses haven't caught on—hotels on the beach just say they are on *la playa*. There is just one main road, so either turn left or right.

The **Fuerte de San Fernando de Omoa** is surprisingly pretty, with stone walls of pink, gray, and deep russett surrounded on all sides by mangroves. The fort was built between 1759 and 1775 to protect the gold and other valuables being shipped back to Spain. It didn't take long, however, for a humiliating defeat. In 1779 the English conquered the fort after a two-day siege, escaping with all booty before the Spaniards could call reinforcements. ⊠ *Omoa,* ☎ *no phone.* 🎟 *L20.* ☉ *Weekdays 8–4, weekends 9–5.*

Dining and Lodging

$ ✕🏨 **Flamingo.** Cool rooms decorated in pine with private terraces overlooking the ocean make this hotel the top choice in Omoa. The sundeck on the beach is a favorite spot for weddings. The friendly Colombian owners really know how to eat, and delicious dishes such as blue crab soup and seafood casserole can't be beat. The tamales may be the best you've ever tasted. ⊠ *La Playa,* ☎ *658–9199,* FAX *658–9288. 10 rooms. Restaurant, pool, cable TV, bar. MC, V.*

$ 🏨 **Hotel Bahía de Omoa.** Across the road from the beach, this spotless little hotel is run by busy Dutch woman who's happy to let you borrow a bike, browse among her books, or putter around in the kitchen. She also hands out local maps and is a great source of information about the area, including boat trips to Guatemala. Into fishing? She knows where to go, and will even loan you a rod and reel. ⊠ *Omoa,* ☎ *658–9076. 4 rooms. Cable TV, bicycles, fishing. No credit cards.*

Tela

92 km (57 mi) northeast of San Pedro Sula.

Garífuna women stride gracefully along the shore with baskets of coconut bread balanced on their heads near Tela, a delightful town on the northern coast. Its sweeping beaches and undisturbed nature reserves have long drawn visitors from around the world. In recent years, young entrepreneurs have made their mark on the town with world-class restaurants and hotels.

The Spanish settled here in 1524—not in Tela, but in the nearby village of Triunfo de la Cruz. Tela itself gained importance centuries later when it served as the main port for the United Fruit Company. When the company moved its base to La Lima, it left behind the interesting **Jardín Botánico Lancetilla** (⊠ 1 km (½ mi) west of Tela). This botanical garden, the second largest in the world, holds more than 1,000 varieties of plants marked by name, country of origin, and date of introduction. Many species of birds have made it their home, and birders come to see a variety of colorful parrots. It's open daily 7–3.

Tela is a great place to learn more about little-known Garífuna culture. Near the Río Tela is the **Museo Garífuna** (⊠ 8a Calle NE, ☎ no phone), which covers everything from musical styles to religious customs. There are also several villages nearby where you can experience Garífuna life firsthand. To the east is **Triunfo de la Cruz,** where you'll find a line of homely little restaurants along the water. Friendly **Tornabé,** to the west, also has a string beachfront eateries as well as a rustic little inn. Beyond Tornabé is **Miami,** a pleasant community on the Laguna de los Micos. This is the most traditional of the villages, consisting mostly of thatched huts.

One of the most geographically diverse nature preserves in the country is **Parque Nacional Jeanette Kawas,** named for a slain environmentalist. The park, also known as Parque Nacional Punta Sal, protects mangrove swamps, tropical forests, shady lagoons, and coral reefs. It is likely you will see as many as 60 howler monkeys having their breakfast if you head out early enough in morning. The males gesticulate from their perches in the treetops, while the females, many with tiny babies, watch from a wary distance. You may also come across white-faced monkeys, some of which have developed a habit of throwing avocado pits at visitors—be ready to duck. Radiantly colored parrot and vine snakes, almost shoelace thin, ripple through the foliage. They are harmless, but be sure to watch your step.

If you take the Los Curumos trail, you can hear the waves as you reach Puerto Caribe, one of the hiding places of the notorious pirate Captain Morgan. Turtles and dolphins swim here in the turquoise waters. If you snorkel you may see barracudas and nose sharks, as well as spindly lobsters taking a slow-motion stroll. A modern day Robinson Crusoe called Don Polo lives near here—alone since a jaguar ate his dogs. He'll be happy to chat if you can manage some Spanish.

You can see Punta Sal jutting out into the ocean from Tela, which might make you think it's quite close. It's actually difficult to reach, so you should considering hiring a guide. It's also a great way to learn about the exotic animal and plant species (there are 14 types of banana here, for example). ⊠ Prolansate, 9 Calle at 3 Av. NE, Tela, ☎ 448–2042. 🖾 L15. ☺ Daily 6–4.

It's essential to hire a guide if you want to visit **Refugio de Vida Silvestre Punta Izopo,** a wildlife refuge east of Tela. It's so easy to get lost in this labyrinth where even locals don't go alone. The best way to see

the refuge is by kayak, letting you navigate the maze of mangroves along the Río Plátano without disturbing the wildlife. You can spot howler monkeys, crocodiles, and iguanas, as well as toucans and parrots that come around late in the afternoon. ⊠ *Prolansate, 9 Calle at 3 Av. NE, Tela,* ☎ *448–2042.* 🖾 *L15.* ☉ *Daily 6–4.*

Dining and Lodging

$–$$ ✕ **Mango Café.** Located on the Río Tela, Mango Café is a great spot for a romantic dinner. Watch the fireflies flit about the lily pads as you enjoy regional dishes like tapado de pescado. Start with the scrumptious garlic bread (served while still warm) or one of the carefully prepared salads. Choose from the selection of wines (sold only by the bottle), beers, or locally made gifiti. If you are heading out on an early morning trip with Garifuna Tours, stop by early to wake yourself up with a steaming cup of coffee. There's also an Internet café and a small B&B. ⊠ *8a Calle NE, above Museo Garífuna,* ☎ *448–2856. No credit cards.*

$ ✕ **Casa Azul.** This cheery little restaurant is a popular evening hangout for tourists, especially since it has a bookstore and a small art gallery. Casa Azul is known for Italian dishes such as pizza and spaghetti and meatballs. The staff is justifiably proud of the "big clean salads." ⊠ *11 Calle, at 6 Av. NE, 1 block north of Parque Central,* ☎ *448–1443. No credit cards.*

$ ✕🏨 **Cesar Mariscos.** Just a stone's throw from the beach, this stylish
★ hotel has rooms with balconies shaded by lush palms. Hand-hewn wood furniture and carefully selected pieces of art add a homey touch. A light and airy reading room on the first floor is popular with adults, while children gravitate to the tiny playground. Truly delicious seafood is served in the romantic restaurant or at shaded tables on the sand. Try the spicy *camarones en salsa jalapeño* (shrimp in a creamy sauce seasoned with peppers). ⊠ *Calle Peatonal Playera,* ☎ *448–2083 or 448–1934,* [WEB] *www.hotelcesarmariscos.com. 15 rooms. Restaurant, bar, Internet, laundry service, playground, airport transfer. AE, MC, V.*

$ ✕🏨 **Maya Vista.** There's a stunning view of the bay from the Maya Vista, which enjoys a vantage point high above the city. Clean and comfortable rooms have wide terraces where you can lounge in a hammock as you enjoy bay breezes. In the popular restaurant, entrées such as Chinese noodles with peppers are tasty and reasonably priced. You can also order wines by the glass—a rarity in this part of the country. The Canadian owners make sure there's a warm, friendly atmosphere. They know what's going on it Tela, so it's good to check with them. ⊠ *8 Calle and 10 Av. NE,* ☎ *448–1497,* [WEB] *www.mayavista.com. 9 rooms. Restaurant, fan, cable TV, bar. AE, MC, V.*

$$ 🏨 **Hotel Villas Telamar.** Once home to executives of the United Fruit Company, this luxurious complex sits on 30 acres right on the Caribbean. The enormous wooden villas, with two or three bedrooms, are perfect for families. Each is filled with beautiful mahogany furniture. The pool and the adjoining grounds are a delight, especially on weekend evenings when an orchestra plays salsa and merengue. The service in the restaurant is depressingly bad. ⊠ *Across the Río Tela,* ☎ *448–2196,* [FAX] *448–2984,* [WEB] *www.telamar.com. 40 rooms, 17 apartments, 38 villas. Restaurant, 2 pools, 9-hole golf course, 4 tennis courts, beach, horseback riding, bar, meeting rooms, playground. AE, MC, V.*

$ 🏨 **Hotel Tela.** With a wide stairway and grand dining room, this breezy hotel feels like a venerable old boarding school. The patios are a great place to relax; one looks inland over the hills, the other to a forest filled with squawking birds. The rooms are spacious, and a fan or two keeps you cool. ⊠ *Calle 9 at 4 Av. NE,* ☎ [FAX] *448–2150. 15 rooms. Restaurant, fans, bar. MC, V*

Nightlife and the Arts

On Friday and Saturday nights, the discos near the market engage in an all-night battle of the sound systems. Follow the noise if you feel like dancing. Salsa and reggae bands (many dreadfully out of tune) often play in the park, and it's fun to join the locals who perch on the concrete ledges to lend a quizzical ear.

Outdoor Activities and Sports

The best beaches are in the nearby Garífuna villages of Tornabé, San Juan, La Ensenada, and Triunfo de la Cruz, all easily accessible from Tela. Farther west and harder to reach are Río Tinto and Miami.

La Ceiba

60 km (37 mi) east of Tela.

The third-largest city in Honduras, La Ceiba was once the country's busiest port. It's named after a huge tree near the dock that sheltered the workers, which should give you an idea of how hot La Ceiba can be. Mild relief is occasionally offered by trade winds off the bay.

You can't miss Pico Bonito, the majestic peak rising behind La Ceiba that turns a deep blue at dusk. **Parque Nacional Pico Bonito** is named after the 7,989-ft peak. Rugged and little explored, Parque Nacional Pico Bonito harbors some amazing primary tropical wet forest. There are 22 rivers that run through the park, meaning there are numerous cold-water pools where you can stop for a dip. Guides see jaguars and ocelots with impressive regularity, although the enormity of the area means you are lucky if you glimpse these fearsome creatures.

The most popular route through the park leads to a waterfall called La Ruidosa (meaning "The Noisy One"). Trails are fairly well maintained, but it is best to go with a guide. They are found through the Fundación Parque Nacional Pico Bonito office in La Ceiba. ⊠ *FUP-NAPIB, Av. República,* ☎ *443–3824,* WEB *www.cohdefor.hn.* ☜ *L100.*

About 27 km (17 mi) west of La Ceiba, the **Refugio de Vida Silvestre Cuero y Salado** is made up of 132 square km (51 square mi) of tropical forest formed by the confluence of the Río Cuero and Río Salado. This is one of the few places in the world where you can see manatees, aquatic creatures once mistaken for mermaids. In addition to these gentle giants, you may also spot white-faced monkeys, crocodiles, turtles, and several species of herons along the canals. The mangroves are best seen by boat, and the park organizes two-hour guided tours.

To get to the park, drive west from La Ceiba, turning right after crossing the Río Bonito. Stop at the railway tracks. From here you can take a small train run by the Fundación Cuero y Salado or a *burra* (a handcart operated by locals) for the remaining 9 km (6 mi). The visitor center has information about the park. ⊠ *Fundación Cuero y Salado, Edificio Ferrocarril Nacional, La Ceiba,* ☎ *443–3525.* ☜ *L165.* ☉ *Weekdays 8–11:30 and 1:30–4:30, Sat. 8–11:30.*

Dining and Lodging

$$–$$$ ✕ **La Plancha.** The town's most popular steak house, La Plancha serves up a 16-ounce *filete especial* that will satisfy the most ravenous diner. There's seafood as well—the shrimp and conch cocktails make a good starter. The service is snappy, whether in the dining room or at the fully stocked bar. ⊠ *Av. Lempira at Calle 9,* ☎ *443–2304. AE, MC, V.*

$$–$$$ ✕ **El Portal.** Among the town's statelier restaurants, El Portal is one of the few places on the mainland where you can satisfy your yearning for Thai food. Start with one of the appetizing soups, then move

on to the barbecued chicken breast or the curried shrimp with rice. The restaurant, in Hotel Colonial, even has a decent wine list. ⊠ *Av. 14 de Julio between 6 and 7 Calle,* ☎ *443–1953 or 443–1678. AE, MC, V.*

$$–$$$ ✕ **Ricardo's.** Some consider this restaurant in the center of La Ceiba to be among the best in Central America. Chef Janet Irias has a taste for traditional fare, but there is always something new on the menu. Choose among the various steak and seafood dishes, served in the pretty dining room or on the leafy terrace. The full salad bar is a nice touch. The service is professional, and the bar is stocked with just about anything you could wish for. ⊠ *Av. 14 de Julio at 10 Calle,* ☎ *443–0468. AE, MC, V. Closed Sun.*

$$ ✕ **Expatriates.** This rooftop bar and grill, known as "Expats," is a gem. Informal and friendly, it is always packed with locals eager to fill you in on what's happening in the area. Heaping portions of charcoal-grilled meats are all delicious, so it may be difficult choosing between fish fillets, chicken wings, or barbecued ribs. The large-screen TV by the bar screens major sports events, and you can buy a wide range of Honduran cigars. ⊠ *End of Calle 12,* ☎ *440–1505. AE, MC, V.*

$ ✕ **Café Giarre.** With a couple of tables outside on the sidewalk and a cozy dining room within, this Italian eatery is becoming very popular. Pretty touches, such as the billowing curtains, abound. The *bruschetta ai pomodori* (toasted bread with tomatoes) makes a tasty starter, especially when followed by the *pasta alla putanesca* (with garlic, capers, and anchovies). Imported beers and wines are great with dinner, and grappa or amaretto brings things to a fine finish. ⊠ *Av. San Isidro at 13 Calle,* ☎ *442–2812. MC, V.*

$$$$ ▦ **Barceló Palma Real.** The only all-inclusive resort on the mainland, the Barceló Palma Real is set on a pristine stretch of beach. The complex holds two hotels, the Barceló Palma Real Beach and the Barceló Palma Real Garden. You can enjoy the amenities at both of these high-spirited establishments. Although walking distance from each other, they are linked by a little train. You can head out for white-water rafting trips, boat rides to Roatán, and hiking at Parque Nacional Pico Bonito. ⊠ *Playa Roma, between La Ceiba and Trujillo,* ☎ *236–9003,* FAX *236–9800,* WEB *www.barcelo.com. 160 rooms. 2 restaurants, fans, in-room safes, pool, beach, tennis court, basketball, 4 bars, convention center, laundry services. AE, MC, V.*

$$$$ ▦ **The Lodge at Pico Bonito.** Set between two mountain-fed rivers, this
★ breathtaking resort brings you unrivaled luxury amid a verdant tropical forest. When you arrive you'll be greeted in the airy lobby with a frothy cocktail served in a coconut shell, then asked when you would like your massage. Your cabin, trimmed in rich mahogany, has a private balcony where a handmade hammock swings in the breeze. Only a few steps beyond the sparkling pool, the jungle overtakes the well-tended gardens. One of the English-speaking biologists will lead you on an early morning tour along the paths to lookout towers and cascading waterfalls. You probably won't spot the jaguars whose howls punctuate the night, but you might see the semi-domesticated ocelot that occasionally visits the lodge. ⊠ *La Ceiba,* ☎ *440–0389,* WEB *www.picobonito.com. 22 rooms. Restaurant, fans, pool, massage, hiking, bar, shop. AE, MC, V.*

$ ▦ **Gran Hotel Paris.** Facing Parque Central, this hotel is a favorite among business travelers. Rooms are airy, with cool ceramic floors. The pool is a true oasis after a dusty day exploring the coast. The poolside bar is a good spot for an evening drink. ⊠ *8a Calle,* ☎ *443–2391 or 443–1643,* FAX *443–1614,* WEB *www.granhotelparis.com. 63 rooms. Restaurant, in-room safes, pool, bar, car rental, travel services. AE, MC, V.*

Nightlife and the Arts

La Ceiba's nightlife is head and shoulders above the rest of the towns along the coast. The clubs are concentrated mostly in Barrio La Isla, east of the estuary. Don't walk alone here at night. **D'Lido** (⊠ Calle 1a) has an inviting beachfront terrace. The music begins at about 10 PM. **La Kosta** (⊠ Calle 1a) is usually packed on Friday and Saturday nights. It opens at 6 PM. **Black and White** (⊠ Av. 5 de Septiembre and Calle 3a) is open every night except Monday, but is especially popular on weekends. A band occasionally takes to the stage.

The disco **El Mussol** (⊠ Calle 1a) has a good sound system playing Latin music. The beachfront bar is a great place for a beer. Popular with a younger crowd, **Cherry's** (⊠ Calle 1a) is always crowded on Friday and Saturday nights. If you want to experience Garífuna culture, **Africa Dance** (⊠ Calle 1a) has dancers gyrating to *punta* music on weekends.

Outdoor Activities and Sports

BEACHES

The closest beach to La Ceiba, **Playa La Barra,** starts beyond Barrio La Isla and continues to the Río Cangrejal. A nicer beach, **Playa de Perú,** is about 10 km (6 mi) east of the city. It's extremely popular on weekends.

WHITE-WATER RAFTING

The Río Cangrejal is one of the top spots in Central America for white-water rafting, offering Class II, III, and IV rapids. Udo Wittemann, the Honduran version of Indiana Jones, can lead you on some lively adventures. He's the owner of **Omega Tours** (⊠ El Naranjo, south of La Ceiba, ☎ 440–0334), which offers rafting and kayaking trips, as well as horseback riding and jungle hiking. **Jungle River Rafting and Adventures** (⊠ Dutch Corner, Calle 1a, ☎ 440–1268) offers half- and full-day rafting trips on the Río Cangrejal, as well as hiking expeditions up Pico Bonito.

Trujillo

160 km (99 mi) east of La Ceiba.

Explorer Christopher Columbus first set foot on the American mainland here, and it's said that he thanked God for delivering him from the *honduras* (loosely translated, it means "deep waters"). That footprint paved the way for the establishment of Trujillo, the country's first capital. Others soon followed. British pirates staked out the Bahía de Trujillo and occasionally raided coastal towns to snag gold bound for Spain. The fine **Fortaleza de Santa Bárbara,** near the central square, will give you the flavor of those days of conflict.

Dining and Lodging

$–$$ ✕ **Café Oasis.** Platters of delicious Cuban food are served up at this pleasant little restaurant. Try the hearty *tajadas delgadas de plátano verde con carne y repollo* (fried green plantains with a meat stew). The portions are ample, so you won't walk away hungry. ⊠ *2a Calle, south of Parque Central,* ☎ *no phone. No credit cards.*

$–$$ ✕ **Restaurant Granada.** One of the oldest establishments in Trujillo, Restaurant Granada specializes in sizzling seafood dishes. There are also plenty of meat dishes made in the local style. ⊠ *2a Calle, south of Parque Central,* ☎ *434–4244. AE, MC, V. No lunch Sun.*

$–$$ ✕ **Rincón de Amigos.** Facing the Caribbean Sea, this open-air restaurant has made quite a splash with the ex-pat community. Sit under the thatched roof and enjoy the excellent pizzas and other Italian fare. There are palapas a few feet from the water if you want to eat right on the beach. ⊠ *Trujillo,* ☎ *no phone. No credit cards. Closed Wed.*

$$ ☎ **Christopher Columbus Beach Resort.** The only resort on the unspoiled beaches of Trujillo, this modern hotel gives you views of the sea or the mountains from your private balcony. Activities including swimming, windsurfing, and fishing from the small private pier. ✉ *Opposite the airport,* ☎ *434–4966,* FAX *434–4971. 69 rooms, 3 suites. Restaurant, fan, cable TV, basketball, volleyball, bar. AE, MC, V.*

$ ☎ **Villa Brinkley.** The nicest hotel in Trujillo looks out on the bay, so every room offers a stunning view from a private terrace. Rooms are trimmed with gorgeous woodwork, while the baths have sunken showers. An elegant patio with a fountain makes it difficult to leave. The restaurant is surprisingly affordable and serves up hearty soups and salads. ✉ *South of Trujillo,* ☎ *434–4444. 20 rooms. Restaurant, 2 pools, bar, Internet. AE, MC, V.*

Caribbean Coast A to Z

AIR TRAVEL TO AND FROM THE CARIBBEAN COAST

La Ceiba is an important transportation hub for travelers headed to mainland communities such as Tela and Trujillo or to the Bay Islands. Taca flies daily to Trujillo. Isleña, Sosa, and Rollins have daily flights to Tegucigalpa, San Pedro Sula, Roatán, and Utila. Isleña and Sosa fly to Guanaja. Atlantic flies to Tegucigalpa, San Pedro Sula, Roatán, Utila, and Guanaja, as well as to Belize City and Managua.

➤ AIRLINES AND CONTACTS: **Atlantic Airlines** (✉ Edificio Caribe, Av. La República, La Ceiba, ☎ 440–2343 or 440–1220, WEB www. atlanticairlines.com.ni). **Isleña** (✉ Av. San Isidro, La Ceiba, ☎ 443–0179 or 443–2344, WEB www.flyislena.com). **Rollins** (✉ 7 Calle, La Ceiba, ☎ 443–3206 or 441–2177). **Sosa** (✉ Av. San Isidro, La Ceiba, ☎ 440–0692 or 441–2512, WEB www.aerolineassosa.com). **Taca** (✉ Av. San Isidro, La Ceiba, ☎ 443–1912 or 441–2519, WEB www.grupotaca.com).

AIRPORTS AND TRANSFERS

Aeropuerto Internacional Golosón is 12 km (7 mi) from La Ceiba.

➤ AIRPORT INFORMATION: **Aeropuerto Internacional Golosón** (✉ Carretera La Ceiba–Tela, La Ceiba, ☎ 441–3025).

BUS TRAVEL WITHIN THE CARIBBEAN COAST

Buses run frequently along the country's northern coast. La Ceiba is unusual in that it has a central bus station, although the deluxe bus companies such as Viana and Hedman have their own terminals.

There are no direct buses from La Ceiba or San Pedro Sula to Tela, but the (supposedly) hourly service by Catisa-Tupsa between San Pedro Sula and La Ceiba stops at Tela, as do the Cotraibal and Cotuc buses that travel from San Pedro to La Ceiba and Trujillo. Expresos del Atlántico offers speedy direct buses between Puerto Cortés and San Pedro Sula, while Impala and Citul offer achingly slow service.

➤ BUS INFORMATION: **Catisa-Tupsa** (✉ Mercado San José, La Ceiba, ☎ 441–2539; ✉ 2 Av. between 5 and 6 Calle SO, San Pedro Sula, ☎ 552–1042 or 550–5199). **Citul** (✉ 4 Av. between 3 and 4 Calle, Puerto Cortés, ☎ 665–0466; ✉ 6 Av. SO, between 7 and 8 Calle, San Pedro Sula, ☎ 553–0070). **Cotraibal** (✉ Barrio El Centro, Trujillo, ☎ 434–4932; ✉ 1 Av. between 7 and 8 Calle, San Pedro Sula, ☎ 557–8470). **Cotuc** (✉ Calle 18 de Septiembre, Trujillo, ☎ 444–2181; ✉ Calle Principal, La Ceiba, ☎ 441–2199). **Expresos del Atlántico** (✉ Parque Central, Puerto Cortés, ☎ no phone; ✉ 6 Av. SO between 7 and 8 Calle, San Pedro Sula, ☎ no phone). **Hedman Alas** (✉ Supermercado Pueblo, highway to Trujillo, La Ceiba, ☎ 441–5347). **Impala** (✉ Barrio San Ramón, Puerto Cortés, ☎ 665–0606; ✉ 2 Av. between 4 and 5 Calle, San Pedro Sula, ☎ 553–3111). **Viana Clase Oro** (✉ Bul. 15 de Septiembre, La Ceiba, ☎ 441–2330).

CAR RENTAL

If you are looking to rent a car along the coast, head to La Ceiba. Most agencies have offices in town and at the airport.

➤ RENTAL AGENCIES: **Avis** (✉ Bul. 15 de Septiembre, La Ceiba, ☎ 441–2802). **Budget** (✉ Col. Miraflores, La Ceiba, ☎ 441–1105 or 441–3398). **Maya** (✉ Col. El Sauce, La Ceiba, ☎ 440–3014 or 443–3071). **Molinari** (✉ Parque Central, La Ceiba, ☎ 443–0055). **Toyota** (✉ Av. San Isidro, La Ceiba, ☎ 443–1975 or 443–1976).

EMERGENCIES

La Ceiba has some of the best hospitals in the country. Hospital Euro Honduras has a 24-hour emergency department staffed with English, German, and French speakers. There is no shortage of good clinics throughout the northern coast. Pharmacies are everywhere, so ask at your hotel which is the nearest.

➤ HOSPITALS: **Clínica Médica** (✉ 2 blocks south of Parque Central, Tela, ☎ 448–0297). **Hospital Euro Honduras** (✉ 1 Calle and Av. Atlántida, La Ceiba, ☎ 443–0244 or 440–0930). **Hospital Salvador Paredes** (✉ Calle Principal Trujillo, ☎ 434–4093). **Hospital Suizo Hondureño** (✉ Prolongación Blvd. 15 de Septiembre, La Ceiba, ☎ 441–2029 or 441–2518). **Hospital Vicente D'Antoni** (✉ Calle de D'Antoni, La Ceiba, ☎ 443–2264).

MAIL AND SHIPPING

All towns along the Caribbean Coast have a centrally located post office. For important packages, La Ceiba has several overnight services.

➤ OVERNIGHT SERVICES: **DHL** (✉ Av. San Isidro, La Ceiba, ☎ 443–2872). **Federal Express** (✉ Bul. 15 de Septiembre, La Ceiba, ☎ 443–1244). **UPS** (✉ Av. 14 de Julio, La Ceiba, ☎ 440–1024).

➤ POST OFFICES: **La Ceiba** (✉ Av. Morazán and Calle del Hospital Vicente D'Antoni, ☎ 442–0024). **Tela** (✉ 4 Av. NE, ☎ 448–2094).

MONEY MATTERS

Because of the number of tourists here, you can easily exchange currency at most communities along the Caribbean Coast. Banks or exchange houses usually offer slightly better rates than your hotel. Except La Ceiba, where transactions are fairly fast, you may not you might not want to bother with waiting in long lines.

➤ BANKS: **Banco Atlántida** (✉ La Ceiba, ☎ 441–4125; ✉ Tela, ☎ 448–2009; ✉ Trujillo, ☎ 434–4830, WEB www.bancatlan.hn). **Banco Ficohsa** (✉ La Ceiba, ☎ 443–4447, WEB www.ficohsa.hn). **Banco Sogerin** (✉ Av. San Isidro, La Ceiba, ☎ 443–4325). **Credomatic** (✉ Av. San Isidro, La Ceiba, ☎ 443–0668, WEB www.credomatic.com).

SAFETY

The coast is fairly laid back, so violent crime is rare. Petty theft, on the other hand, is common. Keep your wits about you, especially when being showered with attention by children. Backpacks are a common target, so don't forget about yours as you walk through crowds.

TAXIS

More than anywhere else in Honduras, taxis along the coast often stop to pick up additional passengers. This will not change your fare, but it might mean that you will not be dropped off first. Fares around La Ceiba are usually no more than 40 lempiras. In Tela fares hover between 10 lempiras and 20 lempiras, rising a bit when you cross the bridge. In Trujillo, some cabbies try to strike a hard bargain. Always check the going rate with locals and stand your ground.

TOUR OPERATORS

Though often expensive, tour operators can make otherwise impossible journeys feasible. In Tela, Garífuna Tours is one of the most-respected tour operators. Run by busy Italian Alessandro D'Agostino, the company has made a name for itself since its inception in 1994 for its trips with trained biologist and local guides. La Moskitia Ecoadventures is among the best regarded in La Ceiba. Birders should contact Gallardo Natural History Tours, run by respected American biologist Robert Gallardo, an expert on birds and butterflies. Also try Caribbean Travel and EuroHonduras Tours.

➤ TOUR COMPANIES: **Caribbean Travel** (✉ Edificio Hermanos Kawas, Av. San Isidro, La Ceiba, ☎ 443–1360). **EuroHonduras Tours** (✉ Edificio Sega, Av. San Isidro, La Ceiba, ☎ 433–3874 or 443–3875). **Gallardo Natural History Tours** (✉ Apdo. 1157, La Ceiba, ☎ 651–4133). **Garífuna Tours** (✉ Calle 9a, Tela, ☎ 448–1069, WEB www.garifuna.hn). **La Moskitia Ecoadventures** (✉ Av. 14 de Julio at Calle 1a, La Ceiba, ☎ 442–0104).

VISITOR INFORMATION

The best information on Honduras is *Honduras Tips,* a free magazine based in La Ceiba. You should find a copy in airports, restaurants, and hotels. Published twice a year, it is also available on-line. It includes a transportation guide featuring current bus and boat schedules.

➤ TOURIST INFORMATION: **Honduras Tips** (WEB www.hondurastips. honduras.com).

THE BAY ISLANDS

By Sandra Sampayo and Gillian Notton

Surrounded by one of the world's largest barrier reefs, the Bay Islands are a dream come true for snorkelers who can come face-to-face with shy sea turtles and divers who can glide along the bottom with graceful eagle rays. It's also irresistible for those who simply want to relax on a palm-fringed beach far from the crowds found in the rest of the Caribbean.

Located off the northern coast of Honduras, the Bay Islands are made up of three larger islands: Roatán, Utila, and Guanaja. There are also more than 60 islets and keys, many of them uninhabited. Truly a tropical paradise, these emerald specks in the azure sea have long attracted an eclectic mix of settlers who make up the spicy cultural soup that flavors life on the islands.

The islands were populated by the robust Pech people when explorer Christopher Columbus first set foot on easternmost island, Guanaja, during his fourth voyage to the region in 1502. He claimed the islands for Spain, and that country soon forced the indigenous people to move to Mexico to work in the gold and silver mines. All the while the Spanish had to fend off pirates like Henry Morgan, who used the islands as a base for raiding Spanish ships in the early 1600s.

The islands were largely uninhabited until the late 18th century, when the British quelled a rebellion by the Garífuna people living on the Caribbean island of St. Vincent. The survivors were moved to Roatán, the largest of the Bay Islands. The Garífuna didn't much care for the island and emigrated to the mainland town of Trujillo, leaving behind one surviving settlement in the community of Punta Gorda.

Residents of the Bay Islands today live much like they have for hundreds of years. They speak a very distinct style of Caribbean-accented English. For work, they fish; for fun, they eat, gossip, and dance (you'll

probably discover their inexplicable fondness for twangy country music).

Roatán

Only about 65 km (40 mi) from end to end, the ribbonlike Roatán is the most populous of the Bay Islands. Most villages are along the water's edge, with rows of modest homes looking directly out to the ocean. The west side of the island has seen much development in the past several years, while the east side is still largely untouched by tourism. A drive into the mountains will reward you with a panoramic view of the entire island.

Coxen Hole

Coxen Hole was named after John Coxen, a buccaneer who lived on Roatán at the end of the 17th century. The town itself, however, wasn't settled until more than a century later. The largest town on the island, it serves as the gateway to Roatán. Here you'll find the airport and the ferry terminal, as well as the island's only ATM. Although it would be a stretch to call this cluster of clapboard houses attractive, the town's rich heritage lends it a unique atmosphere.

DINING

\$\$ ✕ **¿Que Tal? Café** A good spot for a quick and simple meal, this friendly little café serves up salads, sandwiches, and other light fare. Located opposite the main road into Coxen Hole, it also offers Internet access. It's only open until 4 PM, however. ⊠ *Thicket Rd.,* ☎ 445–1007. *No credit cards. No dinner.*

\$-\$\$ ✕ **H. B. Warren.** The most centrally located supermarket on the island, H. B. Warren has a lunch counter where you can sample some delicious fried chicken. It's also a great place for breakfast. ⊠ *Main St.,* ☎ 445–1208. *No credit cards. Closed Sun.*

Sandy Bay
7 km (4 mi) west of Coxen Hole.

On the north coast of the island, Sandy Bay is a laid-back community strung along the sandy beach. It's also the cultural center of Roatán, home to the only museum in the Bay Islands. Here you can find some tantalizing clues to the island's past.

☺ One of the attractions at Anthony's Key Resort, the **Roatán Institute for Marine Sciences** is an educational center that researches bottlenose dolphins and other marine animals. Dolphins trained to leap through hoops and balance balls on their noses perform twice a day, once in the morning and once in the afternoon. For an additional fee you can participate in a "dolphin encounter," which allows you to interact with the dolphins. ⊠ *Anthony's Key Resort,* ☎ 445–1327, WEB *www.anthonyskey.com.* 🖃 *L64.* ☉ *Daily 8:30–5.*

Well worth a visit is the tiny **Roatán Museum,** named one of the best small museums in Central America. The facility, at Anthony's Key Resort, displays archaeological discoveries from Roatán and the rest of the Bay Islands. ⊠ *Anthony's Key Resort,* ☎ 445–1327, WEB *www.anthonyskey.com.* 🖃 *L64.* ☉ *Daily 8:30–5.*

With hundreds of beauties fluttering by, the **Roatán Butterfly Garden** is home to a species native to Honduras. More than a dozen colorful varieties are found here at any given time. Outside the butterfly house you will find a variety of tropical trees, including cashews, hogplums, and breadfruit. ⊠ *West side of Sandy Bay,* ☎ 445–1096, WEB *roatan-island.awwm.com.* 🖃 *L75.* ☉ *Sun.–Fri. 9-5.*

Meet some fine feathered friends at **Tropical Treasures Bird Park,** home to a variety of macaws, parrots, and other exotic birds. Here you'll find species that are native to Honduras as well as those from Central and South America. You can get a close-up look at beauties like the keel-billed toucan. ✉ *Sandy Bay* , ☎ *445–1314,* WEB *roatan-island.awwm.com.* 🎫 *L75.* ⏱ *Tues.–Sun. 10–5.*

DINING AND LODGING

$$$–$$$$ ✕ **Rick's American Café.** Located several stories above the ground, this longtime favorite is reached by a grueling ascent up a flight of steps. Your reward is a spectacular setting in a building that resembles a tree house. The surf and turf menu is pricey, but the collegial atmosphere makes a visit worthwhile. Dinner is served until 9:30 but the bar is open until 11:30. ✉ *Sandy Bay,* ☎ *445–0123. MC, V. Closed Wed.*

$$$ ✕ **Oceanside Inn.** Known throughout the island for its seafood, this place is home to all-you-can-eat lobster dinners that draw crowds every Wednesday between August and February. The dining room is small, lending it a cozy feel. At sunset grab a cocktail and head out to the deck overlooking Anthony's Key and Baileys Key. ✉ *Sandy Bay,* ☎ *445–1552. MC, V.*

$$$$ 🏨 **Anthony's Key Resort.** Nestled on a private key, the low-slung cabanas at this luxury resort put the Caribbean at your doorstep. Ocean breezes waft in through the slatted windows, keeping the simple rooms cool and comfortable. If you prefer, a few come with air-conditioning. Either way, you can enjoy blazing sunsets from your private terrace. Water-taxis ferry you to the rest of the resort. Renowned for its diving operation, Anthony's Key takes you out on six 42-ft boats. The resort also offers kids programs, beach picnics, horseback riding, and a wide range water sports. ✉ *Sandy Bay,* ☎ *445–1003,* FAX *445–1140,* WEB *www.anthonyskey.com. 56 rooms. Restaurant, pool, dive shop, dock, snorkeling, shop, bar. AE, MC, V.*

West End

5 km (3 mi) southwest of Sandy Bay.

One of the most popular destinations for budget travelers, West End offers idyllic beaches stretching as far as the eye can see. One of the loveliest spots is Half Moon Bay, a crescent of brilliant white sand. A huge number of dive shops offer incredibly low-priced courses.

DINING AND LODGING

$$–$$$ ✕ **Eagle Rays Bar & Grill.** Perched out on the pier, this two-story structure has some of the best views of the ocean. No wonder it's a very popular place for locals and travelers alike to watch the sunset. Stop by for a few drinks, or enjoy a seafood dinner before you go out clubbing. Don't forget to try the crispy calamari. ✉ *West End,* ☎ *445–1717. AE, MC, V.*

$$–$$$ ✕ **Tony's.** With a name like Tony's, you'd probably guess this is an Italian restaurant. What you might not know is that the portions here are so big that you'll probably walk away with a doggie bag. Especially tasty is the seafood pasta—the best on the island. Top off your meal with a excellent espresso or cappuccino. ✉ *West End,* ☎ *no phone. MC, V.*

$$ ✕ **Big Blue.** Beautiful menus made of leather, bark, and seashells are a clue that this place on the second floor above a dive shop is something special. The chef was trained in Thailand and imports all his spices, so this food is the real thing. The prawn crackers served with freshly made peanut sauce are enough for four people. Also excellent are the spring rolls with a choice of dipping sauces, the cashew stir-fry, and the lemony snapper. ✉ *West End,* ☎ *445–1531. AE, MC, V. Closed Sun.*

$ ✕ **Boulangerie.** Off the main road, this pleasant little place is run by Frenchmen who import the ingredients for their pain au chocolat. They are up all night baking, so you can pick up a loaf of bread by 6 AM or a bag of croissants by 9 AM. Stop by later in the day for great sandwiches. ⊠ *West End,* ☎ *no phone. No credit cards. Closed Sun.*

$$$$ ✕⊞ **Inn of Last Resort.** The owners of this lovely inn sought to keep the island's natural beauty intact, which is why they built one of the staircases around a huge tree. Nearly hidden in the foliage, the low-slung main building is steps away from a private lagoon where you can relax with a drink as you watch the sunset. The spacious rooms, with honey-color wood walls, have big windows that let in the breeze. The restaurant, cooled by lazily turning ceiling fans, serves international favorites. Should you want to go diving, a pair of 42-ft boats are moored nearby. ⊠ *West End,* ☎ *445–1902,* 𝖥𝖠𝖷 *445–1848,* 𝖶𝖤𝖡 *www. innoflastresort.com. 30 rooms. Restaurant, fans, beach, dive shop, snorkeling, bar, shop. AE, MC, V.*

$$$ ✕⊞ **Luna Beach.** If you ever daydreamed about your own beach house, this lodging may be for you. Here you can have a stunningly designed cabin perched high above the silvery sands of West End. All have two or three bedrooms, making them perfect for families. Louvered windows let tropical breezes blow through your sitting room. If you want to mingle with the other guests, stroll down to the pier jutting out into the ocean. The upscale bar and restaurant have a romantic atmosphere. Enjoy Mediterranean fare as you watch the sun dip below the horizon. ⊠ *West End,* ☎ *445–0009,* 𝖶𝖤𝖡 *www.lunabeachresort.com. 9 houses. Restaurant, fishing. AE, MC, V.*

$$ ✕⊞ **Half Moon Bay Cabins.** These bungalows are away from the rest of the accommodations of West End, giving them a secluded feeling. Overlooking its namesake, the lodging treats you to lovely views of the bay. There is snorkeling and diving off the private dock. The relaxed restaurant draws customers for breakfast, lunch, and dinner. The open-air dining room, surrounded by lush tropical foliage, is a great place to enjoy the breeze. The coconut shrimp is tasty, as is the lobster. ⊠ *North of Half Moon Bay,* ☎ *445–1075,* 𝖥𝖠𝖷 *445–1053,* 𝖶𝖤𝖡 *roatan-island.awwm.com. 14 rooms. Restaurant. AE, MC, V.*

$$ ✕⊞ **Pura Vida.** Popular with divers, this two-story hotel is steps away from the surf. It only takes a few minutes to reach any of 40 different dive sites. Rooms, all of which face the ocean, are clean and comfortable. Judging from the food you might think that the hotel's popular eatery was perched next to the Mediterranean. The family that runs it serves up delicious seafood that calls on their Italian heritage. The atmosphere is convivial—great for people-watching. ⊠ *West End,* ☎ *445–1141,* 𝖶𝖤𝖡 *www.puravidaresort.com. 12 rooms. Restaurant, cable TV, beach, dive shop, snorkeling. AE, MC, V.*

$ ⊞ **Chillies.** Run by a friendly British woman, this clean and comfortable lodging is the destination of most backpackers. In an idyllic setting on Half Moon Bay, it consists of a cluster of cabins with shared baths. If you want more privacy, there are a pair of larger cabins with private baths. ⊠ *Half Moon Bay,* ☎ *445–1214,* 𝖶𝖤𝖡 *www.roatanonline. com/chillies. 11 rooms. Dive shop. No credit cards.*

NIGHTLIFE

It's open every night, but **Fosters** (⊠ West End) is *the* place to go on Friday. In an old house built out over the ocean, it has bars on two levels. Right on the beach you'll find the laid-back **Loafers** (⊠ West End). You can shoot a game of pool on the terrace, join in a volleyball game in the sand, or simply listen to the music. On Wednesday the place goes Mexican, so you can enjoy a heaping plate of tortillas.

Competition among the dive shops is fierce in West End, so check out a few. When shopping around, ask about class size (eight is the maximum), the condition of the diving equipment, and the safety equipment on the dive boat. **Native Sons** (⊠ West End, ☎ 445–1335) is one of the most popular dive shops in town. It's run by a native of Roatán who really knows the area. In business for more than a decade, **West End Divers** (⊠ West End, ☎ 445–1531) has a pair of dive boats. The company is committed to protecting the fragile marine ecology.

The popular **Ocean Connections** (⊠ West End, ☎ 445–1925) is a well-established dive shop. Set over the water, **Sueno del Mar** (⊠ West End, ☎ 445–1717) is below a bar where you can trade stories with other divers.

West Bay

Down the beach from West End is West Bay, where you'll find some of the area's more luxurious resorts and the best beaches on the island. The reef comes quite close to the shore, so you don't even need a boat to see some of the island's most astounding sea life.

DINING AND LODGING

$$–$$$ ✕ **Bite on the Beach.** On a beautiful deck overlooking the beach, the restaurant serves up a wide selection of seafood, including conch, crab, and lobster. The menu changes often, but you'll almost always find favorites like Thai shrimp with peanut sauce. It's easily accessible by water taxi from West Bay. ⊠ West Bay, ☎ no phone. MC, V. Closed Mon.–Wed.

$$–$$$ ✕ **Chez Pascal.** Located at the Island Pearl Lodge, Chez Pascal is run by an animated Frenchman who delights in showing off his culinary skills. With an eclectic atmosphere, it is situated right on the beach. Open only for dinner, it has the only wine cellar on Roatán. ⊠ West Bay, ☎ 991–1858. Reservations essential. MC, V. No lunch.

$$$ ✕⌂ **Mayan Princess.** Set among gardens filled with scarlet hibiscus, these Spanish-style condominiums are along the shore at West Bay. The palm-sheltered beach is just outside your door. If you want to snorkel, the reef is a few yards offshore. The outdoor restaurant is a great spot to quench your thirst or dine on freshly caught seafood. ⊠ West Bay, ☎ 455–5917, FAX 455–5725, WEB www.mayanprincess-roatan.com. 24 rooms. Restaurant, kitchens, microwaves, refrigerators. AE, MC, V.

$$$ ⌂ **Las Rocas.** Between West End and West Bay, this resort has one- and two-story bungalows with private porches overlooking the ocean. Grab a book and relax in one of the hammocks swaying in the breeze. Run by a friendly duo, the dive shop is very popular. ⊠ West Bay, ☎ 445–1841, WEB www.lasrocasresort.com. 9 rooms. Fans, minibars, pool, dive shop. AE, MC, V.

French Harbour

11 km (7 mi) east of Coxen Hole.

The most bustling community on the island, French Harbour is home to one of the largest fishing fleets in the Western Caribbean. The best supermarket on the island, Eldon's, is located at the entrance to the town. It stocks everything you could need for a picnic on the beach or an overnight stay on one of the deserted islets.

DINING AND LODGING

$$$ ✕ **Gio's.** Famous for its king crabs, Gio's is something of an institution on Roatán. Served with lemon butter, the seafood comes in heaping portions. There's a slew of other satisfying seafood specialties, as well as great steaks. Sit in the air-conditioned dining room or on the

terrace overlooking the Caribbean. ✉ *French Harbour,* ☎ *455–5214. AE, MC, V. Closed Sun.*

$$$$ 🏨 **Fantasy Island.** The only resort on southern coast, this sprawling hotel offers accommodations similar to American hotels. At the efficiently run dive shop you can hop aboard any of the six large wooden boats that take you out to the reef. The restaurant is open for lunch and dinner. ✉ *French Harbour,* ☎ *455–5222,* 🆕 *455–5268,* 🌐 *www. fantasyislandresort.com. 87 rooms. Restaurant, minibars, cable TV, tennis court, beach, dive shop, snorkeling, bar. AE, MC, V.*

$$$–$$$$ 🏨 **Palmetto Bay Plantation.** West of French Harbour, Palmetto Bay is a cluster of beautifully designed two- and three-bedroom villas. Rooms feature vaulted ceilings, hardwoods floors, and tiled baths. Set in lovely landscaped gardens, this resort beckons with its glittering pool and private beach. The restaurant offers deliciously prepared seafood. On Saturday night you can grab a beer and dance to the live music. ✉ *Crawfish Rock,* ☎ *991–0811,* 🌐 *www.palmettobayplantation.com. 18 rooms. Restaurant, pool, bar, snorkeling. AE, MC, V.*

$$$ 🏨 **CoCo View.** This hugely popular dive resort is famous for having
★   more repeat business than anywhere else in the Caribbean. That's understandable, as the friendly staff ensures that everyone from newcomers to old pros have dives that are fun and challenging. A quintet of boats carries up to 30 people each to a variety of sites. A few dozen wooden cabins are set out over the ocean, so the sound of the waves will lull you to sleep. Accessible only by boat, the resort is about 5 km (3 mi) east of French Harbour. ✉ *French Harbour,* ☎ *588–4132,* 🆕 *588–4158,* 🌐 *www.cocoviewresort.com. 25 rooms. Restaurant, beach, dive shop, snorkeling, bar. AE, MC, V.*

Utila

The smallest of the Bay Islands, Utila has managed to evade full-scale development. It is small, especially compared to Roatán, and some visitors complain that there isn't much to do. On the other hand, more than a few travelers have planned to drop in for a weekend and ended up staying for a month or more. Locals, with their penchant for storytelling, make visitors feel right at home.

Known for its affordable diving classes, Utila is very popular with backpackers. This does not mean, however, that you'll be roughing it. The resorts here are small but inviting, like the island itself.

DINING AND LODGING

$$ ✕ **The Jade Seahorse.** Looking a bit like a museum, this longtime favorite is decorated with island paraphernalia. The best place to enjoy the big platters of seafood is in the pleasant garden. Stop by for one of the best fresh fruit shakes you'll find on the islands. ✉ *Cola de Mico Rd.,* ☎ *no phone. MC, V. No dinner Sat.*

$ ✕ **Thompson's Bakery.** Without question the most popular place for breakfast, this little establishment sells baked goods hot out of the oven. If you want more substantial fare, try one of the omelets and some fresh orange juice. ✉ *Cola de Mico Rd.,* ☎ *no phone. No credit cards.*

$$$ 🏨 **Laguna Beach Resort.** Perched on the edge of the Caribbean, this resort has bungalows with private decks overlooking the water. The accommodations have a rustic feel, but have amenities such as air-conditioning and private baths. Along with a dive center offering trips to more than 100 underwater wonders, the resort also lets you try your hand at kayaking and other water sports. ✉ *Southeast coast of Utila,* ☎ *425–3239,* 🌐 *www.utila.com. 14 rooms. Restaurant, pool, beach, dive shop, snorkeling, bar. AE, MC, V.*

$ ⊞ Mango Inn. Set amid breadfruit and banana trees, this wooden lodge has generously proportioned rooms with porches where you can relax in a hammock. The restaurant serves up light fare, including a tasty grilled chicken sandwich. There's a pretty garden where you'll find barbecues on the weekends. Homemade ice cream and sorbet are big draws, along with real espresso, cappuccino, and other coffee drinks. ⊠ *Cola Mico Rd.,* ☎ *425–3243,* FAX *425–3327,* WEB *mango-inn.com. 23 rooms. Restaurant, cable TV, beach, dive shop, snorkeling, shop. MC, V.*

NIGHTLIFE

You'll find **Bar in the Bush** (⊠ Past the Mango Inn) in the middle of a tropical forest. It's the noisiest spot on the island. The **Tropical Sunset Bar** (⊠ at the Seafree Resort) is a stone's throw from the airport. It is open until midnight during the week and until 3 AM on weekends. The bar offers the only draft beer on Utila.

OUTDOOR ACTIVITIES AND SPORTS

Warm water, great visibility, and thousands of colorful fish make Utila a popular destination. Add to this a good chance of seeing a whale shark and you'll realize why so many people head here each year. The **Bay Islands College of Diving** (⊠ Utila Lodge, ☎ 425–3143) is one of Utila's top facilities. Classes are small, meaning you'll get more one-on-one attention. If you're looking for a one-stop dive center, look no further than **Ron's World** (⊠ Cross Creek Hotel, ☎ 425–3134). The bar has great music, and the restaurant is open for breakfast, lunch, and dinner.

Guanaja

Guanaja, once populated by the Paya people, has rolling hills covered with evergreens. Explorer Christopher Columbus named it Pine Island when he came across it in his fourth and final voyage to the Americas in 1502. Guanaja Town, also known as Bonacca, is on a small cay off the mainland. Since boats must negotiate shallow canals, Bonacca has been called the "Venice of Honduras." Although the winding roads and bridges make Guanaja Town seem like a maze, the town is so small you can't get lost. There are no no cars here, making the island seem as removed from civilization as you can get.

DINING AND LODGING

$$ ✕ Pirate's Den. Locally caught seafood is the draw here, along with excellent chicken and beef dishes. Stop by on Friday for the weekly barbecue. ⊠ *Bonacca,* ☎ *453–4308. No credit cards.*

$ ✕ The Best Stop. A favorite among the locals, this little bakery has a selection of tasty breads, pastries, pies, and cakes every morning. If you want more substantial fare, it makes the best subs in town. ⊠ *Bonacca,* ☎ *453–4523. No credit cards.*

$$$$ ⊞ Posada del Sol. One of the most well-regarded resorts on the island, this Spanish-style inn is set in a beautifully manicured garden overlooking the sea. A dramatic mountain peak serves as the backdrop. You won't run out of things to do—besides diving and snorkeling, you can take a dip in the pool, play a few games of tennis, or pamper yourself in the full-service spa. The resort has one of the friendliest staffs on the Bay Islands. ⊠ *Guanaja,* ☎ *435–4505,* WEB *www.posadadelsol.com. 23 rooms. Restaurant, pool, spa, beach, dive shop, snorkeling, bar. MC, V.*

$$ ⊞ Bayman Bay Club. On the pristine northwestern shore of Guanaja, Bayman Bay Club is popular among divers and nondivers alike. Set on 100 acres of untouched forest, the resort consists of wooden cabanas perched on the hillside overlooking the private beach. Each has a terrace with great views of the ocean. The restaurant, featuring both island and international fare, is a popular place to enjoy the spectacular sunsets. ⊠ *Guanaja,* ☎ *995–5512,* WEB *www.baymanbayclub.com*

20 rooms. Restaurant, fans, beach, dive shop, snorkeling, bar, library, shop, laundry service. MC, V.

The Bay Islands A to Z

AIR TRAVEL TO AND FROM THE BAY ISLANDS

From North America, Taca flies nonstop from Houston and Miami to Roatán. Isleña offers daily flights from San Pedro Sula, Tegucigalpa, and La Cieba to Roatán. Isleña and Sosa also offer flights between La Cieba and Guanaja, while Sosa flies from La Cieba to Utila.

➤ AIRLINES AND CONTACTS: **Isleña** (☎ 445–1833 on Roatán; 445–4208 on Guanaja). **Sosa** (☎ 445–4359 on Guanaja; 445–3161 on Utila). **Taca** (☎ 445–1387 on Roatán).

AIRPORTS AND TRANSFERS

About 1½ km (1 mi) from Coxen Hole, Roatán International Airport is the destination for all international flights and most domestic flights headed to the Bay Islands. You can also fly into the smaller airports on Guanaja and Utila.

➤ AIRPORT INFORMATION: **Aeropuerto Internacional Roatán** (✉ Coxen Hole, ☎ 445–1874).

BUS TRAVEL WITHIN THE BAY ISLANDS

On Roatán, the minibuses run an hourly service from Coxen Hole east to Oak Ridge and west to West End. All trips cost 10 lempiras.

CAR RENTAL

Renting a car is a popular, if pricey, option on Roatán. The average cost is $35–$40 per day. Well-regarded local companies include Arrendadora de Vehiculos and Sandy Bay Rentals.

➤ LOCAL AGENCIES: **Arrendadora de Vehiculos** (✉ Opposite Roatán International Airport, ☎ 445–1568). **Sandy Bay Rentals** (✉ Sandy Bay, Roatán, ☎ 445–1710).

CAR TRAVEL

The only paved road on Roatán runs the length of the island as far East as Oak Ridge and as far west as West Bay. There are a number of unpaved, unmarked roads leading to various settlements on the southern and northern shores. These are graded from time to time but can be difficult to navigate, particularly if it has been raining.

EMERGENCIES

There is only one private hospital on the Bay Islands. Wood's Medical Centre, open 24 hours, can handle most emergencies. It can also organize transfers to hospitals on the mainland. There are two hyperbaric chambers on the island to treat divers with the bends, one at Fantasy Island and the other at Anthony's Key Resort. These facilities also have medics on call for emergencies.

➤ HOSPITAL: **Wood's Medical Centre** (✉ Coxen Hole, ☎ 445–1080).

MONEY MATTERS

There are a number of banks on Roatán, and most offer cash advance on Visa cards. All have branches in Coxen Hole and French Harbour. Banco Atlántida, in Coxen Hole, has the only ATM on the islands.

➤ BANKS: **Banco Atlántida** (✉ Coxen Hole, ☎ 445–1225). **Banco Futuro** (✉ Coxen Hole, ☎ 455–5643). **Credomatic** (✉ Coxen Hole, ☎ 445–1196).

TAXIS

Roatán is crawling with taxis. Collective taxis, where the driver picks up other passengers along the way, are far less expensive than private

ones. A collective taxi ride from Coxen Hole to French Harbour or to West End should not cost more than 50 lempiras.

TOUR OPERATORS

You can organize a tour of the islands through a travel company like Bay Island Tours, or hire a taxi driver to bring you around.

➤ Tour Company: **Bay Island Tours** (✉ Coxen Hole, ☎ 455–5586).

HONDURAS A TO Z

AIR TRAVEL TO AND FROM HONDURAS

American and Continental have flights to Tegucigalpa and San Pedro Sula from the United States, while Taca flies to both cities from many cities throughout Latin America. Taca also flies nonstop from Houston and Miami to Roatán. From elsewhere in Central America, Atlantic flies to Tegucigalpa from Belize City and Managua. Iberia flies from Madrid to San Pedro Sula.

➤ Airlines and Contacts: **American** (✉ Edificio Palmira, Av. República de Chile, Col. Palmira, ☎ 233–6919 or 232–1415, WEB www.aa.com). **Continental** (✉ Edificio Palic, Av. República de Chile, Col. Palmira, ☎ 220–0988 or 220–0989, WEB www.continental.com). **Iberia** (✉ 12 Calle at 2 Av., San Pedro Sula, ☎ 550–2530 or 668–3216, WEB www. iberia.com). **Taca** (✉ Edificio Interamericana, Blvd. Morazán, Col. Palmira, ☎ 239–0148 or 233–3566, WEB www.grupotaca.com).

AIRPORTS AND TRANSFERS

Most international flights to Honduras land in Tegucigalpa and San Pedro Sula, but visitors to the Caribbean Coast or the Bay Islands can opt to fly directly to La Ceiba and Roatán.

➤ Airport Information: **Aeropuerto Internacional Golosón** (✉ Carretera La Ceiba–Tela, La Ceiba, ☎ 441–3025). **Aeropuerto Internacional Ramón Villeda Morales** (✉ Carretera La Lima, San Pedro Sula, ☎ 668–3260 or 668–4864). **Aeropuerto Internacional Roatán** (✉ Coxen Hole, ☎ 445–1874). **Aeropuerto Internacional Toncontín** (✉ Bul. Comunidad Económica Europea, Tegucigalpa, ☎ 233–1115 or 233–7613).

BUSINESS HOURS

Normal office hours are 8:30 AM–5:30 PM. Government offices usually close for the day at 4:30 PM. Banks close earlier, but many are open on Saturday morning. Many shops close for lunch. In warmer regions, such as San Pedro Sula and all of the Caribbean Coast, businesses commonly open early, close at noon for an hour or two, then reopen in mid-afternoon when temperatures begin to drop.

BUS TRAVEL TO AND FROM HONDURAS

The only buses that run directly to Honduras from neighboring countries at the moment are run by King Quality. They travel from Tegucigalpa to San Salvador, Managua, and Guatemala City and from San Pedro Sula to San Salvador.

➤ Bus Information: **King Quality** (✉ Bul. Comunidad Económica Europea, Tegucigalpa, ☎ 225–5415; ✉ 6a Calle between 7a and 8a Av, San Pedro Sula, ☎ 553–3443).

BUS TRAVEL WITHIN HONDURAS

Wonderful *de lujo* (luxury) buses with air-conditioning and lots of leg room can whisk you between larger cities such as Tegucigalpa, San Pedro, and La Ceiba. Going anywhere else you need patience, as even *primera clase* (first-class) and *directo* (direct) buses stop to pick up passengers along the way. While *servicio a escala* (second-class) buses, the famous

"chicken buses" of Central America, will get you absolutely anywhere, frustrating delays are common.

CAR TRAVEL

A car is the best way to see Honduras, especially if you plan to visit more than one region. Highways linking the major cities are all paved, well marked, and fairly safe. Be careful, though, when you visit. Many roads become streams (or rapids) in the rainy season, especially on the northern coast. Visits to perennially moist national parks, such as Parque Nacional La Tigra or Parque Nacional Celaque, generally require a four-wheel-drive vehicle.

GASOLINE

Gas will run you about $2.50 per gallon. Make sure to fill up frequently in more remote areas, as gas stations are few and far between.

RULES OF THE ROAD

Upon entering the country you must purchase a driving permit if you rent a car.

HEALTH

The worst thing you're likely to encounter in Honduras is a mild case of traveler's diarrhea. If your symptoms don't subside after a few days you may have something more serious, in which case you should see a doctor. Cholera is only a problem in a few isolated areas, but it's wise to watch where and what you eat and drink. Tap water is risky, but bottled water is available everywhere. As for food, avoid raw fruits and vegetables and stay away from cooked dishes if they have been allowed to cool to room temperature.

Malaria is still a problem, particularly in La Mosquitia, although lots of spraying has kept the disease in check. Don't arrive without a strong repellent, preferably one with DEET. Dengue fever, another nasty disease spread by mosquitoes, is one more reason to coat yourself with repellent when you're on the north coast, on the islands, or in the jungles. When locals tell you there are no mosquitoes, there invariably are.

MAIL AND SHIPPING

Any *correo* (post office) can send letters abroad. A letter to the United States takes one to two weeks, while those to Europe and Australia take about a week longer. Postage costs about 70¢. Overnight services such as Federal Express and DHL are found in most larger cities.

MONEY MATTERS

Banks in the major cities will give you cash for major international traveler's checks. U.S. dollars are the most easily convertible currency in Honduras; almost every bank will exchange dollars even if they don't change traveler's checks.

ATMS

Banks in most larger cities have ATMs that accept foreign-issued cards, while those in smaller towns and villages often do not. Before traveling, make sure you have a four-digit secret code for your bank card, as many ATMs will not accept those with five or more digits.

CREDIT CARDS

Credit cards are widely accepted, especially Visa and MasterCard. Most establishments in heavily touristed areas welcome them, but those in more isolated regions may not. When in doubt, make sure to bring enough cash. Most branches of Bancahsa will give cash advances on Visa cards. Credomatic, with offices in Tegucigalpa, San Pedro Sula, and La Ceiba, gives cash advances for MasterCard or Visa.

CURRENCY

The currency is the lempira, abbreviated as L. The government prints 1, 2, 5, 10, 20, 50, 100, and 500 lempira bills. A lempira is made up of 100 centavos, and centavo coins come in denominations of one, two, five, 10, 20, and 50. The rate of exchange (which has been relatively stable in the last five years) used in this book is 16.4 lempiras to US$1.

PASSPORTS AND VISAS

To enter Honduras, everyone needs a passport. Citizens of the United States, United Kingdom, Canada, Australia, and New Zealand no longer need apply for a formal visa. Instead, you will be given a simple form to fill in on the plane or at the border, and receive a 30-day visa that can easily be renewed in almost any town. Extensions of 30 days are always granted as long as you have not exceeded 180 days in the country; in which case you must leave the country for three days before returning. People from other nations can obtain visas from Honduran embassies or consulates.

SAFETY

Pickpocketings and muggings are the most common types of crimes against tourists in Honduras. In larger cities you should do the same as you would in any metropolitan area—leave flashy jewelry and watches at home, keep your camera in a secure bag, and don't handle money in public.

TELEPHONES

There are only 6 million people in Honduras, so you don't need to bother with an area code. From abroad, dial the country code of 52 followed by the seven-digit number. Within Honduras you can drop the country code and simply dial the seven-digit number.

TIPPING

Tipping is not very common in most restaurants. In more elegant eateries you should leave at least 10%. Give porters and other people who handle your baggage the equivalent of $1 per item. It is unnecessary to tip taxi drivers.

VISITOR INFORMATION

The friendly Instituto Hondureño de Turismo in Tegucigalpa is worth a visit for information about the city. It's open weekdays 8:30 AM–4:30 PM. The organization's Web site is also helpful.

➤ TOURIST INFORMATION: **Instituto Hondureño de Turismo** (✉ Edificio Europa, Col. San Carlos, ☎ 222–2124, FAX 222–6621, WEB www.letsgohonduras.com).

6   NICARAGUA

Forget the headlines of the 1980s. Peace
and democracy reign these days in
Nicaragua. You'll find a welcoming people
with a newfound interest in showing off their
surprisingly diverse country, including
Nicaragua's two colonial cities, Granada
and León; the artisan markets of Masaya;
the vast freshwater Lago Nicaragua, with its
unusual looming twin-volcanoed Isla de
Ometepe; a chain of 25 fiercely beautiful
volcanoes, including the delightfully
accessible and cloud-forested Mombacho;
and miles of pristine beaches that you'll
usually have to yourself.

S I PEQUEÑA ES LA PATRIA, uno grande la sueña," read the words on Nicaragua's 100-córdoba bill. Poet laureate Rubén Darío knew his country well when he made that statement: "If your homeland is small, you imagine it large." This New York State–size nation of 5 million people has played a role in history completely out of proportion to its size. A turbulent history, greatly engineered by Cold War politics and natural disasters, grabbed late 20th-century headlines and enticed previous generations of travelers into coming to see what the place was all about. .

For better or for worse—and most people agree it's for the better— Nicaragua is being tamed, the lion tamer wielding a whip of democratic capitalism. The past is mostly the past here, much to everyone's relief, and a new generation of travelers is discovering a new Nicaragua. No longer an exasperating country to visit due to lack of tourism infrastructure, Nicaragua has developed a genuine interest in showing itself off to the world. The country has simplified entry requirements, streamlined banking procedures, opened new lodgings of all stripes, and taken a Madison Avenue approach to marketing itself. And a decade plus of peace and democracy hasn't hurt either.

Everyone comes away with a favorite part of Nicaragua. The country has two of Latin America's finest, though lesser known, colonial cities, León and Granada, historic rivals, but today good-natured competitors for your tourist dollar. About an hour from Managua, the Pacific Ocean works away at miles of desolate, unspoiled beaches. The enormous freshwater Lake Nicaragua and its islands, large and small, dominate the southern half of the country. The north-central region's pleasant climate and forested mountains around Matagalpa fuse to create the ideal hiking environment. On the Atlantic Coast you'll find Afro-Caribbean culture in full swing replete with reggae and Caribbean-accented English. No one lists Managua, arguably the world's most peculiar capital, as their favorite place in the country, but even this city, badly wounded some three decades ago, is experiencing a renaissance of its own.

Today you'll find an economically struggling but friendly country, where travelers are still rare enough to incite curiosity. Roads are therefore pleasantly uncrowded, or are crowded with bicycles, oxcarts, and horses rather than cars. Both foreign investors and exiled Nicaraguans of all political persuasions are buying or reclaiming property all over the country. The tourist industry, though lacking the organization of Costa Rica's finely tuned tourism machine—and that's exactly a strong selling point according to the country's growing number of fans—is getting off the ground. Nicaragua's fractured history and traditional lack of visitors have left it in a bit of a time warp. One Granada restaurant proprietor, herself a Spanish transplant, compares Nicaragua to the Spain she remembers 50 years ago: children play soccer in relatively automobile-free streets. People leave their doors open and sit out on the sidewalks enjoying evening breezes and neighborly conversations. With each passing year, however, more services of the modern world appear and visitor numbers are ever increasing. But for the moment, you'll experience an exhilarating feeling of standing on the edge, before the boom, of being in on a secret the rest of the world has not yet uncovered.

The future looks good for the country, but then history was rarely kind to Nicaragua. Columbus claimed this territory for the Spanish crown in 1502, paving the way for two major colonial settlements—Granada,

on the shore of Lake Nicaragua in the south, and León, in the north. Granada, which had access to the Atlantic via the Río San Juan, continued to prosper as a trading and commercial center, but León didn't fare as well.

The longtime rivalry between intellectual, liberal León and wealthy, conservative Granada set the stage for a century and a half of turbulence from which the country has still not quite recovered. León, anxious to thwart Granada's economic dominance, supported invasion by maniacal 19th-century U.S. invader William Walker and his ragtag mercenary army of *filibusteros* (filibusters). Walker made Nicaragua his unwilling candidate for a fiefdom state in Central America. The ensuing civil war and a revolving door of leaders culminated in a period of occupation by the United States Marines in the early 20th century. They encountered fierce resistance from nationalist leader Augusto César Sandino, one of the country's most revered historical figures, and his "crazy little army," as the U.S. press dubbed them.

The U.S. military departed in 1935, leaving in place one Anastasio Somoza, the first of the three Somozas who would rule the country for the next 44 years. The marines also left in place a trained *Guardia Nacional* (National Guard), the leader's personal army. The Somoza family appropriated for itself most of Nicaragua's prime property and commercial interests, while the country itself remained mired in poverty. Aid poured in following a 1972 earthquake that razed the center of Managua, but little of the assistance found its way beyond the Somoza family's pockets.

A popular revolution in 1979 toppled the Somoza dynasty and put in place the revolutionary government of Daniel Ortega and the *Frente Sandinista de Liberación Nacional* (Sandinista National Liberation Front), or FSLN. The U.S. government, fearful of the Sandinistas' growing rapprochement with the Soviet bloc, supported an insurgence of *contrarevolucionarios* (Contras), supporters of the former Somoza government, keeping the country in conflict for the next decade. The war, the shambled economy, and the ruined infrastructure prevented the Sandinistas from fully implementing their plans to improve the level of literacy, education, and medical care of the ordinary Nicaraguan. Exhausted by war and fed up with the nearly universally despised Sandinista military draft and curtailment of freedoms, Nicaragua voted in a conservative, business-backed coalition led by Violeta Chamorro in democratic elections in 1990. The Sandinistas remain today the major opposition party in the always lively world of Nicaraguan politics.

With a "pro-business" government now in power, the rich, many of whom fled to the United States during the rule of the Sandinistas, have gradually trickled back, along with their *dinero* after a socialist-free decade. Many have returned to reclaim businesses and property confiscated by the Sandinista government and handed over to state cooperatives and *campesinos* (rural folk). The conflict over this property is still one of the most divisive issues in Nicaraguan politics.

The government of current president Enrique Bolaños, only the third democratically elected leader in Nicaragua's history, faces a mountain of problems. Nicaragua has an annual economic growth of 4%, Central America's highest, but critics charge the apparent economic boom and the accompanying frenzy of construction, especially in Managua, is an artificial one. Official unemployment figures stand at 12%, but soar to four times that in some northern parts of the country. Currency devaluations and budget cuts have hit the poor the hardest. It is estimated that one half of Nicaraguans live below the poverty level.

Nicaragua remains today one of those glass-half-empty or glass-half-full places. Though conditions are improving all the time, it's not quite yet the smooth sailing for travelers that you'll find in neighboring Costa Rica. But that Nicaragua functions as well as it does, given its unusual history, is a tribute to the determination of its citizens. Nicaraguans welcome visitors with genuine interest and joy, seeing them as a sign of the country's reentry into the international community. And you'll meet fellow travelers who all smack their heads and say, "I'd have come here sooner, if I'd only known."

Pleasures and Pastimes

Arts and Markets

Great buys can be had all over Nicaragua, but the best shopping town is Masaya, Nicaragua's artisan and folklore center, between Managua and Granada. A lively, scruffy market competes with a more sterile but easier-to-navigate one. In both places, look for shoes, leather goods, hammocks, pottery, and paintings—the country is full of artists making lively, colorful paintings in the style first developed in the Solentiname archipelago in Lake Nicaragua, where Father Ernesto Cardenal (later Minister of Culture in the Sandinista government) founded a commune and trained farmers and laborers in various crafts.

Beaches

For a country with two long coastlines, Nicaragua has surprisingly few developed beaches. Those you can access will not disappoint however. The Pacific coast is ideal for windsurfing and sailing, and is developing a following in the surfing world. San Juan del Sur, just north of the Costa Rican border, sways to that casual expat beach-town beat. Close to Managua, Montelimar houses the country's only flashy seaside resort. Nearby Pochomil, as well as Poneloya (near León) are more local–oriented beaches. The Caribbean coast and Corn Islands have good diving, but lack decent equipment rentals—snorkeling is a better option here—and access is difficult from the country's western half. The country's "third coastline," enormous Lake Nicaragua, gives rise to inland beaches, too. The lake's Ometepe island contains several, Playa Santo Domingo being its most popular.

Coffee

Nicaragua may lack the worldwide prominence in coffee circles enjoyed by Guatemala and Costa Rica, and, yes, you'll often be given instant when you order a cup in a restaurant here. But the cool highlands near northern Matagalpa and El Crucero in the south produce fine arabica beans whose packages will fit nicely in your suitcase to take back home. The Selva Negra Mountain Resort, near Matagalpa, is a hotel on a sustainable coffee plantation. It's a chance to see the life and times of the beverage that poet Rubén Darío called "a black liquor . . . with as many problems and as many poems as a bottle of red wine."

Colonial Towns

Historic rivals, conservative southern Granada and liberal northern León, both founded in 1524, have kept their architectural heritages largely intact and are two of Latin America's lesser known, but well-preserved colonial cities. Granada has fared the better of the two, having suffered less damage than León during the revolution and the Contra war. Granada also simply possesses more available wealth for restoration, but León is making a valiant effort to catch up.

Dining

Nicaraguans favor rice and beans with meat, fish, or chicken; salads are usually made of cabbage with tomatoes and a vinaigrette-style dress-

Nicaragua

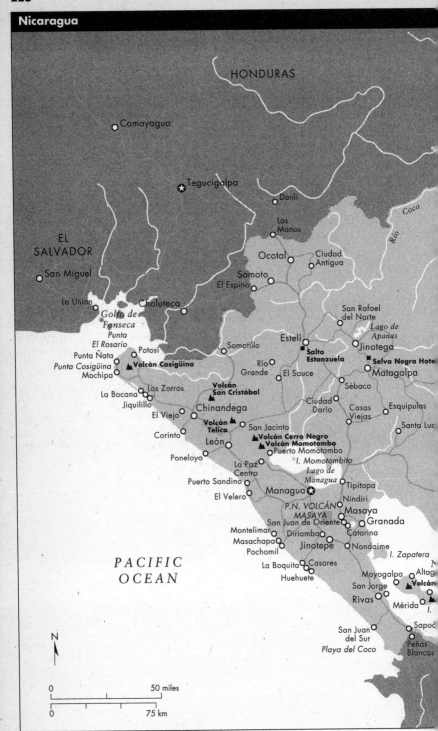

HONDURAS

Comayagua

Tegucigalpa

Danlí

Los
Manos

EL
SALVADOR

Ocotal

Ciudad
Antigua

San Miguel

Somoto

El Espino

San Rafael
del Norte

La Unión

Choluteca

Somotillo

Estelí

Lago de
Apanas

Golfo de
Fonseca
Punta
El Rosario

Potosí

Salto
Estanzuela

Jinotega

Punta Ñata
Punta Cosigüina
Mochipa

Volcán Cosigüina

Río
Grande

El Sauce

Selva Negra Hote

Matagalpa

Los Zorros

Volcán
San Cristóbal

Sébaco

Esquipulas

La Bocana
Jiquilillo

Chinandega

Ciudad
Darío

Casas
Viejas

Santa Luc

El Viejo

Volcán
Telica

San Jacinto

Corinto

León

Volcán Cerro Negro
Volcán Momotombo
Puerto Momotombo

Poneloya

La Paz
Centro

I. Momotombito
Lago de
Managua

Tipitapa

Puerto Sandino

El Velero

Managua

Nindirí

P.N. VOLCÁN
MASAYA

Masaya

Granada

Montelimar

San Juan de Oriente

Catarina

Masachapa
Pochomil

Diriamba

Jinotepe

Nandaime

I. Zapatera

La Boquita

Casares

Moyogalpa

Altag

Huehuete

Volcán

San Jorge

Rivas

Mérida

I.

PACIFIC
OCEAN

San Juan
del Sur
Playa del Coco

Sapoá

Peñas
Blancas

N

Coco

Río

N

0   50 miles

0   75 km

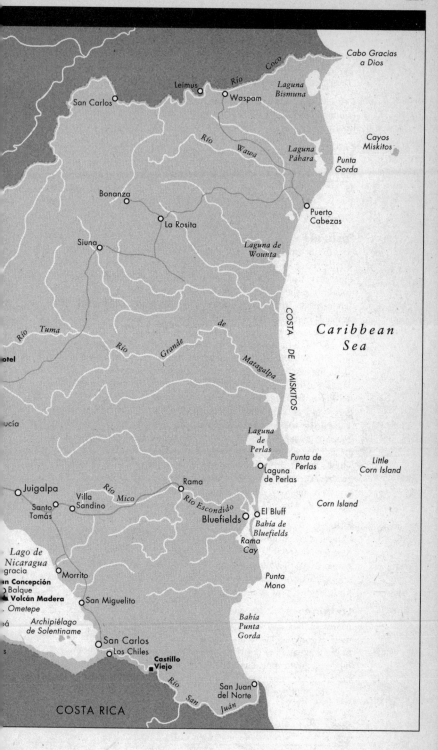

ing; and rice and beans usually reappear as the ubiquitous mix of the two, *gallo pinto* (literally, spotted rooster), at breakfast the next day. Two favorite dishes are *nacatamales,* corn tamales filled with chicken or pork, and *vigorón,* pork rind and cabbage served with steamed yuca. Near the coast, fresh fish is abundant and relatively cheap. It is usually served smothered in garlic (*al ajillo*) or tomato sauce (*entomatado*).

Flor de Caña, some of the best rum in the world, is produced near Chinandega: C$70 gets you a big bottle. Victoria, Toña, and Premium are the three locally brewed beers.

CATEGORY	COST*
$$$$	over C$205
$$$	C$140–C$205
$$	C$70–C$140
$	under C$70

*per person, for a main course at dinner

Festivals

Nicaragua operates at half speed during **Semana Santa,** the Holy Week preceding Easter in March or April, and closes down completely Thursday and Friday of that week. León is the place to be if you're not joining the rest of the crowds who flock to the beaches. The city decorates its streets with colored sawdust designs depicting religious scenes. These are then trampled under the foot of elaborate Good Friday processions. July 19 is **Revolution Day** in Nicaragua, celebrating the 1979 fall of the Somoza dictatorship. The Sandinistas put on rallies in most communities; Managua, León, and Matagalpa host three of the largest. Supporters deck out in red-and-black Sandinista bandanas—though these days you'll see some designer jeans and Winnie-the-Pooh T-shirts among the crowd as well—listen to speeches by party leaders, sing revolutionary songs, and throw back a few beers. The **Purísima,** or Feast of the Immaculate Conception, is celebrated in Nicaragua on December 8. The big celebration is the night before, when crowds parade through the streets, most notably in León and Granada. They stop at homes, enacting the age-old tradition known as the *gritería,* shouting, "*¿Quién causa tanta alegría?* (Who causes so much joy?) The response from those who come out of their homes? *¡La concepción de María!* (The Immaculate Conception of Mary!).

Hiking

Hiking is Nicaragua's best outdoor activity. Some good spots include Masaya National Park, Isla de Ometepe, and the countryside near Matagalpa. All of the volcanoes, and their crater lakes, make for good hikes and swims, too. Check on volcanic activity before setting off: lava is no fun when you're running from it.

Lodging

Managua has accommodations in all price ranges; Granada's assortment is somewhat smaller. The choice of hostelry is limited in the rest of Nicaragua, where extremely basic *hospedajes* are most common. The biggest growth spurt has come in smaller, medium-range, family-owned hotels, where spending C$700–C$1,200 buys you a night in some downright charming places.

CATEGORY	COST*
$$$$	over C$2,100
$$$	C$1,400–C$2,100
$$	C$700–C$1,400
$	under C$700

*for a double room, excluding service and 15% tax

National Parks and Volcanoes

Some 18% of Nicaragua's territory is set aside in 76 protected areas with designations such as "national park" or "wildlife reserve," but few have any facilities for visitors. The most visited is Volcán Masaya National Park, established in 1979, which encompasses roughly 20 square km (12 square mi), including the volcano's multiple craters and Lake Masaya. Several other areas have unofficial park or reserve status, which will probably be "upgraded" to national-park status at some point; these include the volcanoes on Ometepe Island—Madera and Concepción—and Volcán Mombacho, not far from Granada. An official wildlife refuge, Chococente has been established to protect a turtle nesting site on the Pacific coast north of San Juan del Sur.

Politics

Few people here would turn the clock back to the 1980s, but most love a lively political debate about the direction the country should take. If your Spanish is up to the task, don't be afraid to listen in, but it's best done outside the confines of the local cantina. Do let your acquaintances take the lead in the discussion. And U.S. citizens need not worry: despite past stormy Nicaraguan–American relations, few people here harbor any animosity against the United States.

Exploring Nicaragua

Most of the country's population inhabits the largely deforested western Pacific lowlands. Highways and public transportation are excellent in the corridor that extends from León in the north to Rivas in the south near the Costa Rican border. Matagalpa anchors north-central Nicaragua's highlands, a cool respite from the year-round sweltering lowland heat. The sparsely populated eastern half of the country is largely impenetrable rain forest. Travel here is by boat or, for those with more money than time, small plane.

Great Itineraries

Here on business? Your itinerary will likely confine you to **Managua.** Otherwise most travelers take a quick glance at the capital, then head immediately to the colonial cities of **Granada** and **León,** with a shopping stop in **Masaya.** If forced to choose between the two, more travelers opt for Granada, it being centered in a region with access to more sights than is León. A few extra days gives you time to explore the Pacific coast beaches, the island of **Ometepe** in Lake Nicaragua, or the cool northern highlands near **Matagalpa.**

IF YOU HAVE 3 DAYS

Three days gives you time for the classic Nicaragua sightseeing tour, one confined to the capital and the south's prime points of interest. After a morning arrival in **Managua,** spend the afternoon visiting the city's sights. Get an early start the next morning and travel by car or express minivan toward Masaya. En route, stop to visit the smoldering volcano crater at **Volcán Masaya National Park,** about 30 minutes southeast of Managua. It's admittedly easier to make that stop if you're in your own vehicle. Then continue the short distance to **Masaya** itself and spend a half day shopping at its two markets. If time permits, make a midday stop for lunch at the *mirador* (lookout point) at **Catarina;** it's well worth the detour from the Masaya–Granada highway. Arrive in **Granada** that evening. Spend the next day exploring the colonial city's churches and attractions and take in a boat cruise of **Las Isletas,** a groups of tiny islands in Lake Nicaragua. Return to Managua the following day, about a 45-minute trip back from Granada.

An extra two days gives you time to see the sights of northern Nicaragua after following the three-day itinerary, above. From **Managua,** at the beginning or end of that trip, head northwest by car or express minivan and take in the colonial sights and churches and museums of **León,** about 75 minutes from the capital. Spend the night here, then get an early morning start the next day for Matagalpa. One-half hour north of the city is the famed **Selva Negra Mountain Resort,** worth a visit, or even better, worth staying the night. Return to Managua the next day, about a two-hour drive from Matagalpa.

Use the extra two days or more to delve into the sights and attractions of southern Nicaragua. Get an early morning start from Granada by car, bus, or taxi and head to **Rivas,** about an hour away. Catch a ferry from nearby San Jorge to **Ometepe,** an hour by boat from the mainland. Tour the island and laze on balmy Playa Santo Domingo. Spend a night and get an early start on an all-day hike to one of the island's two volcanic craters. Catch a late ferry, or an early one the next day back to San Jorge. Alternatively from Rivas, grab a bus or taxi and head for **San Juan del Sur,** about a half hour away. Spend a day exploring the beaches in this area before heading back to Rivas and points north or south toward Costa Rica.

MANAGUA

You likely know the story by now. On December 23, 1972, an earthquake measuring 7.2 on the Richter scale leveled downtown Managua, killing 5,000 and leaving thousands more homeless. (An equally devastating earthquake had rocked the city 40 years before.) Anastasio Somoza and his cohorts couldn't resist pocketing the aid that poured in from around the world. Then came revolution, war, and economic hardship. Turn the clock ahead to 1990 and the election of a conservative city government headed by one Arnoldo Alemán, later to become president. Anxious to divert attention from the old city center and its Sandinista-era associations, Alemán touted the affluent southern part of the city as *La Nueva Managua* (the new Managua). A construction boom of shopping malls, restaurants, hotels, and car dealerships on the city's fringes resulted. The old center remained a surreal expanse of vacant lots and crumbling buildings for almost a quarter century.

Why begin with mention of an earthquake? It, more than any other event, has shaped the appearance of Nicaragua's capital. But anyone who knew Managua during those grim post-earthquake years would scarcely recognize the place today. The old city center is booming again. Shopping malls, monuments, and government buildings have risen from ashes. The overall effect—expanses of land interspersed with monumental buildings—is much like that of Washington, D.C. The hustling, bustling pre-1972 downtown is no more, and will never be again, but people are returning to a part of the city that, until recently, looked like a barren moonscape.

Never intended to be the country's capital, Managua was an 1852 compromise choice between competing political factions, roughly halfway between liberal León and conservative Granada. Present-day Managua sits on the site of an ancient *indígena* (indigenous) fishing village whose inhabitants refused to submit peacefully to Spanish rule. In response, the Spanish destroyed the village.

For better or for worse, this is big-city life, Nicaraguan style. With no nucleus to hold it together, the capital sprawls, seemingly forever,

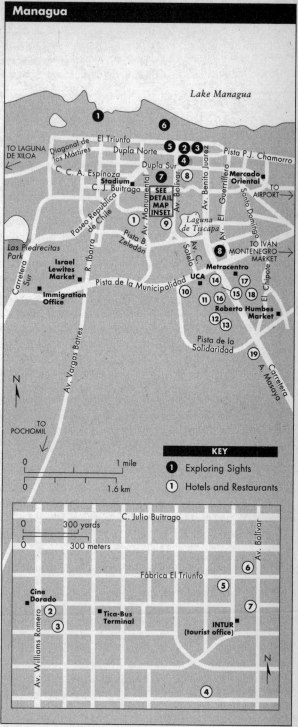

Managua

Exploring

Catedral de la
Inmaculada
Concepción **8**

Catedral de
Santo Domingo **3**

Monumento
al Soldado **7**

Museo Sitio Huellas de
Acahualinca **1**

Palacio Nacional
de la Cultura **4**

Plaza de la
República **2**

Teatro Nacional
Rubén Darío **6**

Tumba de
Carlos Fonseca **5**

Dining

Los Antojitos **7**

Café Mirna **3**

Casa del Café **17**

Cocina de
Doña Haydée **16**

Il Grottino **15**

La Marseillaise **12**

María Bonita **18**

Ristorante
Mágica Roma **6**

San Juan de
la Selva **19**

Lodging

Brandt's Bed
& Breakfast **11**

Casa San Juan **10**

Estancia La Casona . . . **1**

Hotel El
Conquistador **5**

Hotel Inter-Continental
Managua **8**

Hotel Los Felipe **2**

Hotel Los Robles **13**

Hotel Mansión
Teodolinda **4**

Hotel Princess
Managua **14**

Maracas Inn **9**

across vast expanses of open land. And, at some point, every visitor here curses the sheer enormity of the place. Far from the city center, in each of the city's 600 barrios, life of some 1 million Managuans pulses with a dizzying intensity. A couple of days here is plenty, but for those pressed for time, Managua makes a convenient base from which to explore most anything in the León-Granada corridor.

Exploring Managua

Numbers in white bullets in the text correspond to numbers in black bullets in the margins and on the Managua map.

The sprawling capital has few real sights, and the huge open spaces left by the 1972 earthquake make Managua an awful city for walking. That said, most of the must-see sights cluster within easy walking distance of each other around the Plaza de la República in the destroyed city center south of Lake Managua. Immediately south of the center is Barrio Martha Quezada, home to a slew of mostly basic budget lodgings, then Barrio Bolonia and its more fashionable ambience. The famous pyramid-shape Hotel Intercontinental is also nearby, as is a hilltop 54-ft black silhouette of revolutionary leader Sandino, visible from most everywhere in the city. Most of Managua's development rings the old center. Banks and airline offices congregate around Plaza España, south of Martha Quezada. You'll find upscale lodgings and restaurants in the capital's far southern sector, an area anchored by the huge Metrocentro shopping mall.

Managuans give addresses in reference to *cuadras* (blocks) from a landmark: *al sur* (south), *al lago* (toward the lake, or north), *arriba* (up or east, where the sun rises), and *abajo* (down, or west toward the sunset). Beware: the earthquake destroyed a few of those landmarks, but that doesn't stop locals from still referring to them. Addresses on the three main routes heading out of town (Carretera a Masaya, Norte, and Sur) are given by their kilometer distance from the center of Managua. Otherwise street names are scarce, and most directions are based on distances from landmarks.

A Good Walk

Unless you're an archaeology buff and would appreciate a visit to the tiny, out-of-the-way **Museo Sitio Huellas de Acahualinca** ①, begin your walk at **Plaza de la República** ②, the historic heart of pre-1972 Managua. The ruins of the **Catedral de Santo Domingo** ③ front the square's east side. Tour the art and cultural exhibits of the **Palacio Nacional de la Cultura** ④, on the plaza's south. Continue to the square's west side to pay homage to the founder of the Sandinistas at the **Tumba de Carlos Fonseca** ⑤. Head one block north of the square's northwest corner to the **Teatro Nacional Rubén Darío** ⑥. One block south of the plaza's southwest corner takes you to the **Monumento al Soldado** ⑦, a vestige of the Sandinista years. Wrap it up here and take note of the enormous **Catedral de la Inmaculada Concepción** ⑧, when you're near the Metrocentro shopping mall.

TIMING

You can accomplish this waterfront walk in under an hour if you wish only to skim the sights; add another hour for a tour of the Palacio Nacional de la Cultura. (It's closed on Saturday.) Though short, it's a daunting feat in the midday sun. Aim for early morning or late afternoon. Just north of the Teatro Nacional Rubén Darío toward the lake lies a collection of small stands proffering basic food and drink as well as souvenirs. It's a convenient place for a break and a bite to eat.

Sights to See

❽ Catedral de la Inmaculada Concepción. Domino's Pizza magnate Tom Monaghan funded much of the construction in 1993 of this present seat of the Archdiocese of Managua. (Ironically though, a Pizza Hut looms across the highway.) Likened by some to a mosque, others to a nuclear reactor, this mammoth concrete structure could undoubtedly survive an earthquake of the type that devastated its predecessor, the Cathedral of Santo Domingo in the old city center. The hushed devotion of the small *Sangre de Cristo* (Blood of Christ) chapel on the west side of the building contrasts markedly with the cavernous enormity of the main sanctuary. The walk across the huge field to reach the cathedral can be overwhelming in the hot sun, but once you arrive, breezes cool the building's interior. ⊠ *Rotonda Rubén Darío, across from Metrocentro shopping mall.* ⊙ *Daily 8–6.*

❸ Catedral de Santo Domingo. On the plaza's east side stand the poignant ruins of Managua's former cathedral, first badly damaged in a 1931 earth tremor, then destroyed by the 1972 earthquake. The 1929 structure is hauntingly beautiful, with murals and statues still clinging to the walls. The city rescued the ruins in 1995, enclosing them under a glass roof and placing an iron gate at the entrance. The ruins were closed to the public at press time for much needed restoration. No target date has been set for reopening. ⊠ *Plaza de la República, Barrio Santo Domingo.*

❼ Monumento al Soldado. One of Managua's few remaining Sandinista-era monuments inspires pride in some, but embarrassment in others. The fierce-looking socialist-realist statue with no official name or recognition portrays a shirtless soldier with a Kalashnikov rifle in his raised arm, a pickax in the other. The base plaque translates, "Only workers and campesinos will march to the end." An early 1990s bomb blast damaged the work's right leg. ⊠ *Av. Bolívar, Barrio Santo Domingo.*

❶ Museo Sitio Huellas de Acahualinca. Managua's only archaeological site is a small museum housing ancient footprints that are, by most claims, about 10,000 years old. Originally thought to be evidence of an indigenous people fleeing an eruption of nearby Volcán Masaya, these days most believe they were left by people walking at a normal pace. A small exhibit exhausts the known history of these prints and their discovery. The museum is worth a trip only if you're a real archaeological buff. ⊠ *Barrio Acahualinca, about 1 km (½ mi) west of Plaza de la República, on the waterfront,* ☎ *505/266–5774.* ▨ *Free.* ⊙ *Weekdays 8–5.*

❹ Palacio Nacional de la Cultura. Built in 1931, the neoclassic building was the former meeting place of the National Assembly. The calm of the palace's high-ceilinged chambers was disrupted on August 22, 1978, when FSLN commandos, dressed as National Guard soldiers, stormed in and sealed off the building, holding the legislative body hostage for 45 hours, an event regarded as the beginning of the end for the Somoza dictatorship. Renovated in 1994, its orange facade shines once more with quiet elegance. The palace, which rings a beautiful, palm-filled courtyard, houses the **Museo Nacional,** with a small collection of pre-Columbian art and exhibits on natural history, including a display on earthquakes and volcanoes. The museum also houses temporary art exhibitions. ⊠ *Plaza de la República,* ☎ *505/222–2905.* ▨ *C$10.* ⊙ *Sun.–Fri. 8–5.*

❷ Plaza de la República. Ask people what they call this plaza in the heart of the city; their answer belies their politics. Most refer to it by its present

name, Plaza de la República, but to dyed-in-the-wool leftists it will always be Plaza de la Revolución. This plaza and the points nearby have witnessed some of the most memorable events in Nicaraguan history. On July 19, 1979, two days after Somoza fled the country, the plaza was the site of the Sandinista victory celebration. The ocher **presidential palace,** built with aid from the government of Taiwan, fronts the plaza's north side. It's not open to the public. The city constructed a massive fountain in the center of the plaza in 2000. On weekend evenings at 7 and 9, the fountain dances and glows with colored lights as recorded Nicaraguan folk music plays. It's all quite festive, and a reassuring sign that people are coming back to the center city again. ⊠ *Pista P. J. Chamorro (Carretera Norte), at the waterfront, Barrio Santo Domingo.*

❻ Teatro Nacional Rubén Darío. On the north side of the plaza, next to the lake, sits the whitewashed modern theater named for Rubén Darío, Nicaragua's best-known poet. The government-operated institution hosts embassy parties, plays, concerts, and dance performances. In front of the building is a monument and fountain dedicated to Darío, refurbished with funding from Texaco. ⊠ *Plaza de la República, Barrio Santo Domingo,* ☎ *505/222–3630.*

❺ Tumba de Carlos Fonseca. The mango tree–shaded west side of the plaza is the sight of Carlos Fonseca's tomb, one of the founders of the FSLN and its most hallowed leader. Fonseca was killed in 1976 by Somoza's National Guard troops. Blue-and-white Nicaraguan and red-and-black Sandinista banners flutter in a semicircle around the white-stone tomb. An eternal flame tops the structure. ⊠ *Plaza de la República, Barrio Santo Domingo.*

Dining

The quality of the food found in Managua has vastly improved in recent years with an influx of non-Nicaraguan offerings to choose from. Italian cuisine has led the way. Beware of restaurants serving what they call "international" cuisine, which is more often than not an unsuccessful attempt to mimic European and American fare. Hotel restaurants are the worst culprits in this regard.

Prices and Tipping
Expect to pay from C$100–$200 for an entrée at an expensive restaurant. The more basic places will charge C$25–C$50. Lunch specials always give you a better value for your money than the evening meal.

Tipping is expected in upscale restaurants, but the service charge will always be included in the bill. An extra córdoba or two is always a nice gesture. Most servers are minimally compensated.

Reservations and Dress
Reservations are accepted at many nicer restaurants, but are rarely necessary. Peak lunch hours are from 1 to 2. Most people eat dinner between 7 and 9. Sunday is usually the only day without an afternoon closing between lunch and dinner.

Dining in Managua is casual. Jackets and ties are rarely required, even at fancier restaurants. You can get by with shorts during lunch at casual places. Long pants are more appropriate for dinner.

$$$–$$$$ ✕ **La Marseillaise.** René Hauser has tendered elegant air-conditioned
★ French dining out of this rambling old Los Robles house with an art gallery since the days of revolution and right through the Sandinista years. Try the fileta Madagascar (a fillet of beef with green peppers and cognac) or the lobster thermidor, two house specialties. The restaurant

also has a full selection of French, Spanish, Italian, and Chilean wines. ⊠ *4 blocks north of Enitel Villa Fontana, Los Robles,* ☎ *505/277–0224. AE, MC, V. Closed Sun.*

$$$–$$$$ ✕ **San Juan de la Selva.** Renaissance man Vittorio Tassinari (chef, artist, and architect) and his wife, Marí Elizabeth, designed the interior of this place to echo the tropical rain forest. Vines and plants hang from every nook, and the sound of water flowing inside an enormous tank greets you at the door. Seafood is the specialty, prepared with French and Latin influences. The freshwater prawns and fruit-based sauces are something to write home about. ⊠ *Km 5½ Carretera a Masaya, Planes de Altamira,* ☎ *505/277–3055. AE, MC, V. Closed Sun.*

$$–$$$ ✕ **Los Antojitos.** This classy, well-established family restaurant is a wonderful place to sample Nicaraguan haute cuisine. You can eat in the immaculate, air-conditioned dining room or out on a huge terrace overlooking the old city center. Beef is the house specialty, so start with the consommé and move on to the beef fillet *antojitos* (appetizers) for the main course. Without knowing it, you may see some of Nicaragua's political or art celebs sitting next to you. ⊠ *Av. Bolívar, Barrio Bolonia,* ☎ *505/222–4866. AE, MC, V.*

$$–$$$ ✕ **Cocina de Doña Haydée.** Irene and Alicia Espinosa, daughters of the
★ original Doña Haydée, bring 30 years' worth of old family recipes to the porch of an elegant house decorated with Nica artisan work. Their cooking is the perfect introduction to upscale Nica cuisine. Try the *plato surtido,* a sampler platter with a little bit of everything if you can't choose. You'll be serenaded most evenings with local folk music. ⊠ *1 block west of Optica Matamoros, Planes de Altamira,* ☎ *505/270–6100. AE, MC, V.*

$$–$$$ ✕ **Il Grottino.** The place is small—there are just a few tables here—but the service is impeccable, the ambience is elegantly casual, and the pizza can't be beat. Start with the standard list of pizzas on the menu—the napoletano is the most requested—but mix and match any toppings your hear desires. These folks really aim to please. ⊠ *Km 4 Carretera a Masaya, Los Robles,* ☎ *505/277–1790. AE, MC, V.*

$$–$$$ ✕ **María Bonita.** Managua's best Mexican restaurant begins the day early with a breakfast buffet and doesn't stop serving dinner until well into the evening. Try the *carnitas al estilo Michoacán,* lean slices of pork served over plantain leaves. Vegetarians can rejoice: there are many non-meat menu items, a real rarity in Nicaragua. Live music—mariachis and romantic ballad singers—entertain you most evenings on the partially open-air terrace. ⊠ *1½ blocks west of Vicky, across from the San Agustín church, Altamira,* ☎ *505/270–4326. AE, MC, V.*

$$–$$$ ✕ **Ristorante Mágica Roma.** Managua has experienced an invasion of upscale Italian restaurants in recent years, and this place has led the charge. Although it's relatively pricey, dress is fairly casual. The food is tasty: try the amazing version of penne alla vodka (with a bacon, mushroom, and vodka sauce) or one of the many pizzas. There's also a great selection of wine for C$40 a glass and authentic espresso. ⊠ *½ block west of south side of the Hotel Inter-Continental, Barrio Bolonia,* ☎ *505/222–7560. AE, MC, V.*

$–$$ ✕ **Casa del Café.** Perhaps it's because they're also producers of their own El Crucero brand of coffee that makes Casa del Café one the country's few places where you can actually buy good Nicaraguan coffee (C$60 per pound). The vine-covered patio is an excellent spot to sip cappuccino, indulge in some yummy cake or pie, and just hang out. The cornucopia of English and Spanish reading material and knickknacks can justify your lengthy stay. ⊠ *1 block east and 1½ blocks north of Lacmiel, Altamira,* ☎ *505/278–0605. AE, MC, V.*

$ ✕ **Café Mirna.** Sandinistas, Contras, and everyone in between has caught their early morning sustenance through the years at this hole-

in-the-wall restaurant, Managua's longtime breakfast hangout. Mirna and family serve a filling breakfast of pancakes or eggs, beans, and rice. For lunch they'll doll up *comida corriente* (literally "everyday meal") with beef or chicken, rice, beans, and salad. ⊠ *1 block south and 1 block east of Cine Dorado, Barrio Martha Quezada,* ☎ *505/222–7913. No credit cards. No dinner.*

Lodging

There was a time when lodging in Managua meant forking over C$2,000 to stay at the upscale Hotel Inter-Continental or gritting your teeth and bearing one of the decidedly down-at-the-heels hospedajes. No more. Many, though not all, of the budget lodgings have cleaned up their acts and are actually pleasant places to spend the night. Most are clustered in or near Barrio Martha Quezada, just west of the Inter-Continental. With Managua's building boom, the luxury hotels have certainly increased in number, but Managua's biggest surprise is the growth in second-tier hostelries, where spending C$700–C$1,000 gets you clean, decent accommodation in some charming, family-run places.

$$$–$$$$ 🏨 **Hotel Inter-Continental Managua.** Managua's most famous hotel is the centrally located pseudo-Maya pyramid, a city landmark and the haunt of expense-account journalists who covered Nicaragua's turbulent history. The hotel underwent a complete and much-needed remodeling in the late 1990s. The result is a cadre of gleaming, ample-size rooms and a facility with all the amenities a business or leisure traveler expects. ⊠ *Av. Bolívar, Barrio Bolonia,* ☎ *505/222–4151,* ℻ *505/228–3530,* 🌐 *www.interconti.com. 160 rooms, 24 suites. 3 restaurants, room service, in-room data ports, in-room safes, minibars, no-smoking rooms, pool, hair salon, sauna, gym, bar, business services, convention center, travel services, airport shuttle, car rental, free parking. AE, MC, V.*

$$$ 🏨 **Hotel Princess Managua.** This modern colonial style ocher-color hotel is part of the Central American Princess chain. You have all the amenities you'd expect from an international luxury hotel, along with attentive, personalized service sometimes lacking at such lodgings. Rooms are decorated with quiet modern furnishings. ⊠ *Km 4 Carretera a Masaya, Los Robles,* ☎ *505/270–9745,* ℻ *505/278–8444,* 🌐 *www. hotelesprincess.com/managua. 104 rooms. 3 restaurants, room service, in-room data ports, in-room safes, minibars, no-smoking rooms, pool, hair salon, sauna, gym, bar, business services, convention center, airport shuttle, free parking. AE, DC, MC, V.*

$$ 🏨 **Brandt's Bed & Breakfast.** An enormous plant-filled, tiled lobby sprinkled with wicker furniture welcomes you at this hotel that opened in 2001. It's a good medium-range lodging option, with attentive service. The tiled guest rooms are bright, comfortable, and spacious and have enormous windows. Rates include a huge breakfast. ⊠ *1 block west of Galería Casa de Tres Mundos, Los Robles,* ☎ *505/270–2114,* ℻ *505/278–8128,* 🌐 *www.brandtshotel.com.ni. 18 rooms. In-room safes, minibars, laundry service, business services. AE, MC, V.*

$$ 🏨 **Estancia La Casona.** Nicaraguan art hangs on the walls of this cozy hotel, a converted house, on a quiet Barrio Bolonia street. Rooms are clean but plain with air-conditioning and modern baths. Rates include a buffet-style breakfast; lunch and dinner are served for C$60–C$85. ⊠ *5 blocks north and ½ block west of Plaza España, Barrio Bolonia,* ☎ *505/266–1685,* ℻ *505/266–5677,* 🌐 *www.estancialacasona.com. 8 rooms. Restaurant; no in-room phones. MC, V.*

$$ 🏨 **Hotel El Conquistador.** A classy little bed-and-breakfast just up the street from INTUR, in the center of town, El Conquistador has spacious, tile-floor guest rooms decorated with wrought-iron furniture,

combining a colonial and generic-hotel style. Rates include a large breakfast. ⊠ *1 block west and ½ block north of Hotel Inter-Continental, Barrio Bolonia,* ☎ *505/222–4789,* ℻ *505/266–0230,* WEB *www. hotelelconquistador.com. 11 rooms. Cable TV, refrigerators, laundry service, Internet, travel services, car rental, airport shuttle. AE, MC, V.*

$$ 🏨 **Hotel Los Robles.** Nicaraguan furniture and handcrafted furnishings, ★ some new and some restored antiques, adorn this quiet hotel in its namesake southern Managua neighborhood. The building is constructed in the style of a colonial convent with covered interior walkways arranged around a tropical garden and fountain. Rooms are more modern, but the wrought-iron furnishings and small private balconies echo the stylishness of the lodging's common areas. Los Robles proffers a dignified elegance unmatched in Managua. Room rates include an enormous breakfast buffet. ⊠ *4 blocks north of Enitel Villa Fontana, Los Robles,* ☎ *505/267–3008,* ℻ *505/270–1074,* WEB *www.hotellosrobles.com. 14 rooms. Room service, in-room safes, bar, laundry service, business services, Internet. AE, MC, V.*

$$ 🏨 **Hotel Mansión Teodolinda.** This gleaming bright medium-size hotel caters to travelers in town on business. The airy rooms have huge windows and desks (and Internet connection). There's lots of room to spread out and work. All come with a furnished kitchenette. ⊠ *1 block south and 1 block west of INTUR, Barrio Bolonia,* ☎ *505/228–1050,* ℻ *505/228–4908,* WEB *www.teodolinda.com.ni. 37 rooms. Restaurant, room service, in-room data ports, kitchenettes, refrigerators, pool, gym, bar, laundry service, business services, meeting room, free parking. AE, MC, V.*

$$ 🏨 **Maracas Inn.** This is an example of that new breed of medium-range hotels that has sprung up in Nicaragua. The cheery pastel walls of the colonial-style rooms are punctuated by the owner's taste in brightly painted Nicaraguan art. The rate includes a huge breakfast. ⊠ *1 block north and 1½ blocks west of Hospital Militar, Barrio Bolonia,* ☎ *505/ 266–8612,* ℻ *505/266–8982. 12 rooms. Laundry service; no room phones, no room TVs. AE, MC, V.*

$ 🏨 **Casa San Juan.** This quiet, homey guest house is a favorite of exchange groups and NGO delegations; the plant-filled patio is often packed with foreigners excitedly discussing their work in Nicaragua. The rambling building has large, clean basic doubles with bath. An exceptionally friendly staff aids bewildered guests with reserving flights, cars, and minibuses. Three good meals are served daily for C$70–C$90 each. ⊠ *560 Calle Esperanza, Reparto San Juan,* ☎ *505/278–3220,* ℻ *505/267–0418. 12 rooms. Restaurant, travel services, car rental; no room phones, no room TVs. AE, MC, V.*

$ 🏨 **Hotel Los Felipe.** Here's a pleasant, infinitely more upscale alternative to the slew of budget lodgings in Barrio Martha Quezada. Rooms are small and simple, and arranged in a circle motel style around a lush garden. Los Felipe tosses in amenities such as air-conditioning, TV, pool, and a thatch-roof restaurant. You rarely find those in this price bracket. ⊠ *1 ½ blocks west of TicaBus, Barrio Martha Quezada,* ☎ ℻ *505/ 222–6501. 26 rooms. Restaurant, pool, laundry service; no in-room phones. V.*

Nightlife

Managua's nightlife is spread all over the city, making a night on the town a complicated but certainly do-able venture. (Always take a taxi when going out at night.) The capital lacks formal arts events, but you can check *La Prensa* for goings-on at the **Teatro Nacional Rubén Darío** (⊠ near Plaza de la República, Barrio Santo Domingo, ☎ 505/222–3630).

Bars

The semi-open-air **La Curva** (✉ behind the Hotel Inter-Continental, Barrio Bolonia, ☎ 505/222–6876) has occasional live music on weekends along with light Mexican and Nicaraguan food. The gay scene in Managua is limited, but **Loco's** (✉ 1 block north and 1 block west of Montoya statue, Barrio El Carmen, ☎ no phone) draws a mixed gay-straight crowd to an unmarked blue-and-white building for drinks and dancing on weekends. **Hippo's** (✉ 2 blocks west of Hotel Princess Managua, Los Robles, ☎ 505/267–1346) is that back-home beer-and-burger joint that you'd find back in the United States. It doesn't get any better than a pint of Guinness at the **Shannon Irish Pub** (✉ 1 block east and 1 block south of TicaBus, Barrio Martha Quezada, ☎ 505/222–6683). The Irish owner will regale you with stories of his development work here in the 1980s.

Film

Three movie theaters show month-old Hollywood hits. Tickets are C$40. Check *La Prensa,* the daily newspaper, for listings.

THEATERS

Cinemas 1 y 2 (✉ Camino de Oriente shopping center, Km 5 ½ Carretera a Masaya, ☎ 505/267–0964). **Cinemark** (✉ Metrocentro shopping center, ☎ 505/271–9037). **Cinemas Inter** (✉ Plaza Inter shopping center, north of the Inter-Continental, ☎ 505/222–5122).

Music and Dancing

You'll pay a minimal cover charge to get into most upscale places with music and dancing.

An older, local crowd rhumbas, cha-chas, and merengues the evening away at **Edylill** (✉ 1 block north, 5 blocks west of the Montoya statue, Barrio El Carmen, ☎ 505/266–3278). You'll definitely stand out as an outsider, but everyone is very welcoming. A good bet for interesting live Latin and rock music is the **Rancho El Sorba** (✉ Carretera a Masaya, Planes de Altamira, ☎ 505/278–1316). In the same neighborhood as Edylill, **Ruta Maya** (✉ 1½ blocks east of Montoya statue, Barrio El Carmen, ☎ 505/268–0698) hosts pop and Latin musicians.

Outdoor Activities and Sports

If you're a sports fan and you're here sometime between October and April, head to the stadium north of Barrio Martha Quezada to catch a baseball game. Tickets are cheap at C$15. You'll make friends if you deck out in red and blue, the colors of Bóer, Managua's beloved hometown team. If you're less a spectator than participant, it's batter up at **Denis Martínez Sports** (✉ across from the University of Central America, Barrio Jonathán González, ☎ 505/266–7236). Just C$8 gets you 15 balls in a batting cage. You can choose the speed, all the way up to fastball. Use of helmets and bats is free.

Side Trips from Managua

Pochomil and Montelimar

62 km (37 mi) southwest of Managua.

Pochomil, the beach closest to Managua, gets big crowds from December through April and also during Easter week, when Nicaraguans of means head for the beach. At any other time of year, you'll have the place to yourself, especially on a weekday. Pochomil is perfect for day trips from the city, but it has limited accommodations if you want to stay the night. Food is available at the many inexpensive *come-*

BEISBOL SÍ, FÚTBOL NO!

THE MOST COMMONLY PLAYED and watched sport in Latin America is soccer, but Nicaraguans, always content to go their own way, could care less: their passion is baseball. Soccer stadiums are few and far between, but every self-respecting town has a baseball diamond, and terms like *el pícher* and *¡esstrike!* pepper Nicaraguan Spanish. No one seems to know the reason for the "Take me out to the ball game" phenomenon here. Many attribute it to the influence of the long U.S. military occupation during the early 20th century.

Denis Martínez, from Granada, has been Nicaragua's most venerated player ever since he made it to the Major Leagues—the first of six Nicaraguans to do so—as a pitcher for the Cleveland Indians and the Atlanta Braves. Upon his 1999 retirement, Managua renamed its National Stadium for him. Though now a resident of Miami, Martínez makes frequent return trips to Nicaragua in his role as head of the Denis Martínez Foundation, dedicated to providing activities for young people.

But if Martínez is a hero in Nicaragua, then Puerto Rican–born all-star Roberto Clemente can only be called a saint. In the early '70s Clemente played a few times in Nicaragua and developed a rapport with the people. One story claims he was particularly moved when a local boy presented him with his pet lizard. When Clemente heard about the earthquake that leveled central Managua in December 1972, he quickly raised enough funds to fill a chartered plane with food and medicines for the victims. He decided to accompany the relief shipment himself, and tragically died when the plane crashed into the sea just off Nicaragua.

dores lining the *malecón,* the shorefront promenade. The much more upscale 2-km (1-mi) beach of Montelimar was once the exclusive property of the Somozas, then a haven during the Sandinista years for aid workers seeking a little R&R on the sea. Today it houses Nicaragua's only big-time beach resort. Buses to Pochomil depart frequently from Managua's Mayoreo Market, with the last bus back to the capital leaving the beach at 5 PM. A taxi will transport you from Pochomil to Montelimar.

$$$$ ⊞ **Barceló Playa Montelimar Resort and Casino.** Montelimar began life as Somoza's old beach house, but today is completely refurbished and under the management of Spain's Barceló chain. Nicaragua's only all-inclusive resort has magnificent views of the Pacific coastline. You might have time to spend in your brightly furnished, comfortable room or bungalow if you can tear yourself away from the myriad activities, including windsurfing. Look for great off-season deals. ⊠ *Montelimar,* ☏ 505/269–6769, FAX 505/269–7669, WEB *www.barcelo.com/hotels/america/montelim/montili.htm.* 88 rooms, 202 bungalows. 2 restaurants, café, room service, in-room safes, minibars, pools, miniature golf, tennis court, gym, hair salon, sauna, beach, 4 bars, casino, shops, children's programs (6–12), laundry service, business services, meeting rooms, airstrip, car rental, travel services. AE, MC, V.

Corn Islands
90 mins by plane southwest of Managua.

The two Corn Islands (Large and Small) are home to Creole and indigenous Miskito fisherman living a life far removed from the rest of Nicaragua. The people are extraordinarily friendly, the islands are blessed with breathtaking scenery, and the lobster is dirt cheap. Nearly all of the lodging and most of the action are on the big island, although the 45-minute *panga* (a flat-bottomed skiff with an outboard motor) ride to the little island makes for a nice day trip.

Nicaragua's two domestic airlines, La Costeña (☎ 505/285–5131) and Atlantic Airlines (☎ 505/285–5055), have daily 90-minute flights to and from Managua with a stop in Bluefields on the mainland Caribbean coast.

The big island is easily navigated by foot, although a bus circles the island every hour. Taxis to any destination, regardless of distance, will cost C$20. The airstrip runs north–south across the island. The little hump known as Mount Pleasant is on the east side of the airstrip, while Brig Bay is to the west. A water taxi (C$40–C$70 depending on the number of people) connects the two islands.

The best option is the Hotel Bayside (☎ 505/285–5001), located right on the water. Clean, comfortable rooms with air-conditioning are C$420. Its restaurant and bar are also very popular. At the south end of Brig Bay is Hotel Paraíso Club (☎ 505/285–5111, FAX 505/285–5125) with rustic bungalows for C$500. The bar and restaurant are arranged around a landscaped garden.

About 45 minutes from the big island, **Little Corn Island** (often called the Islita by locals) remains a nearly undeveloped tropical paradise. For C$250 you can hire a panga from the dock on Brig Bay for the entire day. Carry a supply of water, food, and mosquito repellent. **Casa Iguana** (casaiguana@mindspring.com) is the lodging here. Allow a week for a reply, as the e-mail message will be printed and sent via boat. It has basic rooms for C$280.

Beaches are the star attraction on both islands. On the big island, Brig Bay and Long Bay (from Brig Bay, cross the airstrip then head east on path) have excellent swimming. If it's a hike you're craving, Mount Pleasant offers good views. You can rent snorkeling gear from the Hotel Bayside.

Managua A to Z

AIR TRAVEL
The capital's Aeropuerto Internacional de Managua sits 11 km (7 mi) east of the city center on the Carretera Norte, the highway to Tipitapa. The airport bank (open weekdays 8:30–noon and 1 to 4, and Saturday 8:30 to noon) may not be open when you arrive, but you can pay for everything with U.S. dollars until you get to a bank or *casa de cambio* (money exchange). Airport taxis charge an outrageous C$250 (about $18 U.S.) to take you into town. Walk across the highway and flag one down instead; you should pay no more than C$100.

➤ AIRPORT: **Aeropuerto Internacional de Managua** (✉ Km 11 Carretera Norte, east of Managua, ☎ 505/233–1624).

BUS TRAVEL
Three of Managua's markets double as bus stations. Two bear an official name, as well as the old Sandinista-era moniker, which most residents still use. The main bus depots are Roberto Huembes Market

(renamed Mercado Central), Israel Lewites Market (Mercado Bóer), and Mercado Mayoreo (no name change here—it was constructed post-1990). Express minivans, seating 15–20 passengers, connect the capital with Granada, León, Masaya and Rivas for about 20% above the regular bus fare of about one U.S. dollar.

ISRAEL LEWITES MARKET
Buses serve León (1½ hrs) every half hour, from 5 AM to 7:30 PM.

MAYOREO MARKET
Buses depart to Matagalpa (2½ hrs) every half hour, from 4 AM to 5:30 PM; Estelí (3 hrs) every half hour, 4 AM to 5 PM.

ROBERTO HUEMBES MARKET
Buses serve Masaya (1 hr) every 30 minutes, from 5 AM to 7 PM; Granada (2 hrs) every 15 minutes, 5 AM to 7 PM; and Rivas (3½ hrs) every half hour, 4:30 AM to 6 PM.

PARKING LOT ACROSS FROM UNIVERSITY OF CENTRAL AMERICA
Express minivans depart from here for Masaya (½ hr) and Granada (¾ hr), as soon as the vehicle fills up (never a long wait), continuously throughout the day and early evening.

ENGLISH-LANGUAGE BOOKS
The Center for Global Education has a good library of books on Central American history and politics. The English-speaking staff is also very helpful.
➤ RESOURCES: **Center for Global Education** (✉ from Estatua Montoya, 1 block east, 1 block south, and ½ block west in building labeled Casa Jaime Mayer, ☎ 505/268–2319).

INTERNET
Kafé@Internet is a Web café with walk-in Internet access. It has branches near the city center and on the Carretera a Masaya. Access is C$39 per hour.
➤ INTERNET RESOURCES: **Kafé@Internet** (✉ 109 yards south of Casa del Obrero, Barrio Martha Quezada, ☎ 505/864–2700; ✉ Km 5 Carretera a Masaya, Los Robles, ☎ 505/270–5670).

MAIL AND SHIPPING
Correos de Nicaragua, open Monday to Saturday 7 to 7, has airmail, express mail, telex, telegraph, and fax services. Its headquarters in Managua is just west of Plaza de la República, near the lake—look for the ugly building with a large antenna. Even if you're not a stamp collector, stop in the Oficina de Filatelia (Office of Philately) to see how the politics of Nicaraguan stamps have changed through the years.

DHL is open weekdays 8 to 6:30, and Saturday 8 to 1; it ships packages internationally. Passus Velox, the local FedEx affiliate, is open weekdays 8–6:30, and Saturday 8 to 1.
➤ MAIL SERVICES: **Correos de Nicaragua** (✉ Palacio de Correos, 1 block west of Plaza de la República, ☎ 505/222–2048). **DHL** (✉ 1 block north of Hotel Inter-Continental, Barrio Bolonia, ☎ 505/228–4081). **Passus Velox (FedEx)** (✉ Km 5 Carretera a Masaya, ☎ 505/278–7323).

MONEY MATTERS
You can change cash here at any bank or casa de cambio around town. Rates vary little from place to place, and most casas de cambio keep similar hours to banks. Any branch of Bancentro or Banco de Finanzas (BDF) will cash American Express traveler's checks and are generally open Monday–Friday 8 to noon and 2 to 4, as well as Saturday morning. The only one of these that is centrally located is the branch

of BDF across from the west side of the Hotel Intercontinental. Multicambios, open weekdays 9 to 5 and Saturday 9 to noon, cashes American Express traveler's checks more quickly than banks and charges no commission on conversion to córdobas. Viajes Atlántida, open weekdays 8:30 to 5 and Saturday 8:30 to noon, is the local American Express affiliate. It sells traveler's checks and replaces lost checks and cards, but will not cash the checks. Look for an ATM machine (*cajero automático*) not at a bank but at a gas station convenience store. Machines at large Esso, Shell, or Texaco stations on highways headed out of town are affiliated with the Plus or Cirrus systems, and occasionally will give cash against an American Express card.

➤ MONEY RESOURCES: **Multicambios** (✉ Plaza España, ☎ 505/266–8879). **Viajes Atlántida** (✉ 1 block east and ½ block north of Plaza España, ☎ 505/266–8720).

TELEPHONES

The Empresa Nicaragüense de Telecomunicaciones (Enitel) is the semi-privatized telephone company with headquarters currently housed in the post office, just west of Plaza de la República, near the lake. Its offices, open daily 7 AM to 10 PM, provide local and international telephone service. Smaller Enitel offices are scattered throughout Managua, including one at the Huembes market. Relatively new to Managua are pay phones. They accept prepaid phone cards sold at most Enitel buildings and some stores (look for *tarjetas telefónicas* signs) or 1-córdoba coins. Dial 112 for information.

➤ PHONE SERVICE: **Empresa Nicaragüense de Telecomunicaciones** (Enitel; ✉ Palacio de Correos, 1 block west of Plaza de la República, ☎ 505/222–2048).

TRANSPORTATION AROUND MANAGUA

BY BUS

Buses in Managua, all recycled U.S. school buses, are great fun, run frequently, and go everywhere, but aren't for the faint of heart. The only way to figure out the bus system is to ask one of the locals (ideally one waiting at a bus stop). There's little time to ask the driver when the bus arrives; most come to kind of a rolling stop at best. A conductor, usually a teenage boy, will help push you into the packed bus. Buses begin running early in the morning and continue at 10-minute intervals until 6 PM, when they start running a little less often. Service stops around 10 PM. Rides cost only C$2. Come prepared with small change. Guard your possessions diligently; the vehicles are notorious for pickpockets who administer what seasoned travelers call "the Managua massage."

BY CAR

Managua's lack of a city center, its enormous sprawl, and the country's relatively few motor vehicles make for surprisingly less automobile congestion than in other Central American capitals. Broad highways and boulevards zip traffic along at a lively pace across the vast distances.

BY TAXI

Taxis are the best way to get around Managua: they're ubiquitous—the driver will toot his horn to let you know he's available—fast, and not outrageously expensive. A few clattering Russian Ladas, a vestige of the Sandinista years, remain, but most companies have upgraded their fleets to spiffy new Japanese models. Prices are set by cooperatives; most rides are C$15–C$20 per person during the day and a bit more at night. Ask for the fare before you climb in. Don't be surprised if occasionally other passengers are picked up along the way, as drivers try to carpool passengers headed in roughly the same direction. Tipping is not expected.

ON FOOT

Managua's sprawling distances, open spaces, and intense heat make the capital a terrible walking city. Opt for a taxi instead.

VISITOR INFORMATION

The Instituto Nicaragüense de Turismo (INTUR) operates a tourist information office near the Hotel Inter-Continental. The helpful folks here will try to answer all your questions; it's open weekdays 8 to 12:30 and 1:30 to 5. INTUR also has an airport office open daily but, oddly, it's in the airport departure lounge and only accessible to those waiting for their flight *out* of Nicaragua.

➤ Tourist Information: **Instituto Nicaragüense de Turismo** (INTUR; ⊠ 1 block west of southern side of Hotel Inter-Continental, Barrio Bolonia, ☏ 505/222–3333).

NORTHERN NICARAGUA

The vast, lavish geography of the northwestern lowlands and the central highlands will give you plenty to write home about. The lowlands are dotted with volcanoes—some of which are still active—that make for excellent hikes. To the west, on the sprawling beaches of the Pacific Coast, lie Nicaragua's most overlooked (and underdeveloped) areas. You'll have the beaches to yourself (except during Holy Week), and the surfing here is decent year-round. León, the largest city north of Managua, pulsates with the energy emanating from Nicaragua's largest intellectual center, the Universidad Nacional Autónoma de Nicaragua. As you make your way across the prolific lowlands by way of the broken, winding highways, the stifling heat gradually diminishes. The cordilleras (mountain ranges) of Isabelia and Dariense tower invitingly ahead.

This coffee-growing region has historically attracted farmers who have tattooed the land with a symmetrical patchwork of agricultural plots. Flocks of European settlers who immigrated here in the late 1800s left an indelible imprint: peculiar pockets of brawny, befreckled men and their families are hidden away in the deep valleys of the highest mountains. Many people make the effort to come up here just to visit the Selva Negra Mountain Resort, a 1,400-acre lot of jungly land that's blessed with an almost dizzying mixture of plants, flowers, and wildlife.

The north has always been far to the left on the political pendulum, and these areas were badly bruised during the revolution and Contra war years. Vestiges of these battles can still be seen today. Yet even here, many of the revolutionary murals have been painted over with advertisements for Pepsi and other U.S. products, a more lucrative use of the space.

León

93 km (56 mi) northwest of Managa.

León means "lion" in Spanish, and this city has always exerted a li-onlike presence on Nicaraguan history. As one of Latin America's most prominent colonial cities, León played an influential role in the commercial and intellectual life of Spanish America. Some of the greatest figures in the country's literature and politics lived or studied here, including the great poet Rubén Darío and prominent Sandinistas such as Sílvio Rodriguez, Tomás Borges, and FSLN founder Carlos Fonseca.

Present-day León sits 24 km (15 mi) west of its original location on the northwest shore of Lake Managua. Founded in 1524, the city was destroyed in 1609 by an earthquake caused by the eruption of nearby Volcán Momotombo. The survivors moved west and settled next to

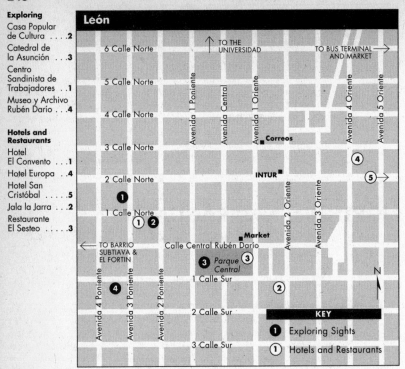

the village of the indigenous Subtiava people. The village still stands today, retaining much of its tradition and folklore.

León, Nicaragua's capital for over 300 years, was important enough to be chosen by the Spanish as the site of Central America's largest cathedral. Construction began in 1746, but didn't end until 1815. The growing rivalry between the Liberals of León and the Conservatives of Granada erupted into bitter conflict in 1821, resulting in 17 battles in the city between 1824 and 1842. León's massive church, however, survived. Many years later, the town again saw fierce fighting during the 1970s revolution against Somoza. Sensing that he was losing control, the dictator ordered the city bombed. Again, the hardy cathedral remained intact.

Though León comes close to approximating a modern city—there are street names and everything—*Leoneses,* like most Nicaraguans, give directions based on distances from landmarks. Fortunately, the city is laid out as a grid, with calles running east–west, and avenidas north–south. The baseline is the intersection of Calle Central Rubén Darío and Avenida Central, at the northeast corner of Parque Central, in front of the cathedral. Most sights are an easy walk from Parque Central.

Though not geared toward sightseeing, the **Universidad Nacional Autónoma de Nicaragua** dominates the city geographically and politically. The country's largest institution of higher education was founded in 1912 and sprawls amorphously north of the city center. Its bookstores, cafés, and ubiquitous copy shops give León that college town feel, Nicaragua style.

Sights to See

Barrio Subtiava. About 11 blocks west of Parque Central, live the Subtiava people, whose ancestors were here long before Columbus arrived.

Here you'll find the church of **San Juan Bautista de Subtiava** (open daily 8:30–11:30), dating from 1700, and the ruins of the even older church of Vera Cruz, which was destroyed by a volcanic eruption in 1835. Semana Santa (Holy Week) is the most colorful time to visit, when residents create an exquisitely beautiful trail of sawdust drawings on the main streets that is then trampled by a procession carrying an images of Christ's Passion.

② **Casa Popular de Cultura.** This small arts museum, with whimsical business hours—you just have to try your luck—contains a tiny collection of paintings by local artists. ⊠ *1 block north and 1½ blocks west of the northwest corner of Parque Central,* ☎ *no phone.* 🎫 *Free.*

③ Taking up an entire city block, the **Catedral de la Asunción,** at Calle Central Rubén Darío and Avenida 1 Pte., is the largest church in Central America. Tradition holds that the architect submitted a smaller, less gradiose blueprint to the Spanish crown fearing that Spain would nix his real intentions. Inside, the high arches and heavy columns lend a feeling of indestructibility. Paintings of the stations of the cross done by artist Antonio Sarra adorn the huge walls. Look for the tomb of poet Rubén Darío at the foot of the statue of Saint Paul, to the right of the altar. A stone lion, representing the city of León, mourns atop the grave.

① **CentroSandinista de Trabajadores.** The first of the Somozas met his demise at what is now the Sandinista Party Center. A plaque on the facade honors the dictator's assassination in 1956 at the hands of the poet Rigoberto López Pérez who posed as a waiter at a government reception. (López himself was immediately shot and killed by Somoza's guards). ⊠ *1 block west and 1½ blocks north of Parque Central's northwest corner,* ☎ *no phone.* 🎫 *Free.* ⊙ *Weekdays 8–4.*

El Fortín. A 19th-century fort once used as a prison by the National Guard sits on a hill a mile south of town and offers good views of León and volcanoes nearby. You can reach it from a dirt road that goes past Subtiava's San Juan Bautista church, about 11 blocks west of Parque Central.

④ **Museo y Archivo Rubén Darío.** The name Darío (1867–1916) may be fairly obscure in the English-speaking world, but throughout Nicaragua it commands instant respect. Rubén Darío, Nicaragua's favorite son and poet laureate, became a leader of Latin American poetry's modernist movement, which rebelled against the ponderous, repetitive verse in vogue at the time. Darío was also famous for his stormy personal life, battling alcoholism and carrying on a series of indiscreet affairs. The museum, in the house where Darío spent his boyhood, includes personal effects and a plaster "death mask" made shortly after the great poet died. ⊠ *3 blocks west of the northwest corner of Parque Central,* ☎ *505/311–2388.* 🎫 *Free.* ⊙ *Tues.–Sat. 8–noon and 2–5, Sun. 9–noon.*

Dining and Lodging

Elegant dining is not León's forte, but as in any college town, you'll never go hungry here. Join the throngs of university students for a quick bite or snack at the eateries dotting the city.

$ ✕ **Jala la Jarra.** The Nicaraguan owners' penchant for Mexican cuisine makes this the best south-of-the-border (but a few countries north of Nicaragua's border) option in town. They dish up chalupas and tacos and usually have live music on weekend evenings. ⊠ *1a Calle SO and Av. 2 O,* ☎ *505/864–2979. MC, V. Closed Mon. No lunch Sun.*

$ ✕ **Restaurante El Sesteo.** An indoor gallery of portraits of Nicaraguan literary figures greets you at this *Leonense* institution, but opt for one of the pleasant outdoor tables overlooking the Parque Central instead.

They make this the place to hang out for hours, late into the evening. The main dishes are a bit pricey, but the tasty ham or chicken sandwiches, amazing club sandwiches, and banana splits are all bargains. ⊠ *East side of Parque Central,* ☏ *505/311–5327. AE, MC, V.*

$$ ▦ **Hotel El Convento.** León's most sumptuous lodging was built only ★ in 2000 in the style of the former San Francisco convent and blends seamlessly with the church next door. Covered interior walkways loop around a large garden and its bubbling centerpiece fountain. The owners have collected 30 years' worth of antiques that furnish the common areas and private rooms. Each tiled room has its own balcony. ⊠ *Calle Rubén Darío, 3 blocks west of cathedral,* ☏ *505/311–7053,* FAX *505/311–7067,* WEB *www.hotelelconvento.com.ni. 32 rooms. Cafeteria, restaurant, room service, bar, laundry service, meeting room, business services. AE, DC, MC, V.*

$$ ▦ **Hotel San Cristóbal.** About a kilometer outside the city limits on the bypass highway, the San Cristóbal is a cool, spacious alternative to the lodgings in town, but just a short taxi ride away. It opened in 2000, but is built in old Nicaragua style, around a courtyard with a central fountain. Modern tiled rooms are simply furnished with wood furniture and flowered drapes and bedspreads. The lower-floor restaurant specializes in Italian cuisine. ⊠ *Carretera Bypass, next to Tropigas,* ☏ *505/311–1606,* FAX *505/311–1608,* WEB *www.sancristobalhotel.com. 30 rooms. Cafeteria, restaurant, room service, pool, bar, laundry service, meeting room, business services. AE, MC, V.*

$ ▦ **Hotel Europa.** The nicest of León's budget lodgings is clean, attractive, and has a staff that aims to please. Rooms, arranged around a courtyard, are small and basic and are bright yellow, bright blue, or bright red. ⊠ *3a Calle NO and 4a Av. NO,* ☏ *505/311–6040,* FAX *505/311–2577. 37 rooms. Restaurant, laundry service; no a/c in some rooms, no TV in some rooms. AE, MC, V.*

Nightlife

The **Casa Popular de Cultura** (⊠ 1 block north and 1½ blocks west of the northwest corner of Parque Central) hosts cultural events some evenings. **Tertulias Leónesas** (León Social Gatherings) provides music and food on the Parque Central each Saturday evening from 6 to midnight.

Outdoor Activities and Sports

Reliable guides can be arranged through the INTUR office for visits to nearby Volcán Momotombo or León Viejo, but you'll be expected to provide a vehicle. Fully escorted excursions to these sites are more easily arranged through a tour operator in Managua. Poneloya is the favorite Leónense beach, about a half-hour west of the city on the Pacific coast.

León A to Z

BUS TRAVEL

León's bus terminal, a dusty field adjoining a market, sits about 1 km (½ mi) northeast of downtown on 6a Calle NE, at 8 Av NE. Express minivans, the fastest option at 90 minutes, leave almost continually for Managua and cost C$20.

CAR TRAVEL

León's about an hour northeast of Managua via one of two routes. The shorter route hugs the shore of Lake Managua and passes through La Paz Centro. A slightly longer route passes through Ciudad Sandino.

EMERGENCIES

➤ EMERGENCY SERVICES: **Ambulance** (☏ 505/311–2089). **Fire** (☏ 505/311–2323). **Hospital Escuela Oscar Danilo Rosales** (⊠ 1 block south

of the cathedral, Calle 2a Sur and Av. 1 Pte., ☎ 505/311–6990). **Police** (☎ 505/311–3137).

INTERNET

Puerto Café Benjamín Linder provides Internet access for C$40 per hour.
➤ INTERNET SERVICE: **Puerto Café Benjamín Linder** (✉ 1a Av. NO and 2a Calle NO, ☎ 505/311–0548).

MAIL AND SHIPPING

The local Correos de Nicaragua, open Monday through Saturday 7 to 7, is across from La Recolección church. A branch of DHL ships packages to international destinations.
➤ MAIL AND SHIPPING SERVICES: **Correos de Nicaragua** (✉ 1a Av. NE and 3a Calle NE, ☎ 505/311–2102). **DHL** (✉ ½ block west of Colegio Mercantil, ☎ 505/311–5219).

MONEY MATTERS

Several banks cluster on the corner of 1a Calle Norte and 1a Avenida Oriente, one block north of the cathedral; they'll change U.S. dollars weekdays 8:30–noon and 2–4, Saturday 8:30–11:30. Bancentro and Banco de Finanzas (BDF) change traveler's checks.
➤ BANKS: **Bancentro** (✉ 1 block north of the cathedral, ☎ 505/311–0991). **Banco de Finanzas** (BDF; ✉ 1 block north of the cathedral, ☎ 505/311–1484).

TELEPHONES

If your hotel room doesn't have a phone, the Empresa Nicaragüense de Telecomunicaciones (Enitel) provides local and international telephone service daily from 7 AM–10 PM.
➤ TELEPHONE SERVICE: **Empresa Nicaragüense de Telecomunicaciones** (Enitel; ✉ northwest corner of Parque Central, ☎ 505/311–7377).

TRANSPORTATION AROUND LEÓN

BY TAXI

León's downtown is easily navigated on foot, but for farther distances, taxis are ubiquitous and inexpensive. A trip from the bus terminal to the city center runs C$8.

VISITOR INFORMATION

The Instituto Nicaragüense de Turismo (INTUR) operates a tourist information office downtown with a helpful, friendly staff.
➤ TOURIST INFORMATION: **Instituto Nicaragüense de Turismo** (INTUR; ✉ 2a Av. NO and 2a Calle NO, ☎ 505/311–3682. ☉ Weekdays 8–12:30 and 2–5.

Volcán Momotombo

29 km (17 mi) east of León.

The near-perfect cone of this volcano—which is best known as the subject of a famous Rubén Darío poem—rises 4,000 ft over the western shore of Lake Managua, and is visible from as far away as the capital. Access is by a bumpy dirt road (which turns muddy in the rainy season) that starts just south of the village of La Paz Centro on the León–Managua highway; look for the sign reading PATRICIÓ ARGÜELLO GEOTHERMAL PLANT. To get here, take one of the buses headed toward Managua and get off at La Paz Centro. From La Paz Centro you can take one of the public-transport trucks to Puerto Momotombo. Technically, you're supposed to have a pass to venture near the geothermal power plant on the volcano's lower slopes. It supplies almost 40% of the country's power. To secure a pass visit the **Empresa Nicaragüense**

de Electricidad (ENEL) office (✉ 1 block north of Casa Nazareth, ☎ 505/266–8756) in Managua's Barrio Martha Quezada. The reward for your troubles, and the arduous four-hour climb, will be a stunning view of the lake and the surrounding country.

León Viejo

30 km (18 mi) east of León.

An interesting day trip from *new* León, the ruined city of León Viejo (Old León) was one of the first two Spanish settlements in Nicaragua. (Granada was the other.) The city was the capital of Spain's colonial province in Nicaragua until a 1610 earthquake, triggered by Volcán Momotombo, leveled it. Now that parts have been excavated—the site was not discovered until 1967—you can make out the cathedral and the plaza central in front of it. In 2000, León Viejo was named a UNESCO World Heritage Site—Nicaragua's first. The ruins suffered much damage during 1998's Hurricane Mitch. Much needed restoration was underway at press time. ✉ *3 km east of La Paz Centro, then 15 km northeast.* 🎫 *C$10.* ⊙ *Daily 8–5.*

Poneloya

23 km (14 mi) west of León.

One of the nicer beaches in Nicaragua, Poneloya is an easy day trip from León. The beach will be yours and yours alone during the week; weekends and holidays, especially Holy Week, are quite another story. Swimmers should be careful of the strong undertow. The seafood restaurants along the beach offer big plates of *camarones al ajillo* (garlic shrimp) for about C$100. You'll find only very basic accommodation here.

En Route   Nicaragua has three border crossings with Honduras: Las Manos (near Somoto) and El Espino (near Ocotal)—both are north of Matagalpa—and El Guasaule, beyond Chinandega north of León. All posts are open daily 8 AM–5 PM. Get an early start and expect delays. Nicaragua and Honduras have engaged in unresolved disputes over territorial waters since 1999. The bickering only affects visitors in the form of long waits at their common border.

Matagalpa

130 km (78 mi) north of Managua.

At just over 3,300 ft, the lush mountains around Matagalpa and its cool climate and reputation for hospitality have attracted large numbers of foreigners for years. In the 1800s, a wave of immigrants—mostly British, German, and French—arrived and established the region's coffee plantations, forcing many of the indigenous farmers off their own land. Years later, the region witnessed a more benevolent invasion of foreigners, who came during the Sandinista years to work on solidarity projects.

The city's heart is staunchly Sandinista. Both Tomás Borges, the lone survivor of the group that founded the FSLN, and Carlos Fonseca, its best-known martyr, were born and raised here. The city is also known for serving one of the best cups of coffee in the country, Matagalpa Roast. You'll find few international-quality hotels and restaurants here, but the region does contain the Selva Negra Mountain Resort, arguably Nicaragua's most famous lodging.

Sights to See

Matagalpa's sole museum makes an interesting visit for fans of Nicaraguan political history. The **Museo Casa Comandante Carlos Fonseca** (⊠ 1 block east of southeast corner of Parque Darío, ☏ no phone) was the home of Carlos Fonseca, the guiding light of the FSLN. Photographs and text tell the story of Fonseca's life, from his childhood to his death in a skirmish with the National Guard in 1976. Its hours are irregular, but you stand a better chance weekdays 9–noon and 2–5; a donation is requested.

If the anachronistic architecture of the Bavarian-style **Selva Negra Mountain Resort** doesn't charm you, then owners Eddy and Mausi Kühl will. After receiving a personal invitation from the Nicaraguan government to come here to grow coffee, Eddy's grandfather emigrated from Germany in 1891. More than 100 years later, Eddy still grows world-famous coffee, and his knowledge of Nicaragua's politics is infinite, as he is a personal friend of many of the country's power brokers. The owners charge C$45 if you want to visit the property, but the fee is applied toward meals or lodging. Come here for a taste of some really fresh coffee, or for the excellent hiking. The 1,500 acres surrounding the hotel house howler monkeys, sloths, minks, ocelots, wild boar, and cougars, as well as 125 species of birds and 85 varieties of orchids. Fourteen different trails wind into the cloudy mountains and around the coffee plantation, and you can even rent a horse for C$45 an hour. ⊠ *Km 140 Carretera Matagalpa–Jinotega,* ☏ FAX *505/ 612–3883,* WEB *www.selvanegra.com.*

Lodging

$ ★ ⌂ **Selva Negra Mountain Resort.** Set in a combination private reserve and working coffee plantation, the "Black Forest" is arguably Nicaragua's most famous hotel. Rooms in the main house are rustic but furnished with flowered spreads and drapes. More luxurious and expensive bungalows ($$$) have one bedroom and private porch with spectacular views. Selva Negra also offers hostel-like accommodations next door. ⊠ *Km 140 Carretera Matagalpa–Jinotega,* ☏ FAX *505/612– 3883,* WEB *www.selvanegra.com. 19 bungalows, 4 chalets, 20 dorm-style bunks. Restaurant, hiking, horseback riding, meeting room; no a/c, no room phones, no room TVs. AE, MC, V.*

Outdoor Activities

HIKING

The hills near Matagalpa contain some stunning scenery. One hiking trail, which begins south of town on the highway (about 60 ft south of pedestrian bridge), climbs 600 ft to **El Calvario,** whose summit has a small shrine dedicated to the crucified Christ and a good view of the valley. An easier excursion leads to the **cemetery** south of town (about 1 km or ½ mi southwest of bus depot), where you can see the town below and visit the grave of aid worker Ben Linder, the only U.S. citizen killed during the Contra war.

Matagalpa A to Z

BUS TRAVEL

Matagalpa's bus depot is at the market in the southwest part of town, next to the river, about a 30-minute walk from Parque Central. A cab ride to the center should cost C$12. From the market, buses leave for Managua (3 hours, C$30) about every 40 minutes 4 AM to 5 PM, with less frequent *expreso* services making the trip in 2 hours. At press time, the future of Expresos del Norte, which ran one luxury express bus to Managua daily, leaving at 4:50 PM, was not certain. Ask your hotel about this route.

CAR TRAVEL

You reach Matagalpa via the Interamerican Highway north from Managua. Watch for the turnoff at Sébaco, 28 km (17 mi) before Matagalpa.

EMERGENCIES

➤ EMERGENCY SERVICES: **Ambulance** (☎ 505/612–2059). **Fire** (☎ 505/612–3167). **Police** (☎ 505/612–3870).

INTERNET

CompuAcSer in the center of town provides walk-in Internet access for C$40 per hour; it's open Monday to Saturday 8 to 8.
➤ INTERNET SERVICE: **CompuAcSer** (✉ 1 block north of Parque Darío, ☎ 505/612–6154).

MAIL AND SHIPPING

The local Correos de Nicaragua, open Monday to Saturday 7 to 7, is across from Parque Darío. A branch of DHL provides package shipping to international destinations.
➤ MAIL SERVICES: **Correos de Nicaragua** (✉ Parque Darío, ☎ 505/612–3880). **DHL** (✉ 1 block west of Teatro Perla, ☎ 505/612–6092).

MONEY MATTERS

The banks cluster a half block south of the Parque Central's southeast corner on a street appropriately called Avenida de los Bancos. Bancentro and Banco de Finanzas (BDF) will change both cash and traveler's checks weekdays 8:30–4:30 and Saturday 8–noon.
➤ BANK INFORMATION: **Bancentro** (✉ Av. de los Bancos, ☎ 505/612–3922). **Banco de Finanzas** (BDF; ✉ Av. de los Bancos, ☎ 505/612–2752).

TELEPHONES

The Empresa Nicaragüense de Telecomunicaciones (Enitel) provides local and international telephone service.
➤ TELEPHONE SERVICE: **Empresa Nicaragüense de Telecomunicaciones** (Enitel; ✉ 1 block east of northwest corner of Parque Central, ☎ 505/612–2999).

VISITOR INFORMATION

The Instituto Nicaragüense de Turismo (INTUR), open weekdays 8 to 12:30 and 1:30 to 5, operates a tourist information office a few blocks south of downtown with a helpful staff.
➤ TOURIST INFORMATION: **INTUR** (✉ 1 block east and ½ block north of Molagüina church, ☎ 505/612–7060).

SOUTHWEST NICARAGUA

The stretch of land between Managua and the Costa Rican border makes up only a sliver of Nicaragua, but aside from Managua it's the most densely populated region in the country. It's one of the most interesting as well. For hundreds of years the isthmus—bounded by the enormous Lago de Nicaragua to the north and the Pacific to the south—has attracted settlers who saw promise in the fertile earth and abundant waters. It has always been the richest part of the country, with Granada, one of the great cities of the colonial Americas, leading the way to prosperity through trade with the rest of America and Europe.

From its wide swaths of unspoiled coastline to its massive volcanoes this corner of Nicaragua is a sampler of the entire country. It draws more travelers than any other region, from dollar-clutching tourists haggling over trinkets at the Masaya craft market to serious volcano-climbers

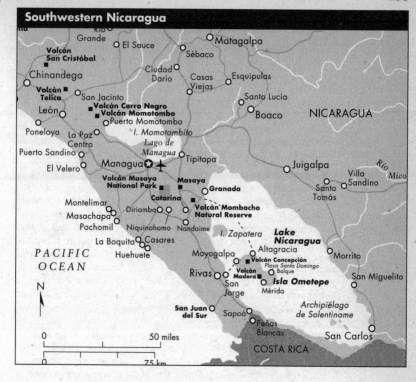

Southwestern Nicaragua

in search of personal epiphany to a growing expatriate population. Whatever brings you here, you'll find the traveling easy and the climate generally cooperative.

Volcán Masaya National Park

23 km (14 mi) southeast of Managua.

The evocative landscapes of Volcán Masaya, also known as Popogatepe ("Mountain That Burns"), suggest a moon with shrubbery—these sterile lava fields slowly turn fertile, invaded by native vegetation and bedecked with thousands of colorful flowers, even orchids, during the dry season. Along with the plants come animals, including coyotes, skunks, raccoons, deer, iguanas, rabbits, and monkeys. Birds are plentiful with flocks of parakeets gamboling within the craters' otherwise toxic confines. Look for them in late afternoon, along with motmots, magpie jays, and woodpeckers.

The turnoff for Parque Nacional Volcán Masaya is 5 km (3 mi) north of Masaya along the main highway from Managua heading toward Granada. It is the country's first, and given its proximity to Managua, most visited national park. A 6-km (4-mi) road leads past a checkpoint (C$45 per car) and up to the steaming Santiago Crater, the largest of four in the volcano.

Stop first at the expansive **Centro de Interpretacion Ambiental** (visitor center), one of Nicaragua's best museums, for an overview of the region's cultural and geological history. There's a lot of fascinating information here, though most of the text is in Spanish. Other exhibits detail the history of volcanic activity in the rest of the country and give a rundown on the local exotic wildlife. As is portrayed in a large painting inside the visitor center, the volcano's eruptions terrorized nearby

tribes for centuries, leading them to develop elaborate rituals of human sacrifice to appease the angry gods.

The edge of the smoldering **Santiago Crater** is just a few feet from the parking lot. The viewpoint from which you can actually see the fire below is closed, but the steaming, sulfuric crater is still an awesome sight. The nearby **Bobadilla Cross**, at the top of 200 stairs, is a replica of one erected by Spanish priests in the 16th century to exorcise the devil. Spanish priests were convinced the crater was the Boca del Infierno—the Mouth of Hell. In their own bizarre sacrificial ritual, the Spaniards lowered several unlucky fools into the crater to retrieve the "boiling gold" they saw there. The last major eruption was in 1852.

The **Coyote Trail** offers intrepid hikers a 5½-km (3½-mi) trek featuring views of petrified lava beds and bird-filled forests en route from the crater's edges to the shores of Lake Masaya. Don't miss the **San Fernando Crater,** inactive for 200 years and now home to a lush forest. It's a good idea to bring water, sunscreen, and a sack lunch if you plan to walk around in the blazing heat. For about C$45 you can hire a guide to fill you in on the park's history, and park rangers can take groups to some caves leading to lava caverns. Both guides and park rangers are available in or around the recreation area, about 1 km (½ mi) from the entrance. ⊠ *Km 23 Carretera Masaya–Managua,* ☎ *505/522–5415 (mailing address: Apdo. NI-1, Nindiri).* 🖃 *C$50.* ☉ *Daily 9–5.*

OFF THE BEATEN PATH	**NIQUINOHOMO -** Sandino groupies will want to visit this village where the general was born and raised. (Appropriately enough, Niquinohomo means "place of the warriors" in Chorotegan.) Sandino's childhood home, across from the church on the main square, is now a museum that is desperate for government funding. Admission is free, but donations are requested. Inside are Sandino's personal effects, rare photos, and text embellishing the life of this legend. Masaya–Rivas buses pass through hourly. ☎ *No phone.* ☉ *Tues.–Sat. 9–noon and 1–5.*

Masaya

29 km (17 km) southeast of Managua.

Some 45 minutes southeast of Managua by car, the city of Masaya offers great shopping, pleasant strolling, and not much else. A half-day trip from Managua or Granada should give you enough time to prowl through the two markets for hammocks, leather goods, weavings, pottery, paintings, and other crafts and to explore the town. Be aware that the market names can be deceiving: the so-called **Mercado Nuevo (New Market)** is the more ramshackle crafts bazaar within the labyrinthine confines of the main city market, five blocks east of the main plaza, known as the Parque 17 de Octubre. The walled older market, the **Mercado Viejo (Old Market),** closer to the center of town, looks like a more modern arts-and-crafts complex, thanks to extensive restoration. Vendors accept dollars or córdobas, and many also take credit cards. An ATM here also gives cash against Plus-affiliated cards. Each Thursday evening, the market hosts *Jueves de Verbena* (Thursday-night festival) with music, food and, of course, shopping by moonlight. The Mercado Viejo also houses Masaya's branch of the **Instituto Nicaragüense de Turismo** (INTUR; ⊠ 1 block east of Parque 17 de Octubre, ☎ 505/552–7615) the government tourist office. It's open daily 8 to 6 and Thursday from 8 AM to midnight; and it's closed one rotating day during the week.

One kilometer (½ mile) south of the Parque 17 de Octubre lies **Monimbó,** a community inhabited by descendants of the indigenous Darianés peo-

ple who proudly cling to their customs and folklore. The neighborhood's colorful murals depict their ancestors' struggle against the Spaniards. During the day, the streets are filled with craftspeople hard at work making baskets, carvings, and leather goods. Check with INTUR in the Mercado Viejo for suggestions of the best workshops to visit.

Catarina

13 km (8 mi) southeast of Masaya.

Watch for the turnoff to Catarina, 16 km (10 mi) along the road from Granada to Masaya—it takes you up to a spectacular *mirador* (lookout point) in this colorful little town overflowing with attractive plant stores. On the back side of town, past the cathedral, a cluster of gaudy souvenir stands (one sells respectable paintings by the young artist manning the stand) and a row of restaurants line the edge of a cliff overlooking the crater lake called **Laguna de Apoyo.** The restaurants are pricey by Nicaraguan standards but well worth the view of Lake Apoyo, Masaya, Granada, and, stretching into the distance, Lake Nicaragua. A different road off the main highway—at Kilometer 38—leads to Laguna de Apoyo itself, where the swimming is good.

Granada

★ *45 km (27 mi) southeast of Managua.*

Once one of the grandest, richest, and most important cities in the Americas, Granada is the *must* on every traveler's itinerary to Nicaragua. The past has not been forgotten here; the city's streets are packed with richly detailed colonial buildings that make it Nicaragua's most architecturally interesting town. Because of its position on the western shore of Lake Nicaragua, Granada played a crucial role in the commercial and trading life of colonial Latin America. Founded in 1524 during the first Spanish expeditions by Francisco Hernández de Córdoba, the city quickly became an important supply link to Spain. Ships entering Lake Nicaragua from the Atlantic via Río San Juan would dock at Granada's port, unload their cargo, and leave with their hulls full of gold mined by conquered tribes. As the region's economy developed and diversified, Granada became the major port for exporting goods to Spain that came from as far away as Guatemala. And the town's elite, whose control of the port brought them enormous wealth, embarked upon a construction campaign that transformed Granada into one of the Americas' classic cities.

As Granada got richer, it got more conservative. By the time Nicaragua gained its independence in the 1820s, a serious schism had developed between Granada's conservatives and León's liberals. With no Spanish master left to police the rivalry, the two cities quickly fell into a battle for power. Granadinos enjoyed the upper hand until American mercenary William Walker, invited by the Liberals, captured the town in 1855. Walker ruled Nicaragua from Granada for nearly two years, until he was driven out by combined Central American forces. During his retreat, the demented colonel ordered the city destroyed, leaving Granada mostly in smoking ruins, and a sign saying, "Here Was Granada."

Granada has survived, and even prospered, through Nicaragua's troubled history. The entire center city has been declared a museum, meaning that no tall buildings will ever be erected in or near the colonial-era downtown. Additionally, every building renovation must follow strict design guidelines intended to maintain the integrity of the existing colonial architecture. Rebuilt, restored, and revived, Granada today carries its conservative heritage proudly, and has reaped the tourism

256

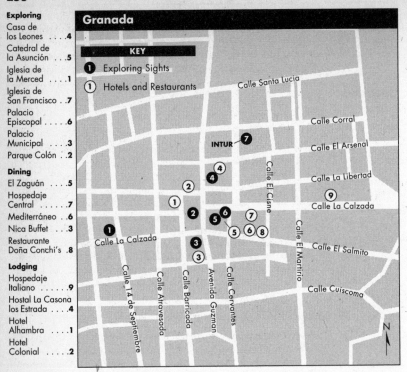

Granada

KEY
1 Exploring Sights
1 Hotels and Restaurants

harvest like no other place in Nicaragua. This is one of the few places in the country where you'll be regularly aware of the presence of other travelers. The city's churches, convents, and horse-drawn carriages attract the crowds, but this is no Colonial Williamsburg. Nicaraguans and investors from Europe, the United States, Costa Rica, and elsewhere have been buying up the city's elegant 18th- and 19th-century homes with large interior patios, renovating them, and transforming them into hotels, restaurants, and trendy boutiques. Many more hold workaday barbershops and billiard halls frequented only by locals. Most remain family homes whose occupants bring their wicker chairs out to the sidewalk to enjoy the cool evening breezes and wish a friendly "*Buenas noches*" to passersby.

Leading the way in signage, streets in Granada do have actual names—romantic sounding, historic names. Calle La Calzada runs east from Parque Colón, the central park. Calle Real Xalteva heads west from the park. But, as elsewhere in Nicaragua, *Granadinos* give addresses in terms of numbers of *cuadras* (blocks) in cardinal directions from a landmark: *norte* (north); *sur* (south); *oeste* or *abajo* (west); and *al lago* (east toward Lake Nicaragua).

Sights to See

Any tour of Granada should start at **Parque Colón,** the city's central park, where you can imagine what Granada must have been like in its glory years. The park was the original site of Granada's central market; today the mango tree–shaded space is quintessential Latin America, a place to greet neighbors or get a shoe shine. Parque Colón is dominated by the **Catedral de la Asunción,** open daily 8 to 6, on its eastern side. Walker burned the original cathedral down in 1857; this structure was completed in 1910. It's a rather imposing example of neo-classical architecture, worth a visit to explore the vivid examples of

religious art within. A July 2000 earthquake caused damage to the building; restoration was underway at press time. The arched and columned

6
3 building to the north of the cathedral is the 1913 colonial-style **Palacio Episcopal,** the seat of Granada's Catholic diocese. The **Palacio Municipal,** the city hall, sits on the south side of the park. On the park's west side sits the wonderful old **Hotel Alhambra,** one of Granada's premier places to spend the night.

The smaller **Plaza de los Leones** adjoins the park on its north side. The obelisk in the center of the plaza honors the heroes of Central Amer-
4 ican independence. On the plaza's east side is the old **Casa de los Leones** (✉ Plaza de los Leones, ☎ 505/552–4176). The building's stone portal dates from 1809 and is the only portion of the structure to survive the fire set by William Walker in 1856. Its inscription, "Long live don Fernando VII," pays homage to the then-Spanish king. It now houses the Casa de Tres Mundos, Granada's art and culture center. It's open daily 8–6 and contains an art gallery, studios, school, library, and café and hosts cultural events.

★ **7** The **Iglesia de San Francisco,** dating from 1529, but rebuilt in 1867 following Walker's fire, has a baroque facade with a system of pediments and symmetrical oval windows. Next door, the **old convent** serves as a museum, with a collection of stunningly carved stone artifacts dating from around AD 800, gathered on the Ometepe and Zapatera islands in Lake Nicaragua. The exhibit includes extensive maps of the archaeological sites on the islands of Ometepe and Zapatera, where the carvings were found. The former convent also hosts temporary art exhibitions and a permanent gallery of Nicaraguan primitivist paintings. Granada's branch of the Instituo Nicaragüense de Turismo (INTUR), the government tourist office, is housed here as well. ✉ *Calle Arsenal and Av. Miguel Cervantes (2 blocks east of Catedral de la Asunción),* ☎ *505/552–5535.* ✉ *C$12.* ☉ *Daily 9–6.*

1 Another church worth visiting is the **Iglesia de la Merced** (✉ 2 blocks west of park's southwest corner). Built in 1781, only its original facade remains. The structure was rebuilt, of course, in 1863 after Walker's retreat. The church has a tower with good views. Ask the caretaker for permission to climb it.

Stroll or take one of the ubiquitous, low-cost horse-carriage cabs (the painfully thin horses are a sorry sight, but locals say it's a parasite, not starvation, that gives them that bony look) down Calle la Calzada to the lakeshore. On the lake, at the end of Calle La Calzada, a warehouse now occupies the foundation of the first fort built by the Spanish in Central America, the **Fuerte de la Muelle.** Little remains except a few old cannons in the park next door. About 109 yards south along the lakeshore is the **Centro Turístico,** a long, shady waterfront park lined with informal, local-patronized discos, restaurants, and other diversions. On weekends, the place fills with families. The park is slated for major redevelopment. A few restaurants will rent boats to tour Las Isletas and Isla Zapatera.

From here it's a few kilometers farther south to **Puerto Aseses** (☎ 505/552–2269), where you can book a boat tour and spend an hour or two cruising through Granada's famed Las Isletas, the 360-odd tiny, plant-bedecked islands that lie offshore. A taxi will take you to Aseses for about C$15 a person.

Dining

Classy dining abounds in this classy old colonial town. A unique Granadino twist to getting out of town for lunch is to take a short boat ride to the nearby Las Isletas, a speckling of 300 islands on the lake

outside the city. A few restaurants scatter among the tiny specks, and you arrange the details at the dock.

$$-$$$ ✕ **Mediterráneo.** Hostess-owner Enriqueta Mateo, unfailingly gracious
★   and well informed, has a worldliness that shines through on the Spanish menu infused with international accents. The paellas are exceptional. A wonderfully romantic atmosphere pervades; the elegantly furnished dining room, done in rosy terra-cotta tones, flanks a lovely interior garden, enhanced by candlelight, plants, and quietly flowing fountains. ⊠ *Calle El Caimito,* ☎ *505/552–6764. AE, MC, V. Closed Mon.*

$$-$$$ ✕ **Restaurante Doña Conchi's.** You can still see bullet holes in the
★   wall, remnants of a botched execution attempt of William Walker by firing squad in this house. But these are happier times. The gracious Doña Conchi hails from Zaragoza and dishes up meats, hams, and fish—the Spanish family cuisine she calls *cocina familiar*—in a lovely garden in back, all to the accompaniment of a whispering fountain. Browse Conchi's artisan creations in the shop while you wait. ⊠ *Calle El Caimito,* ☎ *505/552–7376. AE, MC, V. Closed Tues.*

$ ✕ **Hospedaje Central.** This *very* basic backpackers' lodging has great appeal as an incredibly friendly place to stop for a drink or evening meal. Particularly popular are the all-you-can-eat spaghetti dinners. Informality reigns here: if the small dining room is full, someone will help you carry a table and chairs out to the sidewalk. The Central has become the unofficial information exchange center in town, to which nonguests are welcome. The place is loaded with people who were "only going to visit Nicaragua for a few days" but have decided to stay on longer. ⊠ *Calle La Calzada, 2 blocks east of Parque Colón,* ☎ *505/ 552-7044. No credit cards.*

$ ✕ **Nica Buffet.** U.S. transplants Steve and Ceffie run an old-fashioned breakfast–only diner in the heart of town. They dish up omelettes, pancakes, French toast, and bagels, just like back home. There's more exotic fare on the menu too: Nicaraguan-style gallo pinto or huevos rancheros. It's worth a stop even if your hotel does include breakfast in the room rate. ⊠ *1 block south and ½ block west of Parque Colón, across from Casa Pellas,* ☎ *no phone. No credit cards. Closed Thurs. No lunch or dinner.*

$ ✕ **El Zaguán.** Grilled meat and fish are the order of the day at this semi–open-air courtyard restaurant organized around a centerpiece open grill. Beef, chicken, and the house fish specialty, the freshwater guapote, are prepared Argentine style on the *parrillada* with your choice of barbecue or spicy chimchuri sauce. ⊠ *Behind cathedral,* ☎ *505/552-2522. AE, MC, V. Closed Mon.*

Lodging

There was a time when you only visited Granada as a day trip from Managua. With the increase in number of decent lodgings here in the last five years, you might consider doing Managua as a day trip from Granada instead.

$$ ⊞ **Hostal La Casona los Estrada.** The lobby and restaurant of Granada's most sumptuous lodging ooze colonial elegance and an attention to detail reflecting the owners' impeccable tastes in colonial art. Count on evening entertainment via a Steinway piano in the restaurant while you dine on meats and pastas. The much more modern rooms are pleasantly furnished with splashes of modern Nicaraguan art. ⊠ *½ block west of the Iglesia de San Francisco,* ☎ *505/552-7393,* FAX *505/552-7395,* WEB *www.casonalosestrada.com.ni. 5 rooms, 1 suite. Bar, restaurant, laundry service, meeting room; no room TVs. AE, MC, V.*

$$ ⊞ **Hotel Colonial.** This hotel, with its attentive service, is giving old standby the Alhambra some competition for the "best hotel in Granada" title. Keep your disappointment in check when you walk in: the fu-

turistic tile lobby gives little hint of the colonial-style elegance of the rooms, which have canopied beds and Nicaraguan art. ⊠ *North of Parque Colón,* ☎ *505/552–7581,* FAX *505/552–7299,* WEB *www.nicaragua-vacations.com. 27 rooms. Restaurant, room service, pool, gym, bar, laundry service, meeting room. AE, MC, V.*

$–$$ 🏨 **Hotel Alhambra.** A jewel on Granada's shady Parque Colón, the two-
★   story Alhambra is traditionally the essential Granada spot. The colonnaded, comfortably furnished lobby wraps around an interior courtyard garden with a murmuring fountain. Guest rooms are filled with a hodgepodge of modern desks, lamps, and the like, matched with old carved-wooden cabinets, double beds, and atmospheric pieces. The second-story rooms overlooking the plaza are simply wonderful, though rooms overlooking the pool in back are quieter but smaller. ⊠ *West of Parque Colón,* ☎ *505/ 552–4486,* FAX *505/552–2035. 54 rooms. Café, restaurant, room service, pool, bar, laundry service, meeting room, travel services. AE, MC, V.*

$ 🏨 **Hospedaje Italiano.** Arguably Granada's best value is this hotel run by a friendly Italian couple. Though it hasn't been around for long, it's built in typical Granada style with rooms arranged around a central garden. Rooms have comfy beds, with lots of pillows, white-tiled bathrooms, and shuttered windows that open to the quiet street. Breakfast is served in the large, high-ceilinged lobby, whose walls have a wraparound mural depicting Nicaragua's flamboyant history. ⊠ *Calle La Calzada, 4 blocks east of Parque Colón,* ☎ FAX *505/552–7047. 10 rooms. Laundry service; no room phones, no room TVs. MC, V.*

Nightlife

Raucous nightlife would be unseemly in this gracious old colonial city. Dining and conversation at one of the restaurants are usually the order of the night here. You can step more lively at the string of discos along the waterfront patronized largely by locals, though tourists are welcome, too.

Casa de las Alemanas (⊠ 2 blocks north and 1 block west of Parque Colón, ☎ 505/552–2325) offers quiet conversation over drinks, inside or out on the front terrace. Everyone makes a point to stop for drinks at **Hospedaje Central** (⊠ Calle La Calzada, 2 blocks east of Parque Colón, ☎ 505/552–7044) sometime during their stay here. The city and INTUR sponsor the Friday evening **Noche de Serenatas,** a spectacle of food and music on the Plaza de los Leones just north of Parque Colón. **Tu Bodeguita** (⊠ Calle La Calzada, 2 blocks east of Parque Colón, ☎ 505/883–2015) is a quiet two-story indoor–outdoor bar with a wide selection of appetizers.

Granada A to Z

BUS TRAVEL

Granada's long-distance bus station sits nine blocks west and one block north of Parque Colón, just north of the Hospital San Juan de Dios. Express minivans to Managua leave nearly continually from a small station ½ block south of the southwest corner of Parque Colón.

CAR TRAVEL

Reach Granada from Managua via the Carretera a Masaya. The trip takes about 45 minutes.

EMERGENCIES

➤ EMERGENCY CONTACTS: **Ambulance** (☎ 505/552–2711). **Fire** (☎ 505/ 552–4440). **Hospital San Juan de Dios** (⊠ west side of town, near bus station, ☎ 505/552–2022). **Police** (☎ 505/552–2929).

INTERNET

The largest supply of walk-in Web cafés in the country keeps hourly rates for Internet access (C$30) lower than elsewhere in Nicaragua.

The Binary Base is a particularly friendly spot with freshly squeezed fruit juices to sip and cookies to eat while you surf.

➤ INTERNET SERVICE: **The Binary Base** (⊠ across from San Francisco convent, ☎ no phone).

MAIL

➤ MAIL SERVICE: **Correos de Nicaragua** (⊠ Calle Atravesada, just west of Parque Colón, downtown, ☎ 505/552–3331; ☉ Mon.–Sat. 7–7).

MONEY MATTERS

You can change cash here at any bank around town. Rates vary little from place to place. Any branch of Bancentro or Banco de Finanzas (BDF) will cash American Express traveler's checks and are generally open weekdays 8–noon and 2–4, as well as Saturday morning.

➤ BANK INFORMATION: **Bancentro** (⊠ Calle Atravesada, ☎ 505/552–6555). **Banco de Finanzas** (BDF; ⊠ Calle Atravesada, ☎ 505/552–4005).

TELEPHONES

If your room doesn't have a phone, the Empresa Nicaragüense de Telecomunicaciones (Enitel) provides local and international telephone service.

➤ PHONE SERVICE: **Empresa Nicaragüense de Telecomunicaciones** (Enitel; ⊠ east side of Parque Colón, just north of the cathedral).

TRANSPORTATION AROUND GRANADA

Granada's city center is most enjoyably explored on foot. The city has standard automobile taxis, but more fun are the horse-drawn carriages that locals use as well. An hour-long tour by carriage runs about C$140.

VISITOR INFORMATION

The government tourist office, the Instituto Nicaragüense de Turismo (INTUR), maintains a branch in Granada with an exceptionally helpful staff. It's open weekdays 8 to 12 and 2 to 5.

➤ TOURIST INFORMATION: **Instituto Nicaragüense de Turismo** (INTUR; ⊠ Convento San Francisco, ☎ 505/552–6858).

Volcán Mombacho Natural Reserve

10 km (6 mi) south of Granada.

★ The **Mombacho Volcano,** which looms over Granada, used to be one of those so-close-and-yet-so-far attractions. This unique cloud-forest reserve (the Reserva Natural Volcán Mombacho) was opened to the public with the support of the private Cocibolca Foundation and U.S. aid and has a research station and visitor center at its summit. A well-marked, 2-km-long (1-mi-long) hiking trail surrounds the verdant crater of this dormant volcano, and numerous signs (in Spanish) explain the reserve's diverse flora and fauna—more than 450 species of plants, 87 varieties of orchids, and 118 species of birds—some of which exist nowhere else. At 4,440 ft above sea level, the park has excellent views of the valley and lakes below. The reserve is only 10 km (6 mi) and a cheap taxi ride from Granada; on the Nandaime highway, turn right at the park's entrance and continue another 1½ km (1 mi) to the park entrance. From here it's another 5 km (3 mi) to the trail, hiking up through pretty coffee plantations. If you're tuckered out, ride in the back of the reserve's 20-seat truck to the top. The drive up the steep road takes about 20 minutes. A chilly altitude difference between the volcano summit and the warm lowlands is noticeable; bring a jacket. **Oro Travel** (☎ 505/552–4568) in Granada can arrange transport to the volcano. **Granada's Mombotours** (☎ 505/552–4548) operates a C$490 canopy tour on Mombacho that guides you through the treetops via secure cables and

body harness across 16 platforms. ☎ *505/277–1681.* 🎫 *C$70.* ◷
Thurs.–Sun. 8–5, Tues.–Wed. by reservation only.

Rivas

111 km (67 mi) south of Managua.

Rivas is the capital of Nicaragua's main agricultural region. The last major town before the Costa Rican border, Rivas attracts lots of travelers taking a final look at the country before heading south to Costa Rica. Others stop here because it's convenient to San Juan del Sur, on the Pacific coast, and Isla de Ometepe, in Lake Nicaragua. Rivas owes its place in history to its location a stone's throw from both Lago de Nicaragua and the Pacific Ocean. The town has long been a way station for travelers touring by land or water. Cornelius Vanderbilt made this a major junction for his Accessory Transit Company, which transported passengers between the two coasts of the United States.

Apart from its sleepy streets, Rivas has a couple of sights. The **cathedral,** on the east side of Parque Central, is an open and airy colonial structure. Inside the dome is a painting portraying Catholicism, represented as a fearsome galleon, defeating ships representing Communism and Protestantism. Masonry, depicted as a warrior, lies dead amid the fray. The **Museo de Rivas** (☎ *505/453–0000*) is near the market and exhibits regional pre-Columbian artifacts. It's open weekdays 8:30 to noon and 2 to 5 and costs C$15.

Dining and Lodging

$ ✕🏠 **Hotel Cacique Nicarao.** Rivas's most upscale lodging option is a friendly, family-run place with bright, yet small rooms with exposed brick walls. The patio restaurant serves a mix of burgers, salads, and Nicaraguan cuisine. ✉ *1 block west of the main square,* ☎ *505/453–3234,* 🖷 *505/453–3120. 12 rooms. Restaurant, bar, laundry service. AE, MC, V.*

San Jorge

4 km (2 mi) east of Rivas.

Most people visit this small port town on the shore of Lake Nicaragua to take the boat to Isla de Ometepe. It's also worth a visit to dine at one of the many seafood restaurants with spectacular views of the lake. Buses for Rivas (30 minutes, 60 ¢) leave the dock every half hour 6 AM to 5 PM. Taxis hang around for arriving boat passengers; a ride to Rivas is C$30. The ferry to Moyogalpa on Isla de Ometepe (1 hour, C$35) departs the dock daily at 10:30 AM and 6 PM; on Sunday the boat leaves at noon and 1 PM. The capacity of the tiny wooden craft never ceases to amaze its owners (and its passengers). Even smaller boats also run this route.

En Route Sapoá and Peñas Blancas are, respectively, the Nicaraguan and Costa Rican immigration posts, some 36 km (22 mi) southeast from Rivas. Neither is an actual town with any food or accommodation. Both posts are open daily 6 AM–8 PM. Get an early start: exiting Nicaragua is straightforward, but expect long immigration and customs procedures to enter Costa Rica here.

San Juan del Sur

29 km (17 mi) southwest of Rivas.

After a brief stay in San Juan del Sur, Ernest Hemingway complained that the beer was warm, the music was lousy, and the women were ugly.

Most present-day travelers will leave considerably more satisfied. This is Nicaragua's one quintessential beach town, and it moves at a wonderfully lazy, Jimmy Buffet–type pace. SJDS, as most locals write the long town name, resembles the beach communities just south of here on Costa Rica's Guanacaste coast, but a decade ago, on the brink of discovery. San Juan del Sur and its pretty half-moon beach are tucked between two high headlands, offering shelter for a sweet but ramshackle little town, a small fishing fleet, and the odd pleasure craft. In the last few years a minor influx of European backpackers has inspired the beginnings of a tourist infrastructure, centered on Ricardo's Bar. The beachfront boulevard is lined with open-air seafood restaurants, with a few small hotels across the street or, at most, a block or two inland. This is the place to make your plans for all area activities, from surfing to sportfishing—dozens of pristine beaches lie within half an hour by car or boat.

Dining and Lodging

$$ ✕ **Ricardo's Bar.** Ricardo's is a logical first stop in town, as it offers reliable tourist information, Internet use, boogie-board rental, an English-language book exchange, and good food. Recommended dishes include seafood crepes and Ricardo's special, a chicken breast with shrimp and a cheese sauce. Day and night, the atmosphere is super lively, as travelers' chatter mixes with the sound of the music videos playing on the satellite TV. ⊠ *Waterfront road, 2 blocks west and 3 blocks north of bus stop,* ☎ *505/458–2502. AE, MC, V. Closed Tues.*

$$$ 🏨 **Hotel Casablanca.** The Casablanca has a great location and outstanding, personalized service. Try to stay in the upstairs suite, which has a balcony overlooking the sea across the street. The other rooms are small, though comfortable and air-conditioned. ⊠ *San Juan del Sur,* ☎ *505/458–2135,* 🖷 *505/488–2307,* 🕸 *www.sanjuandelsur.org.ni/casablanca. 14 rooms. Some refrigerators, pool, laundry service; no room phones. AE, MC, V.*

$$ 🏨 **Hotel Colonial.** You don't come across many hotels just one block from the ocean. This, plus the two–story hotel's brick construction, is a rarity in Nicaragua. A little air-conditioning and a shady garden keep things nice and cool. Rooms, with tile floors, are pleasantly furnished, though the bathrooms lack hot water; you probably won't miss it in this heat. Chello, the owner, knows all the local surfing hot spots. ⊠ *From bus stop, 1 block east, ½ block south,* ☎ 🖷 *505/458–2538. 12 rooms. Laundry service; no room phones. AE, MC, V.*

$$ 🏨 **Hotel Villa Isabella.** From the town's modest central plaza it's easy
★ to spot this distinguished hotel—it's the white, colonial-style house with a colorful flower garden out front. The polished hardwood floors, handcrafted wood furniture, walk-in closets, and large bathrooms with black Italian tiles give this hotel a touch of elegance. Continental breakfast is included in the extremely reasonable price. ⊠ *Central plaza, 3 blocks from oceanfront,* ☎ *505/458–2568,* 🖷 *505/458–2549,* 🕸 *www.sanjuandelsur.org/isabella. 7 rooms, 5 with bath. Laundry service; no room phones, no room TVs. AE, MC, V.*

LAGO DE NICARAGUA

Though its western shore is only an hour away from Managua, the Lago de Nicaragua offers some of Nicaragua's most isolated and unspoiled territory. With over 300 islands, many of them uninhabited, and an abundance of aquatic life normally seen only in the ocean, it comes close to being a natural wonder. The lake's unique fish population (including the world's only freshwater sharks) has led scientists to speculate that it was once a large bay that was cut off from the Pa-

cific by a volcanic eruption. As the salinity of the water decreased, the marine life slowly adapted. The people who live in the lake's tiny island settlements are among the friendliest and least harried of all Nicaraguans.

Lago de Nicaragua, the 10th-largest freshwater lake in the world, has played a key role in Nicaragua's history. The Chorotegans arrived here from Mexico early this last millennium as they fled from the war-making Olmecs. They were guided here by an oracle's message that they would settle next to a freshwater sea with two mountains in it. Arriving at the lake, they named it Cocibolca, or "Sweet Sea." The Spanish recognized the lake's strategic value and founded their major settlement, Granada, on its northwestern shore. In the 1800s, the lake made Nicaragua the preferred crossing point between the two oceans, and inspired the idea of a canal linking them. A U.S. company actually began work on the project in 1889, but went bust a few years later. The prospect of a canal here is still occasionally discussed, most recently by a group of Asian investors. The proposal these days is for a so-called "dry canal" that would combine water transport up the San Juan River, through the lake, then transfer to rail for the rest of the trip. Canal or no, the lake has little problem attracting visitors, who are drawn by the volcanoes of Ometepe, the rock drawings of Zapatera, and the work of the primitivist artisans of Solentiname.

Las Isletas

15–60 mins east of Granada by boat.

South of Granada is a group of 300 tiny islands teeming with plant and animal life—and a few *ricos* (rich folks)—who have erected elaborate mansions on their own private islands. Most of the islet specks are privately owned or are being snapped up in Nicaragua's burgeoning real estate boom; a few have bird reserves, small hotels, or restaurants. To tour the islands, head to Puerto Aseses by taxi, just outside Granada, to hire a boat (C$300 per hour). They'll stop at one of the islands for lunch or dinner if you ask, and most likely arrange for a pick-up time. You can expect a meal of rice and fresh-caught fish. On the island farthest from shore is the Fuerte San Pablo, originally built in 1783. Intended as a defense against pirate raids on Granada, the fort underwent restoration in the 1970s and is now quite modern and has an observation deck with commanding views.

Lodging

$$$ 🏨 **Hotel Isleta La Ceiba.** The Isletas' best lodging takes up two of the private island specks. Bungalows, plainly furnished, encircle the open-air dining area and docks. The setting has spectacular views of the lake and the Mombacho volcano. Rates include transportation to and from Puerto Aseses and all meals, and you dine on upscale Nicaraguan cuisine prepared on an open grill, all to the accompaniment of marimba music. ⊠ *Las Isletas,* ☎ *505/266–1018 in Managua,* FAX *505/266–0704 in Managua,* WEB *www.nicaraolake.com.ni. 10 cabins. Restaurant, bar, meeting room; no room phones, no room TVs. AE, MC, V.*

Islas Zapatera and El Muerto

2 hrs southeast of Granada by boat.

Boats from Puerto Aseses are available for day trips to these two islands, about 19 km (12 mi) south of Granada. Both were once rich in archaeological treasures, but many of the best ones were carted off to museums in Managua and Granada. The Iglesia de San Francisco in Granada is actually the best present-day repository of Zapatera's for-

mer archaeological wealth. Zapatera, now protected as the Archipiélago de Zapatera National Park, contains the remains of Sozaofe, an ancient temple. El Muerto, once a sacred burial site, is full of tombs and petroglyphs. Be sure your fare includes the service of a guide. Only Zapatera is inhabited today, and neither island has food or lodging or facilities for visitors.

Isla de Ometepe

★ *1 hr east of San Jorge by boat; 4 hrs southeast of Granada by boat.*

Ometepe, the twin-peaked island mentioned in the oracles' prophecy to the Chorotegans, draws the eye from miles away. Only a few miles off the lake's southern shore just east of Rivas, the island rises dramatically out of the water swathed in greenery that gets richer the closer you get. Ometepe was formed by two volcanoes, Concepción (5,282 ft) and Maderas (4,573 ft), that rose out of the water side by side. The island soil is rich in volcanic ash, which accounts for the heartiness of its plant life. The forests are filled with wildlife, including several species of rambunctious monkeys and beautiful exotic birds. Explorers will have little trouble poking around this wilderness by foot or on horseback. If you're up for a climb, both volcanoes offer incredible views, and Madera (on the island's eastern side) has a hidden crater lake at the top. Also worth exploring are the archaeological sites scattered over the island, including stone carvings and petroglyphs made by the Chorotegans and other tribes.

The volcanoes tower menacingly over the island's villages, which shiver on the shore as far away from the two beasts as possible. Moyogalpa and Altagracia, both served by ferry from the mainland, are the island's main settlements. It's not very hard to get here—just four hours by boat from Granada and an easier one hour from San Jorge. But in many ways, it's a world apart from the rest of the country. Mark Twain described Ometepe as "isolated from the world and its noise," during his 1866 trip here. Indeed, with just 35,000 residents and a scant 300 cars, it still is.

Sights to See

You'll have no trouble learning the lay of the land, as most hotels and restaurants proudly display a map of Ometepe that lists all the pertinent facts about the place. This island is best conceived as two circular islands joined together by a narrow isthmus. Concepción anchors the more developed half; Ometepe's two largest towns are here. Moyogalpa is on the western shore, and Altagracia is on the northeast side near the isthmus that leads east to Madera, the other half of the island. A coast road circles Concepción, linking all of its settlements. Another road runs south of Altagracia across the isthmus and halfway around Madera in either direction.

Beyond exploring the pastoral towns and beaches, the main activity on Ometepe is hiking the two volcanoes. Even if you're not a climber, it's worth walking up their slopes a little way to catch breathtaking views of the island and lake. The trail to the top of Concepción starts near Altagracia and takes about five hours each way. Another trail of similar length and difficulty begins near Moyogalpa. The trail up Madera Volcano, beginning at Balgüe, takes roughly four hours each way. The dazzling crater lake at the top makes it worth the effort. Wildlife abounds—monkeys, birds, sloths—and the views from both peaks are remarkable. A 460-ft waterfall on Madera is the easiest to reach of four known cataracts on the volcano. It is most easily accessed via San Ramón.

The use of a guide is highly recommended for both volcano hikes, as the trails are arduous and not always easy to follow. Your hotel can arrange one. (Avoid the self-appointed guides who offer services at the

docks when you step off the boat.) A great bet, with its knowledgeable bilingual guides, is **Exploring Ometepe** at the Hotel Ometepetl (☎ 505/777–3835) in Moyogalpa. **Julio Castillo** at the Hotel Castillo (☎ 505/552–8744) in Altagracia comes from a long line of Ometepe experts. He can recommend guides, suggest itineraries, and let you peruse *Ometepe: Isla de Círculos y Espirales,* a rare illustrated book on the island's history and archaeology.

Altagracia's main square is decorated with pre-Columbian stone carvings discovered on the island. Near Balgüe, the largest settlement on the Madera side of the island, is a site with dozens of ancient petroglyphs; others can be found between Balgüe and Magdalena. They are thought to date from the 11th–13th centuries, but their spiral etchings are of unknown significance. Ask Julio Castillo in Altagracia for directions. A few beaches east of Altagracia are well worth visiting, including Punta Tagüizapa, which is beautiful and isolated.

Lodging

The island has a smattering of basic, but acceptable lodging options. None would pass for luxury accommodation on the mainland. All serve equally basic but filling meals.

$$ 🏨 **Villa Paraíso.** Facing east across Lake Nicaragua from Playa Santo Domingo, the Paraíso has basic, comfortable accommodations—six rooms in the main building and 11 cabinas, the latter with private baths. The hotel's bar and restaurant overlook the lake, and the staff can help organize volcano and other island tours. ⊠ *Playa Santo Domingo,* ☎ FAX *505/453–4675. 6 rooms with shared bath, 11 cabinas. Restaurant, beach, boating, horseback riding, bar, laundry service; no a/c in some rooms, no room phones. MC, V.*

$–$$ 🏨 **Cari Hotel y Marina.** You can see the Cari from the ferry as you dock in Moyogalpa. Like all of Ometepe's hotels and hospedajes, it has small, clean rooms, some with private baths, at rock-bottom prices. In addition, this hotel rents cars and canoes and leads island tours. If you're feeling mellow, hang out in the open-air restaurant-bar and watch island women do their laundry on washing platforms in the lake. ⊠ *½ block south of dock, Moyogalpa,* ☎ FAX *505/459–4263. 14 rooms, 7 with bath. Restaurant, laundry service, car rental; no room TVs, no room phones. MC, V.*

$ 🏨 **Hotel Castillo.** Julio Castillo continues his late father Ramón's long-held role as unofficial historian and general source of relevant Ometepe information. His one-story hotel encircling a quiet courtyard has clean, comfortable little rooms, within walking distance of Altagracia's petroglyph collection. ⊠ *1 block south and ½ block west of Parque Central, Altagracia,* ☎ FAX *505/552–8744. 15 rooms, 7 with bath. Restaurant, horseback riding; no room TVs, no room phones. MC, V.*

Ometepe A to Z

BY BOAT

Ometepe is linked to the mainland by frequent boat service from Granada and San Jorge near Rivas. Boats from Granada use the dock at Altagracia, while boats from San Jorge dock at Moyogalpa. Small wooden passenger boats from San Jorge (C$20) leave daily at 9 and 11:30 AM and 12:30, 1:30, 2:30, 3:30, 4:30, and 5:30 PM. They return from Moyogalpa at 5:30, 6, 6:30, 7, and 11:30 AM and 1:30 and 3:30 PM. A large car ferry leaves San Jorge daily at 10:30 AM and 2:30 and 5:30 PM; it returns from Moyogalpa at 6:45 AM and 12:30 and 4 PM. It provides a much smoother ride than the smaller boats it you are prone to motion sickness. Large, steel passenger ferries leave Granada on Monday and Thursday at 1 PM. Vehicles may be left in a secure parking facility at the docks in San Jorge.

TELEPHONES

The Empresa Nicaragüense de Telecomunicaciones (Enitel) in Moyogalpa provides local and international telephone service.

➤ PHONE SERVICE: **Empresa Nicaragüense de Telecomunicaciones** (Enitel; ⊠ 3 blocks east, 1 block south of dock, Moyogalpa).

TRANSPORTATION AROUND OMETEPE

Buses (C$6) circle the Concepción half hourly 5 AM to 5 PM in both directions. (These buses give a great whirlwind tour of the island.) No taxis serve the island.

NICARAGUA A TO Z

To research prices, get advice from other travelers, and book travel arrangements, visit www.fodors.com.

AIR TRAVEL

American Airlines flies twice daily between Miami and Managua. Continental Airlines connects Houston and Managua with once-daily flights. Grupo TACA flies once daily between Miami and Managua, as well as connecting Nicaragua's capital with its hub in San Salvador. Nicaraguan airline Sansa flies once daily between Miami and Managua. Panama's COPA connects Managua with other Central American capitals. Spain's Iberia flies to Managua several times weekly from Madrid via Miami.

➤ AIRLINES: **American** (⊠ 1 block south of Plaza España, Barrio Jonathán González, Managua, ☎ 505/266–3900). **Continental** (⊠ Km 4½ Carretera a Masaya, Planes de Altamira, Managua, ☎ 505/278–2834). **COPA** (⊠ Planes de Altamira, Managua, ☎ 505/267–0045). **Grupo TACA** (⊠ Plaza España, Barrio Bolonia, Managua, ☎ 505/266–3136). **Iberia** (⊠ Plaza España, Barrio Bolonia, Managua, ☎ 505/266–4296). **Sansa** (⊠ Plaza España, Barrio Bolonia, Managua, ☎ 505/268–2507).

BUS TRAVEL

TicaBus has service to Tegucigalpa, departing daily at 5 AM (10 hours, C$280); to San José, daily at 5:45 and 7 AM (10 hours, C$140); and to San Salvador, departing daily at 4:45 AM (11 hours, C$350). All buses are roomy and air-conditioned, and you should buy tickets one day before your departure. Service from San Salvador continues north to Guatemala City and Tapachula, Mexico; San José buses continue south to Panama City. Air-conditioned, spacious King Quality buses depart for Tegucigalpa daily at 4:30 AM (10 hours, C$280) and to San Salvador daily (11 hours, C$420). Nicabus departs daily at 6 AM for San José (10 hours, C$280). Transnica leaves for San José daily at 5:30 AM (10 hours, C$140) and for San Salvador daily at 5 AM (12 hours, C$350).

➤ BUS INFORMATION: **King Quality** (⊠ 2 blocks east of Cine Dorado, Barrio Martha Quezada, Managua, ☎ 505/228–1454). **Nicabus** (⊠ 1 block west of Hotel Inter-Continental, Barrio Martha Quezada, Managua, ☎ 505/228–1373). **TicaBus** (⊠ 2 blocks east of Cine Dorado, Barrio Martha Quezada, Managua, ☎ 505/222–6094). **Transnica** (⊠ 1 block east of Rotonda Santo Domingo, Barrio El Carmen, Managua, ☎ 505/278–2090).

BUSINESS HOURS

Normal business and government office hours are 8 AM to noon and 2 PM to 4 PM, weekdays. Banks usually close slightly earlier and are open on Saturday morning. Larger stores in Managua stay open continuously throughout the day. Smaller businesses in the capital, as well as out in the countryside observe a two-hour afternoon break.

CAR RENTAL

Managua is the best place to rent a car, where C$420–C$700 will get you an economy vehicle with air-conditioning and a decent daily mileage allowance. Weekly rentals can be had for as little as C$2,000 and usually include unlimited mileage. All major companies have offices at the airport and in the city. Local firms will usually give slightly better rates than branches of North American chains. Airport rates tend to be higher than the same firm's city branch.

➤ CAR RENTAL AGENCIES: **Budget** (✉ 1 block west of Montoya statue, Barrio El Carmen, ☎ 505/266–6226; airport ☎ 505/263–1222). **Hertz** (✉ Km 4 Carretera Sur, Barrio Batahola Sur, ☎ 505/266–8399; airport ☎ 505/233–1237). **Lugo** (✉ 2 blocks north, 1 block west of Canal 2, Barrio Bolonia, ☎ 505/266–5240; airport ☎ 505/263–2368). **Targa** (✉ 1 block east, 2 blocks north of Av. Bolívar Esso station, Barrio Martha Quezada, ☎ 505/222–4824; airport ☎ 505/233–1176).

CAR TRAVEL

There's less traffic in Managua than in other Central American cities, but this doesn't mean you won't run into congestion, especially during morning and evening rush hours. Directional signing is plentiful on main highways; less so off the beaten path. Street names might exist in cities, but are rarely used, and signing is almost nonexistent. (León is the surprising exception to this rule.) Your own vehicle gives you freedom to stop and go as you please: roadside stands and *miradors* (scenic lookout points) abound, and they're nearly impossible to visit passing through on a bus. Driving at night outside cities and towns is not recommended for several reasons: there is a remote possibility of robbery, but you are more likely to run into cars without headlights and unwitting two- and four-legged pedestrians on the roads.

GASOLINE

Gasoline sells for C$24–C$26 per *galón*. A few self-service pumps get you a discount of C$1 per gallon. Stations are plentiful in major cities. Fill up there if you're heading farther afield.

ROAD CONDITIONS

Major roads in the populated western half of the country are in good shape, but you'll need a four-wheel-drive vehicle to negotiate most smaller roads, especially during the rainy season.

DINING

Managua and Granada have seen an invasion of upscale restaurants in recent years. Basic dining places frequented by locals are often called a *comedor* or *cafetín*. Even in the most expensive places, dining is an informal affair, and reservations are rarely required or needed.

MEALTIMES

Upscale or slightly formal restaurants usually serve lunch until 3, then reopen again for dinner at 6. Comedores and eating places frequented by locals are generally open all day but rarely serve an evening meal.

EMBASSIES AND CONSULATES

The U.S. embassy is open Monday to Wednesday and Friday 10 to 11 and 1:30 to 3:30; the Canadian consulate, Monday to Thursday 2 to 4; and the U.K. consulate 9 to noon and 2 to 4.

➤ EMBASSIES AND CONSULATES CONTACTS: **Canada** (✉ 2 blocks west of Los Pipitos, Barrio Bolonia, Managua, ☎ 505/268–0433). **United Kingdom** (✉ main entrance to Los Robles, 4th house on right, Los Robles, Managua ☎ 505/278–0014). **United States** (✉ Km 4½ Carretera Sur, Barrio Batahola Sur, Managua, ☎ 505/266–6010).

EMERGENCIES

➤ EMERGENCY CONTACTS: **Ambulance** (☏ 128). **Fire** (☏ 115). **Police** (☏ 118).

➤ HOSPITALS: **Hospital Antonio Lenin Fonseca** (✉ Las Brisas, Managua, ☏ 505/266–6547). **Hospital Bautista** (✉ Barrio Largespalda, Managua, ☏ 505/249–7070).

HEALTH

Managua's tap water is reportedly safe to drink but heavily chlorinated. Most travelers stick to bottled water. The intense heat and sun make replenishment with fluids and protection with sunscreen a must.

Malaria remains a problem in parts of the heavily forested eastern half of the country. Take adequate precautions with a preventative medication. Contact the Centers for Disease Control and Prevention for advice on medications and for other health-related matters.

➤ HEALTH CONTACT: **Centers for Disease Control and Prevention** (☏ 877/394–8747, FAX 888/232–3299, WEB www.cdc.gov).

HOLIDAYS

New Year's Day (January 1); Holy Thursday–Easter Sunday (March or April); Labor Day (May 1); Anniversary of the Revolution (July 19); Battle of San Jacinto (September 14); Independence Day (September 15); Feast of the Immaculate Conception (December. 8); Christmas (December 25).

LANGUAGE

Spanish is the official language. Those in the tourist industry will likely speak some English. The typical person on the street will probably know none. A Caribbean-accented English is the lingua franca of the Atlantic coast.

LODGING

International luxury hotel chains, found only in Managua, offer first-world amenities for first-world prices. These places have all the extras, of course—restaurants, pools, shops, and so forth—and are conveniently located. The biggest surprise is a second tier of small, medium-price hotels with clean clean, comfortable accommodations and a far more authentic experience of Nica hospitality. Most budget hotels are called *hospedajes,* or sometimes *casas de huéspedes*; a typical room will have concrete floors, two or three small cotlike beds, and shared bathrooms with cold water. Note, though, that some of these are considerably more comfortable than the average, and some do offer private baths and sometimes even air-conditioning.

CAMPING

Nicaragua has no formal campgrounds, and the countryside, with its thriving insect life, is decidedly inhospitable to campers. Your best bet for camping is the beach, but bring lots of bug repellent and guard your things carefully.

HOSTELS

Nicaragua has no Hostelling International affiliates. Matagalpa's Selva Negra does offer hostel-like accommodation.

MAIL AND SHIPPING

You can buy stamps from any office of Correos de Nicaragua, the country's privatized postal service, but to be sure those cards and letters will actually arrive, you should post them from Managua.

POSTAL RATES

An airmail letter to North America costs C$8.50, and if posted from Managua's central post office—that's your best bet—arrives in about a week. To Europe, you'll pay C$11; delivery takes two weeks.

RECEIVING MAIL

You can receive mail at any town's central post office if addressed to Your Name, Lista de Correos, Correos de Nicaragua, Town, Department. You'll be charged C$2 per item retrieved.

Viajes Atlántida, the American Express affiliate in Managua, will hold mail for cardholders.

COURIER COMPANIES

Anything of value (or valuable looking) should be sent via a courier service. Federal Express and DHL have offices in Managua. DHL has offices in León and Matagalpa.

MONEY MATTERS

ATMS

ATMs (a *cajero automático* in Spanish) are still rare breeds in Nicaragua. Your best bet in finding a Cirrus- or Plus-linked machine is a shopping mall, or a large Esso, Shell, or Texaco gas station convenience store on the highways heading out of Managua, Granada, or León. A very few of these give cash against an American Express card.

CURRENCY

Nicaragua's currency is the córdoba, named after Spanish explorer Francisco Hernández de Córdoba, who founded León and Granada. Locals often refer to the unit of currency as a "peso." Bills come in 10-, 20-, 50- and 100-córdoba as well as 25-centavo denominations. Coins come in 1- and 5-córdoba as well as 50-centavo denominations. The currency is devalued by about 1% a month against the U.S. dollar to keep prices relatively stable in the face of local inflation. At press time, the dollar, the only useful foreign currency here, was equal to roughly 14 córdobas. Córdoba prices are printed with a "C$" in front of the number. Handwritten prices show the $ sign inside the body of the "C." Dollars are also accepted by many stores, hotels, restaurants, and taxi drivers. Most upscale hotels quote prices in dollars, or the prevailing córdoba exchange rate. It is nearly impossible to exchange córdobas outside Nicaragua. Spend or change them before you leave.

CREDIT CARDS

Upscale hotels and restaurants accept credit cards, with Visa being the most widely accepted. MasterCard is a close second; American Express a distant third. Many small businesses add up to 5% on the total if you pay by credit card to offset the high fees they're charged for card transactions.

TRAVELER'S CHECKS

Traveler's checks remain difficult to cash in Nicaragua. All branches of Bancentro and Banco de Finanzas (BDF) will cash American Express checks for a 3% commission and a long wait. Multicambios in Managua will exchange American Express checks to córdobas much more quickly than any bank. Virtually no business accepts traveler's checks as payment.

PASSPORTS AND VISAS

Citizens of the United States and United Kingdom may enter Nicaragua for 90 days, and those from Canada, Australia, and New Zealand for 30 days, with just a passport. Immigration officials ruthlessly enforce a requirement that your passport have at least six months' remaining

validity beyond your exit from Nicaragua. All must purchase a $7 tourist card at the point of entry, payable in U.S dollars only.

SAFETY

Nicaragua has Central America's lowest crime rate, a mantra the tourism industry repeats often, but in a country where many workers make the equivalent of $2 per day, you'll represent enormous wealth. Watch your things carefully. Do not accept tours from random people who you meet on the street, especially on Ometepe. Always go with a verifiable tour guide that is a part of a hotel or organization (with an office and phone).

The Pacific coast beaches have strong currents and undertows, although there are no warning signs or lifeguards. Some remote northern regions near the Honduran border, off the standard tourist itinerary, remain laced with land mines.

TAXES

DEPARTURE TAX

The departure tax for international flights is $25, payable in dollars or córdobas.

VALUE ADDED TAX

A 15% nonrefundable sales tax called the "IGV" is collected on all transactions, but is usually already included in the price sticker you see at stores, bars, and restaurants. It's added to hotel bills.

TELEPHONES

COUNTRY AND AREA CODES

The country code for calling Nicaragua from abroad is 505. There are no city codes within the country.

LOCAL CALLS

All telephone numbers have seven digits. Simply dial that number when making a local call. (Ignore the old city codes still seen on signs and stationery.) Dial a "0" before the seven-digit number when calling another town, or any cellular number starting with "7" or "8." Dial 112 for nationwide directory assistance.

INTERNATIONAL CALLS

The semi-privatized telephone company the Empresa Nicaragüense de Telecomunicaciones (Enitel) has offices in most cities and towns for making international calls. Be aware that many people continue to refer to Enitel by its former name "Telcor." Toll-free international access codes are available for calling the United States, Canada, and the United Kingdom.

➤ ACCESS CODES: **AT&T** (☎ 164). **British Telecom** (☎ 175). **Canada Direct** (☎ 168). **MCI** (☎ 166). **Sprint** (☎ 161).

PUBLIC PHONES

Public telephones are sprouting up around Managua and, to a lesser extent, in other cities. They accept 1-córdoba coins or Publitel phone cards sold at most Enitel offices and many small stores and gas stations. Local calls from a pay phone cost an expensive C$1.95 per minute.

TIPPING

A tip is only expected at pricier restaurants, where it's often included (look for *servicio* on the check). Since most servers receive only minimal compensation, even a córdoba or two is a nice gesture at cheaper restaurants. Taxi drivers are not tipped. Generally, any stranger who offers to do you a favor (like watch your parked car) expects a tip.

TOURS

Careli Tours in Managua is Nicaragua's largest tour operator and specializes in large group excursions. Oro Travel in Granada is a smaller French-owned operation—English is spoken here, too—that gives friendly, attentive service. Tours Nicaragua, a smaller Managua-based operation, is operated by a terrifically fun and friendly Nicaraguan-American couple.

➤ TOUR COMPANIES: **Careli Tours** (☎ 505/278–2572, WEB www.carelitours. com). **Oro Travel** (☎ 505/552–4568, WEB www.orotravel.com). **Tours Nicaragua** (☎ 505/270–7851, WEB www.toursnicaragua.com).

TRANSPORTATION AROUND NICARAGUA

BY AIR

Plane travel to some pretty remote destinations in Nicaragua is easy, if not exactly popular. La Costeña flies from Managua to the Corn Islands and other destinations. Atlantic Airlines connects Managua with Bluefields, Corn Island, and Puerto Cabezas. A typical one-way flight from Managua to Corn Island off the Atlantic coast is about C$670. Check-in at smaller airports is very informal. You're allowed 30 pounds of luggage. Then you hop on the scale and the agent calls out your weight for all within earshot to hear. (They need to know how much weight the small plane is carrying.) The aircraft seats 10 to 15 people. The ride and the view are spectacular, but if you suffer fear of flying, you should probably stay away. Delays and cancellations are common during bad weather.

➤ DOMESTIC AIRLINES: **Atlantic Airlines** (✉ Aeropuerto Internacional de Managua, ☎ 505/222–5787). **La Costeña** (✉ Aeropuerto Internacional de Managua, ☎ 505/263–2142).

BY BUS

Buses are perhaps the best way to see and meet local people. You can actually cross the entire country for about C$70. Trips are usually about C$10 per hour, although express buses charge up to double the normal fare. Even the most far-flung hamlets are usually served by bus (except on the Atlantic coast, where there are few roads). Town markets usually double as bus depots. Most vehicles are vintage school buses from the United States, so don't expect air-conditioning. Overcrowding is common on popular routes, but passengers are usually very polite and friendly and the bus experience as a whole can be exhilarating. Try to get the *expreso* service between major cities if you can. It will shave significant time off your trip. In the south and on the Pacific coast, express service is provided in 20-seat minivans. In the north, it's a full-size bus. Safety is only really an issue on Managua city buses, where pickpockets sometimes work. Most intercity bus routes are serviced daily 5 AM to 6 PM.

VISITOR INFORMATION

The Instituto Nicaragüense de Turismo, or INTUR, is the government tourist office. It has branches in Managua, Bluefields, Carazo, Chinandega, Estelí, Granada, Juigalpa, León, Masaya, and Matagalpa. Ocotal and Rivas are staffed on weekdays. All have dedicated, helpful professionals genuinely interested in making your visit to Nicaragua easier. Printed information is still limited, but come armed with specific questions and these great people will have the answer for you. You can also call the North American toll-free number weekdays 9 to 5 (Eastern Time) for planning information.

➤ TOURISM INFORMATION: **Instituto Nicaragüense de Turismo** (INTUR; ✉ Apartado 5088, Managua, Nicaragua, ☎ 505/222–3333 in Managua; 800/737–7253 in North America; WEB www.intur.gob.ni).

WEB SITES

The daily newspaper, *La Prensa* (WEB www.laprensa.com.ni), is a good source (in Spanish) of daily news about the country. **Nicaragua's Best Guide** (WEB www.guideofnicaragua.com) is a monthly English-language Web magazine with helpful tourism information.

WHEN TO GO

Nicaragua's traditional lack of visitors means there aren't well-delineated high and low seasons. The selection of decent hotels decreases dramatically outside Managua and Granada, so reservations are a good idea year-round.

CLIMATE

Nicaragua's climate varies greatly between regions. The central mountains, regardless of season, remain lusciously cool and agreeable all year long. As for the rest of the country, heat reigns year-round. The wet season lasts from May to November, which is referred to here as *invierno* (winter); it usually rains at least once a day (though not for very long) during these months, and is rarely a hardship. But it can come down for days at a time in October. If you go to the Caribbean coastal lowlands, though, you'll get rained on no matter what time of year it is. The climate in December and January is the coolest, least humid, and least rainy; the hottest, dustiest months are March and April.

The following are the average daily maximum and minimum temperatures for Managua.

Jan.	87F	31C	May	90F	32C	Sept.	86F	30C
	69	21		78	26		72	22
Feb.	87F	31C	June	88F	31C	Oct.	86F	30C
	71	22		75	24		70	21
Mar.	91F	33C	July	87F	31C	Nov.	86F	30C
	73	23		75	14		70	21
Apr.	92F	33C	Aug.	87F	31C	Dec.	86F	30C
	77	25		75	24		69	21

7 COSTA RICA

Costa Rica's beauty would flatter a land ten times as large. The sheer plenty of flora and fauna packed into this tiny nation, combined with a wild variety of climates and landscapes, can make the senses reel. Riding horseback toward simmering volcanoes or tramping through cloud forests, you can daydream about the next day's beach visit or scuba jaunt. Add to the mix luxurious lodges and first-class restaurants, and it's clear why Costa Rica has become one of the hottest destinations in the Western Hemisphere.

H IGH ON THE "MUST VISIT" LISTS of seasoned and armchair travelers, Costa Rica is riding a wave of well-deserved popularity as an ecological wonderland. The mere mention of the country conjures up visions of rain forests, volcanoes, tropical beaches, and exotic wildlife. And it delivers on all these and more. For a country that's about the same size as the state of West Virginia, it's packed with incredible biological diversity, varied landscapes, and a seemingly endless selection of outdoor diversions, from bird-watching and beach trips to rigorous rafting and rain forest hiking adventures.

Costa Rica's raw natural beauty and accessibility gives it a broad range of visitors. Some are "soft adventure" types, looking to explore the wildlife reserves within the country's exemplary system of national parks and perhaps the luxe hotels along the sun-drenched Pacific beaches. (It doesn't hurt that you can also drink the water straight from the tap.) However, the beaches might also be the stomping ground of more serious adventurers on a mission to surf some of North Americas best waters. Whichever type you are, and whether you visit the tropical jungles of the Caribbean coast or the modern cities of the Central Valley, or both, it's apparent that from nearly every angle the country is downright gorgeous. It seems no one is passing up the opportunity to see for themselves.

History explains some of the reasons Costa Rica has managed to avoid the turmoil of the last half century, and has achieved a higher standard of living than its neighbors. Never an important part of the Spanish empire, Costa Rica was largely neglected during the colonial era and experienced most of its growth after independence from Spain. It is consequently a nation of immigrants, who came to work and prospered. Although most Latin American countries remain dominated by families that were granted vast tracts of land by the Spanish Crown, Costa Rica is more of a workingman's republic. Most Costa Ricans—or Ticos, as they call themselves—are middle class by Latin American standards, and are the descendents of independent small farmers. Ticos have a strong sense of national identity and pride themselves first on being Costa Ricans rather than Central Americans, or even Latin Americans.

The country's most impressive quality, however, is its biological diversity, seen in the variety of flora, fauna, landscapes, and microclimates within its frontiers. National parks and preserves cover about 15% of the country and are home to 850 species of birds, 205 species of mammals, 376 types of reptiles and amphibians, and more than 9,000 different species of flowering plants, among them 1,200 varieties of orchids. Landscapes include cool mountain valleys and massive volcanoes emitting tufts of smoke, hilly coffee *fincas* (farms) and flat banana groves, and sultry mangrove forests and palm-strewn beaches.

The many rivers that wind down the country's valleys churn through steep stretches that are popular white-water-rafting routes, and some end up as languid jungle waterways appropriate for both animal-watching and sportfishing. With mile upon mile of beaches backdropped by coconut palms and thick forest, the Caribbean and Pacific coasts are ideal for swimming and sunbathing, and when the sun goes down, many beaches are visited by nesting sea turtles. The oceans that hug those coasts hold intricate coral formations, rugged islands, colorful schools of fish, and plentiful waves, enticing anglers, surfers, and sea kayakers. What more could you want?

Pleasures and Pastimes

Bird-watching

Since the birds of Costa Rica (870 bird species) represent close to 10% of the total species in the world, many visitors to have come here to see our feathered friends. But if you're not one of them, leave yourself open to the experience. The birding here is incredible—especially at dawn and dusk. Tropical birds, including six kinds of toucans, 16 types of parrots and parakeets, and more than 50 varieties of hummingbirds color the forests and gardens, the sightings of which are hard to take for granted.

Dining

While it's possible to order everything from sushi to crepes in Costa Rica, most Ticos have a simple but delicious diet built around rice, beans, and the myriad fruits and vegetables that flourish here. Costa Rican food isn't spicy, and many dishes are seasoned with the same five ingredients—onion, salt, garlic, cilantro, and red bell pepper. Specialties include *arroz con pollo* (chicken with rice), *ensalada de palmito* (heart of palm salad), *sopa negra* (black bean soup), *gallo pinto* (rice with black beans for breakfast), and *casados* (plates of rice, beans, fried plantains, salad, cheese, and fish, chicken, or meat). *Sodas*—inexpensive restaurants comparable to diners—offer these choices for lunch and dinner. The Pacific Coast areas are known for seafood including corvina, a sea bass, yellowfin tuna, dorado, and mahimahi.

When you can, take advantage a *fresco natural*, a fresh-squeezed fruit drink (including carrot, orange, mango, star fruit, and more) that's inexpensive by North American standards. Coffee—which in the countryside may come heavily presweetened—is usually served with steamed milk, if you order it *con leche*. For dessert, *tres leches*, a sinfully rich cake of condensed and evaporated milk and sugar, or flan, a caramel-flavor custard, are customary.

CATEGORY	COST*
$$$$	over $20
$$$	$10–$20
$$	$5–$10
$	under $5

per person for main course at dinner

Lodging

Costa Rica has accommodations to fit every taste and budget, from modern luxury resorts complete with spas to rustic nature lodges with private cabanas surrounded by jungle. Away from cities, hotels in small towns and rural areas aim to be more than just a place to rest your head for the night. Many have nature preserves with hiking trails, butterfly gardens, hot-springs spas, private beaches, and adventure tours. Some employ resident guides who are experts in local flora and fauna and lead interpretive trips. Most visitors stay a night or two in the capital, but the most interesting places to stay are not in San José—although there are some charming colonial homes that have been converted to elegant and mid-price-range inns. Neighboring Escazú and Heredia have several upscale inns with excellent restaurants, which overlook coffee farms and are near the airport.

CATEGORY	COST*
$$$$	over $90
$$$	$50–$90
$$	$25–$50
$	under $25

for a double room, excluding service and tax (16.4%)

Costa Rica

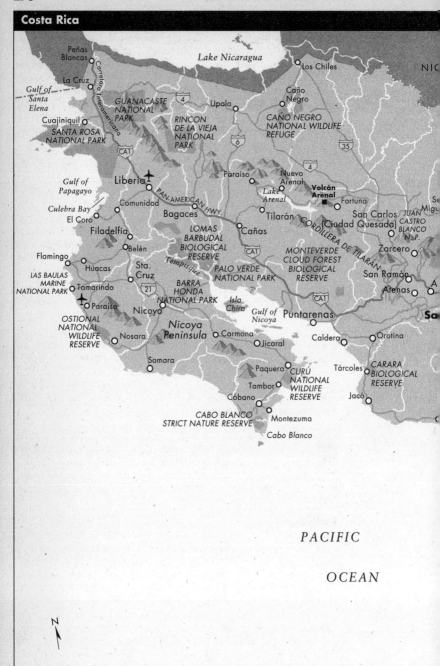

Peñas Blancas

Lake Nicaragua

Los Chiles

La Cruz

Gulf of Santa Elena

Carretera Interamericana

GUANACASTE NATIONAL PARK

Caño Negro

Upala

4

Cuajiniquil

RINCON DE LA VIEJA NATIONAL PARK

CAÑO NEGRO NATIONAL WILDLIFE REFUGE

SANTA ROSA NATIONAL PARK

6

I 35

Paraíso

Nuevo Arenal

4

Gulf of Papagayo

Liberia

CAT

Volcán Arenal

PAN AMERICAN HWY

Lake Arenal

Fortuna

San Carlos (Ciudad Quesada)

JUAN CASTRO BLANCO N.P.

Culebra Bay

El Coro

Comunidad

Bagaces

Tilarán

CORDILLERA DE TILARÁN

Filadelfia

LOMAS BARBUDAL BIOLOGICAL RESERVE

Cañas

Zarcero

Belén

CAT

MONTEVERDE CLOUD FOREST BIOLOGICAL RESERVE

San Ramón

Flamingo

Huacas

Sta. Cruz

Tempisque

PALO VERDE NATIONAL PARK

Atenas

LAS BAULAS MARINE NATIONAL PARK

Tamarindo

21

BARRA HONDA NATIONAL PARK

Isla Chira

CAT

Paraíso

Nicoya

Gulf of Nicoya

Puntarenas

Sa

OSTIONAL NATIONAL WILDLIFE RESERVE

Nosara

Nicoya Peninsula

Carmona

Caldera

Orotina

Jicaral

Samara

Paquera

CURÚ NATIONAL WILDLIFE RESERVE

Tárcoles

CARARA BIOLOGICAL RESERVE

Tambor

Cóbano

Jacó

CABO BLANCO STRICT NATURE RESERVE

Montezuma

Cabo Blanco

PACIFIC

OCEAN

N

0   30 miles

0   45 km

Rain Forests

The lowland rain forests of Costa Rica and the rest of the New World tropics are the most complex biological communities that exist. A typical hectare (2½ acres) of Costa Rican rain forest might be home to nearly 100 species of trees, for example—30 is typical in the richest forests of the United States. In addition to trees, you'll see giant rain forest versions of orchids, epiphytes and other plants common to U.S. households, as well as sloths, monkeys, copious birds, and more.

Filled with giant strangler figs and dripping with moss, Monteverde's private reserve is a good place to hike through primeval cloud forests. Even a quick walk through Manuel Antonio on the way to the beach will reveal all kinds of wildlife. Whenever possible, it's best to walk or hike with a local guide—a good one will point out plants and animals you will surely miss if you go on your own, and will explain the complex interactions between flora, fauna, and climate.

Volcanoes

Nothing in Costa Rica rivals the sheer mass and power of Volcán Arenal, which is often ringed with an ominous haze by day. At night, you can see red hot molten lava oozing from the cone, a flirtatious dance with disaster. In August 2000, an eruption sent poisonous gases spilling down the eastern side of the mountain, killing a tour guide from San José and two tourists from Texas who were watching from a supposedly safe distance. Geologists who scrutinized the area after the tragedy found the popular Tabacón hot-springs resort and a camping area to be in a high-risk zone, but this hasn't stopped visitors from flocking to them. The government has since posted warning signs at the hot springs and various other points around the volcano.

Wildlife

Costa Rica covers less than 0.03% of the earth's surface but contains nearly 4% of the planet's animal species. Flitting around Costa Rica are more than 2,000 species of butterflies, including the huge and incandescent blue morpho. You can expect to see coatis (a long-nose, long-tailed relative of the raccoon), monkeys, and perhaps a sloth or agouti (largish rodent). Sightings of large mammals, including wildcats and tapirs, are extremely rare. On the plus side for most people, you probably won't see any of Costa Rica's 18 species of poisonous snakes either. (Snakes will always try to flee unless cornered or protecting a nest.) Hiring local guides will increase your chances of seeing wildlife.

Exploring Costa Rica

Located in the middle of the country, the capital, San José, is also the center of national political, cultural, and economic life, with a third of Costa Rica's 4 million people living here, in surrounding suburbs, and the neighboring cities of Heredia, Alajuela, and Cartago. To the northeast, in northern Guanacaste and Alajuela, is Volcán Arenal and Monteverde Cloud Forest. Tamarindo is on the Nicoya Peninsula, jutting out into Pacific Coast, and Manuel Antonio National Park, is on the central Pacific coast near San José.

Great Itineraries

IF YOU HAVE 5 DAYS

Don't spend much time in **San José**—instead quickly head to the **Central Valley** and one of the luxe resorts. After a couple nights of R&R, head to the majestic and active **Volcán Arenal,** stopping en route for a soak at **Tabacón** hot springs. After a night in this area, return to San José for a flight to a Pacific Coast beach resort, like **Tamarindo** or **Manuel**

Antonio National Park, or a remote jungle lodge, and spend the rest of your time here.

From **San José** head to one of the **Central Valley** inns for a night or two to acclimatize to Costa's Rica's *pura vida*—the good life—philosophy. Then head to **La Paz Waterfall Gardens** en route to **Volcán Arenal.** Spend a night or two in the area, take a hike, a white-water rafting trip on the **Sarapiquí,** or a bird-watching boat trip through **Caño Negro Wildlife Refuge.** Then continue to **Monteverde Cloud Forest** and consider a canopy tour. Via San José, end your trip with a relaxing stint on the beach—choose the upscale beach areas of **Tamarindo** or **Manuel Antonio National Park,** or one of the less-touristed areas along the Pacific. Note that you can buy one-way tickets back to the capital, if your coastal destination changes.

Add to the 7-day itinerary a trip to the Osa Peninsula or the Atlantic Coast. For details, consult *Fodor's Costa Rica.*

Exploring San José

Downtown San José

A GOOD WALK

Start at the eastern end of the **Plaza de la Cultura** ①, where wide stairs lead down to the **Museo de Oro** ②, whose gold collection deserves a good hour or two. Next to the museum entrance, pop into the Instituto Costarricense de Turismo (ICT tourist office) for a free map, bus schedule, and brochures. Wander around the bustling plaza and slip into the **Teatro Nacional** ③ for a look at the elegant interior and perhaps a cup of coffee in the lobby café. Leaving the theater, you'll be facing west, with the city's main eastbound corridor, Avenida 2, to your left. Walk 1½ blocks west along Avenida 2 to the **Parque Central** ④ and **Catedral Metropolitana** ⑤. Cross Avenida 2 and head north one block on Calle Central to Avenida Central, where you should turn left and follow the pedestrian zone to the small plaza next to the **Banco Central** ⑥. Continue west along the pedestrian zone to the **Mercado Central** ⑦, and shop or browse at your leisure. Head back east two blocks on the Avenida Central pedestrian zone, then turn left on Calle 2, and walk one block north to the green-and-gray stuccoed **Correos** ⑧, the central post office. From there, return to Avenida Central and walk east along the mall back to the Plaza de la Cultura.

From the eastern end of the Plaza de la Cultura, near the Museo de Oro, walk two blocks east on Avenida Central, turn left onto Calle 9, walk one block north, turn right, and slither halfway down the block to the **Serpentario** ⑨, which has an interesting collection of creepy crawlers. Turn left when you leave and head 1½ blocks west on Avenida 1 and one block north to **Parque Morazán** ⑩. Walk across the park— be careful crossing busy Avenida 3—and walk along the yellow metal school building to shady **Parque España** ⑪. On the north side of the park, on Avenida 7, is the modern Instituto Nacional de Seguros (INS) building, whose 11th-floor **Museo de Jade** ⑫ has an extensive American-jade collection and great city views.

From the INS building, continue east on Avenida 7 two blocks, passing the Cancilleria, or Foreign Ministry, and the Embajada de México (Mexican Embassy) on your left; then turn right on Calle 15 and walk a block south to the corner of **Parque Nacional** ⑬. Take a look at the Monumento Nacional at the center of the park, and then head two blocks south to the entrance of the **Museo Nacional** ⑭, housed in the

old Bellavista Fortress. On the west side of the fortress lies the terraced **Plaza de la Democracia** ⑮; from here you can walk west down Avenida Central to return to the Plaza de la Cultura.

TIMING

This walk can take an entire day if you pause to absorb each museum and monument and stop to shop here and there. You can, however, easily split the tour in half: see all the sights west of the Plaza de la Cultura (①–⑧) one day and the remaining places (⑨–⑮) on another. Every stop on this tour is open Tuesday–Friday; if you're here on Monday or a weekend, check the hours listed below to make sure the sights you want to see are open.

SIGHTS TO SEE

❻ Banco Central (Central Bank). Outside the western end of Costa Rica's unattractive, modern federal reserve bank are 10 sculpted figures of bedraggled *campesinos* (peasants). The small, shady plaza south of the bank is popular with hawkers, money changers, and retired men, and can be a good place to get a shoe shine and listen to street musicians. Beware: the money changers here are notorious for circulating counterfeit bills and using doctored calculators to shortchange unwitting tourists. ⊠ *Between Avdas. Central and 1 and Cs. 2 and 4, Barrio La Merced.*

❺ Catedral Metropolitana (Metropolitan Cathedral). To the east of the park stands this not terribly interesting neoclassic structure, built in 1871, with a corrugated tin dome; inside, however, the cathedral has patterned floor tiles and framed polychrome bas-reliefs. The interior of the small chapel (Sagrario) on the cathedral's north side is even more ornate than the cathedral itself, but it's usually closed. Masses are held throughout the day on Sunday starting at 6 AM. ⊠ *Between Avdas. 4 and 2 and Cs. Central and 1, Barrio La Catedral,* ☎ *221–3820.* ⊘ *Weekdays 6 AM–noon and 3–6 PM, Sun. 6 AM–9 PM.*

❽ Correos (Central Post Office). The handsome, carved exterior of the post office, dating from 1917, is hard to miss among the bland buildings surrounding it. There's a display of first-day stamp issues upstairs, from where you can see the loading of *apartados* (post-office boxes) going on below: Ticos covet these hard-to-get boxes, as the city's lack of street addresses makes mail delivery a challenge. A small café on the first floor of the Correos overlooks the bustling pedestrian boulevard and a small park shaded by massive fig trees. Behind the park is the marble facade of the exclusive, members-only Club Unión. The large building behind the Correos is the Banco Nacional, a state-run bank. ⊠ *C. 2 between Avdas. 1 and 3, Barrio La Merced.* ⊘ *Weekdays 8– 6:30, Sat. 8–noon.*

❼ Mercado Central (Central Market). This block-long melting pot is a warren of dark, narrow passages flanked by stalls packed with spices (some purported to have medicinal value), fish, fruit, flowers, pets, and wood and leather crafts. You'll also see dozens of cheap restaurants and snack stalls, including the country's first ice cream vendor. Be warned: the concentration of shoppers makes this a hot spot for pickpockets, purse snatchers, and backpack slitters. ⊠ *Avdas. Central and 1 and Cs. 6 and 8, Barrio La Merced.* ⊘ *Mon.–Sat. 6–6.*

NEED A BREAK?	**Ice cream** is an art in this country, and after a long walk on crowded sidewalks, it may just save your sanity. The crème de la cream is dished out by two prolific chains, Pop's and Wall's (formerly Mönpik). You'll find a Pop's on Avenida Central between Calles 11 and 13. Everyone loves the mango. There are two Wall's on Avenida Central, one at Calle

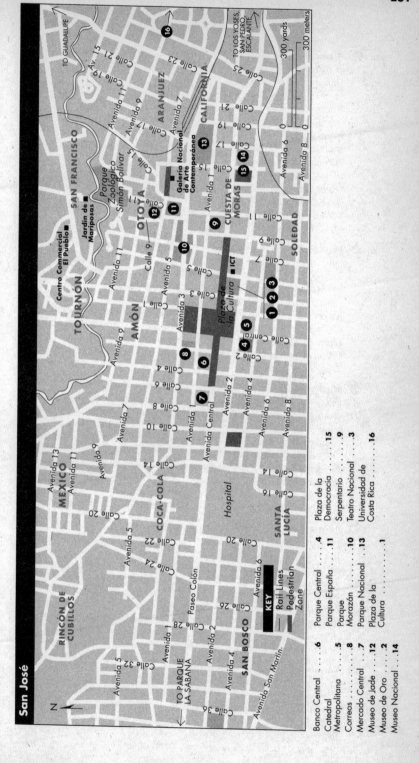

San José

KEY
— Rail Lines
▬ Pedestrian Zone

Banco Central **6**
Catedral
Metropolitana **5**
Correos **8**
Mercado Central ...**7**
Museo de Jade **12**
Museo de Oro **2**
Museo Nacional ...**14**

Parque Central **4**
Parque España ...**11**
Parque
Morazán **10**
Parque Nacional ..**13**
Plaza de la
Cultura **1**

Plaza de la
Democracia **15**
Serpentario **9**
Teatro Nacional ...**3**
Universidad de
Costa Rica **16**

6 and one at Calle Central. Beware the blue *pitufo* (Smurf) flavor but do try the *trits*, a chocolate-swirl sandwich with a crumbly cookie crust.

★ ⑫ **Museo de Jade** (Jade Museum). This is the world's largest collection of American jade—that's "American" in the hemispheric sense. Nearly all the items on display were produced in pre-Columbian times, and most of the jade dates from 300 BC to AD 700. In the spectacular Jade Room, pieces are illuminated from behind so you can appreciate their translucency. A series of drawings explains how this extremely hard stone was cut using string saws with quartz-and-sand abrasive. Jade was sometimes used in jewelry designs, but it was most often carved into oblong pendants. The museum also has other pre-Columbian artifacts, such as polychrome vases and three-legged metates (small stone tables for grinding corn), and a gallery of modern art. The final room on the tour has a startling display of ceramic fertility symbols. ⊠ *11th floor of INS building, Avda. 7 between Cs. 9 and 11, Barrio Carmen,* ☎ *223–5800 or 223–2584.* ☞ *$5.* ⊘ *Weekdays 8:30–3.*

★ ❷ **Museo de Oro** (Gold Museum). The dazzling, modern museum of gold, in a three-story underground building, contains the largest collection of pre-Columbian gold jewelry in Central America—20,000 troy ounces in more than 1,600 individual pieces—all owned by the Banco Central. Many pieces are in the form of frogs and eagles, two animals perceived by the region's pre-Columbian cultures to have great spiritual significance. Most spectacular are the varied shaman figurines, which represent the human connection to animal deities. ⊠ *Eastern end of Plaza de la Cultura, Barrio La Catedral,* ☎ *243–4202.* ☞ *$5.* ⊘ *Tues.–Sun. 10–4:30.*

⑭ **Museo Nacional** (National Museum). Set in the whitewashed colonial interior of the Bellavista Fortress, dating from 1870, the National Museum gives you a quick and insightful lesson in Costa Rican culture from pre-Columbian times to the present. Glass cases display pre-Columbian artifacts, period dress, colonial furniture, and photographs. Outside are a veranda and a pleasant, manicured courtyard garden. A former army headquarters, this now-tranquil building saw fierce fighting during the 1948 revolution, as the bullet holes pocking its turrets attest. ⊠ *C. 17 between Avdas. Central and 2, Barrio La Catedral,* ☎ *257–1433.* ☞ *$5.* ⊘ *Tues.–Sun. 8:30–4:30.*

❹ **Parque Central** (Central Park). Technically the city's nucleus, this simple tree-planted square has a gurgling fountain and cement benches. In the center of the park is a spiderlike, mango-color gazebo donated by former Nicaraguan dictator Anastasio Somoza. Several years ago a referendum was held to decide whether to demolish the despot's gift, but Ticos voted to preserve the bandstand for posterity. Across Avenida 2, to the north, stands the **Teatro Melico Salazar,** San José's second major performance hall (after the Teatro Nacional). The fast-food outlet between the two was once a major movie theater. ⊠ *Between Avdas. 2 and 4 and Cs. 2 and Central, Barrio La Catedral.*

⑪ **Parque España.** This shady little park is one of the most pleasant spots in the capital. A bronze statue of Costa Rica's Spanish founder, Juan Vasquez de Coronado, overlooks an elevated fountain on its southwest corner; the opposite corner has a lovely tiled guardhouse. A bust of Queen Isabel of Castile stares at the yellow compound to the east of the park—once a government liquor factory, this is now the **Centro Nacional de la Cultura** (National Center of Culture). Covering a double block, the complex houses the Ministry of Culture, two theaters, and the extensive **Museo de Arte y Diseño Contemporáneo** (Museum of Contemporary Art and Design), which hosts changing exhibits of

work by artists and designers from all over Latin America. To the west of the park is a two-story, metal-sided school made in Belgium and shipped to Costa Rica in pieces more than a century ago. The yellow colonial-style building to the east of the modern INS building is the **Casa Amarilla,** home of Costa Rica's Foreign Ministry. The massive ceiba tree in front, planted by John F. Kennedy and the presidents of all the Central American nations in 1963, gives you an idea of how quickly things grow in the tropics. A few doors east is the elegant Mexican Embassy, once a private home. ⊠ *Between Avdas. 7 and 3 and Cs. 11 and 17, Barrio Carmen.*

🔟 **Parque Morazán.** Anchored by a neoclassic bandstand, the largest park in downtown San José is somewhat barren, though the tabebuia trees on its northwest corner brighten things up when they bloom in the dry months. Avoid the park late at night, when a rough crowd and occasional muggers appear. Along the southern edge are a public school and two lovely old mansions, both with beautiful facades—one is a private home, the other a prostitute pickup bar. There's a park annex with a large fountain to the northeast, across busy Avenida 3, in front of the metal school building. ⊠ *Avda. 3 between Cs. 5 and 9, Barrio Carmen.*

★ ⓭ **Parque Nacional** (National Park). A bronze monument commemorating Costa Rica's battle against American invader William Walker in 1856 forms the centerpiece of this large and leafy park. The park paths are made of cobblestone rescued from downtown streets, and tall trees shading concrete benches often hide colorful parakeets in their branches. The modern pink building west of the park houses the Registro Público (National Registry) and the Tribunal Supremo de Elecciones (Electoral Tribunal), which keep track of voters and oversee elections. The tall gray building to the north is the Biblioteca Nacional (National Library), beneath which, on the western side, is the **Galería Nacional de Arte Contemporánea,** a small gallery exhibiting the work of contemporary artists, mostly Costa Rican. Quality varies, but since admission is free, it's always worth taking a peek. The walled complex to the northwest is the Centro Nacional de Cultura. Across from the park's southwest end is the Moorish **Asamblea Legislativa** (Legislative Assembly), where Costa Rica's congress meets. Next door is the Casa Rosada, a colonial-era residence now used for Congressional offices, and behind that is a more modern house used by the government for parties and special events. One block northeast of the park is the former Atlantic Railway Station. The park is best avoided at night, despite ample lighting and security patrol. ⊠ *Between Avdas. 1 and 3 and Cs. 15 and 19, Barrio Carmen.*

★ ❶ **Plaza de la Cultura.** This large cement square surrounded by shops and fast-food restaurants is somewhat sterile, but it's a nice place to feed pigeons and buy some souvenirs. It's also a favored performance spot for local marimba bands, clowns, jugglers, and colorfully dressed South Americans playing Andean music. The stately **Teatro Nacional** dominates the plaza's southern half, and its western edge is defined by the venerable Gran Hotel Costa Rica with its 24-hour Café Parisienne. ⊠ *Between Avdas. Central and 2 and Cs. 3 and 5, Barrio La Catedral.*

⓯ **Plaza de la Democracia.** President Oscar Arias built this terraced open space west of the Museo Nacional to mark 100 years of democracy and to receive dignitaries during the 1989 hemispheric summit. The view west toward the dark-green Cerros de Escazú is nice in the morning and fabulous at sunset. The plaza is dominated by a statue of José "Pepe" Figueres, three-time president and leader of the 1948 revolution. Along the western edge jewelry, T-shirts, and crafts from Costa Rica, Guatemala, and South America are sold in a string of stalls. ⊠ *Between Avdas. Central and 2 and Cs. 13 and 15, Barrio La Catedral.*

⑨ Serpentario (Serpentarium). Don't be alarmed by the absence of motion within the display cases here—the inmates are very much alive. Most notorious in this collection of snakes and lizards is the terciopelo, responsible for more than half the poisonous snakebites in Costa Rica. The menagerie includes boa constrictors, Jesus Christ lizards, poison dart frogs, iguanas, and an aquarium full of deadly sea snakes, as well as such exotic creatures as king cobras and Burmese pythons. ⊠ *Avda. 1 between Cs. 9 and 11, Barrio Carmen,* ☎ *255–4210.* ⊡ *$6.* ⊙ *Weekdays 9–6, weekends 10–5.*

★ ③ Teatro Nacional (National Theater). Easily the most enchanting building in Costa Rica, the National Theater stands at the southwest corner of the Plaza de la Cultura. Chagrined that touring prima donna Adelina Patti bypassed San José in 1890, wealthy coffee merchants raised import taxes to hire Belgian architects to design this building, lavish with cast iron and Italian marble. The sandstone exterior is marked by Italianate arched windows, marble columns with bronze capitals, and statues of strange bedfellows Ludwig van Beethoven (1770–1827) and 17th-century Spanish golden-age playwright Pedro Calderón de la Barca (1600–81). The Muses of Dance, Music, and Fame are silhouetted in front of an iron cupola. Given the provenance of the building funds, it's not surprising that frescoes on the stairway inside depict coffee and banana production. The theater was inaugurated in 1897 with a performance of Gounod's *Faust,* featuring an international cast. The sumptuous neo-Baroque interior sparkles thanks to an ongoing restoration project. The theater closes occasionally for rehearsals. The stunning **Café del Teatro Nacional** off the vestibule serves upscale coffee concoctions, good sandwiches, and exquisite pastries. ⊠ *Plaza de la Cultura, Barrio La Catedral,* ☎ *221–1329.* ⊡ *Entry $2.50, performance tickets $4–$40 ($10 average).* ⊙ *Weekdays 9–5, Sat. 9–noon.*

⑯ Universidad de Costa Rica. The University of Costa Rica, in San Pedro east of San José, is a great place to hang out and meet people, especially if your Spanish is pretty good. The open-air gallery at the **Facultad de Bellas Artes** (College of Fine Arts), on the east side of campus, hosts free music recitals on Tuesday nights. If the Serpentario doesn't satisfy your thirst for the yucky, scurry on over to the **Museo de Insectos** (⊠ north of Bellas Artes, in the basement of the Artes Musicales Building, ☎ 207–5318), open weekdays 1–4:45. The $2 admission buys you a good look at dead insects in re-created habitats and information in English and Spanish on everything from insect sex to the diseases these little buggers cause.

Aficionados of Spanish literature should browse around the many off-campus bookstores. Anyone who appreciates cheap grub (you know who you are) will enjoy the vast selection of inexpensive lunch places around the university. Weeknights at the university are mellow, but nearby bars are packed with students and intellectuals on weekends. To get to San Pedro, walk a few miles east along Avenida Central's strip of shops and bars or take a $2 taxi ride from downtown and get off in front of Banco Nacional, beyond the rotunda with the fountain in the middle of it. ⊠ *Avda. Central and C. Central, Barrio Montes de Oca, San Pedro.*

Dining

Wherever you eat in San José, be it a small *soda* (café) or a sophisticated restaurant, dress is casual. Meals tend to be taken early; few restaurants serve past 10 PM. Note that 23% is added to all menu prices—13% for tax and 10% for service. Because a gratuity is included, there's no need to tip; but if your service is good, it's nice to add a little money to the obligatory 10%.

CAFÉS

Costa Rican coffee is strong, and a few places still serve it the old-fashioned way: hot milk in one pitcher and hot coffee in the other. Coffee is not generally taken alone but with bread or a sweet.

$ ✕ **Café Britt Teatro Nacional.** The country's foremost purveyor of gourmet coffee just took over the concession stand at Teatro Nacional. It wins the prize for most relaxed atmosphere. Have a cup of mocha with hazelnut and rest your weary head against cool marble while gazing at the frescoes on the ceiling. Atmosphere comes at a reasonable price here—coffees run anywhere from $1 to $2, depending on how much alcohol or ice cream is added. Sandwiches and cakes will set you back $3 to $4. ⊠ *Teatro Nacional, on Plaza de la Cultura, Barrio La Catedral,* ☎ *221–3262. Closed Sun. Open during evening performances.*

$ ✕ **La Esquina del Café.** Okay, so it looks a little like a tourist trap, and it does have a souvenir shop, but this is the place for cappuccinos and lattes made with frothed milk. The coffee, roasted fresh daily from six different coffee zones of the country, is the smoothest you'll ever drink. It can also be bought in bean form for $10 a kilo. Drinks and pastries are about $1 each. ⊠ *Av. 9 and C. 3 Bis, Barrio Amón,* ☎ *257–9868.*

COSTA RICAN

$$–$$$ ✕ **La Cocina de Leña.** La Cocina serves up traditional Costa Rican fare
★ amid white walls hung with old tools and straw bags to make you feel like you're down on the farm. Popular Tico dishes such as black-bean soup, ceviche, tamales, oxtail with cassava, and plantains cost a bit more here than at small cafés downtown, but the restaurant makes up for the price with live marimba music several nights a week during the high season. Although the kitchen closes at 11, you're welcome to stay as long as the band keeps playing. It is one of the few places that doesn't close during Holy Week. ⊠ *Centro Comercial El Pueblo, Barrio Tournón,* ☎ *223–3704. AE, MC, V.*

$$ ✕ **El Cuartel de la Boca del Monte.** Although it's one of San José's more popular late-night bars, El Cuartel is actually a nice place to have a meal, too. The restored brick walls, wood beams, and simple wood tables lend a rustic feel in one room, and you'll find a more finished room to the left of the entrance, decorated with original art. Best on the menu is arroz con pollo, but you can also order plates of delicious *bocas* (snacks), such as the *plato de gallos* (corn tortillas topped with beef, potatoes, and other fillings) and *piononos* (sweet plantains stuffed with cheese or beans and served with sour cream). ⊠ *Avda. 1 between Cs. 21 and 23, Barrio La California,* ☎ *221–0327. AE, MC, V. No lunch weekends.*

$ ✕ **Mama's Place.** Mama's is a Costa Rican restaurant with a difference: the owners are Italian, so in addition to corvina *al ajillo* (sautéed with garlic) and other staple Tico fare, they serve homemade seafood chowder, traditional pastas, and meat dishes with delicate wine sauces. The brightly decorated coffee shop opens onto busy Avenida 1; the more subdued restaurant is upstairs. At lunchtime, it's usually packed with business types drawn to the delicious and inexpensive daily specials and perhaps the macrobiotic fruit shakes, another menu item that sets this place apart. ⊠ *Avda. 1 between Cs. Central and 2, Barrio del Carmen,* ☎ *223–2270. MC, V. Closed Sun.*

$ ✕ **Manolo's.** This 24-hour eatery has been popular with travelers for years, both for its convenient location on the bustling pedestrian thoroughfare and for its great sandwiches, espressos, and *churros con chocolate* (fried dough with hot fudge sauce). A few outdoor tables allow for some of the city's best people-watching. Inside, however, the place feels more like a diner than a café, down to its plastic-coated menu and its promise of breakfast food at any hour. The owner always prepares a few Spanish favorites in addition to the typical Tico fare, such as *tortilla española* (a

San José Dining and Lodging

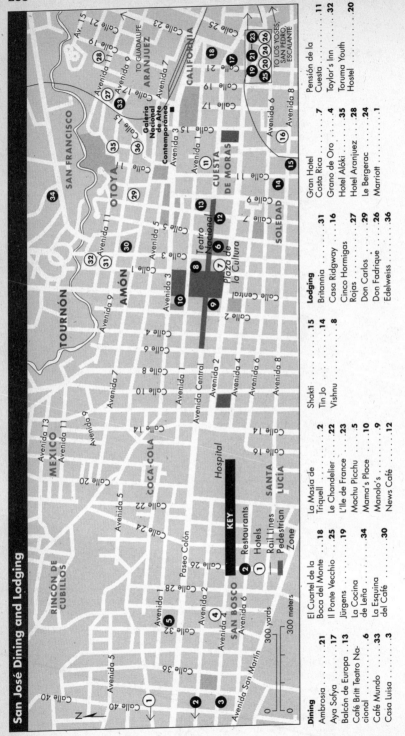

KEY

- **2** Restaurants
- **1** Hotels
- ▬ Rail Lines
- Pedestrian Zone

N

0   300 yards
0   300 meters

Dining

Ambrosia	**21**
Aya Sofya	**17**
Balcón de Europa	**13**
Café Britt Teatro Nacional	**6**
Café Mundo	**33**
Casa Luisa	**3**
El Cuartel de la Boca del Monte	**18**
Il Ponte Vecchio	**25**
Jürgens	**19**
La Cocina de Leña	**34**
La Esquina del Café	**30**
La Masía de Triquell	**2**
Le Chandelier	**22**
L'Ile de France	**23**
Machu Picchu	**5**
Mama's Place	**10**
Manolo's	**9**
News Café	**12**
Shakti	**15**
Tin Jo	**14**
Vishnu	**8**

Lodging

Britannia	**31**
Casa Ridgway	**16**
Cinco Hormigas Rojas	**27**
Don Carlos	**29**
Don Fadrique	**26**
Edelweiss	**36**
Gran Hotel Costa Rica	**7**
Grano de Oro	**4**
Hotel Alóki	**35**
Hotel Aranjuez	**28**
Le Bergerac	**24**
Marriott	**1**
Pensión de la Cuesta	**11**
Taylor's Inn	**32**
Toruma Youth Hostel	**20**

thick potato and onion omelet). ⊠ *Avda. Central between Cs. Central and 2, Barrio La Catedral,* ☎ *221–2041. AE, MC, V.*

ECLECTIC

$$$–$$$$ ✕ **Jürgen's.** Decorated in gold and terra-cotta with leather and wood accents, the dining room of this contemporary and chic restaurant feels more like a lounge than a fine restaurant. In fact, the classy bar with a large selection of good wine and good cigars, is a prominent feature. But the inventive menu, with such delicacies as medallions of roast duck and tuna fillet encrusted with sesame seeds, sets this place apart from the city's more traditional venues. Service here is tops and the feel is trendy and relaxed. ⊠ *800 yards north of the Subaru dealership, on Barrio Dent Blvd., Barrio Dent,* ☎ *283–2239. AE, MC, V. Closed Sun.*

$$$ ✕ **Ambrosia.** The navy-blue canopy in an open-air shopping plaza heralds this chic restaurant. The international menu draws the customers.
★ Expect inventive salads, soups, pasta, and fish dishes. Start with *sopa Neptuna* (a creamy fish soup with tomato and bacon), and follow with either the light fettuccine ambrosia (in a rich cream sauce with ham and oregano) or the corvina *troyana* (covered with a shrimp and tarragon sauce). The dining room is relaxed, with subdued watercolors, crisp white tablecloths, wood and cane chairs, and plants. ⊠ *Centro Comercial de la C. Real, San Pedro,* ☎ *253–8012. AE, DC, MC, V. No dinner Sun.*

$$–$$$ ✕ **Café Mundo.** You could easily walk by this corner restaurant without noticing its tiny sign behind the foliage. Walk in and upstairs, how-
★ ever, and you'll discover an elegant eatery serving meals on the porch, on a garden patio, or in two dining rooms. Chicagoan chef Ray Johnson prepares creative salads, pastas, pizzas, hot and cold sandwiches at lunch, and grill dishes for dinner. Start with the soup of the day and some fresh-baked bread; then opt for penne in a shrimp and vegetable cream sauce or *lomito en salsa de vino tinto* (tenderloin in a red-wine sauce). Save room for the best chocolate cake in town, drizzled with homemade blackberry sauce. ⊠ *C. 15 and Avda. 9, Barrio Otoya,* ☎ *222–6190. AE, MC, V. Closed Sun.*

$$ ✕ **News Café.** Had your fill of rice and beans? You can get a Caesar salad and other American dishes here. Breakfasts and dinner fare are hearty, but the café is most popular at lunchtime and cocktail hour. It's one of the few eateries in the city with covered outdoor seating, and it's in the perfect place for it—right off the pedestrian boulevard's east end. Inside, the wrought-iron chairs, wood beams, and brick walls give the place an old-town tavern feel, though it's actually on the first floor of the 1960s landmark Hotel Presidente. ⊠ *C. 7 and Avda. Central, Barrio La Catedral,* ☎ *222–3022. AE, MC, V.*

FRENCH

$$$$ ✕ **Le Chandelier.** Formal service and traditional sauce-heavy French dishes are part of the experience at the city's classiest restaurant, Le Chandelier. The dining room is elegant, with wicker chairs, a tile floor, and original paintings. The Swiss chef, Claude Dubuis, might start you off with saffron ravioli stuffed with ricotta cheese and walnuts. His main courses include such unique dishes as corvina in a *pejibaye* (peach palm) sauce; hearts of palm and veal chops glazed in a sweet port-wine sauce; or the more familiar *pato a la naranja* (duck à l'orange). ⊠ *1 block west and 1 block south of the ICE building, Los Yoses, San Pedro,* ☎ *225–3980. AE, MC, V. No lunch Sat.*

$$$ ✕ **L'Ile de France.** Long one of San José's most popular restaurants,
★ L'Ile de France is in the Le Bergerac hotel in Los Yoses, where you can dine in a tropical garden courtyard. Chef and proprietor Jean-Claude Fromont offers a fairly traditional French menu with some interesting innovations. Start with the classic onion soup or with *pâté de lapin* (rabbit liver pâté); then sink your teeth into a pepper steak, broiled lamb

with seasoned potatoes, or corvina in a spinach sauce. Save room for the profiteroles, puff pastries filled with vanilla ice cream and smothered in chocolate sauce, or the delicious crème brûlée. ⊠ *Le Bergerac hotel, C. 35 between Avdas. Central and 2, first entrance to Los Yoses, Los Yoses, San Pedro, ☎ 283–5812. Reservations essential. AE, MC, V. Closed Sun. No lunch.*

ITALIAN

\$\$\$ ✕ **Il Ponte Vecchio.** Italian owners have used eclectic artwork and candlelight to help create cozy spaces in which to sip wine and enjoy a quiet meal. Do as many foreign residents who favor the place: After a Caprese salad, tuck into one of the many homemade pasta specialties, such as seafood fettuccine with mussels and shrimp or traditional tomato lasagna. Cream sauces are excellent across the board. Portions are on the small side, so you can be sinful without being sorry. ⊠ *100 yards east and 25 yards north of Fuente de la Hispanidad, San Pedro, ☎ FAX 283–1810. AE, MC, V.*

\$\$–\$\$\$ ✕ **Balcón de Europa.** With old sepia photos and a strolling guitarist that seems to have been working the room for years, Balcón transports you to the era of its inception, 1909. Pasta specialties such as the *plato mixto* (lasagna, tortellini, and ravioli) are so popular that they haven't changed much, either. For something lighter, try the scrumptious heart-of-palm salad or sautéed corvina. ⊠ *Avda. Central and C. 9, Barrio La Catedral, ☎ 221–4841. AE, MC, V. Closed Sat.*

PAN-ASIAN

\$\$–\$\$\$ ✕ **Tin Jo.** You can eat in the Japan, India, China or Thailand rooms
★   at this wide-ranging Asian restaurant with a menu to match its varied dining areas. Tin Jo stands apart from the two other Chinese restaurants on this block with always exceptional food and whimsical decorations that add color to this former residence. Start with a powerful Singapore Sling (brandy and fruit juices) before trying such treats as *kaeng* (Thai shrimp and pineapple curry in coconut milk), *mu shu* (a beef, chicken, or veggie stir-fry with crepes), *samosas* (stuffed Indian pastries), and sushi rolls. ⊠ *C. 11 between Avdas. 6 and 8, Barrio La Soledad, ☎ 221–7605. AE, MC, V.*

PERUVIAN

\$\$–\$\$\$ ✕ **Machu Picchu.** A few travel posters and a fishnet holding crab and
★   lobster shells are the only props used to evoke Peru, but no matter: the food is anything but plain, and the seafood is excellent. The *pique especial de mariscos* (special seafood platter), big enough for two, presents you with shrimp, conch, and squid cooked four ways. The ceviche here is quite different from, and better than, that served in the rest of the country. A blazing Peruvian hot sauce served on the side adds zip to any dish, but be careful—apply it by the drop. ⊠ *C. 32, 150 yards north of Kentucky Fried Chicken, Paseo Colón, ☎ 222–7384. AE, DC, MC, V. Closed Sun.*

SPANISH

\$\$\$–\$\$\$\$ ✕ **Casa Luisa.** The moment you enter this homey, upscale Catalan restaurant, you sense you're in for a special evening. It is eclectic and artful, with wood floors, arresting artwork, soft lighting, and flamenco music in the background. Start the meal with gazpacho or eggplant pâté, accompanied by a glass of top Spanish wine. The wonderful main dishes include rosemary lamb chops, suckling pig, and grilled lobster. Finish with a platter of nuts, dates, and figs drizzled with a wine sauce or the decadent *crema Catalana* with a *brûlée* glaze. Reservations are recommended. ⊠ *Avda. 4 and C. 40, southeast of the Controlaria building, Sabana Sur, ☎ 296–1917. MC, V. Closed Mon.*

$$$ ✕ **La Masía de Triquell.** San José's most traditional Spanish restaurant is appropriately housed in the Casa España, a Spanish cultural center. The dining room follows the theme with a tile floor; wood beams; red, green, and yellow walls; white tablecloths; and leather-and-wood Castilian-style chairs. *Champiñones al ajillo* (mushrooms sautéed with garlic and parsley) make a fine appetizer; *camarones Catalana* (shrimp in a tomato-and-garlic cream sauce) are a standout entrée. The long wine list is strongest in the Spanish and French departments. Reservations are a good idea. ✉ *50 yards west and 150 yards north of Burger King, Sabana Norte,* ☎ *296–3528. AE, DC, MC, V. Closed Sun.*

TURKISH

$$ ✕ **Aya Sofya.** Natives of Istanbul, the chef and one of the owners have imported excellent recipes for red peppers stuffed with spicy beef and rice, eggplant-tomato salad, and other Mediterranean treats. Vegetarians will find a good selection of vegetable and green salads. Desserts include a scrumptious yogurt-and-honey *revani* cake as well as the beloved baklava. Beyond the obligatory evil-eye motif and a few wall hangings, this is a no-frills place, but good food and a friendly staff make it a find. ✉ *Avda. Central and C. 21, Barrio La California,* ☎ *221–7185. MC, V. Closed Sun.*

VEGETARIAN

$ ✕ **Shakti.** Between the baskets of fruit and vegetables at the entrance and the wall of herbal teas, health food books, and fresh herbs for sale by the register, there's no doubt you're in a vegetarian-friendly joint. The bright and airy restaurant serves breakfast and lunch: homemade bread, soy burgers, pita sandwiches (veggie or chicken, for carnivorous dining companions), macrobiotic fruit shakes, and a hearty plato del día that comes with soup, green salad, and a fruit beverage. The *ensalada mixta* is a meal in itself, packed with root vegetables native to Costa Rica. ✉ *Avda. 8 between Cs. 13 and 11, Barrio Lujan,* ☎ *222–4475. Reservations not accepted. No credit cards. No dinner.*

$ ✕ **Vishnu.** Named after the Hindu god who preserves the universe, Vishnu has become a bit of an institution in San José. Even its dining area looks institutional—sterile booths with Formica tables and posters of fruit on the walls—but the attraction is the inexpensive vegetarian food. Your best bet is usually the plato del día, which includes soup, beverage, and dessert, but the menu also offers soy burgers, salads, fresh fruit juices, and a yogurt smoothie called *morir soñando* (literally, "to die dreaming"). ✉ *Avda. 1, west of C. 3, Barrio Carmen,* ☎ *222–2549. Reservations not accepted. No credit cards.*

Lodging

$$$$ 🏨 **Britannia.** Except for the addition of some rooms and the conversion of the old cellar into an intimate international restaurant, this stately pink home with a tiled porch has changed little since its construction in 1910. Rooms in the newer wing are slightly small, with carpeting and hardwood furniture. Deluxe rooms and junior suites in the original house are spacious, with high ceilings and windows on the street side; they're worth the extra money but are close enough to the street that noise might be a problem if you're a light sleeper. ✉ *C. 3 and Avda. 11, Barrio Amón,* ☎ *223–6667,* FAX *223–6411,* WEB *www.centralamerica. com/cr/hotel/britania.htm (mailing address: Apdo. 3742–1000, San José). 19 rooms, 4 suites. Restaurant. AE, MC, V.*

$$$$ 🏨 **Grano de Oro.** Two turn-of-the-20th-century wooden houses on
★ San José's western edge have been converted into one of the city's most charming inns, which is decorated with old photos of the capital and paintings by local artists. A modest restaurant, run by a French chef, is

surrounded by a lovely indoor patio and gardens. The old rooms are the nicest, especially the Garden Suite, with hardwood floors, high ceilings, and private garden. The hotel's sundeck has a view of both the city and the far-off volcanoes. ⊠ *C. 30 between Avdas. 2 and 4, Paseo Colón,* ☎ *255–3322,* FAX *221–2782,* WEB *www.hotelgranodeoro.com (mailing address: 1701 N.W. 97 Ave., Box 025216, SJO 36, Miami, FL 33102–5216). 31 rooms, 3 suites. Restaurant, hot tub. AE, MC, V.*

$$$$ 🏨 **Marriott.** Towering over a coffee plantation west of San José, the
★ stately Marriott evokes an unusual colonial splendor. The building's thick columns, wide arches, and central courtyard are straight out of the 17th century, and hand-painted tiles and abundant antiques complete the historic appearance. Guest rooms are more contemporary, but they're elegant enough, with hardwood furniture and sliding glass doors that open onto tiny Juliet-type balconies. ⊠ *765 yards west of Firestone, off Autopista General Cañas, San Antonio de Belén,* ☎ *298–0000; 800/228–9290 in the U.S.,* FAX *298–0011,* WEB *www. marriotthotels.com/marriott/sjocr. 245 rooms, 7 suites. 2 restaurants, café, lobby lounge, 2 pools, hair salon, driving range, putting green, 3 tennis courts, health club, business services, meeting room, travel services, car rental. AE, DC, MC, V.*

$$$–$$$$ 🏨 **Hotel Alóki.** Guest rooms in this elegant turn-of-the-20th-century manor house surround a covered courtyard restaurant, whose wicker furniture and potted tropical plants spill onto multicolored glazed tiles. The antique furniture, gilt mirrors, and old prints in the rooms make this small, quiet place one of the most tasteful in San José. The Presidential Suite has a large drawing room. Breakfast is included. ⊠ *C. 13 between Avdas. 9 and 11, Barrio Otoya,* ☎ *222–6702,* FAX *221–2533,* WEB *www.tropicalcostarica.com. 6 rooms, 1 suite. Restaurant, bar; no a/c. MC, V.*

$$$ 🏨 **Don Carlos.** As one of the city's first guest houses, Don Carlos has
★ been in the same family for four generations. Most rooms in the rambling villa have ceiling fans, big windows, and original art. Those in the Colonial Wing have a bit more personality, and several newer rooms on the third floor have volcano views. Abundant public areas are adorned with orchids, pre-Columbian statues, and paintings depicting Costa Rican life. The on-site souvenir shop, Boutique Annemarie, has the city's largest selection of crafts and curios. Complimentary cocktails and breakfast are served on the garden patio; the small restaurant serves lunch and dinner. ⊠ *C. 9 and Avda. 9, Barrio Amón,* ☎ *221–6707,* FAX *255–0828,* WEB *www.doncarlos.com (mailing address: Box 025216, Dept. 1686, Miami, FL 33102-5216). 21 rooms, 12 suites. Restaurant, hot tub, travel services; no a/c in some rooms. AE, MC, V.*

$$$ 🏨 **Edelweiss.** Never mind that the interior may look more European than Latin American (one of the owners is Austrian). This elegant little inn has comfortable rooms in a charming area, near the Parque España. Rooms have carved doors, custom-made furniture, and small bathrooms. Most have hardwood window frames and floors; several have bathtubs. Complimentary breakfast is served in the garden courtyard, which doubles as a bar. ⊠ *Avda. 9 and C. 15, Barrio Otoya,* ☎ *221–9702,* FAX *222–1241,* WEB *www.edelweisshotel.com. 27 rooms. Bar, fans; no a/c. AE, MC, V.*

$$$ 🏨 **Gran Hotel Costa Rica.** Opened in 1930, the grande dame of San José hotels remains a focal point of the city and is the first choice of travelers who want to be where the action is. It's a good deal for the money, but the flow of nonguests who frequent the 24-hour casino, Café Parisienne, restaurant, and bar reduces the intimacy quotient to zero. Rooms are large and somewhat lackluster, with small windows and tubs in the tiled baths. Most overlook the Plaza de la Cultura, which can be a bit noisy, and the quieter interior rooms are pretty dark. Breakfast is com-

plimentary. ⊠ *Avda. 2 and C. 3, Barrio La Catedral,* ☎ 221–4000, FAX *221–3501 (mailing address: Apdo. 527–1000, San José). 106 rooms, 4 suites. Restaurant, bar, café, fans, casino; no a/c. AE, DC, MC, V.*

$$$ 🏨 **Taylor's Inn.** As a converted early 20th-century brick house, the inn's old charm makes up for such small flaws as cracking window sills and an uninspiring courtyard garden. Its comfortable, clean rooms and proximity to downtown attractions are also selling points. Rooms upstairs have pleasant views. First-floor rooms have original wood floors and adjoin a central courtyard with a high ceiling and handsome wood beams. Three rooms have bathtubs, a rarity in city hotels. Especially attractive to families is the suite in the front of the inn with a sitting area that connects to a standard double room. ⊠ *Avda. 13, C. 3 Bis, Barrio Amón,* ☎ 257–4333, FAX 221–1475. 12 rooms. Travel services; no a/c. AE, MC, V.*

$$ 🏨 **Cinco Hormigas Rojas.** The name of this whimsical little lodge translates as "Five Red Ants." Behind the wall of vines that obscures it from the street is a wild garden that leads to an interior space filled with original artworks. Color abounds, from the bright hues on the walls right down to the toilet seats. Sure enough, the resident owner is an artist—Mayra Güell turned the house she inherited from her grandmother into San José's most original B&B–cum–art gallery. It's in the historic Barrio Otoya, one of San José's few pleasant neighborhoods, and the room price includes a hearty breakfast. ⊠ *C. 15 between Avdas. 9 and 11, Barrio Otoya,* ☎ FAX 257–8581, WEB *www.crtimes.com/ tourism/cincohormigasrojas/maincinco.htm. 6 rooms, 2 with bath. No a/c, no room phones, no room TVs. AE, MC, V.*

$$ 🏨 **Hotel Aranjuez.** Several 1940s-era houses, with extensive gardens and ★ cozy common areas, constitute this family-run B&B. Every room is comfortable, but each is different—it pays to check out a few, as some have private gardens or little sitting rooms. Aranjuez is a short walk from most San José attractions and offers such perks as discount tour service. The complimentary breakfast buffet makes lunch unthinkable. Reserve well in advance during high season. ⊠ *C. 19 between Avdas. 11 and 13, Barrio Aranjuez,* ☎ 256–1825, FAX 223–3528, WEB *www.hotelaranjuez.com. 35 rooms, 25 with bath. In-room safes, travel services; no a/c. MC, V.*

$$ 🏨 **Pensión de la Cuesta.** Rooms in this laid-back, centrally located wooden villa in sloping Cuesta de Nuñez have hardwood floors, brightly painted walls, and original art. Rooms in back are quieter, but those in front are brighter. You can lounge and read in the sunken sitting area (also used as the breakfast room), which has a high ceiling, a wall of windows, and cable TV. Breakfast is included in the price, and you're welcome to use the kitchen at other times. The nine rooms share four baths. A furnished apartment is also for rent. ⊠ *Avda. 1 between Cs. 11 and 15, Apdo. 1332, Barrio Cuesta de Nuñez,* ☎ 256–7946, FAX 255–2896, WEB *www.arweb.com/lacuesta. 9 rooms without bath, 1 apartment. No a/c, no room TVs. AE, MC, V.*

$ 🏨 **Casa Ridgway.** Affiliated with the Quaker Peace Center next door, ★ Casa Ridgway is the budget option for itinerants concerned with peace, the environment, and social issues in general. Set in an old villa on a quiet street, the bright, clean premises include a planted terrace, a lending reference library, and a kitchen where you can cook your own food. There are three rooms with two bunk beds each, three rooms with single beds, and one with a double bed, all of which share three bathrooms. ⊠ *Avda. 6 Bis and C. 15, Barrio Lujan,* ☎ FAX 233–6168 *(mailing address: Apdo. 1507–1000, San José). 7 rooms without bath. Library, meeting room; no a/c, no room phones, no room TVs. No credit cards.*

Northeast of San José

The small properties beyond downtown, toward the university, offer personalized service and lots of peace and quiet. Plenty of restaurants

and bars are within easy reach, although downtown is a 10-minute cab ride away.

$$$ ✕🖼 **Le Bergerac.** Le Bergerac, surrounded by extensive green grounds,
★   is the cream of a growing crop of small, upscale San José hotels. French owned and managed, it occupies two former private homes and is furnished with antiques. All rooms have custom-made wood-and-stone dressers and writing tables; deluxe rooms have two beds, private garden terraces or balconies, and large bathrooms. The hotel's restaurant, L'Ile de France, is one of the city's best, so dinner reservations are essential, even for guests. Complimentary breakfast is served on a garden patio. ⊠ *C. 35 between Avdas. Central and 2, first entrance to Los Yoses, Los Yoses, San Pedro,* ☎ *234–7850,* 𝔽𝔸𝕏 *225–9103,* 𝕎𝔼𝔹 *www. bergerac.com (mailing address: Apdo. 1107–1002, San José). 18 rooms. Restaurant, meeting room, travel services. AE, MC, V.*

$$$ ✕🖼 **Don Fadrique.** This tranquil, family-run B&B on the outskirts of San José was named after Fadrique Guttierez, an illustrious great-uncle of the owners. A collection of original Costa Rican art decorates the lobby and rooms, most of which have hardwood floors, peach walls, and pastel bedspreads. Several carpeted rooms downstairs open onto the garden. There is also an enclosed garden patio, where meals are served. ⊠ *C. 37 at Avda. 8, Los Yoses, San Pedro,* ☎ *225–8186,* 𝔽𝔸𝕏 *224–9746,* 𝕎𝔼𝔹 *www.centralamerica.com/cr/hotel/fadrique.htm. 20 rooms. Restaurant; no a/c. AE, MC, V.*

$–$$ 🖼 **Toruma Youth Hostel.** The headquarters of Costa Rica's expanding hostel network is housed in an elegant colonial bungalow, built around 1900, in the eastern suburb of Escalante. The tiled lobby and veranda are ideal places for backpackers to hang out and exchange travel tales and enjoy a light complimentary breakfast. Beds on the ground floor are in little compartments with doors; rooms on the second floor have standard bunks. There are also two private rooms for couples. The on-site information center offers discounted tours. ⊠ *Avda. Central between Cs. 29 and 31, Escalante,* ☎ 𝔽𝔸𝕏 *224–4085 (mailing address: 6 Apdo. 1355–1002, San José). 2 rooms without bath, 95 beds in 17 rooms. Dining room; no a/c, no room phone, no room TVs. MC, V.*

Nightlife and the Arts

The Arts

FILM

Films are screened in their original language, usually English, and subtitled in Spanish. There are theaters all over downtown San José, as well as in the malls outside the city. Check the local papers *La Nación* or the *Tico Times* (in English) for current listings.

THEATER AND MUSIC

The baroque **Teatro Nacional** (⊠ Plaza de la Cultura, Barrio Catedral, ☎ 221–1329) is the home of the excellent National Symphony Orchestra, which performs on Friday evening and Sunday morning between April and December. The theater also hosts visiting musical groups and dance companies. San José's second main theater is the **Teatro Melico Salazar** (⊠ Avda. 2 between Cs. Central and 2, Barrio Catedral, ☎ 221–4952). There are frequent dance performances and concerts in the Teatro FANAL and the Teatro 1887, both in the **Centro Nacional de la Cultura** (⊠ C. 13 between Avdas. 3 and 5, Barrio Otoya, ☎ 257–5524). The **Eugene O'Neill Theater** (⊠ Avda. 1, C. 37, Barrio Dent, San Pedro, ☎ 207–7500) at the Costa Rican–North American Culture Center has chamber concerts and plays most weekend evenings. The center is a great place to meet expatriate North Americans. Dozens of

theater groups (most of which perform slapstick comedies) hold forth in smaller theaters around town.

Nightlife

BARS

Outside the hotels, there aren't many places to have a quiet drink—Tico bars tend to be on the lively side. For a little taste of Mexico in Costa Rica, head to **La Esmeralda** (⊠ Avda. 2 between Cs. 5 and 7, Barrio La Catedral), a popular late-night spot where locals enjoy live mariachi music until the wee hours. The second floor of the **Casino Colonial** (⊠ Avda. 1 between Cs. 9 and 11, Barrio Carmen, ☎ 258–2827) is a good place to watch a game. **Mac's Bar** (⊠ Sabana Park S., next to the Tennis Club, Sabana Sur, ☎ 234–3145) is a quiet spot for a drink.

The **Centro Comercial El Pueblo** (⊠ Avda. 0, Barrio Tournón) has a bar for every taste, from quiet pubs to thumping discos. Several bars have live music on weekends; it's best to wander around and see what sounds good. A trendy place to see and be seen is **El Cuartel de la Boca del Monte** (⊠ Avda. 1 between Cs. 21 and 23, Barrio La California), a large bar where young artists and professionals gather to sip San José's fanciest cocktails and share plates of tasty *bocas* (snacks). It has live music Monday and Wednesday night. The **Jazz Café** (⊠ Avda. Central next to Banco Popular, San Pedro) draws big crowds, especially for live jazz on Tuesday and Wednesday nights.

The highly recommended restaurant, **Café Mundo** (⊠ C. 15 and Avda. 9, Barrio Otoya, ☎ 222–6190), is also quiet spot for a drink frequented by gay and bohemian crowds. **El Bochinche** (⊠ C. 11 between Avdas. 10 and 12, Barrio Soledad) is another of San José's upscale gay bars that doubles as a restaurant.

DISCOS

El Tobogan, outside town on the road north to Guápiles, is the place to watch the best in Latin dancing. Its oversize hall is always packed with a mature crowd who swivel to live music on the weekends. For a more international scene, **Planet Mall,** on the top floor of the massive San Pedro Mall, is one of the city's most expensive dance bars. The **Centro Comercial El Pueblo** has two full-fledged discos: Cocoloco has Latin music, and Inifnito plays mostly techno, pop, and funk on one dance floor and Latin music on the other. Across the parking lot from the Centro Comercial El Pueblo is **La Plaza,** a larger, slightly more upscale disco that plays a good mix of pop and Latin music.

Déjà Vu (⊠ C. 2 between Avdas. 14 and 16A, Barrio El Pacífico) is a mostly gay, techno-heavy disco with two dance floors. Take a taxi to and from here; the neighborhood's sketchy. A gay and lesbian crowd also frequents **La Avispa** (⊠ C. 1 between Avdas. 8 and 10, Barrio La Catedral), which has two dance floors and a quieter upstairs bar with pool tables.

Outdoor Activities and Sports

Participant Sports

FITNESS CENTERS AND DAY SPAS

The Radisson Europa Hotel (⊠ Avda. 15 between Cs. Central and 3, next to La Republica newspaper office, Barrio Tournón, ☎ 257–3257) houses the downtown branch of the upscale, full-service gym **Multi Spa,** which offers daily rates (about $4) for drop-ins. Other luxury hotels, like the Aurola Holiday Inn, Marriott, and the Meliá Cariari, have modern gyms for guests only.

The **Harmony Day Spa** at Hotel Amón Plaza (⊠ Avda. 11 and C. 3 Bis, Barrio Amón, ☎ 257–0191) offers massages, manicures, pedicures, and sunburn relief treatments. The hotel also lends its hot tub, pool, and modest exercise equipment to nonguests for about $3 a day.

RUNNING

Once San José's airport but now a eucalyptus-shaded park, **Parque La Sabana,** at the end of the Paseo Colón, is the city's best place to run, with 5-km (3-mi) routes on cement paths. Within the park are a sculpture garden and duck ponds. Free **aerobics classes** on La Sabana's west end start at 9 on Sunday morning and usually draw scores.

WHITE-WATER RAFTING

White-water trips down the Reventazón, Pacuare, Sarapiquí, and General rivers all leave from San José. Nearly half a dozen licensed, San José–based tour companies operate similar rafting and kayaking trips of varying lengths and grades. The Reventazón's Class III and IV–V runs are both day trips, as are the Sarapiquí's Class II–IV runs. You descend the General (Class III–IV) on a three-day camping trip. You can run the Pacuare (Class III–IV) in one, two, or three days, the Sarapiquí (Class II–IV) in one day.

Accommodations for overnight trips on the General or Pacuare River are usually in tents, but Aventuras Naturales and Ríos Tropicales have comfortable lodges on the Pacuare, making them the most popular outfitters for overnight trips on that river. Costa Rica Expeditions runs day trips. The cost is around $75–$95 per day, depending on the river. Two- and three-day river rafting or kayaking packages with overnight stays are considerably more expensive.

Aventuras Naturales (⊠ behind Banco Nacional, Barrio Roosevelt, San Pedro, ☎ 225–3939 or 224–0505, FAX 253–6934) is a popular outfitter with high-adrenaline rafting adventures on the Pacuare, Reventazón, and Sarapiquí rivers. **Ríos Tropicales** (⊠ 50 yards south of Centro Colón, Paseo Colón, San José, ☎ 233–6455, FAX 255–4354) is the largest outfitter running white-water tours in the area. **Costa Rica Expeditions** (⊠ Avda. 3 and C. Central, Barrio María Auxiliadora, San José, ☎ 257–0766, FAX 255–4354) has been offering rafting tours to the Pacuare, Reventazón, and Sarapiquí rivers for more than 20 years.

Spectator Sports

SOCCER

Professional soccer matches are usually played on Sunday morning or Wednesday night in either of two San José stadiums. The **Estadio Nacional** is on the western end of La Sabana park. The **Estadio Ricardo Saprissa** is in the northern suburb of Tibás. Consult the Spanish-language daily *La Nación* or ask at your hotel for details on upcoming games—you simply buy a ticket at the stadium box office. Prices range from $2 to $12—the most expensive are reserved seats in the shade (ask for *sombra numerado*).

Shopping

Specialty Items

ANTIQUES

Antigüedades Chavo (⊠ C. Central between Avdas. Central and 1, Barrio Carmen, ☎ 258–3966) sells mostly furniture but has some smaller antiques. **Antigüedades El Museo** (⊠ Avda. 7 and C. 3 Bis, Barrio Amón, ☎ 223–9552) sells paintings, ceramics, jewelry, and other small items.

BOOKS AND MAPS

Lehmann (✉ Avda. Central between Cs. 1 and 3, Barrio La Catedral, ☎ 223–1212) has some books in English and a stock of large-scale topographical maps. **Librería Internacional** (✉ 330 yards west of Taco Bell, Barrio Dent, ☎ 253–9553) has English translations of Latin American literature and coffee-table books on Costa Rica. **7th Street Books** (✉ C. 7 between Avdas. Central and 1, Barrio La Catedral, ☎ 256–8251) has an excellent selection of new and used books in English and is strong on Latin America and tropical ecology.

COFFEE AND LIQUOR

You can buy coffee in any souvenir shop or supermarket, where you'll get the best price. The best brand is Café Rey Tarrazú; the second-best is Café Britt. Good, fresh-roasted coffee is also sold at **La Esquina del Café** (✉ Avda. 9, C. 3 Bis, Barrio Amón, ☎ 257–9868), which has a great selection of coffee souvenirs and hand-rolled Costa Rican cigars that can be enjoyed at La Esquina's bar and café. Costa Rica's best rum is the aged Centenario—pick up a bottle for about $8. There are also several brands of coffee liqueurs, the oldest of which is Café Rica but the best of which is Britt. Buy these at any of San José's abundant supermarkets and liquor stores.

CRAFTS

Atmosfera (✉ C. 5 between Avdas. 1 and 3, Barrio Carmen, ☎ 222–4322) has three floors of crafts and local art, including wooden bowls, jewelry, and paintings and sculptures by Costa Rican artists. **Galería Namu** (✉ Avda. 7 between Cs. 5 and 7, behind Aurola Holiday Inn, Barrio Amón, ☎ 256–3412) has Costa Rican folkloric art and some of the best indigenous crafts in town. Its inventory brims with colorful creations by the Guaymí, Boruca, Bribri, Chorotega, Hueter, and Maleku peoples from Costa Rica. You'll also find exquisitely carved ivory nut "Tagua" figurines made by Wounan Indians from Panama's Darien region. Take note of carved balsa masks, woven cotton blankets, and hand-painted ceramics.

SOUVENIRS

Boutique Annemarie (✉ C. 9 and Avda. 9, Barrio Amón, ☎ 221–6707) in the Don Carlos hotel has a huge selection of popular souvenirs and CDs of Costa Rican musicians, including Grammy-winning Editus. The boutique carries comical figurines, cards, stationery, and standard, kitschy tourist gear.

The **gift shop** at Aeropuerto Internacional Juan Santamaría has coffee ($5 per pound), and a terrific selection of good-quality merchandise, such as hand-carved bowls and jewelry, Aveda-esque aromatherapy candles, banana paper stationery, and Costa Rica travel books. There's nary another store in the country carrying such desirable items all in one place. But you'll pay U.S. prices.

San José A to Z

AIRPORTS AND TRANSFERS

There are two airports in the San José area—Aeropuerto Internacional Juan Santamaría, 16 km (10 mi) northwest of downtown San José, the destination for all international flights, and Aeropuerto Internacional Tobías Bolaños in Pavas, 3 km (2 mi) west of the city center, from which some domestic flights depart.

➤ AIRPORT INFORMATION: **Aeropuerto Internacional Juan Santamaría** (☎ 443–2942). **Aeropuerto Internacional Tobías Bolaños** (☎ 232–2820).

A taxi from the airport to downtown San José costs around $12. Drivers wait at the airport exit in a startling mass. They do not expect tips, but beware of drivers eager to take you to a particular hotel—their only motive is a hefty commission. Far cheaper (about 40¢), and almost as fast, is the bus marked RUTA 200 SAN JOSÉ, which drops you at the west end of Avenida 2, close to the heart of the city. If you rent a car at the airport, driving time to San José is about 20 minutes, 40 minutes if traffic is heavy or you get lost. Note that some hotels provide a free shuttle service—inquire when you reserve.

BUS TRAVEL TO AND FROM SAN JOSÉ

A handful of private companies operate from San José, providing reliable, inexpensive bus service throughout much of Costa Rica from several departure points (San José has no central bus station).

BUS TRAVEL WITHIN SAN JOSÉ

Bus service within San José is absurdly cheap (30¢–50¢) and easy to use. For Paseo Colón and La Sabana, take buses marked SABANA-CEMENTERIO from stops on the southern side of the Parque Morazán, or on Avenida 3 next to the Correos building. For the suburbs of Los Yoses and San Pedro near the university, take one marked SAN PEDRO, CURRIDABAT, or LOURDES from Avenida Central, between Calles 9 and 11.

CAR RENTAL

It's virtually impossible to rent a car in Costa Rica between December 20 and January 3. Any other time of year, shop around for the best rate.

➤ MAJOR AGENCIES: **Alamo** (✉ Avda. 18 between Cs. 11 and 13, Barrio González-Viques, ☎ 233–7733 or 800/570–0671). **Budget** (✉ Paseo Colón and C. 30, Barrio Paseo Colón, ☎ 223–3284 or 800/224–4627). **Dollar** (✉ Paseo Colón and C. 32, Barrio Paseo Colón, ☎ 257–1585 or 800/800–4000). **Hertz** (✉ Paseo Colón and C. 38, Barrio Paseo Colón, ☎ 221–1818 or 800/654–3001). **National** (✉ 1 km [½ mi] north of Hotel Best Western Irazú, Barrio La Uruca, ☎ 290–8787 or 800/227–7368).

CAR TRAVEL

San José is the hub of the national road system. Paved roads fan out from Paseo Colón south to Escazú and northwest to the airport and Heredia. For the Pacific coast, Guanacaste, and Nicaragua, take the Carretera Interamericana (Pan-American Highway) north (CA1). Calle 3 runs east into the highway to Guápiles, Limón, and the Atlantic coast through Braulio Carrillo National Park, with a turnoff to the Sarapiquí region. If you follow Avenida Central or 2 east through San Pedro, you'll enter the Pan-American Highway south (CA2), which has a turnoff for Cartago, Volcán Irazú, and Turrialba before it heads southeast over the mountains toward Panama.

Almost every street in downtown San José is one-way. Try to avoid driving at peak hours (8 AM–9 AM and 5 PM–6:30 PM), as traffic gets horribly congested. Parking lots, scattered throughout the city, charge around $1 an hour. Outside the city center, you can park on the street, where *cuidacarros* (car guards) usually offer to watch your car for a $1 tip. Even so, never leave shopping bags or valuables inside.

EMERGENCIES

You can dial ☎ 911 for just about any emergency. Your embassy can provide you with a list of recommended doctors and dentists. Hospitals open to foreigners include Clínica Bíblica, which has a 24-hour pharmacy, and Clínica Católica.

➤ EMERGENCY SERVICES: **Ambulance** (☎ 128). **Fire** (☎ 118). **Police** (☎ 117; 127 outside major cities). **Traffic Police** (☎ 222–9245).
➤ HOSPITALS: **Clínica Bíblica** (✉ Avda. 14 between Cs. Central and 1, Barrio El Pacífico, ☎ 257–0466 emergencies). **Clínica Católica** (✉ Guadalupe, attached to San Antonio Church on C. Esquivel Bonilla St., Barrio Guadalupe, ☎ 283–6616).

TOURS

Everyone is setting up tours these days, but a few companies have more experience than most. Prescheduled half-day and full-day bus tours to waterfalls, Central Valley volcanoes, coffee plantations, botanical gardens, and San José sights can be arranged through Eclipse Tours. Aventuras Naturales leads rafting and mountain-biking tours. Costa Rica Expeditions is one of the country's most experienced rafting outfitters. Expediciones Tropical arranges horseback riding tours. Sun Tours and Horizontes will customize natural-history and adventure trips with expert guides to any Costa Rican itinerary. Ríos Tropicales offers rafting, sea-kayaking, and mountain-biking tours. The Rain Forest Aerial Tram takes you floating through the treetops on a modified ski lift. Tropical Bungee runs bungee-jump trips daily from San José to an old bridge on the way to the Central Pacific. For a day trip to the beach at Punta Coral and Isla Tortuga, try Calypso.

The popular coffee tour run by Café Britt, in Heredia, presents the history of coffee harvesting and drinking via skits, a coffee-farm tour, and a tasting. Most of San José's travel agencies can arrange one-day horseback tours to farms in the surrounding Central Valley.
➤ TOUR COMPANIES: **Aventuras Naturales** (✉ Avda. 5 at C. 33, Barrio Escalante, ☎ 225–3939, FAX 253–6934). **Café Britt** (✉ 900 yards north and 400 yards west of Comandancia, Barva de Heredia, Heredia, ☎ 261–0707, FAX 260–1456). **Calypso** (✉ Arcadas building, 3rd floor, next to Gran Hotel Costa Rica, Barrio del Catedral, San José, ☎ 256–2727, FAX 256–6767). **Camino Travel** (✉ C. 1 between Avdas. Central and 1 Barrio del Carmen, San José, ☎ 257–0107, FAX 257–0243). **Costa Rica Expeditions** (✉ Avda. 3 at C. Central, Barrio del Carmen, San José, ☎ 222–0333, FAX 257–1665). **Eclipse Tours** (✉ Villa Tournón, Avda. 0, east side of traffic circle, Barrio Tournón, San José, ☎ 223–7510, FAX 233–3672). **Expediciones Tropical** (✉ C. 3 between Avdas. 11 and 13, Barrio Amón, San José, ☎ 257–4171, FAX 257–4124). **Horizontes** (✉ 150 yards north of Pizza Hut, Barrio Paseo Colón, San José, ☎ 222–2022, FAX 255–4513). **Rain Forest Aerial Tram** (✉ Avda. 7 between Cs. 5 and 7, Barrio Amón, San José, ☎ 257–5961). **Ríos Tropicales** (✉ 50 yards south of Centro Colón, Barrio Paseo Colón, San José, ☎ 233–6455, FAX 255–4354). **Sun Tours** (✉ 200 yards south of Burger King, Barrio La Uruca, San José, ☎ 296–7757, FAX 296–4307). **Tropical Bungee** (✉ Sabana Sur, 100 yards west and 50 yards south of Controlaria, Sabana Sur, San José, ☎ 232–3956).

TAXIS

Taxis are a good deal within the city. You can hail one on the street (all taxis are red with a gold triangle on the front door) or have your hotel or restaurant call one for you, as cabbies tend to speak only Spanish and addresses are complicated. A 3-km (2-mi) ride costs around $2, and tipping is not the custom. Taxis parked in front of expensive hotels charge about twice the normal rate. By law, all cabbies must use their meters—called *marías*—when operating within the metropolitan area; if one refuses, negotiate a price before setting off, or hail another. Cab companies include San Jorge, Coopetaxi and, if you need to go to the airport, Taxis Unidos.

➤ TAXI COMPANIES: **Coopetaxi** (☎ 235–9966). **San Jorge** (☎ 221–3434). **Taxis Unidos** (☎ 221–6865).

TRAVEL AGENCIES

➤ LOCAL AGENT REFERRALS: **Aviatica** (✉ Avda. 1 and C. 1, Barrio del Carmen, ☎ 222–5630). **Galaxy** (✉ C. 3 between Avdas. 5 and 7, Barrio Amón, ☎ 233–3240). **Intertur** (✉ 50 yards west of Kentucky Fried Chicken, Avda. Central between Cs. 31 and 33, Barrio Francisco Peralta, ☎ 253–7503).

VISITOR INFORMATION

➤ TOURIST INFORMATION: **Instituto Costarricense de Turismo** (ICT; ✉ C. 5 between Advas. Central and 2, Barrio del Catedral, ☎ 222–1090) staffs a tourist information office beneath the Plaza de la Cultura, next to the Museo de Oro. Pick up free maps, bus schedules, and brochures weekdays 9–12:30 and 1:30–5.

CENTRAL VALLEY

Distinctive hotels in the Central Valley hills offer what the capital can't—quiet and luxurious accommodations surrounded by awesome volcanoes and working coffee *fincas* (farms). The Valley is a no-less convenient base for heady excursions: Peer into the crater of a volcano, marvel at rushing waterfalls, wander through butterfly gardens, or visit colonial-era towns that prosper thanks to the *grano de oro* (golden bean).

Heredia

9 km (6 mi) north of San José.

With a population of around 30,000, Heredia is the capital of one of Costa Rica's most important coffee provinces and perhaps the country's best-preserved colonial town. It bears witness, however, to how little preservation can mean in an earthquake-prone country: Heredia has lost many of its colonial structures over the years. Still, the city retains a historic feel, with old adobe buildings scattered throughout downtown, and you'll see more in the charming nearby villages of Barva de Heredia, Santo Domingo, and San Rafael de Heredia.

The tree-studded **Parque Central** holds some colonial appeal. At the park's eastern end stands the impressive stone **Catedral de Heredia,** dating back to 1797, whose thick walls, small windows, and squat buttresses have kept it standing through countless quakes and tremors. Unfortunately, the church's stained-glass work has not fared as well. The park has a simple kiosk and a cast-iron fountain imported from England in 1897. ✉ *Parque Central,* ☎ 237–0779. ☉ *Daily 6–6.*

Surrounding the park are some interesting buildings. The 1843 barrel-tile-roof **Casa de la Cultura** often houses art exhibits. Behind the brick **Municipalidad** (municipal building) stands a strange, decorative tower called the fortín, or small fort.

Between Heredia and Barva is the **Museo de Cultura Popular** (Museum of Popular Culture), an early 20th-century farmhouse built with an adobe-like technique called *bahareque.* Run by the National University, the museum is furnished with antiques and surrounded by a small garden and coffee fields. An inexpensive, open-air lunch restaurant serves authentic Costa Rican cuisine and can be a lively spot on weekends, when a more extensive menu is sometimes paired with marimba music and folk dancing. ✉ *Between Heredia and Barva, follow signs for right turn,* ☎ 260–1619. ▣ *$2.* ☉ *Daily 9–4, restaurant daily 11–2. No credit cards.*

☺ The producer of Costa Rica's most popular export-quality coffee, **Café Britt,** offers a lively tour of its working coffee plantation, which highlights Costa Rica's history of coffee cultivation through a theatrical presentation. (You have to see it to believe it.) Take a short walk through the coffee farm and processing plant, and learn how professional tasters distinguish a fine cup of java in a coffee-tasting session from a not-so nice one. On an additional tour ($10) you can learn how espresso beans are roasted and then make your own cappuccino after lunch. ✉ *900 yards north and 400 yards west of the Comandancia, Heredia,* ☎ *260–2748,* FAX *260–1456.* ✉ *$20, $27 with transportation from San José.* ◷ *Dec.–May, tours daily at 9, 11, and 3; June–Nov., tours daily at 11.*

☺ The guided tour of **INBio Parque** is an excellent introduction to three of the country's ecosystems before you head out to see them for real. After watching short videos, wander trails through climate-controlled wetlands and out to tropical dry forest. Along the way, stop at the butterfly farm, snake and insect exhibits, and a bromeliad garden. English-speaking guides end the tour with a discussion on biodiversity and INBio (Biodiversity Institute). A pleasant restaurant serves typical Costa Rican fare and an extensive bookstore and shop has eco-friendly souvenirs. ✉ *400 yards north and 250 yards west of Shell gas station in Santo Domingo, Heredia,* ☎ *244–4790.* ✉ *$16.* ◷ *Daily 8–5.*

The small community of **Barva de Heredia,** about 2 km [1 mi] north of Heredia proper, has a wonderful Parque Central surrounded by old Spanish-tiled adobe houses on three sides and a white stucco church to the east. Flanked by royal palms, the stout, handsome church dates from the late 18th century; behind it is a lovely little garden shrine to the Virgin Mary. On a clear day you can see verdant Volcán Barva towering to the north, and if you follow the road that runs in front of the church, veering to the right, you'll reach the village of Sacramento. Here the road turns into a steep, dirt track leading to the Barva sector of Braulio Carrillo National Park.

Lodging

$$$$ 🏨 **Finca Rosa Blanca Country Inn.** There's nothing common about
★ this luxurious little B&B overlooking coffee farms; you need only step through the front door of the Gaudíesque main building to marvel at its soaring ceiling, white-stucco arches, and polished wood. Each guest room is different, but all have original art, local hardwoods, and colorful fabrics. The spacious, two-story suite is out of a fairy tale, with a spiral staircase leading up to a window-lined tower bedroom. Out on the grounds—planted with tropical flowers and shaded by massive fig trees—are two villas, each with two bedrooms. Four-course dinners are optional. ✉ *Barrio Jesus, 6 km (4 mi) west of Santa Barbara de Heredia,* ☎ *269–9392,* FAX *269–9555,* WEB *www.fincarosablanca.com (mailing address: SJO 1201, Box 025216, Miami, FL 33102-5216). 6 rooms, 2 villas. Dining room, pool, horseback riding, travel services, airport shuttle; no a/c. AE, MC, V.*

$$$ 🏨 **Hotel Bougainvillea.** Here you'll soon forget that you're only 15 min-
★ utes from San José. Set amid the coffee farms of Santo Domingo de Heredia, the Bougainvillea has extensive grounds filled in with tall trees and brightened by one of the country's most impressive bromeliad gardens. The spacious, carpeted guest rooms are furnished with local hardwoods; the tiled bathrooms come with tub and hair dryer. Decorating the lobby and excellent restaurant are original pre-Columbian pieces and paintings by local artists. ✉ *Guápiles Hwy. to Tibas exit, then road to Santo Domingo, and follow signs,* ☎ *244–1414,* FAX *244–1313,* WEB *www.bougainvillea.co.cr (mailing address: Apdo. 69–2120,*

San José). 76 rooms, 4 suites. Restaurant, bar, pool, hot tub, sauna, tennis court. AE, MC, V.

Alajuela

20 km (13 mi) northwest of San José.

Despite being Costa Rica's second-largest city (population 50,000) and a mere 30-minute bus ride from the capital, Alajuela has a decidedly provincial air. Architecturally it differs little from the bulk of Costa Rican towns: it's a grid plan of low-rise structures painted in primary colors. Alajuela's picturesque **Parque Central** is filled with royal palms and mango trees, has a lovely fountain imported from Glasgow, and cement benches where locals gather to chat. Surrounding the plaza is an odd mix of charming old buildings and sterile cement boxes. The large, neoclassic **cathedral,** badly damaged by a 1990 earthquake, has interesting capitals decorated with local agricultural motifs and a striking red dome. The interior, though spacious, is rather plain except for the ornate dome above the altar. ⊠ *C. Central between Avdas. 1 and Central,* ☎ *441–0769.* ☉ *Daily 8–6.*

To the north of the park stands the **old jail,** which now houses the local offices of the Ministry of Education—an appropriate metaphor for a country that claims to have more teachers than police.

Alajuela was the birthplace of Juan Santamaría, the national hero who lost his life in a battle against the mercenary army of U.S. adventurer William Walker (1824–60) when the latter invaded Costa Rica in 1856. A statue of the youthful Santamaría stands in Alajuela's **Parque Juan Santamaría,** one block south of the Parque Central.

Juan Santamaría's heroic deeds are celebrated in the **Museo Juan Santamaría,** one block north of Parque Central. The museum contains maps, compasses, weapons, and paintings, including an image of Walker's men filing past to lay down their weapons. The colonial building that houses the museum is more interesting than the displays, however. ⊠ *C. 2 and Avda. 3,* ☎ *441–4775.* ☞ *Free.* ☉ *Tues.–Sun. 10–6.*

☙ Spread over the lush grounds of **Zoo Ave** (Bird Zoo) is a collection of large cages holding macaws, toucans, hawks, and parrots, not to mention crocodiles, monkeys, and other interesting critters. The zoo runs a breeding project for rare and endangered birds and mammals, all of which are destined for eventual release. An impressive mural bordering part of the facility shows Costa Rica's 850 bird species painted to scale. To get here, head west from the center of Alajuela past the cemetery; then turn left after the stone church in Barrio San José. Kids under 10 get in for $2. ⊠ *La Garita de Alajuela,* ☎ *433–8989.* ☞ *$9.* ☉ *Daily 9–5.*

☙ The **Finca de Mariposas** (Butterfly Farm), in the suburb of La Guácima, offers a regular lecture on the ecology of these delicate insects and gives you a chance to observe and photograph them up close. In addition to an apiary exhibit, the farm's several microclimates keep comfortable some 40 rare species of butterflies. Try to come here when it's sunny, as that's when butterflies are most active. The farm offers transportation from San José for $10. ⊠ *From San José, turn south (left) at the intersection past Cariari Hotel, then right at church of San Antonio de Belén, then left, and then follow butterfly signs,* ☎ *438–0115.* ☞ *$15.* ☉ *Daily 8:30–5.*

OFF THE
BEATEN PATH   **LA PAZ WATERFALL GARDENS** – Self-guided brick-lined trails through this landscaped high-elevation park lead past five magnificent rushing waterfalls—the park's main attractions. Arm yourself with a raincoat, as it's

easy to get sprayed upon from the observation decks, which put the cascades within arm's reach. The main trail from the visitor center, complete with an attractive gift shop and open-air cafeteria with a view, leads first to a huge multilevel butterfly observatory and continues past a garden where hummingbird feeders attract swarms of the playful little birds. Take an alternate trail through a fern and orchid garden before winding back to the visitor center for hot tea or coffee. A free shuttle van transports you from the trail exit and back to the main building, if you'd prefer to avoid the hike back uphill. The tour takes about 1½ hours. ⊠ *On the road to Poás Volcano, turn right at the sign to Poasito and continue for 1½ km (1 mi). Turn left at the sign for Vara Blanca, continue for 5 km (3 mi); it's 20 km (12 mi) from Alajuela,* ☎ *482–2720,* WEB *www. waterfallgardens.com.* ⊠ *$24.* ⊙ *Daily 8:30 –4.*

Lodging

$$$$ ⊞ **Villas Pura Vida Retreat Center.** Yoga classes and workshops are as much a part of the stay as the accommodations themselves. A weekly rate includes two daily yoga classes, tours, tranfers, all meals, and one massage. If you like privacy, upgrade to the minimalist Japanese pagoda, with a Balinese-style outdoor shower and its own hot tub and sun deck. Three suites and a villa have large windows and bamboo furniture, and more creature comforts than the unique "tentalows" or luxury tents set within surrounding tropical gardens. A stay in the carpeted tents (furnished with a chair, night tables, and small wood desk) is meant to strengthen the connection with the outdoors, which means you're up with the sun, when the first yoga activity begins. The retreat serves delicious and healthy meals, and the spa offers many treatments from massage to guided meditation. ⊠ *700 yards south of cantina Salon Apolo 15, Pavas de Carrizal,* ☎ *392–8099,* FAX *483–0041,* WEB *www.puravidaspa.com (mailing address: Apdo. 1112, Alajuela 4050; reservations: R & R Resorts, Box 1496, Conyers, GA 30012,* ☎ *888/767–7375). 45 tent bungalows, 3 suites, 1 villa, 1 pagoda. Dining room, spa, travel services; no a/c, no room phones, no room TVs. AE, MC, V.*

$$$$ ⊞ **Xandari.** The tranquil and colorful Xandari is a strikingly original
★ inn. Its bold design is the brainchild of a talented couple—he's an architect, she's an artist. Contemporary pueblo-esque villas, along a ridge overlooking Alajuela, are spacious, with plenty of windows, colorful paintings, creatively placed tile showers, large terraces, and secluded lanais (sunbathing patios). Ultra villas are independent; the two Prima villas share one building. The attractive restaurant serves lowfat food, using some ingredients grown on the grounds. The slow enjoyment of meals is emphasized. A trail through the hotel's forest reserve winds past five waterfalls. ⊠ *3 km (1.8 mi) north of Alajuela, turn left after small bridge, follow signs,* ☎ *443–2020,* FAX *442–4847,* WEB *www.xandari.com (mailing address: Apdo. 1485–4050, Alajuela). 17 villas. Restaurant, bar, 2 pools, hot tub, spa; no a/c, no room TVs. AE, MC, V.*

$$$ ⊞ **Orquideas Inn.** Once the home of a coffee farmer, this Spanish-colonial residence has some quirky additions that make it a lively retreat in otherwise tranquil surroundings: a bar dedicated to Marilyn Monroe, an outdoor grill-your-own steak house, and a geodesic dome that contains one of the hotel's four suites. Standard rooms have terra-cotta tile floors, Guatemalan bedspreads, and paintings by Central American artists. Rooms in a newer wing are more in keeping with a tropical theme, with bamboo headboards and colorful floral bedspreads. Pet toucans, parrots, and macaws inhabit the wooded grounds, which means there's lots of squawking by the light of day. ⊠ *5 km (3 mi) west of cemetery,* ☎ *433–9346,* FAX *433–9740 (mailing address: Apdo. 394, Alajuela). 29 rooms, 4 suites. Restaurant, bar, pool. AE, MC, V.*

NORTHERN GUANACASTE AND ALAJUELA

The red lava of Volcán Arenal and the green cloud forests of Monteverde loom over Costa Rica's northernmost reaches. This amazingly diverse region also takes in Caño Negro's remote, bird-filled waters; the wind-surfing mecca of Laguna de Arenal; dusty, deforested uplands with cowboys and grazing cattle; jungles alive with birds, monkeys, and butterflies; and sparkling Pacific Coast beaches. And if you want to make like a bird, don't pass up the chance to glide through the treetops on one the north's famed canopy tours.

La Fortuna

40 km (25 mi) east of Volcán Arenal, 10 km (6 mi) northwest of San Carlos.

At the foot of towering, overpowering Volcán Arenal, the small farming community of La Fortuna de San Carlos (commonly called La Fortuna) attracts visitors from around the world. The town overflows with restaurants, hotels, and tour operators. It's also the best place to arrange trips to the popular Caño Negro National Wildlife Refuge, since the town is on the road to that protected area. Tours vary in price and quality, so ask around, but all provide an easier alternative than bussing up north to Los Chiles and hiring a boat to take you down through the rain forest on Río Frío.

Besides offering access to a multitude of outdoor adventures, La Fortuna also provides you with the opportunity for some serious soaking and pampering. Where else can you lounge in a natural hot-springs waterfall with a volcano spitting fireballs overhead? Kick back at the **Tabacón Resort,** a busy day spa and hotel, with gorgeous gardens, waterfalls, mineral water soaking streams (complete with subtle ladders and railings and average 39°C (102°F), swimming pools, swim-up bars, and dining facilities, all in a florid Latin interpretation of grand European baths. Nonguests of the hotel can purchase a day pass and move on. The best deal is to sign up for a zip-through-the-trees canopy tour ($45), the price of which includes access to the waters. If you're seeking an Iskandria Spa treatment, it's best to make an appointment a day in advance. ✉ *13 km (8 mi) northwest of La Fortuna on highway toward Nuevo Arenal,* ☎ *460–2020 or 256–1500,* FAX *221–3075,* WEB *www.tabacon.com.* ✉ *Entry $17, 45-min massage $40, mud-pack facial $20.* ☾ *Daily noon–10. MC, V.*

If Tabacón is full or if you want a less expensive spa alternative, head to **Baldi Termae.** The complex's seven hot-spring-fed pools vary in temperature but share views of Volcán Arenal. There's also a swim-up snack bar. ✉ *4 km (2½ mi) west of La Fortuna,* ☎ *479–9651.* ✉ *$10.* ☾ *Daily 10–10.*

A pleasant but steep day hike from La Fortuna takes you to the 54-m- (177-ft-) high waterfall **Cataratas de La Fortuna.** The 6-km (4-mi) walk to the falls begins off the main road toward the volcano; look for the yellow billboard marking the entrance. If you've got your own wheels, double-check road conditions in the rainy season. If you don't feel like walking, several operators in La Fortuna will take you to the falls by car or on horseback.

Dining

$–$$ ✕ **La Choza de Laurel.** The tantalizing chicken turning on the rotisserie and the cloves of garlic and bunches of onions dangling from the

roof always draw in passersby to this open-air Costa Rican–style restaurant near the center of town. These folks open early; it's a great place to grab a hearty breakfast on your way to the volcano. ⊠ *100 m northwest of town church,* ☎ *479–9231. MC, V.*

$–$$ ✕ **Rancho la Cascada.** You can't miss its tall, palm-thatch roof in the center of town. The festive upstairs contains a bar, whose large TV, neon signs, and flashing lights give it the appropriate ambience. Downstairs, the spacious dining room—decorated with foreign flags—serves basic, mid-priced Costa Rican fare as well as hearty, American-style breakfasts. ⊠ *Across from northeast corner of Parque Central,* ☎ *479–9145. AE, MC, V.*

$–$$ ✕ **La Vaca Muca.** It isn't a posh place, but the food is good and the servings are generous. The exterior is draped with foliage, and the interior has turquoise paneling and bamboo aplenty. Try the casado heaped with chicken, beef or fish, rice, beans, fried egg, fried banana, and cabbage salad—easily enough for two. ⊠ *2 km (1 mi) west of La Fortuna,* ☎ *479–9186. V. Closed Mon.*

$ ✕ **Soda La Parada.** It's always busy but never crazy. Grab an open-air seat alongside the locals, under the canvas tarp (from which hangs a huge color TV), and let the waiters in neon-lime shirts bring you a fresh carrot-and-orange juice, a beef or chicken empanada, or one of the tasty casados. You and your wallet will leave full. ⊠ *Across from town church and regional bus stop,* ☎ *479–9546. No credit cards.*

Lodging

$$$$ ⊞ **Tabacón Resort.** Without question, Tabacón, with its impeccably land-
★ scaped gardens and hot-spring rivers at the base of Volcán Arenal, is one of Central America's most compelling resorts. The hot springs and lovely spa customarily draw visitors inland from the ocean with no regrets. All rooms have tile floors, a terrace or patio, and big bathrooms. Some have volcano views; others overlook the manicured gardens. The suites are some of the country's finest lodgings, with tile floors, plants, beautiful mahogany armoires and beds, and two-person Jacuzzi tubs. The hotel's intimacy is somewhat compromised by its scale and its popularity with day-trippers, so the hotel has some private areas (including a dining room and pool) for overnight guests only. ⊠ *13 km (8 mi) northwest of La Fortuna on highway toward Nuevo Arenal,* ☎ *256–1500,* 🅵🅰🆇 *221–3075,* 🆆🅴🅱 *www.tabacon.com (mailing address: Apdo. 181–1007, San José). 73 rooms, 9 suites. Restaurant, 3 bars, dining room, cable TV, 9 pools, outdoor hot tub, mineral baths, spa, airport shuttle (fee). MC, V.*

$$$–$$$$ ⊞ **Arenal Observatory Lodge.** Once you're arrive at the end of the winding road leading to the lodge, originally founded by Smithsonian researchers in 1987, you're as close as anyone should be to an active volcano, a mere 1⅘ km (1½ mi) away. The isolated lodge is fairly rustic, emphasizing that outdoor activities are what it's all about. Rooms are simply furnished, but comfortable (comforters on beds are a cozy touch), and most have stellar views. After a hike, take a dip in the "infinity" pool or 12-person Jacuzzi, which face tall pines one side and the volcano on the other. The dining room, which serves tasty and hearty food, has great views of the volcano and lake. ⊠ *3 km (2 mi) east of dam on Laguna de Arenal; from La Fortuna, drive to Tabacón Resort and continue 4 km (3 mi) past the resort to turnoff at base of volcano; turn and continue for 9 km (5½ mi),* ☎ 🅵🅰🆇 *695–5033,* ☎ *290–7011 in San José,* 🅵🅰🆇 *290–8427 in San José,* 🆆🅴🅱 *www.arenal-observatory.co.cr (mailing address: Apdo. 13411–1000, San José). 35 rooms, 2 suites. Restaurant, pool, outdoor hot tub, horseback riding, laundry service; no room phones, no room TVs. AE, MC, V. CP*

$$$–$$$$ ⊞ **Montaña de Fuego Inn.** Set on a manicured grassy roadside knoll, this highly recommended collection of cabins affords utterly spectacular views of Volcán Arenal. The spacious, well-made hardwood structures are notable for their large porches. All rooms have ceiling fans and rustic decor. The friendly management can arrange tours of the area. ⊠ *8 km (5 mi) west of La Fortuna,* ☎ *460–1220,* FAX *460–1455,* WEB *www.montanadefuego.com. 52 cabinas. Restaurant, pool, hot tub, laundry service. AE, MC, V.*

$$$ ⊞ **Arenal Country Inn.** It doesn't quite approximate an English country inn, although it is a bit charming. Each brightly furnished, modern room has two queen-size beds and a private patio. The lush grounds have great views of the Arenal volcano. Rates include a big breakfast served in the restaurant, an open-air converted cattle corral. You can take lunch and dinner there as well. ⊠ *1 km south of church of La Fortuna, south end of town,* ☎ *479–9670,* FAX *479–9433,* WEB *www. costaricainn.com. 20 rooms. Bar, restaurant, in-room safes, minibars, pool, laundry service, meeting room, travel services; no room TVs. AE, MC, V.*

$$$ ⊞ **Las Cabañitas Resort.** Each of the red-roof cabinas here has a terrace that looks out over landscaped grounds toward the volcano; have a seat in a rocking chair and enjoy the view. Inside, you'll find solid wood furnishings and quilted bedspreads. ⊠ *1 km (½ mi) east of La Fortuna,* ☎ *479–9400,* FAX *479–9408 (mailing address: Apdo. 5–4417, La Fortuna). 30 cabinas. Restaurant, bar, pool, laundry service; no room phones, no room TVs. AE, MC, V.*

$$$ ⊞ **Chachagua Rain Forest Lodge.** At this working ranch, intersected by a sweetly babbling brook, you can see caballeros at work, take a horseback ride into the rain forest, and look for toucans from the open-air restaurant, which serves beef, milk, and cheese produced on the premises. Each cabina has a pair of double beds and a deck with a picnic table. Large, reflective windows enclosing each cabina's shower serve a marvelous purpose: birds gather outside your window to watch their own reflections while you bathe and watch them. The lodge is 3 km (2 mi) up a rough track—four-wheel drive is recommended in rainy season—on the road headed south from La Fortuna to La Tigra. ⊠ *12 km (7 mi) south of La Fortuna,* ☎ *231–0356,* FAX *290–6506,* WEB *www.novanet.co.cr/chachagua (Apdo. 476–4005, Ciudad Cariari). 15 cabinas. Restaurant, bar, pool, sauna, tennis court, horseback riding, casino, meeting rooms; no room phones, no room TVs. AE, MC, V.*

$$$ ⊞ **Lomas del Volcán.** You'd think you were right on top of the volcano, but Arenal is really a reassuring 6 km (4 mi) away. You need a four-wheel-drive vehicle to get here, but once you do, you can luxuriate in the splendid isolation. The simple cabins have hot water and come with two beds and throw rugs. Each has a volcano-viewing porch. ⊠ *Road entrance 1½ km (1 mi) west of La Fortuna,* ☎ *393–1361,* FAX *479– 9770,* WEB *www.lomasdelvolcan.com. 8 cabins. Fans, refrigerators; no a/c, no room phones, no room TVs. AE, MC, V.*

$$$ ⊞ **Luigi's Lodge.** Every one of this hotel's rooms has a stunning view of the volcano: it's the only lodging in the center of town able to make that claim. Rooms also have high wooden ceilings and stenciled animal drawings. The green-and-white tiled bathrooms have bathtubs, a rarity in Costa Rica. The adjoining restaurant serves pizza. ⊠ *200 m northwest of town church,* ☎ *479–9636,* FAX *479–9898,* WEB *www.luigislodge.com. 22 rooms. Restaurant, pool, hot tub, gym. AE, MC, V.*

$$$ ⊞ **Tilajari Hotel Resort.** As a comfortable base from which to have outdoor or adventure tours, this 35-acre resort with a butterfly garden and orchard is a good choice. The hotel organizes horseback tours through its own rain forest preserve, kayak tours in the river that nudges up against the property, as well as other area tours. "Papaya on a stick"

feeders hang outside the open-air dining room, attracting an array of raucous toucans and parrots to entertain you while you sip your morning coffee. The modest guest quarters have river-view balconies and satellite TV; family suites have lofts. Tilajari is a half hour outside of town, and there's no shuttle service. ⊠ *San Carlos Valley, outside Muelle (follow signs), about 25 km (15 mi) from La Fortuna,* ☎ *469–9091,* FAX *469–9095,* WEB *www.arenallodge.com (mailing address: Apdo. 81, San Carlos, Alajuela). 60 rooms, 16 suites. Restaurant, bar, 2 pools, outdoor hot tub, 6 tennis courts, horseback riding, Ping-Pong, laundry service, meeting rooms. AE, MC, V.*

$$ 🛏 **Cabinas Los Guayabos.** A great budget alternative to the more expensive lodgings lining the road to the volcano is this group of basic but spotlessly clean cabins managed by a friendly family. The units have all the standard budget lodging furnishings, but each comes with its own porch facing Arenal, ideal for viewing the evening spectacle. ⊠ *9 km (5½) west of La Fortuna,* ☎ *460–6644. 5 cabins. No a/c, no room phones, no room TVs. No credit cards.*

$$ 🛏 **Hotel San Bosco.** Covered in blue-tile mosaics, this two-story hotel ★ is certainly the most attractive and comfortable in the main part of town. Two kitchen-equipped cabinas (which sleep 8 or 14 people) are a good deal for families. The spotlessly clean, white rooms have polished wood furniture and firm beds and are linked by a long veranda lined with benches and potted plants. You pay a little more for air-conditioning. ⊠ *220 m north of La Fortuna's gas station,* ☎ *479–9050,* FAX *479–9109,* WEB *www.arenal-volcano.com. 34 rooms, 2 cabinas. Pool, hot tub, laundry service; no room phones. AE, MC, V.*

$$ 🛏 **La Pradera.** La Pradera, a roadside restaurant beneath a high thatched roof, has 10 comfortable guest rooms, all with high ceilings, spacious bathrooms, and verandas in a building next door. Two have Jacuzzis. Beef eaters should try the restaurant's steak with jalapeño sauce—a fine, spicy dish. ⊠ *About 2 km (1 mi) west of La Fortuna,* ☎ *479–9597,* FAX *479–9167. 10 rooms. Restaurant; no a/c in some rooms. AE, MC, V.*

Outdoor Activities and Sports

CANOPY TOURS

Want a bird's-eye view of the trees? Let the professionals at the **Original Canopy Tour** (⊠ Tabacón Resort, 13 km [8 mi] northwest of La Fortuna on highway toward Nuevo Arenal, ☎ 460–2020 or 256–1500, FAX 221–3075, WEB www.canopytour.com) show you the canopy from a new perspective. You'll be securely strapped into a rock-climbing harness and attached to a pulley and horizontal zip line. Well-trained guides then send you whizzing between trees that stand about 100 m (328 ft) over the streams of Tabacón. (If it's a small tour, they may even be able to snap a picture of you.) Since a tour requires a certain amount of fearlessness, it's not for everyone, but it's for more folks than you might think. While it's not rigorous per se, it's certainly exhilarating and unique. Tours are at 7:30 AM, 10 AM, 1:30, and 4. The price of a tour ($45) includes admission to Tabacón hot springs for the day.

FISHING

The eastern side of Laguna de Arenal has the best freshwater fishing in Costa Rica, with guapote aplenty, although it is difficult to fish from the shore. Arenal Observatory Lodge is one of many hotels and tour companies in the area offering boats and guides.

HIKING

To take the 6-km (4-mi) day hike from La Fortuna to the **Cataratas de la Fortuna,** look for the yellow entrance sign off the main road toward the volcano. After walking 1½ km (1 mi) and passing two bridges, turn

right and continue straight ahead until you reach the river turnoff. You'll go 10 or 15 minutes down a steep but very well constructed step trail that has a few vertiginous spots along the way. Swimming in the pool under the waterfall is fairly safe. You can work your way around into the cavelike area behind the cataract for an unusual rear view, but you'll have to swim in turbulent waters and/or hike over slippery rocks. A $2 fee is collected at the head of the trail, which is open daily 7–4.

HORSEBACK RIDING

If you're interested in getting up to Monteverde from the Arenal–La Fortuna area without taking the grinding four-hour drive, there's an alternative: the ever-ingenious Suresh Krishnan, a transplant from California, offers a wonderful adventure out of his tour agency, **Desafío Tours** (⊠ Central plaza [Apdo. 37–4417], La Fortuna, ☎ 479–9464, WEB www.desafiocostarica.com)—a 4½-hour guided horseback trip around the southern shore of Lake Arenal with continuing service to Monteverde. The trip involves taxi service on both ends, as well as a boat ride across Laguna de Arenal. They'll take your luggage and drive your car up there if need be, all for $65 per person. You leave La Fortuna at 7:30 AM and arrive in Monteverde around 2:30 PM. **Eagle Tours** (⊠ north of gas station, La Fortuna, ☎ 479–9091) has horseback rides to Monteverde, with the caveat that rainy conditions and poor trail conditions could cancel the trip. Note that many other agencies in La Fortuna and Monteverde offer rides over a muddy, poorly maintained trail. Some riders have returned with stories of terrified horses barely able to navigate the way. It's best to avoid other tours.

RAFTING

Several La Fortuna operators offer Class III and IV white-water trips on the Río Toro. The narrow shape of this river requires the use of special, streamlined, U.S.-made boats that seat just four and go very fast.

Desafío Expeditions (⊠ Central plaza [Apdo. 37–4417], La Fortuna, ☎ 479–9464, WEB www.desafiocostarica.com) has trips on the Río Toro for $59 per person.

SPELUNKING

Sunset Tours (⊠ Across from Desafío Expeditions, La Fortuna, ☎ 479–9415) will take you to the Venado Caverns for $25, including an English-speaking guide, entrance fee, boots, and a lantern. Prepare to get wet and muddy.

Caño Negro National Wildlife Refuge

91 km (57 mi) northwest of La Fortuna.

A lowland rain forest reserve in the far northern reaches of Alajuela, Refugio Nacional de Vida Silvestre Caño Negro covers 62 square km (38 square mi). Caño Negro has suffered severe deforestation over the years, but most of the Río Frío is still lined with trees, and the park's vast lake is an excellent place to watch such waterfowl as the roseate spoonbill, jabiru stork, and anhinga, as well as a host of resident exotic animals. In the dry season, you can ride horses; but the visit here chiefly entails a wildlife-spotting boat tour. Caño Negro can be reached from the Nuevo Arenal–La Fortuna area, or you can approach via Upala (a bus from here takes 45 minutes). Visiting with a tour company is the best way to see the park. ☎ $6. ☉ *Daily 7–4.*

Sunset Tours (☎ 479–9415), in La Fortuna, runs daylong tours down the Río Frío to Caño Negro for $45. Bring your jungle juice: the mosquitoes are voracious. Camping is permitted or you can stay in basic lodging for around $10, including meals.

Volcán Arenal

★ *17 km (11 mi) west of La Fortuna, 128 km (80 mi) northwest of San José.*

If you've never seen an active volcano, Arenal makes a spectacular first—its perfect conical profile dominates the southern end of Laguna de Arenal. Night is the best time to observe it, as you can clearly see rocks spewing skyward and red-hot molten lava enveloping the top of the cone. Phases of inactivity do occur, however, so it's wise to check ahead. The volcano is also frequently hidden in cloud cover, so you may have to stay more than one day to get in a good volcano-viewing session.

Arenal lay dormant for 400 years until 1968. On July 29 of that year an earthquake shook the area, and 12 hours later Arenal blew. Pueblo Nuevo to the west bore the brunt of the shock waves, poisonous gases, and falling rocks; 80 people perished. Since then, Arenal has been in a constant state of activity—eruptions, accompanied by thunderous grumbling sounds, are sometimes as frequent as one per hour. An enormous eruption in 1998 put the fear back into the local community and led to closure of Route 42 and the evacuation of several nearby hotels. This earth-shaking event reminded everyone what it really means to coexist with an active volcano.

Though folks here still do it, hiking is not recommended on the volcano's lower slopes; in 1988 two people were killed when they attempted to climb it. History repeated itself in 2000 with the death of an American traveler and her guide who were hiking on the lower slopes in a supposedly safe area. The conventional wisdom in these parts is that it's still safe to approach from the south and west, within the national park, although many recommend enjoying the spectacle from no closer than any of the lodges themselves.

Nuevo Arenal

40 km (25 mi) west of La Fortuna.

There's little reason to stop in Nuevo Arenal itself. Off the main road, the pleasant, if nondescript, *nuevo* town was created in 1973 to replace the original Arenal, flooded when the lake was created. If you're staying overnight in the area make sure you find a hotel with a view of the volcano. On the north shore, between the dam and the town of Nuevo Arenal, there's one short stretch of road still unpaved, potholed, and at times quite dangerous; beware of deep, tire-wrecking washouts at all times. This stretch adds a bone-jarring hour to an otherwise lovely drive with spectacular lake and volcano views all the way.

Five kilometers (3 miles) east of Nuevo Arenal, the elegantly organized **Jardín Botánico Arenal** (Arenal Botanical Gardens) exhibits more than 2,000 plant species from around the world. Countless orchids, bromeliads, heliconias, and roses; varieties of ferns; and a Japanese garden with a waterfall are among the many floral splendors laid out along well-marked trails. An accompanying brochure describes everything in delightful detail; well-placed benches and a fruit-and-juice stand provide resting places along the paths. ☎ 694–4273. ☒ $5. ☉ Daily 9–5.

Lodging

$$$–$$$$ ⊞ **Arenal Lodge.** Surrounded by macadamia trees and rain forest, this modern white bungalow is high above the dam, midway between La Fortuna and Nuevo Arenal. You need four-wheel drive to negotiate the steep 2-km (1-mi) drive, but the hotel will ferry you from the bottom. Bedroom suites, some in a newer annex, are pleasantly furnished, with

pretty green-tile baths; there are also cheaper, smaller, darker rooms without volcano views. Interiors are finished in natural wood, with walls of louvered windows. Hilltop chalets have floor-to-ceiling windows and kitchenettes. Perks include use of bicycles, a small snooker table, breakfast with the price of a room, and a free hour of horseback riding. ⊠ *18½ km (11½ mi) west of La Fortuna, past the Arenal Dam, then 2 km (1 mi) north,* ☎ *383–3957,* WEB *www.arenallodge.com (mailing address: Apdo. 1139–1250, Escazú,* ☎ *228–3189,* FAX *289–6798). 6 rooms, 18 suites, 10 chalets. Dining room, hiking, horseback riding, fishing, library, Internet, laundry service. AE, MC, V.*

$$$ 🏨 **Hotel Joya Sureña.** In the midst of a working coffee plantation, this Canadian-owned property with variously sized suites occupies a rather imposing three-story hacienda-style building surrounded by tropical gardens. It's fairly luxurious for up-country Costa Rica. Extensive trails in and around the place bring a rich diversity of plant, animal, and bird life to view. ⊠ *1½ km (1 mi) down a rocky road that leads east from Nuevo Arenal,* ☎ *694–4057,* FAX *694–4059. 28 rooms. Restaurant, pool, hot tub, massage, sauna, health club, hiking, boating, fishing, laundry service. AE, MC, V.*

$$$ 🏨 **Lake Coter Eco-Lodge.** This ruggedly handsome mountain hideaway tucked into cloud forest offers lots to do, thanks to the setting. The lodge offers canopy tours on-site, hikes on 29 km (18 mi) of trails, kayaking and sailing on Laguna de Arenal, and an extensive stable of horses for trail rides through the cloud forest. Stay in comfortable ridgetop cabinas, if they're available. Clean, basic rooms are attached to the main brick-and-hardwood reception building, which has a friendly bar, dining facilities, a fireplace, and a pool table. ⊠ *3 km (2 mi) up a rough track off north shore of Laguna de Arenal,* ☎ *694–4480 or 440–6768,* FAX *694–4460 or 440–6725,* WEB *www.ecolodgecostarica.com. 23 rooms, 14 cabinas. Restaurant, bar, hiking, horseback riding, boating, laundry service, meeting room. AE, MC, V.*

Shopping

Toad Hall (☎ 381–3662), an eclectic store on the road between Nuevo Arenal and La Fortuna, sells everything from indigenous art to maps to recycled paper. The owners can give you the lowdown on every tour and tour operator in the area; they also run a deli-café with stunning alfresco views of the lake and volcano. Toad Hall is open daily 8:30–5.

En Route   If your bones can take it, a very rough track leads from Tilarán via Cabeceras to Santa Elena, near the Monteverde Cloud Forest Biological Reserve, doing away with the need to cut across to the Pan-American Highway. You may well need a four-wheel-drive vehicle—inquire locally about the present condition of the road—but the views of Nicoya Peninsula, Lake Arenal, and Volcán Arenal reward those willing to bump around a bit. Note, too, that you don't really save much time—on a good day, it takes about 2½ hours as opposed to the 3 required via Cañas and Río Lagarto on the highway.

Monteverde Cloud Forest Biological Reserve

★   *35 km (22 mi) southeast of Tilarán, 167 km (104 mi) northwest of San José.*

In proximity to several fine hotels, the private Reserva Biológica Bosque Nuboso Monteverde is one of Costa Rica's best-kept reserves, with well-marked trails, lush vegetation, and a cool climate. The area's first residents were a handful of Costa Rican families fleeing the rough-and-ready life of nearby gold-mining fields during the 1940s. They were joined in the 1950s by Quakers from Alabama who came in search of peace, tranquillity, and good grazing, but the cloud forest that lay above their

Monteverde and Santa Elena

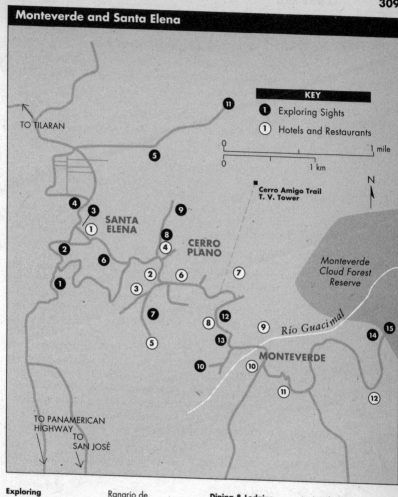

KEY

● Exploring Sights

① Hotels and Restaurants

TO TILARAN

SANTA ELENA

CERRO PLANO

Cerro Amigo Trail
T. V. Tower

Monteverde
Cloud Forest
Reserve

Río Guacimal

MONTEVERDE

TO PANAMERICAN
HIGHWAY
TO
SAN JOSÉ

0 _____ 1 mile
0 _____ 1 km

N

dairy farms was soon to attract the attention of ecologists. Educators and artisans followed, giving Monteverde and its "metropolis," the village of Santa Elena, a mystique all their own.

The collision of moist winds with the continental divide here creates a constant mist whose particles provide nutrients for plants growing at the upper layers of the forest. Giant trees are enshrouded in a cascade of orchids, bromeliads, mosses, and ferns, and, in those patches where sunlight penetrates, brilliantly colored flowers flourish. The sheer size of everything, especially the leaves of the trees, is striking. No less astounding is the variety: 2,500 plant species, 400 species of birds, 500 types of butterflies, and more than 100 different mammals have so far been cataloged at Monteverde. A damp and exotic mixture of shades, smells, and sounds, the cloud forest is also famous for its population of resplendent quetzals, which can be spotted feeding on the *aguacatillo* (like an avocado) trees; best viewing times are early mornings from January until September, and especially during the mating season of April and May. Other forest-dwelling inhabitants include hummingbirds and multicolor frogs.

For those who don't have a lucky eye, a short-stay aquarium is in the field station; captive amphibians stay here just a week before being released back into the wild. Although the reserve limits visitors to 100 people at a time, Monteverde is one of the country's most popular destinations and gets very busy, so come early and allow a generous slice of time for leisurely hiking to see the forest's flora and fauna; longer hikes are made possible by some strategically placed overnight refuges along the way. At the entrance to the reserve you can buy self-guide pamphlets and rent rubber boots; a map is provided when you pay the entrance fee. A two-hour guided night tour starts each evening at 7:30. Note that the Monteverde settlement has no real nucleus; houses and hotels flank a 6-km (4-mi) road from Santa Elena until you arrive at the reserve's entrance. ☎ 645–5122, WEB *www.cct.or.cr.* ✉ *Reserve $12, guide $15.* ☉ *Daily 7–4.*

☾ Greet 30 species of live Costa Rican reptiles and amphibians at the **Serpentario Monteverde.** ✉ *Outside Santa Elena on road to Monteverde,* ☎ *645–5238.* ✉ *$3.* ☉ *Daily 8–5.*

★ ☾ Only in Monteverde would visitors groove to the nightlife at the **Ranario de Monteverde,** an exhibition of 25 species of frogs, toads, and other amphibians. Bilingual biologist-guides take you through a 45-minute tour of the terrariums in the facility outside Santa Elena. For the best show, come around dusk and stay well into the evening when the critters become more active and much more vocal. ✉ *600 yards southeast of Supermercado La Esperanza,* ☎ *645–6320.* ✉ *$8.* ☉ *Daily 9–8:30.*

Several conservation areas that have sprung up near Monteverde make attractive day trips, particularly if the Monteverde reserve is too busy. The **Reserva Santa Elena,** west of Monteverde, has a series of trails that can be walked alone or with a guide. ✉ *6 km (3½ mi) north of Santa Elena,* ☎ *645–5390,* WEB *www.monteverdeinfo.com.* ✉ *$8.* ☉ *Daily 7–4.*

With tours operating out of the El Sapo Dorado hotel (☎ 645–5010), the **Reserva Sendero Tranquilo** invites you to hike 200 acres containing four different stages of cloud forest, including one area illustrating the results of cloud-forest devastation. ✉ *3 km (2 mi) north of park entrance,* ☎ *645–5010.* ✉ *$20 (2-person minimum, 10-person maximum).*

☾ The **Jardín de las Mariposas** (Butterfly Garden) displays tropical butterflies in three enclosed botanical gardens with stunning views of the Golfo de Nicoya. A guided tour helps you understand the stages of a

EYES AFLIGHT IN COSTA RICA

If you visit a Costa Rican cloud forest, you'll probably have your eyes peeled for the emerald toucanet or the three-wattled bellbird, but if you're here between October and April, you'll actually be just as likely to see a Kentucky warbler. Experienced birders shouldn't be surprised to see that some of their feathered friends from home made similar vacation plans, but many people probably don't realize that when northern birds fly south for the winter, they don't all head to Miami.

Seasonal visitors are just part—about a quarter—of the amazing avian panorama in Costa Rica. Nearly 850 bird species have been identified here, more than the United States and Canada have between them—all in an area about half the size of Kentucky. The country is consequently a mecca for amateur ornithologists, who flock here by the thousands. Though the big attractions tend to be such spectacular species as the keel-billed toucan and resplendent quetzal, it is the diversity of shape, size, coloration, and behavior that makes bird-watching in Costa Rica so fascinating.

The country's avian inhabitants range in size from the scintillant hummingbird, standing a mere 2½ inches tall and weighing just over 2 grams, to the long-legged jabiru stork, which reaches a height of more than 1⅓ m (4 ft) and a weight of 14 pounds. The diversity of form and color varies from such striking creatures as the showy scarlet macaw and the quirky purple gallinule to the relatively inconspicuous, and seemingly ubiquitous, clay-color robin, which is, surprisingly enough, Costa Rica's national bird. These robins may look a bit plain, but their song is a melodious one, and since the males sing almost constantly toward the end of the dry season—the beginning of their mating season—local legend has it they call the rains, which play a vital role in a nation so dependent on agriculture.

Foreigners tend to ooh and ah at the sight of those birds associated with the tropics: parrots, parakeets, and macaws; toucans and toucanets; and the elusive but legendary quetzal. But there are many other, equally impressive species flitting around, such as the motmots, with their distinctive racket tails; oropéndolas (golden orioles), which build remarkable hanging nests; and an amazing array of hawks, kites, and falcons.

On the color scale, the country's tanagers, euphonias, manakins, cotingas, and trogons are some of its loveliest plumed creatures, but none of them match the iridescence of the hummingbirds. Costa Rica hosts 51 members of the hummingbird family, compared to the just one species for all of the United States east of the Rocky Mountains. A bit of time spent near a hummingbird feeder will treat you to an unforgettable display of accelerated aerial antics and general pugnacity.

You just might find that the more you observe Costa Rica's birds, the more interesting they get. Bird-watching can be done everywhere in the country—all you need is a pair of binoculars and a copy of *A Guide to the Birds of Costa Rica*, the excellent field guide by Stiles and Skutch. Wake up early, get out into the woods or the garden, focus those binoculars, and you'll quickly be enchanted by the beauty on the wing.

butterfly's life. The private **bird farm** next door has several trails through secondary forest. More than 90 bird species have been sighted here, from the crowned motmot to the resplendent quetzal. ⊠ *Near Pensión Monteverde Inn (take right-hand turnoff 4 km [2½ mi] past Santa Elena on road to Monteverde; continue for 2 km [1 mi]),* ☎ *645–5512.* ⊠ *$7.* ⊙ *Daily 9:30–4.*

Dining and Lodging

$$-$$$ ✕ **De Lucía.** Cordial Chilean owner José Belmar is the walking, talking (five languages) menu in this elegant restaurant. He's always on hand to explain with enthusiasm such masterfully prepared dishes as sea bass with garlic sauce and orange chicken. All the entrées are served with an impressive assortment of grilled vegetables and fried plantains. The handsome wooden restaurant with red mahogany tables is given a distinct South American flavor by an array of Andean tapestries and ceramics. An excellent dessert choice is the *tres leches* (a rich cake of condensed and evaporated milk and sugar) with decaf coffee—a novelty in Costa Rica. ⊠ *Off main road between Santa Elena and Monteverde, on turnoff to Jardín Mariposa,* ☎ *645–5337. AE, MC, V.*

$$-$$$ ✕ **Pizzería de Johnny.** Everyone makes it to this stylish but informal place with candles and white tablecloths during a visit. The Monteverde pizza, with the works, is the most popular dish, and pastas, sandwiches, and a fine wine selection round out the menu. ⊠ *1½ km (1 mi) from Santa Elena on road to reserve,* ☎ *645–5066. V.*

$-$$ ✕ **Jungle Groove Café.** This is nightlife, Monteverde-style—never raucous, but on the quiet side, with good food and soft music amid a lush garden setting. Miami native and owner Miriam Merino mixes Tico cuisine with mild Cuban spices. Try the fajita-like mixed *gallos*, warm tortillas with spicy meat and vegetable fillings. And Miriam sets a new standard for tapas with her seven-layer Cuban-style nachos. ⊠ *50 yards northeast of CASEM,* ☎ *645–6270. MC, V.*

$$$-$$$$ ✕▥ **Hotel El Sapo Dorado.** Having begun life as a nightclub, the Golden Toad became a popular restaurant and then graduated into a very pleasant hotel. Geovanny Arguedas's family arrived here to farm 10 years before the Quakers did, and he and his wife, Hannah Lowther, have built secluded hillside cabins with polished paneling, tables, fireplaces, and rocking chairs. The restaurant is renowned for its pasta, pizza, vegetarian dishes, and sailfish. ⊠ *6 km (4 mi) northwest of park entrance,* ☎ *645–5010,* 𝔽𝔸𝕏 *645–5180,* 𝚆𝙴𝙱 *www.cool.co.cr/usr/sapodorado (mailing address: Apdo. 9–5655, Monteverde). 30 rooms. Restaurant, bar, massage, laundry service. AE, MC, V.*

$$$ ✕▥ **Fonda Vela.** Owned by the Smith brothers, whose family was among
★ the first American arrivals in the 1950s, these steep-roof chalets have large bedrooms with white-stucco walls, wood floors, and huge windows. Some have markedly better views of the wooded grounds, so specify when booking. The most innovatively designed of Monteverde's hotels is also one of the closest to the reserve entrance. Local and international recipes, prepared with flair, are served in the dining room or on the veranda. ⊠ *1½ km (1 mi) northwest of park entrance,* ☎ *645–5125,* 𝔽𝔸𝕏 *645–5119,* 𝚆𝙴𝙱 *www.fondavela.com (mailing address: Apdo. 70060–1000, San José,* ☎ *257–1413,* 𝔽𝔸𝕏 *257–1416). 40 rooms. Restaurant, bar, refrigerator, horseback riding, meeting room; no a/c, no room phones, no room TVs. AE, MC, V.*

$$$ ✕▥ **Hotel Belmar.** Built into the hillside, Hotel Belmar resembles two tall Swiss chalets and commands extensive views of the Golfo de Nicoya and the hilly peninsula. The amiable Chilean owners have designed both elegant and rustic rooms, paneled with polished wood; duvets cover the beds, and half the rooms have balconies. In the dining room, you can count on adventurous and delicious *platos del día*

(daily specials) of Costa Rican and international fare. ⊠ *4 km (2½ mi) north of Monteverde,* ☎ *645-5201,* FAX *645-5135,* WEB *www. centralamerica.com/cr/hotel/belmar.htm (mailing address: Apdo. 17-5655, Monteverde, Puntarenas). 34 rooms. Restaurant, bar, basketball, laundry service; no a/c, no room TVs. V.*

$$–$$$$ 🏠 **El Establo Mountain Resort.** Mixing old and new, The Stable began life as just that, a stable near the road, remodeled and apportioned into comfortable rooms with basic furnishings. A newer pink building perches on the hill above with large suites with wood-and-stone walls. Some contain lofts; all come with amenities rarely seen up here, such as bathtubs, cable TV, in-room phones, and enormous windows with views of the Golfo de Nicoya. ⊠ *3½ km (2 mi) northwest of Monteverde,* ☎ *645-5110,* FAX *645-5041,* WEB *www.hotelestablo.com. 50 rooms. Restaurant, bar, cable TV, pool, hot tub. AE, MC, V.*

$$$ 🏠 **Trapp Family Lodge.** Take a whiff in this cozy lodge and you can imagine yourself in a lumberyard. The enormous rooms, with wood paneling and ceilings, have lovely furniture marvelously crafted from—you guessed it—wood. The architectural style is appropriate, as the lodge is surrounded by trees, a 10-minute walk from the park entrance. It's the closest to the reserve. The friendly Chilean owners are always around to provide personalized service. ⊠ *On main road from park,* ☎ *645-5858,* FAX *645-5990,* WEB *www.trappfam.com (mailing address: Apdo. 70-5655, Monteverde). 20 rooms. Restaurant, bar; no smoking, no a/c, no room phones, no room TVs. V.*

$$–$$$ 🏠 **Arco Iris Lodge.** You can't tell that you're in the center of town at this tranquil spot, with its cozy cabins set among 4 acres of birding trails. Cabin decor ranges from rustic to more plush, but all come with porches. Start your day with a delicious breakfast buffet, including homemade bread, granola, and marmalades. This is an "ecolodge," so many of the kitchen's ingredients come from its own organic garden. The laid-back German management can provide good advice about how to spend your time in the area. ⊠ *75 yards south of Banco Nacional, Santa Elena,* ☎ *645-5067,* FAX *645-5022,* WEB *www.arcoirislodge.com. 10 cabins. Horseback riding, laundry service; no a/c, no room phones, no room TVs. AE, MC, V.*

$$ 🏠 **El Bosque.** Convenient to the Bajo del Tigre nature trail and Meg's Stables, El Bosque's quiet, simple rooms are grouped around a central camping area with a volleyball court. A bridge crosses a stream and leads to the hotel, which serves brick-oven pizzas on its a veranda. ⊠ *2½ km (1½ mi) from Santa Elena on road to reserve,* ☎ *645-5158,* FAX *645-5129 (mailing address: Apdo. 5655, Santa Elena). 26 rooms. Restaurant, volleyball, laundry service; no a/c, no room phones, no room TVs. AE, MC, V.*

$$ 🏠 **La Colina.** This Colorado ranch-style place is a longtime Monteverde standby. Rust colors and earth tones prevail in the rooms, which are accentuated with the occasional wagon wheel and old western trunk. A hearty American-style breakfast is included in the rates, and it will keep you going until your evening dinner. The friendly management offers discounts for extended stays. ⊠ *300 yards south of Cheese Factory,* ☎ *645-5009,* WEB *www.lacolina.com. 11 rooms, 6 with bath. Restaurant, hot tub; no a/c, no room phones, no room TVs. V.*

$ 🏠 **Pensión Monteverde Inn.** The cheapest Monteverde inn is quite far from the park entrance, on a 28-acre private preserve. The bedrooms are basic, but they have stunning views of the Golfo de Nicoya and have hardwood floors, firm beds, and powerful, hot showers. Home cooking is served by the chatty David and María Savage and family. Their dog, Bambi, will warm up to you, too. ⊠ *5 km (3 mi) past Butterfly Garden (on turnoff road), Monteverde,* ☎ *645-5156,* FAX *645-5945. 8 rooms. Dining room; no a/c, no room phones, no room TVs. No credit cards.*

Outdoor Activities and Sports

CANOPY TOURS

One of the most unique ways to explore the rain forest canopy is on an exhilarating canopy tour. Be sure to ask questions about safety of all canopy tour companies and be prepared to walk away if the trip doesn't look professionally handled.

You can visit the Monteverde cloud forest treetops courtesy of the **Original Canopy Tour** (⊠ 50 yards west of La Esperanza Supermarket, ☎ 645–5243; 257–5149 in San José, WEB www.canopytour.com), which has 11 platforms in the canopy—the company's longest tour—that you arrive at using a cable-and-harness traversing system and another that you climb 13 m (42 ft) inside a strangler fig tree to reach. This location also has a Tarzan Swing. Several knockoff tours, with uneven reputations, have sprung up around Costa Rica, also calling themselves "canopy tours." This one, which calls itself "the original," is top-notch. The tours last 2½ hours and are held at 7:30 AM, 10:30 AM, and 2:30 PM. The cost is $45.

Perhaps the idea of being in the tree canopy appeals to you, only you suspect the rock-climbing gear and zip line route are not for you? **Sky Walk** (⊠ across from Banco Nacional, ☎ 645–5238, WEB www.skywalk.co.cr) lets you walk between treetops, up to a height of 42 m (138 ft), by way of five hanging bridges connected from tree to tree. Imposing towers are also used as support although they somewhat mar the landscape. The hour-long walk can be done anytime between 7 and 4 daily and costs $12. Tours with an English-speaking guide leave at 8 and 1—be sure to make reservations. At the same facility is the more adventurous **Sky Trek**, which uses rock-climbing gear, zip lines, and has seven platforms and longer cables between them than the Original Canopy Tour. Tours cost $35 and leave at 7:30, 9:30, 11:30, 1:30, and 2. The company provides cheap transport to and from hotels when called a few hours in advance.

HIKING

The Monteverde Conservation League's **Bajo del Tigre trail** (follow signs along the highway to Monteverde, ☎ 645–5003, WEB www.acmonteverde.com), in the Bosque Eterno de los Niños, makes for a gentle, 1½-km (1-mi) hike through secondary forest. Admission to the trail is $5, and it's open daily 8–4:30.

HORSEBACK RIDING

Meg's Stables (⊠ on main road, halfway between Santa Elena and Monteverde, ☎ 645–5029) offers horseback riding for everyone from toddlers to seasoned experts. Guided rides through the Monteverde area cost around $10 an hour, with prices dropping for longer rides. Reservations are a good idea in high season.

Shopping

In Monteverde, the **Comité de Artesanas de Santa Elena y Monteverde** (CASEM; ☎ 645–5190), an artisans' cooperative open next door to the El Bosque hotel-restaurant, sells locally made crafts, mostly by women, and English books. The **Hummingbird Gallery** (☎ 645–5030), outside the reserve entrance, sells books, gifts, T-shirts, great Costa Rican coffee, prints, and slides by nature specialists Michael and Patricia Fogden, as well as watercolors by nature artist Sarah Dowell.

Northern Guanacaste and Alajuela A to Z

AIR TRAVEL

Central American airline Grupo TACA offers a few flights from abroad into Liberia's Daniel Oduber International Airport. Various charters

serve the airport on changing schedules as well. If your destination lies in Guanacaste, make sure your travel agent investigates the possibility of flying into Liberia instead of San José—you'll save some serious hours on the road.

CARRIERS

SANSA, the domestic division of Grupo TACA, and Travelair fly to Liberia from San José daily. SANSA serves the small airstrip outside of La Fortuna from San José on a charter basis only.
➤ AIRLINES AND CONTACTS: **Grupo TACA/SANSA** (✉ C. 42 and Avda. 3, San José, ☎ 296–0909). **Travelair** (✉ Aeropuerto Internacional Tobías Bolaños, ☎ 220–3054).
➤ AIRPORTS: **Aeropuerto Internacional Daniel Oduber** (✉ 5 km [3mi] west of Liberia, ☎ 296–0909).

BOAT TRAVEL

Desafío Expeditions in La Fortuna and Monteverde provides a fast, popular three-hour transfer between the communities. The taxi–boat–taxi service costs $25 one-way.
➤ BOAT INFORMATION: **Desafío Expeditions** (✉ Central plaza, 50 m [164 ft] north of Banco Nacional, La Fortuna, ☎ 479–9464, WEB www. desafiocostarica.com).

BUS TRAVEL

Fantasy Bus's air-conditioned point-to-point shuttles connecting Arenal with San José and Tamarindo are preferable to buses, although buses cover most areas at a reasonable price. Buses in this region are typically large, clean, and comfortable, but often crowded Friday–Sunday. Don't expect air-conditioning, and even supposedly express buses marked *directo* often make some stops.

Auto Transportes San José–San Carlos buses leave San José for the three-hour trip to San Carlos from Calle 12 between Avenidas 7 and 9, daily every hour 5 AM–7:30 PM. The company runs three buses daily from this same station in San José to La Fortuna, near Arenal, at 6:15, 8:40, and 11:30 AM. From San Carlos you can connect to Arenal and Tilarán. The company also has buses for Los Chiles (Caño Negro), which depart from Calle 12, Avenida 9, daily at 5:30 AM and 3:30 PM; the trip takes five hours. Transmonteverde makes the five-hour trip to Monteverde, departing weekdays at 6:30 AM and 2:30 PM. This route is notorious for theft; watch your bags.
➤ BUS INFORMATION: **Auto Transportes San José-San Carlos** (☎ 256–8914 or 460–5032). **Transmonteverde** (☎ 222–3854).

CAR RENTAL

A few of the high-end resorts on the beach will arrange car rentals. Otherwise, it's best to rent cars in San José or on the Nicoya Peninsula.

CAR TRAVEL

Road access to the northwest is by way of the paved two-lane Pan-American Highway (Carretera Interamericana, CA1), which starts from the west end of Paseo Colón in San José and runs northwest through Cañas and Liberia and to Peñas Blancas (Nicaraguan border). The drive to Liberia takes about three to four hours. Turnoffs to Monteverde, Arenal, and other destinations are often poorly marked—drivers must keep their eyes open. From the easterly zone of Arenal and the Cordillera de Tilarán (La Fortuna), you can head west by way of the road, badly potholed in sections, around Laguna de Arenal. The Monteverde (Santa Elena) turnoff is at Río Lagarto, about 125 km (78 mi) northwest of San José. (From here, an unpaved 30-km [19-mi] track snakes dramatically up through hilly farming country; it takes 1½ to 2 hours

to negotiate it, less by four-wheel-drive vehicle. At the junction for Santa Elena, bear right for the reserve.)

The turnoff for Tilarán and the northwestern end of Laguna de Arenal lies in the town of Cañas. At Liberia, Highway 21 west leads to the beaches of the northern Nicoya Peninsula. To reach San Carlos, La Fortuna, and Caño Negro from San José, a picturesque drive (Highway 35) takes you up through the coffee plantations and over the Cordillera Central by way of Sarchí and Zarcero.

ROAD CONDITIONS

Four-wheel-drive vehicles are recommended, but not essential, for most roads. (If you don't rent a four-wheel-drive vehicle, at least rent a car with high clearance—you'll be glad you did.) The most important thing to know is that short drives can take a long time when the road is potholed or torn up. Plan accordingly. Most minor roads are unpaved and either muddy in rainy season or dusty in dry season—the pavement holds out only so far, and then dirt, dust, mud, potholes, and other impediments interfere with driving conditions and prolong hours spent behind the wheel.

The Pan-American Highway (CA1) and other paved roads run to the Nicaraguan border; paved roads run west to small towns like Filadelfia and La Cruz. The roads into Rincón de la Vieja are unpaved and very slow; figure on an hour from the highway, and be prepared to walk the last half mile to the Las Pailas entrance. The road into Santa Rosa National Park is smooth going as far as the ruins of La Casona. Beyond that, it gets dicey and very steep in places. The national park service encourages you to walk, rather than drive, to the beach. A couple of dirt roads lead into various sections of Guanacaste National Park.

EMERGENCIES

In case of any emergency, dial 911, or one of the specific numbers below.
➤ EMERGENCY SERVICES: **Fire** (☎ 118). **Police** (☎ 911). **Traffic Police** (☎ 227–8030).

ENGLISH-LANGUAGE MEDIA

Librería Chunches in Santa Elena maintains a good selection of books, magazines, and day-old U.S. newspapers in English.
➤ ENGLISH-LANGUAGE BOOKSTORES: **Librería Chunches** (⊠ 50 yards south of Banco Nacional, Santa Elena).

LANGUAGE

Though isolated, Monteverde's large expatriate population makes it a good place to find English speakers. Elsewhere, those connected with large tourist establishments are likely to speak English.

MAIL, SHIPPING, AND INTERNET

Privatized Correos de Costa Rica provides reasonable postal service from this region, though you're better off waiting to post those cards and letters from San José. Public Internet access is not widespread in this part of the country. Expect to pay about $3–$4 per hour of access time.
➤ POST OFFICE: **Correos de Costa Rica** (⊠ 50 yards north of police station, La Fortuna; 50 yards downhill from La Esperanza Supermarket, Santa Elena [Monteverde]).
➤ INTERNET CAFÉS: **Desafío Expeditions** (⊠ Central plaza, La Fortuna, ☎ 479–9464, WEB www.desafiocostarica.com). **Tranquilo Comunicaciones** (⊠ 150 yards downhill from La Esperanza Supermarket, Santa Elena [Monteverde], ☎ 645–5831).

Playa Tamarindo and Playa Longosta

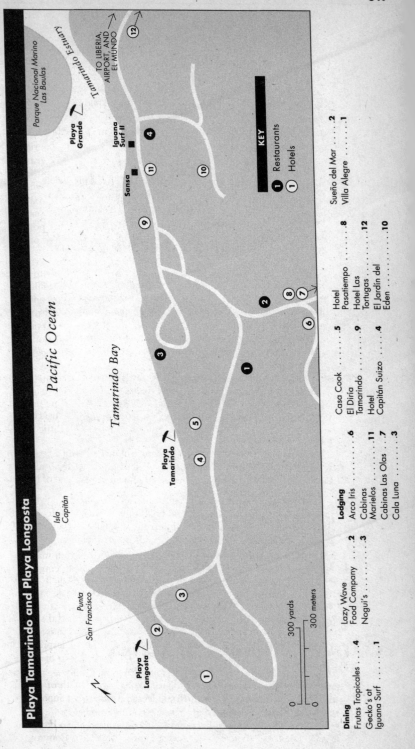

317

Parque Nacional Marino
Las Baulas

Tamarindo Estuary

TO LIBERIA,
AIRPORT, AND
EL MUNDO

Playa
Grande

Iguana
Surf II

Sansa

Pacific Ocean

Isla
Capitán

Punta
San Francisco

Tamarindo Bay

Playa
Tamarindo

Playa
Longosta

KEY

❶ Restaurants

① Hotels

0   300 yards
0   300 meters

Dining
Frutas Tropicales 4
Gecko's at
Iguana Surf 1
Lazy Wave
Food Company ...2
Nogui's 3

Lodging
Arco Iris 6
Cabinas
Marielos 11
Cabinas Las Olas ...7
Cala Luna 3

Casa Cook 5
El Diriá
Tamarindo 9
Hotel
Capitán Suizo 4

Hotel
Pasatiempo 8
Hotel Las
Tortugas 12
El Jardin del
Eden 10

Sueño del Mar 2
Villa Alegre 1

MONEY MATTERS

Most larger tourist establishments are prepared to handle credit cards. Changing U.S. dollars or traveler's checks is possible at the few offices of Banco Nacional scattered throughout the region, but lines are long. Take care of getting local currency with your ATM card back in San José before venturing out here.

➤ BANKS: **Banco Nacional** (✉ Pan-American Highway, La Cruz, ☎ 679–9296; ✉ Central Plaza, La Fortuna, ☎ 479–9022; ✉ 50 yards north of bus station, Santa Elena [Monteverde]), ☎ 645–5027; ✉ Central Plaza, Tilarán, ☎ 695–5255; ✉ 100 yards north of church, Zarcero, ☎ 463–3838).

SHUTTLE VANS

Alternatives to public buses exist. Fantasy Bus has daily service between San José and Arenal. Comfortable, air-conditioned vans leave various San José hotels at 8 AM and return at 2 PM. Tickets cost $21 and must be reserved a day in advance. Fantasy Bus also connects Arenal to Tamarindo on the Nicoya Peninsula.

➤ INFORMATION: **Fantasy Bus** (☎ 800/326–8279 in Costa Rica only).

TOURS

Tikal Tours runs highly informative weeklong eco-adventure tours in Santa Rosa and Arenal. The excellent Horizontes specializes in more independent tours with as few as eight people, including transport by four-wheel-drive vehicle, naturalist guides, and guest lectures. Reputable, organized, and knowledgeable Sun Tours guides can customize trips or recommend some popular stops in the area and some that are off the map.

➤ TOUR COMPANIES: **Horizontes** (✉ 150 yards north of Pizza Hut, Paseo Colón, San José, ☎ 222–2022). **Sun Tours** (✉ Cerro Plano, next to Pizzeria de Johnny, Monteverde, ☎ 645–6328 or 296–7757 in San José). **Tikal Tours** (✉ Avda. 2 between Cs. 7 and 9, San José, ☎ 223–2811).

VISITOR INFORMATION

The ubiquitous TOURIST INFORMATION signs around La Fortuna and Monteverde are really storefront travel agencies hoping to sell you tours rather than provide unbiased sources of information.

The tourist office in San José has information covering the northwest, including maps, bus schedules, and brochures. It's next to the Museo de Oro, beneath the Plaza de la Cultura, and is open weekdays 9–12:30 and 1:30–5. In Liberia, the Casa de la Cultura is officially open weekdays 8–noon and 1:30–5 and Saturday 8–noon and 1:30–4, but it often doesn't adhere to this schedule.

➤ TOURIST INFORMATION: **Casa de la Cultura** (✉ 3 blocks from Central Plaza, Liberia, ☎ 666–4527). **Instituto Costarricense de Turismo** (ICT; ✉ C. 5 between Advas. Central and 2, Barrio del Catedral, San José; ☎ 222–1090).

NICOYA PENINSULA BEACHES

On this sun-drenched Pacific protrusion, expatriate California surfers wander endless golden beaches, coatimundis caper, monkeys howl in dry tropical forests, and turtles ride in on nocturnal high tides to lay their eggs. Combined with a burgeoning number of high-end resorts, these natural wonders make Nicoya a microcosm of Costa Rica.

Tamarindo

37 km (23 mi) west of Filadelfia.

Tamarindo is a lively town with a great variety of restaurants, bars, and hotels at all price levels. Surfing is the main attraction here—Tamarindo hosted the 2002 International Billabong Professional Surfing Tournament—for the young crowd that parties hard at beachfront bars after a day riding the waves. An older crowd is attracted by the upscale, beachfront hotels south of the bustling town center. Developmental hustle is everywhere, evidenced by the presence of condo projects and mini–strip malls. Still, Tamarindo remains appealing because it's virtually self-contained: its beaches are great for snorkeling, boating, kayaking, diving, surfing, and just plain swimming; there are estuaries north and south of town for bird- and animal-watching; and there are two turtle-nesting beaches nearby—Playa Langosta to the south, and Playa Grande to the north. With an airstrip outside town, Tamarindo is also a convenient base for exploring all of Guanacaste. Except for some sections through the middle of town, the very dusty road is in dire need of repaving. The sickly sweet smell in the air is from the molasses mixture poured on the roads to keep down the dust in the dry season.

El Mundo de la Tortuga. To learn about the life cycle of the leatherbacks and the threats they face, visit this creative turtle museum in Playa Grande. Audio tours (in English, Spanish, German or French) are 30 minutes long and lead you through the interactive exhibits. The museum also conducts excellent turtle tours, which often occur late at night, sometimes till 3 AM, depending on turtle sightings. ⊠ *On road to Hotel Las Tortugas,* ☎ *653–0471.* 🖃 *$5.* ☺ *Late Oct.–end Mar., daily 4 PM–after midnight.*

Parque Nacional Marino Las Baulas. North of Tamarindo, across an estuary, this marine park and beach protects the long **Playa Grande.** This beach hosts the world's largest visitation of nesting leatherback turtles (nesting season is October through April). Playa Grande is also a great surf spot. Environmental activist Lewis Wilson, also the owner of the Hotel Las Tortugas, struggled for a decade to get Las Baulas established and has a true understanding of the importance of balancing the oft-conflicting needs of locals, turtles, and tourists. An evening spent discussing ecotourism with him is a real education. The adjacent **Tamarindo Wildlife Refuge,** a mangrove estuary with some excellent bird-watching, has been under some developmental pressure of late. Just south of Tamarindo, accessible by dirt road, is the **Río San Francisco,** with an estuary system that's also rich in bird life. Unlike Tamarindo, it's free of motorboats. *3 km (2 mi) north of Tamarindo,* ☎ *653–0423,* 🖃 FAX *653–0458,* WEB *www.cool.co.cr/usr/turtles.*

Dining

$$–$$$ ✗ **Gecko's at Iguana Surf.** This rustic, thatch-roof restaurant brimming with trickling fountains is attached to a surf shop and is very popular with local American families. Chef John Szilasi bakes his own bread and bread sticks studded with spicy seeds. His menu revolves around fresh local ingredients, such as tuna, calamari, and lobster. The chocolate cake here is famous and sells out quickly; a good backup dessert is the Brandy Freeze. ⊠ *Beside Iguana Surf, on the road to Playa Langosta,* ☎ *653–0334. No credit cards. Closed Mon.–Tues.*

$$–$$$ ✗ **Nogui's.** Also known as the Sunrise Café, Nogui's is considered by local aficionados to have Tamarindo's freshest and most reasonably priced seafood—although even it is getting expensive. Only a dirt road separates Nogui's alfresco plastic tables and chairs from the beach. There are great salads and shrimp tacos for lunch; the full seafood menu is only available at dinner. The langostino is highly recommended, as is

the swimsuit selection in the adjacent shop. ⊠ *South of Zullymar, on Tamarindo circle,* ☎ *653–0029. AE, MC, V.*

$$ ✕ **Lazy Wave Food Company.** For serious food at laughable prices, visit ★ this casual, open-air restaurant built around a giant dead tree. Chéf Derek Furlani from Toronto entertains customers at the open-kitchen counter with his dry wit as he chops, swirls, and sautés fresh local ingredients. The eclectic menu changes daily. At lunch, there may be chunks of seared tuna with a heap of his signature crispy, hand-cut shoestring fries and blanched green beans swirled in sesame oil. For dinner, there may be a warm conch salad. Desserts are standouts, too. ⊠ *Beside Hotel Pasatiempo, behind the storefronts,* ☎ *no phone. No credit cards.*

$ ✕ **Frutas Tropicales.** Waiters hose down the road to dampen the dust that would otherwise smother this busy street-side eatery. The plastic tables and chairs stay full for a reason—the restaurant dishes out Costa Rican food at Costa Rican prices to travelers of every shape and description. The food is nothing fancy, but the casados and breakfasts are tasty and substantial. The menu includes U.S.-style hamburgers and fries, and great *frutas tropicales* (tropical fruit drinks). ⊠ *Main road, toward north end of town,* ☎ *653–0041. AE, MC, V.*

Lodging

$$$$ 🏨 **Casa Cook.** These one-bedroom, hardwood-detailed cabinas just off Tamarindo's beach are owned by a retired American couple, Chuck and Ruthann Cook. Each cabina has a full kitchen, its own water heater, a queen-size sofa bed in the living room, a queen bed in the bedroom, and screened doors and windows. The *casita* (literally, a small house)—a 550-square-ft, one-bedroom apartment—has a private bath, kitchen, living room, and outside eating area. Air-conditioning is $10 extra per night. ⊠ *On road to Playa Langosta, north of the Hotel Capitán Suizo,* ☎ *653–0125,* FAX *653–0753,* WEB *www.tamarindo.com/cook. 3 cabinas, 1 casita. Fans, in-room safes, cable TV, kitchenettes, pool, beach; no-smoking. AE, MC, V.*

$$$$ 🏨 **El Diria Tamarindo.** A shady tropical garden right next to the beach eliminates the need to stray far from Tamarindo's first high-end hotel. Rooms in the contemporary three-story building with pre-Columbian design motifs have tile floors and modern furniture, and each has a spacious balcony. Try to avoid the rooms facing the noisy main road. The thatched rotunda bar and restaurant overlook a large rectangular pool. ⊠ *800 yards before Tamarindo center; next to the shopping center,* ☎ *653–0031,* FAX *653–0208,* WEB *www.tamarindodiria.co.cr (mailing address: Apdo. 476–1007, San José,* ☎ *258–4224). 123 rooms. Restaurant, bar, in-room safes, cable TV, minibars, 2 pools, casino, laundry service. AE, MC, V.*

$$$$ 🏨 **Hotel Capitán Suizo.** Steps from a relatively quiet stretch of ★ Tamarindo's gorgeous beach, these elegant, balconied bungalows (part of a small, upscale chain of inns) are set in a lushly landscaped garden, and surround a large, shady pool. The stunning, multilevel rooms have high, angled ceilings and amusing flourishes of color on the walls. A beautifully decorated and subtly lit restaurant serves contemporary cuisine and hosts beach barbecues. Monkeys and birds visit the Swiss Captain's place, so the price of your room includes some wildlife. Diving and kayaking trips can be arranged. ⊠ *Right side of road toward Playa Langosta (veer left before circle),* ☎ *653–0075 or 653–0353,* FAX *653–0292,* WEB *www.hotelcapitansuizo.com. 22 rooms, 8 bungalows. Restaurant, in-room safes, refrigerators, pool, horseback riding, boating, fishing, laundry service. AE, MC, V.*

$$$$ 🏨 **El Jardín del Eden.** The only drawback to the "Garden of Eden" (this one, anyway) is that it's not right on the beach. Instead, the two-tier, Mediterranean-style, pink building is among a lush hillside gardens.

Rooms have carved hardwood furniture or oversize bamboo furniture, and elegantly styled bathrooms. All rooms have ocean views, and two beautiful pools provide the missing water element. The thatch-roof restaurant prepares a variety of fresh seafood dishes and outstanding steaks. ⊠ *From Hotel El Milagro on main road, turn left, go 200 yards, then right for 200 yards uphill, (mailing address: Apdo. 1094–2050, San Pedro),* ☎ *653–0137,* FAX *653–0111,* WEB *www.jardindeleden.com. 18 rooms, 2 apartments. Restaurant, 2 bars, fans, in-room safes, cable TV, refrigerators, 2 pools, hot tub, laundry service; no a/c. AE, MC, V.*

$$$ 🏨 **Hotel Las Tortugas.** Who would have thought that architecture could be shaped by turtles? Indeed, the comfortable rooms here were built with them in mind. Guest room windows do not overlook the nesting beaches, since light interferes with the turtles' nighttime rituals. The rooms are otherwise quiet, with good beds, stone floors, and stucco walls. Owner Louis Wilson offers long-term rentals in apartments with kitchenettes or basic housing for turtle volunteers. The restaurant serves healthful, high-quality food. The surf is good but it sometimes has dangerous rip currents, at which times you can retreat to the turtle-shape pool. Local guides lead turtle tours at night, and the hotel also offers canoe trips in the nearby Tamarindo Wildlife Refuge. ⊠ *Las Baulas Marine National Park, 3 km (2 mi) north of Tamarindo,* ☎ *653–0423,* ☎ FAX *653–0458,* WEB *www.cool.co.cr/usr/turtles (mailing address: Apdo. 164, Santa Cruz de Guanacaste). 11 rooms, 7 apartments. Restaurant, pool, boating, laundry service; no room phones. V.*

$$$ 🏨 **Hotel Pasatiempo.** One of the better bargains in Tamarindo, the hotel's cabinas, each named after a Guanacaste beach, are scattered around the nicely landscaped grounds and the pool; each has a patio with a hammock, simple wooden furnishings, and a unique hand-painted mural. Sherbet-color suites have one bedroom and a pull-out sofa in the living room. The Yucca Bar frequently hires local musicians—a bonus if Costa Rica's otherwise slow nightlife leaves you restless—and a wide-screen satellite TV provides sports fans with their periodic fix. Water sports, a sailing cruise, and other activities are easily arranged. ⊠ *Off the dirt road to Playa Langosta, 200 yards from beach behind Tamarindo circle,* ☎ *653–0096,* FAX *653–0275,* WEB *www.hotelpasatiempo.com. 11 cabinas, 2 suites. Restaurant, bar, some cable TV, pool, laundry service. AE, MC, V.*

$$ 🏨 **Arco Iris.** This wonderful small hotel is on the hill behind the Tamarindo circle. The four cheery, wildly imaginative cabinas are painted in primary colors and decorated along distinct themes. One has two bedrooms and a kitchen. In the past aerobics, kick-boxing, or yoga sessions have been taught on-site, and in case it all gets to be too much, there's also a masseuse. At press time, however, it was unclear whether these unique services will be continued under a new owner. ⊠ *Follow signs past Hotel Pasatiempo and go up hill to the right,* ☎ *653–0330. 4 cabinas. Some kitchenettes; no a/c, no room phones. No credit cards.*

$$ 🏨 **Cabinas Marielos.** In high season Tamarindo presents few decent bargain rooms; among the best are the cabinas here, which have a slightly Alpine look. They're in two wings, flanking a colorful flower garden well back from the noise and dust of the road. Guests sometimes share their meals in the common kitchen. The atmosphere is surprisingly serene. Note that the water doesn't get terribly hot except in the three newest air-conditioned rooms. ⊠ *Across the main dirt road from the beach, north of the town center (follow signs),* ☎ FAX *653–0141. 20 rooms. Laundry service; no a/c in some rooms, no room phones. AE, MC, V.*

Outdoor Activities and Sports

BOATING, SURFING, AND KAYAKING

Iguana Surf (⊠ on the road to Playa Langosta, ☎ FAX 653–0148) has information for surfers and visitors. Iguana Surf rents surfboards,

Boogie boards, and snorkeling equipment at their second location, **Iguana Surf 2**, right on the beach. Naturalists lead tours into the bird-watching haven of the nearby San Francisco estuary, which might include an encounter with a troop of howler monkeys. Snorkeling tours by kayak or motorboat are also available.

SPORTFISHING

A number of fishing charters in Tamarindo cater to saltwater anglers. The best among them is probably **Tamarindo Sportfishing** (☎ 653–0090), run by Randy Wilson, who has led the way in developing catch-and-release techniques that are easy on the fish. Wilson has roamed and fished the Guanacaste waters for 25 years now, and he knows where the big ones lurk. His boat, the *Talking Fish,* is equipped with a marlin chair and a cabin with a shower. Full days run $975, half days $575.

Playa Langosta

2 km (1 mi) south of Tamarindo.

Playa Langosta, a leatherback-turtle nesting beach, is less protected than the beach at Tamarindo. As a result, informal viewings with private guides are a lot cheaper here than the more organized Playa Grande turtle tours. Big, well-shaped river-mouth waves near the north end of the beach make it popular with surfers. But with lots of expensive, private villas and refined B&Bs, Playa Langosta is fast becoming an upscale, gentrified extension of Tamarindo.

Quite separate, geographically and atmospherically from Langosta, **Playa Avellanas,** 32 km (20 mi) to the south, is a beautiful 1-km (½-mi) stretch of pale-gold sand with rocky outcroppings, a river mouth, and a mangrove swamp estuary. You have to drive inland to Villa Real to get from one to the other. Locals claim there are eight surf spots when the swell is strong.

Dining and Lodging

$$$$ ✕☷ **Cala Luna.** A labyrinth of high hibiscus hedges leads to large, luxe, ocher-color rooms, with king-size beds and alcoves softly lit with signature moon sconces. Oversize bathrooms have dolphins cavorting on walls around curved bathtubs for two. The private villas each have their own small pool; two larger, and glorious pools are for shared use. Overlooking one is the pretty Cala Moresca restaurant. The chef leans toward Mediterranean cuisine: red snapper with a lime–caper butter accompanied by tabouli and hummus. The exotic fruit plate (part of the free Continental breakfast) is a work of art, and all the food is reasonably priced. ✉ *Across from Sueño del Mar,* ☎ *653–0214,* ℻ *653–0213,* ⓦⓔⓑ *www.calaluna.com. 20 rooms, 21 villas. Restaurant, bar, in-room safes, cable TV, 2 pools, massage, snorkeling, fishing, bicycles. AE, MC, V.*

$$$$ ☷ **Sueño del Mar.** A garden gate opens onto a dreamy world of intimate
★   gardens and patios adorned with frescoes and antique tiles. Seashells are embedded in window frames and strung together in mobiles. The adobe-style house, which descends down a stepped passageway, contains three double rooms with high, queen-size beds and Balinese showers open to the sky. There's also a casita with its own kitchen and a breezy, book-filled honeymoon suite upstairs. A lavish breakfast is served on the patio looking onto a tiny garden pool. Or you can take your morning coffee a few steps down to the desert-island beach. Air-conditioning is $10 extra. ✉ *150 yards south of Capitan Suizo, turn right for 50 yards, then right again for about 100 yards to entrance gate (across from back of Cala Luna Hotel),* ☎ ℻ *653–0284,* ⓦⓔⓑ *www.tamarindo.com/sdmar. 3 rooms, 1 suite, 1 casita. Restaurant, pool, horseback riding, snorkeling, boating, fishing, bicycles, laundry service; no room phones. V.*

$$$$ ⊞ **Villa Alegre.** Owned by congenial and helpful Californians Barry
★ and Suzye Lawson, this homey but very sophisticated Spanish-style B&B
has a lovely location, close to a stand of trees and a somewhat rocky
but swimmable beach. Rooms are furnished with souvenirs from the
Lawsons' travels to Japan, Russia, Guatemala, and other lands. Each
room has a private patio. The lavish gourmet breakfast is included in
the price. The hotel often plans and hosts weddings. ⊠ *Playa Langosta,
south of Sueño del Mar,* ☎ *653–0270,* FAX *653–0287,* WEB *www.
tamarindo.com/alegre. 7 rooms, 2 villas. Fans, no-smoking rooms,
pool; no room phones. AE, MC, V.*

$$$ ⊞ **Cabinas Las Olas.** Frequented mainly by surfers, these spacious
glass and stone cabinas in an airy forest behind Playa Avellanas should
also appeal to bird-watchers, animal lovers, and naturalists. Monkeys
and other critters lurk around this isolated spot, which has expansive
grounds with trees galore. An elevated boardwalk leads from the cab-
inas to the beach through a protected mangrove estuary. The three-
meal restaurant, complete with an adjacent outdoor video bar, serves
reasonably priced food. ⊠ *20 km (12 mi) south of Tamarindo, in Playa
Avellanas,* ☎ *233–4455 or 382–4366,* FAX *222–8685,* WEB *www.
cabinaslasolas.co.cr (mailing address: Apdo. 1404–1250, Escazú). 10
cabinas. Restaurant, bar, dive shop, boating, bicycles, laundry service;
no a/c, no room phones. AE, MC, V.*

Playa Negra

44 km (27 mi) south of Playa Langosta.

Americans—surfers at least—got their first look at Playa Negra in *The
Endless Summer II,* which featured some dynamite sessions at this spec-
tacular rock-reef point break. Surfing cognoscenti will dig the waves,
which are almost all rights and often beautifully shaped. Surfer cul-
ture is also apparent in the wave of casual restaurants, health-food bak-
eries, Internet cafés, and bikini shops springing up along the road. A
roadside tent bazaar sells sarongs and crafts.

Lodging

$$$ ⊞ **Hotel Playa Negra.** From sunny lawns strewn with lush plantings,
★ this collection of round, brilliantly colored, thatch-roof cabinas face the
ocean. Inside, cooled by ceiling fans, the cabinas have built-in sofas and
beautiful tile bathrooms. The ocean is good for swimming and snorkeling, with tidal pools, swimming holes, and rock reefs providing shelter. And for surfers, with a good swell running, this is paradise found.
There is also a surfing school, as well as Boogie board classes. The restaurant serves deftly prepared Latin and European dishes. ⊠ *Go north on
dirt road out of Paraiso and follow signs carefully at forks in the road,*
☎ *658–8034,* FAX *658–8035,* WEB *www.playanegra.com. 10 cabinas.
Restaurant, bar, in-room safes, pool, horseback riding, volleyball, surfing, laundry service; no a/c, no room phones. AE, MC, V.*

$$ ⊞ **Mono Congo Lodge.** Mono Congo translates as "howler monkey,"
and those noisy but endearing creatures have been plentiful here. But
a new luxury-housing complex developed by the hotel owner is tak-
ing over this part of the beach and may scare away some of the wildlife.
The shaded, three-story hardwood lodge has comfortable seating areas,
a communal kitchen, and four guest rooms, with bathrooms down the
hall. Decent waves, boards for rent, and rustic, comfortable accom-
modations still make this a good surfing holiday spot. ⊠ *50 yards north
of La Plaza football field in Los Pargos,* ☎ FAX *382–6926 (mailing ad-
dress: Apdo. 177–5150, Santa Cruz). 4 rooms share 2 baths, 1 house.
Tennis court, horseback riding, surfing, laundry service. No credit
cards.*

Playa Junquillal

2 km (1 mi) south of Paraiso

Junquillal (pronounced hoon–key–*yall*), to the south of Playa Negra, is a long 3-km (2-mi) stretch of uninterrupted beach, with calm surf and only one hotel on the beach side of the road. This is one of the quieter beaches in Guanacaste and a real find for seekers of tranquillity.

Dining and Lodging

$$$ ✕ **La Puesta del Sol.** Food aficionado Alessandro Zangari and his wife
★ Silvana have created what he modestly calls "a little restaurant in my home." But regulars drive all the way from San José just to enjoy the haute-Italian menu at this dinner-only restaurant. Alessandro spares no expense or effort to secure the best ingredients: Every year he travels to Italy to buy truffles in season. The softly lit patio restaurant, tinted in tangerine and deep blue, evokes a Moroccan courtyard. All the pasta is made from scratch, of course; the ravioli *boscaiolo* contain a woodsy trio of cremini, porcini, and Portobello mushrooms. ⊠ *North of the beach, Playa Junquillal,* ☎ 658–8442. *No credit cards. Closed May–June and Sept.–Oct. No lunch.*

$$$ ⌂ **Guacamaya Lodge.** Secluded Guacamaya, on a breezy hill, has ex-
★ pansive views of surrounding countryside and a river estuary below and is ideal for bird-watching. Swiss siblings Bernie and Alice Etene have a delightful compound, with flocks of visiting parrots and cranes rising up from the estuary. The landscaping around the pool is exceptional, with chenille plants trailing velvety pink tails and tall gingers blazing vibrant red torches. The three-meal restaurant serves excellent, reasonably priced food. In addition to spacious cabinas, with lovely fabric curtains and bedspreads and lots of windows to let in the cooling breezes, there's an airy, well-equipped modern house with a full kitchen. ⊠ *300 yards off Playa Junquillal,* ☎ FAX 653–0431 or 658–8431, WEB *www.guacamayalodge.com (mailing address: Apdo. 6, Santa Cruz).* 6 *cabinas, 1 house. Restaurant, bar, pool, volleyball, playground, laundry service; no a/c, no room phones. AE, MC, V.*

$$$ ⌂ **Hotel Iguanazul.** This isolated beachfront resort on a bluff has a pool, a three-meal restaurant and bar, and 3 km (2 mi) of beach stretching south. Rooms (two per cabina) have wood-beam ceilings, tile floors, and are simply furnished, with two double beds. The hotel itself is looking a little tired, but the fabulous surf of Playa Negra is 10 minutes away, and there's often decent surfing in front of the hotel. Air-conditioned rooms cost more, but breakfast is free for all. Satellite TV is available in a recreation room. ⊠ *North end of Playa Junquillal,* ☎ 658–8124, FAX 653–0123, WEB *www.iguanazul.com (mailing address: Apdo. 130–5150, Santa Cruz).* 24 *rooms. Restaurant, bar, fans, in-room safes, pool, volleyball, beach, recreation room, laundry service; no a/c in some rooms, no room phones. AE, MC, V.*

$$$ ⌂ **Land Ho! at Hotel Villa Serena.** Cape Cod comes to Costa Rica—
★ American owners Olive and John Murphy have created a tropical version of New England, with shell-motif quilts and wall stencils, and hooked rugs with palm trees. Rooms are spacious and comfortable; for the ultimate in romance, ask for No. 10, a round room with an ocean view. There's a large pool in a lovely, landscaped garden and a full-service day spa. To reach the terrace restaurant overlooking the beach, you'll pass a collection of Costa Rican student art, some of it for sale. ⊠ *Across the dirt road from Playa Junquillal,* ☎ FAX 658–8430, WEB *www.land-ho.com.* 12 *rooms. Restaurant, pool, spa, horseback riding, snorkeling, boating, fishing; no a/c, no room phones. AE, MC, V. Closed Oct.*

Tambor

20 km (14 mi) south of Curú National Wildlife Refuge, 27 km (17 mi) south of Paquera.

In the back of the large half-moon Bahía Ballena, Tambor is undergoing a land-sale frenzy similar to that at Tamarindo—you can see a golf course and housing development from the road, and signs of further development all around them. The area's luxe resort hotels have gotten a lot of press, thanks to *Temptation Island,* which filmed episodes here. The resorts arrange plenty of activities, but you could break out on your own. The hike from Tambor around the Piedra Amarilla point to Tango Mar Resort is about 8 km (5 mi) long, and the trees along the way resound with the throaty utterings of male howler monkeys. You can fly to Tambor from San José.

Along a dusty road are interesting souvenir shops, a supermarket, a SANSA office, and an adventure-tour office as well as restaurants and hotels. **Cóbano,** 12 km (7½ mi) to the west, is a bustling crossroads with supermarkets, a bank, restaurants, shops, a gas station, and even an ice-cream parlor.

Lodging

$$$$ ⊞ **Barceló Playa Tambor & Casino.** This Spanish-owned mega-complex was one of Costa Rica's first all-inclusive resorts; the price includes all food, alcoholic drinks (local brands), and the use of sports equipment, including kayaks and catamarans. You can partake of lots of activities around the resort's grassy grounds. But be prepared to share with up to 1,200 other guests during high season. The airy although fairly standard rooms have spacious bathrooms, hair dryers, and some have coffeemakers. ⊠ *South of Tambor village, on the main road,* ☎ *683–0303,* FAX *683–0304,* WEB *www.barcelo.com. 402 rooms. 2 restaurants, 3 bars, snack bar, cable TV, pool, hair salon, massage, 3 tennis courts, aerobics, beach, casino, dance club, Internet, laundry service, travel services. AE, MC, V.*

$$$$ ⊞ **Tambor Tropical.** Perhaps you've seen this collection of five cabinas,
★ which surround a pool in the palm trees off Playa Tambor in Bahía Ballena, when it was featured on the TV series *Temptation Island?* The remarkable buildings are made from strips of local hardwoods arranged in attractive diagonal patterns. Each comfortable and spacious (1,000-square-ft) cabina has a living room, bedroom, bathroom with hot water, and fully equipped kitchen. Friendly staff members go out of their way to be helpful. ⊠ *Follow main street of Tambor toward water (hotel fronts beach),* ☎ *683–0011,* FAX *683–0013,* WEB *www.tambortropical.com (reservations: 867 Liberty St. NE, Box 12945, Salem, OR 97301,* ☎ *503/365–2872,* FAX *503/371–2471). 10 rooms. Restaurant, bar, kitchens, pool, hot tub, horseback riding, beach, Internet; no a/c, no room phones. AE, MC, V.*

$$$$ ⊞ **Tango Mar Resort.** Chosen as an ideal tropical location for the
★ *Temptation Island* TV series, this alluring hotel is perfect for the part, with palm-thatch cabins on stilts. They look rustic on the outside but are pure luxury inside. Rooms in the main hotel are luxurious, too, with private balconies and sea views; some have whirlpool baths. The breezy Cristobal restaurant serves international cuisine and has an ocean view. On the grounds are a lushly landscaped, spring-fed pool, a spectacular beachfront waterfall, and an immaculate golf course. The hotel is fronted by a good surfing wave. ⊠ *2 km (1 mi) west of Tambor (mailing address: Apdo. 1–1260, Escazú),* ☎ *683–0001; 289–9328 in San José,* FAX *683–0003,* WEB *www.tangomar.com. 6 villas, 18 rooms, 12 suites. 2 restaurants, 2 bars, in-room safes, cable TV, some kitchenettes, re-*

frigerators, pool, some in-room hot tubs, 9-hole golf course, 2 tennis courts, hiking, horseback riding, beach, boating, fishing, Internet. AE, DC, MC, V.

Montezuma

7 km (4½ mi) southeast of Cóbano, 45 km (28 mi) south of Paquera.

Montezuma is beautifully positioned on a sandy bay, hemmed in by a precipitous wooded shoreline. At the bottom of the hill, the funky town center is a pastel cluster of new-age health-food cafés, trendy beachwear shops, and jaunty tour kiosks mixed in with older Tico *sodas* (casual eateries) and noisy open-air bars. Montezuma has been on the international vagabond circuit for years, attracting surfers and alternative-lifestyle types, and some unsavory characters as well. But now you are as likely to meet older, outdoorsy European tourists as dreadlocked surfers.

The main attraction for everybody is the beach that stretches across one national park and two nature preserves to the north, leading to a spectacular beachfront waterfall. Just over a bridge, 10 minutes south of town, a slippery path patrolled by howler monkeys leads upstream to two waterfalls, the second one an impressive 33 m (108 ft) high with a thrilling **swimming hole.** Do not jump or dive from the waterfalls. There are no signs posting the danger and some young people inadvertently jumped to their deaths in 2002.

Dining and Lodging

$$ ✕ **Playa Los Artistas.** This creative open-air Italian restaurant on the beach specializes in Mediterranean recipes for fresh seafood. Driftwood tables, lamps, and other rustic touches provide a romantic yet casual atmosphere. Try the carpaccio *de atun,* a raw tuna appetizer seasoned with oregano and garlic. ✉ *300 yards south of town, past Los Mangos Hotel,* ☎ *no phone. No credit cards. Closed Sun. No lunch.*

$ ✕ **Cafe Iguana.** This funky café, subtitled *La Esquina Dulce* (The Sweet Corner), serves up real Italian espresso, fresh fruit juices, and baked goods from 6 AM on. Check out the impressive selection of huge muffins and dessert breads, including such exotic flavors as mango and pineapple. The overstuffed sandwiches, made on fresh, crusty home-baked bread, are big enough for two. Wooden stools on a terrace make perfect perches for watching the passing parade of *todo el mundo* Montezuma. ✉ *Town center, Montezuma,* ☎ *no phone. No credit cards.*

$$$ ▥ **Cabinas El Sano Banano.** This colony of eight tropical igloo-like cabins huddles in the woods north of town close to the beach. Each cozy, domed bungalow sleeps two and has a refrigerator. A two-story building has three air-conditioned suites, with kitchens above, and three double rooms below. Adding to the Smurf-world fantasy is the pool, with curvy mounds that form a series of waterfalls. There is no restaurant, but it's a 10-minute walk into town with its many food options. ✉ *On the beach, north of Montezuma, main road,* ☎ *642–0638,* FAX *642–0068,* WEB *www.elbanano.com. 3 rooms, 3 suites, 8 bungalows. Some kitchenettes, refrigerators, pool, hiking, beach, laundry service; no a/c in some rooms, no room phones. AE, MC, V.*

$$$ ▥ **Hotel El Jardín.** Climbing the hill above town, this Italian-owned
★ hotel has panoramic ocean views. True to its name, the cabins are scattered around a garden lush with flowering gingers and populated by indigenous stone-sculpture people. Teak paneling and furniture, stained-glass pictorial panels, and terraces with hammocks give this hotel style as well as comfort. ✉ *Main road, entering Montezuma,* ☎ *642–0548,* FAX *642–0074,* WEB *www.hoteleljardin.com. 15 rooms, 2 houses with kitchens. Fans, refrigerators; no a/c in some rooms, no room phones. No credit cards.*

$$$ 🏠 **Nature Lodge Finca Los Caballos.** A spirited Canadian woman runs this charming, small hotel high on a hill. The open-air restaurant and reception area both have bird's-eye views of ocean and valley below. Designed with a southwestern U.S. motif, the rooms have pastel walls decorated with stencils of lizards and frogs. A two-bedroom bungalow, formerly the owner's house, is set apart from the hotel and accommodates up to four. The owner leads wonderful horseback tours and often invites guests to accompany her to rodeos. ✉ *3 km (2 mi) north of Montezuma,* ☎ FAX *642–0124,* WEB *www.naturelodge.net (mailing address: Apdo. 22, Cóbano de Puntarenas). 7 rooms, 1 bungalow. Restaurant, fans, pool, horseback riding; no a/c, no room phones. AE, MC, V.*

$$–$$$ 🏠 **Hotel Amor de Mar.** Take the time to walk 10 minutes south of town
★ to find this ruggedly handsome, two-story natural-wood hotel surrounded by trees and a grassy lawn stretching to the ocean. Great breakfasts and immediate access to the waterfall hike make this perhaps the finest little hotel in Montezuma. The rooms, with wood paneling, are comfortable and simply furnished. The dining room serves breakfast and lunch only. ✉ *South of town on beach road,* ☎ FAX *642–0262,* WEB *www.amordemar.com. 11 rooms, 9 with bath. Dining room, beach, laundry service; no a/c, no room phones. V.*

$$ ✕🏠 **El Sano Banano Restaurant and B&B.** Montezuma's original nat-
★ ural-food source has grown more sophisticated and now includes fish and chicken on its healthful but delicious menu. It's hard to believe that the sinfully rich-tasting chocolate mousse tart is made with tofu. A battalion of ceiling fans keeps the air moving in the renovated, spacious, adobe-style restaurant. It's open for breakfast from 7 AM but if you come for dinner around 7:30 PM, you can take in a nightly free movie. Attached to the restaurant is a new B&B annex, with air-conditioned rooms decorated in Mexican style with private baths for $50 a night. ✉ *Main road, Montezuma,* ☎ *642–0638,* FAX *642–0068,* WEB *www.elbanano.com. 3 rooms, 3 suites, 8 bungalows. Restaurant, cable TV, pool, Internet. AE, MC, V.*

Nicoya Peninsula Beaches A to Z

AIR TRAVEL

Liberia has a tiny international airport, Aeropuerto Internacional Daniel Oduber. Small airstrips (and sometimes an adjacent building or shelter) are in Tamarindo, Tambor and a few others coastal resort areas.

CARRIERS

SANSA flies daily from Juan Santamaría International Airport to Tamarindo, Tambor, Playa Carrillo, Punta Islita, and Nosara. Travelair leaves from Aeropuerto Internacional Tobías Bolaños in Tibás, a northern suburb of San José, to fly to Liberia, Tamarindo, Playa Carrillo, Punta Islita, and Tambor.

➤ AIRLINES AND CONTACTS: **Aeropuerto Internacional Daniel Oduber** (☎ 668–1032 or 296–0909, Liberia). **SANSA** (☎ 296–0909 Liberia airport, FAX 666–1017; 656–0131 in Sámara; ☎ 653–0012 in Tamarindo; 683–0015 in Tambor; WEB www.flysansa.com). **Travelair** (✉ Apdo. 8–4920, ☎ 220–3054, FAX 220–0413, WEB www.travelair-costarica.com).

BOAT AND FERRY TRAVEL

At press time it was unclear how the Taiwan Friendship Bridge will affect the river's passenger-and-car ferry routes at Puerto Moreno.

Car ferries run by Naviera Tambor and the Asociación de Desarrollo Integral Paquera (formerly Ferry Peninsula) connect Puntarenas with

Paquera, with continuing bus service to Montezuma. The trip takes 1¼-hours and the car ferries leave six times daily, between 5 AM and 8:15 PM, with an equal number of return trips. The Puntarenas–Playa Naranjo car ferry, run by Cooantramar, takes 1½ hours, departing daily at 3:15, 7, and 10:50 AM and 2:50 and 7 PM.

A passenger-only *lancha* (launch), run by the Asociación de Desarrollo Integral de Paquera, leaves Puntarenas for Paquera three times daily, at 6 and 11 AM and 3:15 PM, from a hard-to-find small dock west of the Banco Nacional near the market. On the Paquera side, launches leave for Puntarenas on the same schedule. Bus links and cabs are available at the Nicoya end of the ferry lines.

Note that these schedules are subject to change between the high and low seasons and during holidays. Expect long waits on all car ferries in high season and holiday weekends. To avoid a longer than necessary wait and to get up-to-the-minute schedules, always call ahead.

➤ BOAT AND FERRY INFORMATION: **Asociación de Desarrollo Integral de Paquera (formerly Ferry Peninsular)** (car ferry and passenger-only launch between Puntarenas and Paquera, ☎ 641–0118 or 641–0515). **Coonatramar** (car ferry to Playa Naranjo, ☎ 661–1069). **Naviera Tambor** (car ferry to Paquera, run by Barceló hotel company, ☎ 661–2084).

BUS TRAVEL TO AND FROM THE NICOYA PENINSULA

Bus service connects the larger cities to each other and to the more popular beaches, but forget about catching a bus from beach to beach; you'll generally have to backtrack to the inland hubs of Nicoya and Liberia unless you take a minibus, which may take just a long as a bus, although it should be more comfortable. Given the unpredictability of bus schedules, bus conditions, and the changes to road travel with the new bridge across the Río Tempisque, it's best to fly into the airport nearest your resort and stay put for a bit of time until you're ready for another part of the country altogether.

BUS ROUTES

For Tamarindo, a 5½-hour trip, buses run by Empresa Alfaro leave daily at 6 AM and 3:30 PM from Calle 14 at Avenida 5.

Tralapa runs a daily bus from San José to Junquillal at 2 PM from Calle 20, Avda. 3, taking 51//2 hours. There's also a daily bus from Santa Cruz to Junquillal.

Buses currently run to Montezuma from Paquera, via Cóbano, six times daily between 6:15 AM and 6:15 PM, returning six times between 5:30 AM and 4:30 PM; but inquire about the latest schedule for this route before you set off.

MINIBUS ROUTES

For $21, you can ride on the comfortable, air-conditioned Greyline Fantasy Tours minibuses that connect San José, Liberia, Tamarindo, and other destinations in Guanacaste. The Greyline bus from San José to Tamarindo and Liberia begins picking up passengers from hotels daily around 6 AM. The return leaves Tamarindo around 2 PM and passes through Liberia around 3:30 PM.

➤ BUS INFORMATION: **Empresa Alfaro** (☎ 222–2666 or 685–5032 in Nicoya). **Greyline Fantasy Tours** (☎ 223–4650). **Tralapa** (☎ 223–5859 or 680–0392).

CAR RENTAL

It's best to stick with the main rental offices in San José because they have more cars available and you're more likely to reach an English-speaking agent on the phone; some have local satellite offices. There

are also a few local rental agencies. Alamo offers pickup and car delivery in Liberia. Budget has branches in San José and also 6 km (4 mi) west of Liberia's airport. Economy and Alamo now offer cars in Tamarindo. Elegante also offers cars in Tamarindo. Sol Rentacar is in front of Hotel El Bramadero in Liberia.

➤ INTERNATIONAL AGENCIES: **Alamo** (✉ 2 km [1.2 mi] north of the Liberia airport, Liberia, ☎ 668–1111 or 800/462–5266; Hotel Diría, Tamarindo, ☎ 653–0727 or 653–0357). **Budget** (✉ 6 km [4 mi] southwest of Liberia airport, Liberia, ☎ 668–1024 or 668–1126; Tamarindo Vista Villas Hotel, Tamarindo, ☎ 653–0829). **Economy** (✉ 5 km [3 mi] south of Liberia on road to airport, Liberia, ☎ 666–2816 or 666–7560; on the main road entering Tamarindo, across from Restaurant Coconut, Tamarindo, ☎ 653–0728).

➤ LOCAL AGENCIES: **Elegante** (✉ C. 10 between Avdas. 13 and 15, San José, ☎ 257–0026). **Sol Rentacar** (✉ Liberia, ☎ 666–2222).

CAR TRAVEL

The northwest is accessed via the paved two-lane Pan-American Highway (CA1), which begins at the top of Paseo Colón in San José. The new bridge across the Río Tempisque, scheduled to open in late 2002 or early 2003, should cut down travel time considerably to the Pacific beaches south of Liberia. Ferries will continue to run from Puntarenas to Paquera and Playa Naranjo for access to destinations on the Gulf of Nicoya side of the peninsula.

Paved roads run down the spine of the Nicoya Peninsula all the way to Playa Naranjo, with just a few unpaved and potholed stretches. Once you get off the main highway, the pavement holds out only so far, and then dirt, dust, mud, potholes, and other factors come into play. The roads to Playa Sámara and Playa del Coco are paved all the way; every other destination requires some dirt-road maneuvering. If you're headed down to the coast via unpaved roads, be sure to get advance information on road conditions. Take a four-wheel-drive vehicle if possible.

If you want to drive be prepared to spend some serious time in the car. The road to Nicoya's southern tip is partly paved and partly just gravel, and it winds up and down and around various bays. Some roads leading from Liberia to the coast are intermittently paved. As you work your way toward the coast, pay close attention to the assorted hotel signs at intersections—they may be the only indicators of which roads to take to your lodging.

EMERGENCIES

In case of any emergency, dial 911, or one of the specific numbers below.
➤ EMERGENCY SERVICES: **Fire** (☎ 118). **Police** (☎ 118). **Red Cross Ambulance** (☎ 128).

TOURS

In addition to the following major agencies, most hotels can organize guided tours for you.

Ríos Tropicales, a high-quality adventure tour company, runs excellent multiday sea-kayaking trips that leave from Curú National Wildlife Refuge and meander among the islands of the Gulf of Nicoya. The company also leads river-rafting trips throughout the country and a float trip for bird-watchers down Guanacaste's Río Corobicí. Day trips to the idyllic Isla Tortuga in the Gulf of Nicoya are very popular, and Calypso Tours has been leading them longer than anyone else. The excellent Horizontes specializes in more independent tours with as few as eight people, including four-wheel-drive transport, naturalist guides, and guest lecturers.

➤ TOUR COMPANIES: **Calypso Tours** (✉ Avda. 2 between Cs. 1 and 3, San José, ☎ 256–2727, FAX 256–6767, WEB www.calypsotours.com). **Horizontes** (✉ 150 yards north of Pizza Hut Paseo Colón, San José, ☎ 222–2022, FAX 255–4513, WEB www.horizontes.com). **Ríos Tropicales** (✉ 50 yards south of the Centro Colón on Calle 38 in San José, ☎ FAX 233–6455, WEB www.riostropicales.com).

VISITOR INFORMATION

The tourist office in San José has information on Guanacaste and the peninsula.

CENTRAL PACIFIC COAST BEACHES AND MANUEL ANTONIO NATIONAL PARK

With the attractions that probably drew you to Costa Rica—lush tropical forests, palm-lined beaches, and hospitable terrain for an array of outdoor activities—there's really no need to explain why this coastal area has become so popular. Manuel Antonio National Park protects an indented stretch of coastal rain forest and idyllic white-sand beaches. Despite the fact that the region's protected areas are among the smallest in the country, they are vibrant habitats with an amazing variety of flora and fauna, including such endangered species as the scarlet macaw and the Central American squirrel monkey. Ideal conditions for snorkeling, world-class sportfishing surfing, sea-kayaking, horseback riding, rafting, hiking, and bird-watching abound—all within 160 km (100 mi) of San José.

Quepos

23 km (14 mi) south of Parrita, 174 km (108 mi) southwest of San José.

With a population of around 12,000, Quepos is the largest and most important town in this corner of Costa Rica. It owes its name to the tribe that inhabited the area when the first visiting Spaniard, Juan Vásquez de Coronado, rode through the region in 1563. It's not certain whether those Indians were called Quepos or Quepoa, but we do know that they lived by a combination of farming, hunting, and fishing until the violence and disease that accompanied the Spanish conquest wiped them out.

For centuries following the Spanish conquest, the town of Quepos barely existed, but in the 1930s the United Fruit Company put it on the map, building a banana port and populating the area with workers from other parts of Central America. The town thrived for a decade, until Panama disease decimated the banana plantations around 1945. The fruit company then switched to (less lucrative) oil palms, and the area slipped into a prolonged depression. Only in the last decade have tourism revenues lifted the town out of its slump—a renaissance owed to natural causes, the beauty of the nearby beach and Manuel Antonio National Park. The town today, though still a bit seedy and down-at-the-heels owing to the vestiges of its Banana Port past, draws a number of expats for the world-class sportfishing. The nightlife moves along at a good clip and some of the bars pace themselves just as well during the day. As Hemingway said of drinking in the morning, it must be noon somewhere in the world.

If you're traveling with children and/or have a keen interest in flora, you may want to visit the **Jardín Gaia**, an orchid garden and butterfly farm. Call in advance to set up a tour of the botanical project, which houses more than 1,000 orchid species. Admission is free for kids

under 12. ⊠ *Left side of road to Manuel Antonio, 2½ km (1½ mi) east of Quepos,* ☎ *777–0535.* ☜ *$5.* ⊙ *Daily 9–4.*

Dining and Lodging

$$–$$$ ✕ **El Banco Bar.** It's a cozy spot that specializes in Mexican food, but you can also get good steaks and seafood. Wide-open windows overlooking the street and a funky, relaxed atmosphere, make this an easy place to sit and watch the world go by for the entire afternoon. This is also a popular nightspot for the expat crowd. ⊠ *In town, in front of Hotel Ramos,* ☎ *777–0478. AE, MC, V.*

$$–$$$ ✕ **El Gran Escape.** A favorite with sportfishermen—"You hook 'em,
★ we cook 'em"—The Great Escape menu ranges from broiled shrimp with a tropical sauce to the catch of the day prepared in any of a half dozen ways. Seating is scattered between an old wooden building, patio, and second-floor bar. In the back is the popular Epicentro Bar, which draws young crowds late into the night. ⊠ *Southwest corner of Quepos waterfront,* ☎ *777–0395. V. Closed 2 wks in June.*

$–$$ ⊞ **Hotel Malinche.** One block west of the Quepos bus station, this small hotel has two kinds of rooms, both of which are a bargain. Newer, air-conditioned rooms are carpeted and have large tile baths with hot-water showers. The older rooms, cooled by ceiling fans, cost about half as much; those on the ground floor are nicer, with white tile floors and baths, while those on the second floor have wooden floors and are slightly smaller. ⊠ *Avda. Central, ½ block west of bus station,* ☎ *777–1833,* ℻ *777–0093. 29 rooms. Some fans; no a/c in some rooms. AE, MC, V.*

Nightlife

The popular disco **El Arco Iris** (☎ 777–0449), built over the estuary north of the bridge, gets packed on weekends and holidays. American expats gather beneath the ceiling fans of **El Banco Bar** (☎ 777–0478), on Avenida Central, to watch U.S. sports on TV or listen to live rock and roll. **Byblos** (☎ 777–0411), on the way to Manuel Antonio, has a small casino. The **Epicentro Bar** in El Gran Escape restaurant (☎ 777–0395) draws a young crowd looking for good music. There is a small casino on the ground floor of the **Hotel Kamuk** (☎ 777–0811) in Quepos. A popular watering hole with younger travelers is **Tiburón** (☎ 777–3337), upstairs behind the bus station, where wild murals cover the walls and reggae is usually blasting on the stereo.

Outdoor Activities and Sports

HORSEBACK RIDING

Lynch Travel (⊠ Behind the bus station, Quepos, ☎ 777–1170) can arrange two horseback tours: a three-hour ride to a scenic overlook and an all-day trip to the Catarata de Nara, a waterfall that pours into a natural swimming pool. **Rain Maker** (⊠ Hotel Sí Como No, Manuel Antonio, ☎ 777–3565) leads an exclusive horseback excursion through the pristine rain forest of a private reserve in the mountains, as well as a fascinating walk through suspended bridges over the forest canopy. Other guided tours of the 1,500-acre reserve include hikes to waterfalls and natural pools.

SPORTFISHING

The southwest has some of Costa Rica's finest deep-sea fishing, and Quepos is one of the best points of departure. Fewer boats troll these waters than troll off Guanacaste, and they usually catch plenty of sailfish, marlin, wahoo, mahimahi, roosterfish, and yellowfin tuna. **Garobo Tours** (☎ 777–3566) offers full- and half-day fishing trips out of Quepos. **Bluefin Tours** (☎ 777–2222) can customize fishing trips from Quepos. **Lynch Travel** (⊠ Behind the bus station, Quepos, ☎ 777–1170) arranges sportfishing excursions from the Quepos area.

WHITE-WATER RAFTING

There are three white-water rivers near Quepos, but they have rather limited seasons. The Parrita is a mellow route (Class II–III), perfect for a first rafting trip; it's navigable in rafts from May to January, after which it drops so low that you can only float in two-person inflatable "duckies." The Naranjo (Class III–IV) requires some experience and can only be run from June to December. The Savegre (Class II–III) is fun: it flows past plenty of rain forest and wildlife and is passable from June to March, but landslides sometimes limit access. **Iguana Tours** (⊠ next to the soccer field, ☏ FAX 777–1262) is the oldest rafting outfitter in Quepos and also runs sea-kayaking tours. **Amigos del Río** (⊠ about 2 km on the road to Manuel Antonio from Quepos, ☏ 777–0082) leads trips down all the Quepos area's rivers.

Manuel Antonio

3 km (2 mi) south of Quepos, 179 km (111 mi) southwest of San José.

Once you're here, it's not hard to see why Manuel Antonio has become one of Costa Rica's most famous destinations: you need only contemplate one of its views of beach, jungle, and the shimmering Pacific dotted with rocky islets. Spread over the hill that separates Quepos from Manuel Antonio National Park, the town of Manuel Antonio is surrounded by dozens of hotels and restaurants, scattered along the road between Quepos and the park. The best hotels are near the top of the hill, as the views are most spectacular; and since there is nearly as much rain forest around these hotels as in the nearby national park, most of the wildlife in the park can also be spotted near the hotels.

As the road approaches the national park, it skirts the lovely, palm-lined strand of **Playa Espadilla**, which stretches north from the rocky outcropping that borders the park. The beach is popular with sunbathers, surfers, volleyball players, and vacationing Ticos; beware of deadly rip currents when the waves are large.

Dining

$$$–$$$$ ✕ **Gato Negro.** Though seafood reigns here (as it does all over town), this open-air restaurant at the top of the hill stands out thanks to its Italian chef, who has a flair for international cooking. The extensive menu combines classic Italian preparations with innovative dishes like spaghetti *a lo scoglio* (mixed seafood pasta) and penne *con salmone e gamberi* (pasta with salmon and shrimp). Breakfast and lunch are also served in the Mediterranean-style dining room, with a terra-cotta tile floor. ⊠ *Next to Hotel Casitas Eclipse,* ☏ *777–1728. AE, MC, V.*

$$$ ✕ **Karolas.** In the forest below Barba Roja, with tables on two simple patios surrounded by greenery, Karolas is easily Manuel Antonio's most attractive, intimate restaurant at night. At any time of day, it compensates its lack of ocean view with quality cuisine, particularly fresh fish and shrimp dishes. The homemade desserts are top-notch—leave room for a piece of macadamia pie. Reservations are recommended. ⊠ *Main road, at the top of the hill,* ☏ *777–1557. AE, MC, V.*

$$ ✕ **Barba Roja.** Perched near the top of the hill, with sweeping views of the Manuel Antonio shoreline, Barba Roja is one of this town's oldest and most popular restaurants. The dining room is furnished with dark hardwoods and decorated with colorful prints. Food takes a close second to atmosphere; try the daily fish specials or, at lunchtime, the excellent sandwiches. Desserts are delicious as well. Breakfast is popular, but the view is most impressive at sunset. ⊠ *Main road, before the top of the hill,* ☏ *777–0331. AE, MC, V. No lunch Mon.*

$ ✕ **Café Milagro.** The only place in town serving banana bread and home-roasted coffee, Café Milagro doubles as a souvenir shop and meeting

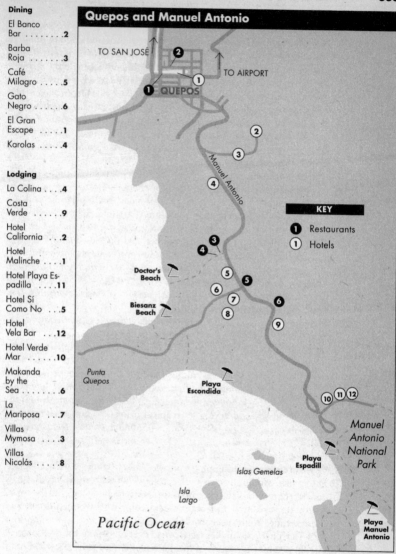

Quepos and Manuel Antonio

TO SAN JOSÉ

TO AIRPORT

QUEPOS

Manuel Antonio

KEY

Restaurants

Hotels

Doctor's
Beach

Biesanz
Beach

Punta
Quepos

Playa
Escondida

Manuel
Antonio
National
Park

Islas Gemelas

Playa
Espadill

Isla
Largo

Pacific Ocean

Playa
Manuel
Antonio

place right off the road to the national park and Playa Espadilla. The atmosphere is decidedly North American, and the consistently good breakfast food—available all day—keeps locals and travelers coming back for seconds. The café also sells local and international newspapers here and at its sister locale in Quepos. ⊠ *Main road at top of the hill, in front of Hotel Casa Blanca,* ☎ *777–0794. AE, MC, V.*

Lodging

$$$$ ✕▥ **Hotel Sí Como No.** Designed to damage as little of the forest as possible, this modern, eco-friendly place was built to use solar power, energy-efficient air-conditioning systems, and very little hardwood. The hotel has its own nature reserve. The rooms are a good size and bright—some have ocean views—and have stained-glass windows in the bathrooms. The blue-tile pool has an artificial cascade, water slide, and swim-up bar; there's also a poolside grill, a formal Costa Rican restaurant, and a small movie theater. ⊠ *Top of the hill, opposite Café Milagro,* ☎ *777–0777; 800/282–0488 Ext. 300 in the U.S.,* ℻ *777–*

1093, WEB *www.sicomono.com. 58 rooms. 2 restaurants, 2 bars, grill, some kitchenettes, minibars, 3 pools, hot tub, cinema. AE, MC, V.*

$$$$ ✕⊡ **Makanda by the Sea.** If you've got an occasion coming up, give
★ yourself the gift of a stay at Makanda, a secluded luxury retreat on a
rain-forested hill, with its own infinity pool and ocean views through
the trees. Tropical fruit trees, which regularly attract troops of monkeys and colorful birds, conceal the handful of villas from each other.
All villas have high roofs, hammocks, couches, modern kitchenettes,
phones, and modem lines. The poolside restaurant serves some of the
best food in town. ⊠ *1 km (½ mi) west of La Mariposa,* ☎ *777–0442,*
FAX *777–1032,* WEB *www.makanda.com. 5 villas, 4 studios. Restaurant,
fans, kitchenettes, minibars, pool, beach. AE, MC, V.*

$$$$ ✕⊡ **La Mariposa.** Set high on a promontory, Manuel Antonio's classi-
★ est hotel has the best view in town, perhaps in Costa Rica: a sweeping panorama of verdant hills, pale beaches, rocky islands, and the
shimmering Pacific. The main building is a white, Spanish-style villa
over an open-air dining room and pool area, with swim-up bar. The
older, secluded, split-level units are perched on the edge of the ridge
and have sitting rooms, balcony bedrooms, and conservatory bathrooms
alive with plants. ⊠ *Top of the hill, west of the main road at the Café
Milagro,* ☎ *777–0355; 800/416–2747 in the U.S.,* FAX *777–0050,* WEB
*www.lamariposa.com. 14 rooms, 22 suites, 4 villas. Restaurant, bar,
pool, some in-room hot tubs. AE, MC, V.*

$$$$ ⊡ **Costa Verde.** You might well spot squirrel monkeys, sloths, and iguanas right outside your room, since the builders of this place were careful to damage the forest as little as possible—although it may be
surprising to see the imported train car, which serves as the hotel's reception area. The spacious studios have tile floors, large beds, tables,
chairs, air-conditioning, and kitchenettes. All rooms have ceiling fans,
lots of screened windows, and large balconies. The open-air restaurant
serves good seafood and killer tropical drinks. ⊠ *Southern slope of
hill, near park,* ☎ *777–0584,* FAX *777–0560,* WEB *www.hotelcostaverde.
com. 44 rooms. 2 restaurants, fans, bar, kitchenettes, 2 pools; no a/c
in some rooms. AE, MC, V.*

$$$$ ⊡ **Hotel California.** Just uphill from the Villas Mymosa, this lovely place
has stylish, modern rooms with attractive wood furnishings and balconies that overlook the large pool area, surrounding jungle, or the coast.
The hotel is painted a pleasant cream color with wooden doors and
Mediterranean-blue accents. The poolside bar and restaurant are run
by a Tico chef who makes fresh bread every morning for breakfast. A
gift shop shows the work of local artists. ⊠ *Left from the main road
about, about 2 km from Quepos,* ☎ *777–1234,* FAX *777–1062,* WEB *www.
hotel-california.com (mailing address: Apdo. 159, Quepos). 22 rooms.
Restaurant, bar, pool, hot tub. AE, MC, V.*

$$$–$$$$ ⊡ **Hotel Playa Espadilla.** This hotel and preserve is a short walk from
the beach and national park entrance to Espadilla. (The owners' land
was declared part of the park decades ago, but they were never paid
for it, so they petitioned the government to create a private preserve.)
Two cement buildings hold simple but spacious rooms with tile floors
and kitchenettes. A blue-tile pool and bar are covered by a barrel-tile
roof in back. You can also opt for one of the smaller, cheaper cabinas
across the street. ⊠ *1 block east of beach,* ☎ FAX *777–0903,* WEB *www.
espadilla.com (mailing address: Apdo. 195, Quepos). 16 rooms, 16 cabins. Restaurant, bar, kitchenettes, pool. AE, MC, V.*

$$$–$$$$ ⊡ **Villas Mymosa.** These tasteful, incredibly spacious condos are simple, clean, inviting, and well worth the not-excessive price. Second-floor
rooms have the best views of mountains and estuaries to the north. High
barrel-tile ceilings, clever irregular architectural details, and oversize private balconies with tables and hammocks make the already commodi-

ous quarters feel even larger. All rooms have kitchenettes and futons or daybeds. Outside, the grounds are less charming, though there are a few intimate spaces. ⊠ *Up side road from Mimo's Aparthotel,* ☎ 777–1254, FAX 777–2454 *(mailing address: Apdo. 271–6350, Quepos). 8 rooms, 2 suites. Restaurant, bar, kitchenettes, pool. AE, MC, V.*

$$$–$$$$ 🏠 **Villas Nicolás.** There's a certain serenity to the rooms in these Mediter-
★ ranean-style villas that sets them apart from other options in this price range. Narrow walkways between whitewashed, garden-lined villas lead to attractive split-level rooms built on a cliff, the higher of which have wonderful Pacific views. Half the units have well-equipped kitchens; all have terra-cotta floors and oversize balconies furnished with a dining table, chairs, and hammocks. Waterfalls unite two small pools. ⊠ *Top of the hill, near La Mariposa,* ☎ 777–0481, FAX 777–0451, WEB *www. villasnicolas.com. 18 rooms. Restaurant, kitchenettes, pool. AE, MC, V.*

$$$ 🏠 **Hotel Verde Mar.** Also known as La Casa del Sol, this whimsical hotel off the main road borders the rain forest and offers direct access to the beach. The rooms, all in one long cement building, have colorfully artistic interiors and windows on each end overlooking surrounding gardens and wild foliage. There's a pool in back, from which a wooden catwalk leads through the woods and out to the shore. ⊠ *½ km (¼ mi) north of park,* ☎ 777–1805, FAX 777–1311, WEB *www.verdemar. com (mailing address: Apdo. 348, Quepos). 20 rooms. Kitchenettes, pool, library, travel services. AE, MC, V.*

$$–$$$ 🏠 **La Colina.** The cement tower of this B&B on the Quepos side of Manuel Antonio's hill has the nicest rooms, with tile floors, big windows, and balconies. Smaller rooms without views are less expensive; there are also two cozy apartments. Next to the split-level pool is the thatched-roof, open-air restaurant, where complimentary breakfast, a light lunch menu, and nightly dinner specials are served. The friendly American owners are happy to book tours and help you with travel arrangements. ⊠ *North side of hill,* ☎ 777–0231, FAX 777–1553, WEB *www.lacolina.com. 11 rooms, 2 apartments. Restaurant, bar, fans, pool. AE, MC, V.*

$$–$$$ 🏠 **Hotel Vela Bar.** Set a hundred yards back from Playa Espadilla on a paved road, this low-key hotel has rooms of varying size and with various views; all have white stucco walls decorated with framed tapestries, terra-cotta floors, and ceiling fans. A casita sleeps four and is a good value for a group. The open-air restaurant set beneath a high, circular roof is popular with nonguests for its selection of fresh seafood, vegetarian, and meat entrées. ⊠ *Next to Hotel Playa Espadilla,* ☎ 777–0413, FAX 777–1071, WEB *www.velabar.com. 8 rooms, 1 casita, 1 studio apartment. Restaurant, bar. AE, MC, V.*

Nightlife and the Arts

Costa Verde's owner just opened **El Avión** (☎ 777–0548), a great sunset place on the top of the hill. The bar's centerpiece is a 1954, C-123 Fairchild Provider airplane used by Ollie North and his compatriots in Nicaragua's Contra War. **Barba Roja** (⊠ main road, before the top of the hill, ☎ 777–0331) has a bit of a bar scene to complement the dining and is a favorite among Manuel Antonio's older crowd. **Billfish Bar** (⊠ Byblos Hotel, across from Villas Nicolás, ☎ 777–0411), is another relaxed place to have a nightcap in Manuel Antonio. **Byblos Hotel** (⊠ Top of the hill, ☎ 777–0041) is also home to the only casino in Manuel Antonio. The **Costa Verde** (☎ 777–0548) hosts live jazz and reggae in a bar-and-Internet café off the road to Manuel Antonio National Park. **Mar y Sombra** (⊠ across from Villas Nicolás, ☎ 777–0510), a restaurant on the beach, becomes an open-air disco on weekend evenings and is the most popular place for late-night lounging in Manuel Antonio. **Torumoco** (⊠ 2 km [1 mi] from Quepos on the road to Manuel Antonio, ☎ no phone) has a spectacular sunset view and

is a perfect place to escape the crowds of travelers that pack Manuel Antonio's other bars in high season.

Outdoor Activities and Sports

HORSEBACK RIDING

Malboro Stables (☏ 777–1108) rents horses and leads customized guided tours through the forest around Manuel Antonio. **Equus** (☏ 777–0001) provides mounts and leads you through Manuel Antonio's forest and beach.

SEA-KAYAKING

Iguana Tours (☏ 777–1262) runs sea-kayaking adventures to the islands of Manuel Antonio National Park, which requires some experience when the seas are high, and a mellower paddle to the mangrove estuary of Isla Damas, where you might see monkeys, crocodiles, and plenty of birds.

SKIN-DIVING

Playa Manuel Antonio, inside the national park, is a good snorkeling spot, as is Playa Biesanz, near the **Hotel Parador** (600 yards south of Makanda by the Sea). During high season, **Lynch Travel** (☏ 777–1170) in Quepos offers scuba diving for experienced divers only, around the islands in the national park.

SWIMMING

Manuel Antonio's safest swimming area is the sheltered second beach in the national park, Playa Manuel Antonio, which is also great for snorkeling. When the surf is up, rip currents are a dangerous problem on Playa Espadilla, the long beach north of the park. Riptides are characterized by a strong current running out to sea; the important thing to remember if you get caught in one of these currents is not to struggle against it but instead to swim parallel to shore. If you can't swim out of it, the current will simply take you out just past the breakers, where its power dissipates. If you conserve your strength, you can then swim parallel to shore a bit, then back into the beach. Needless to say, the best general policy is not to go in deeper than your waist when the waves loom large.

Shopping

There's no shortage of shopping in this town, between the T-shirt vendors near the national park and the boutiques in major hotels. You'll find little in the way of local handicrafts, however; goods here are similar to those in San José, at slightly elevated prices. **La Buena Nota** (☏ 777–1002), to the right on the southern slope of the hill, is one of the oldest and largest souvenir shops in town; it also sells used books and international newspapers and magazines.

Manuel Antonio National Park

5 km (3 mi) south of Quepos, 181 km (112 mi) southwest of San José.

Parque Nacional Manuel Antonio, though small (6½ square km [2½ square mi]), is one of the most popular protected areas in Costa Rica. A tropical storm that hit Manuel Antonio several years ago toppled many of the park's largest trees, but there's still plenty to see here, including three beaches; rain forest with massive ficus, cow kapok, and gumbo-limbo trees; mangrove swamps; marshland; and coves that hold submerged rocks and an abundance of marine life, such as coral formations. Manuel Antonio is home to two- and three-toed sloths, green and black iguanas, capuchin monkeys, agoutis (large jungle rodents), and nearly 200 species of birds. It is also one of the two places in Costa Rica where you can see squirrel monkeys.

The park entrance is at the end of the road to the Hotel Playa Espadilla. Here you will find the ranger station and maps for the trails that take you through the rain forest. The first beach after the ranger station, **Playa Espadilla Sur,** is the longest and least crowded, since the water can be rough. At its southern end is a tombolo (isthmus formed from sedimentation and accumulated debris) leading to a steep, forested path that makes a loop over **Punta Catedral,** offering a good look back at the rain forest. The path also passes a lookout from which you can gaze over the blue Pacific at some of the park's 12 islands; among them, **Isla Mogote** was the site of pre-Columbian Quepos Indian burials. The lovely strand of white sand east of the tombolo is **Playa Manuel Antonio,** a small, safe swimming beach tucked into a deep cove. At low tide you can see the remains of a Quepos Indian turtle trap on the right—the Quepos stuck poles in the semicircular rock formation, which trapped turtles as the tide receded. The bay is good for snorkeling, with nearby coral formations. Walk even farther east and you'll come to the rockier, more secluded **Playa Escondido.**

Be careful of *manzanillo* trees (indicated by warning signs)—their leaves, bark, and applelike fruit secrete a gooey substance that irritates the skin. And don't feed or touch the monkeys, who have seen so many tourists that they sometimes walk right up to them and have been known to bite overly-friendly visitors. Because Manuel Antonio is so popular (the road between the park and the town of Quepos is lined with hotels), the number of people allowed entrance on any given day is limited to 600; come as early as possible, especially during the dry season. Plans are in the works to add some 10 km (6 mi) of beach at the southern end of the park. ☎ 777–0654. ⌧ $6. ☉ *Tues.–Sun. 7–4.*

Central Pacific Coast A to Z

AIR TRAVEL
Most travelers find the 30-minute flight between San José and Quepos preferable to the 3-hour drive or 3½-hour bus trip.

CARRIERS
SANSA flies eight times daily between San José and Quepos in the high season, four in the low season. Travelair also has eight daily flights between San José and Quepos in the high season, four in the low season.
➤ AIRLINES AND CONTACTS: **SANSA** (☎ 777–0683 in Quepos; 221–9414 in San José). **Travelair** (☎ 777–1170 in Quepos; 220–3054 in San José).

BUS TRAVEL
Express buses operated by Transportes Delio Morales depart from San José's Coca-Cola bus station daily for the 3½-hour trip to Quepos and Manuel Antonio National Park at 6 AM, noon, and 6 PM, returning at 6 AM, noon, and 5 PM. Buses heading *toward* San José can drop you off at the airport, but you need to ask the driver ahead of time. Local buses make the short trip from Quepos to Manuel Antonio every half hour daily from dawn till dusk, with a few more runs after dark.

CAR RENTAL
There are two car-rental agencies in Jacó and one in Quepos.
➤ MAJOR AGENCY: **Economy** (☎ 643–1719 in Jacó).
➤ LOCAL AGENCY: **Elegante** (☎ 643–3224 in Jacó; 777–0115 in Quepos).

CAR TRAVEL
The quickest way to get to this region from San José is to take the Carretera Inter-Americana (Pan-American Highway, CA1) west past the

airport to the turnoff for Atenas, turn left (south), and drive through Atenas to Orotina. The coastal highway, or Costanera, heads southeast from Orotina to Tárcoles, Jacó, Hermosa, and Quepos and is well marked. A paved road winds up the hill from Quepos to Manuel Antonio National Park.

The well-marked, newly paved Costanera connects Orotina with Carara Biological Reserve, Tárcoles, Jacó, Playa Hermosa, and Quepos. The drive from Quepos to Manuel Antonio National Park takes about 15 minutes.

EMERGENCIES

In case of an emergency, dial 911 or one of the specific numbers below.
➤ EMERGENCY SERVICES: **Ambulance** (☎ 777–0116). **Fire** (☎ 118). **Police** (☎ 117 in towns; 127 in rural areas). **Traffic Police** (☎ 222–9245).

TOURS

The *Okeanos Aggressor* makes all-inclusive 9- and 10-day guided dive trips to Cocos Island, one of the best dive spots in the world. Transfers to and from San José are provided from Puntarenas. Cruceros del Sur offers a seven-day natural-history cruise through Costa Rica's central and south Pacific regions and some islands off Panama aboard the *Temptress,* a 63-passenger ship. The *Undersea Hunter* also leads 10-day dive trips to Cocos Island.

Any number of agencies can help you arrange land-bound tours. Camino Travel can help you plan tours to Manuel Antonio. Cosmos Tours can also help plan a stay in Costa Rica's central Pacific region. Costa Rica Expeditions specializes in rafting and nature tours to Carara Reserve and other points of interest in the central Pacific region. Horizontes also specializes in nature tours to Carara Reserve as well as Manuel Antonio National Park and has expert guides.

Fantasy Tours leads an array of tours from Jacó, among them hikes in Carara Biological Reserve, boat trips on the Río Tárcoles, horseback rides, kayak outings, and cruises to Isla Tortuga. Jacó Adventures offers an unforgettable crocodile- and bird-watching tour.

In Quepos, Lynch Travel offers a wildlife-watching boat trip to the Isla Damas Estuary, guided tours of the national park, several horseback trips, river rafting, kayaking, sportfishing, and more. Iguana Tours specializes in sea-kayaking and white-water rafting. The Eco-Era Foundation runs an invigorating jungle hike to a waterfall in its private reserve and a less strenuous bird-watching and conservation tour. Rain Maker leads horseback rides, hikes, and canopy tours in its private reserve.
➤ TOUR COMPANIES: **Camino Travel** (✉ between Avdas. Central and 1, at C. 1, San José, ☎ 257–0107, FAX 257–0243). **Cosmos Tours** (✉ 50 yards north and 50 yards east of Centro Cultural Norteamericano Coastarricense, ☎ 234–0607, FAX 253–4707). **Costa Rica Expeditions** (✉ Avda. 3 and C. Central, San José, ☎ 222–0333, FAX 257–1665). **Cruceros del Sur** (✉ across from Colegio Los Angeles, Sabana Norte, San José, ☎ 232–6672, FAX 220–2103). **Eco-Era Foundation** (✉ Manuel Antonio, ☎ 777–1661). **Fantasy Tours** (✉ Best Western Jacó Beach Hotel, ☎ 643–3032). **Horizontes** (✉ 150 yards north of Pizza Hut Paseo Colón, ☎ 222–2022, FAX 255–4513). **Iguana Tours** (✉ across from soccer field, Quepos, ☎ 777–1262). **Jacó Adventures** (☎ 643–1049). **Lynch Travel** (✉ behind bus station, Quepos, ☎ 777–1170). *Okeanos Aggressor* (✉ 1–17 Plaza Colonial, Escazú, ☎ 556–8317 or 877/506–9738 in the U.S., FAX 556–2825). **Rain Maker** (✉ Hotel Sí Como No, Manuel Antonio, ☎ 777–0850). *Undersea Hunter* (✉ San Rafael de Escazú, 600 yards north and 50 yards west of Rosti Pollos, ☎ 228–6535, FAX 289–7334).

The tourist office in San José has information on the central Pacific region. Lynch Travel in Quepos can also give general advice.

➤ VISITOR INFORMATION: **Lynch Travel** (behind bus station, Quepos, ☎ 777–1170).

COSTA RICA A TO Z

AIR TRAVEL

From New York, flights to San José last 5½ hours nonstop, 6–7 hours via Miami; from Los Angeles, 8½ hours via Mexico; from Houston, 3½ hours nonstop; from Miami, 3 hours. Ask a travel agent about charter options in addition to major carriers.

Domestic flights are the most economical mode of transportation in the country. Costa Rica's two domestic airlines, SANSA and Travelair, fly daily to Quepos, Tamarindo, Tambor, and many others. SANSA flies from Juan Santamaría International Airport, near Alajuela. Travelair leaves from Tobias Bolaños Airport, in the San José suburb of Pavas. One-way fares range from $44 to $75. Pick an early morning domestic flight, as clouds and rain prevent many from going later in the day.

Note that domestic flights have a luggage weight limit of 11.3 kg (25 pounds)—*including* carry-ons—as the planes are tiny. Excess weight, if safety permits, is charged by the pound.

CARRIERS

➤ DOMESTIC AND CENTRAL AMERICAN AIRLINES: **Copa** (☎ 506/223–7033). **Grupo Taca** (☎ 506/296–0909). **Lacsa** (☎ 506/296–0909). **SANSA** (☎ 506/221–9414 or 506/441–8035). **Travelair** (☎ 506/220–3054).

➤ TO AND FROM THE U.S.: **American** (☎ 800/433–7300). **Continental** (☎ 800/231–0856). **Copa** (☎ 506/222–6640). **Delta** (☎ 800/221–1212). **Grupo TACA** (☎ 800/535–8780). **Lacsa** (☎ 800/225–2272). **Mexicana** (☎ 800/531–7921). **United** (☎ 800/241–6522). **US Airways** (☎ 800/428–4322).

➤ TO AND FROM THE U.K.: **American Airlines** (☎ 0345/789–789). **British Airways** (☎ 0345/222–111). **Iberia** (☎ 0171/830–0011). **United Airlines** (☎ 0845/844–4777). **Virgin Atlantic** (☎ 01293/747–747).

AIRPORTS

The major gateway to Costa Rica is Aeropuerto Internacional Juan Santamaría, on the outskirts of San José, near Alajuela. Besides the larger airports listed here, the other places where planes land aren't exactly airports. They more resemble a carport with a landing strip, at which a person with a SANSA clipboard arrives just minutes before a plane is due to land or takeoff. The informality of domestic air service means you might want to purchase your domestic airplane tickets in advance, although you can buy them when you're in the country or directly from the SANSA Web site, too.

➤ AIRPORT INFORMATION: **Aeropuerto Internacional Daniel Oduber** (☎ 506/668–1032 in Liberia). **Aeropuerto Internacional Juan Santamaría** (☎ 506/443–2622 or 506/443–2942 in San José). **Aeropuerto Internacional Tobías Bolaños** (✉ Pavas, 3 km [2 mi] west of San José, ☎ 506/232–2820).

AIRPORT TRANSFERS

All international passengers arriving in San José are funneled out one tiny doorway to an underground fume-filled parking area, which is flanked with hordes of tour operators waiting for arriving visitors and cab drivers calling out "taxi?" If you're on a tour, you need only look

for a representative of your outfitter with a sign that bears your name. Others should take an orange cab, called *taxi unidos,* which only work from the airport; avoid *collectivos,* or minivans—they're almost the same price as a taxi, the van is almost always crammed with other passengers, and you'll have to make stops at their hotels. It's also safe to take any red or orange cab identified with a number and which has a meter. Avoid *pirates* or unregulated cabs.

BOAT AND FERRY TRAVEL

Regular passenger and/or car ferries connect Puntarenas with Playa Naranjo, Tambor, and Paquera, on the south end of the Nicoya Peninsula. These ferries take you to the southern and mid-Nicoya Peninsula. Traditionally, to get to Guanacaste, a car ferry crossed the Río Tempisque, about a one-hour drive northwest from Puntarenas, every 20 minutes from 5 AM to 11 PM in the high season (December–April), hourly in the green season (May–December). However, the new Río Tempisque bridge, officially called the Taiwan Friendship Bridge, is slated to open here at the end of 2002. The bridge, it is hoped, will eliminate the wait of up to three hours common for the 15-minute ferry trip.
➤ INFORMATION: **Arco Iris Passenger Ferry** (506/661–1084). **Puntarenas–Playa Naranjo Ferry** (☎ 506/661–1069). **Río Tempisque Ferry** (506/661–8105). **Zancudo Ferry** (506/776–0012).

BUS TRAVEL

Reliable, inexpensive bus service covers much of the country. Several different private companies leave San José from a variety of departure points. Buses range from huge, modern, air-conditioned beasts with lead-foot drivers, bathrooms, and an occasional movie to something a little less new and a whole lot sweatier and crowded. For schedules and departure locations for your destination of choice, *see* Bus Travel *in* the A to Z sections of the appropriate section.

Tickets are sold (cash only) at bus stations and on the buses themselves. The only way to reserve a seat is to buy your ticket ahead of time or, depending on the route, simply show up early for departure. On longer routes, buses stop midway at modest restaurants. Near the ends of their runs many nonexpress buses turn into large taxis, dropping passengers off one by one at their destinations; to save time, take a *directo* (express) bus.
➤ CENTRAL VALLEY BUS COMPANIES: **Empresarios Unidos** (☎ 506/222–0064). **Sacsa** (☎ 506/591–0636). **Transtusa** (☎ 506/222–4464). **Tuasa** (☎ 506/222–5325).
➤ NORTHERN GUANACASTE AND ALAJUELA BUS COMPANIES: **Tralapa** (☎ 506/221–7202). **Transportes La Cañera** (☎ 506/223–4242). **Transportes Tilarán** (☎ 506/222–3854).
➤ NICOYA PENINSULA BUS COMPANIES: **Empresa Alfaro** (☎ 506/685–5032). **Empresarios Unidos** (☎ 506/222–0064). **Pulmitan** (☎ 506/222–1650).
➤ CENTRAL PACIFIC BUS COMPANIES: **Transportes Delio Morales** (☎ 506/223–5567). **Transportes Jacó** (☎ 506/223–1109).

BUSINESS HOURS

Most state banks are open weekdays 9–3, and many are open Saturday morning. Several branches of Banco Nacional are open until 6. Private banks—Scotia, Banco Banex, and Banco de San José—tend to keep longer hours and are usually the best places to change U.S. dollars and traveler's checks.

Pharmacies throughout the country are generally open 8 AM–8 PM. There are 24-hour gas stations near most cities, especially along the Pan-American Highway. Most other stations are open from about 7 to 7, sometimes until midnight.

Most of Costa Rica's public museums are closed on Monday. Shops are open weekdays 8–6 and Saturday 8–1.

CAR RENTAL

Costa Rica is not an ideal place to drive—in San José, traffic is bad and car theft is rampant (look for guarded parking lots or hotels with lots); in rural areas, roads are often unpaved or dotted with potholes. The greatest deterrent of all might be the extremely high rental rates ($45 a day and $290 a week for an economy car with air-conditioning, manual transmission, and obligatory insurance) and gas prices (about $1.50 per gallon).

If you decide to go for it, consider whether you'll need a standard vehicle, fine for most destinations, or a *doble-tracción* (four-wheel-drive), which is often essential during the rainy season. These can cost roughly twice as much as an economy car and should be booked well in advance. If you plan to rent any kind of vehicle between December 15 and January 3, or during Holy Week, reserve several months ahead of time.

Costa Rica has around 50 international and local car-rental firms, the larger of which have several offices around San José. At least a dozen rental offices line San José's Paseo Colón, and most large hotels have representatives. For a complete listing, look in the local phone directory once you arrive, under *alquiler de automóviles*.

➤ LOCAL AGENCIES: **Ada** (☎ 506/233–7733). **American** (☎ 506/221–5353). **Avis** (☎ 506/293–2222). **Budget** (☎ 506/255–4750). **Dollar** (☎ 506/257–1585). **Economy** (☎ 506/231–5410). **Elegante** (☎ 506/257–0026). **Hertz** (☎ 506/221–1818). **Hola** (☎ 506/231–5666). **National** (☎ 506/290–8787).

CAR TRAVEL

Keep in mind that mountains and poor road conditions make most trips longer than you'd normally expect. Domestic flights are often a better option.

EMERGENCY SERVICES

In Costa Rica, 911 is the nationwide number for accidents. Traffic police are scattered around the country, but Costa Ricans are very good about stopping for people with car trouble. Local car-rental agencies can give you a list of numbers to call in case of accidents or car trouble.

PARKING

Park overnight in a locked garage or guarded lot, as Central American insurance may hold you liable if your rental car is stolen. Most hotels, barring the least expensive, offer secure parking with a guard or locked gates, as car theft is rife.

RULES OF THE ROAD

Be prepared for harebrained passing on blind corners, tailgating, and failure to signal. Watch, too, for two-lane roads that feed into one-lane bridges with specified rights of way. And finally, look out for potholes, even in the smoothest sections of the best roads. The highway speed limit in Costa Rica is usually 90 kph (54 mph), which drops to 60 kph (36 mph) in residential areas. Seat belts are required, though drunk-driving laws tend to be less severe than in other parts of the world. You may not drive out of Costa Rica in a rental car.

CUSTOMS AND DUTIES

Customs officials at San José's international airport rarely examine tourists' luggage, but if you enter by land, they'll probably look through your bags. Visitors entering Costa Rica may bring in 500 grams of tobacco, 3 liters of wine or spirits, 2 kilograms of sweets and chocolates,

and the equivalent of $100 worth of merchandise. Two cameras, six rolls of film, binoculars, and electrical items for personal use only are also allowed.

EMBASSIES
The British Embassy handles inquiries for citizens of Australia and New Zealand.
➤ CONTACTS: **British Embassy** (✉ Centro Colón, Paseo Colón between Cs. 38 and 40, Barrio Paseo Colón, ☎ 258–2025). **Canadian Embassy** (✉ Oficentro La Sabana, Sabana Sur, next to tennis club, Sabana Sur ☎ 296–4149). **United States Embassy** (✉ in front of Centro Comercial del Oeste, Apdo. 920–1200, Pavas, ☎ 220–3939).

EMERGENCIES
Costa Ricans are usually quick to respond in emergencies. In a hotel or restaurant, the staff will usually offer immediate immediate assistance, and in a public area, passersby can be counted on to stop and help.
➤ EMERGENCIES: **General emergencies** (☎ 911). **Ambulance** (☎ 128). **Police** (☎ 117; 127 outside cities).

GAY AND LESBIAN TRAVEL
As a result of its history of tolerance, Costa Rica has attracted many gay people from other Latin American nations and consequently has a large gay community. San José and Manuel Antonio are probably the most gay-friendly towns, with some gay-and-lesbian bars and hangouts. The beach at the northern end of Playa Espadilla in Manuel Antonio National Park is a small, secluded cove known as a gay nude beach. There are no anti-gay laws. The informal Gay and Lesbian Guide to Costa Rica Web site, www.hometown.aol.com/GayCRica/guide.html, has some good travel information, including hotels that are listed with the Costa Rican Gay Business Association.

HEALTH
ENGLISH-SPEAKING DOCTORS
Many of the doctors at San José's Clinica Biblica and Clinica Catolica, and Escazú's CIMA Hospital speak English well, and some studied medicine in the United States. Many of these clinics have 24-hour *farmacias* (pharmacies).
➤ LOCAL MEDICAL HELP: **CIMA Hospital** (✉ next to PriceSmart, Escazú, ☎ 506/208–1000). **Clinica Biblica** (✉ Avda. 14 at C. 1, San José, ☎ 506/257–5252). **Clinica Catolica** (✉ San Antonio Guadalupe, ☎ 506/283–6616).

FOOD AND DRINK
Costa Rica's tap water is drinkable, and most food and water here are sanitary. In rural areas, you run a mild risk of acquiring Montezuma's Revenge (traveler's diarrhea) and leptospirosis (another disease borne in contaminated food or water that can be treated by antibiotics if detected early). Although it may not be necessary, you can stay on the safe side and watch what you eat—avoid ice, uncooked food, and unpasteurized milk (including milk products), and drink bottled water.

HAZARDS
Unless you're visiting the hot, humid regions of the Atlantic Lowlands, Osa Peninsula, and Southern Pacific, you won't need an insect repellant. Sunscreen and a hat are a must year-round. Beach vacationers should be aware of riptides. Several tourists drown in them every year. If you see waves, ask the locals where it's safe to swim; if you're uncertain, don't go in deeper than your waist. If you get caught in a rip current, swim parallel to the beach until you're free of it, and then swim back to shore.

HOLIDAYS

National holidays are known as *feriados*. On these days government offices, banks, and post offices are closed, and public transport is restricted. Except for those in hotels, most restaurants and many attractions close between Christmas and New Year's Day and during Holy Week (Palm Sunday–Easter Sunday). Those that do stay open might not sell alcohol between Holy Thursday and Easter Sunday.

2003 dates: New Year's Day; February 12, Shrove Tuesday; April 11, Juan Santamaría Day; March 29–31, Good Friday–Easter Sunday; May 1, Labor Day; July 25, Annexation of Guanacaste; August 2, Virgin of the Angels (Costa Rica's patron saint); September 15, Independence Day; October 12, Columbus Day (Día de la Raza); Christmas.

LANGUAGE

Spanish is the official language, although tour guides and many people also speak English, especially along the Caribbean coast. Learn the rudiments of polite conversation before you go, and bring a phrase book with you. When possible, choose the more formal phrasing, such as *¿Cómo está usted?* (How are you?) and *Mucho gusto* (You're welcome/My pleasure) rather than the North American or Mexican *¿Cómo está?* or *De nada,* which are not done here.

The English-language weekly the *Tico Times,* published every Friday, has local news and information on entertainment and travel.

MAIL AND SHIPPING

International mail can take up to three weeks to arrive in Costa Rica (occasionally it never arrives at all). Within the country, mail service is even less reliable. Outgoing mail is marginally quicker, especially when sent from San José. Always use airmail for overseas cards and letters. Mail theft is a chronic problem, so do not mail checks, cash, or anything else of value.

OVERNIGHT SERVICES

If you need to send important documents, checks, or other noncash valuables, use an international courier service. "Overnight" shipments to most North American cities take two days, to Britain, three, and to Australia and New Zealand, four or five.

RECEIVING MAIL

You can have mail sent poste restante (*lista de correos*) to any Costa Rican post office. There is no house-to-house mail service—indeed, no house numbers—in Costa Rica; most residents pick up their mail at the post office itself. In written addresses, *apartado,* abbreviated *apdo.,* indicates a P.O. box.

Anyone with an American Express card or traveler's checks can receive mail at the American Express office in San José.

MONEY MATTERS

All prices in this chapter are quoted in U.S. dollars.

The Costa Rican currency, the colón (plural: colones), is subject to continual, small devaluations. At press time, the colón had topped 350 to the dollar, 307 to the Euro, 219 the Canadian dollar, 187 to the Australian dollar, and 121 to the New Zealand dollar. Banks in Costa Rica won't change Australian or New Zealand dollars, so these currencies should be changed to U.S. dollars before arrival.

The cabbies at Costa Rica's international airport accept dollars and most hotels change them, so it's not necessary that you buy colones before you leave for Costa Rica.

A 750-milliliter (¾-liter) bottle of Coca-Cola, costs U.S. 65¢–95¢; cup of coffee, 50¢–95¢; bottle of beer, $1–$1.50; sandwich, $2–$3; daily U.S. newspaper, $1.25–$2.25. Sumptuous dinners in finer hotels and restaurants will run you closer to U.S. prices.

ATMS

If you bring some cash (U.S. currency) with you and use country-wide ATMs, you can get by without traveler's checks and avoid the paying a currency-exchange commission.

CREDIT CARDS

Credit cards are accepted at many major hotels and restaurants, but plenty of properties, some in the expensive range, still require payment in cash. Some businesses add a surcharge (around 5%) to the bill if you pay with a credit card, or give you a 5%–10% discount if you pay in cash.

CURRENCY EXCHANGE

For the most favorable rates, change money through banks. Avoid people on the city streets who offer to change money. They're notorious for shortchanging people and passing counterfeit bills.

PASSPORTS AND VISAS

Passports, but no visas, are required for Canadian, American, and British citizens visiting Costa Rica for stays up to 90 days. Citizens of Australia and New Zealand may visit with a passport for 30 days (and once you're here, you can go to the Migracion office in La Uruca and extend the visa to 90 days).

SAFETY

Crime is not a serious problem in Costa Rica, although thieves can easily prey on tourists who don't know their whereabouts and standout. Don't bring anything you can't stand to lose and don't wear expensive jewelry or watches. Use hotel room safes for passports, airline tickets, or other valuables when possible. Be especially alert in San José and on buses. Wallets go in your front pocket. Beware of anyone who seems overly friendly, aggressively helpful, or disrespectful of your personal space.

Car theft is common; always roll up car windows and lock car doors when you leave your car, and don't leave your valuables in sight. Park in designated parking lots or accept the offer of men or boys who ask if they can watch your car while you are gone. Give them the equivalent of a dollar when you return.

TAXES

Visitors pay a $17 airport departure tax at Juan Santamaría Airport. (This fee may be going up to $21.) Buy your exit stamp inside the airport from someone with airport-employee identification.

VALUE-ADDED TAX

All Costa Rican businesses charge a 13% sales tax, and hotels charge an extra 4% tourist tax. Tourists do not get refunds on sales tax paid in Central American countries.

TELEPHONES

The Costa Rican phone system is very good by the standards of other developing countries. However, phone numbers change and are handed out willy-nilly and phone books are not updated regularly.

AREA AND COUNTRY CODES

The country code for Costa Rica is 506. There are no area codes. Phoning home: the country code for the United States and Canada is 001, Australia 61, New Zealand 64, and the United Kingdom 44.

DIRECTORY AND OPERATOR ASSISTANCE

In Costa Rica, dial ☎ 113 for domestic directory inquiries and ☎ 110 for domestic collect calls.

INTERNATIONAL CALLS

Costa Rica's *guía telefónica* (phone book) lists the rates for calling various countries. To call overseas directly, dial 00, then the country code, the area code, and the number. Calls to the United States and Canada are discounted on weeknights between 10 PM and 7 AM and on weekends; calls to the United Kingdom are only discounted on weekends, from Friday at 10 PM to Monday at 7 AM.

It's cheapest to call from a pay phone using an international phone card, sold in shops; call from a pay phone using your own long-distance calling card; or call from a telephone office. Dialing directly from a hotel room is very expensive, as is recruiting an international operator to connect you.

LOCAL CALLS

Pay phones are abundant, though they always seem to be in use. Some phones accept coins; others require phone cards, which are sold in various shops.

➤ TELEPHONE OFFICES: **Radiográfica Costarricense** (✉ Avda. 5 between Cs. 1 and 3), open weekdays 8 AM–7 PM and Saturday 8 AM–noon, also has phone, fax, and Internet facilities.

PHONE CARDS

Costa Rica has two kinds of phone cards: domestic cards, which record what you spend, and international cards, which have codes that you have to punch into the telephone. Both cards are sold in an array of shops.

TIME

Costa Rica is in the Central Standard time zone, and observes Daylight Savings.

TIPPING

Restaurant bills include a 13% tax and 10% *propina* (tip) —sometimes these amounts are included in prices on the menu, and sometimes they aren't. Additional gratuity is not expected; but people often leave something extra when service is good. Leave a tip of about 50¢ per drink for bartenders, too.

In hotels, if you're not toting your bags to your room, tip the person who does $1 per bag; give more in $$$$ hotels. At the end of your stay, leave the equivalent of at least $2 per night for maid service.

Give about $10 per day to naturalist guides, who show you the sloths and special hiking trails you'd never find on your own. Give less to guides on bigger tours, or if they're affiliated with the hotel or lodge where you're staying.

VISITOR INFORMATION

Instituto Costarricense de Turismo in San José staffs a tourist information office beneath the Plaza de la Cultura, next to the Museo de Oro. Pick up free maps, bus schedules, and brochures weekdays 9–12:30 and 1:30–5.

➤ COSTA RICA TOURISM OFFICES: **Instituto Costarricense de Turismo** (ICT; ✉ C. 5 between Advas. Central and 2, Barrio del Catedral, San José, ☎ 222–1090, WEB www.tourism-costarica.com). **North America** (☎ 800/343–6332). **United Kingdom** (✉ 47 Causton St., London SW1P 4AT, ☎ 020/7976–5511, FAX 020/7976–6908).

WEB SITES

Start with www.costarica.tourism.co.cr and www.infocostarica.net/english for general information. For current events, check out the English-language *Tico Times* on-line at www.ticotimes.net and *La Nación's* English-language "supersite" www.incostarica.net. To explore nature-tour options, see the commercial sites at www.horizontes.com and www.expeditions.co.cr.

WHEN TO GO

The most popular time to visit Costa Rica is the dry season—locally called *verano* (summer)—which runs from mid-December through April. From mid-December until early February in particular, you have the combined advantages of good weather and lush vegetation.In the rainy season, *invierno* (winter), which is May through mid-December, beaches are often wet in the afternoon but sunny and dry in the morning. Much of Costa Rica gets some sunny weather in July, August, and early September.

CLIMATE

Central America's climate varies greatly between the lowlands and the mountains. Tropical temperatures generally hover between 70°F and 85°F. Guanacaste, on the more arid Pacific coast, is perhaps Costa Rica's hottest region, with frequent temperatures in the 90s during the dry season. Drink plenty of bottled water to avoid dehydration.

SAN JOSÉ

Average daily high and low temperatures:

Jan.	75F	24C	**May**	80F	27C	**Sept.**	79F	26C
	58	14		62	17		61	16
Feb.	76F	24C	**June**	79F	26C	**Oct.**	77F	25C
	58	14		62	17		60	16
Mar.	79F	26C	**July**	77F	25C	**Nov.**	77F	25C
	59	15		62	17		60	16
Apr.	79F	26C	**Aug.**	78F	26C	**Dec.**	75F	24C
	62	17		61	16		58	14

MANUEL ANTONIO

Average daily high and low temperatures:

Jan.	91F	33C	**May**	91F	33C	**Sept.**	91F	33C
	72	22		73	23		72	22
Feb.	91F	33C	**June**	90F	32C	**Oct.**	90F	32C
	72	22		73	23		72	22
Mar.	91F	33C	**July**	90F	32C	**Nov.**	91F	32C
	73	23		72	22		72	22
Apr.	91F	33C	**Aug.**	90F	32C	**Dec.**	91F	33C
	73	23		72	22		72	22

8 PANAMA

Panama is more than a canal. It is also the pristine Darién jungles, the cool rain forest mountain lodges, the sun-kissed shores and exotic Afro-Antillian culture of the Caribbean coast—and Panama is also it's origins, evinced in timeless villages of indigenous peoples. The country is rediscovering itself and the visitor is the beneficiary.

MISTAKEN IMPRESSIONS OF PANAMA ARE COMMON even among travelers who are well acquainted with the rest of Central America. At first glance, Panama City may seem much like the Western urban melee you're probably trying to escape, but if you take the time to explore it, you'll discover a rich history, vibrant culture, and a wildly diverse population that includes indigenous peoples, Spanish, and African, among other ethnicities. Even with its familiar American presence in the late twentieth century, the truth is that the country's top destinations date further back than this influence and Panama's natural sights remain largely untouched by tourism. These exceptional destinations include lush, tropical isles of the Bocas del Toro archipelago; the monumental volcano, mountains, and surrounding wildlife of Chiriquí province; the colonial towns of Portobelo and Casco Viejo in Panama City; and the villages of the Kuna, Emberá, and other indigenous peoples. And if you think you can find another Panama Canal, well, good luck.

Of course, Panama is most famous for its canal linking the Atlantic and the Pacific oceans. Built by the United States and well worth a visit, that monumental project is one of the world's great engineering marvels. The canal, together with Panama's role as the crossroads between North and South America, prompted the label *el puente del mundo* ("the bridge of the world"). Ever since Vasco Nuñez de Balboa first "discovered" the Pacific Ocean by crossing the Panamanian isthmus, Panama has witnessed a constant stream of foreigners traveling from one ocean to the other.

Of all Panama's visitors, the United States distinguishes itself as champion usurper amid a competitive field. Since 1850, the United States has intervened militarily in Panama 18 times. (The most recent example of U.S. intervention included the removal of Manuel Noriega.) The U.S. government has exerted such influence over Panama's development that in many ways the nation resembles a U.S. colony more than an independent nation. U.S. greenbacks are the official currency, and the northwestern province of Bocas del Toro is largely owned by the Chiquita banana company. Panamanians have also heartily embraced U.S. consumerism: Nike shoes and McDonald's outlets are everywhere.

It was the United States that helped bring about Panama's independence from Colombia in 1903, after Colombia refused a proposal that would have granted the United States control over a 5-km (3-mi) zone on either side of the canal. The United States then signed a treaty with the new government of Panama, represented by Philippe-Jean Bunau-Varilla, a Frenchman left over from the 1880s bankrupt canal project of Ferdinand de Lesseps (also of Suez Canal fame). The treaty was negotiated and passed into law without a word of Spanish spoken or a single Panamanian signature. The treaty granted the United States the territory on either side of the canal "in perpetuity" (i.e., forever), and the right to occupy lands outside the Canal Zone whenever such action was deemed "vital to the maintenance and defense of the waterway." Over the decades, Panamanian opposition to the "in perpetuity" clause grew steadily, and anti-American sentiment came to a head in 1964 with a series of riots and the temporary suspension of diplomatic relations. Panamanian strongman Omar Torrijos Herrera led an international campaign to make the canal Panamanian, and in 1977, he and U.S. President Jimmy Carter signed two treaties outlining the gradual relinquishment of the canal. Panama finally gained control of the canal on December 31, 1999.

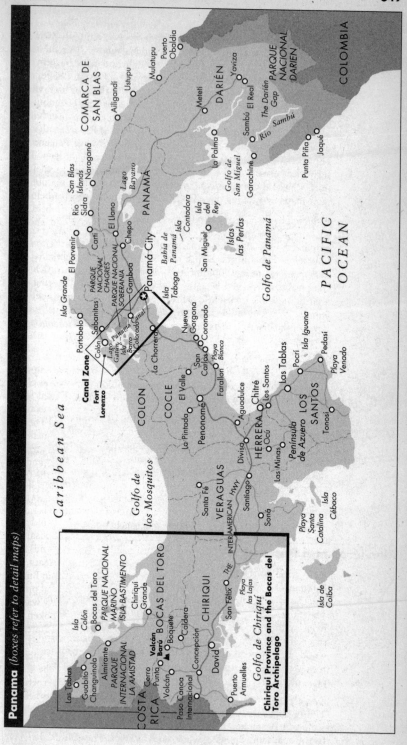

Panama (boxes refer to detail maps)

349

A few years after signing the treaty, Torrijos Herrera died in a plane crash, and the void he left in Panama's military government was soon filled by Manuel Noriega: a CIA informant who eventually got on the bad side of his old friend Uncle Sam. Noriega, whose CIA retainer and general's salary were apparently not enough, had other business ventures as varied as selling guns to Nicaraguan rebels and helping out the Colombian cocaine cartels. It was the latter that got him indicted in the United States, which eventually led to President George Bush's invasion of Panama in December of 1989. "Operation Just Cause," as the military action was called, left thousands of Panamanians dead or wounded and entire neighborhoods in rubble. While Panama City burned, Noriega fled to the local Vatican embassy. After agreeing to surrender, Noriega was taken to Miami, where he was convicted of drug trafficking and has since lived in a federal prison. All Panamanians are more than happy to put this chapter of the nation's history behind them.

Although the invasion of Panama was disastrous for its citizenry, Noriega's departure did give new life to a process of democratization demanded by the Panama Canal treaties. Arnulfo Arias was elected president for the third time just as the canal was to be turned over to the Panamanians in 2000. But Arias never had a chance to see his accomplishment realized because he died of a terminal illness shortly after taking office. His wife, Mireya Moscoso, who became the first woman president in Panama, presided over the grand event. Panama now, for the first time in its entire history, does not have a foreign power in residence.

At the moment, Panama is blissfully seeking its own identity, and, at the same time, welcoming overseas investment to boost the country's industries. New infrastructure like a multimillion dollar airport will go up in the city of Colón to boost business in the Free Trade Zone.

Tourism has been big on the agenda since the U.S. military pulled out. Fifty thousand Americans previously based in the Canal Zone played a part in fueling the local travel industry. Since they departed, the country has had to work hard at attracting visitors to replace them. The result is truly amazing. Beautiful, upscale resorts and inns are the norm of the new countrywide tourism boom. The Panama Tourism Board has an international promotion campaign underway for the first time, so Americans' awareness of Panama as a tourist destination is bound to rise as the word on the country's assets gets out.

Pleasures and Pastimes

Arts and Markets

Handmade clothing and beautiful handicrafts can be found at markets and shops in Panama City and in some of the the outlying provinces. The indigenous Kuna people produce stunning *molas,* squares made from multiple layers of bright cloth with designs from nature hand stitched into them. The Emberá carve intricate figures from hardwoods and a wood known as vegetable ivory. The Guaymí are famous for *chaquiras,* breastplate-type necklaces made from hundreds of tiny glass beads.

Beaches

The best beaches are along the Caribbean in the Bocas del Toro archipelago. It's here that transparent waters enfold coral-ringed islands, with palm-studded, white-sand beaches. The islands also have superb snorkeling and diving. Near Panama City is Isla Taboga; there are beach resorts along the Pacific, and a couple of out-of-the-way beaches on the road to Portobelo.

Colonial Towns

Portobelo has impressive ruins of a major fortress-city built by the Spaniards to protect cargoes of precious goods headed for Spain. It was eventually destroyed by the English. There are still vestiges of once-magnificent buildings at Old Panama, which was destroyed by the pirate Henry Morgan in the 17th century. The "new" city, replete with narrow streets and wrought-iron balconies, went up where Casco Viejo stands today. The Cathedral, churches, and Presidential Palace overshadow the once-grand buildings, some of which are currently undergoing renovations.

Dining

Panama City has the largest selection of restaurants that appeal to sophisticated tastes. Many international restaurants also include some traditional *criollo,* or Panamanian dishes, which rely heavily on chicken, beef, and corn and tend, like much of the local cuisine, to be a bit greasy by North American standards. If you don't mind a bit of *grasa* (fat), however, try Panamanian *carimañolas,* which are fried snacks made of diced and spiced meat surrounded by sticky yucca paste; *hojaldras,* which are crunchy, bubbly fried breads (the perfect quick breakfast food); and *bollos,* which are long corn tamales that come in many flavors. Also sample the local tortillas—thick yellow-corn disks that are very different from their Mexican counterparts. Other great snack foods include meat-filled empanadas and ceviche. *Chichas* (tropical fresh-fruit drinks) are usually available to wash it all down. Do not eat from street stands, even if the food looks appetizing. Hygiene is not always up to U.S. standards.

When you sit down for a proper meal, the grease level drops considerably. *Ropa vieja* (literally "old clothes"), one of the most popular Panamanian dishes, consists of shredded flank steak in a sauce of onions, peppers, and spices. *Mondongo* (tripe) is another popular dish. Chicken is prepared in myriad ways: *Sancocho* is a chicken stew made with vegetables, spices, and starchy roots like yucca and naimey; *arroz con pollo,* is rice with chicken and is served everywhere; *pollo guisado* is chicken stewed in a red sauce.

Plenty of fresh seafood is served around Bocas del Toro, and though local cooks aren't terribly inventive with it, a few resident foreigners are: Chinese and Italian foods are available on the islands. The Darién and San Blas are another story altogether: Stick to bland choices when dining here.

The accepted currency is the U.S. dollar, also called the balboa.

CATEGORY	COST*
$$$$	over $15
$$$	$10–$15
$$	$5–$10
$	under $5

*per person, for a main course at dinner

Festivals

Carnaval is Panama's biggest party, especially in Las Tablas on the Azuero Peninsula; it's celebrated the five days prior to Ash Wednesday, and Tuesday is the high point. Otherwise, Panama goes crazy with minor *ferias* (festivals); you're bound to come across one during your trip. Some of the most popular regional celebrations are the Festival de Flores y Café in Boquete in late January; the Feria Internacional de David in David on March 19; the Feria Internacional de Azuero in Los Santos at the end of April; Corpus Christi in Los Santos in June; Fiesta de los Congos at the end of August on the Caribbean Costa Arriba; Feria

del Mar in Bocas del Toro in mid-September; Festival de la Mejorana in Guararé at the end of September; and the Celebración del Cristo Negro in Portobelo at the end of October.

Lodging

More luxury hotels and inns have appeared in the last two years, a result of the government's push to accelerate tourism development. The Canal Zone is going through a building boom with upscale properties popping up in or near national parks and other forest reserves. Chiriquí has some of Panama's nicest hotels, on former coffee plantations. These include many small, eco-friendly and strikingly attractive newcomers on Bocas del Toro. The most charming inns on the mainland are nestled in stunning mountain valleys, at the side of the towering volcano, or in the middle of lush forest. Reservations in this area are a must during Panamanian holidays. The town of Bocas del Toro itself has an overabundance of hotel rooms and relatively low rates. Alternatives to Bocas are Bastimentos, Carenero, and Solarte, just across the bay.

The accepted currency is the U.S. dollar, also called the balboa.

CATEGORY	COST*
$$$$	over $150
$$$	$100–$150
$$	$50–$100
$	under $50

*for a double room, excluding service and 10 % tax

Snorkeling and Scuba Diving

Whether you're an experienced scuba diver itching to plumb the depths or are anticipating a first attempt at snorkeling, Bocas del Toro has what you need. The points, cays, and submerged reefs in this vast lagoon host an array of marine life that ranges from lugubrious sea turtles to hyperactive tropical fish. The ocean off Panama's Caribbean coast is home to almost 75 different species of coral and an even greater variety of sponges, around which lurk countless vibrantly colored invertebrates, rays, lobsters, and hundreds of fish species. Portobelo, closer to Panama City, also has some excellent dive spots.

White-Water Rafting

The country's best white-water rafting is found in Chiriquí. Two rambunctious rivers wind their way down out of the Chiriquí highlands, theoretically inviting rafting year-round. However, good rafting is not always a sure bet during the January-to-April dry season. The Río Chiriquí has some Class II–III rapids during the dry season. In the wettest months, October to December, the water level rises and the river gets wilder, with some Class IV rapids. The more remote Chiriquí Viejo provides an invigorating Class IV white-water trip with some Class II–III sections for novices.

Exploring Panama

The S-shape country lies between two oceans and is divided by mountains; it's a mere 80 km (48 mi) at its narrowest and a skinny 190 km (114 mi) at its widest. The Caribbean skirts the northern coast and the Pacific Ocean borders the southern coast. To the far east lies Darién and its impenetrable jungle. Beyond it is Colombia. The country's west or Chiriquí Province is high and mountainous, home to a volcano and an international park shared with Costa Rica. Farther north in Chiriquí, the Bocas del Toro archipelago has charming islands and cays. Las Tablas, the main city on the southern Azuero peninsula, is also home to numerous beaches and tiny islands. Rounding the top of the S-curve

is the duty-free zone of Colón, the small colonial enclave of Portobelo with its centuries-old fortresses, and the San Blas Islands, inhabited by the Kuna Indians. The Panama Canal cuts across the middle of the country in a flat and narrow portion of land.

Great Itineraries

IF YOU HAVE 3 DAYS

Spend your first day sightseeing in **Panama City** and tour the **Panama Canal.** The next morning, drive or take a tour to **Portobelo** to see the fort. In the afternoon, leave Panama City and fly to Isla Colón on **Bocas del Toro** for the night. Wake up early and make for a long beach day at **Isla Bastimentos** or one of the beaches, such as Carenero, or Solarte in Isla Bastimentos National Marine Park, where you can dive or snorkel. Fly back to Panama City in the late afternoon.

IF YOU HAVE 5 DAYS

Follow the 3 Day Tour and on Day 4 take a boat tour from Bocas del Toro to Isla de Pájaros or nearby Boca del Drago. On the 5th day, fly to **David** on an early morning flight, rent a car, and head for the mountain air of **Boquete,** which has a good selection of lodging. Go for a bird-watching hike or pre–dawn drive up **Volcán Barú.** The next morning, drive to David and catch the first flight to Panama City.

IF YOU HAVE 7 OR MORE DAYS

On Day 6, after overnighting in Boquete, get a pre-dawn start to drive up Volcán Barú to catch the sunrise from the summit or go bird–watching, whichever one you didn't do the day before. Move on to **Cerro Punta,** which is higher and thus cooler. Stop off at the Los Quetzales hotel and join a tour of the **Amistad International Park** forests. Or go white-water rafting, from Boquete or Cerro Punta. (Book in advance for the Amistad Park tour and rafting.) If time's no object, take a trip, via the capital, to the **San Blas Islands,** where beaches and indigenous culture blend to create a gorgeous finale to your vacation.

PANAMA CITY

More than half the country's 2.8 million citizens live in Panama City, which borders the canal and is the country's transportation hub. It also lies near some of the most accessible rain forest in the world, marked by the two national parks, with lush foliage growing right up to the edge of the concrete sprawl.

The original Panama City was founded in 1519, the first city founded by Europeans on the Pacific Coast of the Americas. It was from here that Francisco Pizarro sailed south to conquer the Inca Empire in 1532, and it was to here that he brought his plunder en route to Spain. Panama quickly became a key point in the Spanish colonies, with most of the gold and silver captured in South America being shipped to Panamá Viejo (Old Panama), carried across the isthmus on mule trains, then loaded onto galleons for the trip across the Atlantic. The city grew into one of the richest in the continent, and that wealth soon attracted the attention of pirates. In 1671, it was sacked and completely destroyed by the English pirate Henry Morgan. (The ruins of Panamá Viejo show just how devastating this attack was.)

Two years later, the city relocated to a narrow peninsula, which was deemed easier to defend. Although this section of the city, now known as Casco Viejo (literally Old Shell) is somewhat grimy and run-down, the government has started restoring the area beginning with buildings close to the Parque Mayor and Presidential Palace. The result is nothing short of stunning, with buildings reflecting their magnificent

354

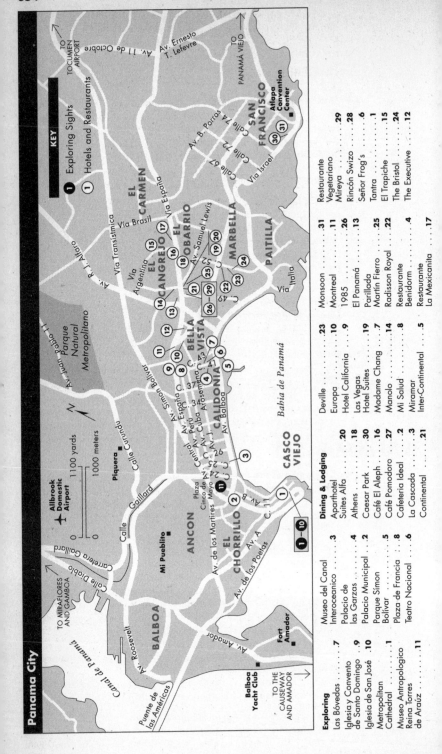

Panama City

KEY

● Exploring Sights ...... ●

● Hotels and Restaurants ... ●

past. Unfortunately, the work is donkey slow, and you often view a dilapidated slum next to a meticulously restored colonial mansion. Here, among the crumbling walls, the city rings with vibrancy: soccer balls bounce off the ruins of 300-year-old cathedrals, families barbecue on the cobblestone streets, and barbers set up shop on sidewalks where passersby can casually take a seat and get a haircut.

The baroque facades and iron grill work of Casco Viejo appear frozen in time, while the rest of the city is vaulting into the 21st century. Gleaming silver skyscrapers tower over Vía España, where you can shop for some of the finest (and cheapest) goods in the world, and where restaurants serve an eclectic spectrum of cuisines. The constant flow of international traffic through the canal continually brings both wealth and a vibrant influx of people into the city.

Exploring Panama City

Populated for almost five centuries, Panama City has an incredibly rich history. It's a sprawling urban area, stretching for 10 km (6 mi) along the Bahía de Panamá on the Pacific coast. Most of the city is served by three roughly parallel east–west streets. Avenida Balboa runs along the Pacific Ocean and passes the Atlapa Convention Center and Paitilla Airport, changing names twice (first to Vía Israel and then to Vía Cincuentenario) before turning inland at the ruins of Panamá Viejo. Vía Transístmica runs out of the city across the isthmus, eventually reaching Colón. Vía España is sandwiched between the two and is packed with banks, restaurants, and fancy shopping malls. The transport hub is the Plaza Cinco de Mayo on Avenida Central, in the western part of the city; from here you can catch almost any city bus.

If you navigate the city using a map, watch closely: sometimes one street will have two or three names. Avenues with numbers are colloquially referred to by their officially forsaken names. For example, Avenida 3 Sur is Justo Arosemena, and Avenida 6 Sur is Balboa. Using this logic, Avenida 4a should be called Nicanor de Obarrio, but locals refer to it as Calle 50. Neighborhoods, too, are only loosely defined. Streets often have no signs, and there is no such thing as a number on a building, so do as the locals do and steer yourself by major landmarks: Plaza Cinco de Mayo, Plaza Santa Ana, or Vía España.

Casco Viejo and Santa Ana

The narrow cobblestone streets, wrought-iron balconies, and intricate cornices in Casco Viejo invoke visions of Panama's glorious history as a major trade center. It's here also that you can appreciate the beautiful blending of Spanish colonial, neoclassical, and art nouveau architecture.

Santa Ana on the other hand, is mainly distinguished by a long pedestrian mall which runs from the north end of Casco Viejo at Plaza Santa Ana along Avenida Central to the Plaza Cinco de Mayo. The mall was dedicated to the firemen who strove to extinguish the fire from an explosion at a gunpowder warehouse in 1914.

A GOOD WALK

Starting at the Plaza Mayor in Casco Viejo, note the lovely **Metropolitan Cathedral** ① on the west side of the square. Also on the square is the ornate **Palacio Municipal** ②, home of the Museo de la Historia de Panamá. The stately **Museo del Canal Interoceanico** ③ is next door. Two blocks north on Calle 5 you can see the **Palacio de las Garzas** ④, if the security guards let you get that far. Walk one block south and another east to check out the colonial church and statue of Símon Bolívar, "Liberator of Latin America," at **Parque Símon Bolívar** ⑤. Just beyond is the beautifully restored **Teatro Nacional** ⑥.

Continue walking out to the point, where you'll find the former dungeons, **Las Bóvedas** ⑦, and the beautiful shady park in front of them called the **Plaza de Francia** ⑧. Wander back to Avenida A, and one block west to Calle 3, where you'll find the ruins of the **Iglesia y Convento de Santo Domingo** ⑨. Just inside the entryway is the earthquake-resistant Arco Chato. Farther up Avenida A, on the corner of Calle 8, is the **Iglesia de San José** ⑩. Veer over to Avenida Central and follow it north about a mile (either walking or catch a cab) to the **Museo Antropologico Reina Torres de Araúz** ⑪, named for the museum's founder and Panama's leading anthropologist.

TIMING AND PRECAUTIONS

You can easily explore these neighborhoods in three hours if all you do is skim by the buildings and plazas. If you do it in-depth, actually touring the museums and other buildings, allow four to five hours. Note that museums are closed on Monday, and some of the churches may only be open during services. Casco Viejo and Santa Ana can be dicey to walk around in at night. If you end up in the area after dark, grab a cab to return to your hotel; you can hail one around the plazas and main avenues.

SIGHTS TO SEE

★ ⑦ **Las Bóvedas.** It translates into "old dungeons" but the area once notorious for staving off pirate attacks has been gentrified. A walkway, which curves around a point with a marvelous view of the ocean and city, dips down onto a street where the actual dungeons used to be. Built in the late 1600s, after the city center relocated to Casco Viejo, the dungeons were thick-walled cubicles that filled with water as the tide came in. During high tide water levels might reach a prisoner's torso. Of course, during the heat of summer, the inside was a living hell. Anyone on the wrong side of the Spanish crown was sent here. In the 1980s, the Panama Tourist Board initiated the renovation of 11 cells, which became an art gallery, and a French restaurant called "Las Bóvedas" and a handicrafts shop opened. Now guided tours, covering the site and the rest of Casco Viejo, are given by students and depart from the National Institute of Culture next to the restaurant. ⊠ *Bottom of Av. Central, near the tip, Casco Viejo,* ☎ *no phone.* ▨ *Free.* ⊙ *Daily 11–6. No tours Mon.*

⑨ **Iglesia y Convento de Santo Domingo** (Santo Domingo Church and Convent). A 17th-century place of worship, the church and seminary now lie in ruins. What's still left at the entrance to the once-grand religious complex is the Arco Chato or "stubby arch" that has been standing unsupported for three centuries. It was used as proof that the country was not subject to earthquakes, tipping the scales in favor of Panama over Nicaragua for a transoceanic canal. ⊠ *Av. A and Calle 3, Casco Viejo,* ☎ *no phone.* ▨ *Free.*

⑩ **Iglesia de San José** (Church of San José). The church is the resting place for a famous golden altar, the most ornate piece of craftsmanship in an otherwise plain church, which is supposedly the only valuable object left behind by the pirate Henry Morgan when he razed the old city. According to conflicting legends, either a wily priest painted the altar black or clever nuns covered it with mud to discourage its theft. Not only did Morgan not pilfer it, he donated money to the priest for a new altar because he thought it was ugly. ⊠ *Calle 8 and Av. A, Casco Viejo,* ☎ *no phone.* ▨ *Free.*

① **Catedral Metropolitan** (City Cathedral). Built between 1688 and 1796, this cathedral has the distinction of surviving an earthquake almost one hundred years later. The belfry, made of mother-of-pearl, holds the bell

of the first cathedral built at Panama Viejo, and the interior has a good example of a religious painting from the well-respected Seville school of painting from Spain. ⊠ *Av. Central and Calle 7, Casco Viejo,* ☎ *no phone.* ☉ *Daily 7–7.*

OFF THE
BEATEN PATH

MI PUEBLITO – It might seem too touristy to some, but the Panamanians love this hilltop attraction and living museum. Tile-roofed houses set around a small courtyard are intended to depict life in a "typical" Panamanian village in the 1800s. A guide wearing a *pollera* (an intricately stitched dress) will take you around various refurbished rooms and to a lovely exhibit of clothing worn in the country's interior. A small on-site restaurant is a good deal and offers an incredible city view. Take a taxi, which should run $3. ⊠ *Off Av. de los Mártires and Calle Jorge Wilbert, Ancon,* ☎ *507/228–7154.* ☎ *50¢.* ☉ *Daily 10–10.*

⓫ **Museo Antropologico Reina Torres de Araúz** (The Reina Torres de Araúz Anthropological Museum.) Built into an old train station, this museum named for and founded by Panama's major anthropologist, has artifacts dating back thousands of years and spanning numerous cultures. Most impressive is its collection of stone statues and pre-Columbian painted ceramics. One small room is filled with exquisite gold bells, pendants, and bracelets fashioned in the shape of fantastic insects, reptiles, and other creatures. All the signs are in Spanish, but the admission price includes an English-speaking guide. At press time many exhibits were closed during the museum's renovations. ⊠ *Plaza Cinco de Mayo, Santa Ana,* ☎ *507/262–8338.* ☎ *$2.* ☉ *Tues.–Sat. 10–4, Sun. 10–3.*

❸ **Museo del Canal Interoceanico.** Panama's best museum, in the former post office building, is dedicated to the country's biggest attraction. A series of elaborate educational exhibits traces the history of the project, from France's first disastrous attempt to dig a canal to the signing of the treaty giving control back to Panama. It also looks at the canal's current operation. A collection of artifacts, paintings, photographs, and videos provides a thorough look at the history and importance of that monumental ditch. ⊠ *Plaza Mayor, Casco Viejo,* ☎ *507/211–1649.* ☎ *$2, free Sun. morning.* ☉ *Tues.–Sun. 9:30–5:30.*

❹ **Palacio de las Garzas** (Palacio Presidential). The neoclassical lines of the stunning, white presidential palace stand out against the skyline of Casco Viejo. This glorious building is where the president of the country has executive offices and security is tight. So tight, in fact, that it's not open for touring unless you write a letter to the national tourism board (*see* Visitor Information *in* Panama City A to Z for the address) beforehand requesting a visit. Without a pass, you can get a good side view of it from Avenida Alfaro just as it approaches the palacio. ⊠ *Av. Alfaro, 2 blocks north of Plaza Mayor, Casco Viejo.*

❷ **Palacio Municipal** (City Hall). The mayor of Panama City and his staff inhabit this white colonial building which, in former days, was the seat of the legislature for the country. Within its confines is the **Museo de la Historia de Panamá**, which traces the history of the country from the explorations of Christopher Columbus to the present day. ⊠ *Plaza Mayor, Casco Viejo,* ☎ *no phone.* ☎ *50¢.* ☉ *Weekdays 8:30–3:30.*

❺ **Parque Símon Bolívar** (Símon Bolívar Park.) A monument to the "liberator of Latin America" graces the park. Decorative friezes mark the important events in his life. The colonial churches of San Philip Neri, San Francisco, and the San Francisco Monastery, which are undergoing restoration or have already been restored under government order, are also worth a look. The churches are most likely to be open on Sunday, when Mass is celebrated. ⊠ *Av. B and Calle 8, Casco Viejo.*

★ ❽ **Plaza de Francia.** Constructed by Leonardo de Villanueva, this walled plaza at the end of the Casco Viejo peninsula is dedicated to the Frenchmen who perished in the 19th century while trying to build the canal. A series of plaques and statues intertwined among the beautiful flowering trees recounts the arduous task with names of prominent personalities involved. Of note is Dr. Carlos Finlay, a Cuban physician who discovered that yellow fever, which killed thousands of workers, originated from a mosquito bite. The view from the Plaza on a clear day of Panama Bay, the Amador Causeway, and part of the Darién is truly heart stopping and worth the visit alone. The infamous dungeons of Las Bóvedas lie on one side; a small, pleasant park, which hosts musical events, is below the plaza on the other. Appropriately enough, the French Embassy has taken up residence across from the Plaza. ⊠ *Bottom of Av. Central, near the tip, Casco Viejo.*

❻ **Teatro Nacional** (National Theater). The interior of the 1907 theater is truly posh, with muraled ceilings, gold balconies, and glittering chandeliers—a little bit of Europe in the middle of Panama City. After serving as a convent for cloistered nuns and, later, an army barracks, the building was remodeled by Italian architect Genaro Ruggieri. Paintings inside by Panamanian artist Roberto Lewis depict Panama's history via Greek mythology. While you're here, check out what's playing, as the national symphony orchestra is often in town. ⊠ *Av. B, at the waterfront, Casco Viejo.* ⊘ *Tues.–Sat. 9:30–4:15, Sun. 1:30–4:15.*

Dining

The best restaurants are concentrated in an area along Vía España, Vía Argentina, and Calle 50. Java junkies rejoice: Just about every restaurant grinds its own beans and makes every cup to order with an espresso machine.

Prices and Tipping

A typical entrée at an expensive restaurant runs about $12 while a main dish at a less expensive place will go for around $5. Sunday brunch buffets are all-you-can-eat affairs that will save you money. It's customary to tip at least 10% of the bill. Rarely is the tip included.

Reservations and Dress

Reservations are required only at the best restaurants, however, the 1st and 15th of each month are big spending days in Panama, when most people receive their paychecks. Jackets and ties are rarely required, even at fancier restaurants. However, shorts are not considered appropriate unless the restaurant is very casual.

Casco Viejo and Santa Ana

Although dominated by fast-food joints and greasy spoons, newer upscale restaurants are slowly moving in. Around Avenida B, between Calles 13 and 14, you'll find the best dim sum south of San Francisco. In Chinatown you'll see stores selling roast whole ducks, dried fungus, and animal parts labeled in Chinese.

$$$–$$$$ ✕ **Tantra.** This exotic new restaurant near the Presidential Palace claims it's for lovers, taking its name from the Hindu expression of spiritual love. (Although they may have gotten the worldly and otherworldly mixed up.) The tongue-in-cheek menu warns that its Mediterranean cuisine is an aphrodisiac. Dishes have such names as "the fruits of passion" (sautéed sea scallops and asparagus), and "sweet and sour bewitchery" (duck breast with a ginger-scallion sauce). ⊠ *Hotel Colonial, Plaza Cathedral, Casco Viejo,* ☎ *507/262–8788. AE, MC, V.*

$ ✕ **Cafeteria Ideal.** This simple cafeteria underneath the Hotel Ideal serves hearty, meaty lunches for around $2.50 a plate, which is why it is usually packed from noon to 2 PM. The menu is pretty basic, but the food is less greasy than most comparable area places. Open 24 hours, this is the perfect place to catch breakfast after a night on the town. ✉ *Calle 16, 2 blocks west of pedestrian mall, Santa Ana,* ☎ *507/262–2085. No credit cards.*

Calidonia and Bella Vista

This area is safer to walk around than the Casco Viejo/Santa Ana neighborhoods. Restaurants here are slightly scattered, but many are good and have moderate-to-low prices.

$$–$$$$ ✕ **Madame Chang.** One of the top dishes, served with the verve and flair the elegant restaurant prides itself on, is whole baked fish in red sauce made to look like bunches of grapes. Try the crayfish rolls for starters followed by lobster in ginger sauce or fish wrapped in mustard leaves. For vegetarians, there's eggplant stuffed with tofu. ✉ *Calle 48, next to Señor Frog's, Bella Vista,* ☎ *507/269–1313. AE, MC, V.*

$$–$$$ ✕ **Señor Frog's.** Panama hasn't been the same since the invasion of this zany Mexican chain, which caters to the most animalistic of party animals. Waiters dance in the aisles while serving up generous portions of ribs, burgers, and drunken chicken (chicken marinated in beer). "World Famoso" is the bilingual slogan, and you can't miss the giant green frog splayed across one side of the building. Put on your dancing shoes from Thursday through Saturday when a DJ plays Latin mixed with bolder American disco music. ✉ *Calle 48, near Av. Balboa, Bella Vista,* ☎ *507/213–9119.*

$–$$$ ✕ **Caffé Pomodoro.** This cozy Italian bistro with lovely patio dining serves seven varieties of homemade pastas, plus Italian sandwiches on focaccia, and a good selection of entrées. Only the daily specials, like grilled swordfish in a fresh tomato cream sauce with Provençal herbs, can displace these winning choices. For dessert pair the homemade Sicilian ice cream with espresso. Several dozen different vintages, including Italy's finest, are served at the popular Wine Bar next door. ✉ *Vía Venetto, at the corner of Calle Eusebio A. Morales, Bella Vista,* ☎ *507/269–5836. AE, MC, V.*

$–$$$ ✕ **La Cascada.** For an adventure, head to the self-proclaimed "biggest" restaurant in Panama. Giant blue-and-yellow mushroom lights bloom between the tables, many of which overlook a carp-filled canal fed by a giant artificial waterfall. The seafood-heavy menu is an imposing 16-page tabloid that reads like a trashy novel ("If you like to buy a fresh natural red rose for your female companion," it says, "look page No. 12"). Portions are huge: the paella easily feeds two. ✉ *Av. Balboa, at Calle 25, Bella Vista,* ☎ *507/262–1297. No credit cards.*

$$ ✕ **Restaurante Benidorm.** It's no coincidence that this 24-hour restaurant around the corner from the Hotel Soloy is packed so much of the time—the food is consistently good and the portions are generous. Chicken, fries, salads, and even paella and filet mignon are offered. Wash it all down with a mug of draft beer for a mere 75¢. ✉ *Calle 30 Este between Avs. Perú and Cuba, next to Hotel Acapulco, Calidonia,* ☎ *507/226–8467. No credit cards.*

$ ✕ **Mi Salud.** "My Health" was founded by a Catholic nun and is the place to go for a meatless meal in Calidonia. The restaurant serves about a half dozen hot dishes cafeteria style. You can get heaping plates of any three and a fruit drink for less than $4. Mi Salud also bakes whole wheat bread and cakes, but the ice cream and frozen yogurt are probably the most provocative things on the dessert menu. ✉ *Calle 31, near Av. Balboa, Calidonia,* ☎ *507/225–0972. No credit cards. Closed Sun.*

El Cangrejo and El Obarrio

Most of the outstanding restaurants, which cater to a sophisticated international clientele, are found here in the commercial and banking center of the city.

$$$–$$$$ ✕ **1985.** The service is formal and the French cuisine is complemented
★ by an excellent wine cellar. The sauces shine in such dishes as corvina in a creamed spinach sauce, tenderloin in green peppercorn sauce, and tender veal medallions and chanterelles in wine sauce. You can choose your vintage from among fine French, German, and Chilean imports. ⊠ *Eusebio A. Morales, next door to the Rincón Swizo, El Cangrejo,* ☎ *507/263–8541. AE, MC, V. No dinner weekends.*

$$–$$$$ ✕ **Parillada Martín Fierro.** This place is for serious carnivores who like their steaks big, tender, and juicy. The meat is flown in daily from the United States and comes with a hot baked potato and salad, which you round up yourself from the salad bar. Grilled slabs of beef served Argentinian-style with *chimichuri* sauce (a spicy meat mariande) is another popular dish. The most expensive item is a 3-pound lobster, which will set you back around $30. ⊠ *21 Calle Eusebio A. Morales, El Cangrejo,* ☎ *507/264–1927. AE, MC, V.*

$$–$$$ ✕ **Monsoon.** Monsoon sweeps through Southeast Asia, serving Thai,
★ Korean, Chinese, and Vietnamese dishes. In most cases the attentive waitstaff cooks meals at your table. You can't go wrong with fu-na soup (with finely sliced fish fillet), pad Thai, or moo shu pork served with flour tortillas. For vegetarians, 10 vegetables of the day can be stir-fried with tofu. ⊠ *Caesar Park hotel, Vía Israel, Calle 77, San Francisco,* ☎ *507/270–0477. Reservations essential. AE, MC, V. No lunch.*

$$–$$$ ✕ **Rincón Swizo.** Chef Willie Digglemann started his successful restaurant empire when he opened here in a wooden chalet, just like the ones back home in Switzerland. Classic dishes like breaded Wiener schnitzel stuffed with ham and cheese and cheese raclette are the most popular dishes. The menu also includes seafood. ⊠ *Calle Eusebio A. Morales, next to the Hotel Suites Las Vegas, El Cangrejo,* ☎ *507/263–8310. AE, MC, V. No dinner weekends.*

$–$$$ ✕ **El Trapiche.** Eat like the locals do and you'll be pleasantly surprised
★ at the food as well as the prices. Typical Panamanian dishes like ropa vieja accompanied by *patacones* (fried plantains), corn fritters, or hojaldras are served fresh and in generous portions. An old sugarcane press, flowered tablecloths from the Anzuero provinces, and waitresses who wear stylized folk dress create a folksy Panamanian feel. You can eat indoors, alfresco, or get it to go. ⊠ *Vía Argentina, 2 blocks off Vía España, El Cangrejo,* ☎ *507/269–4353. No credit cards.*

$$ ✕ **Athens.** Athens offers delightful Greek food that's meant to please both discriminating vegetarians and carnivores. Try the pita *tsatsiki* (yogurt and cucumbers) with olives wrapped in homemade pita bread or a scrumptious Greek salad. Carnivores can dine on sliced beef or chicken with yogurt, tomatoes, and cucumbers stuffed in various types of homemade bread. ⊠ *Calle 57, 2 blocks south of Vía España, Obarrio,* ☎ *507/223–1464. No credit cards. Closed Tues.*

$–$$ ✕ **Restaurante La Mexicanita.** One of the city's best restaurants is
★ owned and managed by a Mexican expat and occupies a former home on busy Calle 50. The ample menu includes everything from soft tacos to *mole poblano* (a spicy chili sauce made with chocolate). It's all authentic—they've even got Mexican beer and $3 margaritas. ⊠ *42 Calle 50,* ☎ *507/213–8952. No credit cards. Closed Mon.*

$ ✕ **Restaurante Vegetariano Mireya.** The wide selection of entrées changes every day, but they're always tasty and meat-free. Mireya also has the city's best salad bar. Choose your food from the cafeteria line, then eat in the air-conditioned dining room. ⊠ *Calle Ricardo Arias,*

down the street from Hotel Continental, El Cangrejo ☎ *507/269–1876. No credit cards. Closed Sun.*

$ ✗ **Café El Aleph.** Panama's budding young poets, artists, and musicians exchange ideas over crepes and cappuccino at this superb café/art gallery/bar. Try the flavored coffees or a vegetarian sandwich. This is also one of the city's more popular nightspots, often presenting good films, live music, and other entertainment. ⊠ *Vía Argentina at Vía España, El Cangrejo,* ☎ *507/264–2844. No credit cards.*

$ ✗ **Manolo.** You can usually find some good sweets to accompany the java in this café-restaurant. If you sit outside, it's a great place to watch the world go by no matter what you drink. ⊠ *Vía Venetto, near Hotel El Panamá, El Cangrejo,* ☎ *507/269–5414. No credit cards.*

Lodging

Calidonia and Bella Vista

This area is close to the restaurants and nightlife of El Cangrejo and Vía España, which is a definite plus. Many of the budget and modestly priced hotels fill up on weekends, when Panamanian couples move in. Stays in the $ category can be as low as $25 a night with a private bath.

$$$$ ▢ **Miramar Inter-Continental.** The rooms in this sleek, modern, 25-story high-rise are on the waterfront and have knockout bay views. Business travelers favor this place for its ample convention-size meeting space, executive floors, and business center. A concierge and room service ensure you want for nothing. Rooms are decorated in comfortable soft beige tones and have three phones and huge windows. The location is along Avenida Balboa, one of the most beautiful streets in the city. ⊠ *Miramar Plaza, on Av. Balboa, Bella Vista,* ☎ *507/214–1000; 800/327–0200 in the U.S.,* FAX *507/223–4891,* WEB *www.miramarpanama.com. 206 rooms. 2 restaurants, in-room data ports, in-room safes, minibars, cable TV with movies and video games, pool, health club, hair salon, marina, 2 bars, shops, dry cleaning, concierge, car rental, travel services, business center, meeting rooms, helipad, free parking. AE, MC, V.*

$$$ ▢ ★ **The Executive.** Because it's one of the best deals around, the Executive is always full. Close to banks and restaurants, it has just the right amount of services to make your stay hassle free. Rooms have lots of good light and a small refrigerator, stocked with free soft drinks, coffee, and tea. Walls are stark white and bedspreads are a loud pink-and-green, which is the only thing that seems off here. The staff is warm and there's a 24-hour restaurant on-site with a decent reputation. A Sunday brunch for $8 is popular with locals. ⊠ *Calle 52 and Calle Aquilino de la Guardia, Bella Vista,* ☎ *507/265–8011 or 507/264–3989; 800/528–1243 in the U.S.,* WEB *www.theexecutivehotel.com. 96 rooms. Restaurant, in-room data ports, refrigerators, cable TV, pool, gym, bar. AE, MC, V.*

$ ▢ **Europa.** This spiffy, salmon-color hotel on Vía España is a heartbeat away from restaurants, banks, and travel agencies. It has most comforts found in more expensive hotels—including air-conditioning, room service, and covered parking—at a fraction of the price. It's a favorite of Central American business travelers who cluster in the large art-deco lobby or the elegant dining room. All rooms have good mattresses and go for $35 for a single and $39 for a double. The hotel will also book you on a fishing or boat tour to Contadora Island for $40. ⊠ *Vía España, across the street from the Bella Vista Theater, Bella Vista,* ☎ *507/263–6369,* FAX *507/263–6749. 103 rooms. Restaurant, cable TV, pool, bar, meeting rooms. MC, V.*

$ ⊞ Hotel California. This place on the Vía España is a short walk from the restaurants of El Cangrejo. Some of the spacious, bright, clean rooms have views of the bay. Rooms in back are much quieter. The hotel has its own restaurant and bar, serving some acceptable lunch specials, but there are definitely better places to eat in the area. ⊠ *Vía España, at Calle 43, Bella Vista,* ☎ *507/263–7736 or 507/263–8140, 60 rooms. Restaurant, cable TV, laundry service. AE, MC, V..*

$ ⊞ Montreal. There are two selling points here—the great location on Vía España and the tiny rooftop pool. There's also a decent restaurant downstairs. Although rooms are on the small side, they have TVs, phones, and air-conditioning. Avoid rooms in the front facing the busy street. ⊠ *Vía España, at Av. Justo Arosemena, Bella Vista,* ☎ *507/263–4422. 94 rooms. Restaurant, cable TV, pool, laundry service, free parking. MC, V.*

El Cangrejo

North of Vía España, this neighborhood is a busy commercial center with lots of restaurants and shops.

$$$ ⊞ El Panamá. Panama's first luxury hotel, the venerable El Panamá, still has rooms big enough for 20 instead of 2 and at one time hosted every visiting VIP to the country. Although the new owners whitewashed the memorabilia left over from its 1950s heydays, the hotel still has some architectural charms. Plus, everything from a large convention center to check-in counters for airlines adds convenience if you're looking to find everything under one roof. A shopping area resembles a small mall, and there's a first-class casino. The only nostalgia is provided by the U.S. military types who gather here for seminars as in days of old. ⊠ *Vía España and Calle Eusebio A. Morales, El Cangrejo,* ☎ *507/269–5000,* ℻ *507/223–6080,* 𝗪𝗘𝗕 *www.elpanama.com. 340 rooms. 3 restaurants, in-room safes, cable TV, minibars, hot tub, sauna, steam room, bar, dance club, casino, shops, dry cleaning, concierge, meeting rooms, business center, car rental, helipad, travel services, children's program (3–11), free parking. AE, MC, V.*

$$ ⊞ Continental. A new tower added some pizzazz to the hotel, a favorite with Latin-American tourists. The open-air lobby sweeps onto a busy street and makes a perfect perch for people-watching, especially when Carnaval rolls around. Newer rooms have desks, floral bedspreads, tile floors, bathtubs, and in-room VCRs. There's a 24-hour business center, a popular casino for after hours, and a restaurant specializing in barbecue. The attractive inner lobby is dripping in gilded French mirrors and late-19th-century furniture. Service can be slow. ⊠ *Vía España and Calle Ricardo Arias, El Cangrejo,* ☎ *507/203–9999,* ℻ *507/263–4247. 336 rooms. 2 restaurants, cable TV, some in-room safes, pool, dance club, casino, bar, dry cleaning, business center, free parking. AE, MC, V.*

$$ ⊞ Las Vegas Hotel Suites. A good choice for families or for long stays, this hotel has suites with two queen beds, full kitchens, and a full-fledged dining table. One studio suite comes with a microwave and free breakfast in place of a kitchen. The noise from the street can disturb the peace and quiet of the day, but you can't beat the price or location just steps from a major banking and shopping area. A popular Italian restaurant and wine bar is on the bottom floor. ⊠ *Calle 55 and Calle Eusebio A. Morales, El Cangrejo,* ☎ *507/269–0722,* ℻ *507/223–0047,* 𝗪𝗘𝗕 *www. lasvegaspanam.com. 89 suites, 1 studio. Restaurant, wine bar, kitchens, cable TV, Internet, free parking. AE, MC, V.*

$ ⊞ Aparthotel Suites Alfa. Although it's surrounded by prime restaurants and shops, this hotel is not much to look at. Most suites are spacious and nondescript, with a separate bedroom and kitchen-and-dining area. The lobby is small and funky with a teeny bar and piano for who-

ever wants to tickle the keys. The receptionist is usually wearing a baseball cap. ⊠ *Vía España and Calle Ricardo Arias, El Cangrejo,* ☎ *507/ 203–6754. 65 rooms. Kitchens, microwaves, cable TV, free parking. MC, V.*

El Obarrio, Marbella, and San Francisco

South of Vía España, El Obarrio is Panama's vibrant banking district. Marbella, south of El Obarrio, has chic shops with designer clothes, fine restaurants, and a score of embassies. San Franciso, to the east, has Panama City's convention center, ALTAPA, and the offices of the Panama Tourist Board (IPAT).

$$$$ 🖫 **The Bristol.** Built with an English manor in mind, The Bristol is gor-
★ geous and classy, much like a European boutique hotel. Selling points are personalized service and attention to detail. This carries through to the rooms, with high ceilings, handsome hardwood furniture, live plants, robes, and a marble bathroom. A writing desk with a fresh orchid, fax machine, and CD player can be turned into an office with the addition of a computer and printer. Other services include a 24-hour concierge, room service, your own business cards, and coffee or tea with your wake-up call. ⊠ *Av. Aquilino de la Guardia, between Calle 50 and Vía España, El Obarrio,* ☎ *507/265–7844; 800/323–7500 in the U.S.,* FAX *507/265–7829,* WEB *www.thebristol.com. 55 rooms. 2 restaurants, cable TV, in-room safes, in-room VCRs, gym, bar, dry cleaning, concierge, business services, meeting rooms, Internet, travel services, free parking. AE, MC, V.*

$$$–$$$$ 🖫 **Caesar Park.** Fidel Castro (who went to the laundry to shake hands
★ with the workers) and King Juan Carlos of Spain have stayed at this Westin-owned hotel. Four exceptional restaurants including a Thai bistro and the town's best health club are here, too (it has a TV in the sauna). Rooms are attractively appointed with a rust-and-turquoise color scheme, large desks, three phones, coffeemakers, and ironing boards. An elegant casino is open 22 hours a day, and the hotel has its own airline check-in counter, food court, and duty-free shops. ⊠ *Vía Israel and Calle 77, across from the ALTAPA convention center, San Francisco,* ☎ *507/270–0477; 800/325–5555 in the U.S.,* FAX *507/226–4262,* WEB *www.caesarpark.com. 353 rooms. 4 restaurants, in-room safes, 3 tennis courts, pool, health club, spa, casino, dry cleaning, concierge, meeting rooms, business center, Internet, shops, travel services, car rental, airport transfers (fee), children's program (ages 5–12). AE, MC, V.*

$$$–$$$$ 🖫 **Deville.** One of a few small, elegant boutique hotels in the city, the Deville suites have an eclectic mix of fine antique furnishings, with mostly Asian and French pieces. Beds are to die for, with fluffy goose down pillows and Egyptian cotton sheets; bathrooms have Italian marble everywhere. In-room high-speed modem connections and fax machines (plus a business center downstairs) make it a good choice when you've got work to do. The restaurant has a bona fide French chef, who turns out good French-Mediterranean cuisine. ⊠ *Av. Beatriz Cabal, near Calle 50 Este, Marbella,* ☎ *507/206–3100,* FAX *507/206–3111,* WEB *www. devillehotel.com.pa. 33 suites. Restaurant, cable TV, in-room VCRs, exercise equipment, bar, dry cleaning, concierge, business center, meeting rooms, free parking. AE, MC, V.*

$$$–$$$$ 🖫 **Radisson Royal.** Built into the capital's World Trade Center, the Radisson is near embassies, fashionable boutiques, and good restaurants. Rooms are nicely set up with free in-room coffee, two queen beds, three phones, a desk, and small dining table. The cozy lobby bar has live Caribbean music Wednesday evenings, the gym has an on-site trainer, and there's a DHL office on the premises. ⊠ *Calle 53 and Av. 5a B sur, World Trade Center, Marbella,* ☎ *507/265–3636,* FAX *507/265–3550,* WEB *www.radisson.com. 112 rooms, 16 suites. 2 restaurants, in-room*

safe, cable TV with video games, pool, tennis court, gym, hot tub, massage, sauna, steam room, 2 bars, concierge, helipad, car rental, travel services, meeting rooms, business center, free parking. AE, MC, V.

Nightlife

For nightlife listings, check out the *The Visitor* magazine. Buses run until 10 PM, so plan on getting a taxi back to your hotel.

Bars and Music

The underground **Casa de Cerveza** (⊠ Vía España, east of Vía Argentina, El Cangrejo, ☎ 507/223–1959) is a no-frills bar that plays Latin music. **Pavo Real** (⊠ Calle 51, near Calle Ricardo Arias, El Cangrejo, ☎ 507/269–0504) is a British-style pub in the banking district. It has live music, mostly classic rock on Wednesday and jazz on Friday. It's a good place to meet other English-speakers. **Ralph's Pool Place** (⊠ Vía Argentina, at Calle 52, El Cangrejo, ☎ 507/262–2065) has sort of a gringo sports-bar set up. Sunset cocktails taste great at the rooftop bar of the **Hotel Costa Sol** (⊠ Vía España at Av. Federico Boyd, El Cangrejo, ☎ 507/227–1522). If you don't want to hit the bars, you can attend poetry readings or see live music or alternative films at **Café El Aleph** (⊠ Vía Argentina at Vía España, El Cangrejo, ☎ 507/264–2844), a casual, coffee-house setting.

Casinos

Gambling is a popular pastime in Panama City, and there are casinos all over the place, ranging from fancy to seedy. The nicest ones are in the Caesar Park and El Panamá hotels.

Dance Clubs

All dance places play a mix of American pop, salsa, merengue, and reggae. Cover charges are between $5 and $15, and usually include two drinks or even an open bar.

Bacchus (⊠ Calle Elvira Mendez, off Vía España, El Cangrejo, ☎ 507/263–9005) is probably the most agreeable of the lot, with pool tables and dartboards in a glass-walled room if you're tired of the huge, air-conditioned dance floor. Expect to find a wild mix of young people dancing same-sex salsa at **Boy Bar** (⊠ off Vía Ricardo Alfaro, El Dorado, ☎ 507/230–3128), sometimes called El Garage, one of the city's most popular gay clubs. It's open Friday–Sunday 9 PM until the wee hours of the morning, and charges a $5 cover. **Dreams** (⊠ Jardines Comerciales, Hotel El Panamá, Vía España, El Cangrejo, ☎ 507/269–4248) is a massive, split-level place with light shows and a waterfall between the bar and dance floor, but it has never been quite as popular as Bacchus or Patatus. **Patatus** (⊠ Calle 50 and Av. Federico Boyd, El Cangrejo, ☎ 507/264–8467) is a popular dance bar, slightly smaller than Bacchus, but with a similar crowd of young Panamanians. You can dance to Latin and U.S. hits Thursday through Saturday at the wild and hip **Señor Frog's** (⊠ Calle 48, near Av. Balboa, Bella Vista, ☎ 507/213–9119).

Folk Dancing

Tinajas (⊠ Av. 3 A Sur near Av. Frederico Boyd, El Cangrejo, ☎ 507/269–3840), a slightly upscale restaurant specializing in Panamanian cuisine, has Panamanian folk dancing Tuesday, Thursday, Friday, and Saturday. The hour-long show starts at 9 PM and costs $5, plus a one-drink minimum. You can often enjoy folk dancing for free on weekends at Mi Pueblito and less frequently at Panamá Viejo. Check out the local tourist paper, *The Visitor,* for special events.

Outdoor Activities and Sports

Panama City offers a wealth of activities for outdoorsy types, including the largest chunk of urban rain forest in the world. **ANCON Expeditions** (⊠ Calle Elvira Mendez, Edificio El Dorado, El Dorado, ☎ 507/269–9414) has an excellent selection of day tours to protected areas near the capital, plus longer excursions to five field stations scattered around the country. **Iguana Tours** (⊠ Av. Porras, across from Parque Omar, between Calles 72 and 73, San Francisco, ☎ 507/226–8738) uses such specialists as marine biologists and Smithsonian researchers as guides. **Pesantez Tours** (⊠ Av. Balboa, Paitilla, ☎ 507/263–8771) runs day tours from and around the capital, including to the Indian settlements along the Chagres River.

Beaches

The closest beach with clear water is found on **Isla Taboga,** a 90-minute ferry ride from the city (☞ Isla Taboga *in* Canal Zone, *below*).

Shopping

Shopping has been a tradition ever since Panama became a trade center more than 400 years ago. Today, fashionable shops that sell top-quality European and American brands for less than in the United States can be found in the Marbella neighborhood at the World Trade Center, in high-end hotels, and along Calle Ricardo Arias and Vía España.

Even if you're not interested in buying, take a walk around one of the city's three major **craft markets,** open daily 9–6. The rows of stalls filled with native handicrafts are great places to browse and get to know the culture. *Molas* (embroidered cloths) tend to be substantially cheaper at the market nearest **Plaza Cinco de Mayo** (⊠ behind Museo Antropologico Reina Torres de Araúz, Santa Ana). The market at **Panamá Viejo,** next to the tower, tends to have more of the country's other coveted items and fewer molas, such as masks from Chitré and Los Santos, pottery from La Arena, and baskets from the Darién. The newest of the three markets, called **Centro Municipal de Artesanias Panameñas** (⊠ at Calle Arnulfo Arias, formerly Balboa Rd., a half block from Calle Ramon Levy, El Cangrejo), is staffed entirely by friendly Kuna tribe members who sell their molas sewn into dresses, bags, pot holders, T-shirts, and every other imaginable item. Many of the Kunas dress in Western apparel, but often older women still model their traditional attire as it was originally worn.

La Central, a pedestrian-only section of Avenida Central (⊠ between Plaza Santa Ana and Plaza Cinco de Mayor, Colón), is packed with shops and street vendors offering especially good deals on imported watches, camera equipment, electronics, jewelry, fabrics, and clothing. A little bargaining can get you the same price you'd pay in duty-free.

Panama City A to Z

AIR TRAVEL

Panama City's airport, Aeropuerto Internacional de Tocumen, 26 km [13 mi] northeast of Panama City, is the gateway into the country. All U.S. carriers fly direct into Panama City and several Panamanian carriers have service from here to the interior. Domestic flights go through Albrook Airport (north of downtown).

➤ AIRPORTS: **Aeropuerto Internacional de Tocumen** (⊠ Off Via España, 26 km (13 mi) east of city center, ☎ 507/238–4322 or 507/263–8777). **Albrook Airport** (⊠ Carratera Guillard and Corredor Norte, north of Ancón, ☎ no phone).

BUS TRAVEL

If you don't mind a little jolting and pressing the flesh (literally) with the locals, buses (of the school bus variety) are a cheap (15¢) way to get around the city. They're also the best entertainment around. Each wildly painted or billboard-bearing bus has its destination and route painted broadly across the windshield. The word to remember when you want to get off is *parada* (stop). You pay your fare as you get off. The central bus stop is Plaza Cinco de Mayo; from here you can catch buses to both airports and almost everywhere else in the city. Buses run consistently until about 10 PM, with some routes running as late as 1 or 2 AM. Buses to the former Canal Zone leave from the SACA terminal, one block north of Plaza Cinco de Mayo.

CAR TRAVEL

Driving a car in Panama City is not an undertaking for the meek, but renting a car can be an excellent way to explore the countryside. Rental cars are $30–$40 a day, four-wheel-drive vehicles start at $53. (*See* Panama A to Z for agencies.)

EMERGENCIES

National police (☎ 104). **Fire department** (☎ 103). **Ambulance** (Red Cross, ☎ 507/228–8127).

MAIL

Small *correos* (post offices) are scattered all over the city. The main post office, Correos Nacional, can hold mail for you when it's mailed to its *poste restante* (general delivery) address: Entrega General, Zona 3, Panamá, República de Panamá, Central America. The main correos is open weekdays 7–5:30 and Saturday 7–5; DHL is open weekdays 8–5.

➤ COURIER SERVICES: **DHL** (✉ Radisson Hotel, World Trade Center, Calle 53 and Av. 5a B sur, Marbella, ☎ 507/265–3636).

➤ POST OFFICE: **Correos Nacional** (✉ At the end of Av. Balboa, at Central Peatonal, Santa Ana, ☎ 507/262–1831).

SAFETY

Certain parts of Panama City are not safe to walk around in, especially at night. The most dangerous area is El Chorrillo, which was hard-hit by the U.S. invasion: almost the entire neighborhood was burned down in 1989, and where ramshackle wood tenements once were, characterless pastel cement projects now hold sway. Unfortunately, neighboring Santa Ana, which borders the Casco Viejo, and parts of Calidonia are also dicey. If you stay in Casco Viejo, take a taxi at night.

TELEPHONES

You'll find telephones just about everywhere but lots of them are out of order. Those at hotels, banks, and big department stores are generally in working order. Phone cards are a handy and inexpensive way to make calls. You can buy one from any pharmacy or hotel gift shop in several denominations. Cable and Wireless, an international calling center, is open daily 7:30 AM–9:30 PM.

➤ TELEPHONE COMPANY: **Cable and Wireless** (✉ Calle Eusebio A. Morales, near Hotel Continental, Marbella, ☎ 507/264–8104).

TOURS

Most major travel agencies offer city tours and day trips. Gray Line runs the gamut from a city highlights tour, a nightlife tour, to diving trips, visits to national parks, and a partial Canal transit. Shirley Eco Tours runs soft adventure tours, sojourns to indigenous villages, and other trips, all from an eco-friendly perspective.

➤ Tour Companies: **Gray Line Panama Tours** (☎ 507/206–3300). **Shirley Eco Tours** (☎ 507/613–8223).

TAXIS

Fares are based on a zone system. The official charge is $1.25 per zone plus 25¢ for each additional person. Most trips around town cost up to $3. All cabbies have to carry a map with zones and fares on it, which you can consult. Cabbies will usually pick up several passengers if they're headed the same direction, so be prepared to share. Tips are not expected.

VISITOR INFORMATION

The **Instituto Panameño de Turismo** (IPAT; ✉ Atlapa Convention Center, Vía Israel, across the street from the Marriott Caesar Park Hotel) publishes a brochure titled "Conjunto Monumental Historico de Panamá," which has some background information and small maps of Panamá Viejo, Casco Viejo, and Portobelo.

THE CANAL ZONE

From 1904, only one year after Panama declared its independence from Colombia, until the treaties began to take effect in the 1980s, the United States controlled and maintained a large area along both sides of the canal—approximately 48 km (30 mi) wide—that included a number of military bases and housing for canal workers and military families. Since 1999, when Panama gained full control of the canal, all 10,000 of the foreign workers and military personnel have departed, leaving the installations in the hands of the Panamanian Army.

These days, the government is trying to attract private investment in electricity, water, and telecommunications projects in the Canal Zone. As a bonus, it can offer the use of some of the $4 billion worth of buildings and infrastructure the United States left behind. The first container transshipment center in Latin America, which will transport ship's containers by land from the Atlantic to the Pacific, is already open. A certain amount of cash is collected in tolls as boats pass through the canal. Tolls are based on weight, and the average is about $30,000 per ship. The unsuspecting Richard Halliburton was charged 36¢ when, in 1928, he swam through the canal.

One of the biggest pushes in the Canal Zone is tourism, and the government has earmarked nearly $516 million for tourism development through 2005. New luxury hotels are constantly opening and many more are scheduled to follow. (This trend is also encouraging hotel investment in Panama City, which has added several new luxury lodgings over the last couple of years.) The area draws sightseers because its forests, along with those of several nearby national parks, are protected as a watershed to feed the huge lakes that provide the water to raise and lower ships on the canal. So while the area's star attraction may be the canal itself, the waterway is flanked by some of the most accessible rain forests anywhere in the world. In fact, just minutes from the capital, Carretera Gamboa, a smooth, paved road, winds through Soberanía, a completely undeveloped forest filled with a mind-boggling diversity of tropical flora and fauna.

The Panama Canal

Stretches from southwest Panama City to north to Colón.

Connecting the Pacific Ocean and the Caribbean Sea, the Panama Canal runs 80 km (50 mi) from southwest Panama City across the narrowest part of the isthmus, passing through Lago Gatún, an enormous

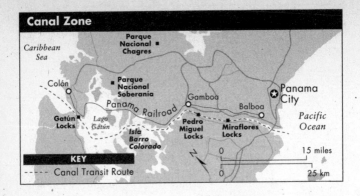

Canal Zone

Caribbean
Sea

Parque
Nacional
Chagres

Colón

Parque
Nacional
Soberanía

Gamboa

Panama
City

Balboa

Pacific
Ocean

Panama Railroad

Gatún
Locks

Lago
Gatún

Isla
Barro
Colorado

Pedro
Miguel
Locks

Miraflores
Locks

KEY

- - - - Canal Transit Route

0   15 miles

0   25 km

artificial lake created by the damming of the Río Chagres. The first
ship traversed the Panama Canal in 1914 after 10 years of construction—and a little international wheeling and dealing—by the United
States. The canal is just minutes from the city and can easily be toured
as a morning or afternoon trip.

Spain developed plans for a canal here as early as the 16th century. In
the 1880s, France started serious work under Ferdinand de Lesseps (the
architect responsible for Suez), but his Compagnie Universelle du
Canal Interocéanique went bankrupt in 1889. Soon after, the Americans took over and completed the canal at a cost of $352 million, a
staggering sum at that time. Its cost was more than just dollars, though.
Especially during the French years, workers on the canal dropped like
flies from disease. Malaria, yellow fever, bubonic plague, beriberi, and
typhoid felled as many as 25,000 people during the 30-odd years of
construction—that's 500 deaths for every mile of the canal.

Despite the unconscionable death toll, there's no getting around the
fact that this is one amazing piece of engineering. The amount of dirt
excavated for the canal could have filled a train stretching three times
around the equator. Under de Lesseps's original plan, which called for
an ocean-level canal, even more dirt would have been dug out. American engineers found his plan unfeasible. Instead, they opted for a lock
system that would raise and lower ships over the terrain of the isthmus. They constructed three sets of locks—Miraflores, Pedro Miguel,
and Gatún—each measuring 1,000 ft by 110 ft.

The locks act as aquatic elevators by opening doors that let the lock
either fill with water or drain. As the water level rises, a ship is raised
(or conversely, lowered). Each door of each lock weighs 80 tons, yet
they float and thus require only about 40 watts of power to open and
close. Gravity does all the necessary water transfer, so the locking process uses no pumps. "Panamax" ships are designed specifically for the
canal to maximize the cargo capacity. Watching a ship 106 ft wide and
950 ft long passing with only inches to spare is probably the most awesome sight on the canal. A future project calls for widening the canal
at its narrowest point so as to allow two ships coming in opposite directions to pass each other. A scenic trip on the historic Panama Canal
Railroad, the only operating train service in Central America, follows
alongside the Canal, and is a good way to get from the capital to
Panama's Atlantic coast. It dates to 1850, when thousands of gold seekers heading for California sought intercontinental transportation. The
Panama Society (WEB www.pancanalsociety.org) has information on the
railroad and other historical aspects of the Canal and the country.

If you've rented a car, drive towards Gamboa or Paraíso to the Miraflores Locks. Follow the signs to the visitor center, where bilingual guides explain what's happening over loud speakers as you watch the ships passing through.

Amador

Directly south of Panama City.

Amador, a series of former islands connecting the Causeway in the Canal Zone to the mainland, used to be the headquarters of Fort Amador when the U.S. military was running the Canal. Now, it's being transformed into a tourism development. No wonder. The impressive view of the Bridge of the Americas, Panama City, and the entrance to the Canal is truly worth a trip here. It's also a fantastic place for watching the sunset. Among the new attractions are restaurants, a modern-looking cruise-ship terminal, and a small shopping mall. A Hilton hotel with villas and suites overlooking the Pacific is under construction using the former underground rocket warehouse as its entrance. To get here, head west from Panama City to the Bridge of the Americas and turn left onto Calle Amador.

Dining and Lodging

$$–$$$$ ✕ **Café Barko.** Since it's in a replica of the deck of an old Spanish galleon, "ships ahoy" could be the motto here in. House specials cover fish and seafood, including a grilled miniature Atlantic lobster, but menu items also draw from the land—steaks, salads, and even hamburgers. The extensive wine list offers 90 vintages from around the world. Congenial owner Abraham Hasky works the crowd to make everyone feel at home. Come evening, diners can shake it up with salsa, jazz, and 1970s dance music. ⊠ *Isla Flamenco, Calzada de Amador,* ☎ *507/314–0000. MC, V.*

$$–$$$ ✕ **Las Pencas.** This place started out as a bike rental shop, and as Amador developed, so did it. The view of the bay and passing ships from the dining terrace is lovely—just ask the office workers who pack the place at lunch. Top menu items include grilled salmon and brochette of lobster, or you can choose a chicken, beef, or pasta dish—the portions are huge. Top it off with a frosty beer or glass of wine. The bicycle shop is still in business if you want to take a spin after you eat. ⊠ *Calle Boulevard, Causeway de Amador across the street from Plaza Iberamericana,* ☎ *507/211–3671. AE, MC, V.*

$$ ⊡ **Country Inn & Suites Panama Canal.** The homey lobby, which welcomes you with a bowl of apples, a fireplace, pot of hot coffee, and checkered-cloth chairs, more resembles rural Pennsylvania than Panama but it sells. This Carlson-chain hotel has rooms with a view of the Canal or the garden and all come with a complimentary buffet breakfast. Standard doubles, junior suites with microwaves, one-bedroom suites, and a whirlpool suite make up the room inventory. A branch of the popular T.G. I. Friday's serving burgers, fries, and steaks is next door. ⊠ *Calles Amador and Pelicáno, on the Amador Causeway,* ☎ *507/211–4500; 888/201–1746 in the U.S.,* FAX *507/211–4501,* WEB *www.countryinns.com. 47 rooms, 40 suites, 1 apartment. Restaurant cable TV, tennis court, pool, gym, hot tub, sauna, spa, laundry facilities, meeting rooms, travel services, free parking, airport shuttle (fee). AE, MC, V.*

Isla Taboga

90-min ferry ride south of Panama City.

The "Island of Flowers," as Isla Taboga is known, is an excellent day or overnight trip from Panama City, reached by an enjoyable 90-

minute ferry ride. Taboga itself is a beautiful, tranquil isle, with a charming little village and pretty beaches washed by aquamarine waters. On weekends the main beach often has an excess of radios and screaming kids, but during the week it's almost deserted. The nicest beach lies within the grounds of the Hotel Taboga, which charges nonguests $5 to use it. However, the hotel gives you $5 in play money that you can use for food and drink at the overpriced snack bar, which makes it fairly worthwhile. If you bring along your snorkeling gear, you may see some big fish not far from shore. A trail near the hotel entrance leads to a smaller, more isolated beach that most tourists never see. (Follow it as it veers left and runs along the back fence.) Another option is to hike to the top of the nearby hill, which is topped by a huge white cross. On a clear day you'll get a dazzling view of the town, the bay, and even Panama City in the distance.

Ferries leave twice a day from Pier 7 in Balboa. Once you're on the island, you'll be able to walk everywhere. You can easily see everything on a day trip, except for the thousands of frogs that come out only at night. If you stay the night, you'll quickly discover that lodging on Taboga is expensive for what you get, though not outrageous. **Hotel Chu** (⊠ left of pier, ☎ 507/250–2035) is an old wooden building on the water, where simple rooms run $19 for a single and $24 for a double. The restaurant serves decent Chinese food ($5–$8). The pretty **Hotel Taboga** (⊠ right of pier, ☎ 250–2122) has a big beach, swimming pools, and large, air-conditioned rooms that run $66 for a double.

Isla Barro Colorado

Northwest of Panama City, in the Panama Canal

The island of Barro Colorado in Lago Gatún (a lake in the middle of the canal) was created when the Río Chagres was dammed during construction of the Panama Canal. Today it's a center for environmental research, and only a few visitors are allowed at a time with permission from the Smithsonian Tropical Research Institute (STRI). On your way out to the island, you pass over a surreal underwater forest of trees submerged when the dam was built. Also lost in the depths are the remains of the first railroad on the isthmus. The underwater world is the exclusive territory of Lago Gatún's famous peacock bass, a species introduced to the area as an experiment that went awry. The invasive latecomer now dominates all the indigenous species of fish. When the lake flooded the surrounding jungle, many large mammals retreated to the safety of the island, so there's a much larger concentration of monkeys, coatis, agoutis, and other jungle animals here than in other areas, and they're much less frightened of people.

The **Smithsonian Tropical Research Institute (STRI)** (☎ 507/227–6022, WEB www.stri.org), which administers the Barro Colorado preserve and grants permission to visit, takes groups to the island on Tuesday, Saturday, and Sunday. The $32 tour is well worth it, since the English-speaking guides do an excellent job of pointing out the flora and fauna. These tours tend to fill up five months to a year ahead of time, so your best bet is to call when you arrive in Panama City and ask if there have been any cancellations, which are frequent enough. At press time, the Smithsonian was planning to increase the number of tours. If you can't get in with the Smithsonian, consider a trip with Iguana Tours or with Gray Line Panama Tours. Both can arrange for your visit, which at $90 is more expensive, but it actually takes in more wildlife. No matter how you get here, be sure to wear long pants, shoes, and socks to combat the island's mean chigger population.

Parque Nacional Soberanía

25 km (16 mi) northwest from Panama City.

Soberanía is one of the planet's most accessible rain forests. Its protected territory of 54,000 acres of tropical jungle is about 25 km (16 mi) from Panama City. Within that lush wilderness live more than 100 species of mammals—including the howler monkey, tamandua anteater, and jaguarundi—and more than 350 bird species. Here you can spot the endangered (and shamelessly carnivorous) harpy eagle, Panama's national bird. The 17-km (11-mi) **Camino del Oleoducto (Pipeline Road)**, which heads north out of Gamboa toward the park, is one of the best bird-watching spots in the world. You can head up that paved road on foot or bicycle, or if you take a tour, in a car. About 10 km (6 mi) past the Miraflores Locks, surrounded by the national park, is **Jardín Botánico Summit** (Summit Botanical Garden, ☎ 507/232–4854), with more than 15,000 plant species, nature trails, and a zoo. Locked in its cages are all those monkeys, birds, and jaguars that may elude you on your hike. Although the zoo is a bit small, it has some rare animals, such as the impressive harpy eagle. You can while away your time in the fragrant gardens, or stray from the cages to see such wild animals as agoutis, as well as parrots and other birds in the nearby forest. On weekends you can rent bicycles just inside the entrance for $2 an hour. The gardens are open weekdays 8–4, weekends 8–5.

The **Sendero el Charco,** on the right about 1 km (½ mi) past the botanical gardens is another excellent route for seeing animals, although it can get seriously muddy during the rainy months. ("Charco," by the way, means puddle.) The trails can be reached on a Gamboa bus, which leaves from the Plaza Cinco de Mayo terminal in Panama City, although you'll see and understand a lot more if you go with an experienced guide. Pesantez Tours, Iguana Tours, and ANCON Expeditions all run guided trips to Soberanía. (A public bus ride is a hotter, more crowded way to get here.) The best time to see animals is first thing in the morning or early evening; these are also the coolest times to hike in the jungle. Be sure to wear shoes with good traction, and bring insect repellent. If you're driving from the capital, take Carretera Gaillard north towards Miraflores Locks and the town of Paraíso. There is a formal entrance and ranger station with maps, information, and camping permits. ✉ *Ranger station, Gamboa,* ☎ *507/229–7885.* 🏷 *Free, $1 for Jardín Botánico Summit.* ☉ *Daily 8–5.*

Parque Nacional Chagres

35 km (22 mi) north from Panama City.

If you yearn to visit one of the region's primitive tribes but don't want to battle mud, jungle, and hordes of insects, you should visit the Chagres National Park. In the park, part of the region's protected watershed, the mountains still harbor jaguar and wild boar, which the Emberá hunt just as they have for hundreds of years. These gentle people, who migrated here from the Darién in the 1970s, live in thatched huts and spurn most modern conveniences. Adhering to tradition, the men wear loincloths and women wrap themselves in bright-color cloth skirts and no tops, covering their breasts with large necklaces.

You need a vehicle to get to the park, where you pay a $3 entrance fee. You also must call the tribe a few days in advance (☎ 507/685–3009 cell phone) so they can send a dugout canoe to transport you to the village. If you come on your own, the tribe charges $45 for one person or $30 each for two or more. **Pesantez Tours** (☎ 507/223–5374) also provides an English-speaking guide and transportation; it's about

$125 per person for a party of two for the day outing (the price goes down the more people you have). The Emberás provide a lunch of grilled peacock bass—that's it—and demonstrate traditional folk dances. You can take all the photos you want and chat up the village leader, Atliano Flacco, who's very forthcoming about the customs of the tribe. After lunch, his cousin, Miguel, conducts a tour of the area's medicinal plants. In spite of catering to tourists, this place has a pretty authentic feel to it. If you fall under its enchantment and want to stay longer, you can sleep in a bare-bones "guest hut" above the rushing river for $25–$32 a night, including meals.

Dining and Lodging

The new hotels are spectacular, surrounded by amazing rain forest filled with wildlife. Some are converted U.S. military installations, which makes them even more surprising.

$$$$ ✕🖭 **Canopy Tower Ecolodge.** What looks like a giant soccer ball is actually a funky minilodge built above the rain forest in an abandoned radar tower. (The Audubon Society gave it a top ranking as one of ten spectacular eco-hostels in the world.) The movie *The Tailor of Panama* was filmed here. Rooms are rustic, small, and basic with cement floors, beds with mosquito netting, and small white bathrooms. Suites are bigger and nicer. But the spartan rooms are ignored by the serious conservation groups who come here to bird-watch. You can climb to the top deck for a thrilling view of the Canal and Panama City. All meals (prepared by an outstanding chef) and two nature tours—one at night—are included in the price. ⊠ *Carretera Gamboa, about 1 mi northeast of Summit Park,* ☎ *507/264–5720; 800/722–2460 in the U.S.,* 🖩 *www.canopytower.com. 10 rooms, 2 suites. Restaurant, library, free parking; no a/c, no room phones, no room TVs. AE, MC, V.*

$$$$ ✕🖭 **Gamboa Rainforest Resort.** Surrounded by 340 acres of wilderness, the hotel cascades down a hill overlooking the Panama Canal,
★   and has its own monkey island, an observation tower for catching toucans, and an aerial tram to get you there. This has to be adventure at its most luxurious. Rooms have rattan furniture, bright-color bedspreads, big bathrooms, plus terraces slung with hammocks. Former U.S. military apartments built in the 1930s have been refurbished into villas. You can also choose a sportfishing, wildlife, or all-inclusive package. The on-site restaurant serves fish and meat dishes prepared with international flair. ⊠ *Carretera Gamboa, 17 mi from Panama City,* ☎ *507/314–9000; 877/800–1690 in the U.S.,* 🖷 *507/314–9020,* 🖩 *www.gamboaresort.com (mailing address: Box 7338, Zone 5, Panama City). 107 rooms, 45 villas. 3 restaurants, cable TV, spa, boating, fishing, 2 bars, shops, dry cleaning, travel services, business services, convention center, airport shuttle (fee), free parking. AE, MC, V.*

$$$$ ✕🖭 **Meliá Panamá Canal.** The Meliá was built into the former School of the Americas, which has a more benign use now than when it was known as a controversial U.S. military training academy. Perched above Lago Gatún, the hotel's interior is grandiloquent with an Old Spain motif. Handsome hand-carved wooden furniture and handicrafts from Mexico decorate the rooms and lobby, which also has a four-story atrium. Rooms have two queen beds and large marble bathrooms with fancy soaps and shampoos. You'll pay more here than in the other area hotels, but the sounds of the jungle animals at night from your open window are truly bewitching. ⊠ *Res. Espinar Colón, 1 yard from Colón,* ☎ *507/470–0495; 800/336–3542 in the U.S. and Canada,* 🖷 *507/470–0427,* 🖩 *www.solmelia.com. 310 rooms. 2 restaurants, cable TV, in-room safe, 2 tennis courts, pool, 3 bars, dry cleaning, concierge, meeting rooms, travel services, free parking, airport shuttle (fee). MC, V.*

Colón

80 km (50 mi) northwest of Panama City.

With unemployment around 40%–50%, Colón is a wasteland, which the average traveler should avoid, even though it's marked on every map and has what appears to be a good location. Such is the desperation in Colón that not even in daylight or crowds are you safe from muggings. It's a great pity, not only for the residents of Colón, who are almost entirely descendants of African slaves or Jamaicans brought for railroad and canal work, but for Panama as a whole. In the early 20th century, Colón was an important shipping center and one of the world's most beautiful ports. If you visit downtown Colón today, you'll see the decaying remnants of what was once a gorgeous city, with wide boulevards and stylish old buildings, all now completely dilapidated. There are efforts to revive the town, though. A new **cruise ship pier** and Radisson hotel complex have opened in the nicer and safer part of the city and plans for a multimillion-dollar international airport and the largest container port in the world have been announced.

Behind huge walls, impervious to the surrounding blight, is the **Zona Libre,** a duty-free microcity with huge international stores drawing in $4 billion a year. It sells mainly to retailers, so you only get good prices if you buy in bulk. However, tourists can get a four-day pass by showing their passports. If you buy anything, you are required to have it sent to your hotel; you should allow 24 hours for delivery. Small shops do not accept credit cards. With all that money pouring into the Zona Libre and with so much poverty just outside the gates, you might sympathize a little with those Colón residents. Guard your belongings, even during the day. The Zona Libre is on the eastern edge of the city; take a taxi (from your transportation hub) rather than attempting to walk. It's open weekdays 9–5, but tourists are not allowed inside after 3 PM.

Canal Zone A to Z

The Canal Zone is not a city per se but a former U.S. military zone broken up into bases, administrative office, schools, and dormitories, which are taking on a life of their own as hotels or institutions of higher learning. Thus, most major services like hospitals, car rental, banks, and mail and shipping (although you can post letters or postcards from your all hotels in the Zone) are still handled from Panama City. The only way to traverse the Zone is by road, and a car will get you any place you have to go. Hotels usually have taxis to provide transportation to Panama City, Colón, or the airport.

BY BOAT
BOATING THE PANAMA CANAL
The best way to see the canal is from a boat, which is why you might want to consider signing up for a tour. Pesantez and Argo Tours run one or two ocean-to-ocean trips each month. These voyages, at $135 per person, have the best view of Gaillard Cut, where engineers had to slice through solid rock to get across the isthmus, as well as the jungle-cloaked islands of Lago Gatún. The other option is the half-day tour, which takes you through the Miraflores Locks for $90 per person. These tours are only offered on weekends.

Another way to get see the canal is to tour Isla Barro Colorado, which lies within the canal route, in Lago Gatún. A third and inexpensive and convenient option is to take the ferry out to Isla Taboga, at the canal's Pacific entrance, passing big ships en route.

➤ CANAL TOURS INFORMATION: **Argo Tours** (✉ Pier 18, Balboa, Canal Zone, ☎ 507/228–4348). **Pesantez** (✉ Av. Balboa, Paitilla, Panama City, ☎ 507/263–8771).

FERRY TO ISLA TABOGA

The ferry costs $8 per person round-trip. Boats leave for Taboga on weekdays at 8:30 AM and 3 PM (return trips at 10 AM and 4:30 PM), on weekends at 8:30 and 11:30 AM and 4 PM (return trips at 10 AM, 2:30 PM, and 5 PM). To reach the ferry dock in Balboa, take a cab to Pier 7.

BY CAR

The canal is accessible from Panama City via Carretera Gaillard and Madden.

BY TRAIN

The Kansas City Railroad restored the original transcontinental railroad which first started running in 1850 to carry seekers of gold to California during the Gold Rush of 1849. The Panama Canal Train Co. has observation cars for viewing the Canal and leaves the train station in Corozal, in Panama City, at 7:15 AM and departs from Colón, the line's terminus, at 5:15 PM in the afternoon. It runs once a day weekdays only and costs $20 one-way, $35 round trip.

➤ TRAIN STATION INFORMATION: **Panama Canal Train Co.** (✉ Calle Corozal, Ancon, Panama City, ☎ 507/317–6070 in Panama City; ✉ Calle Mt. Hope, Cristobal, Colón, ☎ no phone).

THE CARIBBEAN COAST

Coral reefs, colonial ruins, and the predominant Afro-Caribbean culture make Panama's Caribbean coast an exciting place to visit. This is where people from Panama City come to enjoy white-sand beaches and creole lobster and conch concoctions. Scuba diving around the colonial town of Portobelo is a big part of the coastal commerce, too. One of the area's main cultural attractions is the dance performances, known as **congos.** Men wear elaborate costumes covered with beads, feathers, and mirrors and dance to wild drum music. These displays are performed in many towns along the coast, but the most spectacular is in Portobelo on the town's Patron Saint Day (March 20), as well as at New Year's and during Carnaval.

Fort San Lorenzo

40 km (25 mi) west of Colón.

Perched on a cliff overlooking the mouth of the Chagres River are the ruins of the ancient Spanish Fort San Lorenzo, which was destroyed by pirate Henry Morgan. To get here you must drive through some serious rain forest (where the U.S. Army's old jungle-warfare training site was located). The cliff it's perched on offers a stunning view of the vast jungle and the Caribbean coast. Unfortunately, tours to the remote fort are infrequent. If you have a vehicle, drive toward Colón, veering left past Fort Davis to the Gatún Locks. After driving across the canal, veer right on the main road, following it to Fort Sherman, where you may have to check in with a Panamanian Army guard (just tell him you're headed to Fort San Lorenzo). The gates here close at 4 PM, so it's best to arrive before 1 PM to give you enough time to get to San Lorenzo and back. Stay on the main dirt road through the jungle (the side roads are, for the most part, marked with signs saying stuff like AMBUSH TRAINING SITE–STAY OUT). Bring a flashlight to explore the nifty nooks and crannies. Cover yourself with bug repellent or risk being devoured. There's no admission charge to get in.

48 km (30 mi) northeast of Colón.

Sitting on a clear-water bay bordered by jungle, Portobelo ("beautiful port") lives up to the name it was given by explorer Christopher Columbus. It harbors some of Panama's most interesting colonial ruins, with rusty cannons still lying in wait for an enemy assault and decaying fortress walls yielding to the advancing jungle—and is a UNESCO World Heritage Site. Invoking the translation of Panama as "the place of abundant fish," this coastal town is also known for its national marine park and the Coiba National Park islands, both of which draw scuba divers. On the approach from Sabanitas are two tidy beaches, Playas María Chiquita and Langosta; the former has black sand. Be sure to bring food along from Sabanitas or elsewhere as not much is available in Portobelo.

Whole sections of the **old walls** of the city, instead of being carefully preserved, have been used to build ramshackle houses. Here you'll see a 16th-century customs house that now holds a museum and the church that contains the **Cristo Negro** (Black Christ), which legend says saved the town from a terrible scourge of cholera. In the late-October Celebración del Cristo Negro, the statue is clothed in sumptuous velvet and bejeweled cloaks and is carried through the streets in a procession of the faithful. A new museum in the restored Casa de la Aduana (Customs House) is being built in town to honor Cristo Negro the rest of the year. Portobelo also comes alive on Patron Saint Day (March 20), with festivals, parades, and congo dancing. If you're not scuba diving, you can easily see the entire town on a day trip, or during a stop on your way to Isla Grande.

Scuba Diving and Snorkeling

The town hops with divers here for the reefs and underwater wildlife at **Portobelo National Park.** In fact, you'll see several dive centers along the road just before you reach town, and they all run boats out to nearby coral reefs (with 50-plus coral species), the many wrecks (this area is filled with them, some centuries-old), and several tiny uninhabited islands. Typical trips may include Buenaventura Island (for shallow and deep dives); Drake Island, named for Sir Frances Drake, who shipwrecked and died here; and semi-submerged Salmedina Reef. Look for sergeant majors, yellowtail snappers, schoolmasters, and blue tangs.

Most local outfitters charge $30 to rent diving equipment, $5 per tank, $5 for snorkel, mask, and fins, and $4 per boat ride. Several of them also have dorm-style sleeping quarters for $8 to $10. You need to be certified to dive, but, if you don't mind the risk, these places also offer quick and inexpensive certification courses. **Aquatic Park** (☏ 507/448–2175) has weekend packages that include meals, accommodations, and instruction if needed. Trips with **Diver's Haven** (☏ 507/448–2003) include dives, meals, accommodations, and instruction. If you want to plan in advance, **Iguana Tours** (☏ 507/226–8738) runs daily scuba trips from Panama City, which include meals and a tour of Portobelo's colonial sights. **Scuba Portobelo** (☏ 507/261–3841) has been around awhile and has an established reputation as a local outfitter.

★ The town is also a point of departure for dive trips to the spectacular **Coiba National Park islands,** a former penal colony that was restricted to visitors until recently, and is now being touted as the new Galapagos, and as the hemisphere's biggest land mass of virgin forest on an island. Sea creature sightings may include sailfish, tarpon, tuna, turtles, dolphins, and whale sharks (in December and January). **Padama Twin Oceans Dive Center** (☏ 507/448–2067, ⟨WEB⟩ www.padamatwinoceans.com) runs the trips, and the dive masters used to work for the Smithsonian Institute before setting up shop here, offering certification courses as well as dive tours.

Isla Grande

10-min boat trip from La Guaira; 25 km (15 mi) from Portobelo.

A smashing little island, with sparkling white-sand beaches framed by towering palm trees, and just off the Caribbean coast, **Isla Grande** has a town so small you don't need addresses, or even directions, to find your way to the half dozen hotels. Only a couple hundred people live on the laid-back island, making a living by fishing or taking part in the tiny tourism industry. A dirt road facing south is the main coastal thoroughfare, with hotels and restaurants predominately serving seafood. A cement-paved road crosses the island to the north shore. The rest of the island is rather impassable, although there are paths to the beaches and the surfing area. Although the island is quiet during the week, it can become crowded on weekends.

To get here from Portobelo, it's a short ride to the tiny town of La Guaira, the jumping-off point for the island. Boats arrive regularly for the 10-minute trip across the strait ($1).

The island's big resort is **Bananas Village** (☎ 507/263–9510 or 507/263–9766, FAX 507/264–7556, WEB www.bananasresort.com); it has the infrastructure and amenities you might want (transfers, in-room air-conditioning, a pool, and activities), and a predictable resort-y feel. Rates are $75 per night. The spacious grounds of the **Hotel Isla Grande** (☎ 507/225–6721) overlook the western end of the island, where bungalows shaded by coconut palms go for $60. **Villa Ensueño** (☎ 507/269–5819), with a view of Isla Grande's famous cross on top of a coral reef, has air-conditioned rooms for $44–$55.

Since Isla Grande has little in the way of beaches, and the surrounding reef has suffered years of abuse, it's worthwhile to organize a group and hire a boat for a day trip to other nearby beaches and reefs.

THE PACIFIC COAST

Dotted with small agricultural communities and traditional horse farms, the stretch of coast south of Panama City toward the Azuero Peninsula is awakening to the possibilities of tourism. Part of its charm is the small-town flavor that permeates it. The Interamerican highway runs through it from Panama City and eventually connects with the western-bound Pan American highway that goes to Costa Rica and beyond.

Coronado

80 km (50 mi) south of Panama City.

This area started out as a country club for the well-heeled. Then a golf green designed by Tom Fazio was added, and soon after a horseback riding center. At the same time, an exclusive residential complex took root and, today, there's a small shopping center a mile down the road. It's always been a country escape for Panama City residents, and the hope seems to be that visitors from farther afield will want to visit, too.

Dining and Lodging

$$$$ ✕🏨 **Coronado Hotel & Resort.** Red-tile roofs and lovely curved archways reflect a colonial hacienda architectural style at this place that started out as country club. Then the equestrian club and professional golf course were added, so today it's a super-luxury hotel. The nearby airfield will get you to Albrook airport in Panama City in 12 minutes—it's that close to the capital. The high-ceilinged suites are extra roomy, with nice wicker furniture, tile floors, and enough sofa beds to accommodate a large family. The sleeping area is separated from the rest of the suite by a louvered

door. The beach club, which is a few miles away, can arrange windsurfing and kayaking trips. ⊠ ☎ *507/264–3164; 800/267–6465 in the U.S.,* FAX *507/223–8513,* WEB *www.coronadoresort.com. 77 suites. 2 restaurants, cable TV, 18-hole golf course, pool, gym, hot tub, massage, spa, billiards, horseback riding, dance club, 2 bars, children's program (infants–age 12), laundry services, business services, meeting rooms. AE, DC, MC, V.*

El Valle

100 km (62 mi) south of Panama City, 27 km (17 mi) north of the Interamerican Highway (turnoff between Coronado and Playa Blanca).

In a high valley surrounded by lush mountains, about 16 km (10 mi) inland from the coast, El Valle is abundantly verdant and full of flowers. It's known for its **handicrafts market** that gets packed with city goers on the weekends, who come to search out the latest design in soapstone sculptures for which it is famous. Much like dropping down the magic hole into Wonderland, El Valle is also well known for a small **forest** of square-trunk trees (really!), golden frogs (the famous *sapo rubios* of Panama), and unusual wild (nonedible) mushrooms. But most of all, adventure seekers flock here to **El Chorro Macho** park to fly over the treetops attached to a zipline cable. Five platforms along the way allow for stopping and taking in the flora and fauna, and guides accompany participants at all times. Canopy tours are led by **Canopy Adventures** (☎ 507/983–6547) and cost $40 a person. Trips are ongoing throughout the day.

There are plenty of small inns and places to eat in the area. You can stay overnight at the rustic **Hotel Campestre** (⊠ Off Calle Mata Ahogado, at the far eastern end of town, ☎ 507/983–6146, WEB www.hotelcampestre.com), which has 40 large rooms surrounded by a peaceful garden, each for $30 a night.

Playa Blanca

115 km (170 mi) south of Panama City, 25 km (16 mi) south of Coronado.

This area is one of the newest to be developed for tourism. It had previously been a highly restricted (and isolated) military zone when former heads of the country Omar Torrijos and Manuel Noriega had residences here. The beautiful beachfront property stretches for miles and has already attracted several hotel developers. It also has its own landing strip for small planes and a few commercial flights which shuttle people back and forth to Panama City.

Dining and Lodging

$$$$ ×🏨 **Royal Decameron Costa Blanca.** The price is right at this Colombian-owned all-inclusive resort, already known and loved by Canadians and Italians. It's constantly adding facilities like a casino and convention center that opened in May 2001, perhaps to attract Americans. A golf course is also on the agenda. A big draw to the hotel is its mile-long beach and six speciality restaurants serving á la carte meals (Japanese, Lebanese, Thai, Italian, seafood, Spanish). Rooms are spread along garden walkways in four-story buildings and the place is big enough so you can have some space alone if you want to. Myriad activities include free scuba lessons, diving and snorkeling, use of kayaks, paddle boats, banana boats, and day trips are available. ⊠ ☎ *507/993–2255 or 507/214–3535,* FAX *507/993–2415 or 507/214–8059. 600 rooms. 7 restaurants, 3 snack bars, cable TV, in-room safes, 2 tennis courts, 2 pools, beach, boating, jet skiing, horseback riding, travel agency, dance club, casino, 6 bars, children's program (4–12), convention center, airport shuttle (free). AE, DC, MC, V.*

CHIRIQUÍ PROVINCE

Panama's southwest corner is a land of rolling plains, green mountain valleys, raging rivers, and luxuriant forests. It's dominated by the peaks of the Cordillera de Talamanca, which extends southeast from Costa Rica into Panama and defines the province's northern edge. The upper slopes of this range are covered with thick cloud forest, kept wet by the mist that the trade winds regularly push over the continental divide. That mist not only keeps the landscape green, but it creates the perfect conditions for rainbows and feeds countless streams and boulder-strewn rivers. Two valleys set high on either side of Volcán Barú—Panama's highest peak—offer cool mountain climates and intense exposure to nature, while the rolling lowlands are hot and almost completely deforested.

The province consequently reflects Panama's varied cultural spectrum, which includes half a dozen indigenous ethnicities, a mestizo majority, and the descendants of immigrants from all over the world. During the colonial era, Chiriquí was still the realm of indigenous peoples, who descended from various ethnicities but whom the Spanish invaders collectively dubbed the *Guaymí*—a name that has stuck to this day. The Spaniards introduced cattle to the region, and as ranching took hold, the area's forests receded. In the 19th century, banana and sugar plantations were established in the lowlands, and the rich soil of the mountain valleys was dedicated to more lucrative crops such as coffee, fruit, and vegetables. This agricultural development meant that indigenous territory shrank considerably—the majority of Chiriquí's native inhabitants now live in the mountains to the east—but it made the province fairly affluent and gave it a certain amount of independence.

Chiricanos are a hardworking, traditional people—with a rich folkloric heritage—who fly their red-and-green provincial flag with more vigor than the national banner. The independent nature of the Chiricanos probably has something to do with distance from the Panamanian capital and canal. You may be fortunate enough to experience some local folk music and dance in Chiriquí, and you're almost certain to hear some popular Panamanian *típica* music, which is similar to Colombian *cumbia* but adds accordions and ululating vocals.

David

438 km (280 mi) west of Panama City.

The provincial capital of David is of little aesthetic use to travelers, but it is the local transportation hub. Serving as political and economic center for a vast agricultural area, which produces Panama's best coffee, the town is well equipped with banks, car-rental agencies, and a small airport. Not only do Chiriquí's scattered inhabitants come here to take care of business, but Costa Ricans sometimes travel to David on shopping trips, as most imported items are considerably cheaper in Panama than in Costa Rica; thus, the busy boulevards near the town center are lined with a variety of modern shops and other enterprises. Wander past some of the clothing and department stores and you may notice a peculiar habit of Panamanian salesmen: clapping and shouting about the merchandise and walking along next to passersby, telling them personally to come into the store and buy something.

Though David was founded almost 400 years ago, no buildings survive from the colonial era; there's hardly even anything left from the 19th century. This is a fairly modern, grid-plan city centered on the shady Parque Cervantes and skirted by the Pan-American Highway. It's not terribly attractive, and its lowland location makes for steamy

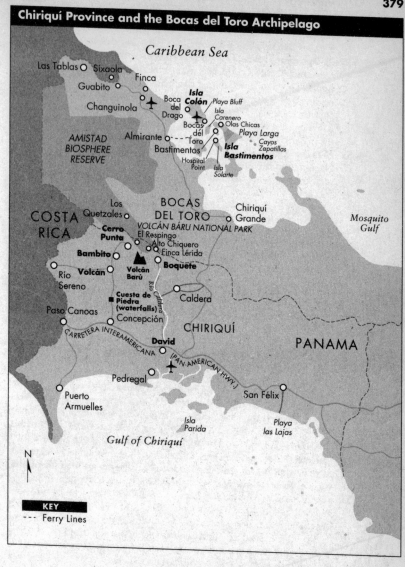

Caribbean Sea

Las Tablas
Sixaola
Finca
Guabito
Changuinola
Boca del Drago
Isla Colón
Playa Bluff
Isla Carenero
Bocas del Toro
Olas Chicas
Playa Larga
Almirante
Bastimentos
Cayos Zapatillas
Isla Bastimentos
Hospital Point
Isla Solarte

AMISTAD BIOSPHERE RESERVE

COSTA RICA

Los Quetzales
BOCAS DEL TORO
Chiriquí Grande
Mosquito Gulf

Cerro Punta
VOLCÁN BÁRU NATIONAL PARK
El Respingo
Alto Chiquero
Finca Lérida
Bambito
Volcán
Volcán Báru
Boquete

Río Sereno
Cuesta de Piedra (waterfalls)
Río Caldera
Caldera

Paso Canoas
Concepción
CHIRIQUÍ
PANAMA

CARRETERA INTERAMERICANA
David
(PAN-AMERICAN HWY.)
Pedregal
San Félix
Playa las Lajas

Puerto Armuelles
Isla Parida

Gulf of Chiriquí

N

KEY
--- Ferry Lines

temperatures, but David can be a convenient base for one-day white-water rafting trips, boat tours of the mangroves and islands in the Gulf of Chiriquí, or day hikes on Los Quetzales Trail through the forest on the northern slope of Volcán Barú.

If you have some extra time here, pop into the **Museo José de Obaldía,** which has displays on Chiriquí's pre-Columbian cultures and colonial history. ⊠ *Av. 8 Este and Calle A Norte,* ☎ *507/775–7839.* 🖃 *$1.* ☉ *Tues.–Sat. 8:30–4:30.*

Dining and Lodging

$$–$$$ ✕ **Mar del Sur.** The best seafood in David is served at this Peruvian
★ restaurant. It's in a former home on the north end of town, a few blocks from the bus station. The dining area has tile floors, wooden ceilings, arched doorways, and a few posters and paintings of Peru. Appetizers include ceviche, *chicharón de calamar* (deep-fried squid), and *papas a la huancaina* (boiled potatoes in a cream sauce). The entrées, like the

picante de langostinos (prawns in a spicy cream sauce) and the corvina prepared six different ways, are delicious. ⊠ *Calle J Norte and Av. 4 Oeste,* ☎ *507/775–0856. AE, MC, V. Closed Sun. and daily 3–6.*

$–$$$ ✕ **Churrascos Place.** This open-air restaurant two blocks from Parque Cervantes serves a good selection of inexpensive food and is open 24 hours. The plant-lined dining room has a red-tile floor, a high sloping ceiling, and a bar on one end. The menu is pretty basic, with several cuts of beef, fish fillets, rice with chicken, soups, and sandwiches. Main courses come with a simple salad. ⊠ *Av. 2 Este and Calle Central,* ☎ *507/774–0412. No credit cards.*

$–$$ ✕ **Pizzería Gran Hotel Nacional.** Across the street from the Gran Hotel Nacional (in the same building as the hotel's discotheque), this place serves decent pizza (17 kinds) and an ample selection of meat, seafood, and pasta dishes. Decor is pretty basic, but the place is clean and air-conditioned, and service is good. The hotel's nearby multicinema and casino make this complex a hot spot at night; the hotel itself is not recommended for overnight stays. ⊠ *Av. Central and Calle Central,* ☎ *507/775–1042. AE, MC, V.*

$ ☷ **Hotel Alcalá.** The Alcalá stands on a busy street near the market, a few blocks from Parque Cervantes. Its shiny, modern rooms still manage to exude a certain coziness, even though they lack personality. For peace and quiet, be sure to ask for a room away from the street. ⊠ *Av. 3 Este at Calle D Norte,* ☎ *507/774–9020,* 𝔽𝔸𝕏 *507/774–9021,* 🆆🅴🅱 *members.tripod.com/hotelalcala. 57 rooms. Restaurant, cable TV, bar, free parking. AE, MC, V.*

$ ☷ **Hotel Castilla.** The three-story Castilla's dark-green rooms provide a cool, air-conditioned oasis in the middle of a sweltering city. All rooms have tiled floors and exceptionally comfy beds. You might be tempted to spring for one of the corner minisuites, which have a dining area, refrigerator, and private balcony, but their location, overlooking the busy street, makes them a tad noisy. ⊠ *Calle A Norte at Parque Cervantes,* ☎ *507/774–5236,* 𝔽𝔸𝕏 *507/774–5246. 62 rooms, 6 suites. Restaurant, some refrigerators, bar, laundry service, free parking. AE, MC, V.*

$ ☷ **Hotel Occidental.** Step back into the 1970s at this budget hotel, which faces Parque Cervantes. The Occidental's cafeteria jumps at lunchtime, with locals traveling from across town for hearty Panamanian food at a great price. The hotel has kept up its harvest-gold leather furniture and orange-and-brown detail well, giving the interior a relatively clean look. The beige guest rooms are air-conditioned and comfortable and come with expected amenities such as telephones and cable TV. ⊠ *Calle 4, in front of Parque Cervantes,* ☎ *507/775–4068,* 𝔽𝔸𝕏 *507/775–7424. 60 rooms. Cafeteria, free parking. AE, MC, V.*

Outdoor Activities and Sports

Marina de Pedregal (☎ 507/721–0071) offers sportfishing charters to the Gulf of Chiriquí or trout-fishing excursions to the mountains. David-based **Marco Devilio** (☎ 507/775–3830) can hook you up with ocean or mountain-stream fishing excursions.

To escape the heat, head to the *balneario* (swimming hole) just north of town, across the bridge from the *cervecería* (brewery) on the road to Boquete. This simple hole in the Río David is fed by a small waterfall. Check out the on-site open-air bar. It's packed on weekends and holidays but is usually quiet the rest of the week.

Boquete

38 km (24 mi) north of David.

This pretty and pleasant little town of wooden houses and colorful gardens sits 3,878 ft above sea level in the verdant valley of the Río

Caldera. Trade winds blow over the mountains and down through this valley during much of the year, often bringing a mist that keeps the area green and makes rainbows a common sight. The mountains above town still have plenty of trees on them, great for bird-watching, and the roads and trails heading into the hills can be explored on foot, mountain bike, horseback, or four wheels. Most recently, it's become a small Mecca for U.S. retirees, who are drawn by the ideal climate, inexpensive living, and squared-away personality of the town.

You'll also probably see Ngwobe, or Guaymí, who migrate here from the eastern half of Chiriquí to work the orange and coffee harvests, which together span the period from September to April. Tidy homes and abundant blossoms make Boquete a nice place for a stroll; you can make a short loop by walking north until you come to a fork in the road, where you veer right, passing the Hotel Panamonte and crossing the Río Caldera. Turn right after crossing the river and follow it south past the flower-filled fairgrounds to another bridge, which you cross to return to the town square. If you drive to Boquete, be sure to stop at the **Tourist Information Center,** 1 km (½ mi) south of town on the road to David, for information on local sights and a splendid view of the Boquete Valley. Look for it on the right as you climb the hill into town.

Just north of town—as you veer left at the sign for the Hotel Panamonte—is **Mi Jardín es Su Jardín** (My Garden Is Your Garden), the private yet public garden of an eccentric millionaire. Cement paths wind past flower beds ablaze with color, and all kinds of bizarre statues of animals and cartoon characters make this place a minor monument to kitsch. ⊠ *½ km (¼ mi) north of town, south of Café Ruiz,* ☎ *no phone.* ⊡ *Free.* ⊙ *Daily 9–5.*

The processing plant of **Café Ruiz,** also north of town, offers a 15-minute tour of its roasting and packaging operations and a taste of its coffee. If you have a deep interest in coffee, call ahead of time and reserve a private tour of the family farm in the mountains above town, where you'll get a close look at the cultivation, harvest, and processing of the golden bean. Not surprisingly, this is the best place in Boquete to buy coffee. ⊠ *North of Mi Jardín es Su Jardín,* ☎ *507/720–1392.* ⊡ *Free.* ⊙ *Mon.–Sat. 8–11:30 and 1:30–4.*

★ At 11,450 ft above sea level, **Volcán Barú National Park** is literally the area's biggest attraction. The park protects the upper slopes and summit of Volcán Barú and encompasses significant patches of cloud forest. Inside the cloud forest is a wealth of bird life, including three-wattled bellbirds, resplendent quetzals, and the rare volcano junco, which lives at the top. The road to the summit begins in Boquete; a large sign marks the route one block north of the main road. It's paved for the first 7 km (4½ mi), after which it becomes a rough and rocky dirt track that requires four-wheel drive for the remaining 14 km (9 mi). Tours to the summit run from $50 to $150 a day for groups of up to three people; cheaper guided hikes include transportation to and from the end of the paved road. ⊡ *$5.*

Other distractions include bird-watching, horseback riding, and mountain biking in the hills above town; hiking through the forest to several waterfalls; white-water rafting; and visiting the hot springs and pre-Columbian petroglyphs in the nearby village of **Caldera.**

Dining and Lodging

The fancier hotels in town require reservations, but the others welcome drop-ins.

$$ ✕ **La Casona Mexicana.** Run by a local woman who lived in Mexico for many years, this colorful place serves a limited selection of popular Aztec taste treats. The burritos are pretty standard, but the tacos are made with soft corn tortillas; tostadas and sopas have fried tortillas. The rooms of this old wooden house are painted wild colors and decorated with Mexican souvenirs. The building is on the left as you enter town. ✉ *Av. Central,* ☎ *no phone. No credit cards.*

$–$$ ✕ **Santa Fe Bar and Grill.** This hexagonal eatery has become Boquete's quintessential gringo hangout, which may or may not be what you're looking for in Panama. But there's no denying that the southwestern-style barbecue dishes right off the grill are scrumptious. The big glass windows and vaulted wooden ceiling enclose a friendly, informal setting that includes the dining area and a bar that serves great margaritas. The banana splits alone are worth the trip. ✉ *East side of bridge next to fairgrounds,* ☎ *507/720–2224. MC, V.*

$ ✕ **Pizzería La Volcánica.** This simple restaurant on Boquete's busy main drag serves decent pizza at amazingly low prices. You can build your own pie with impunity, as they charge only by size, not by number of toppings. ✉ *Av. Central, 45 m (50 yards) south of Parque Central,* ☎ *no phone. No credit cards. Closed Mon.*

$$$–$$$$ 🏨 **Los Establos.** This new small-and-chic inn with a stirring view of
★ the cloud-capped volcano started out as a horse stable. Now the classy, light-filled rooms (all different and all named after a horse) have rattan furniture, animal-skin rugs, wood ceilings, Panamanian handicrafts and antiques, and paintings gleaned from all parts of the globe. You can stroll through the garden on the coffee plantation grounds or escape to the tree house deck. Charming bilingual manager Claudia Lombardo makes personalized service a reality for the smart guests who choose to stay here. Breakfast is included. ✉ *In hills northeast of town, near El Explorador (follow signs), Jaramillo Arriba,* ☎ FAX *507/ 720–2685. 6 rooms. Dining room, in-room safe, some cable TV, miniature golf, hot tub, mountain bikes, horseback riding, hiking, laundry service, Internet, car rental, airport shuttle, free parking; no room phones, no kids under 14. AE, MC, V.*

$$ 🏨 **La Montaña y el Valle Coffee Estate Inn.** These three charming bun-
★ galows in the center of a small coffee estate offer peace and privacy. Units have a spacious sitting room with dining table, fully stocked kitchenette, and large bedrooms with dehumidifiers to keep mold and mildew away. Big windows and ample balconies with lounge chairs frame vistas of the forested valley below and of massive Volcán Barú. Bird-watchers can follow footpaths through tropical gardens, coffee plants, and forest patches. The friendly Canadian owners can serve delicious dinners (with vegetarian options) by candlelight in your bungalow. ✉ *In hills northeast of town, near El Explorador (follow signs), Jaramillo Arriba,* ☎ FAX *507/720–2211,* WEB *www.coffeeestateinn.com. 3 suites, 3 campsites. Some cable TV, kitchenettes, laundry service, free parking; no room phones, no kids under 10. DC, MC, V.*

$$ 🏨 **Panamonte.** It's easier to picture this country inn in rural New England, but the Collins family, of North American origin, opened in Panama (in 1946) instead. Painted baby-blue, the wooden main building has a lobby with a collection of colonial art, an elegant restaurant (to-die-for meals), a bar, and several guest rooms; rooms in the newer, cement units behind it are more spacious and private, though not nearly as charming. A yellow house across the street has additional rooms. The large bar in back has a fireplace and wonderful garden views. ✉ *Av. 11 de Abril, right at fork after town,* ☎ *507/720–1327,* FAX *507/ 720–2055). 19 rooms. Restaurant, mountain bikes, hiking, horseback riding, bar, laundry service, free parking; no room phones, no room TVs. AE, MC, V.*

$$ ⊞ **Villa Marita.** Spread along a ridge about five minutes north of Boquete, these attractive yellow *cabañas* (cabins) share a gorgeous view of the valley, volcano, and nearby coffee farms through bay windows. Inside, each has two bright rooms: a bedroom and a smaller sitting room with a couch that doubles as an extra bed. The dining room is on the second floor of a cement building behind the bungalows. Interestingly, rates drop $10 after your first night. Hiking and horseback tours are available. A lounge has cable TV. ⊠ *Alto Lino, 4 km (2½ mi) north of Boquete* ☎ *507/720–2165,* FAX *507/720–2164,* WEB *www.panamainfo.com/marita. 7 bungalows. Restaurant, laundry service, free parking; no room phones, no room TVs. MC, V.*

$ ⊞ **Pensión Marilos.** The small, clean rooms in this family-run lodge are the best deal in Boquete, perhaps in all of Panama. All have tile floors and windows, and most have private bathrooms. Access to kitchen facilities, the Internet, and a small library help you feel right at home, and the hospitable owner is quick to help arrange tours. The *pensión* is on the corner of two quiet side streets a few blocks south of Parque Central. ⊠ *Calle 6 Sur and Av. A Este,* ☎ *507/720–1380. 7 rooms, 5 with bath. Library, Internet. No credit cards.*

$ ⊞ **Pensión Topas.** Owned by a young German couple, this small lodge sits in the corner of their backyard. Rooms are spacious and attractive, with tile floors, large windows, firm beds, posters, and original paintings. Four rooms open onto a covered terrace with a few tables where you can enjoy a hearty German breakfast overlooking the yard and small pool. The separate mountain house–cum–art studio houses a few guest rooms and a small café with views of the Pacific coast. ⊠ *Behind Texaco station; turn right after station, then right at first corner,* ☎ *507/720–1005). 7 rooms, 5 with bath. Café, pool, free parking. No credit cards.*

Outdoor Activities and Sports

BIRD-WATCHING

The forested hills above Boquete are perching grounds for abundant and varied avian life, including such polychrome critters as collared redstarts, emerald toucanets, sulfur-winged parakeets, and about a dozen species of hummingbirds and their relatives. This is also one of the world's best places to spot the legendary quetzal, especially between January and May. The **Panamonte** (☎ 507/720–1327) offers bird-watching on its private farm, where you're practically guaranteed to see a quetzal during the dry season. The waterfall hike offered by **Expediciones Tierras Altas** (☎ 506/720–1342) also passes through prime quetzal territory. The trip to the top of **Volcán Barú** takes you to higher life zones with bird species not present in Boquete.

HIKING

The **Sendero los Quetzales,** the footpath to Cerro Punta, heads through the forest along Río Caldera, crossing the river several times, and then over a ridge to El Respingo in the hills above Cerro Punta. This 6-km (4-mi) hike is easier if you start in Cerro Punta, and a guided trip offered by **Expediciones Tierras Altas** (☎ 507/720–1342) includes transportation to El Respingo and pickup at Alto Chiquero.

The hike to the summit of **Volcán Barú** is considerably more demanding, more than twice as long, and much steeper than the Sendero los Quetzales. Leave a car or arrange to be dropped off and picked up at the entrance to the national park, 14 km (9 mi) from the summit. Bring lots of water and warm, waterproof clothing. **Expediciones Tierras Altas** (☎ 507/720–1342) leads hikes up Barú and, as an alternative, a much easier tour on a farm above town, where you visit several waterfalls hidden in the forest. **Río Monte Ecological Tours** (☎ 507/720–1327)

also arranges hikes up Barú. If you're not up to the hike, you can still opt for a sunrise jeep tour that deposits you on the summit.

Volcán

60 km (36 mi) northwest of David, 16 km (10 mi) south of Cerro Punta.

A breezy little town at a crossroads, Volcán is spread along the road on a plain south of Barú, in an area that lost its forests long ago. The highland areas of Boquete, Bambito, and Cerro Punta are all so close to the volcano that you can't see it in its entirety from any of them; but from Volcán, weather permitting, you can often admire that massive peak and the mountains beyond it. Like Bambito and Cerro Punta, Volcán was settled largely by immigrants from Switzerland and Yugoslavia in the early 20th century. It's a good place to stay if you want to hike up the volcano's southern side, a grueling trip for which you'll want to get up before dawn. If that's not your cup of tea, use Volcán as a base for day trips to the Cerro Punta area, which has much more to see and do. Though it's often windy, Volcán tends to be warmer than either nearby Bambito or Cerro Punta, which can get very chilly at night.

Several miles south of Volcán, a few small lakes known as Las Lagunas are surrounded by some of the last bits of standing forest in the area. These are too remote to reach on foot, however, and the last stretch of road is too rough for anything but a vehicle with four-wheel drive.

OFF THE
BEATEN PATH

CUESTA DE PIEDRA WATERFALLS – There are several waterfalls in a valley below Cuesta de Piedra, a small community on the road to Volcán about 20 km (12 mi) north of Concepción. Since the cascades are in a restricted area belonging to the national electric institute, IHRE, you can only visit them with a guide from Cuesta de Piedra. Hire one through the Restaurante Porvenir (☎ 507/770–6088)—talk to Eneida or Leonel, and be prepared to haggle over the price (aim for around $30 a day). If you're driving, the **Mirador Alanher,** on the left side of the road shortly after Cuesta de Piedra, is a good place to stop for a *batido* (fruity milk drink)—papaya and *zarzamora* (blackberry) are the usual flavors—hot chocolate, or coffee. Just don't forget to climb the stairs to the *mirador* (lookout) itself.

Lodging

$$–$$$ ⬚ **Hotel Dos Ríos.** This two-story wooden building west of town is managed by Barceló Hotels of Spain. Large rooms (four different kinds) have wood floors and ceilings and small, tile baths. Two larger bungalows on the far end of the building have sitting areas and lots of windows. A large restaurant in front has a new menu of Italian cuisine, and although the bar next door is a bit on the ugly side, a large window lets you gaze at the volcano while you sip your martini. The hotel can arrange early morning transport to the foot of the volcano and a guide to the summit. ✉ *2 km (1 mi) west of Volcán on main road,* ☎ *507/771–4271. 15 rooms, 2 bungalows. Restaurant, some TV, playground, bar, shop, laundry service, meeting room, airport shuttle (fee), free parking; no room phones. AE, MC, V.*

Bambito

6 km (4 mi) north of Volcán, 10 km (6 mi) south of Cerro Punta.

It's not really a town . . . Bambito consists of a series of farms and homes scattered along the narrow valley on the western side of Volcán Barú, down which the Río Chiriquí Viejo winds. The terrain is marked by sheer rock walls, trees clinging to steep hillsides, and suspension bridges

spanning the boulder-strewn river. Trade winds whip down through the valley for much of the dry season, keeping it fairly cool, but it gets more sun than the Cerro Punta area. Small coffee and vegetable farms line much of the road, and several roadside stands sell local vegetables and fruit preserves. This is a lovely spot and makes a good base for exploring the mountains around Cerro Punta or rafting on the Río Chiriquí Viejo.

Lodging

$$$–$$$$ ☆ **Hotel Bambito.** This full-service Alpine–style resort overlooks the Bambito Valley and surrounding mountains from its idyllic pastoral setting. Rooms have attractive hardwood floors, high ceilings, and large tile bathrooms. Junior suites have balconies, and master suites have bedroom lofts. The cozy lobby has a fireplace and a small exhibit of pre-Columbian art; next door is a posh restaurant specializing in mouthwatering pastas and trout, which you are invited to catch yourself at the hotel's stocked pond. All manner of adventure activities are available including, but not limited to, kayaking, rappelling, and a more leisurely orchid tour. ⊠ *On the highway to Cerro Punta, Bambito,* ☎ *507/771–4265,* 𝖥𝖠𝖷 *507/771–4207,* 𝖶𝖤𝖡 *www.chiriqui.com/bambito. 47 rooms, 2 cabanas. Restaurant, 2 tennis courts, pool, hot tub, gym, spa, mountain bikes, miniature golf, table tennis, volleyball, hiking, horseback riding, shop, bar, laundry service, meeting rooms, free parking. AE, DC, MC, V.*

Cerro Punta

78 km (48 mi) northwest of David, 16 km (10 mi) north of Volcán.

This valley known as "Panama's breadbasket" has some splendid bucolic scenery with its patchwork of farms, some clinging to steep slopes, and an extensive ranch that raises dairy cattle and Thoroughbred horses. The area is also known for its succulent fruits, especially strawberries, blueberries, raspberries, and pineapples, which are served in *batidos,* a smoothie made with water or milk. Several foliage-clad rocky formations tower over the rolling landscape, one of which gives the valley its name (Pointy Hill). The upper slopes of the mountains that ring the valley still have most of their forest cover, and it's home to countless birds and other wildlife. Since the trade winds regularly push clouds over the continental divide and into the valley, Cerro Punta is often swathed in mist, which keeps it verdant year-round and makes for frequent rainbow sightings.

Because it's considerably higher than Boquete, Cerro Punta can get rather chilly when the sun goes down or gets stuck behind the clouds. The temperature sometimes drops down near 40°F (4°C) at night, so you'll want to bring warm clothes and a waterproof jacket.

La Amistad International Park is the single largest protected area within La Amistad Biosphere Reserve: it covers more than 2,007 square km (775 square mi) from cloud forests down to sultry lowland jungles. The name Amistad—Spanish for "friendship"—refers to the park's binational status; Panama's Parque Internacional La Amistad is contiguous with Costa Rica's Parque Nacional La Amistad, slightly smaller than its Panamanian twin and harder to visit.

Two trails lead into the forest near the ranger station at Las Nubes, which is a 20-minute drive along a dirt track that ventures into the mountains above Cerro Punta. Turn left after the Hotel Cerro Punta, then left at the next intersection, then follow that road to the park, keeping to the left after you drive through the gate. The road is rough and fit only for vehicles with four-wheel drive; if you don't have one, hire

a four-wheel-drive taxi to take you to the park entrance (it should cost about $5). **Hotel Bambito** (☎ 507/771–4265) can arrange guided La Amistad tours. A 2-km (1-mi) trail makes a loop through the forest, and a second trail scales a ridge, complete with views of the valley, en route to a nearby waterfall (roughly two hours round-trip).

Another way to explore that park's forest is to visit the private reserve belonging to **Los Quetzales** (☎ 507/771–2182, FAX 507/771–2226, WEB www.losquetzales.com), which lies up a rough, four-wheel-drive–only road from the Guadelupe neighborhood. You must be accompanied by one of the reserve's guides, who charge each person $3 per hour; they can take you to waterfalls and possibly help you spot quetzals. The reserve entrance is about a 30-minute hike from where the bus stops; ask for directions at the hotel.

Anyone with even the slightest interest in orchids will want to visit **Finca Drácula** (⊠ on the road to Los Quetzales reserve ☎ 507/721–2223), named after the Dracula orchid, one of the many rare species found here. The farm has one of Latin America's largest collections of orchids, among them a prizewinner which sells for $25,000. Also exhibited are hundreds of orchids from different parts of Panama and the world, as well as a laboratory where rare orchids are reproduced using micro-propagation methods. It's open weekdays 9–3 and costs $7. It's a 1½-hour trip on a 4-wheel-drive-only road from the Guadelupe neighborhood; a sign about an hour into the road marks the turnoff; be prepared for an even bumpier ride for about 20 minutes to the finca.

Dining and Lodging

$$–$$$$
★ ✕🏨 **Los Quetzales.** Cerro Punta's best hotel is hidden from the world on a private 600-acre reserve in the Amistad cloud forest. (A bumpy jeep ride over two rivers will get you here.) Among the accommodations are three two-story wood cabins, each with several beds and futons, a kitchen, a woodstove, hot water (there's a generator)—and its own hiking guide. Rooms don't have electricity, and lighting is by kerosene lantern. A cement duplex (a good deal for a small group) holds cheaper two-bedroom apartments with no kitchen and an outdoor bathroom. The hotel has rooms and dormitories in a ski-lodge atmosphere; its restaurant serves the best pizza and international cuisine in town. ⊠ *Altos de Guadelupe,* ☎ *507/771–2182,* FAX *507/771–2226,* WEB *www.losquetzales.com. 10 rooms, 4 cabins, 3 dormitories. Restaurant, hot tub, spa, hiking, horseback riding, bar, free parking, airport transfers (fee); no a/c, no room TVs, no room phones. MC, V.*

$ ✕🏨 **Hotel Cerro Punta.** This cozy lodge has great views of the surrounding farms and distant peaks, along with hearty food. Rooms are on the small side, with worn wooden floors, picture windows, and tiled baths. The restaurant serves basic Panamanian food; daily specials are your best bet, washed down with a fruit smoothie. The grounds are planted with flowers, which attract an amusing cast of hummingbirds to the scene you can take in from comfortable patio chairs. ⊠ *Calle Principal, across from the Shell station,* ☎ FAX *507/771–2020. 10 rooms. Restaurant, laundry service, bar, parking (free); no room phones, no room TVs. MC, V.*

Outdoor Activities and Sports

BIRD-WATCHING

The region's various feathered friends can be spotted all around the valley, especially near the streams and rivers that flow into and out of it. Several roads head off the main loop around the valley floor, all leading to prime bird-watching territory. The trails into the national parks bring you to the vast expanses of wilderness that border the valley, but the best birding area in **Cerro Punta** is probably the private nature re-

serve, **Los Quetzales** (☎ 507/771–2182, ℻ 507/771–2226), 🌐 www. losquetzales.com).

HIKING

A decent selection of trails heads into the mountains around Cerro Punta, ranging from short paths through the woods to the six-hour trek around the back of Volcán Barú to Boquete. Several trails also explore the cloud forests of **La Amistad International Park,** both near the ranger station and within the private reserve at Los Quetzales. The most challenging and rewarding hike out of Cerro Punta is the 6-km (4-mi) trek over the northern slope of **Volcán Barú,** from El Respingo to Alto Chiquero, high in the hills above Boquete. The hardest part, in fact, might be getting back to Cerro Punta, which lies about four hours by bus from Boquete. The last buses from Boquete and David leave at 6 PM, which means it's safer to take the hike while based in David, since it gives you a few more hours to get back to your hotel. Guides are available for this hike, as is transport back to Cerro Punta, though it can be expensive.

Chiriquí Province A to Z

AIR TRAVEL

To reach Chiriquí by plane, you can fly into David's Enrique Malek Airport (via Changuinola) from Bocas del Toro or from Panama City. Aeroperlas and Mapiex fly at least once a day between David, Changuinola, and Bocas del Toro.

➤ CARRIERS: **Aeroperlas** (☎ 507/721–1230). **Mapiex** (☎ 507/721–0841 or 507/775–0812).

BUS TRAVEL

Utranschiri has daily buses from Panama City to David, departing Panama City from the new Albrook Bus Terminal 16 times a day starting at 6:15 AM and departing David daily from the main terminal at 6:45 AM. Utranschiri is luxury service with air-conditioning, bathroom, video movies, reclining seats, and an attendant. The bus trip takes nine hours.

Buses travel regularly between David—leaving from the main bus station on Avenida del Estudiante, the extension of Avenida 2 Este, six blocks from Parque Cervantes—and the following destinations: Cerro Punta, Bambito, and Volcán every 30 minutes from 5 AM to 6 PM, a two-hour trip; and Boquete, every 30 to 60 minutes from 5 AM to 6 PM, a one-hour trip.

➤ BUS INFORMATION: **Utranschiri** (✉ Albrook Bus Terminal, Panama City, ☎ 507/232–5803; ✉ Av. del Estudiante, David, ☎ 507/775–0585).

CAR RENTAL

All rental agencies in David offer four-wheel-drive vehicles.

➤ MAJOR AGENCIES: **Avis** (✉ Enrique Malek Airport, ☎ 507/774–7075). **Dollar** (✉ Av. 7 Oeste at Calle F Sur, ☎ 507/775–1667 or 507/774–3385). **Hertz** (✉ Av. 20 at Calle F Sur, ☎ 507/775–6828). **National** (✉ Enrique Malek Airport, ☎ 507/774–3462).

CAR TRAVEL

Renting a car is the best way to explore Chiriquí, as the roads are in good repair and David has several rental agencies. The road to Boquete heads straight north out of David, no turns required. To reach Volcán, drive west on the Pan-American Highway to the town of Concepción—a collection of modern buildings 24 km (15 mi) west of David—where you turn right. The road to Bambito and Cerro Punta, on the right in Volcán, is well marked.

EMERGENCIES

➤ EMERGENCY SERVICES: **Ambulance** (☎ 507/775–2161). **Fire** (☎ 103). **Hospital** (☎ 507/775–4221 in David). **Police** (☎ 104).

TELEPHONES

To make international calls, either dial the international operator at 106, or go to the Cable and Wireless office to pay in cash.

➤ CONTACT: **Cable and Wireless** (✉ Calle C Norte and Av. Cincuente-naria).

TOURS

Boquete's Expediciones Tierras Altas offers a variety of day trips including bird-watching, hiking, taking jeep trips up Volcán Barú, and visiting the nearby hot springs and pre-Columbian sites of Caldera. Río Monte Ecological Tours, also in Boquete, offers bird-watching tours to Finca Lérida and four-wheel-drive-vehicle trips up Barú Volcano. Chiriquí River Rafting is the local specialist in white-water rafting.

➤ TOUR OPERATOR RECOMMENDATIONS: **Chiriquí River Rafting** (☎ 507/720–1505; 507/225–8949 in Panama City, FAX 507/720–1506, WEB www.panama-rafting.com). **Expediciones Tierras Altas** (☎ 507/720–1342). **Río Monte Ecological Tours** (☎ 507/720–1327).

VISITOR INFORMATION

The IPAT (the regional tourist office), on the second floor of a corner building across from Parque Cervantes, is open weekdays 8:30–4:30.

➤ TOURIST INFORMATION: **IPAT** (✉ Av, 3 de Noviembre and Calle A Norte, David, ☎ 507/775–5120, WEB www.panamatours.com/ipat/ipat_home.htm).

BOCAS DEL TORO ARCHIPELAGO

The isolated cluster of islands known as Bocas del Toro—in the northwest corner of Panama, in a province of the same name—has some spectacular scenery, a wealth of natural assets, and a laid-back, Caribbean atmosphere. The province includes a large piece of the mainland as well, but this part of mainland Panama is nothing special—it's the Chiquita Republic, an area virtually blanketed with banana plantations. The real interest for travelers lies offshore, on the islands where you'll find the capital city, also called Bocas del Toro.

The archipelago was "discovered," or at least visited, by Christopher Columbus in 1502. The islands' original inhabitants were Guaymí Indians, and they're still around in isolated villages and intermingled with African-Caribbeans and Hispanics in the larger towns. The language, too, is an interesting mix called Guari-Guari, a patois English with traces of Spanish and indigenous languages. The source of the region's odd name, which translates as "Mouths of the Bull," is lost to legend. One theory is that the area was named after an Indian chief called something like Bokatoro, who ruled the area when the first Europeans arrived.

Bocas del Toro is experiencing something of a tourist boom that may actually have had bureaucratic beginnings: thousands of foreigners living in Costa Rica on tourist visas have to leave the country for 72 hours every 90 days, and many of them eventually wind up on Bocas. These temporary refugees quickly discover that the islands are a very cool place: offbeat, out of the way, and possessed of great beaches, supreme diving, and mellow locals. The islands have also been inscribed in the annals of pop culture—in Spain, France, and Italy, at least—as the setting for those countries' editions of the television megahit *Survivor*.

A VOICE IN THE WILDERNESS

Perhaps it's just good public relations, but Costa Rica gets the lion's share—well, the jaguar's share—of attention in this part of the world when it comes to conservation efforts. You rarely hear much about Panama as a green destination—maybe because of the relative dearth of visitors—but this country has some 30% of its territory set aside as protected lands and surpasses Costa Rica in biodiversity. Panama counts some 950 bird species, 100 more than its northern neighbor, and the country is home to 100-plus animal varieties found nowhere else in the world.

As in Costa Rica, scarce funding, lack of personnel, and weak environmental law all hinder conservation efforts in Panama. And as in Costa Rica, it is through the dauntless efforts of private organizations that the real work takes place. First among these is the Asociacion Nacional para la Conservación de la Naturaleza (National Association for Conservation of Nature), better known by its acronym ANCON.

Founded in 1985, ANCON began as a staff of two operating out of a small office in Panama City's Bank of Boston with a donation of $35,000 from The Nature Conservancy. Then and now, the organization has been the proverbial voice crying in the wilderness, never missing a beat, even through the difficult years of the Noriega regime and subsequent U.S. invasion. ANCON purchases large tracts of land for conservation and reforestation projects, and work with farmers and landowners to educate them in the ways and means of environmentally friendly, sustainable development.

ANCON Expeditions was born as the organization's tourism arm with a twofold purpose: to inform locals and visitors alike of the country's biodiversity, and to inject much needed funding into ANCON's conservation efforts. With guides recognized as the country's best, travelers can transit the Panama Canal, learn about the country's colonial history, visit Kuna indigenous communities in the San Blas Islands, or explore the wilds of the eastern Darién province. In Bocas del Toro, ANCON operates small, rustic waterfront accommodations and ferries visitors around the archipelago on its expedition boat, the *Bocas Endemic,* leading bird-watching, hiking, and snorkeling excursions.

If you're in the mood for a working vacation, you can pitch in as a volunteer with ANCON's sea turtle conservation efforts. The work is tough—you'll participate in turtle census counts and help clear trash and litter from turtle nesting sites—and the pay is nil, of course, but the rewards are great. For more information, contact **ANCON Expeditions** (☎ 507/757–5226, WEB www.anconexpeditions.com).

Isla Colón

21 km (13 mi) north of Chiriquí Grande.

A look at a map of the archipelago shows Isla Colón, named after the explorer himself (Cristóbal Colón), to be quite an odd piece of geography. The town of **Bocas del Toro,** sometimes called Bocas, sits on a little headland connected to the island's main bulk by an isthmus that gets no wider than a hundred yards. In the early 20th century, Bocas del Toro was the third-largest city in Panama. It was the hub of the banana business, dominated by the U.S.'s United Fruit Co., and the elegant wooden homes of banana barons, some of which can be seen today, lined the town's waterfront and main streets. That prosperity was ephemeral, however: when a fungal disease began to destroy the region's banana crop during the 1930s, the fruit company abandoned the region for nearly two decades.

Bocas del Toro has begun to pull out of an extended period of economic depression. The renaissance has largely been the result of a tourist boom. During the annual **Feria,** a fair normally held in September or October, Panamanians crowd into Bocas by the hundreds. Along the right side of the isthmus road are dozens of simple structures that house beer shacks, restaurants, and exhibits during the Feria, standing empty the rest of the year. Behind those shacks is the **town beach,** which is unfortunately sometimes littered. The island has much nicer beaches, though you'll want to rent a bike or hire a taxi to visit them.

If you follow the road for several miles, veering right at the fork, you'll reach **Playa Bluff,** a long swath of golden sand backed by thick foliage and washed by aquamarine waters. Four species of endangered sea turtles nest here from March to October, including the leatherback turtle, one of the largest reptiles in the world. Local guides can take you to the beach at night during nesting season.

Veer left at the fork and you'll cross the middle of the island to the other side, where there's a little village called **Boca del Drago.** Between the two villages called Bocas, the island is mainly jungle. The rain forest here is home to such animals as armadillos, pacas, several types of frogs, boa constrictors, two- and three-toed sloths, raccoons, coatis, and monkeys. At the center of the island is a large grotto with bats and a shrine to the Virgin Mary—bring a flashlight! The island is pretty big, so plan on a long bike ride to cross it, or take a taxi, which should cost about $30.

At the Mangrove Inn you can pick up the free newsletter, Islas de Bocas, published by local diving expert Angel Gonzales Diaz. This simple publication includes a local map and gobs of useful info.

★ Bocas is a good place to catch a boat out to the real draw of these islands: **Isla Bastimentos National Marine Park.** There are dozens of great diving and snorkeling spots around here, especially around the two **Cayos Zapatillas.** Panama's National Authority on the Environment (ANAM) charges a $10 admission fee for the Cayos Zapatillas, which you should pay at its office on Calle 1 in Bocas before leaving for the cays. Since that fee increases the cost of an excursion, most of the boat drivers in Bocas take people to other good **dive spots** outside the marine park, which include Hospital Point, on Isla Solarte, and Coral Island and Olas Chicas, on Isla Bastimentos.

DINING AND LODGING

$$–$$$ ★ ✕ **Buena Vista Bar & Grill.** The back deck, which sits right over the water, is the town's most pleasant place to have a meal. Ceiling fans turn above the tables, plants hang here and there, and the view lives

up to its name. The menu lists such gringo favorites as pork chops, filet mignon, and sandwiches made with imported meats and cheeses. You can also order a box lunch to carry over to the national park. Sports events play on a large TV over the bar, which is famous for its frozen margaritas and popular with the area's growing population of expatriate Americans. ⊠ *Calle 1, where it splits from Calle 3 (main street),* ☎ *507/757–9035. MC, V. Closed Tues.*

$$–$$$ ✕ **La Ballena.** Just behind the Gobernación, La Ballena ("The Whale") is a popular little joint with a colorful interior that's usually complemented by good music during the high season. A few tables in front overlook one of this little town's somnolent side streets and a garden patio next door. The Italian owners offer an ample selection of salads, pastas, and fresh seafood; dishes include pasta with a lobster sauce and steak *a la pizzaiola* (in a tomato sauce). They also rent bicycles, arrange horseback tours, rent apartments, and give general travel advice. ⊠ *Av. F between Cs. 2 and 3,* ☎ *507/757–9089. MC, V.*

$$ ✕ **Blue Moon.** Blue Moon dishes up light fajitas, burritos, and quesadillas in an informal, open-air setting on a dock overlooking the water. You'll gain back any calories you saved on the main course with the Chocolate Frangelico cheesecake or banana split. For breakfast try the huevos rancheros, accompanied by breads and an ample fruit plate. ⊠ *Calle 3, north of ferry dock,* ☎ *no phone. No credit cards. Closed Tues. No lunch.*

$–$$ ✕ **Heike's.** The eponymous German chef-owner of this small restau-
★ rant on the main drag happily whips up everything from chicken curry to a tasty meatless dish to which she's given the laconic name "Vegetarian Food." The restaurant itself is a narrow affair with a colorful interior, two tables overlooking the street, and a few more on a tiny garden patio in back. Heike and her Panamanian husband only serve dinner, but they stay open until the last person leaves. ⊠ *Calle 3, across from Gobernación on the central park,* ☎ *507/757–9708. No credit cards. No lunch.*

$–$$ ✕ **Kuna.** Don't let its ramshackle appearance fool you; this place serves great food, especially breakfast, at excellent prices. The Kuna Indian family that runs the joint knows what its North American clientele wants and has mastered the art of pancake and omelet preparation. Instead of toast, they serve *hojaldra* (a flaky puff of fried dough), the perfect accompaniment to coffee. The cooks are wizards with seafood and specialize in lobster dishes. Large groups should stop in to place orders a few hours in advance. ⊠ *Av. Norte and Calle 3,* ☎ *no phone. No credit cards.*

$$$$ ▥ **Punta Caracol Acqua Lodge.** This sensational new lodge at water's
★ edge at the far end of Isla Colón is turning heads as well as spearheading a trend for eco-friendly hotels. Built by Spanish investors, the hotel, accessible only by boat, has five two-story wood cabanas with private walkways built on stilts over the ocean. The lodge's emphasis is on personalized service and it *does* deliver. Cabanas have a large canopy bed and two twin beds, plus a high thatched-roof ceiling and hand-carved furniture. A room includes breakfast and dinner created from a Panamanian/Catalan menu devised by the friendly Bordas family who operate the hotel. ⊠ *Calle 3 between Avs. F and G,* ☎ *507/612–1088 or 507/676–7186,* 🕸 *www.puntacaracol.com. 5 cabanas. Restaurant, dive shop, fishing, mountain biking, horseback riding, bar, laundry service, free airport shuttle; no a/c, no room phones, no room TVs. MC, V.*

$$–$$$ ▥ **Hotel Swan's Cay.** The biggest and fanciest hotel in Bocas, Swan's Cay was built by an Italian family that also has an inn on the Lago di Garda in Italy. Their Panama property is a two-story wooden complex with interior courtyards and a bit of artwork that evokes old Italy. The

furniture in the carpeted guest rooms was also brought over from the old country. No wonder it's a favorite with film crews from the Spanish *Survivor* series. The nicest rooms have small balconies. The large restaurant serves mainly pastas, pizzas, and Panamanian food. ⊠ *Calle 3, between Avs. F and G,* ☎ *507/757–9090,* FAX *507/757–9027,* WEB *www.bocas.com/swamkey.htm. 48 rooms. Restaurant, pool, bicycles, fishing, bar, laundry service. AE, MC, V.*

$$ ★ 🏨 **Cocomo on the Sea.** For around $50 per night, this small, homey place offers Bocas's best waterside accommodations. Its spacious rooms have day beds, hardwood floors, and white walls decorated with tropical prints. All rooms have air-conditioning, but ceiling fans and lots of windows give you the option of letting the ocean breeze cool things down. The breeziest spot here is the porch in back, which hangs over the water and is well furnished with chairs and hammocks. The friendly American owners serve a sumptuous complimentary breakfast on the veranda and will arrange tours. ⊠ *Av. Norte, at Calle 6,* ☎ FAX *507/757–9259,* WEB *www.panamainfo.com/cocomo. 4 rooms. Fans, laundry service; no room phones, no room TVs. MC, V.*

$$ 🏨 **Hotel Laguna.** With its carved wooden balconies and sidewalk café, the Hotel Laguna looks like it was picked up from an Alpine village and dropped into the heart of Bocas. The rooms have local-hardwood furniture, modern black fixtures, and small windows. Downstairs rooms have tile floors; upstairs rooms, wood floors. All have colorful Peruvian bedspreads and orthopedic mattresses. The brightest and nicest of quarters is the suite which comes with a refrigerator. ⊠ *Calle 3 between Avs. D and E,* ☎ *507/757–9091,* FAX *507/757–9092,* WEB *www.bocas.com/laguna.htm. 17 rooms. Restaurant, cable TV, bar, laundry service. MC, V.*

$$ 🏨 **Mangrove Inn.** A short boat trip from town takes you to this collection of buildings on the edge of a mangrove forest. Buildings are propped over the water on stilts and connected to each other by a series of docks. Primarily a dive resort, with all the equipment and a resident dive master, the inn is just a short swim from a decent reef; dive packages include meals and boat transportation to the province's best dive sites. The inn is a good spot even if you just want to snorkel, swim, and relax. The blue-and-white wooden cabins have bunks, double beds, and small bathrooms. ⊠ *Mangrove Beach; office at Calle 3, at central park,* ☎ FAX *507/757–9594,* WEB *www.bocas.com/bocavent.htm. 4 cabins. Restaurant, dive shop, bar, laundry; no a/c, no room phones, no room TVs. No credit cards.*

$ ★ 🏨 **Hotel La Veranda.** This delightful inn one block from the water embodies all the charm of its Caribbean setting, from the playful sponge-painted patterns on the walls to the vintage furniture, high wood-paneled ceiling, and oversize windows. The artistic Canadian owner pays great attention to detail, using braided-rope rugs and bamboo blinds to create a true-to-form Caribbean retreat. Guest rooms vary in size, personality, and privacy, so ask what's available when you reserve. All rooms have fans and comfortable beds draped in mosquito netting. If you're lucky, you'll get to try the owner's Panamanian chocolate, made from the local crop. ⊠ *Av. G at Calle 7,* ☎ FAX *507/757–9211,* WEB *www. laverandahotel.com. 4 rooms, 2 with bath. Fans, travel services; no a/c, no room phones, no room TVs. MC, V.*

Outdoor Activities and Sports

SCUBA DIVING AND SNORKELING

There are three dive centers on Isla Colón and at least a half dozen people who lead snorkeling excursions. Bocas has a great variety of coral—almost 75 different species, plus sponges and small invertebrates. You're also likely to see rays, colorful tropical fish, and sometimes sea

turtles or even dolphins. The most famous snorkel spot is the reef around the **Cayos Zapatillas,** which is vast and packed with varied marine life; but the $10 parks fee makes this the most expensive option. A no-fee alternative to Cayos Zapatillas is **Coral Island,** a smaller isle outside the national park. Another option not far from Bocas, good if you're short on time or money, is **Hospital Point,** where an impressive coral and sponge garden extends down a steep wall into the blue depths. **Olas Chicas,** on the northern coast of Isla Bastimentos, is another sublime spot. If you stay in Bocas, it's cheaper to bike or hike out to the reef off Paunch or, better yet, the point on the far end of Playa Bluff.

Bocas Water Sports (⊠ Calle 3, ☎ FAX 507/757–9541) offers a variety of boat dives and nonscuba excursions, including trips to its Red Frog camping area on a beach on Isla Bastimentos. **J & J Boat Tours** (⊠ Calle 3, ☎ 507/757–9565) leads trips to about a dozen dive spots and can customize private tours. **Starfleet Eco-Adventures** (⊠ Calle 1, ☎ 507/ 757–9630) leads scuba and snorkeling excursions on a private catamaran and has inexpensive certification courses.

You can also negotiate a ride to any local attraction with one of the dozens of freelance boatmen in and around town, though you might want to get a small group together to make it affordable. Dive trips usually cost about $15 a head if you go with a group.

SURFING

There are a few surfers in Bocas but no boards for rent, so you'll have to bring your own. Bocas hosts an international surf competition in December, and has several good spots: the point off Isla Colón's Playa Paunch, the northern tip of Isla Carenero, and the first beach on Isla Bastimentos, across the island from the town of Bastimentos.

TURTLE-WATCHING

CARIBARU (⊠ Calle 3, ☎ 507/757–9488), a local conservation group with a small office in front of the town library, runs nightly guided tours to Playa Bluff during peak nesting season (March–October) for a small donation.

Isla Bastimentos, Carenero, and Solarte

24 km (15 mi) north of Chiriquí Grande.

Bocas town on Isla Colón is hardly what you'd call an urban jungle, but three nearby, sparsely populated spots in the archipelago offer even quieter, get-away-from-it-all alternatives to the main island. Water taxis connect Isla Bastimentos, Carenero, and Solarte with Isla Colón. The ride to Carenero takes about 5 minutes, to Bastimentos and Solarte, about 15 minutes.

From Bocas, you can see and hear a few lively bars just a stone's throw away on **Isla Carenero,** but appearances are deceiving: the tiny island isn't as developed as it seems at first. Home to a couple of small lodgings, Carenero offers a perfect balance between being close enough to Bocas to access its attractions but far enough away for a sense of retreat.

★ Three kilometers (2 miles) east of Bocas town is **Isla Bastimentos.** Its greatest attraction is probably the golden beach on the island's northern side, a 30-minute hike from town on a dirt path. Known locally as the **First Beach,** this lovely strand, backed by thick vegetation, is a surf spot when the ocean is rough and has decent snorkeling around the point to the left when the ocean is calm. It's just one of several sparkling beaches that line the island's northern shore.

The northern coast of Bastimentos Island also has one of the region's best dive sites: **Olas Chicas,** also known as Polo's Beach after Polo, the friendly hermit who lives here (and who is also known as "Beach Doctor"). Boat operators in Bastimentos and Bocas offer snorkeling trips to Olas Chicas, which can even include a lunch of fresh-caught seafood prepared by Polo for $6.

An easy place to visit is the funky little town of **Bastimentos,** also called Old Bank, on the island's southwestern end. Its hundreds of small houses are packed together on a hillside overlooking a quiet bay, populated by friendly, Guari-Guari–speaking residents. Among other things, Bastimentos is the home of an authentic little calypso band with a not-too-original name: the Beach Boys of Bastimentos (there is actually another calypso band in Bocas, also called the Beach Boys, which is considerably better but performs much less regularly). When the Beach Boys aren't blasting their music over the bay, Bastimentos is a tranquil, unspoiled place, with a few small hotels that provide interesting alternatives to staying in Bocas. Small boats regularly carry people between the towns of Bocas and Bastimentos, leaving Bocas from the dock next to the Commercial Chow Kai store and Bastimentos from the fruit-company dock. The ride costs $2 each way.

★ Centered on Bastimentos Island just across the lagoon from Bocas, the **Isla Bastimentos Marine National Park** (Parque Nacional Marino Isla Bastimentos) protects an important sea-turtle nesting beach and a significant expanse of rain forest housing ospreys, iguanas, parrots, and tiny poison dart frogs. Composed of coral reefs, white-sand beaches, and dozens of small cays and islets, the park offers such diversions as skin diving, beachcombing, viewing copious wildlife, enjoying sea-turtle nesting events, and, potentially, windsurfing and surfing.

The best place to skin-dive within the park is around the **Zapatillas Cays**—two atolls southeast of Bastimentos. When the ocean is calm, visibility is quite good around the cays, revealing an impressive array of sponges and corals that includes immense brain-coral formations. Of course, such a colorful coral garden is home to countless tropical fish, from tiny angelfish to larger parrot and trigger fish, and a great diversity of rays. The caves at the reef's edge often attract massive snappers, drums, moray eels, and sometimes sleeping sharks; if you have time to look closer you may discover delicate starfish, shrimp, octopi, and still other invertebrates.

Playa Larga, the park's long beach, is an important nesting area for several species of sea turtles, which arrive here at night from March to September to bury their eggs in the sand. Unfortunately, this beach is almost impossible to visit at night, which makes Isla Colón's Playa Bluff the best option for turtle-watching.

South of Bastimentos, the more remote **Isla Solarte** (shown as Cayo Nancy on many older maps) houses a small Guaymí population and one hotel. Hospital Point, in the strait between Solarte and Carenero, is one of the archipelago's premier dive sites. It's named for a former island hospital that was built to quarantine yellow fever patients during Bocas del Toro's banana heyday.

Lodging

$$ Buccaneer Resort. After sailing the high seas for 25 years, owners Thom and Rick settled on a beach on the east side of Carenero. Small one-bedroom units with individual screened porches are contained in a single building. Larger, separate, octagonal-shape cabins containing bedroom–living room suites are scattered between the beach and the forest. Cabins or rooms are all simply furnished with beds and tables.

Screened windows keep the bugs out, but let the cool breezes pass through. The beachside seafood restaurant is reserved for guests, but you can call for a reservation if you're staying elsewhere. ⊠ *Isla Carenero,* ☎ FAX *507/757–9042,* WEB *www.buccaneer-resort.com. 12 rooms. Restaurant, bar; no a/c. MC, V.*

$$ 🏨 **Casa Acuario.** In a previous life, this two-story building jutting out over the water was a fueling station for boats. Four spacious, airy rooms offer you wooden floors, colorful bedspreads and drapes, ceiling fans (in addition to air-conditioning), and tiled showers. The large wooden deck is the perfect place to while away the afternoon. The owners are proprietors of J&J Boat Tours, so transport to Isla Colón is never more than a quick phone call away. ⊠ *Isla Carenero,* ☎ FAX *507/757–9505. 4 rooms. Fans; no room phones. No credit cards.*

$$ 🏨 **Solarte del Caribe Inn.** Friendly owner Steve Hartwig is bound to come down to the pier as you step off the boat—there's no other way to get here—to accompany you up to this rambling hillside plantation-style house. Cool breezes ventilate the interior. Rooms contain queen-size beds, ceiling fans, and hot-water baths and are decorated with wood and wicker furniture and Panamanian art. A huge, healthy breakfast and transport to and from Isla Colón are included in the rates. Steve can arrange for diving and fishing tours with island locals. ⊠ *Isla Solarte,* ☎ *507/697–1115. 7 rooms. Fans, bar; no a/c. No credit cards.*

$ 🏨 **El Limbo.** Surrounded by a private 35-acre reserve at edge of Isla Bastimentos National Marine Park, El Limbo's rustic, low-ceilinged beachside cabins are accented by brightly colored, indigenous-style drapes and bedspreads, and simple wood furniture. Rates include breakfast and dinner—seafood is the favorite—as well as transport between Bocas airport and this remote north-side Bastimentos setting. ⊠ *Isla Bastimentos,* ☎ FAX *507/750–9888; 507/260–6208 in Panama City,* WEB *www.ellimbo.com. 10 rooms. Restaurant, bar; no a/c, no room phones, no room TVs. No credit cards.*

Bocas del Toro Archipelago A to Z

AIR TRAVEL
You can fly Aeroperlas or Mapiex airlines on a daily flight to Bocas del Toro from Panama City and David via Changuinola. The airstrip is in the town of Bocas del Toro on Isla Colón.
➤ CARRIERS: **Aeroperlas** (☎ 507/757–8341). **Mapiex** (☎ 507/757–9841).

BIKE TRAVEL
Several places in Isla Colón rent bicycles—Hotel Swan's Cay, Hotel Laguna, and La Ballena Restaurant—providing a good way to reach the island's beaches.

BOAT AND FERRY TRAVEL
Water taxi is the most common means of transport between Almirante on the mainland and Bocas del Toro. (To get to Almirante from Chiriquí Grande, also on the mainland coast, just zip up the mainland highway.) Water taxis make the 20-minute trip hourly from 6 AM to 6 PM. There are two companies, headquartered about 100 yards apart in Almirante; and the 20-passenger boats leave once they fill up, so sign up at one that has more people waiting. In Bocas, taxis leave from a cement dock near the police station on Calle 1 and from another dock a few blocks south of Le Pirate Restaurant. A car ferry runs between Almirante and Bocas on Wednesday, Friday, and Sunday, but it's much slower than a water taxi, and it's pricey.

Individually chartered, motorized dugouts are the usual means of interisland travel, though there's at least one sailboat for charter in

Bocas. Boats to Bastimentos and Solarte leave fairly regularly from the dock next to the Commercial Chow Kai store, charging $2 per person. Plan on $1 for the short jaunt to Carenero.

BUS TRAVEL

Several buses depart Panama City for Almirante daily from the new bus terminal at Albrook. It's a 9-hour trip each way. The Almirante bus stop, at the David turnoff from Carretera Changuinola, in front of a restaurant, is about a 10-minute taxi ride to the docks. From here water taxis run hourly to Bocas del Toro. Several daily buses also leave David every 20 minutes from the main terminal on Avenida del Estudiante for a 3½-hour trip to Almirante.

A small bus crosses Isla Colón every Monday, Wednesday, Friday, and some weekends, leaving Boca del Drago at 7 AM and Bocas del Toro at 1 PM.

➤ BUS INFORMATION: **Almirante Bus** (☎ 507/774–0585 in David).

CAR TRAVEL

You won't see much in the way of auto traffic here, though a few cabs cruise around Bocas. You can take a taxi from Bocas to Boca del Drago for about $25 round-trip, or to the closer Playa Bluff for about $10 round-trip. You can also rent a car in Changuinola and bring it over on the car ferry, but this is not recommended, as the most desirable spots can only be reached by boat.

EMERGENCIES

➤ EMERGENCY SERVICES: **Fire** (⊠ Calle 1 and Av. Norte, Bocas del Toro, ☎ 103). **Hospitals** (☎ 507/757–9201 in Bocas; 507/758–8295 in Changuinola). **Police** (⊠ next to IPAT building on waterfront, Bocas del Toro, ☎ 104).

MAIL, INTERNET, AND SHIPPING

The post office in the town of Bocas del Toro is at Calle 3 and Calle 2. Internet service at Don Chicho in Bocas del Toro, next to the restaurant of the same name, costs 5¢ a minute.

➤ INTERNET CAFÉ: **Internet Don Chicho** (⊠ Calle 3, ☎ FAX 507/757–9829).

MONEY MATTERS

There's a branch of the Banco Nacional de Panama in Bocas, on Avenida F between Calles 1 and 2; they'll cash traveler's checks but cannot give cash advances on credit cards. An ATM machine next to the Taxi 25 building allows cash withdrawals from Visa, MasterCard, and Cirrus- and Plus-affiliated bank accounts.

TELEPHONES

For information, dial 102, or for the international operator, dial 106. Public telephones are scattered throughout town, including Bocas's airport, Parque Simón Bolívar, Hotel Bahía, Hotel ANCON, and the Cable and Wireless office.

TOURS

Three dive shops and several local fishermen offer one-day excursions to the Cayos Zapatillas, Hospital Point, Olas Chicas, and other popular snorkeling sites for about $15 per person including equipment. Some other boatmen dock next to the Commercial Chow Kai store and are usually willing to negotiate a price. Always confirm that there are life vests on board before you set out.

ANCON Expeditions offers bird-watching, snorkeling, and hiking expeditions throughout the islands and the opportunity to participate in

its volunteer turtle conservation projects. Bocas Aventuras (formerly Turtle Divers) leads boat trips to Isla de Pájaros, Boca del Drago, a Teribe indigenous village in the rain forest, and a Guaymí indigenous village. Transparente Tours specializes in snorkeling excursions to all the local dive sites. Starfleet Eco-Adventures features diving and snorkeling excursions on a private catamaran, as well as hiking on Isla Bastimentos. Bocas Water Sports has a variety of dive trips and a day trip to its Red Frog camp on Isla Bastimentos.

➤ TOUR OPERATOR RECOMMENDATIONS: **ANCON Expeditions** (☎ 507/ 757–5226; 507/269–9415 in Panama City, FAX 507/264–3713, WEB www.anconexpeditions.com). **Bocas Aventuras** (☎ FAX 507/757–9594). **Bocas Water Sports** (☎ FAX 507/757–9541). **Starfleet Eco-Adventures** (☎ FAX 507/757–9630). **Transparente Tours** (☎ FAX 507/757–9172 or 507/757–9600).

VISITOR INFORMATION

You can get information on Bocas lodging and summer volunteer projects on Long Beach involving turtle rescue a local Isla de Bocas Web site. The Bocas branch of the Panamanian Tourist Board (IPAT) is in Bocas, on Avenida D at Calle 1. For information on Isla Bastimentos Marine National Park, stop by ANAM (Autoridad Nacional del Ambiente or National Authority on the Environment).

➤ TOURIST INFORMATION: **ANAM** (✉ Calle 1, ☎ 507/757–9244). **Panamanian Tourist Board (IPAT)** (✉ Av. D at Calle 1, Bocas del Toro). **Isla de Bocas** (WEB www.bocas.com).

SAN BLAS

20-min flight from Panama City.

Also known as Kuna Yala, Panama's northeastern Caribbean coast is a stretch of some of the most beautiful green-forested mountains and reef-encircled islands on the planet. It's also a trip to another cultural world. This area is owned and administered exclusively by the Kuna people, who essentially run it as an autonomous republic. Here, anyone who's not Kuna (including Panamanians) is a *waga* (foreigner). From the time you step off your boat or plane, you'll be subject to the laws, folkways, and mores of the Kuna people.

When Christopher Columbus arrived on the Caribbean coast in 1502, most of the Kuna lived on the mainland in what is now eastern Panama and northwestern Colombia. When the Spanish began their conquest of the Americas, the Kuna managed to distance themselves and thus maintained their language and customs. Several hundred years ago, they began migrating to the islands of San Blas—this not only protected them from diseases that ravaged mainland villages (particularly malaria), but it also saved their culture and society from Spanish domination.

When Panama attempted to take over the region in the 1920s, the Kuna rebelled. Thanks to some backing from the U.S. military, they managed to establish an independent province governed by their own laws and customs. Today, Kuna Yala (Land of the Kuna), as they call San Blas, is one of the most culturally intact communities of native peoples in the Americas. There are now Kuna villages on about 40 of the more than 350 San Blas islands, the rest of which are covered with either Kuna coconut plantations or jungle.

A trip to San Blas is exactly the kind of cross-cultural adventure that foreign travel should be. The Kuna are proud of their culture and happy to share it with outsiders. Be aware, however, that you are expected to follow their rules and that they demand respect of their culture and

laws. Some islands won't even allow you to step off the boat, while at others you'll be asked to register with local authorities. Most people visit the western end of the province, around El Porvenir, which is regularly overrun by tourists and has consequently become pretty commercialized. Nevertheless, it still offers beautiful beaches shaded by coconut palms, superb snorkeling, and exposure to the way of life and unique culture of a fascinating people.

Dining and Lodging

The province's three best-value hotels are on or near El Porvenir and are owned and operated by Kuna people. The price of a room at any one includes three meals (often fresh lobster for dinner), use of snorkeling gear, and boat trips to nearby islands for diving and sunbathing or to see villages. The least expensive, and most rustic, is the **Hotel San Blas,** on the island of Nalunega (☎ 507/262–5410), with 15 rooms, all with shared bath. The property is owned by the venerable Luis Burgos, who charges $27 per person for a thatched hut with a sand floor or a room in a nearby building. The **Hotel Porvenir** (☎ 507/226–2644 or 507/270–1748), with eight rooms, all with private bath, is on the island of the same name, which is also the location of a landing strip. It charges $35 for a single ($60 for a double) for small rooms with cement floors. The **Hotel Anai** (☎ 507/239–3025), with 30 rooms, all with private bath, is on nearby Wichub Huala Island and has nicer rooms than Hotel Porvenir and charges $55 per person. A much better option in the $ price range is **Kuanidup** (☎ 507/227–7661 or 507/227–1396), with 10 rooms, all with shared bath, which charges $70 per person for thatched huts on a private island near Río Sidra, surrounded by great snorkeling and communities that have seen fewer tourists.

Shopping

The Kunas of San Blas are famous for their molas, multilayered, hand-stitched panels in a dizzying assortment of colors that depict animals, mythical scenes, or abstract patterns. Some simple patches sell for as little as $1, while more complex designs can go for more than $50. Besides molas, the Kunas design intricate gold necklaces and bracelets, which—when wrapped around the arms or legs—form interlocking patterns.

San Blas A to Z

AIR TRAVEL

The easiest way to get to San Blas is to fly. ANSA and Aerotaxi have daily flights to almost a dozen airstrips scattered along the coast. The closest is El Porvenir ($57 round-trip) and the farthest is Puerto Obaldía ($90 round-trip). If you plan to island-hop, you'll want to buy a one-way ticket, so you can board a plane at any of those tiny airports.
➤ AIRLINES: **Aerotaxi** (☎ 507/264–8644). **ANSA** (☎ 507/226–7891).

BY BOAT

If you're thinking about hiring a private boat to go between islands, keep in mind that may cost a minimum of $50 a person for an hour. It can be cheaper to wait at the airstrip and ask pilots if they can take you to nearby islands.

EMERGENCIES AND TELEPHONES

The larger islands have *Centros de Salud* (health centers), which will treat you for a minimal charge. There's one phone in the region, on the island of El Porvenir, but police stations on larger islands have radios to call for help in an emergency.

MONEY MATTERS

Change all the money you'll need into cash before you get here; you won't find any banks.

THE DARIÉN

Crisscrossed by rivers and blanketed by thick jungle, Darién is Panama's largest and most isolated province. The Panamerican Highway stops 48 km (30 mi) short of the Colombian border—this is the only break in its path from Alaska to Tierra del Fuego—and beyond it lies the Darién Gap, a wild and beautiful area that holds dozens of tribal villages and the incomparable **Parque Nacional Darién,** covering 1.5 million acres along the border. For the adventurer, nature-lover, or anyone interested in indigenous culture, the jungles and villages of the Darién are nonpareil.

The Darién is also inhabited by the Waunan and Emberá people, who live in stilt houses in villages scattered along the region's main rivers, hunting and practicing small-scale agriculture. In isolated villages, the men often wear loincloths while the women don colorful skirts and lots of necklaces. Both men and women often paint their faces and bare chests with a black dye made from charcoal and plant juices, which serves both as decoration and protection from biting insects. These tribes share two *comarcas* (reservations): Comarca Cemaco, to the north of the highway, and Comarca Sambú, which runs along the Sambú River in the southern part of the province. In addition to the Emberá and less-numerous Waunan communities, the Darién also has a few Kuna villages (Paya, Ucurgantí, and Púcuro).

The Darién's major towns are completely different from the tribal villages and are inhabited mostly by Cimarrones, Spanish-speaking descendants of slaves who escaped during the colonial era. The towns of Yaviza, La Palma, El Real, Pinogana, and Boca de Cupe are largely inhabited by Cimarrons and Latinos who have migrated from other parts of Panama or Colombia. About half the native people, mostly the younger ones, speak Spanish. If you don't know any Spanish, you'd better bring a phrase book, because English is not spoken.

The most hassle-free way to go is via a high-adventure ANCON Expeditions excursion that provides all food, guides, and sleeping arrangements. The 14-day Darién Explorer Trek begins in La Palma after an easy flight from Panama City. A lot of the tour follows a network of rivers—and travel by dugout canoe—with land forays into steaming jungle with exuberant vegetation and never-seen-before wild birds. Indian villages host the group at various points and offer traditional indigenous dances and a peek at handicrafts. Lodging varies from ranger stations with bunk beds and river bathing to ANCON camps with cold showers amidst the lush rain forest. An abandoned gold mining camp and a visit to a harpy eagle nesting site provide other singular experiences. Call for prices.

Lodging

$$$$ ✕🏨 **Tropic Star Lodge.** If you want to turn your Darién adventure into a sports fishing trip, this is the way to go—and in comfort. More than 150 world fishing records have been broken in these waters teeming with black, blue, and striped marlin. There's 15 cabin rooms with three more units in The Palace, a private home on the mountainside reached by a cable car. No radios or phones disturb the tranquility of the place, although there's a VCR available for viewing fishing videos. Rooms have two double beds and memorable views of the bay. Access is by charter plane, boat, or commercial jet (charter flights cost $315 roundtrip from Panama City). A minimum 1-week stay is required and all meals are included. ⊠ *Punta Piñas, on Piñas Bay, 150 mi south of Panama City,* ☎ *507/232–8375; 800/682–3424 in the U.S,* FAX *507/232–8377,* WEB *www.tropicstar.com. 18 rooms. Restaurant, pool, massage, beach, fishing, bar, laundry service. MC, V. Closed Oct.–Nov.*

The Darién A to Z

AIR TRAVEL

From Albrook Airport, Aeroperlas has flights to Jaque, Garachiné, Sambú, La Palma, and El Real ($70–$80 round-trip).

➤ AIRLINES: **Aeroperlas** (☎ 507/269–4555).

TOURS

ANCON Expeditions, based in Panama City has field stations in Punta Patiño, near La Palma, and Cana, on the edge of Darién National Park. ANCON also runs two-week trans-Darién expeditions.

➤ TOUR CONTACTS: **ANCON Expeditions** (✉ ☎ 507/269–9414, WEB www.anconexpeditions.com).

PANAMA A TO Z

AIR TRAVEL

International flights arrive at Aeropuerto Internacional de Tocumen, about 26 km (13 mi) northeast of Panama City, and domestic flights go through Albrook Airport, north of downtown. Tocumen has a tourist-info center, 24-hour luggage storage, car-rental agencies, and a Cable and Wireless calling center. Albrook has small domestic planes that give you a stunning view of the jungle. Domestic flights are a good way to cut travel time way down, and are practically the only way to visit San Blas and much of the Darién. Aerotaxi flies to San Blas and Mapiex flies to David. Aeroperlas covers the rest of the interior. ANSA serves the Darién and San Blas Islands. Domestic flights are from $60 to $110 round-trip.

➤ INTERNATIONAL CARRIERS: **American** (☎ 507/269–6022). **British Airways** (☎ 507/236–8335). **Continental** (☎ 507/263–9177). **COPA** (☎ 507/227–5000). **Delta** (☎ 507/263–3802). **Iberia** (☎ 507/227–2505). **United** (☎ 507/269–8555).

➤ DOMESTIC CARRIERS: **Aeroperlas** (☎ 507/269–4555). **Aerotaxi** (☎ 507/264–8644). **ANSA** (☎ 507/226–7891). **Mapiex** (☎ 507/270–0377).

AIRPORT TRANSPORTATION

Buses to Tocumen (about 30¢) run frequently from the terminal north of Plaza Cinco de Mayo, but it can be a hassle to hoist your luggage onto them. Depending on traffic, it can take anywhere from 45 to 90 minutes to reach the airport. A **taxi** to and from Tocumen is $12–$27, depending on the size of the taxi, the time of day (evenings are more expensive), and whether the driver goes by way of the toll road, which cuts down on driving time. To get into the city from the airport, you can take a **colectivo,** a big, van that carries groups for $8 per person.

BUS TRAVEL

Buses and minibuses are a clean and comfortable option in Panama City, though they often have distorted stereos blasting and a couple of routes have onboard videos. Not only do buses connect Panama City with the country's major towns, but there is also regular service between those towns, so you can pretty much go where and when you want. All buses are privately owned and operated, so there's no organized way to find out schedules except by asking around. Similarly, rates are not set in stone, but you can estimate $1–$2 per hour of travel. The most expensive bus ride is less than $25 (Panama City to Changuinola in Bocas del Toro). Panama City is the biggest transport hub and serves all points accessible by road. To get to smaller cities and beaches, you'll need to catch minibuses out of regional transit hubs.

Utranschiri has daily buses from Panama City to David, departing Panama City from the new Albrook Bus Terminal 16 times a day start-

ing at 6:15 AM and departing David daily from the main terminal at 6:45 AM. Utranschiri buses are air-conditioned, and have a bathroom, video movies, reclinable seats, and an onboard attendant. The trip takes nine hours.

Buses travel regularly between David—leaving from the main bus station on Avenida del Estudiante, the extension of Avenida 2 Este, six blocks from Parque Cervantes—and the following destinations: Cerro Punta, Bambito, and Volcán every 30 minutes from 5 AM to 6 PM, a two-hour trip; and Boquete, every 30 to 60 minutes from 5 AM to 6 PM, a one-hour trip.

➤ BUS INFORMATION: **Almirante Bus** (☎ 507/314–6228). **Utranschiri** (☎ 507/232–5803 in Panama City; 507/775–0585 in David).

BY BIKE

If you plan to tour the country on a bike, be aware that you'll be sharing the road with drivers who view yielding as a sign of weakness. Instead, rent a mountain bikes in tourist towns such as Boquete and Bocas del Toro, which are actually quite conducive to biking.

BY BOAT

In the archipelagos of San Blas and Bocas del Toro and much of the Darién, boats are the only way to get between points A and B. Bocas has a structured system, with private boats island-hopping fairly regularly and inexpensively. In the Darién, where people wind their way up narrow waterways in dugouts with outboard motors, rides can be expensive ($60–$200), so you're better off going with a tour company.

BUSINESS HOURS

Some businesses start as early as 8 or 8:30 in the morning, closing at 5 or 6. Banks are typically open 8:30–2:30, but many ATMs are open 24 hours. Restaurants are generally open until 10:30 PM, given that dinner in Panama is eaten later than in the rest of Central America.

CAR TRAVEL

Panama may have the best roads in Central America and amazingly helpful signs that make it easy to find your way around the countryside. Gas isn't too expensive (around $1.50 a gallon), and rental prices range from $30 a day for a sedan to $50 for a 4 x 4. Cars can be rented in Panama City and David.

In exchange for good signs, you'll have to deal with aggressive local drivers, who will mow you down without touching the brake, then sue you for denting their grill with your head. Even worse are bus and taxi drivers.

Be prepared for lots of traffic in Panama City during work hours. The mostly two-lane road from Panama City to the town of Colón is a nightmare between 8 and 9 in the morning and 5 to 6 in the afternoon because of rush-hour traffic. Two highways going north and south out of the city somewhat alleviate the congestion.

➤ MAJOR AGENCIES: **Avis** (✉ Vía Venetto, El Cangrejo, ☎ 507/264–0722). **Budget** (✉ Edificio Wonaga 1B and Calle D, El Cangrejo, ☎ 507/263–8777). **Hertz** (✉ Hotel Caesar Park, Vía Israel and Calle 77, San Francisco, ☎ 507/264–1111). **National** (✉ Edificio Wonaga 1B and Calle D El Cangrejo, ☎ 507/265–2222).

➤ LOCAL AGENCIES: **Gold** (✉ Calle 55, El Cangrejo, ☎ 507/223–5745). **International** (✉ Vía Venetto, El Cangrejo, ☎ 507/264–4540).

Customs and Duties

You may import 500 cigarettes (or 500 grams of tobacco) and three bottles of alcohol duty-free. Panamanian customs can be very strict;

even if you are only making an airline connection, make sure your papers are in order. Prescription drugs should always be accompanied by a doctor's authorization. When departing the country by land, travelers are not allowed to export any duty-free items. Duty-free items, by law, have to be shipped to a foreign address if the buyer is departing the country by land.

DINING

DRINKS

Chichas (fresh-fruit drinks) are popular and come in a kaleidoscope of flavors: *maracuya* (passion fruit), *tamarindo* (a sour, brown-seed coating), *maíz* (corn), *zarzamora* (blackberry), *saril* (a small, tart red fruit), and *guanabana* (a white-pulped fruit also known as soursop). Panamanian beers are nothing to write home about, although there are two local dark brews: H B (pronounced "ah-chay bay") and Steinbock.

MEALTIMES

Breakfast is anywhere from 7:30 to 9; lunch may begin as early as noon in some restaurants; dinner is around 8 or 9 at night.

RESERVATIONS AND DRESS

Dress is informal in Panama, although shorts are not appropriate. Reservations are usually not necessary unless it's the 15th or 30th of each month when all Panamanians crowd restaurants and nightspots, especially the first Friday and Saturday, following pay day.

EMBASSIES AND CONSULATES

Most embassies in the capital open at 8:30 and close by noon.
➤ CONTACTS: **British Embassy** (✉ Calle 53, 4th floor of Torre Swiss Bank, Marbella, ☎ 507/269–0866). **Canadian Embassy** (✉ 1st floor of the World Trade Center, Calle 53 Este, Marbella, ☎ 507/264–9731). **U.S. Embassy** (✉ Calle 37 and Av. Balboa, ☎ 507/225–6998).

EMERGENCIES

The Clinica Bella Vista is a private clinic with English-speaking doctors. The Centro Médico Paitilla is the country's best, and most expensive, hospital. To take advantage of Panama's socialized medical system, head to the public Hospital Santo Tomás.

Two chains of 24-hour supermarket/pharmacies—Arrocha and Rey—have numerous branches: A convenient Arrocha farmacia is just off Vía España at the Banco Continental building.
➤ CLINICS AND HOSPITALS: **Centro Médico Paitilla** (✉ Av. Balboa and Calle 53, near Paitilla Point, ☎ 507/265–8800). **Clinica Bella Vista** (✉ Av. Perú and Calle 38, Calidonia, ☎ 507/227–1266). **Hospital Santo Tomás** (✉ Av. Balboa at Calle 34 Este, ☎ 507/227–4122).
➤ EMERGENCY CONTACTS: **National police** (☎ 104). **Fire department** (☎ 103). **Ambulance** (Red Cross, ☎ 507/228–8127).

ENGLISH-LANGUAGE BOOKSTORES

Librería Argosy, a virtual clearinghouse of info on local cultural events, is owned by the jovial Gerasimos Kanelopulos. He carries a wide stock of intellectual stimulants in a number of languages, including an amazing selection in English. The shop is open Monday–Saturday 9–12:30 and 2–6. Any of the Gran Morrison stores have departments with English-language books.
➤ BOOKSTORE CONTACT: **Librería Argosy** (✉ Vía Argentina at Vía España, Obarrio, ☎ 507/223–5344).

MAIL AND SHIPPING

A letter to the United States costs 35¢; to Europe or Australia it's 45¢. Letters take a long time to arrive—up to two months. If you hope to

receive mail while you're in Panama, remember that mail is most often delivered to post offices. Home delivery is available, but most people consider it unreliable. Most *correos* (post offices) will hold mail addressed to: [Name on your passport], Entrega General, [city], [province], República de Panamá. There's a Panama City, Florida, so be sure to include the "República," unless you want some sun-loving retiree knowing all your business.

MONEY MATTERS

ATMS

ATM machines, found all over Panama City and in David, can be used for cash advances on most MasterCard and Visa cards, although you may have to get your PIN authorized for use abroad. The major banks with ATMs are Banco del Istmo, Banco General, and Banco Nacional de Panama. The American Express office, open weekdays 8–5 and Saturday 8–2:30 also has services for its cardholders.

➤ BANK SERVICES: **American Express** (⊠ Agencia de Viajes Fidanque, Calle 50, Obarrio, Panama City, ☎ 507264–2444).

CURRENCY

Panama's national currency is the U.S. dollar, interchangeably referred to as dólares or balboas. All the bills come in standard American denominations, although Panama also mints its own version of nickels, dimes, and quarters.

CREDIT CARDS

All major credit cards like American Express, MasterCard, and Visa are accepted at most places in major cities. Some even accept Diners Club.

CURRENCY EXCHANGE

Convert your money into U.S. dollars before you arrive in Panama; it's the accepted currency and everything else is hard to change. If you're stuck, Panacambios exchanges currency from all over the world, but at very poor rates. Otherwise, most international banks have branches here and will change their own currency into dollars, although it's a hassle worth avoiding if possible.

➤ CURRENCY EXCHANGE: **Panacambios** (⊠ Ground floor of Plaza Regency, on Vía España, Obarrio, ☎ 507/223–1800).

TRAVELER'S CHECKS

Make sure to carry your traveler's checks in American dollars. American Express checks can be changed without a commission at offices of the Banco del Istmo, although it's easier to use them to pay for rooms, meals, and merchandise, since they are widely accepted and the change is always in dollars. Banco General will change Visa and MasterCard traveler's checks with a 2% commission.

PACKING

Pack as little as possible, if you're going on small planes, which have weight restrictions. Besides your regular vacation wear, bring sturdy boots or hiking shoes, sandals, a bathing suit, a rain-resistant light-weight coat, insect repellent, sunscreen, a flashlight, and, if you're going to Darién, the list will grow to include a mosquito net, some sort of water purifier, and lots of plastic bags. So much for packing light.

PASSPORTS AND VISAS

The Panamanian consulate-general advises that all visitors obtain visas, issued by consulates and embassies throughout Central and North America. Technically, U.S. and Canadian citizens only need tourist cards ($5), which are issued at border posts and at the airport ticket counter. Citizens of Australia and New Zealand must obtain visas, while citizens of the United Kingdom only need a valid passport.

Visas are free and good for up to 90 days; officially everyone needs an onward or return ticket and proof of solvency, though the requirement is not always enforced if you're arriving by air.

➤ LOCAL CONTACTS: **Ministerio de Hacienda y Tesoro** (for expired visas: ✉ Calle 35 at Av. Perú, Panama City, ☎ 507/227–3060). **Oficina de Migración** (for visa extension: ✉ Av. Cuba and Calle 29, Panama City, ☎ 507/225–8925).

TAXES

There's a value added tax of 10% on luxury items and in restaurants and hotels. Visitors departing by air are charged an exit tax of $20.

TELEPHONES

From any phone in Panama you can use a direct-dial number to reach an English-speaking operator who will place a collect or calling-card call. Panama's country code is 507. An international, Spanish-speaking operator can be reached by dialing 106.

➤ DIRECT-DIAL SERVICE: **AT&T** (☎ 109). **MCI** (☎ 108). **Sprint** (☎ 115).

TIPPING

A 10% tip is normal in restaurants unless service has been extraordinarily good, in which case you can tip more. Taxi drivers are not tipped. Tip bell boys and skycaps $1 a bag (even if they don't have a uniform). Tip tour guides $10 per day.

TOURS

Panama has some very professional guides and travel professionals who will take you just about any place you want to go or customize a trip for you. ANCON Expeditions has some of the country's best eco-adventure trips, as well as terrific day trips, and educational volunteering opportunities. Pesantez travels to the Emberá communities, runs Panama Canal tours, and others. Gamboa Tours specializes in ecotourism with trips to the rain forest reserves. Panama Travel Experts has good sports fishing tours.

➤ TOUR COMPANIES: **ANCON Expeditions** (✉ Calle 50, opposite Floristería Marbella, El Cangrejo. ☎ 507/264–8100 or 507/269–9415, WEB www.anconexpeditions.com). **Gamboa Tours** (WEB www.gamboaresort.com). **Helipan Corp–Helicopter Tours** (☎ 507/315–0452, WEB www.helipan.com). **Panama Star Tours** (☎ 507/265–7970, WEB www.panamastar.com). **Panama Travel Experts** (☎ 507/265–5324 or 877/836–5300, WEB www.panamatravelexperts.com). **Pesantez** (☎ 507/263–8771, WEB www.pesantez-tours.com).

VISITOR INFORMATION

The English-speaking staff at Instituto Panameño de Turismo is helpful—the Web site's in Spanish—and open weekdays 8:30–4:30, but the main Panama City office is far from everything but Panamá Viejo. (To find it, go through a metal door in back of the Atlapa Convention Center.) If you go, make sure you pick up a copy of *Panama, It's the Trip,* a digest-size guide with useful information in English and good maps. You're better off visiting the various provincial branches, which have much of the same literature, and the staff can give you useful information about local attractions and services. Panama Tourism Board is a private company with a Web site that's better than anything the government offers. Other resources include *The Visitor,* a small, free paper, which can be found at most hotels and travel agencies, and *Panama Planner* , an excellent new tourist magazine, available at large hotels.

➤ VISITOR INFORMATION CONTACTS: **Instituto Panameño de Turismo** (IPAT; ✉ Atlapa Convention Center, Vía Israel, across from the Marriott Caesar Park Hotel, San Francisco, ☎ 507/226–7000, WEB

www.ipat.gob.pa). **Panama Tourism Board** (☎ 507/315–0609; 800/231–0568 in the U.S., FAX 507/315–0504, WEB www.panamainfo.com).

WHEN TO GO

The dry season (December–March) is the best time to visit Panama, but the rains the rest of the year aren't much of an inconvenience unless you're trying to reach the Darién. The best time to visit Darién is immediately following the rainy season, December or January, since the jungle is lush and the rivers are high enough to navigate deep into the jungle. San Blas hosts huge cruise ships during the dry season, so you may want to visit in the rainy season or consider avoiding the touristy area around El Porvenir. Bocas del Toro, in the northwest, goes through two dry/rainy cycles annually: February to April is dry, May to July is wet, August to October is dry, and November to January is wet. (Keep in mind that in Bocas "dry" doesn't mean no rain, it just means less rain.) September is regarded as the best month to visit Bocas del Toro. There's no time of year when Panama is overrun with tourists, but the dry season is also when Panamanian students are on vacations, so resorts and beaches are most crowded.

INDEX

NOTES

NOTES

NOTES

Fodor's Key to the Guides

America's guidebook leader publishes guides for every kind of traveler. Check out our many series and find your perfect match.

Fodor's Gold Guides
America's favorite travel-guide series offers the most detailed insider reviews of hotels, restaurants, and attractions in all price ranges, plus great background information, smart tips, and useful maps.

Fodor's Road Guide USA
Big guides for a big country—the most comprehensive guides to America's roads, packed with places to stay, eat, and play across the U.S.A. Just right for road warriors, family vacationers, and cross-country trekkers.

COMPASS AMERICAN GUIDES
Stunning guides from top local writers and photographers, with gorgeous photos, literary excerpts, and colorful anecdotes. A must-have for culture mavens, history buffs, and new residents.

Fodor's CITYPACKS
Concise city coverage with a foldout map. The right choice for urban travelers who want everything under one cover.

Fodor's EXPLORING GUIDES
Hundreds of color photos bring your destination to life. Lively stories lend insight into the culture, history, and people.

Fodor's POCKET GUIDES
For travelers who need only the essentials. The best of Fodor's in pocket-size packages for just $9.95.

Fodor's To Go
Credit-card–size, magnetized color microguides that fit in the palm of your hand—perfect for "stealth" travelers or as gifts.

Fodor's FLASHMAPS
Every resident's map guide. 60 easy-to-follow maps of public transit, parks, museums, zip codes, and more.

Fodor's CITYGUIDES
Sourcebooks for living in the city: Thousands of in-the-know listings for restaurants, shops, sports, nightlife, and other city resources.

Fodor's AROUND THE CITY WITH KIDS
68 great ideas for family days, recommended by resident parents. Perfect for exploring in your own backyard or on the road.

Fodor's ESCAPES
Fill your trip with once-in-a-lifetime experiences, from ballooning in Chianti to overnighting in the Moroccan desert. These full-color dream books point the way.

Fodor's FYI
Get tips from the pros on planning the perfect trip. Learn how to pack, fly hassle-free, plan a honeymoon or cruise, stay healthy on the road, and travel with your baby.

Fodor's Languages for Travelers
Practice the local language before hitting the road. Available in phrase books, cassette sets, and CD sets.

Karen Brown's Guides
Engaging guides to the most charming inns and B&Bs in the U.S.A. and Europe, with easy-to-follow inn-to-inn itineraries.

Baedeker's Guides
Comprehensive guides, trusted since 1829, packed with A–Z reviews and star ratings.

At bookstores everywhere.   www.fodors.com/books